Hip Hop around the World

Hip Hop around the World

An Encyclopedia

VOLUME I: A–L

Melissa Ursula Dawn Goldsmith and
Anthony J. Fonseca, Editors

GREENWOOD™

An Imprint of ABC-CLIO, LLC
Santa Barbara, California • Denver, Colorado

Library of Congress Cataloging-in-Publication Data

Names: Goldsmith, Melissa Ursula Dawn, editor. | Fonseca, Anthony J., editor.
Title: Hip hop around the world : an encyclopedia / Melissa Ursula Dawn Goldsmith
     and Anthony J. Fonseca, editors.
Description: Santa Barbara, California : Greenwood, [2019] | Includes
     bibliographical references and index.
Identifiers: LCCN 2018009510 (print) | LCCN 2018011517 (ebook) |
     ISBN 9780313357596 (ebook) | ISBN 9780313357589 (hardcover : set : acid-free paper) |
     ISBN 9781440849466 (hardcover : vol. 1 : acid-free paper) | ISBN 9781440849473
     (hardcover : vol. 2 : acid-free paper)
Subjects: LCSH: Rap (Music)—Encyclopedias. | Hip-hop—Encyclopedias.
Classification: LCC ML102.R27 (ebook) | LCC ML102.R27 H56 2018 (print) |
     DDC 782.42164903—dc23
LC record available at https://lccn.loc.gov/2018009510

ISBN: 978-0-313-35758-9 (set)
        978-1-4408-4946-6 (vol. 1)
        978-1-4408-4947-3 (vol. 2)
        978-0-313-35759-6 (ebook)

23 22 21 20 19   1 2 3 4 5

This book is also available as an eBook.

Greenwood
An Imprint of ABC-CLIO, LLC

ABC-CLIO, LLC
130 Cremona Drive, P.O. Box 1911
Santa Barbara, California 93116-1911
www.abc-clio.com

This book is printed on acid-free paper ∞

Manufactured in the United States of America

*In memory of Duane Robinson, our wonderful neighbor and friend.
We will miss your smile. The Academy of Music was lucky
to have had you all those years.*

Contents

List of Entries

Guide to Related Topics

ARTISTS

Above the Law

Aceyalone

Afrika Bambaataa

Akon

Allen, Harry

Ant Banks

Antipop Consortium

Anwar, Joni

Ashanthi

Ashanti

Asia One

Awadi, Didier

Babyface

Bahamadia

Banks, Azealia

Beastie Boys

Ben Sharpa

Beyoncé

Big Daddy Kane

Big Pun

Birdman

Black Eyed Peas

Blige, Mary J.

Bliss n' Eso

Blondie

The Bomb Squad

Boogie Down Productions

Brand Nubian

Briggs

Brotha Lynch Hung

Brothablack

Brown, James

Bubba Sparxxx

Bubbles

Busta Rhymes

Campbell, Don

Chance the Rapper

The Chemical Brothers

Christie Z-Pabon

Chuck D

C-Murder

Coldcut

Common

Company Flow

Compton's Most Wanted

Coolio

Crazy Legs

C-Real

Cut Chemist

Cypress Hill

Da Brat

Daara J

CONCEPTS

COUNTRIES

Afghanistan
Albania
Algeria
Angola
Argentina
Australia
Austria
The Bahamas
Bangladesh
Barbados
Belarus
Belgium
Benin
Bermuda
Bolivia
Bosnia and Herzegovina
Botswana
Brazil
Brunei
Bulgaria
Burkina Faso
Cambodia
Cameroon
Canada
Cape Verde
Chile
China
Colombia
Congo
Costa Rica
Croatia
Cuba
Cyprus
Czech Republic
Denmark
The Dominican Republic

East Timor
Ecuador
Egypt
El Salvador
Equatorial Guinea
Estonia
Ethiopia
Fiji
Finland
France
Gabon
The Gambia
Germany
Ghana
Greece
Guadeloupe
Guatemala
Guinea-Bissau
Haiti
Hungary
Iceland
India
Indonesia
Iran
Iraq
Ireland
Israel
Italy
Ivory Coast
Jamaica
Japan
Jordan
Kazakhstan
Kenya
Korea
Kuwait

Laos

Latvia

Lebanon

Lesotho

Libya

Lithuania

Macedonia

Madagascar

Malawi

Malaysia

The Maldives

Mali

Malta

Martinique

Mauritius

Mexico

Mongolia

Montenegro

Morocco

Mozambique

Myanmar

Namibia

Nepal

The Netherlands

New Zealand

Niger

Nigeria

Norway

Oman

Pakistan

Palestine

Panama

Peru

The Philippines

Poland

Portugal

Puerto Rico

Romania

Russia

Samoa

Saudi Arabia

Senegal

Serbia

Sierra Leone

Singapore

Slovakia

Slovenia

Somalia

South Africa

Spain

Sri Lanka

Sudan

Swaziland

Sweden

Switzerland

Syria

Taiwan

Tanzania

Thailand

Togo

Trinidad and Tobago

Tunisia

Turkey

Uganda

Ukraine

The United Kingdom

The United States

Venezuela

Vietnam

The Virgin Islands

Yemen

Zambia

Zimbabwe

STYLES

Bounce
Breakdancing
Brick City Club
Celtic Hip Hop
Chap Hop
Chicano Rap
Chopper
Christian Hip Hop
Clowning
Crip Walk
Crunkcore
Cumbia Rap
Dirty Rap
Dirty South
Dubstep
Gangsta Rap
G-Funk
Glitch Hop
Graffiti Art
Grime
Hardcore Hip Hop
Hip Hop Dance
Hip House
Horrorcore
Industrial Hip Hop
Jerkin'
Krumping
Kwaito
Lyrical Hip Hop
Mafioso Rap
Merenrap
Miami Bass
Motswako
Neo Soul
Nerdcore
New Jack Swing
Political Hip Hop
Popping and Locking
Reggae
Reggaetón
The Robot
Snap
Trap
Trip Hop
Uprock

Preface

Hip Hop around the World is a comprehensive reference on global hip hop culture. Its main audience is high school and college/university students, but we hope that it will appeal to educators, researchers, scholars, journalists, aficionados, interested laypersons, and hip hop practitioners themselves. Its focus is, like hip hop itself, primarily music; however, other aspects of hip hop culture—art, dance, fashion, literature, education, cultural movements, marketing, and global history—are also addressed through the source's entries, appendices, references, and front matter. *Hip Hop around the World* has over 450 entries that fall under the umbrella topics artists, concepts, countries, and styles. Entries suggest further reading, listening, and/or viewing about specific subject matter.

Musicians, dancers, band names, concepts, and countries for entries were suggested by some of the scholars (see Acknowledgments) who contributed to these two volumes. We started with that list and amended it as we discovered influential and historically important people and concepts. The length of an entry is based on the size of the artist's contribution to hip hop. For countries, we decided that complete inclusion was necessary to give a full picture of the global hip hop scene; therefore, even countries where hip hop is just getting a foothold, as well as countries where it is outlawed and practiced only underground (and therefore is more difficult to document), are included.

Since this is a book on a global phenomenon, many of the band, song title, and album title names are in other languages. We did the best we could to translate, either literally or roughly, taking into account idioms when possible, all names in other languages. We also consulted native speakers. We appreciate the help of our colleagues (noted in the Acknowledgments) in this endeavor.

HOW TO USE THESE VOLUMES

Entries are arranged alphabetically. A list of entries is provided at the beginning of each volume, and dictionary-style running heads at the top of each page assist in locating entries. For a list of entries arranged by subject, see the "Guide to Related Topics" section, located after the list of entries in each volume. Individual entries direct readers to related entries through "*See also*" listings, which appear at the end of the entries. In the index, page numbers for main entries appear in **bold** type for easy identification and location.

We attempted to supply inclusive birth and death dates for all people mentioned in these two volumes as well as dates when bands, dance crews, record labels, and movements began and ended. Such a practice helps to give context to the names to which dates are applied, allowing readers to infer at a glance a person's, band's, dance crew's, or record label's contemporary events and entities, thus supplying one form of historical context.

In cases where we could not discover a hip hop artist's real name, we note that person as anonymous. Though we tried to avoid anonymous artists (because of the problem of verifying his or her facts), in some cases we could not; some artists have chosen to remain anonymous for political and personal reasons and have hidden their identities well.

As mentioned, we attempted to include all birth and death (and start and end) dates. To do this, we consulted music databases such as *WorldCat*, *MusicBrainz*, *Discogs*, *IMDB*, and *AllMusic* as well as biographical encyclopedias. In cases where variant dates existed, we took the one most agreed on by the most recent sources. When finding a date was not possible, we denote this with either an *n.d.* designation, which means that no date could be found, or with an *asterisk (*)* after the date, if that date had to be inferred. For example, a 2016 interview that refers to a living person as 25 years old would lead to an inference of that person's being born around 1991, which would be represented as follows: (1991*–). In a case where an entire date range had to be inferred (both birth and death or start and end dates), the asterisk is placed outside the parentheses that enclose the entire date range, as follows: (1992–2016)*.

TYPES OF ENTRIES

Several kinds of entries can be found in this encyclopedia: Beyond artists, concepts, countries, and styles, medium-sized and lengthy entries such as "Australia," "Fashion," "Gangsta Rap," "India," "Horrorcore," "Political Hip Hop," "Public Enemy," "Reggae," "Tanzania," and "Trip Hop" have subheadings that are also indexed. "Bhangra," under "India," for example, is a specific kind of traditional music and dance from India that has led to *bhangra-beat*, which combines traditional Punjabi music with hip hop.

ADDITIONAL FEATURES

A chronology of significant moments in global hip hop follows the Introduction in volume 1. The timeline traces hip hop not only as its development unfolded in the United States, where it started, but as it spread internationally. Among many details, it includes interactions between American and international artists, emerging subgenres and techniques, first crews, debut recordings, and accomplishments that have entered the mainstream. It also shows how several artists have appeared often during hip hop's development.

Following the entries in volume 2 are five appendices, a glossary, and a selected bibliography. Appendix 1, "Frequently Mentioned Hip Hop Artists," lists the stage names or nicknames, real names, birth dates, and place of births of these artists. With the exception of artists' entries, names in this appendix are abbreviated to stage name and years for the purpose of conciseness and readability. Appendix 2, "The 100 Most Influential Global Hip Hop Record Labels," lists names of labels, their years of operation, and their locations.

When compiling a list of videos, the editors observed that many artists do not have financial access to quality music video filmmaking as experienced in most first-world countries. Therefore, Appendix 3, "Editor-Recommended Top Hip Hop Music Videos Worldwide," rather than claiming to list the most important videos, offers music videos that employ appealing visual and narrative elements or creative use of resources. Appendix 4, "Hip Hop Films and Documentaries," lists full-length motion pictures and documentaries that either focus on hip hop or use hip hop as a backdrop. Appendix 5, "Countries with Severely Restricted Underground Activity," lists countries in which governments restrict underground activity so much that hip hop is greatly threatened there and little or no verifiable activity exists.

The glossary provides vocabulary and definitions that often appear in hip hop and music as well as in this book. Finally, the selected bibliography includes books focusing on hip hop and lists of journals and periodicals that frequently cover hip hop.

Acknowledgments

Our contributors include hip hop scholars, ethnomusicologists, musicologists, comparatists, literary specialists, theatre and film scholars, communications and rhetorical studies scholars, anthropologists and sociologists, historians, and professional writers and editors as well as music industry, dance, and theatre practitioners. This is a fitting group of scholars given hip hop's interdisciplinary nature: it is not merely a music phenomenon but a series of dance, art, sociopolitical, fashion, teaching, and literary movements. Hip hop is an all-encompassing lifestyle that goes well beyond its music. Because of this, this large project required a great deal of organization, painstaking attention to detail, and handling what seemed at times like endless streams of real-time information on musicians, dancers, scholarship, and even language studies.

The support that we have received from ABC-CLIO was invaluable to accomplishing and refining our vision and writing. We are grateful to acquisitions editors Rebecca Matheson and Catherine M. Lafuente. Becky was our first contact and walked us through the project's initial steps, and Catherine answered all our questions and kept us informed (and encouraged) as we got toward the midpoint and end of the project. Throughout the project, we worked with development editor Patrick Hall, who made suggestions on every draft of the book's manuscript and gave sage advice whenever we had writing questions—all with thoughtfulness, efficiency, and a much-needed sense of humor.

We thank hip hop scholar and musicologist Felicia Miyakawa and hip hop aficionado Teresa Sessions Peacock, who offered suggestions on entries based on reading early (and very rough) drafts of this project's lists of potential subjects. They asked important questions that helped us further shape the book. We appreciate early correspondence, contributor recommendations, and/or project suggestions made to us by Phil Ford, Travis L. Gosa, John Howland, Loren Kajikawa, Jennifer Roth-Burnette, Amanda Sewell, Marie Sumner Lott, Scott Warfield, and Paige A. Willson. The world is a large place, and neither editors nor contributors could have traveled extensively everywhere hip hop has been. Without the help of contacts from around the world who have provided cultural and historical information as well as advice on translations and rendering idiosyncratic phrases in English, this book would not have been nearly as comprehensive. Here we would like to thank Neha Chitrakar, Howard Fredrics, Xiomara Demeterio Glyndmeyer, Kheng Keow Koay,

Babacar M'Baye, and Champika Ranasinghe as well as Latvian rapper and producer ansis (Ansis Kolmanis).

We are especially grateful to Danielle Keyes for her thorough work as fact-checker. Danielle provided an extra pair of editorial eyes throughout the entries and appendices. Her patience throughout the process of continually updating names, dates, and places helped make the professionalism of this book a reality. The timeline included here would not have been possible without her hard work and keen eye.

We also appreciate Valerie Lavender and Steve Berlin, Jim and Pat Gallant, Amy Baker, and Latisha Rocke; our colleagues at the Music Department at Westfield State University and Elms College Alumnae Library; our students in music appreciation, world music, and freshmen year seminar; and everyone who lives in the little blue Victorian house. These friends graciously filled much-needed breaks with good conversation and encouragement. Finally, we wish to express our gratitude to our favorite writing haven, Northampton, Massachusetts's La Fiorentina, in our humble opinion the best little pastry shop in the world.

Introduction

Hip hop may have begun in the United States, but hip hop culture has global roots. During hip hop's formative years, exchanges between artists from the United States and artists who were either in other countries or part of the American immigrant experience took place. This resulted in fusions such as jazz and slam poetry, American (rooted in West African and European) and Latin American dance, and graffiti and fine art—all of which led to the emergence of hip hop culture's basic elements: music that uses rap and beatmaking; dance that includes breakdancing (b-boying and b-girling), popping and locking, clowning, krumping, roboting, and other moves and styles; graffiti ranging from lettering and stenciling to highly detailed spraying techniques; fashion that functions and serves as expression for those living within hip hop culture; literature that focuses on hip hop elements and history but may also embrace writings by proponents of Black Nationalism, the Nation of Islam, or the Five Percent Nation; and education that emphasizes hip hop—its arts and approaches to life—while prioritizing those who have felt like second-class citizens in the mainstream formal classroom (e.g., minorities, immigrants, and the poor).

A brief exploration of hip hop's early history shows how quickly globally related interactions within the culture took place. The Last Poets (1968–), a band from Harlem, New York, was one of hip hop music's earliest influences, using rapping, emceeing, and beatboxing. Though personnel changed early on, the band's activities were an exchange among African American, West African, and Puerto Rican cultures and music, as well as among members who were strongly involved in black and Puerto Rican nationalist movements. In brief, hip hop dance's formative years show several cultural exchanges. By the early 1970s on the West Coast, a dance crew known as the Lockers had been founded by African American and Italian American choreographers Don Campbell (1951–) and Toni Basil (Antonia Christina Basilotta, 1943–), merging street dancing (such as popping and locking) and funk dance moves with more formalized jazz and modern dance. By the mid to late 1970s, breakdancing crews such as Rock Steady Crew (RSC, 1977–) had emerged in the Bronx, also revealing an exchange between African American and Puerto Rican artists. At this time, graffiti was beginning to be perceived as art rather than just vandalism, with central figures such as Fab Five Freddy (1959–), Lee Quiñones (George Lee Quiñones, 1960–), and Jean-Michel Basquiat (1960–1988) being celebrated at New York City art gallery shows. Beyond stencil, lettering, and spray techniques, graffiti art could combine pop and expressionist art, or orishas and iconic images of Malcolm X or Martin Luther King Jr., among other kinds of elements. Meanwhile, deejaying and turntablism developed, emerging first with DJ Kool Herc (aka Kool DJ Herc, DJ Kool Herc, Clive Campbell, 1955–), whose family immigrated from Kingston, Jamaica, to the Bronx when he was 12 years old. Inspired by the Jamaican sound systems, dancehall deejaying, and use of two turntables, Kool Herc figured out how to stretch the duration of a breakbeat, giving dancers more time with their favorite segment of funk music, and initiated both vocal deejaying and turntablism techniques in the United States.

Hip hop's fastest global reach was to countries where Americans could bring artifacts like sound recordings and films, disseminate music, or teach elements of hip hop like breakdancing. Graffiti was the only exception, since it can be traced back to ancient times in many parts of the world. These countries show that having access and an openness to street art was the most important factor for hip hop's immediate popularity. Puerto Rico and countries in the Caribbean such as Jamaica are just a few examples of countries where American hip hop became popular close to the same time as its emergence in the United States; however, both American Samoa and Samoa (known as Western Samoa until 1997) also had a very early interest in and exposure to hip hop that was fortified by New Zealand's interest in hip hop.

A second and much larger fertile ground for hip hop's reception was a set of countries that already had a music industry and were active in a global exchange of music, especially with hits. For example, the first commercial release of a rap song, the Sugarhill Gang's (1979–1985, 1994–) "Rapper's Delight" (1979), not only charted at No. 36 on the Billboard Hot 100 and became the first hip hop song to reach the Top 40 in the United States; between 1979 and 1980, it also charted in a Top 5 position in Austria, Belgium, Canada, France, Germany, Israel, the Netherlands, Norway, South Africa, Sweden, Switzerland, and the United Kingdom. In addition, the song reached Top 40 positions in Australia, Ireland, and New Zealand. The single album, which went double Platinum in the United States, attained Platinum status in Canada, Gold in Spain, and Silver in the United Kingdom. Two songs and their music videos released shortly after "Rapper's Delight" helped solidify the international presence of rap in popular music: Blondie's (1974–1982, 1997–) "Rapture" (1980) from the United States and Malcolm McLaren's (1946–2010) "Buffalo Gals" (1982) from the United Kingdom. "Rapture" was No. 1 on the Billboard Hot 100 in the United States and reached the Top 40 in every country where "Rapper's Delight" charted in addition to Finland. "Buffalo Gals" had much less of a chart reach, never making it to the Billboard Hot 100 but charting on Billboard's Hot Dance/Club Play at No. 33. It still found Top 40 chart positions in the United Kingdom, Australia, Austria, Switzerland, Germany, Ireland, New Zealand, and Sweden. Though it was not as successful as "Rapper's Delight" and "Rapture," the video became frequently broadcast on television. MTV, which began in 1981 in the United States, was aired in most of the same countries where these songs were hits. Music videos for "Rapture" and "Buffalo Gals" included turntablism, breakdancing, and graffiti art. These videos introduced elements of hip hop to youth worldwide and showed how these elements could be fused with other musical styles.

At this time, both Blondie and McLaren were new wave artists with their roots in punk rock. Hip hop and punk music shared an affinity for do-it-yourself art, protesting (for example, against governments or capitalism), and consciousness raising.

By at least a year, the music videos for "Rapture" and "Buffalo Gals" predated the releases of the first American full-length motion pictures featuring hip hop culture: *Wild Style* and *Flashdance* (both 1983) as well as *Beat Street, Breakin'*, and *Breakin' 2: Electric Boogaloo* (all 1984). These films offered visual and aural aesthetic stimuli of hip hop in much the same way as their music video precursors. The international distribution of these films helped American hip hop to spread further and become popular in countries that had access to them. Like audiocassettes, videocassettes were artifacts of hip hop that could be shipped, exchanged, bootlegged, pirated, and sold. These motion pictures became popular in countries where these films could easily be shown in movie theatres or on VHS players at home but also in countries that posed more challenges to their access and restrictions to freedom of expression. The popularity of these films also helped hip hop spread to more countries in Africa, East Asia, India, Southeast Asia, and South America. Some countries whose own hip hop scenes were inspired by easily attainable copies of these films were Barbados, Brazil, Denmark, Greece, Iceland, India, Italy, Japan, and the Virgin Islands. Countries that posed resistance to gaining access to or showing these films yet still felt an impact from them included Argentina, China, Nigeria, Uganda, and former Yugoslavia. Meanwhile, American hip hop music's entry into South Africa, in addition to the dancing, graffiti, fashion, and other cultural aspects of these films, spread to countries and lands that were heavily influenced (politically, culturally, and musically) by South Africa. These countries and lands were also members of the Southern African Development Community (1960s–) and include present-day Botswana, Lesotho, Namibia, Swaziland, and Tanzania. Though other nearby countries like Angola, Mozambique, and Zimbabwe were also strongly influenced by South Africa, civil wars and regimes that were hostile to freedom of expression disrupted or prevented American hip hop from emerging there early on.

Restrictions of freedom of expression, civil wars, political tensions, and economic disparity were not the sole causes of a delay in American hip hop's reach to some countries. Sometimes dominating musical tastes were responsible. Ironically, in these countries, the popularity of rock and reggae—both genres that musicians so readily fused with rap and beatmaking—dominated musical preferences so much that hip hop remained an alternative music. Examples include places where American hip hop made an early appearance, such as Argentina, Australia, Austria, Iceland, Ireland, Jamaica, South Africa, and former Yugoslavia, but also places where American hip hop appeared slightly later in the mid-1980s, countries like the Bahamas, Bangladesh, Costa Rica, Cuba, the Dominican Republic, Ghana, Hungary, Sri Lanka, and Thailand. In addition to being dominated by American rock, Jamaican reggae, and these countries' own rock and reggae music, the public's tastes were dictated by popular music that developed within the country or region. For example, modernized *cumbia* (a dance music that began in 1940s Colombia) dominated popular music tastes in countries like Colombia, Costa Rica, and El Salvador. Some countries that have experienced the harshest restrictions on freedom of expression in music also favor rock. A few examples include Belarus (which also has a preference for punk), Cambodia, and Ethiopia (which has not only its own rock but also its own jazz).

Nonetheless, in some places, elements of hip hop other than music had a strong initial influence. For example, breakdancing found more popularity than rap music in Madagascar, where American hip hop culture reached in the 1980s. Several rap musicians began as breakdancers and graffiti artists. Norway, for example, is known for having hip hop musical acts that maintain simultaneous involvement in graffiti art.

MAKING HIP HOP ONE'S OWN

The spread of American hip hop and cultural exchanges are just part of the story of global hip hop. Some countries' artists responded by using American vernacular and adapting previously composed beats in their music as well as by learning American breakdancing footwork and moves. Examples of this activity could be found by the mid to late 1980s in countries such as Botswana, Brazil, Bulgaria, Ghana, Greece, India, Jamaica, Pakistan, South Africa, Vietnam, and former Yugoslavia. As influential as early American hip hop was to artists, the need to make the music one's own grew at a varying pace. Many artists from around the world had to consider the reach of their own music, facing the decision of whether to use English—and shortly afterward, other languages popularly spoken in their countries, such as French, Spanish, and Portuguese—or even their own vernacular (street language, idioms, and regional dialects).

Still, the use of American urban vernacular and English was initially favored, and likewise, American lyrical content, from the inner-city concerns of gangsta rap to themes such as partying, acquiring bling, and finding romance and sex, was initially appealing. But in countries such as Puerto Rico, France, and Portugal, the need to make hip hop local and part of an authentic cultural identity tied to regional dialect was strong. Panama was the home of reggaetón, which fused reggae, dancehall, soca, and hip hop into its own sound, but Puerto Rico embraced it as its own and furthered its development and popularity, using Spanish texts. French hip hop, which employed the French language and focused more on political and socially conscious lyrical content than did early American rap, became more influential than American hip hop in French-speaking countries worldwide. Another influence on French hip hop came from its African artists who made names for themselves as French immigrants, such as Senegalese-Chadian rapper MC Solaar (Claude M'Barali, 1969–). French hip hop, which emerged by 1983, became popular in countries such as Belgium, Cameroon, Canada, Congo, Gabon, Guadeloupe, Lebanon, Martinique, the Netherlands, Nigeria, Senegal, and Vietnam. Though having a far smaller impact than French or American hip hop, by the late 1980s and into the early 1990s, Portuguese hip hop had had significant impact in other countries. Known as hip hop Tuga, it was popular in Angola, Brazil, Cape Verde, Guinea-Bissau, and Mozambique, where Portuguese is the official language or considered a common language. Part of its influence occurred because of diaspora activity in Lisbon, where Angolan and Mozambican and other acts first encountered hip hop before taking it back to their home countries.

As with reggaetón in Panama and Puerto Rico, using a native language is not the only way countries make hip hop their own—fusing hip hop with native music or other kinds of local popular music is also a way for artists in various countries to give hip hop a sound associated with its place of creation. For example, Ghanaian hip hop (called GH rap), which opted for English with American urban vernacular, though pidgin English (combining English with Ghanaian dialects), Twi, and Ga are often used, incorporated American-inspired beats and musically had a softer sound than American hip hop because of its fusion of reggae with rap. By the early 1990s, Ghanaian hip hop acts had started to combine elements of modernized Ghanaian highlife, a guitar band musical style with roots tracing back to the 1920s (it fused American swing jazz and rock with Jamaican ska and Congolese soukous, derived from Congolese rumba). The result was a new hip hop style called *hiplife*. Reggae's influence on hip hop has been especially strong in the Caribbean, Africa, parts of South America, and Oceania.

Beyond country identification or authenticity, the need for making hip hop local has been felt especially in communities living on the margins, particularly those consisting of immigrants and indigenous populations. For example, hip hop culture quickly became popular among urban indigenous populations living in Melbourne and Sydney, Australia. Part of the reason for hip hop's popularity for indigenous or aboriginal urban Australians was their self-identification with the "blackness" of the genre. Rap was also seen as a tool for disseminating a political message, as youth were able to musically criticize local living conditions and discrimination as well as confront social and economic inequality. Since the 1980s, indigenous hip hop— consisting of both indigenous music and indigenous-related lyrical content—has had a strong presence in Australia and New Zealand. It is at present experiencing increased activity in other countries such as Bolivia, Canada, Colombia, Ecuador, Finland, Mexico, Mongolia, and the United States, the birthplace of rap. Many more countries have hip hop scenes influenced by indigenous musical elements. Rather than focusing on an indigenous-related message, rap acts that employ indigenous musical elements often use instrumentation and traditional performance practice to give their sound an identity based on place. Just some examples include Algeria, Burkina Faso, Cameroon, Congo, Costa Rica, Egypt, El Salvador, the Gambia, Iceland, India, Ireland, Israel, Ivory Coast, Morocco, and Senegal.

In immigrant communities, rap music was appealing for numerous reasons. Sometimes it was used to teach a new language; sometimes it became a history and sociology lesson for immigrant youth, enabling them to relate to native youth in their new home countries. The music also provided a point of entry into a larger hip hop arts scene and enabled immigrant cultures to use hip hop culture as a political tool. Immigrants also found ways to make hip hop their own, as something slightly different from even that of their new country. For example, Stockholm, Sweden's immigrant communities took an early interest in recreating hip hop music as a unique, immigrant-based experience. After an initial wave of hip hop acts in English, by the early 1990s, Swedish hip hop was being recorded not only in Swedish but in Rinkeby Swedish—a local dialect that is a pidgin language, with loanwords from American English slang—as well as from Arabic, Kurdish, Italian, Persian, Spanish, and Turkish languages. Rinkeby Swedish became a youth-based vernacular usually spoken only in those immigrant communities, yet early acts rapped in Rinkeby Swedish, most notably the Latin Kings (TLK, 1991–2005), which had members of Chilean or Venezuelan descent. Many countries have hip hop scenes that are dominated by immigrant and diaspora acts. For example, Germany is the home to most Turkish hip hop acts (and most early German rappers were Turkish), Belgium is home to many Congolese hip hop acts, and Portugal is home to many Angolan hip hop acts.

Hip hop music produced by artists of nomadic descent is also popular in many countries. Identifying as being on the continuum between indigenous and immigrant and sometimes embracing an otherness, these hip hop acts employed their own language and/or fused their various countries' traditional musical styles with rap. For example, Romani hip hop acts can be found in Austria, the Czech Republic, Denmark, and Hungary, and elements of Romani music (formally called gypsy music) have had a broader reach—it can be heard in hip hop from as far away from Europe as Ecuador.

FULL CYPHER/FULL CIRCLE

In the 21st century, studying hip hop poses the same challenge as studying other kinds of music. Its global history should come as no surprise to researchers, yet global scholarship is relatively new and in constant need of real-time updating that is both locally inclusive and constantly conscious of hip hop's American beginnings, specifically the genre's earliest lyrical themes. Contemporary hip hop is informed by global exchanges, and today these exchanges are appreciated by music fans more than ever. Choice of language gives rap an identification with a place and culture, and both artists and audiences have even become interested in freestyle performed in different languages and dialects, the incorporation of traditional music instruments in instrumentation, and the fusion of diverse world music styles. In addition, traditional modifications to hip hop dance or fusions of graffiti art with global art movements, as well as with folk and established styles, have experienced an increase in activity and popularity.

Hip Hop around the World draws attention to global exchanges in hip hop, from its roots to present-day practices, thus contributing to modern scholarship—by gathering information about hip hop activity in over 140 countries. Countries where hip hop is not performed or restricted are also addressed, since it is just as important for a global history to account for those who do not or cannot participate in a culture as it is to include all active participants. This global history also gives attention to countries such as Croatia and Kenya that have previously had hip hop activity but are presently experiencing restrictions because of laws imposed by new regimes. Though coverage of 140 countries is extensive, the intention is not to be exhaustive. There are countries that are too small in land mass and/or population where significant hip hop activity is not present, and these countries have not been covered here. Some examples are commonwealth states and realms such as Antigua and Barbuda, Belize, and Seychelles.

While we realize that books that study vibrant, evolving cultures are outdated as soon as they are printed, we hope that these two volumes will help scholars by updating global hip hop studies to 2018.

Chronology

1968

In the United States, the Last Poets is formed in Harlem, New York, and the group uses rapping, MCing, and beatboxing, becoming one of hip hop music's earliest influences.

1971

In the United States, hip hop dance crew the Lockers is formed in Los Angeles.

1973

In the United States, DJ Kool Herc performs turntablism for the first time as a DJ MCing at parties in housing projects in the Bronx, New York, after developing and honing turntablism techniques to elongate musical breaks using disco, funk, soul, and rock albums; he promotes this sound by modifying speakers in his car, which he drives around the Bronx.

1974

In the United States, poet and singer Gil Scott-Heron releases "The Revolution Will Not Be Televised," a three-minute spoken-word track that is the prototype for sociopolitical rap music.

1977

In the United States, Rock Steady Crew is established in the Bronx, New York, and the Electric Boogaloos is formed in Fresno, California.

1979

In the United States, New Jersey–based Sugar Hill Records is founded and releases the first recorded rap song, the Sugarhill Gang's "Rapper's Delight," which contains the words "hip hop" as the name of the music genre (between 1979 and 1980, "Rapper's Delight" charts in the United States, Canada, Austria, Belgium, France, Germany, Ireland, the Netherlands, Norway, Sweden, Switzerland, the United Kingdom, Australia, and New Zealand); Mercury Records releases Kurtis Blow's "Christmas Rappin'," which sells half a million copies; the Fatback Band releases "King Tim III (Personality Jock)," a song that includes rap; and the Sequence becomes the first female group to release a rap single, "Funk You Up." In the Philippines, Manila singer and comedian Dyords Javier records a rap song called "Na Onseng Delight," a parody of "Rapper's Delight."

1980

In the United States, Kurtis Blow's "The Breaks" becomes the first certified-Gold rap record; Blow becomes the first rapper to appear on *Soul Train*, thereby giving rap national television exposure; Lady B records "To the Best Y'all" and becomes the first recorded female rapper; and Kool Moe Dee of the Treacherous Three introduces speed rapping (a precursor to chopper style) on "The New Rap Language." In the Philippines, Vincent Dafalong records the country's first serious rap song.

1981

In the United States, the first song containing rap to reach No. 1 on the Billboard Hot 100, New York punk and new wave band Blondie's "Rapture," is released and its video played on MTV; New York City–based Tommy Boy Music is founded; and Grandmaster Flash and the Furious Five release "Wheels of Steel," the earliest example of a rap record that employs turntablism and sampling. In France, the Paris City Breakers become the country's first breakdancing crew.

1982

Haitian rapper Master Dji records the first Creole rap song, "Vakans" ("Vacation"), and tours Europe with Afrika Bambaataa and Rock Steady Crew.

1983

In the United States, Def Jam Recordings is founded in Queens, New York; Los Angeles's KDAY (93.5 FM) hires Greg Mack from KMJQ (102.1 FM) in Houston as music director, and he makes it the first hip hop music radio station; PBS releases the hip hop documentary *Style Wars*; and *Flashdance* is released, featuring break-dancing by American street dancers and choreographers Crazy Legs and Frosty Freeze, with Puerto Rican street dancer and choreographer Ken Swift. In France and the United Kingdom, Crazy Legs and Rock Steady Crew go on the Roxy Tour, the first international hip hop tour, with Afrika Bambaataa and Fab Five Freddy. In New Zealand, the first song that fuses contemporary Māori folk music with hip hop is recorded.

1984

In the United States, the hip hop dance films *Beat Street* and *Breakin'* are released.

1985

In the United States, the Roxanne Wars begin with Roxanne Shanté's recording of "Roxanne, Roxanne"; Boogie Down Productions debuts; and members of the Chicago Bears, as the Chicago Bears Shufflin' Crew, release "The Super Bowl Shuffle," a braggadocio rap that hits the Billboard Hot 100 and gets heavy rotation on MTV. In Russia, the group Chas Pik records the country's first rap album. In the United Kingdom, the first DMC World DJ Championships take place as a DJ mixing battle (scratching would be introduced into the competition in 1986).

1986

In the United States, Salt-N-Pepa debut; Ruthless Records is formed in Compton, California, by Eazy-E and Jerry Heller; Run-D.M.C. covers Aerosmith's "Walk This Way" on its album *Raising Hell* (the song reaches No. 4 on the Billboard Hot 100); and the Bridge Wars continue with Boogie Down Productions' "South Bronx," which contains lyrics that diss the Juice Crew. In Bulgaria, the first rap song, "This Is a Fake Love," is released by MC Guinness.

1987

In the United States, Juice Crew member MC Shan responds in the Bridge Wars with "Kill That Noise"; Spoonie Gee releases his debut album, produced by Marley Marl; and the Beastie Boys' "(You Gotta) Fight for Your Right (to Party)" reaches No. 7 on the Billboard Hot 100 (the album *Licensed to Ill* would be certified Diamond). In Barbados, DiKK becomes one of the nation's first rapping crews.

1988

In the United States, Public Enemy releases its studio album *It Takes a Nation of Millions to Hold Us Back* on New York's Def Jam Recordings (in 1989, Spike Lee releases the film *Do the Right Thing*, which prominently features Public Enemy's "Fight the Power"); Atlanta-based Ruff Ryders Entertainment is founded; MC Hammer releases the album *Feel My Power*, which goes Platinum; U.K. native Slick Rick releases his solo debut on Def Jam Recordings; and MC Lyte releases *Lyte as a Rock*, the first album by a solo female MC. In New Zealand, Upper Hutt Posse becomes the first entirely indigenous group to have a hip hop hit.

1989

In the United States, MTV's *Yo! MTV Raps* begins, introducing rap music videos through television; Ruthless Records' N.W.A. releases its studio album *Straight Outta Compton*, ushering in the age of gangsta rap; both Queen Latifah and Roxanne Shanté release debut albums; and the Billboard Hot Rap Tracks chart is established, later to become Hot Rap Singles and then Hot Rap Songs. In South Korea and Malaysia, rap is introduced by Hong Seo-beom and rap crew Krash Kozz, respectively. In the United Kingdom, Coldcut releases its debut album.

1990

In the United States, A Tribe Called Quest debuts; Will Smith of DJ Jazzy Jeff & the Fresh Prince gets national exposure with the TV series *The Fresh Prince of Bel-Air*, which uses a rap as its theme song; 2 Live Crew's album *As Nasty as They Wanna Be* is outlawed by a judge in Florida; Vanilla Ice's "Ice Baby" becomes the first rap song to top the Billboard Hot 100; No Limit Records is founded by Master P in Richmond, California (and soon moved to New Orleans); and *Newsweek* magazine puts rapper Tone Lōc on its cover as the face of "rap rage." In South Korea, Madagascar, and Sweden, Hyun Jin-young (of the band Wawa), MCM Boys, and Just D, respectively, release the country's first rap album.

1991

In the United States, Death Row Records is founded in Los Angeles by discontented rappers from Ruthless Records and Suge Knight, and one of those discontented rappers, Dr. Dre, joins Death Row (he will later become the genre's preeminent producer); Swing Mob, an Imprint of Elektra, is created in Portsmouth, Virginia, by Jodeci member DeVante Swing, and Missy Elliott and Timbaland join Swing Mob; *Doo Bop*, an album that fuses jazz with rap, by bebop, cool jazz, and jazz-rock fusion trumpeter Miles Davis, is released posthumously; Tupac Shakur and Cypress Hill both release debut albums; *New Jack City*, starring Ice-T, is released and becomes a box-office hit; and *Boyz n the Hood*, which features rapper Ice Cube, is released. In India, Peru, and Yugoslavia, Baba Sehgal, Golpeando la Calle, and MC Buffalo, respectively, introduce hip hop.

1992

In the United States, Dr. Dre releases his first solo album, *The Chronic*, on Death Row Records, introducing G-funk; and Wu-Tang Clan, Mary J. Blige, TLC, and the Notorious B.I.G. debut. In Greece/Cyprus, the first rapping crew, Vaomenoi Esso, begins self-releasing in Greek Cypriot, and Active Member releases the first hip hop album in Greek. In the Netherlands and Romania, Osdorp Posse and Vorbire Directa, respectively, introduce rap and hip hop.

1993

In the United States, Bad Boy Records is founded by Puff Daddy; Dr. Dre produces Snoop Dogg's debut album; KRS-One releases his solo debut; MC Lyte becomes the first solo female rapper to achieve Gold certification and a Grammy nomination; and Kirk Franklin releases *Kirk Franklin and the Family*, an album that combines hip hop with gospel music.

1994

In the United States, Da Brat becomes the first solo female rap artist to have a certified-Platinum album and single. In Tanzania and the United Kingdom, Hard Blasters, Tricky, and Urban Species release debut albums.

1995

In the United States, Eazy-E dies of AIDS, and Ruthless Records begins a death spiral. In Sri Lanka, Brown Boogie Nation, likely the country's first hip hop group, is formed. In Estonia, the Gambia, Hungary, Macedonia, and Senegal, debut rap albums are released by Cool D, Black Nature, R.A.C.L.A., the Most Wanted, and Positive Black Soul, respectively.

1996

In the United States, Tupac Shakur is murdered in the East Coast–West Coast feud; Jay-Z and Lil' Kim release debut solo albums. In Croatia and Iceland, Tram 11 and Quarashi, respectively, become the first rap crews. In the Czech Republic, Chaozz's debut rap album is certified Platinum. In Israel, the first hip hop radio show debuts. In South Korea, T.I.P. Crew becomes the first b-boy squad. In Macedonia, the first hip hop recording label, Dolina Na Senkite, is formed. In Martinique, Nèg Lyrical releases the first Antillean Creole rap album.

1997

In the United States, the Notorious B.I.G. is murdered in the East Coast–West Coast feud; Erykah Badu and Missy Elliott debut; American Yemeni Hagage Abul-Gowee Masaed releases "Yemen," introducing Yemen to rap; and Rapper LL Cool J wears a FUBU hat in a Gap commercial and raps the phrase "For us by us on the low," which promotes FUBU and ushers in the era of hip hop fashion companies. In Chile, Tiro de Gracia signs with EMI to release its debut album. In France, MC Solaar releases the first Platinum-certified French hip hop album. In Iceland and Mongolia, Multifunctionals and Enkhtaivan, respectively, introduce rap and hip hop.

1998

In the United States, Geto Boys debuts and popularizes horrorcore. In the United Kingdom, Imogen Heap releases her debut album. In China, Montenegro, and Peru, Cui Jian, Rambo Amadeus, and Droopy G, respectively, introduce rap and hip hop music.

1999

In the United States, Lauryn Hill releases her solo studio album, *The Miseducation of Lauryn Hill*, which wins four Grammy Awards and sells nearly six million copies; Hill is featured on the cover of *Time* magazine with the caption "Hip Hop Nation—After 20 Years—How It's Changed America"; Eminem, Lil Wayne, Mos Def, and 50 Cent debut; Aceyalone begins collaborating on jazz poetry in Los Angeles; and Billboard creates the Hot R&B/Hip-Hop Singles & Tracks chart. In Canada, Shebang! becomes the first b-girl crew. In Japan, J-pop star Hikaru Utada releases a multi-Platinum debut album, which includes hip hop songs. In Nigeria, Lakal Kaney releases the first rap Nigerien album. In Thailand, pop idol Joni Anwar releases his solo hip hop debut.

2000

In the United States, Jill Scott and Ludacris debut; Leroy F. Moore Jr. establishes Krip Hop, a disability hip hop movement in Berkeley, California. In Burma, Myanmar, Nepal, and Slovenia, the first hip hop albums are released by Sai Kham, Acid, Rappaz Union, and KlemenKlemen, respectively.

2001

In the United States, J Dilla debuts. In Iceland and Korea, the first hip hop albums in each country's native tongue are released by Sesar A and Verbal Jint, respectively. In Slovenia, the first freestyle rap championships are organized.

2002

In the United States, Grandmaster Flash and the Furious Five's "The Message" becomes the first hip hop recording chosen by the Library of Congress for the National Recording Registry; the Roots becomes the first hip hop band to perform at the Lincoln Center in New York City; and Eminem wins an Oscar for Best Original Song for "Lose Yourself." In Australia, 1200 Techniques debuts. In Cuba, the Ministry of Culture establishes the Cuban Rap Agency to further develop and promote hip hop locally and internationally. In Iran, Salome MC becomes the first female hip hop artist and producer. In Sri Lanka, BnS signs with Sony BMG.

2003

In the United States, 50 Cent releases his first album, which debuts on the Billboard 200 at No. 1. In Nigeria, M.I. returns to pursue a rap career. In Saudi Arabia, the first hip hop concert is held. In Senegal, Daara J debuts. In Uganda, members of Bataka Squad help found the Uganda Hip Hop Foundation.

2004

In the United States, Kanye West and Akon debut; Massive Monkees becomes the first American b-boy crew to win an international title. In Korea, Dynamic Duo releases *Taxi Driver*, the best-selling Korean hip hop album to date. In Norway, rap duo Jaa9 and OnklP releases its debut album.

2005

In the United States, nerdcore is introduced by MC Frontalot. In the Maldives and Mozambique, Black Prison 8 and SIMBA, respectively, introduce hip hop. In South Africa, Tumi and the Volume debut, and Tuks Senganga wins Best Rap Album at the South African Music Awards. In the United Kingdom, M.I.A. debuts.

2006

In the United States, Death Row Records goes bankrupt; Gnarls Barkley debuts; Three 6 Mafia wins an Oscar for its song "It's Hard Out There for a Pimp," from the film *Hustle and Flow*; and Queen Latifah becomes the first hip hop artist to be awarded a star on the Hollywood Walk of Fame. In Nigeria, Jesse Jagz debuts.

2007

In the United States, Grandmaster Flash and the Furious Five become the first hip hop group to be recognized and inducted into the Rock and Roll Hall of Fame; Trinidadian American Nicki Minaj debuts; Krip Hop Nation is established and makes efforts for disabled hip hop artists to share their music on a global level.

2008

In the United States, Thai American rap crew Thaitanium releases the album *Flip Side*, the band's first global album release. In Indonesia, Batik Tribe combines hip hop with gamelan. In Nigeria, Naeto C's debut album sells over a million copies.

2009

In Ghana, Sarkodie and Skillions debut. In South Africa, Die Antwoord debuts. In the United Kingdom, chap hop is introduced by Mr. B The Gentleman Rhymer in the parody song "Chap Hop History," and Professor Elemental releases his debut album.

2010

In the United States, Nicki Minaj becomes the first female solo artist to have seven singles simultaneously chart on the Billboard Hot 100. In Canada, Drake debuts. In Canada and Somalia, Somali Canadian K'Naan has his 2009 song "Wavin' Flag" chosen as Coca-Cola's promotional anthem for the 2010 FIFA World Cup.

2011

In the United States, Kendrick Lamar debuts. In Saudi Arabia, *Laisch Hip-Hop* becomes the first hip hop radio program.

2012

In the United States, a holographic image of Tupac Shakur performs with Snoop Dogg at Coachella; and Talib Kweli releases his solo debut. In Albania, the first hip hop festival is created. In Cambodia, Yab Moung Records becomes the first hip hop label. In Ghana and Saudi Arabia, C-Real, El, and Arabian Knightz release long-awaited debut hip hop albums (C-Real and El are from Ghana). In South Korea, PSY releases "Gangnam Style," the first video to reach 1 billion YouTube views. In the United Kingdom, Barbados-based rap crew Cover Drive have a hit album with *Bajan Style*.

2013

In the United States, Mix Master Mike becomes the first turntablist to perform at the John F. Kennedy Center for the Performing Arts for the Kennedy Center Honors. In the Maldives and Morocco, Dizzy DROS and Magumathi, respectively, release debut albums. In Sri Lanka, Ashanthi becomes the first female hip hop artist to release a globally distributed album.

2014

In Burma, Hlwan Paing releases an electrodance-fused hip hop debut album.

2015

In the United States, Lin-Manuel Miranda's *Hamilton: An American Musical* popularizes rap music for the Broadway stage. In Cameroon, Stanley Enow releases his debut album.

2016

In Ecuador and Martinique, Mateo Kingman and Kalash, respectively, release debut albums.

2017

In the United States, Nicki Minaj surpasses Aretha Franklin for having more songs charted on the Billboard Hot 100 than any other female artist; Kanye West's studio album, *The Life of Pablo* (2016), becomes the first streaming-only album to attain Platinum status; and Cardi B becomes the first solo female rapper since Lauryn Hill in 1998 to top the Billboard Hot 100 with her song "Bodak Yellow."

2018

In the United States, the Kennedy Center in New York City celebrates the 35th anniversary of *Wild Style* with a screening and dance party featuring Grand Wizard Theodore and Grandmaster Caz.

A

Above the Law

(aka A.T.L., 1989–, Pomona, California)

Above the Law (A.T.L.) is an American West Coast rap and G-funk band that was associated with Eazy-E's (1964–1995) Ruthless Records label (1986–) and the Tommy Boy label (1981–). The band's members, Cold 187um (aka Big Hutch, Gregory Fernan Hutchison, 1967–), DJ Total K-Oss (Anthony Stewart, n.d.), KMG the Illustrator (Kevin Gulley, 1969–2012), Go Mack (Arthur Goodman, n.d.), and sometime member Kokane (Jerry B. Long Jr., 1969–) produced a debut album, *Livin' Like Hustlers* (1989), which featured guest appearances from members of the legendary rap band N.W.A. (1986–1991). The album also featured production from Dr. Dre (1965–) on the songs "Murder Rap" and "The Last Song." Cold 187um and Dr. Dre worked on the tracks and influenced one another, both eventually claiming to have created G-funk. Both worked toward the style simultaneously, although Cold 187um was the first to publicly release it: *Livin' Like Hustlers* featured songs that hinted toward G-funk (a mix of vintage funk, soul, and rap) and was released at a time when Dr. Dre was between labels, having left Ruthless Records for rival Death Row Records (1991–2009), which would release his solo debut *The Chronic* in 1992, the same year as A.T.L.'s *Black Mafia Life* (1992), both competing to be called the first G-funk album. Some argument can be made that A.T.L.'s song "4 the Funk of It" from the EP *Vocally Pimpin'* (1991) is also a precursor to G-funk, and many consider its third album, *Uncle Sam's Curse* (1994), a classic G-funk album.

By the time Above the Law released *Uncle Sam's Curse*, which contained the rap anthem "Black Superman," it had achieved a reputation as one of gangsta rap's hottest acts. The band released nine studio albums in all, four of which charted in the Top 20 of the Hot R&B/Hip-Hop Songs chart—*Black Mafia Life* reached No. 6 and was certified Platinum. Eight of its albums charted in the Billboard 200. In 1990, the band participated in the West Coast Rap All-Stars collaborative song "We're All in the Same Gang." *Livin' Like Hustlers* spawned two minor hits, "Untouchable" and "Murder Rap"; the latter, which featured a modified sample from Quincy Jones's (1933–) *Ironside* (1967–1975) theme, was licenced for video games and film.

After Eazy-E's death, the band was dropped from Ruthless and moved to Tommy Boy, which released its next three albums, *Time Will Reveal* (1996), *Legends Worldwide* (1997), and *Legends* (1999). After the band had a brief stint with Death Row, where Cold 187um served as house producer, Cold 187um formed his own label, West World Records (1999–2014)*, to release the band's seventh and eighth albums. Besides its influence on gangsta rap, A.T.L. is remembered for causing some controversy with its commercials for *Uncle Sam's Curse*, which depicted images of the hate group the Klu Klux Klan with burning torches and contained a scene where Uncle Sam takes an African American infant from its mother.

Rumors of a new A.T.L. album and of unreleased songs recorded before main lyricist KMG's 2012 death persist as of 2018.

Anthony J. Fonseca

See also: Gangsta Rap; G-Funk; The United States

Further Reading

Diallo, David. 2010. "From Electro-Rap to G-Funk: A Social History of Rap Music in Los Angeles and Compton, California." In *Hip Hop in America: A Regional Guide*, edited by Mickey Hess, vol. 1, chap. 10. Santa Barbara, CA: Greenwood.

Westoff, Ben. 2016. *Original Gangstas: The Untold Story of Dr. Dre, Eazy-E, Ice Cube, Tupac Shakur, and the Birth of West Coast Rap*. New York: Hachette Book Group.

Further Listening

Above the Law. 1994. *Uncle Sam's Curse*. Ruthless Records.

Aceyalone

(Edwin Maximilian Hayes Jr., 1970–, Los Angeles, California)

Aceyalone is an American rapper, poet, and songwriter who records alternative, experimental, and trip hop as well as jazz rap. He was important to the development of 1990s Los Angeles alternative hip hop that resisted the popular West Coast gangsta rap scene. Alternative and jazz hip hop artists opted for intimate venues such as cafés, workshops, and sidewalks, recalling the beat poetry happenings that took place in the 1950s and 1960s. Aceyalone's lyrical content focuses on aspirations, losing inhibitions, romance, and challenging the mind. At times, his lyrics seem akin to nerdcore, as in "The Guidelines" from *A Book of Human Language* or when expressing the need for one's own space in "Five Feet" from *Accepted Eclectic* (2001), both of which use scientific metaphors and metatextuality.

Most of Aceyalone's recordings have received critical acclaim. His solo albums *Accepted Eclectic*, *Love and Hate* (2003), and *Magnificent City* (2006) charted on Billboard's Independent Albums at Nos. 36, 31, and 43, respectively. *Magnificent City* also peaked at No. 39 on Billboard's Top Heatseekers chart. The single "A Beautiful Mine" was arranged and adapted as the opening-credits theme song for the American television series *Mad Men* (2007–2015).

EARLY GROUPS, PROJECTS, AND SOLO ALBUMS

Aceyalone grew up with future rapper and producer Myka 9 (aka Myka Nyne, Mikah 9, or Microphone Mike, Michael Troy, 1969*–). While in high school in the late 1980s, the two, with rapper Self Jupiter (Ornette Glenn, 1970–), formed the short-lived MC Aces (1987–1988)*, a precursor to their Freestyle Fellowship

(1991–1993, 1998–), at open-mic nights at the Good Life Café, a health-food store and restaurant in South Central Los Angeles. Freestyle Fellowship added former high school friend, rapper, and musician P.E.A.C.E. (Mtulazaji Davis, n.d.).

Freestyle Fellowship rapped over jazz, sometimes incorporating R&B and funk, and honed its skills at double-time rapping—rhyming to a slower beat to accommodate multisyllabic words and/or longer lines. The group released the studio albums *To Whom It May Concern* (1991) and *Innercity Griots* (1993) but went on hiatus when Self Jupiter served prison time. The group reunited afterward, recorded more albums, and continues to record as of 2018.

Meanwhile, starting in 1994, Aceyalone and rapper Abstract Rude (Aaron Pointer, n.d.) began the open-mic workshop Project Blowed (1994–) and its related hip hop collective. An alternative to gang and drug activity, the workshop hosts rap battle and open-mic events, freestyle rapping, slam poetry, alternative hip hop, and spoken-word art. Two compilation albums, *Project Blowed* (1995) and *Project Blowed: 10th Anniversary* (2005), resulted from these workshops.

Like 1950s and 1960s California writers, Aceyalone, Myka 9, and Abstract Rude collaborated on jazz poetry between Los Angeles and San Francisco, forming Haiku D'Etat (1997–). Their eponymous debut release (1999) features San Francisco Bay Area musicians. Their second album, *Coup de theatre* (2004), was less successful. Aceyalone has also had a concurrent prolific solo recording career with his studio albums. In addition to the aforementioned albums, he has released *All Balls Don't Bounce* (1995), *A Book of Human Language* (1998), *Hip Hop and the World We Live In* (2002), *Lightning Strikes* (2007), *Aceyalone and the Lonely Ones* (2009), *Leanin' on a Stick* (2013), *Action* (2015), and *Mars* (2016), as well as compilation albums, and made many appearances.

Melissa Ursula Dawn Goldsmith

See also: The United States

Further Reading

Bradley, Adam, and Andrew Dubois, eds. 2010. "Freestyle Fellowship." Under "Part 3: 1993–99: Rap Goes Mainstream" in *The Anthology of Rap*, pp. 387–94. New Haven, CT: Yale University Press.

Lee, Jooyoung. 2009. "Escaping Embarrassment: Face-Work in the Rap Cipher." *Social Psychology Quarterly* 72, no. 4: 306–24.

Further Listening

Aceyalone. 2000. *Accepted Eclectic*. Ground Control Records.

Aceyalone. 2006. *Magnificent City*. Decon.

Afghanistan

Afghanistan had no hip hop scene until 2002 as a result of the Taliban government's (1996–2001) control of radio stations, its ban of the Internet, and its condemnation of music for entertainment. With the institution of a new government under President Hamid Karzai (1957–) in 2002, an Afghan popular music scene began to emerge. By the second decade of the 21st century, hip hop had begun to reshape

Male Afghan teenagers breakdance on knotted rugs during the Sound Central Festival at the French Cultural Center in Kabul. A sign of Afghanistan's emerging hip hop culture since the end of the Taliban government, the Sound Central Festival features live music, as well as graffiti art and hip hop dance showcases. (MASSOUD HOSSAINI/ AFP/GettyImages)

Afghan youth culture. By 2013, hip hop was part of the global music curriculum at Afghanistan's National Institute of Music. The 2013 Sound Central Festival, featuring alternative arts at the French Cultural Center in Kabul, included live performances by hip hop artists such as Ramika Khabiri and Arash Strange (n.d.) and bands such as 143Band (aka Paradise and Diverse, 2008–), Farhad and Matin (aka FM Rap Band, n.d.), and Face Off (n.d.), founded by Abdul Basir Shakeri (n.d.) and Taqi Mohammdai (n.d.), as well as graffiti artists Dark Artery (Abul Qasem Foushani, 1987–) and Shamsia Hassani (1988–). Afghan rap (or AFG rap) has grown explosively on the Internet and includes such artists as Mahmoud Rezai (n.d.), Ali Janjal (n.d.), Aref King (n.d.), Cool AFG Boys (n.d.), and Yasin Guli (n.d.).

As the Afghan hip hop scene grew, women rappers came to the fore. Sonita Alizadeh (1997*–) raps about forced marriage (often of underage girls), violence against women, and the Taliban's ban on women's education. Her 2014 Internet release "Brides for Sale" brought international attention and the opportunity to pursue an education in the United States. A German and Swiss documentary of her life, *Sonita* (2015), won two awards at the 2016 Sundance Film Festival. Paradise Sorouri (1989*–), considered Afghanistan's first female hip hop artist, began rapping while a refugee in Iran. In 2008, Sorouri formed 143Band with boyfriend and fellow rapper Diverse Marwi (1988*–). Both are featured in the Afghan documentary *Hip Hop Kabul* (2013) and, since its filming, are based in Berlin. Soosan Firooz (aka Susan Feroz, 1989*–), an Afghan rapper and television actress, appears in videos wearing jeans and often no headscarf as she delivers lines that challenge traditional views on Afghan women. Another musician, Aryana Saeed (1985–), is a singer from Afghanistan's capital, Kabul, who fuses feminist-themed hip hop with pop. Ramona Khabiri (1995*–), hip hop artist and student at Kabul University, raps for voter turnout and women's rights. She describes backlash from fellow students and threats from the Taliban over her music and her message.

The earliest Afghan hip hop artists brought skills and sensibilities acquired while they were refugees in other countries. DJ Besho (aka DJ Diamond, Bezhan Zafarmal, 1988*–) fled with his family during the Afghan Civil War (1992–1996), immigrating to Germany, where he developed his gangsta-style rapping skills and persona. He considers Tupac Shakur (1971–1996), Vanilla Ice (1967–), and 50 Cent (1975–) his main influences. DJ Besho raps primarily in the Dari language and is intent on shaping a new Afghan cultural identity—encouraging Afghanistan's youth to see themselves first as friends and brothers united in rebuilding and improving their country. The anonymous Los Angeles–based Awesome Qasim (n.d.) raps in Farsi, Pashto, and English and aims to reinforce patriotic values. His 2015 Internet release "Askar Afghan" showed support for Afghan security forces.

Jennifer L. Roth-Burnette

See also: Bliss n' Eso; Davy D; Filmmaking (Documentaries); Graffiti Art

Further Reading

Nordland, Rod, and Fatima Faizi. 2017. "For Afghan Pop Star, Mullahs Aren't Showstoppers." *The New York Times*, August 20, A4.

Stein, Eliot. 2016. "Afghanistan's First Female Rapper: 'If I Stay Silent, Nothing Will Change.'" *The Guardian*, December 1.

Afrika Bambaataa

(aka Afrika Bambaataa Aasim, Kevin Donovan, 1957–, Bronx, New York)

Afrika Bambaataa was a towering figure in New York hip hop and African American culture in the 1970s and 1980s. As the founder of the Universal Zulu Nation (1973–), a loose collection of African American street youths in Harlem, New York, he was highly instrumental in channeling the attention of New York's most notorious gangs through more creative outlets, setting the foundation for what later became known as hip hop culture. By 1980, Afrika Bambaataa was one of the best-known DJs in New York, alongside such luminaries as Grandmaster Flash (1958–) and DJ Kool Herc (1955–). Since that time, hip hop culture has become a global phenomenon and the Universal Zulu Nation has spread overseas.

GANG INVOLVEMENT AND THE UNIVERSAL ZULU NATION

In the years before he founded the Universal Zulu Nation, Afrika Bambaataa was a member and warlord for one of South Bronx's largest and most dangerous gangs, the Black Spades (1968–). In this position, he was central in enforcing the

1971 ceasefire between the city's black and Latino gangs in an era that saw escalating gang violence across the United States. His success with the Universal Zulu Nation was a product of his elevated position, his interest in black liberation, and his personal belief in Islam. His adopted name, which has been claimed to translate as "Chief Affection," was borrowed from a 19th-century Zulu chief who lived in pre-apartheid South Africa, and his Universal Zulu Nation was inspired by the code of honor demonstrated by the black participants of the English and American film *Zulu* (1964). He was known for regularly reviewing the teachings of Elijah Muhammad (1897–1975), a leader of the Nation of Islam, who mentored such black-rights dignitaries as Malcolm X (1925–1965) and Muhammad Ali (Cassius Marcellus Clay Jr., 1942–2016).

As part of the Universal Zulu Nation's activities, Afrika Bambaataa organized block parties. These evening parties were the meeting place for artists who practiced four of the core components of hip hop culture: DJing (turntabling), MCing (rapping), b-boying (breakdancing), and producing graffiti art. These activities, over time, provided a countertide to the violence of the gang era, and as a major figure in this community, Africa Bambaataa became tied not only to the artistic discoveries taking place but also to the positive social change this new creative direction inspired. By the early 1980s, he was himself highly respected as a DJ and had formed several well known DJ crews, including the Jazzy Five (1975–1981)* and Soulsonic Force (1980–). Early singles appeared in 1980 in conjunction with Soulsonic Force and Cosmic Force (n.d.). These included two versions of "Zulu Nation Throw Down." His most influential track, however, came in 1982 with "Planet Rock," a track produced in collaboration with Soulsonic Force. His "Jazzy Sensation," with the Jazzy Five, was released in 1981.

Afrika Bambaataa found inspiration in techno-rock groups such as the German ensemble Kraftwerk (1970–) and the Japanese group Yellow Magic Orchestra (1977–), which can be heard in "Planet Rock." His affinity for techno-rock set the tone not only for "Planet Rock," for which he sampled Kraftwerk's "Trans-Europe Express" (1977), but also for future hip hop and electro-dance trends. "Planet Rock" used only electronic instruments (a TR 808 drum machine, a synthesizer, and a vocoder) under its hip hop vocals and introduced esoteric references to Kraftwerk's "Numbers" as well as "The Mexican" by the English rock group Babe Ruth (1970–1976, 2005–), based on Italian film composer Ennio Morricone's (1928–) melody "Per qualche dollar in più" ("For a Few Dollars More") from the spaghetti Western film of the same title (1965). The song features brief rapped statements and pre-planned lyrics traded between Afrika Bambaataa and the other vocalists and sung over a funky, synthesized bass paired with an aural laser effect. The group uses call-and-response passages with the audience and later leads it in a simple sing-along about the need to "rock" continuously. Several times in the song, the words "planet rock" are sung through a vocoder. Blending Jamaican dancehall bass with synthesized disco beats and techno-rock electronica, the song introduced rap to techno, funk, and drum synthesizers. Afrika Bambaataa's 1983 single, "Looking for the Perfect Beat," continued this trend.

This style, which he called "electro-funk," was enormously influential on the development of rap and electronic dance music over the following decades, with the song not only reaching the top of the U.S. soul and dance charts but also taking the hip hop creative world by storm and changing the trajectory of popular music.

INFLUENCE AND LEGACY

Afrika Bambaataa's influence on hip hop culture and its music is monumental, and his blend of funk, electro-pop, and obscure rock have been responsible for setting into motion some versions of hip hop as we know it today. Still, though he has released numerous tracks and albums and though he was featured in the 1984 American hip hop film *Beat Street*, his star fell somewhat over the decades, and he never again enjoyed the same level of musical acclaim he did in the early 1980s. Although his influence has been less pronounced since the 1980s, it has been nonetheless potent; his support of hip hop culture and creativity at its nascence encouraged an incredible amount of musical variety, and his nurturing of the Universal Zulu Nation was pivotal in turning gang culture into creative culture in the 1970s.

Jessica Leah Getman

See also: Gangs (United States); Nation of Islam; The United States; The Universal Zulu Nation

Further Reading

Chang, Jeff. 2005. "Soul Salvation: The Mystery and Faith of Afrika Bambaataa" and "Zulus on a Time Bomb: Hip Hop Meets the Rockers Downtown." In *Can't Stop Won't Stop: A History of the Hip Hop Generation*, chap. 5 and 8. New York: Picador.

Lamotte, Martin. 2014. "Rebels without a Pause: Hip Hop and Resistance in the City." *International Journal of Urban and Regional Research* 38, no. 2: 686–94.

Further Listening

Afrika Bambaataa. 1986. *Planet Rock: The Album*. Tommy Boy.

Akon

(Aliaume Badara Thiam, 1973–, St. Louis, Missouri)

Akon is a Senegalese American hip hop and popular music artist who lived in Senegal until he was seven years old, when his parents, Mor Thiam (Mor Dogo Thiam, 1941–) and Kiné Thiam (n.d.), relocated to the United States. From humble beginnings, Akon has become one of the most successful singers and entrepreneurs in modern hip hop. His songs, albums, and other products have had record sales, while his philanthropic works have transformed the lives of thousands around the world. Akon's 2006 album, *Konvicted*, was certified triple Platinum in the United States alone by November 2007. His 2008 album, *Freedom*, was certified Platinum and remained on the Billboard 200 for many weeks after its release. Akon's popularity is not restricted to the United States; he has become a star in Africa and Europe, where fans have been mesmerized by his mixture of hip hop and techno with occasional reggae.

Akon's youth was troublesome, as he was arrested several times for crimes such as receiving stolen vehicles. In 1998, at age 25, he submitted a guilty plea for felony

Senegalese-American rapper Akon is best known for his Platinum albums *Konvicted* (2006) and *Freedom* (2008), which fuse hip hop, techno, and reggae. Though questioned about exaggerating his past in prison, Akon continues to use his convict image to motivate others serving prison time to better themselves, and, through his Konfidence Foundation, he has led efforts for improving lives in both the United States and Africa. (Carrienelson1/Dreamstime.com)

gun possession. He was sentenced to three years' probation. Together, the arrests also led to some jail time; however, Wyclef Jean (1969–) gave Akon the opportunity to prepare and release his 2004 debut album *Trouble*, which went viral. Akon tapped into his jail experience in his first single, "Locked Up," turning it into an early example of his use of a prison sentence as a theme—prison was later transformed to become a central image in his ideological, musical, and commercial messages and endeavors.

Akon founded KonLive Distribution (2006–) and Konvict Clothing (2007–), which have both had major successes. By 2008, however, the media and fans confronted Akon for exaggerating his past in prison for the purpose of marketing. He nevertheless continues to use his name as well as convict image and persona to remind himself about his experience and to help motivate others who either are serving or have served time in prison.

Akon has recorded hit songs with such American icons as Snoop Dogg (1971–), Michael Jackson (1958–2009), Whitney Houston (1963–2012), Gwen Stefani (1969–), Lionel Richie (1949–), and Lady Gaga (1986–) but also with other international legends, such as Amadou & Mariam (Amadou Bagayoko, 1954–, and Mariam Doumbia, 1958–) of Mali, Shaggy (1968–) of Jamaica, and Youssou N'dour (1959–) of Senegal. Akon's closest collaborator is Haitian American hip hop and reggae star Jean, with whom he recorded the 2007 hit song "Sweetest Girl (Dollar Bill)."

From the lessons learned in his past, Akon has developed a social consciousness, a sense of cosmopolitanism, and a confidence and conviction in his personal responsibility to uplift other people. For this purpose, he also created the Konfidence Foundation in 2007, an organization aimed at improving the lives of people in Africa and the United States, and, in 2014 he launched Lighting Africa, a project that seeks to provide electricity to millions of people that need it.

Babacar M'Baye

See also: Fashion; Gangsta Rap; Senegal; The United States

Further Reading

Boone, Mary. 2008. *Akon.* Hockessin, DE: Mitchell Lane.

Smith, Emily. 2013. *The Akon Handbook: Everything You Need to Know about Akon.* Aspley, Australia: Emereo.

Further Listening

Akon. 2006. *Konvicted.* Universal Motown/Street Records.

Albania

Albania is a Southeast European nation with a population of approximately three million people. Tirana, its largest city, has more than 800,000 inhabitants. Musicians from Albania, Kosovo, Macedonia, and Montenegro (which all recognize Albanian as an official language), as well as rappers from countries in which Albanians now reside, such as Germany, Switzerland, the United Kingdom, and the United States, helped turn the Albanian hip hop scene into a robust one, especially after French hip hop artists created the first Albanian hip hop festival in 2012. Kosovo's rap scene emerged in the 1990s with early rap groups such as W.N.C. (aka White N—s Clan, n.d.). One of the most prominent early rappers was Getoar Selimi (aka Ghetto Gold, 1982–), who later cofounded the popular rap group Tingulli 3nt (Sound 3nt, 1996–). Albanian hip hop culture has had a large impact on urban youth, despite the government's onetime censorship of radio and television—Albania went from being a Nazi German protectorate to a socialist republic under Enver Hoxha (Enver Halil Hoxha, 1908–1985, in office 1941–1985) to a democratic republic in 1991. The government's loosening of its hold over culture in 1991 allowed hip hop to take root.

Other prominent hip hop bands have included Ritmi i Rrugës (loosely, Rhythm of the Street, 1995–2004), a rap duo from Kosovo that released three studio albums, including *Përjetësisht* (*Eternally*, 2004), and Etno Engjujt (aka Etnon, 1997–), a name that calls attention to the ethnic music incorporated in its songs. In its seven albums, which include *The Dynasty* (2002), *The Best of Albarap* (2003), *Vitamin E* (2005), and *10she* (2007), Etno Engjujt combines ethnic Albanian music with hip hop rhythms and raps about such issues as ethnic and national pride as well as lighter themes such as partying and dancing. The duo models itself on West Coast hip hop, incorporating R&B-style singing into its rap songs.

As of 2018, the most famous Albanian rap group is Banda Butuesi (Butterfly Band, 1997–), which uses chopper rapping and bases its music style on the highly symphonic and dramatic U.S. East Coast sound, with almost no incorporation of traditional Albanian music. Albanian rap groups based in other countries include O.T.R. (On Top of the Rest, 2014–). Composed of Albanians from London who migrated back to Albania in the early 2000s, O.T.R. is led by Noizy (Rigels Rajku, 1986–), an extremely popular Albanian gangsta-style rapper with seven studio albums to his credit. The New York City–based Bloody Alboz (aka T.B.A., 2005–) is an Albanian rap group led by one of Albania's first and most popular rappers, Rebeli (aka Unikkatil, Viktor Palokaj, 1981–), who models his rap songs after the more atmospheric U.S. West Coast G-funk and Southern styles and uses complex instrumentation, including traditional Albanian instruments.

Anthony J. Fonseca

See also: Gangsta Rap

Further Reading

Elezi, Gentian, and Elona Toska. 2017. "Rapping into Power: The Use of Hip Hop in Albanian Politics." In *Hip Hop at Europe's Edge: Music, Agency, and Social Change*, edited by Milosz Miszczynski and Adriana Helbig, chap. 1. Bloomington: Indiana University Press.

Tochka, Nicholas. 2017. "Cosmopolitan Inscriptions? Mimicry, Rap, and Rurbanity in Post-Socialist Albania." In *Hip Hop at Europe's Edge: Music, Agency, and Social Change*, edited by Milosz Miszczynski and Adriana Helbig, chap. 9. Bloomington: Indiana University Press.

Further Listening

The Bloody Alboz. 2005. *Prezenton the Bloody Alboz*. Conqueror Records.

Algeria

Algeria, the 10th-largest country in the world, is a sovereign North African semi-presidential republic. Its capital and most populous city is Algiers, located in the country's far north. The main style of Algerian music is *raï*, a combination of Western music and Bedouin (nomadic Arab peoples who inhabit North Africa's desert regions) music concerned with social issues. Such music was made famous by Khaled (Khaled Hadj Ibrahim, 1960–), a native of Oran who immigrated to France in 1986 and had seven Top 10 hits (including three No. 1 songs) on the French Syndicat National de l'Édition Phonographique (SNEP) album charts. Other styles based on Arabo-Andalusian music—classical Arabic, Bedouin, and Berber music—exist, as do some popular forms of Westernized music.

Events leading up to the Algerian Civil War (1991–2002), as well as the war itself, disrupted hip hop in Algeria. The war broke out because of conflict between the Islamic Salvation Front (FIS), an Islamic fundamentalist party, and the ruling National Liberation Front (FLN), an Algerian and Arab nationalist democratic socialist party. During the early 1990s, supporters of the FIS evolved into several armed groups, such as the Armed Islamic Group (GIA), who between 1992 and 1998 conducted civilian massacres that also targeted journalists and tourists in Algeria as well as terror attacks that spread to France.

Algerian hip hop music has therefore been defined mainly by native Algerian bands and diaspora musicians living in France. Algerian rap can be traced to 1988, when a military massacre of protesting citizens inspired rap crews Intik (1988–2001) and Le Micro Brise le Silence (MBS, The Microphone Breaks the Silence,

1988–2011) to form. Led by these two pioneer bands, rap became a big underground scene. Inspired by Public Enemy (1982–) and French rapper Imhotep (Pascal Perez, 1960–), Intik, a rap and hip hop quartet, went on to release two albums in Darija (Algerian Arabic creole) and French, *Intik* (1999) and *La victoire* (2001). Its sound involves synthesized versions of traditional Algerian music combined with funk, hip hop, rap, and reggae, and its laid-back raps are interspersed with Jamaican-style reggae interludes and Algerian melodies. Using traditional string instruments, synthesizers, and turntables against a hip hop beat, MBS rapped and sang songs critical of the Algerian government in Arabic and French and went on to produce five albums: *Ouled al bahdja* (translated as *Children/Tribe of the Radiant One* but also a nickname for USM Alger, an Algerian football club campaign, 1997), *Hbibti aouama* (*My Lover Is a Good Swimmer*, 1998), *Le micro brise le silence* (1999), *Wellew* (*They Have Returned*, 2001), and *Maquis bla sleh* (*Marquis without Weapons*, 2005).

Algerian diaspora hip hop acts include Paris-born Rim'K (Abdelkrim Brahmi-Benalla, 1978–), L'Algérino (aka L'Algé, Samir Djourhlel, 1981–), Médine (Médine Zaouiche, 1983–), Sinik (aka Malsain, l'Assassin, or S.I.N.I.K., Thomas Idir, 1980–), and Zaho (Zahera Darabid, 1980–). Rim'K, whose family is from Barbacha, Algeria, was raised in the Parisian suburb of Vitry-sur-Seine. He released six solo albums between 2004 and 2018, five of which, *L'enfant du pays* (*Child of the Country*, 2004), *Maghreb United* (2009), *Chef de famille* (*Head of the Family*, 2012), *Monster Tape* (2016), and *Fantôme* (*Ghost*, 2017), have peaked in the SNEP Top 10. Marseille-born L'Algérino, whose family came from Khenchela, Algeria, started singing and rapping at age 11 and quickly began releasing mixtapes. His style involves African- and reggae-infused autotuned singing, and his debut album, *Les derniers seront les premiers* (*The Last Will Be the First*, 2005), was relatively successful, but it was his next three efforts, *Mentalité* (2007), *Effet miroir* (*Mirror Effect*, 2010), and *C'est correct* (*It's Correct*, 2011), that thrust him into the spotlight.

Le Havre–born Médine (Médine Zaouiche, 1983–) raps and performs spoken-word poetry in Kabyle, an Afroasiatic language, and is a practicing Muslim whose songs emphasize the hardships of being Muslim in the Western world. Sinik is a French-language American-style mobb rapper and record label owner whose father is Algerian; he is known for his diss battles and clashes with other rap artists. Canadian-based Zaho (Zahera Darabid, 1980–) is a female Algerian pop and neo soul singer-songwriter who immigrated to Montreal in 1999 and released her debut album *Dima* (*Always* in Arabic) in 2008.

Anthony J. Fonseca

See also: France

Further Reading

Davies, Eirlys E., and Abdelali Bentahila. 2006. "Code Switching and the Globalization of Popular Music: The Case of North African Rai and Rap." *Multilingua* 25, no. 4: 367–92.

Moser, Keith. 2013. "Franco-Maghrebi Rap and Benyoucef's *Le nom du père*." *CLCWeb: Comparative Literature and Culture* 15, no. 4: 9.

Further Listening
Intik. 1999. *Intik.* Saint George Records.
MBS. 1999. *Le micro brise le silence.* Universal Music.

Allen, Harry

(1964–, Brooklyn, New York)

Harry Allen is an American journalist and activist, best known for his publicist role with Public Enemy (1982–), which nicknamed him their media assassin. Allen's primary role was to deal with mainstream media. He specialized in spinning media missteps, such as in 1989 when, shortly after the release of *It Takes a Nation of Millions to Hold Us Back*, rapper Professor Griff (Richard Griffin, 1960–) gave an interview to the *Washington Times* in which he expressed both homophobic and anti-Semitic ideas. Allen was responsible for defusing the tension created by Griff's comments with the goal of keeping Public Enemy in good standing with the media. An early adopter of technology, including the fax machine and the Internet, Allen used all tools at his disposal to disseminate information. By the early 1990s, he had created a hip hop newsletter called *Rap Dot Com* that he disseminated via email; he also advocated the commercial distribution of music online. Allen argued against the claim that African American people were alienated from technology, suggesting that African Americans actually sought out technology and used it in surprising and unexpected ways.

During the early 1980s, Allen formed friendships and professional relationships with a number of people who would go on to become major figures in American hip hop, including Bill Stephney (n.d.), a college radio DJ who befriended Chuck D (1960–) around the time Public Enemy was founded and became president of Def Jam Records (1983–); Dr. Dré (André Brown, 1963–), host of *Yo! MTV Raps*; and other future members of Public Enemy and the Bomb Squad (1986–), including Flavor Flav (1959–). Allen made a brief appearance in "Don't Believe the Hype," a single on *It Takes a Nation of Millions to Hold Us Back*. In the track, Flavor Flav calls out Allen and asks about the band's reputation, to which Allen responds, "Don't believe the hype." He has also made spoken-word cameos on other Public Enemy tracks: "More News at 11" (1991) and "Harry Allen's Interactive Superhighway Phone Call to Chuck D" (1994).

As a writer, Allen has contributed articles on hip hop to a number of respected media outlets, including *Essence*, *Spin*, *Village Voice*, and *Wired*. In 1992, he created the Rhythm Cultural Institute, a nonprofit organization dedicated to promoting hip hop music and culture. Since 2014, he has served as an adviser to the Archives of African American Music and Culture (AAAMC) at Indiana University, Bloomington.

Amanda Sewell

See also: The Bomb Squad; Public Enemy; The United States

Further Reading
Chang, Jeff. 2005. *Can't Stop Won't Stop: A History of the Hip Hop Generation.* New York: Picador.

Harrington, Richard. 1989. "Public Enemy's Rap Record Stirs Jewish Protests." *The Washington Post*, December 29, D4.

Myrie, Russell. 2008. *Don't Rhyme for the Sake of Riddlin': The Authorized Story of Public Enemy.* New York: Canongate.

Angola

Angola is a South African country that won its independence from Portugal in 1975, putting into power a one-party state that is Marxist-Leninist. Independence sparked the Angolan Civil War (1975–2002), when the Soviet-backed People's Movement for the Liberation of Angola (MPLA) was victorious. Since 2002, Angola has become a presidential unitary state. Hip hop in Angola, known as rap Angolano, was imported from America in the late 1980s. Angolan hip hop fuses African beats with Caribbean music such as Jamaican reggae and Angolan *kuduru* (a popular music that developed in the 1980s in Luanda). It combines drum machine beats, sometimes sampled Trinbagonian soca and Guadeloupean zouk, and Portugese lyrics. Portugese hip hop, commonly called hip hop Tuga, has also been influential on Angolan hip hop. Rappers prefer Portugese, the country's official language, but they sometimes use American vernacular. Rap Angolano is used for social activism and is often critical of government corruption and the resulting socioeconomic disparity; therefore, many Angolan hip hop artists work under aliases only.

Luanda, Angola's capital city, is the main center for hip hop, and mostly black Africans (Ovimbundu and Ambundu) participate in rap music creation. Notable 1990s pioneering Luandan rappers include Kool Klever (Nelson Rosa, n.d.), Nelboy Dastha Burda (n.d.), Das Primeiro (The First, Rui da Silva, 1968–), and Angolan Portugese Ikonoklasta (Henrique Luaty da Silva Beirão, 1981–) as well as the group Pobres Sem Culpa (Poor without Guilt, 1990s–2000s*). Because of the Angolan Civil War, many musicians have established and/or continue careers in exile. For example, in the late 1990s, pioneering Luandan rapper Mutu Moxy (aka Intelektu, Genio Lyricista*, 1977*–) immigrated to Johannesburg and then Cape Town before settling in the 2000s in France. Intelektu raps in Portugese, fuses hip hop with jazz and soul, and uses boombap production values. Notable Angolan hip hop artists who have made their careers in South Africa include Tribo Sul (Tribe of Soldiers, 1992*–), a pioneering Lugandan trio who rap in Portugese and English and who since 1999 have lived in exile in Cape Town, and Jamayka Poston (1976–), who was born in Malange and grew up in Luanda. Poston is now an MC for Conquering Lions (2003*–), which performs in Portugese.

The duo Hemoglobina (2000–), which is based in Moscow and raps in Portugese, was in the group Wave Gang (1999*) in Luanda, which released the first Angolan mixtape, *Ruas de Luanda* (*Streets of Luanda*, 2000). Conductor (Andro Carvalho, n.d.), from Luanda, was based in Lisbon as a member of the electronic dance and techno fusion project Buraka Som Sistema (Buraca Sound System, 2006–2016) before returning home to form Conjunto Ngonguenha (2002–) with Ikonoklasta, among other MCs. Post-Angolan Civil War rap activity has increased with such acts as MCK (aka Mc K, Katro, Katrogi Nhanga Lwamba, 1981–), Yannick Afroman

(Yannic Manuel Ngombo, n.d.), Phay Grand (n.d.), Dmaster DJ (Silvestre Marcos Azevedo da Encarnação, 1991–), DJ Pastrana (Evandro Franco, n.d.), and Gaia Beat (1992–).

Angolan rappers, however, are still persecuted. Ikonoklasta and MCK were jailed, and Angolan police have beaten their fans. Their lyrical content has focused on informing listeners about atrocities conducted by the Angolan government as well as protesting government corruption, making revolutionary calls to action to rise against the government, and articulating the need for sociopolitical change in Angola. Some of these rappers have called the Angolan government "Babylon," which suggests the same meaning that Jamaicans use in their reggae songs against the wealthy, corrupt, and greedy people who are often in positions of power.

Melissa Ursula Dawn Goldsmith

See also: Portugal

Further Reading

Moorman, Marissa J. 2014. "Anatomy of Kuduro: Articulating the Angolan Body Politic after the War." *African Studies Review* 57, no. 3: 21–40.

Sheridan, Garth. 2014. "Fruity *Batidas*: The Technologies and Aesthetics of Kuduro." *Dancecult: Journal of Electronic Dance Music Culture* 6, no. 1: 83–96.

Further Listening

Intelektu. 2005. *Verbalogia.* Vocab Lab.

MCK. 2012. *Proibido ouvir isto* (*Forbidden to Hear This*). Diferencial Produções/Masta K Produsons.

Ant Banks

(Anthony Banks, 1966–, Oakland, California)

Ant Banks is an American rapper, beatmaker, and producer who got his start in the Oakland, California, area by creating beats for various MCs and producing their albums independently on his short-lived Raw Dog Records label (1988–1989)*, not to be confused with the Jacksonville, Florida–based Raw Dog Records (n.d.). He is rumored to have sold hundreds of thousands of off-label albums in the Oakland and San Francisco Bay areas out of the trunk of his car before becoming a major-label songwriter and performer on the New York City–based Jive Records (1981–) label, for which he produced three albums.

Ant Banks's interest in music began at an early age, when he became a member of his school band and a multi-instrumentalist. Using a Casio digital keyboard, he started to create funk beats, at first emulating George Clinton (1941–) before trying his hand at original compositions. His hip hop career began when he worked with Oakland lyricist and rapper M.C. Ant (Anthony Jerel Thomas, 1970–1999), producing the album *The Great* (1988).

Ant Banks has four solo albums, *Sittin' on Somethin' Phat* (1991), *The Big Badass* (1994), *Do or Die* (1995), and *Big Thangs* (1997), as well as two albums with his group T.W.D.Y. (aka Ant Banks Presents T.W.D.Y., 1999–2000), *Derty Werk* (1999) and *Lead the Way* (2000). His funk-influenced basslines (with lots of slap bass) are considered influential by many hip hop and electronica artists, including MC Ren (Lorenzo Jerald Patterson, 1969–) and Daft Punk (1993–). His sound is defined by heavy use of synthesizer and keyboard and singsong rap style that can best described as old-school gangsta rap. As of 2018, Ant Banks has over 170 production credits to his name.

Anthony J. Fonseca

See also: The United States

Further Reading

Campbell, Kermit E. 2005. "Can't Knock the Hustle? The Gangsta Ethos from Stag-O-Lee to Snoop D-o-double-g." In *Getting' Our Groove On: Rhetoric, Language, and Literacy for the Hip Hop Generation*, chap. 3. Detroit, MI: Wayne State University Press.

Ciccariello-Maher, George, and Jeff St. Andrews. 2010. "Between Macks and Panthers: Hip Hop in Oakland and San Francisco." In *Hip Hop in America: A Regional Guide*, edited by Mickey Hess, vol. 1, chap. 11. Santa Barbara, CA: Greenwood.

Further Listening

Ant Banks. 1994. *The Big Badass*. Jive.

Antipop Consortium

(aka Tri-Pinnacle, 1997–2002, 2007–, New York City, New York)

Antipop Consortium is an American alternative and experimental hip hop group that also records IDM (intelligent dance music). Its studio albums include *The Isolationist* (1999), *Tragic Epilogue* (2000), *Shopping Carts Crashing* (2001), *Arrhythmia* (2002), *Antipop vs. Matthew Shipp* (2003), and *Fluorescent Black* (2009), with the last receiving the strongest critical acclaim. Antipop Consortium has also released the EP *The Ends against the Middle* (2001), among several singles and remix albums. It collaborates with other hip hop artists, such as DJs Vadim (n.d.), Logic (Jason Kibler, 1972–), Krush (Hideaki Ishi, 1962–), and Dee Nasty (Daniel Bigeault, 1960–), as well as avant-garde and free-jazz pianist, composer, and bandleader Matthew Shipp (1960–), American bassist and record label owner Bill Laswell (1955–), and U.K. trip hop band Attica Blues (1995–).

In 1997, rappers Beans (Robert Edward Stewart II, 1971–), High Priest (aka Hprizm, Kyle J. Austin, n.d.), and M. Sayyid (Maurice Greene, n.d.) met producer Earl Blaize (n.d.) at a poetry slam in New York City. With members developing production skills, the group released its earliest singles and two albums on Dan the Automator's (Daniel M. Nakamura, 1966–) record label 75 Ark (1996–2001), which specialized in experimental hip hop, including the U.K. indie raga rock and alternative dance band Cornershop's (1991–) *When I Was Born for the 7th Time*. Antipop Consortium's approach to hip hop consisted of stream-of-consciousness rapping and heavy use of electronica, creating electro-rap. In 2000, Antipop Consortium signed with Warp Records (1989–), which specialized in a variety of electronica, including IDM, music with a dance beat that derived from acid house, U.K. breakbeat, and Detroit techno music, yet with the cerebral sense that appeals to listeners of ambient music. Though the group had just a cult following, its sound was appealing to indie rock listeners. In 2001, Antipop Consortium performed in Europe to open for Radiohead on its *Amnesiac* tour.

By 2002, Antipop Consortium had disbanded, primarily to work on separate projects but also because of creative differences. Beans began his solo career with his solo debut album *Tomorrow Right Now* (2003), also produced by Warp. High Priest collaborated with various artists, such as West Coast alternative hip hop rapper Aceyalone (1970–), and formed Airborn Audio (2002–) with M. Sayidd. But despite whatever creative differences existed, each worked on psychedelic-sounding hip hop, and the group reunited in 2007 and recorded its latest album two years later on Big Dada Recordings (1990–), a U.K. label owned by English electronica, house, hip hop, and trip hop (downtempo) duo Coldcut (1986–).

Melissa Ursula Dawn Goldsmith

See also: The United States

Further Reading
Freeman, Phil. 2003. "Perfect Strangers." *Jazziz* 20, no. 11: 42.
Kot, Greg. 2002. "The Hip Hop Underground Mixes It Up." *Chicago Tribune*, April 28, 7.1.

Further Listening
Antipop Consortium. 2009. *Fluorescent Black*. Big Dada Recordings.

Anwar, Joni

(aka Joni Raptor, 1981–, Bangkok, Thailand)

Joni Anwar, of Indonesian Scottish ancestry, is a Thai pop, R&B, and hip hop singer as well as songwriter and actor. Although he did not emerge on the music scene until 1994, he began his career in entertainment by acting in television commercials for products such as Ovaltine (a milk-flavoring product) and Bata (footwear and fashion accessories). His music career began when he (as Joni Raptor) and Kenyan rapper Louis Scott (1982–) formed the rap and R&B boy band duo Raptor (1994–1998) in Bangkok and signed with RS Public Company Limited (RS Promotion, 1976–), a Thai entertainment company that handles multimedia, digital, and physical distribution, copyright collection, and concert bookings. Raptor had a hit with "Kid Thung Ter," and its second album, *WAAB Boys* (1996), went Platinum.

After becoming a teen icon and trendsetter in fashion as a member of Raptor, which disbanded in 1998, Anwar went solo, first performing on his younger brother Anan's (1986–) eponymous debut album. As a solo singer, Joni Anwar's most popular albums are *Bad Boy* (2000), *Free Man* (2002), and *Outtaspace* (2003). The song "Go Now" (2002) was named Record of the Year by 104.5 FAT Radio, as was the song "Outtaspace." Anwar then went to New York to work on an album called *Katsue* (2004) with producer, DJ, and singer Montonn Jira (aka Jay, 1978*–). He has since been semiretired from music.

Anwar's films include *Ahingsa—Jikko mee gam* (aka *Ahingsa* [*Karma—Stop to Run*], 2005), a teen comedy-thriller concerned with romance and clubbing. His music is a cross between smooth R&B and soul and high-energy synth-pop–infused hip hop with a strong Bollywood influence.

Anthony J. Fonseca

See also: Thailand

Further Reading

Anon. 2007. "Going Underground." Under "Lifestyle" in *Phuket Gazette* (Thailand), September 8–14, 18.

Sinlapalavan, Budsarakham. 2012. "Fun and Games with Raptor." *The Nation* (Bangkok), April 24.

Argentina

Argentina, a South American republic, is the largest Spanish-speaking country in the world. Its music is based on native traditional forms, such as the *tango, chacarera,* and *chamamé,* although folk, rock, pop, and classical are popular. Argentine popular music (rock nacional) has many forms: rock, pop, ska, reggae, funk, folk, blues, and hip hop. Early Argentine rock was influenced by British rock, but by the mid-1960s, localization of the music had begun to occur. Vox Dei (1967–1981,

In the 1980s and 1990s Afro-Argentine reggae singer and rapper Fidel Nadal popularized hip hop with his Buenos Aires rasta-punk band, Todos Tus Muertos (All Your Dead), which he founded in 1984. But by the time he started his prolific solo recording career in 2000, Nadal had focused more on reggae and other kinds of Latin music, including cumbia, opting for a gentler sound. (Pedro González Castillo/LatinContent/Getty Images)

1986–) became the country's biggest rock band, recording 10 albums. Argentine reggae is popular, with notable artists such as roots reggae band Los Cafres ("The Unfaithful" in Arabic, 1987–) and singer Fidel Nadal (1965–), who not only sings but raps in his upbeat reggae. Rap was brought to Argentina in the 1980s by American hip hop films such as *Wild Style* (1983), but generally speaking, very little hip hop is currently being produced in Argentina. Electronic music became popular in the 1990s, and DJs such as Diego Ro-K (Diego Roca, n.d.), Hernán Cattáneo (1983–), and Bad Boy Orange (Eduardo La Forgia, n.d.) began to flourish.

The capital, Buenos Aires, is the center of Argentinian hip hop, and preferred rapping texts are in Spanish. Rap recordings are becoming more common, but as recently as 2013, rap artists had recorded only 30 albums in Buenos Aires, mainly to share on social networking sites. Early Argentine rap artists include Illya Kuryaki and the Vanlderramas (1991–) and Sindicato Argentino del Hip Hop (1992–). Grammy-winning Sindicato is a hip hop trio that infuses its hip hop beats with funk; Illya Kuryaki and the Vanlderramas is a duo that synthesized hip hop–style beats with funk. Groups such as these paved the way for other 1990s Argentine rap acts, such as Actitud María Marta (aka Hardcore, 1995–) and Mustafa Yoda (n.d.). Actitud María Marta is a socially conscious all-female hip hop quintet whose beats show a Latin American and Jamaican influence; Yoda started out as a pioneer freestyle rapper and member of the group La Organización (1998–) but became a label owner.

Second-generation hip hop acts include Emanero (Federico Andres Giannoni, 1988–), Kris Alaniz (1989*–), and Koxmoz (2002–). Emanero, a rapper and actor known for clever, tongue-twisting verses as well as catchy choruses that have a mainstream appeal, began rapping in his teens and released his first demo in 2004. Alaniz is a female rapper who combines gangsta beats with bossa nova and soul. Koxmoz (2002–), a rap group that blends hip hop with electronica, creates raps that are known for being edgy and erudite. The younger generation of Argentinian hip hop musicians is a combination of skilled rappers who use introspective and playful rhymes and craft tongue-twisting verses and those who master catchy, singsong choruses.

Anthony J. Fonseca

See also: Chile; Germany

Further Reading
Castillo-Garsow, Melissa, and Jason Nichols. 2016. *La Verdad: An International Dialogue on Hip Hop Latinidades*. Columbus: Ohio State University Press.
Kane, Stephanie C. 2009. "Stencil Graffiti in Urban Waterscapes of Buenos Aires and Rosario, Argentina." *Crime, Media, Culture* 5, no. 1: 9–28.

Further Listening
Actitud María Marta. 2008. *Con perfume revolución* (*With Perfume Revolution*). Conciencia Organizada Con Sexto Sentido.
Emanero. 2014. *Tres.* S-Music/Haciendo Bulla.

Further Viewing
Bercetche, Segundo, Diane Ghogomu, and Sebastián Muñoz, dirs. 2014. *Buenos Aires Rap*. Buenos Aires, Argentina: Self-released.

Ashanthi

(Ashanthi De Alwis, 1981*–, Colombo, Sri Lanka)

Ashanthi is a Sinhalese rapper, singer-songwriter, and sound-recording producer from Colombo, Sri Lanka's capital city. Called by many the queen of Sri Lankan hip hop, she is the only female Sri Lankan rapper with an international recording contract, having signed in 2006 with Universal Music Group (1996–). Her style combines rap, pop, R&B, and traditional Sinhalese music. Inspired by Beyoncé (1981–), the Black Eyed Peas (1995–), and Jessie J (Jessica Ellen Cornish, 1988–), her musical style has mainstream appeal, resembling uplifting old-school rap and favoring texts about romantic heartbreak. Ashanthi's vocal range is soprano.

Ashanthi's father, Antoinette de Alwis (n.d.), is a professional pop and jazz vocalist. Ashanthi herself grew up formally studying and singing classical, jazz, and Broadway music as well as traditional Sinhalese songs. In 2000, she rapped as a crewmember for the most internationally successful Sinhalese hip hop duo, BnS (Bathiya and Santhush, 1998–). She then became part of the short-lived pop and R&B duo Ashanthi 'n' Ranidu (2001–2002) and released under the Sony (1929–) label *Oba Magemai* (2002), an album of Sinhalese and English songs that were mostly composed by Ranidu (Ranidu Lankage, 1982–). The title track peaked at No. 1 on the Sri Lanka song chart.

By 2002, Ashanthi was pursuing a solo career, rapping in both Sinhalese and English. She sang on television and radio commercials for Coca-Cola, Tang, and Marmite, among others, and toured worldwide. With Universal, she has since released *Sandawathuren* (*Water from the Moon*, aka *Seethala Wathuren, I'm Getting Wet*, 2006), *Rock the World* (2013), and *Daas Panawa* (*Both Eyes [on] Panawa*, 2014). *Rock the World* was her first English album. It features the single "Let's Give Peace a Chance," written by Ashanthi in both English and Sinhala, featuring Hindi vocals by Indian playback and pop singer Benny Dayal (1984–).

Since 2010, she has owned Ethno Entertainment Audio and Visual Productions and Ashanthi's School of Music in Colombo. In 2013, she became the first female Sri Lankan hip hop artist to release a globally distributed album in English. Also in 2013, Ashanthi was the subject of harsh public criticism for her homage to "Gangnam Style," subtitled "English R&B Remix." This YouTube single sampled South Korean hip hop artist PSY's (1977–) international viral video hit "Gangnam Style" (2012).

Melissa Ursula Dawn Goldsmith

See also: PSY; Sri Lanka

Further Reading

Anon. 2012. "Grabbing the World's Attention with Pop, Rock, and Soul." *Daily News* (Colombo, Sri Lanka), September 21.

Anon. 2017. "Hip Hop Phenomenon." *Daily News* (Colombo, Sri Lanka), July 25.

Saucier, Paul Khalil, and Kumarini Silva. 2014. "Keeping It Real in the Global South: Hip Hop Comes to Sri Lanka." *Critical Sociology* 40, no. 2: 295–300.

Further Listening

Ashanthi. 2006. *Sandawathuren* (*Water from the Moon*, aka *Seethala Wathuren, I'm Getting Wet*). Universal Music.

Ashanthi. 2013. *Rock the World.* Universal Music.

Ashanti

(Ashanti Shequoiya Douglas, 1980–, Glen Cove, New York)

Ashanti is an American R&B, pop, and neo soul singer-songwriter, dancer, model, actress, and record producer. She is best known for her hit song "Foolish" (2002), which reached No. 1 on Billboard's Hot 100, as well as for her successful collaborations with notable hip hop artists and work with Disney (1923–). Ashanti's vocal range is lyric soprano, and most of her songs focus on love, relationships, fame, and overcoming adversity.

She had a few false starts in music, first with Bad Boy Records (1993–), then with Jive Records (1981–) and Epic Records (1953–), but in 2001 Ashanti asked Irv Gotti (Irving Domingo Lorenzo Jr., 1979–) of Murder Inc. Records (1997–), which became the INC Records (2004–), to produce her studio demos; he asked her to compose lyrical R&B responses to several rappers' calls and to appear on a few albums. Ashanti's first Billboard Hot 100 hits were therefore appearances on American rapper Ja Rule's (Jeffrey Atkins, 1976–) "Always on Time" and American rapper Fat Joe's (Joseph Antonia Cartagena, 1970–) "What's Luv" (both 2001).

Her success continued with *Ashanti* (2002), which was certified triple Platinum and peaked at No. 1 on the Billboard 200 albums chart. *Ashanti* also won the 2003 Grammy Award for Best Contemporary R&B Album. *Soul Train* (1971–2006) awarded Ashanti their Aretha Franklin Award for Entertainer of the Year. Her *Chapter II* (2003) also went Platinum despite an FBI investigation of Murder Inc. Records.

In 2004, she released her third Platinum album, *Concrete Rose*—its title was based on Tupac Shakur's (1971–1996) posthumously published poetry collection *The Rose That Grew from Concrete* (1999)—and in 2005 and 2008, she released *Collectibles by Ashanti* (a remix album of *Concrete Rose*) and *The Declaration*. The following year, Murder Inc. Records ended Ashanti's contract, but in 2014, she returned to hip hop with *Braveheart* under her own production label, Written (2013–).

Melissa Ursula Dawn Goldsmith

See also: The United States

Further Reading

Norment, Lynn. 2005. "Ashanti: Answers Critics and Doubters." *Ebony* 60, no. 5: 154–56, 159, 161.

Wiltz, Teresa. 2002. "Hip Hop's Ashanti, Getting No R-E-S-P-E-C-T." *The Washington Post*, August 17, C01.

Further Listening

Ashanti. 2004. *Concrete Rose*. INC Records.

Asia One

(Anonymous, 1971–, Denver, Colorado)

Asia One, considered one of the best-known b-girls in the world, is committed to introducing hip hop dance and culture to youth worldwide. Growing up in Denver with a father from China and a mother from the United States, Asia One did not believe she fully belonged to either culture. As a teenager, she turned to drugs but then discovered hip hop, and breakdancing became her creative outlet. She opened Denver's first hip hop shop and workspace, La Casa del Fonk (1991/1992–1993). Here she helped build Denver's hip hop community with fellow dancers, such as Denver-born Fienz (Delfino Rodriguez, 1973–). In 1994, she moved to San Diego and then Los Angeles, where she danced with Bronx-based Rock Steady Crew (RSC, 1977–) and Universal Zulu Nation's (1973–) Mighty Zulu Kweens (n.d.). Her main b-girl contemporaries were also from New York: Honey Rockwell (Ereina Valencia, n.d.) from the Bronx and Rokafella (Ana García, 1971–) from Harlem. That same year, Asia One established B-Boy Summit, which was originally formed as a community event to enable her crew to find places to dance. In 1997, she established No Easy Props, an organization and dance crew that sets hip hop dance standards as well as provides after-school hip hop educational programs and classes in Los Angeles. At times, No Easy Props has included legendary hip hop dancers as instructors, such as Rock Steady Crew's (1977–) Crazy Legs (1966–). Since the 2000s, No Easy Props has had a European chapter.

Asia One's hip hop activism includes engaging youth in hip hop culture and educating those interested in aspects of hip hop dance, especially battling (when dancers challenge each other aggressively) and a metatextual understanding of the culture (she calls it "overstanding"). Fueling her hip hop activism are instances such as the 1999 B-Boy Summit at Venice Beach, California, in which participants were arrested and detained for dancing. She understands that hip hop can be used as an empowerment tool to create global change.

Asia One excels at slow moves and freezes, air and side chairs, and cleanness in overall technique. Her own fascination with battling stems from believing that despite training, winning the battle is also about the moment. She has danced in many videos by various bands, including the Black Eyed Peas (1995–) and A Tribe Called Quest (1985–1998, 2006–2013, 2015–). Asia One also produces hip hop dance videos.

Melissa Ursula Dawn Goldsmith

See also: Battling; Breakdancing; Hip Hop Dance; Rock Steady Crew; The United States; The Universal Zulu Nation

Further Reading

García, Ana "Rokafella." 2005. Introduction to *We B*Girlz* by Nika Kramer and Martha Cooper. New York: powerHouse Books.

Goddess, Rha, and JLove Calderón, eds. 2006. "Holding the Planet: Motherhood, Mother U.S." In *We Got Issues: A Young Woman's Guide to a Bold, Courageous, and Empowered Life.* Novato, CA: New World Library.

Further Viewing

Calderón, JLove, dir. 2013. *Asia One: Expect the Unexpected.* Los Angeles: JLove Calderón and Asia One.

Australia

Australia, a country in Oceania, is the sixth-largest country in the world by landmass. Hip hop emerged there in the early 1980s, after television broadcasts of music videos such as Blondie's (1974–1982, 1997–) "Rapture" (1981) and Malcolm McLaren's (1946–2010) "Buffalo Gals" (1982) introduced rap, turntablism (in "Rapture" as a visual image only), graffiti, and breakdancing. Hip hop was immediately taken as the culture of disadvantaged urban populations—mostly poor immigrant and indigenous youth. The earliest hip hop scenes were in Sydney, Melbourne, and Perth, with the earliest b-boy crews, Bigg Noiz Krew (1980*–) and Wickid Force Breakers (1980*–), emerging in Melbourne.

In 1606, Dutch explorers discovered Australia, originally naming it Nieuw-Holland. In 1770, Great Britain claimed the eastern half of Australia, and by 1788, it was sending settlers to New South Wales via penal transportation. Six self-governed colonies federated in 1901 as states to form the Commonwealth of Australia, a federal parliamentary constitutional monarchy. Prior to European colonialism and Great Britain's settlement efforts, Australia had been home to about 250 diverse indigenous Australian groups. Through European conflict, land theft, transmission of infectious diseases, utilization and destruction of resources (for example, the 1850s gold rush), and government-sanctioned efforts to thin, relocate, and assimilate indigenous Australians, this population has dwindled to just 145 groups, with 13 nonendangered languages remaining.

On February 13, 2008, a public government apology was issued to the Stolen Generations, Australian Aboriginal, and Torres Strait Islanders (culturally and ethnic Melanesians related to indigenous Papua New Guineans), who were forcibly removed between 1871 and 1970. Surviving indigenous Australians include the Anangu, Aranda, Koori, Murri, Ngunnawal, Nyungar, Tiwi, Wangai, Yamatji, and Yolngu peoples. Majority populations are mostly white, while minority populations are Indian, Chinese, and indigenous. Populations are concentrated in eastern coastal urban cities such as Sydney, Melbourne, Brisbane, Adelaide, and the capital, Canberra. Perth, on the southwest coast, is the main exception.

As of 2018, over one-quarter of Australia's population are immigrant expatriates. Most are from England, New Zealand, China, India, the Philippines, and Vietnam. English is the official language, and Australians, including most indigenous Australians, speak British English. Australian Aboriginal English has also developed, borrowing phrases and grammatical structures from indigenous Australian languages.

Traditional musical practices that have become well known over time include ceremonial music that employs instruments such as the *bilma* (clapsticks that establish a beat) and didgeridoo (a long aerophone that requires circular breathing and makes onomatopoetic sounds and that indigenous Australians refer to by regional names—for example, the Aranda in Alice Springs call it the *Iipirra*). Indigenous Australian instruments have been used often in popular music. The Sydney alternative rock band Midnight Oil (1976–2002, 2016–2017), for example, has used a didgeridoo in live performances of its song "The Dead Heart" (1987). Other kinds of traditional music include Celtic-inspired folk music such as bush ballads, of which Australia's unofficial national anthem, Banjo Paterson's (Andrew Paterson, 1864–1941) "Waltzing Matilda" (written in 1895, published in 1903), is an example.

EARLY HIP HOP IN AUSTRALIA

With an established music industry, including the Australian Recording Industry Association's (ARIA, 1983–) Charts (1988–), Australia was fertile ground for rock, pop, soul, R&B, reggae, and other kinds of popular music. In 1987, Mighty Big Crime's (1987–1988*) "16 Tons," a rendition of Merle Travis's (1917–1983) 1946 country hit about a coal miner, became Australia's first hip hop release. A year later, the first Australian compilation album was released. *Down Under by Law* included tracks by Mighty Big Crime, the alternative funk rock and disco band Swoop (1991–1999), and Sydney-based Westside Posse (aka Sound Unlimited, 1990–1994), whose members were of Russian as well as mixed-Spanish and Filipino descent; Westside Posse rapped about racism, poverty, and overcoming adversity. The group's single, "Saturday," from its studio album *A Postcard from the Edge of the Underside* (1992), featured members of the pioneering hip hop and ragga rap group Def Wish Cast (DWC, 1989–1995, 2002–), whose debut studio album was *Knights of the Underground Table* (1993).

Other 1990s acts included Sydney's South West Syndicate (1992–2003); Melbourne's Bias B (Adam Stevens, n.d.), Brad Strut (Brad Itter, n.d.), and Pegz (aka MC Pegasus, Tirren Staaf, 1977–); Lismore's Skunkhour (formerly Skunk, 1991–2001); and Canberra's Koolism (aka Tribe Ledda L, 1992–). London-born MC Opi (1971–), of Australian Irish Celtic and Ghanaian descent, appeared on Australian pop and R&B artist Christine Anu's (1970–) hit rendition of Australian rock-acoustic singer-songwriter Paul Kelly's (1955–) "The Last Train" (1994). MC Opi was the first female rapper in Australia to receive national recognition through ARIA.

Though Virgin Records (1972–) produced the earliest hip hop, Capital Records (1942–) soon created an offspring company, Obese Records (1995–2016), headed by Pegz. Obese became Australia's largest hip hop label, with studios and stores in Melbourne. One of its artists, Hilltop Hoods (1994–), from Adelaide, became the country's most famous and influential hip hop act. Hilltop Hoods incorporated jazz, funk, electronica, rock, and punk into hip hop. Five of Hilltop Hoods' seven studio albums were ARIA-certified Platinum. These included *The Calling* (2003), *The Hard Road* (2006), *State of the Art* (2009), *Drinking from the Sun* (2012), and *Walking under Stars* (2014). *The Hard Road* won Hilltop Hoods the honor of becoming the first Australian hip hop group to have a No. 1 hit on the ARIA Albums Chart. Lyrical content focused on urban and suburban life, social and economic injustice, racial inequality, American celebrity, ageism, and antiwar sentiments. Hilltop Hoods was involved with the collaborative-turned-collective Certified Wise Crew (2000*–), which linked its members to other Obese-produced Adelaide hip hop acts such as Vents (aka Vents One, Vents Uno, Joseph Lardner, 1983–) and Funkoars (1999–). Meanwhile, Koolism, a duo consisting of MC and lyricist Hau Latukefu (Langomie-Hau Latukefu, 1976–), of Tongan descent and from Queanbeyan, Australia, and producer, musician, and turntablist DJ Rampage (aka Danielsan Ichiban, Daniel Elleson, 1975–), from Auckland, New Zealand, emerged. As of 2018, Koolism is best known for its second album, *Part Three: Random Thoughts* (2004), which won an ARIA music award. Lyrical themes include Polynesian pride, family, war and terrorism, braggadocio, and survival. Though their music includes some electronica and other instruments, Koolism's sound often resembles American old-school hip hop.

Though it developed further in New Zealand with Urban Pacifika, Pacific Island hip hop was also recorded in Sydney. Just one example is Sydney-born rapper 6 Pound (Charles Lomu, n.d.). Fiji-born MC Trey (Thelma Thomas, n.d.) focuses beyond Pacific Island hip hop. Much earlier New Zealand Urban Pacifika acts, such as Sisters Underground (1990–1995) and the Otara Millionaires Club (OMC, 1992–2010), had hits both at home and in Australia.

Melbourne's 1200 Techniques (1997–2005) fused hardcore hip hop with funk, jazz, electronica, breakbeat, ragga, rock, soul, and drum and bass. The trio's music was retro and old-school, using gangsta raps that focused on Melbourne street life, violence, and poverty. Contemporary acts included Mexico-born but Sydney-based rapper, songwriter, MC, and radio personality Maya Jupiter (Melissha Martinez, 1978–); Lebanese Australian rapper, programmer, and actor Sleek the Elite (Paul Nakad, 1975–); Melbourne's hip hop, electronica, and neo soul producer Plutonic Lab (Leigh Ryan, n.d.); and North Perth rapper Drapht (aka Paul Reid, Paul Gary James Ridge, 1982–).

Sydney also produced the groups Bliss n' Eso (BnE, Bliss n' Esoterikizm, 2000–) and the Herd (2001–), while Melbourne produced the groups TZU (1999–) and Hyjak N Torcha (2000–); Perth produced the crew Downsyde (1996–). By the early 2000s, BnE had become internationally known through its 2004 studio album *Flowers in the Pavement*, which included "Hip Hop Blues," a track produced by contemporary group Hilltop Hoods' Suffa (Matthew David Lambert, 1977–). Two of BnE's studio albums were certified Platinum: *Running on Air* (2010) and *Circus in the Sky* (2013). The band focused on street life, sex, partying, and drugs—but it also began to introduce issues such as the evils of mass consumerism, and it preached music as salvation. The Herd became famous for its live shows and incorporation of acoustic instruments such as piano, accordion, clarinet, guitars, and bass. One of its DJs and producers, Traksewt (Kenny Sabir, 1975*–), founded the prolific hip hop label Elefant Traks (1998–).

CURRENT HIP HOP

Many pioneering acts are still active, including Drapht and Downsyde. MC Layla (Layla Rose Hanbury, 1982–), who is married to Downsyde's Dazastah (Darren Reutens, n.d.), belongs to the Obese Records collective Syllabolix (SBX, Syllaboliks, 2000*–), which also has its own label, SBX (2000–). In 2005, the Hilltop Hoods Initiative was created in collaboration with Arts SA to financially assist new South Australian hip hop artists in manufacturing and distributing a recording on compact disc. Since 2008, Hilltop Hoods has recorded on its own Adelaide-based label, Golden Era Records (2008*–). Koolism's Latukefu's solo career includes the studio albums *Let It Be Known* (2014) and *The No End Theory* (2015), the latter fusing jazz, R&B, and new jack swing with hip hop. He collaborates with Hilltop Hoods, among others, on EPs and mixtapes. As Dan Elleson, Koolism's DJ Rampage has written, produced, and collaborated on tracks recorded by Australian hip hop artists such as Mnemonic Ascent (1999–2015). More recent acts include Split Syndicate (2005–), Horrorshow (2006–), Astronomy Class (2006–), Thundamentals

(2008–), Dialectrix (aka D-Trix, Ryan Leaf, n.d.), the Tongue (Xannon Shirley, 1997*–), Muph & Plutonic (2004–), Gully Platoon (2008–), M-Phazes (Mark Landon, 1983–), Matty B (Matthew Victor Barrett, n.d.), Koi Child (2014–), and Kerser (Scott Barrow, 1987–). Five of Kerser's seven studio albums peaked in the Top 10 on the ARIA Albums Chart. Another recent artist is Shahrooz Raoofi (1979*–), a prolific Australian hip hop, electro-house music producer of Iranian descent who now resides in London.

As of 2018, the most internationally famous Australian hip hop act is Dirty South–influenced rapper Iggy Azalea (1990–), from Sydney, who between 2012 and 2015 was the focus of several hip hop controversies, which included accusations of white appropriation of black music, hypersexualization, and lack of skills. Iggy Azalea's studio album *The New Classic* (2014) peaked at No. 3 on the Billboard 200 and No. 1 on Billboard's Top R&B/Hip Hop Albums and Top Rap Albums. It also spawned a No. 1 hit, "Fancy," and went Platinum.

ABORIGINAL HIP HOP

Since Australian hip hop's pioneering days, indigenous activity and identity have been essential. Wickid Force Breakers, Mnemonic Ascent, and South West Syndicate, among many other acts, included indigenous Australian members. More important, lyrical content and efforts to support indigenous Australian hip hop continue well into the 21st century. Brothablack (1978–) is a Sydney-based indigenous (of the Yiman Tribe) hip hop performer, rapper, breakdancer, beatboxer, actor, and indigenous youth educator and advocate who was a founding member of South West Syndicate before having his solo career. Brothablack's music is best described as old-school rap with highly energized vocal deliveries accompanied by heavy guitars and turntablism. His debut solo studio album was *More Than a Feeling* (2006). In 2007, he collaborated with Hilltop Hoods to draw attention to indigenous mortality rates.

The group Local Knowledge (2002–2006) and its descendants the Last Kinection (2006–) and Street Warriors (2007*–) formed a grassroots movement focusing on the poverty, unemployment, and discrimination that indigenous Australians experience. CuzCo (2006–) is a hip hop, R&B, and reggae fusion duo that heightens awareness of aboriginal rights. Briggs (1986–), an indigenous (Yorta Yorta) Australian rapper, record label owner, comedy writer, and actor from Shepparton, became known after Hilltop Hoods took him on its 2009 European tour. He established Bad Apples Music (2015–), a record label that focuses on indigenous hip hop artists and music. His solo albums include *The Blacklist* (2010) and *Sheplife* (2014). As part of the duo A.B. Original (2014–), he released the studio album *Reclaim Australia* (2016). Briggs's musical themes include racism and economic inequality, and he has been a prominent activist against blackface. His aggressive, fast-paced raps often use stream-of-consciousness lyricism and wordplay, accompanied by such vocalizations as trills and stutters that he uses for effect. Briggs has a penchant for metal-style guitars set against an intricate interplay of samples and beats, making his songs diverse and complex. Other indigenous Australian acts include Morganics

(Morgan Lewis, n.d.), from Sydney; Little G (Georgina Chrisanthopoulos, 1986*–), from Melbourne; and Nathan Lovett-Murray (1982–), from Heywood.

Melissa Ursula Dawn Goldsmith

See also: Bliss n' Eso; Briggs; Brothablack; Hilltop Hoods; Iggy Azalea; MC Opi; New Zealand; 1200 Techniques; The United States

Further Reading

Dunbar-Hall, Peter, and Chris Gibson. 2004. *Deadly Sounds, Deadly Places: Contemporary Aboriginal Music in Australia.* Sydney, Australia: University of New South Wales Press.

Maxwell, Ian. 2003. *Phat Beats, Dope Rhymes: Hip Hop Down Under Comin' Upper.* Middletown, CT: Wesleyan University Press.

Mitchell, Tony. 2003. "Indigenizing Hip Hop: An Australian Migrant Youth Subculture." In *Ingenious: Emerging Youth Cultures in Urban Australia*, edited by Melissa Butcher and Mandy Thomas, pp. 198–214. North Melbourne, Victoria, Australia: Pluto Press.

Morgan, George, and Andrew Warren. 2011. "Aboriginal Youth, Hip Hop, and the Politics of Identification." *Ethnic and Racial Studies* 34, no. 6: 925–27.

Warren, Andrew, and Rob Evitt. 2012. "Indigenous Hip Hop: Overcoming Marginality, Encountering Constraints." In *Creativity in Peripheral Places*, edited by Chris Gibson, chap. 11. London: Routledge.

Further Listening

Hilltop Hoods. 2006. *The Hard Road.* Obese.

Kerser. 2016. *Tradition.* ABK Records.

Last Kinection, The. 2011. *Next of Kin.* Elefant Traks.

Thundamentals. 2017. *Everyone We Know.* High Depth.

Austria

Austria's hip hop scene emerged in Vienna, its capital, in the early 1980s. The first Austrian rapper was singer-songwriter Falco (Johann Hölzel, 1957–1998), who recorded pop and new wave. Falco had many international hits, most notably "Rock Me Amadeus" (1986), which reached No. 1 on the Billboard Hot 100, and "Vienna Calling" (1985), which peaked at No. 18. Falco, who never referred to himself as a rapper, preferred performing in Austrian German with some English. In contrast, another pioneering act from Vienna, an electronica/hip hop group, the Moreaus (aka Creatures, 1986–1991), featured Sugar B (Martin Forster, n.d.), who rapped in English.

From 1867 until 1918, the Austro-Hungarian Empire was a major European power, collapsing at the end of World War I (1914–1918). After the First Austrian Republic (1919–1934) and a brief interwar period under Fascist leadership, Austria became part of Greater Germany (and the Greater Germanic Reich) until the end of World War II (1939–1945). Since 1945, the Second Republic of Austria has been a democracy, and since 1955, Austria has been independent and neutral. The vast majority of its peoples are Austrian, followed by small minorities of former Yugoslavians, Germans, Turks, and other ethnic groups. The country's official language is Austrian Standard German, which shares syntax, words, and phrases with the Bavarian dialect.

Vienna has been an important center for Western classical music. Composers such as Joseph Haydn (1732–1809), Wolfgang Amadeus Mozart (1756–1791), Ludwig van Beethoven (1770–1827), Franz Schubert (1797–1828), and Arnold Schoenberg (1874–1951) lived and developed their music in the city. Musical influences include Romani music, such as Hungarian *Csárdás* (folk dance music). Viennese traditional music includes *Waltzes*, *Ländlers* (both are dance music), and *Schrammelmusik* (ensemble music played by double-necked guitar and accordion), which were influenced by immigrants from Hungary, Bavaria, Moravia, and Slovenia. Yodeling is a shared musical tradition between Austria, Bavaria, and Switzerland. By the end of the 20th century, popular music preferences favored Austrian pop and rock. Though its music industry is small, the country has established its own Austrian singles and albums charts (Ö3 Austria Top 40, 1968–).

EARLY AUSTRIAN HIP HOP

Hip hop music from Vienna and other Austrian cities was recorded more often once Schönheitsfehler (Blemish, 1992–2005), the first commercially successful hip hop act, whose single "F—You" (1993) charted in Germany, established its own recording label, Duck Squad (1993–). Schönheitsfehler helped groups such as Texta (1993–), from Linz, and Total Chaos (1993–), from Innsbruck, record their first albums. Texta employed humor and rap using the Upper Austrian (Linzer) dialect. Its debut studio album, *Gediegen* (*Solid*, 1997), was followed by *SexDrugsAndHipHop* (2000), which peaked at No. 20 on the Austrian Longplay Charts. Lyrical content reflected a German focus on American-inspired gangsta themes, but Austrian rap also protested against local right-wing political activity, xenophobia, and racism and made comical references to Austrian culture. Fünfhaus Posse (Five-House Posse, 1993–), from Vienna, stood out for fusing hip hop with jazz-influenced beats. After the 2000s, the group opted to rap texts in Standard Austrian German to attain a larger audience.

Other acts included Aphrodelics (1995–), Kaputtnicks (1995*–), Hidden Nation Crew (1995–), and Rückgrat (Backbone, 1997–2005). Meanwhile, Texta and Total Chaos formed the supergroup Kaleidoskop (2001–2002) with the Bavarian band from Freising, Blumentopf (Flowerpot, 1992–2016). Turntablism and instrumental hip hop gained popularity with the Viennese turntablist crew Waxolutionists (1997–) and the Moreaus' DJ DSL (Stefan Biedermann, 1969–), a pioneering instrumental hip hop and trip hop producer. Another notable turntablist crew, the Phonosapiens (2005*–), from Innsbruck, records downtempo instrumental trip hop, dubstep, funk, and jungle music.

THE 2000s AND BEYOND

Hip hop musicians who began in the 2000s included Viennese acts such as the duo Penetrante Sorte (2002–) and rappers Kamp (aka Alois, Kamp MC, Florian

Kampelmühler, 1982–) and MadoppelT (Matthias Leitner, 1983–), as well as Linzer acts such as boombap collective Markante Handlungen (Striking Actions, 2001–2007) and rapper Chakuza (Peter Pangerl, 1981–). By the mid-2000s, Austrian German had become the rap language for irony and humor and was used (over Standard German) for Austrian gangsta and message rap. Die Vamummtn (The Dummies, 2006–2016) was a hardcore Viennese rap crew whose 2008 amateur-made music video "Krocha Hymne" went viral on YouTube; it became the first national hip hop hit since 2003. Die Vamummtn pioneered slangsta, a portmanteau of slang and gangsta, creating a new music scene in Vienna.

Another gangsta rap act is the duo Tracks—taz (2010–2015), whose debut and second albums *Oldaah pumpn muas's* (*It's Gotta Pump, Dude*) and *Prolettn felan längaah* (aka *Scullies Celebrate Longerrr*), both released in 2011, peaked at No. 1 on the Austrian Albums Chart. By the late 2000s, West Coast gangsta rap–influenced Brenk Sinatra (Branko Jordanović, 1979–) emerged as a prolific Viennese music producer, DJ, and instrumental hip hop composer. Other artists included rapper Kayo (aka Nicholas Stage, Alexander Pressl, n.d.) from Linz, who works with DJ Phekt (Alexander Härtl, 1979–), as well as rapper, DJ, producer, and radio host Trishes (Stefan Trischler, n.d.), from Innsbruck. Several pioneering acts remain active. For example, Texta is involved with Markante Handlungen and formed the instrumental hip hop and bass music project group Restless Leg Syndrome (2017) with Viennese DJ and producer Chrisfader (Christian Fleischmann, n.d.). Texta's rapper Skero (aka Skero One, Martin Skerwald, 1972–) collaborates with Brazilian-born and Vienna-based producer, DJ, and singer Joyce Muniz (1983–). As of 2018, DJ DSL is based in Hamburg, where he focuses on creating remixes.

Immigrant acts have also had national success. For example, Tehran-born and Viennese-raised rapper and producer Nazar's (Ardalan Afshar, 1984–) albums *Camouflage* (2014) and *Irreversibel* (2016) peaked at No. 1 in Austria and Nos. 2 and 7 in Germany. Nazar worked on the single "Fallen" ("Fall") with Swiss-born singer-songwriter and producer RAF 3.0 (aka Raf Camora, Raf0Mic, Raphael Ragucci, 1984–), of Austrian and Italian descent. The most successful female artist in Austria is Schwetzingen, Germany–born rapper, slam poet, and writer Mieze Medusa (Doris Mitterbacher, 1975–), who records with DJ and producer Tenderboy (Philipp Diesenreiter, n.d.).

Melissa Ursula Dawn Goldsmith

See also: Gangsta Rap; Germany; Hardcore Hip Hop; Horrorcore

Further Reading

Hafez, Farid. 2016. "Political Beats in the Alps: On Politics in the Early Stages of Austrian Hip Hop Music." *Journal of Black Studies* 47, no. 7: 730–52.

Ondrej, Daniel. 2011. "Ethnicity, Transnational Communication, and Consumerism among the Hip Hop Subcultures in Vienna." In *The Ethnically Diverse City*, edited by Frank Eckardt and John Eade, pp. 509–534. Berlin: BWV.

Further Listening

Nazar. 2016. *Irreversibel*. Universal Music Group/Chapter One.

Restless Leg Syndrome. 2017. *Rooted*. Duzz Down San Rec.

Texta. 2016. *Nichts dagegen, aber* (*Do Not Mind*). Tonträger Records.

Awadi, Didier

(aka DJ Awadi, Didier Sourou Awadi, 1969–, Dakar, Senegal)

Didier Awadi is one of the most prominent figures of African hip hop. With Senegalese rapper Doug E-Tee (aka Duggy Tee, Amadou Barry, 1971–), Awadi cofounded Positive Black Soul (PBS, 1989–) in Dakar, one of the first Senegalese rap groups. Both Awadi and Doug E-Tee come from the stable middle-class areas of Dakar's Sicap Amitié 2 and Sicap Liberté 6 residential districts, but the new sociocultural revolution they launched reached youth throughout Africa.

As a solo act, Awadi released *Sunugaal* (2006) and, as part of PBS, numerous successful albums, including *Parole d'honneur—Kaddu Gor* (*A Man's Word—Kaddu Gor*, 2001*), *Un autre monde est possible* (*Another World Is Possible*, 2004*), *Présidents d'Afrique* (*African Presidents*, 2007), and *Ma revolution* (*My Revolution*, 2012*), which all attest to his community-based activism and contain uplifting messages. Awadi has earned numerous awards, including the Prix RFI Musiques du Monde (2003), the Tamani d'Or du Meilleur Rappeur Africain (2004), and the Chevalier de l'Ordre des Arts et des Lettres (2005, given by both France and Senegal); these awards recognize the original quality of his music beginning as early as his PBS mixtape *Boul falé bou bés* (*Don't Care! Brand New*, 1994), especially his combining of American rap rhythms of groups such as N.W.A. (1986–1991) and Run-D.M.C. (1981–2002) with Senegalese rhythms and the rhythms of superstars such as Omar Péne (1956–), Aby N'dour (n.d.), Baba Maal (1953–), Pape Niang (1988–), and Yaye Aminata Fall (1930–2002).

Identifying themselves as the voice of a generation, Awadi and Doug E-Tee aimed to do their best to represent the "boul falé," young Senegalese disillusioned by the poverty, unemployment, despair, and corruption that confronted them during the 1990s. The duo spoke to urban youth to guide them through media falseness toward the real contemporary Africa. Urban youth experienced a modern Africa destabilized by corrupt political leadership (of its many nations) and beholden to what they considered to be uncaring, opportunistic foreign financial institutions, such as the International Monetary Fund (IMF) and the World Bank. These youth felt their countries were being run by make-believe leaders who cared nothing for the people who elected them. Consequently, most young Senegalese developed an attitude of having no *bras longs* (connections); therefore, they gave up on legal means of influencing the leadership in their country, as they saw it as a pariah rather than as a step toward development.

Awadi continues to spread his political messages—and play a major role in the evolution of Senegalese and African hip hop. Despite the breakup of PBS, he remains close with Doug E-Tee. The two reunited for a highly attended August 2009 concert at the Cices, Dakar, and a 2014 album, *Positive Black Soul: 25 Years*. Moreover, Awadi remains engaged in social activism, often expressed when he performs at national and international festivals. He has collaborated with many international artists, including Afropop singer and songwriter Salif Keita (1949–), of Mali, and reggae singer and songwriter Tiken Jah Fakoly (Doumbia Moussa Fakoly, 1968–), of Ivory Coast.

Babacar M'Baye

See also: Political Hip Hop; Positive Black Soul; Senegal

Further Reading

Lo, Sheba. 2014. "Building Our Nation: Senegalese Hip Hop Artists as Agents of Social and Political Change." In *Hip Hop and Social Change in Africa*, edited by Msia Kibona Clark and Mickie Mwanzia Koster, chap. 2. Lanham, MD: Lexington Books.

Tang, Patricia. 2012. "The Rapper as Modern Griot: Reclaiming Ancient Traditions." In *Hip Hop Africa: New African Music in a Globalizing World*, edited by Eric Charry, chap. 3. Bloomington: Indiana University Press.

Further Reading

Positive Black Soul. 1994. *Boul falé bou bés* (*Don't Care! Brand New*). No label.

B

Babyface

(Kenneth Brian Edmonds, 1959–, Indianapolis, Indiana)

Babyface is an American R&B and new jack swing songwriter, singer, producer, and entrepreneur/businessman. He began as a member of the groups ManChild (1974–1980) and the Deele (1981–1993, 2007–). He left the latter to work as a singer and producer with producer and fellow Deele member L.A. Reid (Antonio Marquis Reid, 1955–), who went on to handle R&B and hip hop benchmark acts such as Paula Abdul (1962–), Boyz II Men (1985–), Whitney Houston (1963–2012), and TLC (1990–). Babyface won 11 Grammy Awards; won BMI Songwriter of the Year in 1989, 1990, 1991, and 1995; received two double-Platinum album certifications with *Tender Lover* (1989) and *For the Cool in You* (1993); and won an NAACP Lifetime Achievement Award. Babyface and Reid cofounded LaFace Records

American singer-songwriter and record producer Babyface is a Grammy Award–winning artist whose musical styles include hip hop, R&B, pop, and new jack swing. In 1989 he cofounded Atlanta-based LaFace Records with L.A. Reid, which gathered the talents of Dallas Austin, Daryl Simmons, Kayo, and Organized Noize as in-house producers. (Randy Miramontez/Dreamstime.com)

(1989–2001). Babyface also cofounded Edmonds Entertainment (aka Babyface Entertainment, 1997–). Today, the Reid/Babyface team is considered one of the most prolific producer and songwriter teams in the history of popular music. At one point, the production duo had six singles in the R&B Top 10 at one time.

FROM PRODUCTION TO SINGER/SONGWRITER

Babyface learned guitar at a young age and sang in various bands until landing a spot in the funk group ManChild, at which point he decided he needed to learn keyboard to be successful at music. He joined Reid's group, the Deele, and began producing with Reid—the two were asked to write and produce for other bands and soon got bigger clients. Their break came writing for Bobby Brown (1969–). In 1989, the two formed the LaFace label in Atlanta, and in 1990, they were honored as the BMI Pop Songwriters of the Year. Despite his self-definition as more of a writer than a musician or singer, Babyface's second solo album, *Tender Lover*, produced the hit "Whip Appeal." In 1993, Babyface's song "End of the Road," performed by Boyz II Men, became one of the best-selling singles of all time and broke long-standing chart records, earning him a Grammy as producer (he won the Grammy for Producer of the Year from 1995 to 1997).

Around this time, Babyface began to deprioritize his role in LaFace to concentrate on a solo career. His third album, *For the Cool in You*, featured the hit "When Can I See You?" He teamed with Boyz II Men again in 1995 to produce the hit "I'll Make Love to You," again breaking into the Billboard Hot 100. Also in 1995, Babyface received five Grammy Awards, including one for Best Male R&B Vocal Performance. His next production project, the soundtrack for the 1995 American film *Waiting to Exhale*, produced several hits. His fourth solo album, *The Day*, was well received by critics but did not enjoy the same financial success as his previous albums.

In 1997, he cofounded Babyface Entertainment, a film production company. *Soul Food* (1997), its first film, spawned a double-Platinum soundtrack. In 2000, Babyface cofounded Babyface Sports Group, which provided agent representation for professional athletes. He released more solo albums: *Face 2 Face* (2001), *Grown and Sexy* (2005), *Playlist* (2007), and *Return of the Tender Lover* (2015). In 2014, Babyface released a Grammy Award–winning duet album with Toni Braxton (1967–) titled *Love, Marriage and Divorce*.

Anthony J. Fonseca

See also: New Jack Swing; The United States

Further Reading

Chaney, Cassandra. 2014. "The Tears of Black Men: Black Masculinity, Sexuality, and Sensitivity in R&B and Hip Hop." In *Hyper Sexual, Hyper Masculine? Gender, Race, and Sexuality in the Identities of Contemporary Black Men*, edited by Brittany C. Slatton and Kamesha Spates, chap. 8. New York: Routledge.

Grem, Darren E. 2006. "'The South Got Something to Say': Atlanta's Dirty South and the Southernization of Hip Hop America." *Southern Cultures* 12, no. 4: 55–73.

Hilburn, Robert. 1997. "Cover Story: Crown Prince of Pop: At 38, Babyface Has Won Six Grammys and Is Nominated for Another Dozen, but Does He Mind His Work Being Tagged 'Commercial'? Not One Bit." *Los Angeles Times*, February 23, 5.

Further Listening
Babyface. 1989. *Tender Lover.* CBS.
Babyface. 1993. *For the Cool in You.* Epic.

Bahamadia

(Antonia Reed, 1976–, Philadelphia, Pennsylvania)

Bahamadia is a Philadelphia-based DJ and MC. In the 1980s, she began her career by working with Philadelphia's own DJ Ran (Randy Gaskins, 1969*–) as well as MC Guru (Keith Edward Elam, 1961–2010) and the East Coast hip hop duo Gang Starr (1986–2006). Bahamadia developed her characteristically smooth, flowing rap, which she alternates with jazz- and R&B-influenced singing. In 1993, she recorded her first single, "Funk Vibe," inspiring MC Guru to help her attain a record deal with Chrysalis Records (1969–). She has since released four albums: *Kollage* (1996), *BB Queen* (2000), *Good Rap Music* (2006), and *Here* (2015). In 1996, her singles "I Confess" and "Three the Hardway" (*Kollage*) both peaked at No. 11 on Billboard's Hot Rap Songs and at No. 45 on Billboard's Hot R&B/Hip Hop Songs. She has remained part of the Philadelphia hip hop scene while touring internationally, achieving an international fan base with the songs "Total Wreck" (1994), "Uknow-howwedu" (1995), and "Here" (2015).

Because she had to wait out her contract with Chrysalis, which became a subsidiary of EMI (1931–2012), Bahamadia's solo career was put on hold. She frequently appears as a guest artist, collaborating with Erykah Badu (1971–), the Herbaliser (1995–), Jedi Mind Tricks (1993–), Queen Latifah (1970–), and another Philadelphia act, the Roots (1987–), among others. In 2000, she began her own recording label, B-Girl Records (2000–), in Philadelphia. She has been an advocate for women involved in hip hop production and management.

Melissa Ursula Dawn Goldsmith

See also: Gang Starr; The United States

Further Reading
Bradley, Adam, and Andrew Dubois, eds. 2010. "Bahamadia." Under "Part 3: 1993–99: Rap Goes Mainstream" in *The Anthology of Rap*, pp. 335–37. New Haven, CT: Yale University Press.
Hess, Mickey. 2010. "The Sound of Philadelphia: Hip Hop History in the City of Brotherly Love." In *Hip Hop in America: A Regional Guide*, edited by Mickey Hess, vol. 1, chap. 7. Santa Barbara, CA: Greenwood.

Further Listening
Bahamadia. 1996. *Kollage.* Chrysalis.

The Bahamas

The Bahamas, located north of Cuba and Hispaniola and southeast of Florida, is an archipelagic state comprising over 700 islands, cays, and islets within the Atlantic Ocean. Since 1973, the Commonwealth of the Bahamas has been an independent commonwealth under England. Bahamians were introduced to hip hop by the mid-1980s through tourists and traveling citizens. The major hip hop center is in its capital city, Nassau, which until then aired Jamaican reggae and dancehall, American R&B and rock, and Trinbagonian calypso, soca, and *rapso*, as well as two kinds of Bahamian music, *junkanoo* and *rake 'n' scrape*. Bahamian hip hop is usually fused with reggae and junkanoo and more recently has incorporated soca; bands are more emphasized than individual rappers. One exception is Nassau rapper Avalanchee (Avalanchee Yaj, n.d.), who combines uplifting hip hop with reggae and gospel, releasing tracks through streaming services.

The most famous Bahamian hip hop group is Nassau's Baha Men (1980–), who fuse modernized junkanoo with hip hop, reggae, soca, and dance pop. The band's studio albums *I Like What I Like* (1997), *Doong Spank* (1998), *2 Zero O-O* (1999), *Who Let the Dogs Out?* (2000), *Move It Like This* (2002), *Holla!* (2004), and *Ride with Me* (2015) employ hip hop, and their smash hit "Who Let the Dogs Out?" (2000) combines modernized junkanoo with hip hop elements. It peaked at No. 40 on the Billboard Hot 100; however, it reached No. 2 on the U.K. Singles Chart and No. 1 in Australia and New Zealand. In 2001, it won a Grammy Award for Best Dance Recording. Also from Nassau, Willis and the Illest Bahamas Reggae Band (2008–) fuses reggae, dancehall, and dubstep with hip hop. The band's lyrical content focuses on tolerance, acceptance, and love. In 2011, Willis and the Illest released its eponymous album, though it is still best known for its live concerts on New Providence.

Melissa Ursula Dawn Goldsmith

See also: Dubstep; Reggae

Further Reading

Rommen, Timothy. 2009. " 'Come Back Home': Regional Travels, Global Encounters, and Local Nostalgias in Bahamian Popular Musics." *Latin American Music Review* 30, no. 2: 159–83.

Strauss, Neil. 2000. "An Island Breeze Revives a Dream: At Long Last, a Bahamain Band Has a Hit on Its Hands." *The New York Times*, August 28, E1.

Thompson, Krista A. 2011. "Youth Culture, Diasporic Aesthetics, and the Art of Being Seen in the Bahamas." *African Arts* 44, no. 1: 26–39.

Further Listening
The Baja Men. 2000. *Who Let the Dogs Out?* S-Curve Records.

Bangladesh

Bangladesh, the world's eighth most populous nation and the third-largest Muslim-majority country, is a south Asian parliamentary democracy whose largest cities include its capital, Dhaka, as well as its biggest port city, Chittagong. Bangladesh's citizenry is 98 percent Bengali, and its Bengali Muslims make up a large part of the population. Bangladesh has been a cosmopolitan Islamic republic and was at one point part of British India, with a war for liberation and independence occurring in 1971. Bangladeshi hip hop, which emerged in 1992 with rapper Ashraf Babu (n.d.), is influenced not by English but by American artists, mainly because hip hop did not come into its own until 2000, when American television programs and CDs became available and, combined with social networking, enabled musicians to disseminate their songs.

Traditional Bangladeshi music consists of religious and secular songs, many based on ragas (melodic modes or scales in Indian classical music) and Hindustani classical music, in the Bengali language. Some of its styles include *baul*, a sparsely accompanied solo music; *bhandari, gazir gaan, hason raja, kirtan*, and *shyama sangeet*, all devotional musics; *bhatiali* and *sari*, both maritime musics; *dhamail, gombhira*, and *jhumur*, based on dance; *ghazal* and *lalon*, which introduce philosophy and religious ideas; and *jari* and *kavigan*, both battling musics—the latter being between two poets, a form that appears similar to rap battling. Modern songs are put under the umbrella term *adhunik* (short for *adhunik sangeet*, or modern music); these include film songs (including *filmi music*), pop, and rock music, the latter having been introduced in the early 1970s by bands such as Spondan (1972–) and Uccharon (1973–)*. As of 2018, rock, nicknamed Bangla or Bangla music, dominates popular musical tastes.

Queens, New York–based Bangladeshi American rap group Stoic Bliss (2004–) was the first Bangladeshi-oriented hip hop band to sign on a major label, with its 2006 album *Light Years Ahead* being made available in Bangladesh and selling 250,000 copies its first year. In 2006, the pioneering Bangladeshi hardcore rap group Deshi MCs (aka E.N.L. Crew—E.N.L. for "enlightenment," 2005–) released its first album *Banned*, followed in 2009 by *Banned Version 2.0*.

Beginning first as a commercial enterprise, Bangladeshi hip hop has evolved to also include an urban, sociopolitical underground rap scene in cities such as Dhaka and Chittagong (especially in its Rangamati District). In addition to urban and sociopolitical themes, Bangladeshi hip hop has focused on street violence and gangsta rap themes (called Bangla gangsta rap), drugs (especially marijuana), partying, and self-esteem. As a result of diaspora, one Bangladeshi artist who has become popular in the United States is hip hop, electronica, rock, and R&B singer-composer Fuad (Fuad al Muqtadir, 1980–), who is based in New York City. Recently, hip hop has been kept alive in Bangladeshi nightclubs by acts such as Dhaka-based DJ Rahat (Rahat Hayat, n.d.), who has also released eight albums that feature Bangladeshi hip hops acts. A couple of successful later acts have been Dhaka-based Theology of Rap (T.O.R., 2007–) and the first mainstream female Bangladeshi rapper, Amzii Khan (Amani Khan, 1993–).

Anthony J. Fonseca

See also: Gangsta Rap; India; Pakistan

Further Reading

Farzana, Kazi Fahmida. 2011. "Music and Artistic Artefacts: Symbols of Rohingya Identity and Everyday Resistance in Borderlands." *Austrian Journal of South-East Asian Studies* 4, no. 2: 215–36.

Henderson, David. 2013. "Three Minutes on Music from Bangladesh." *World Literature Today* 87, no. 3: 7.

Further Listening
Deshi MCs. 2006. *Banned.* G-Series.
Deshi MCs. 2009. *Banned Version 2.0.* G-Series.

Banks, Azealia

(1991–, New York City, New York)

Azealia Banks is an American rapper, singer-songwriter, and actress known for her self-released (via social media) breakthrough hip house single "212" (2011), her critically acclaimed EP *1991* (2012), her mixtape *Fantasea* (2012), and her album *Broke with Expensive Taste* (2014), the last peaking at No. 30 on the Billboard 200. Banks followed her debut album with self-released singles and her second mixtape *Slay-Z* (2016).

Banks is also known for criticizing Iggy Azalea (1990–) and Macklemore (Benjamin Hammond Haggerty, 1983–), white rappers who she argues appropriate black music to gain unwarranted recognition over more talented black rappers. Banks, who is openly bisexual, is known for a hard-hitting rapping style, producing confrontational texts on how black women are objectified and sexualized, especially by white men. She uses a lot of expletives, internal rhymes, and humor, and her lyrics express pride in being from New York City. Her rapping and speaking voice is higher than her strong contralto singing voice, which she uses to create contrasting lyrical passages. Though she raps quickly and is youthfully stylish, Banks's sound and style come closer to Missy Elliott (1971–) and a mature Miley Cyrus (Destiny Hope Cyrus, 1992–) than to Nicki Minaj (1982–).

Banks grew up in Harlem, New York, where she developed early interests in musical theatre, singing, dancing, and acting. By age 10, she had begun winning auditions for off-Broadway musical productions, and by 14, she was attending the Fiorello H. LaGuardia High School of Music and Art and Performing Arts. At 16, Banks dropped out of high school to focus on becoming a hip hop recording artist. Under the stage name Miss Bank$, she self-produced and released several tracks, including "Seventeen" (2009), which sampled English electronic band Ladytron (1999–). Though this effort led to a development deal with XL Recordings (1989–), after a year, Banks parted from the label over artistic differences.

By 2010, Banks had dropped her stage name and released more tracks, including "L8R" (2010), through social media music outlets. In 2011, Banks moved to Montreal and made the video for "212," which features her rapping and singing over DJ Lazy J's (aka Basto, Jef Martens, 1975–) electro-house "Float My Boat" (2009). The video for "212" went internationally viral, and the song peaked at No. 7 in Ireland, 12 in the United Kingdom, and 14 in the Netherlands.

In 2012, a still unsigned Banks went back to New York to work with English producer Paul Epworth (1974–). She self-released her debut mixtape *Fantasea*, while "212" had an additional release on the EP *1991*, on the Interscope Records label (1989–). Though *1991* was first released in the United Kingdom, the album peaked at No. 133 on the Billboard 200 in the United States. In 2014, after breaking off with Interscope and Polydor Records (1913–), Banks released *Broke with Expensive Taste*, first on iTunes, then in 2015 on the Prospect Park label (2008–). As of 2018, she plans to release a third mixtape, *Fantasea II: The Second Wave*, and her second studio album, tentatively titled *Business and Pleasure*.

Melissa Ursula Dawn Goldsmith

See also: Iggy Azalea; Political Hip Hop; The United States

Further Reading

Dawkins, Marcia Alesan. 2013. "Shady 2.0." Coda in *Eminem: The Real Slim Shady. Hip Hop in America*, pp. 167–72. Santa Barbara, CA: Praeger.

Hawkins, Stan. 2016. *Queerness in Pop Music: Aesthetics, Gender Norms, and Temporality.* New York: Routledge.

McNally, James. 2016. "Azealia Banks's '212': Black Female Identity and the White Gaze in Contemporary Hip Hop." *Journal of the Society for American Music* 10, no. 1: 54–81.

Further Listening

Banks, Azealia. 2014/2015. *Broke with Expensive Taste.* Azealia Banks Records/Prospect Park.

Barbados

Barbados, a British commonwealth island nation in the Caribbean, has popular, diverse music tastes that include American jazz and rock, Trinbagonian calypso and soca, and Jamaican reggae, ragga, and ska. In addition, Barbados originated its own popular music, *spouge*, in the 1960s. This fusion of ska with calypso was influenced by American and British Isles spirituals, hymns, and sea shanties, with cowbell and bass guitar for main instrumentation—in addition to a trap set, electronic instruments, and later the trumpet, trombone, and saxophone.

Hip hop emerged in Barbados in the mid-1980s when traveling tourists and citizens introduced hip hop music and films. By the late 1980s, hip hop was being played at touristy discotheques. Elements of reggae and soca are often fused with Barbadian hip hop, which has produced many internationally renowned artists. Rapping texts are in English with a West Indies dialect that also includes American, British English, and Bajan creole. Lyrical themes include partying, economic disparity, the frustrations of island youth, and self-improvement (including elements of gospel). Since 2004, Barbados's capital city and hip hop center, Bridgetown, has hosted the Barbados Hip Hop Festival.

DiKK (1987–1990*) from Bridgetown is one of the earliest Barbadian rapping crews. In 1988, DiKK recorded *Reason with My Rhyme*—the first rap album in the Caribbean. Rapper, singer-songwriter, producer, and actor Magnet Man (anonymous, n.d.), from Christ Church, fuses hip hop with R&B, soca, ragga, neo soul, and American and Latin pop. Since 2003, Magnet Man has performed worldwide with notable hip hop artists Busta Rhymes (1972–) and Shaggy (1968–), among others. The four-piece fusion band Cover Drive (2010–) records hip hop, reggae, R&B, dancehall, soca, electronic dance music, and Caribpop. Cover Drive's opening-act engagement for R&B and reggae singer-songwriter Rihanna's (1988–) Loud Tour (2011) led to a publishing deal with Sony (1929–) and a recording deal with Polydor Records (1913–). Its debut studio album *Bajan Style* (2012) peaked at No. 14 on the U.K. Albums Chart and has produced several hits in the United Kingdom. Cover Drive's second studio album is *Fall Forward* (2017).

In addition, many Barbadian-born hip hop acts have established themselves elsewhere. Most famous are singer-songwriters Rihanna and Shontelle (Shontelle

Layne, 1985–) as well as rapper, beatboxer, and producer Doug E. Fresh (1966–) and DJ, turntablist, and mixer Grandmaster Flash (1958–). Both Grandmaster Flash and Doug E. Fresh are pioneering hip hop artists in American hip hop. The 1966 independence of Barbados prompted the latest Barbadian diaspora, producing several first-generation hip hop artists, such as London-born R&B singer-songwriter Shaznay (Tricia Marie Lewis, 1975–) and Toronto-born rapper, singer-songwriter, record producer, and director Tory Lanez (Daystar Peterson, 1992–) as well as legendary American singer-songwriter, DJ, and producer Afrika Bambaataa (1957–) and rapper, singer-songwriter, producer, director, actor, and model A$AP Rocky (Rakim Mayers, 1988–).

Melissa Ursula Dawn Goldsmith

See also: Afrika Bambaataa; Doug E. Fresh; Grandmaster Flash; Reggae; Rihanna

Further Reading

Best, Curwen. 2003. "Reading Graffiti in the Caribbean Context." *Journal of Popular Culture* 36, no. 4: 828–52.

Best, Curwen. 2012. "The Digital Nation." In *The Popular Music and Entertainment Culture of Barbados: Pathways to Digital Culture*, chap. 9. Lanham, MD, Toronto, and Plymouth, England: Scarecrow.

Further Listening

Cover Drive. 2012. *Bajan Style.* Polydor.

Battling

Battling has existed in rap music, beatboxing, breakdancing, and turntablism since their formative years. Battles take place informally on street corners or formally on a concert or battle stage. The events provide a space for artists to confront their peers through showcasing their art. Worldwide, police, who misinterpret the confrontational aspect of battling as gang-related activity or find youth gatherings suspicious, have often disrupted hip hop battles, sometimes arresting artists involved in their competitions.

Rap battling, which employs a style of delivery called freestyle, is an improvisational method of rapping that can be accompanied by a basic instrumental beat, a sample, or beatboxing, or can be delivered a capella. In freestyle battling, two rappers use either prepared lyrics or stream-of-consciousness on-the-spot songwriting to create lyrics, sometimes with no particular subject or structure and sometimes challenging the opposing rapper's skills while bragging about their own skills. The goal is to diss the opposing rapper through clever lyrics and wordplay. Either the audience (sometimes called the battle's cipher or cypher) or an appointed competition judge evaluates these rhymed lyrics, at which point a winner is declared. As a musical style, freestyle rap is comparable to improvisational jazz.

Old-school rapper Big Daddy Kane (1968–) was one of the first to attempt to define freestyle, calling it a rhyme that was free of style and usually full of braggadocio. He differentiated between rhymes created at the moment (improvised) and those the rapper prepared for the battle. Rapper Kool Moe Dee (1962–) followed up with a new definition, arguing that old-school freestyle was improvisational rapping based on a script, versus new-school freestyle, rap created on the spot. Some current rappers, such as Eminem (1972–), are considered freestyle experts. To prove that a freestyle rap is being created in the moment, rappers will often refer to places and objects in their immediate setting or will take suggestions on lyrics from the crowd, although most freestyle rappers have template rhymes at the ready to use as filler. As of 2018, freestyle battles are usually entered with some written lyrics, with improvisation incorporated, making it possible for rappers to create intricate rhymes and insults. Freestyling can also be used as a songwriting method for albums or mixtapes.

Breakdance (aka b-boying, b-girling, or breaking) battles can be solo- or team-oriented and, like rap battles, can happen informally on street corners or formally at staged competitions, with international tournaments where teams represent their home countries. Because breakdancing began on urban streets with Puerto Rican and African American b-boy crews (and later b-girl crews) in New York City, it is often referred to as street dancing. B-boy and b-girl battles are a combination of prepared material and improvisation (although less improvisation is used than with rap battling due to the nature of team dancing). These battles are social events, where teams interact with each other and with the judges and spectators, often incorporating humor in the form of subtle jabs at opposing teams' skills.

Breakdancing is athletic and gymnastic in nature and is made up of major kinds of movement: uprock (aggressive or intimidating moves that mimic fighting), toprock (standing-position moves that emphasize footwork), downrock (floor-based moves that incorporate hands or head, as well as feet, for support), power moves (acrobatics), and freezes (suddenly stopping an acrobatic move and holding a frozen position for as long as possible). Although it involves moves from funk dance styles such as popping, locking, and electric boogaloo, it differs from those styles in its equal emphasis on floor-work acrobatics and non-footwork-related gymnastics, such as handstands, headstands, and flips onto the back, as well as because it does not emphasize the flow between the feet and hands the way that funk dances do (making it less smooth and better suited for solo improvisation). In team battles, most emphasis is on each dancer's solo work, although some of the better teams incorporate highly synchronized multidancer moves into a soloist's entrance and exit (the moves dancers do when they enter or leave the dancing circle). In time, breakdancing battles have become international, with some of the best crews hailing from the United States, France, Japan, and South Korea. Though not as popular as rap battles or b-boy/b-girl competitions, beatboxing championships are held annually and are judged in the same fashion, by both audience reaction and expert judges.

For turntablism, one of its most important formal battles traces back to 1985 when the first DMC World DJ Championships took place in London. The London remix label DMC (Disco Mix Club, 1983–) established this competition, which soon afterward had regional and national competitions that led into the World Championships. During its first year, this competition was a DJ mixing battle, but in 1986, scratching was introduced. During a DMC Championship battle, elimination rounds last for two minutes while final sets receive six minutes. In both, DJs perform routines that exhibit a team or individual's scratching, mixing, and DJing techniques (including selecting and switching albums), as well as choreographed combinations of these techniques, using any kind of stylus (record needle). Rules for turntablism in less formal competitions more closely resemble those seen in freestyle or hip hop dance battles. For example, ciphers (aka cyphers, a circular formation around competitors) form to allow observers and judges to watch closely and to allow competitors to take turns. Another example is sudden-death rounds, which may be determined by the audience as much as by a battle competitor's or team's accomplishments.

Anthony J. Fonseca and Melissa Ursula Dawn Goldsmith

See also: Breakdancing; Hip Hop Dance; MC; Turntablism

Further Reading

Alim, H. Samy, Jooyoung Lee, and Lauren Mason Carris. 2011. "Moving the Crowd, 'Crowding' the Emcee: The Coproduction and Contestation of Black Normativity in Freestyle Rap Battles." *Discourse & Society* 22, no. 4: 422–39.

Choi, Seokhun. 2017. "The Marionette: Intermedial Presence and B-Boy Culture in South Korea." *Theatre Research International* 42, no. 2: 132–45.

Dodds, Sherril. 2016. "Hip Hop Battles and Facial Intertexts." *Dance Research* 34, no. 1: 63–83.

Katz, Mark. 2006. "Men, Women, and Turntable: Gender and the DJ Battle." *The Musical Quarterly* 89, no. 4: 580–99.

Katz, Mark. 2012. "Turntablism: 1989–96." In *Groove Music: The Art and Culture of the Hip Hop DJ*, chap. 5. New York: Oxford University Press.

Sato, Hahoko, Hiroyuki Nunome, and Yasuo Ikegami. 2016. "Key Motion Characteristics of Side-Step Movements in Hip Hop Dance and Their Effect on the Evaluation by Judges." *Sports Biomechanics* 15, no. 2: 116–27.

Further Viewing

Fitzgerald, Kevin, dir. 2005. *Freestyle: The Art of Rhyme.* New York: Palm Pictures.

Beastie Boys

(1980–2012, New York City, New York)

Beastie Boys was an American hip hop, rap, and hard rock band formed in the early 1980s in New York City. It was best known as one of the great crossover successes in early hip hop, bringing the genre to a wider audience. The band's lineup was consistent throughout its tenure, with New York City drummer and vocalist Mike D (Michael Diamond, 1965–) and guitarist and vocalist Ad-Rock (Adam Horovitz, 1966–) joining forces with Brooklyn bassist and vocalist MCA (Adam Yauch, 1964–2012). According to Mike D, the name Beastie Boys stands for "Boys Entering Anarchistic States towards Internal Excellence." The band came into prominence after working with disc jockey DJ Double R turned producer Rick Rubin (Frederick Jay Rubin, 1963–), cofounder of Def Jam Records (1983–). The band's first studio album went multi-Platinum, and four of its albums reached No. 1 on the Billboard 200. The albums *Ill Communication* (1994) and *Hello Nasty* (1998) debuted at No. 1; the former was introduced by one of the band's most popular singles and music videos, "Sabotage." The Beastie Boys' rap was characterized by intentional, often kitschy humor, sophomoric lyrics, liberal sampling, worldly references, and a crossover technique that featured elements of hard rock. This technique influenced a generation of artists, including American rapper Eminem (1972–), American alternative rock band Rage against the Machine (1991–2000, 2007–2011), and English alternative rock band Blur (1988–2003, 2008–). In 2012, the Beastie Boys were inducted into the Rock and Roll Hall of Fame.

EARLY MUSICAL EFFORTS

The Beastie Boys began as a hardcore punk quartet with drummer Kate Schellenbach (1966–), who would later join the alternative all-female rock band Lucious Jackson (1991–2000, 2011–), appearing in early performances. In 1982, the Beastie Boys released an eight-song, 11-minute EP, *Polly Wog Stew*, on the Rat Cage (1982–2003) label. In 1983, the group made inroads into hip hop with the 12-inch Rat Cage single "Cooky Puss," a reference to a Carvel ice cream cake. New York City is often referenced in the band's songs, with mentions of specific companies, streets, neighborhoods, and landmarks in Brooklyn and Manhattan. "Cooky Puss" features excerpts of crank phone calls, samples, and scratching over a beat loop. After the Beastie Boys had gained some commercial success, the two early releases, *Polly Wog Stew* and *Cooky Puss*, were repackaged in 1994 as *Some Old Bullshit*, which included two songs recorded live on *Noise the Show* (1981–1982), which aired on New York University's WNYU station. The band became popular after collaborating with Rubin and his Def Jam label. Def Jam went on to produce LL Cool J (1968–), Public Enemy (1982–), and Run-D.M.C. (1981–2002) as well as the heavy metal band Metallica (1981–) and the alternative funk-rock fusion band Red Hot Chili Peppers (1983–). In 1985, the Beastie Boys got its big break when Madonna (1958–) asked them to open for her Virgin Tour. The trio played six songs in a 30-minute set. On the strength of this exposure, the band's first studio album, *Licensed to Ill* (1986), went multi-Platinum and led to seven subsequent studio albums, the aforementioned *Ill Communication* and *Hello Nasty*, as well as *Paul's Boutique* (1989), *Check Your Head* (1992), *To the 5 Boroughs* (2004), *The Mix-Up* (2007), and *Hot Sauce Committee Part Two* (2011). *Licensed to Ill*, *Ill Communication*, *Hello Nasty*, and *To the 5 Boroughs* all went to No. 1.

Licensed to Ill featured their breakout hit, "Fight for Your Right," and introduced the band's sampling from disparate rock sources, including Led Zeppelin (1968–1980), AC/DC (1973–), Black Sabbath (1968–2006, 2011–), and Kool and the Gang (1964–), among others. In subsequent albums, particularly *Paul's Boutique*, the use of samples expanded to include such varied source material as James Brown (1933–2006), Public Enemy, the Beatles (1960–1970), Joni Mitchell (Roberta Joan Anderson, 1943–), and the Sugarhill Gang (1979–1985, 1994–). The Beastie Boys eventually severed ties with Def Jam over royalty payments and moved to Los Angeles to produce *Paul's Boutique* for Capitol Records (1942–), a critical—but not immediate—commercial success. They subsequently started their own Capitol subsidiary label, Grand Royal (1992–2001), and produced a Los Angeles–based clothing line called X-Large (1991–2012*).

OTHER INTERESTS AND POLITICS

In the 1990s, the members of the group became increasingly active in global concerns. The highlight of the band's activism occurred when MCA began studying Tibetan Buddhism and, on a visit to Tibet in the early 1990s, spoke with refugees who had suffered human-rights abuses at the hands of the Chinese government. Determined to increase awareness of these abuses and contribute proceeds from certain projects to the cause, the Beastie Boys performed in 1994's Tibetan Freedom Concert. By the late 1990s, all members of the Beastie Boys had returned to New York City, culminating in one of their most commercially successful albums, *Hello Nasty.*

Despite another smash single, "Intergalactic" (1998), financial concerns led to the shuttering of the Grand Royal label in 2001. *To the 5 Boroughs*, a "love letter" to a New York City that had suffered in the terrorist attacks of September 11, 2001, was the band's most New York–centric album since *Licensed to Ill.* It also marked a return to their roots, with a simpler style of rapping over beats, balanced against political concerns with the administration of George W. Bush (1946–, in office 2001–2009), specifically criticizing U.S. foreign policy post-9/11. Soon after the group's induction into the Rock and Roll Hall of Fame in 2012, MCA died from cancer of the parotid salivary gland. The surviving members confirmed they would not continue musical activity under the name Beastie Boys.

Christine Lee Gengaro

See also: Mix Master Mike; Turntablism; The United States

Further Reading

Hess, Mickey. 2007. "Beastie Boys." In *Icons of Hip Hop: An Encyclopedia of the Movement, Music, and Culture*, edited by Mickey Hess, pp. 91–116. Westport, CT: Greenwood Press.

Stratton, Jon. 2008. "The Beastie Boys: Jews in Whiteface." *Popular Music* 27, no. 3: 413–32.

Further Listening

Beastie Boys. 1986. *Licensed to Ill.* Def Jam Recordings/Columbia.

Beastie Boys. 1998. *Hello Nasty.* Grand Royal.

Beastie Boys. 2004. *To the 5 Boroughs.* Capitol Records.

Beatboxing

Beatboxing is the practice of making drum and synthesizer sounds using the mouth and nose, as well as drumming with the hands on parts of the torso and neck. It is a way of creating a beat when no instrumentation is available, as with street rap battling. Skilled beatboxers can create both a beat and a melodic line simultaneously.

Now considered the best beatboxer in early rap music, Doug E. Fresh (Douglas E. Davis, 1966–) was a New York–based beatboxer, rapper, dancer, and radio personality who was musically active during the 1980s. Known as the human beatbox, he emulated the sounds of drum machines, tap dancing, percussion instruments, and synthesizers by using only his mouth, throat, and a microphone. He appeared in the

American film *Beat Street* (1984) and later was the founder of Doug E. Fresh and the Get Fresh Crew (1985–2003), which included Slick Rick (aka MC Ricky D, Richard Martin Lloyd Walters, 1965–). American rapper and beatboxer Biz Markie (Marcel Theo Hall, 1964–) was a member of Juice Crew and worked closely with his friend Big Daddy Kane, who wrote lyrics. In 1986, rapper DMX (Earl Simmons, 1970–) also began beatboxing. Also in the United States, Barbados native Grandmaster Flash (Joseph Saddler, 1958–) introduced the idea of the synthesized beatbox, a manually operated, custom-rigged drum machine.

Internationally, beatboxing appeared in Togo around the same time as rapping and turntablism in the 1980s. In the early to mid-1990s, Motswana and South African hip hop, known as *motswako*, employed beatboxing as well as sampling, drum machine beats, turntablism, and hip hop instrumentation. In addition to concerts and emcee battles,

Beatboxers often refine their skills through hours of busking or street performance. This teenage beatboxer, performing in 2016 in the city center of Milan, works on his vocal techniques by making beats and creating sound effects to pre-recorded music. (Alberto Masnovo/Dreamstime.com)

festivals may showcase beatboxing, such as Burkina Faso's Ouago/Waga Hip Hop Festival, which hosts residencies for musicians who lead workshops on beatboxing and sampling. Since the 2000s, Ethiopian musicians have fused hip hop with traditional Amharic music called *fukera*, beatboxing to its oration. Rapper Basy Gasy (Malagasy Gun, 2012–) fuses hip hop and slam poetry with reggae, ragga, and electronica, employing beatboxing, guitars, and percussion. Singaporean hip hop music also includes beatboxing.

Beatboxing battles are currently held internationally (in Germany) every three years, the last having been in 2015, with champions being recognized for their accuracy in imitating instruments, their speed, and their creativity. Current champions as of 2018 are Mael Gayaud (n.d.) of France and Kaila Mullady (n.d.) of the United States. The current crew champion is Beatbox Collective (n.d.), out of England.

Anthony J. Fonseca

See also: Doug E. Fresh; Grandmaster Flash; Juice Crew

Further Reading

Kuch, Andreas, and Indra Tedjasukmana. 2016. *Beatbox Complete: Sounds, Patterns, and Styles*. English ed. Innsbruck, Austria: Helbling Verlag.

Proctor, Michael, Erik Bresch, Dani Byrd, Krishna Nayak, and Shrikanth Narayanan. 2013. "Paralinguistic Mechanisms of Production in Human 'Beatboxing': A Real-Time Magnetic Resonance Imaging Study." *Journal of the Acoustical Society of America* 133, no. 2: 1043–54.

Shanks, David. 2010. "Uptown, Baby! Hip Hop in Harlem and Upper Manhattan." In *Hip Hop in America: A Regional Guide*, edited by Mickey Hess, vol 1., chap. 2. Santa Barbara, CA: Greenwood.

Further Listening

Doug E. Fresh. 1995. *Play*. Gee Street.

Various Artists. 2001. *Beat Boxing, Vol. 1.0: The Mystery of Beatboxing*. Jive.

Belarus

Belarus is an Eastern European country, sharing its borders with Russia, Ukraine, Poland, Lithuania, and Latvia. The hip hop community in Belarus is small and dislocated because of severe censorship imposed by the administration of President Alexander Lukashenko (1954–), who has been president since 1994. Official culture dominates the music industry in Belarus, with the government blacklisting politically active bands and arresting those who stage underground protest concerts and events. Although there are two official languages in Belarus, Belarusian and Russian, most Belarusian rap is sung in Russian.

In 2005, a law was passed mandating that 75 percent of all music broadcast in Belarus must be Belarusian in origin; since then, all lyrics are carefully checked. Despite the government's vetting of rap, Basowiszcza, the biggest Belarusian music festival, held in the Polish town of Grodek (not far from the border with Belarus), is dominated by rock and punk rock and provides an outlet for Belarusian rappers. Belarusian rap groups include Nestandartnii Variant (Non-Standard Variant, 1998–), S.E.V.E.N. (n.d.), and Deti Indigo ("Indigo Children," n.d.). Meanwhile, Minsk-based Nestanda Records (2010s–) features LSP (Little Stupid Pig, Oleg Savchenko, 1989–) and Bezz and Junior (n.d.).

The dominant official musical style tends to be bubblegum pop sung in Russian, not hip hop or rap. Many Belarusian musicians, especially hip hop artists, have therefore moved to Poland or Russia to continue their careers. For example, Minsk-born Bianca (Tatyana Eduardovna Lipnitskaya, 1985–) performs and releases albums in Russia. Her collaborator Seryoga (Sergey Vasilyevich Parhomenko, 1976–) released his first album, *Zagubili Ljalju* (*Lost Lyalya*, 2003), in Russia and Belarus, but soon after moved to Ukraine; in 2013, he became a Ukrainian citizen. Those who remain in Belarus are driven to the underground scene.

The rapper Krou (n.d.) from the band Čhyrvonym Pa Bielamu (aka CPB, Red and White, 2006–2008) raps in Belarusian, with politically charged pro-Belarusian, anti-Soviet, and anti-Lukashenko lyrics. A music project called Partyzanskaya Szkola (Partisan School) also produced hip hop music in protest of the Lukashenko regime in 2006 (especially the Belarusian song "Ne," meaning "No"), and as a result, many of Partyzanskaya Szkola's members were jailed.

Terry Klefstad

See also: Russia

Further Reading

Lovas, Lemez, and Maya Medich. 2006. *Hidden Truths: Music, Politics, and Censorship in Lukashenko's Belarus.* Copenhagen: Freemuse.

Wines, Michael. 2001. "Street Theater and Graffiti: Belarus Dissidents Make News by Making Noise." *New York Times*, August 19.

Belgium

Belgium is bilingual and bicultural. The northern region, Flanders, shares linguistic and cultural roots with the Netherlands; the southern region, Wallonia, shares its roots with France. On an individual level, these linguistic and cultural roots have historically overshadowed Belgian national identity. As the hip hop scene incorporates artists from former Belgian protectorates and other nationalities, those voices are woven into a fabric that is either Francophonic or Flemish and/or Dutch speaking. The Netherlands' Dutch hip hop, which came to be called Nederhop, is also an influential part of the Belgian hip hop scene. Wallonian hip hop, in the French language, is often characterized by a smooth, flowing delivery, natural to the lingual centrality of vowels, nasals, and soft consonants. Flemish hip hop, in Flemish and related dialects, tends toward a crisper and often more punctuated sound that capitalizes on the comparatively harder and more numerous consonants.

Like most hip hop cultures, Belgian hip hop emerged in urban centers, bringing together Belgians of Wallonian and Flemish backgrounds, as well as others who have roots in the former Belgian territories of central Africa and immigrants from the Middle East and South America. By the second decade of the 21st century, Internet, radio, and club personalities such as DJ Emiliot (anonymous, n.d.), who podcasts the *El DJ Loco Show* (2006–), were offering lively hip hop mixtape assortments with commentary that drew a wide Belgian following. Meanwhile, releases and tours by artists such as the anonymous Krhymes (n.d.), whose raps blend Flemish and English rhymes with a heady old-school and jazz sound, have unleashed a new era of urban rap in Belgium.

Belgian hip hop began in the late 1980s when the R.A.B. Posse (whose name stands for Rien à Branler, loosely translated as "We Don't Give a F—") appeared in Brussels as a crew of over 50 members who were focused on graffiti art and tagging. R.A.B. Posse gave rise to the band De Puta Madre (1990–), meaning "excellent" in Spanish slang, whose founding members, DJ Grazzhoppa (Wim Verbrugghe, 1972–), MC Pee Gonzalez (Pablo Gonzalez, n.d.), and Smimooz (Mathias J. Smimoez, 1973–) achieved worldwide success. DJ Grazzhoppa had won DJ battles in Belgium and at the European and World levels in the 1990s and in 2003 formed DJ Grazzhoppa's DJ Bigband with 12 turntablists. MC Pee Gonzalez was already known for his street art, and Smimooz (Mathias J., 1973–) was on the road to becoming the beatmaker and producer for many regional hip hop artists. Another well known group, Starflam (1990–2005, 2015–), illustrates the fluid nature of many Belgian hip hop groups: its membership circulated in and out from Liège, Brussels, the Democratic Republic of Congo, and France. The group's name has changed over time from H-Posse (early 1990s) to Malfrats Linguistik (Linguistic Gangstas, 1993–2007) to the anagram Starflam (1996).

Several Belgian hip hop artists reach wider audiences. Benny B (Abdel Hamid Gharbaoui, 1968–), who was criticized for mixing house music and hip hop, released the chart-topping single "Vous êtes fous!" ("You're All Crazy," 1990), which was accompanied by a sepia-toned video of b-boys and a turntablist in action. The video popularized breakdancing and turntablism, sparking the country's artistic appreciation of these aspects of Belgian hip hop culture much in the same way that graffiti has become appreciated as urban art. Castro (Wannes van de Welde, 1977–), from Ghent, released the EP *Herfst 2057/De mening is verdeeld/Eens* (*Autumn 2057/ The Mind Is Divided/Once,* 2000) and the album *Shockgolf* (2003), both featuring rhymes in Flemish, making them accessible to Dutch-speaking Nederhop audiences. Krewcial (Pascal Garnier, n.d.) juxtaposed keyboard-based musical hooks against a distorted, gangsta-style vocal delivery, rapping in American slang. Brussels-based Pitcho (Laurent Womba Konga, 1975–) originally from Kinshasa, Democratic Republic of Congo, rhymed in French and rapped about the plight of immigrants. His 2003 hit "Ma part du ghetto" ("My Part of the Ghetto") brings to light the hardship and imprisonment people feel when trapped in urban poverty.

Jennifer L. Roth-Burnette

See also: Congo; France; The Netherlands

Further Reading

Mertens, Jamina, Wouter Goedertier, Idesbald Goddeeris, and Dominique De Brabanter. 2013. "A New Floor for the Silenced? Congolese Hip Hop in Belgium." *Social Transformations: Journal of the Global South* 1, no. 1: 87–113.

Verbeke, Martin. 2017. "Represent Your Origins: An Analysis of the Diatopic Determinants of Non Standard Language Use in French Rap." *International Journal of Francophone Studies* 20, nos. 3–4: 209–36.

Further Listening

Castro. 2003. *Shockgolf.* DKR.

Starflam. 2015. *A l'ancienne: Classics, rares and nédits* (*Old Fashioned: Classics, Rarities, and Unreleased*). Warner Music Group.

t'Hof van Commerce. 2005. *Ezoa en niet anders* (*Ezoa and No Other*). Plasticine.

Various Artists. 1998. *9 MM Parabellum M.Ceez.* 9mm Recordz.

Ben Sharpa

(Kgotso Semela, 1979–, Johannesburg, South Africa)

Ben Sharpa is a South African underground hip hop rapper and producer. He grew up in South Africa and the United States and then returned to South Africa in 1993 to establish himself as a hip hop force, at one point meeting Eminem (1972–) during Eminem's Anger Management Tour (2000–2005). In 2006, Ben Sharpa headlined the Tri-Continental Hip Hop Festival that toured South Africa. He is known throughout Africa as a skilled lyricist and rapper.

Born in the Soweto, Johannesburg, ghetto during Apartheid (1948–1991), Ben Sharpa witnessed both hardships and the revolution they caused. His family took voluntary exile in Chicago. As a teen, he moved back to South Africa to witness the first free post-apartheid elections, bringing his love of American rap with him.

In 1996, he joined with Snazz D (aka Snazz the Dictator, Julian Du Plessis, 1977–) and Krook'd tha Warmonga (Isaac Chokwe, n.d.) to create the rap crew Audio Visual (1996–), which eventually folded into the collective GroundWorks (2001–). This collective produced a self-released untitled promotional album (2002) and a self-released studio album, *Demolition: The MeStory* (2002).

His career began in 2002, when he won a freestyle battle competition, which led to a London meeting with Eminem, whose rap style he favors in his own songs. In 2007, he fell into a diabetic coma and was not expected to survive, but he did. In 2008, he released *B. Sharpa*, his debut studio album, containing dubstep-infused hip hop, and did his first European tour, playing in Austria, Belgium, England, the Netherlands, and Switzerland (he has done 16 European tours since then).

He has released a second album, *4DLS (Fourth Density Light Show)* (2012), and one EP, *The Sharpaganda Theory: Lesson 1* (2008). His lyrics tend to focus on social issues, such as police brutality, government corruption, and the problems of teenage pregnancy, although he also writes songs about spirituality.

Anthony J. Fonseca

See also: Political Hip Hop; South Africa; The United States

Further Reading

Anon. 2010. "Midem: Cape of Good Hope." *Music Week*, January 30, 30.

Künzler, Daniel. 2011. "South African Rap Music, Counter Discourses, Identity, and Commodification beyond the Prophets of da City." *Journal of Southern African Studies* 37, no. 1: 27–43.

Molebatsi, Natalia, and Raphael d'Abdon. 2007. "From Poetry to Floetry: Music's Influence in the Spoken Word Art of Young South Africa." *Muziki: Journal of Music Research in Africa* 4, no. 2: 171–77.

Further Listening

Ben Sharpa. 2008. *B. Sharpa.* Pioneer Unit.

Ben Sharpa. 2012. *4DLS (Fourth Density Light Show).* Jarring Effects/Pioneer Unit.

Benin

Benin is a West African, mainly Roman Catholic nation whose population of roughly 11 million people of 42 ethnic groups lives mainly on its southern coastline in either Porto-Novo or its largest city, Cotonou, which is also its capital. It is a tropical, agricultural nation whose official language is French, with some indigenous Fon and Yoruba being spoken. During the 17th century, its region was known as the Slave Coast because of the Trans-Atlantic slave trade. In 1960, the country (at that time named Dahomey) gained full independence from France. This led to a series of coups and military governments. In 1991, the current multiparty governing structure was created.

Despite its music industry's setback in 1972 when the Kérékou (1972–1991, 1996–2006) government instituted curfews and inhibited musical expression, the country became important to the African music scene because of Grammy Award–winning Beninese Afropop superstar Angélique Kidjo (1960–), who also records reggae, jazz, gospel, and world music fusion. In the 1970s, funk became popular in Benin, with acts such as Nel Oliver (1948*–) creating Afro-*akpala*-funk and the Orchestre Poly Rythmo de Cotonou (1966–) releasing over 50 funk and roots music albums. Hip hop, or urban music, was introduced into the Beninese music in a 1992 concert by French Senegalese–Chadian rapper MC Solaar (1969–).

Hip hop acts from Benin include the trio Sakpata Boys (1995*–), known for its chants and elements of Beninese *vodou*; Diamant Noir (Dark Diamond, n.d.), whose debut album *Faux freres, vrais jumeaux* (*Fake Brothers, True Twins*, 2005) has been influential; and rapper and singer-songwriter Dibi Dobo (n.d.).

Anthony J. Fonseca

See also: MC Solaar; France

Further Reading

Amuzu, Evershed K., and John Victor Singler. 2014. "Codeswitching in West Africa." *The International Journal of Bilingualism* 18, no. 4: 329–45.

Washington, Teresa N. 2014. "Rapping with the Gods: Hip Hop as a Force of Divinity and Continuity from the Continent to the Cosmos." *Journal of Pan African Studies* 6, no. 9: 72–100.

Bermuda

Bermuda, a British Overseas Territory, is a major destination for American tourism because of its proximity to the United States and Puerto Rico. Bermuda's hip hop is largely tourist-driven, produced in countries such as Jamaica, the United States, or the United Kingdom. It is influenced by American hip hop and house; Jamaican reggae, dancehall, and raga; Trinbagonian soca; and Puerto Rican reggaetón, all of which—in addition to other music, such as American jazz, rock, and pop and Bahamanian *junkanoo* (parade music)—overshadow it. Clubs, radio airplay, battle events, open-mic sessions, popular music festivals, and breakdancing workshops are public venues for participating in Bermudian hip hop. It was not until the 2000s that distinct Bermudian hip hop emerged. Since then, the center of hip hop activity has been Bermuda's capital city, Hamilton. Nearly all the country's rappers are black, and their texts are in Bermudian English, peppered with urban British and American vernacular English.

Until 2018, the Bermudian hip hop scene had been made up almost entirely of young, new artists rather than established musicians. Rapper, singer, percussionist, and DJ Kidd Clazzic (Jahroy Richards, 1996*–), from Hamilton, has edgy rapping texts that range from light gangsta rap (e.g., comradeship and loyalty) to uplifting messages about local pride. Kidd Clazzic has been recording in the United States and tours in concerts throughout the Caribbean. In 2016, he self-released his debut studio album *Kidd vs. Everybody* through SoundCloud. Female rapper Imari Wade (1987–) began rapping in 2008, won a national rap battle in 2013, and has performed and recorded in Kingston, Jamaica. Wade's singles have appeared on Bermuda radio stations. The notable exception to this youth-only movement is rapper, singer-songwriter, and DJ Bento (aka Bento BDA, Matthew Bento, n.d.). After growing up in a musical family in Bermuda, Bento attended Berklee College of Music and began a recording career in London. He toured with American hip hop and R&B singer-songwriter and dancer Chris Brown (1989–), American producer Dallas Austin (1970–), and English hip hop collective WSTRN (2015–), among others. Bento has released two studio EPs, *The Deep* (2014) and *Trapitalist* (2016).

Melissa Ursula Dawn Goldsmith

See also: Reggae; Reggaetón

Further Reading

Pinckney, Warren R. 2000. "Toward a History of Jazz in Bermuda." *The Musical Quarterly* 84, no. 3: 333–71.

Rivera, Raquel Z., Wayne Marshall, and Deborah Pacini Hernandez. 2009. *Reggaetón*. Durham, NC: Duke University Press.

Beyoncé

(Beyoncé Giselle Knowles, 1981–, Houston, Texas)

Beyoncé is an American singer of R&B and pop, but she has also recorded hit hip hop songs. As of 2018, she has won 22 Grammy Awards, and all six of her solo studio albums have been certified Platinum or multi-Platinum. If her R&B trio Destiny's Child (1997–2006) and her own hits are added together, Beyoncé is one of the best-selling and most acclaimed music artists in global music history.

As the standout soprano in Destiny's Child, Beyoncé also pursued solo projects, starting in 2000 with an appearance on New York–based female rapper and Jay-Z (1969–) protégé Amil's (Amil Kahala Whitehead, 1973–) "I Got That" and in 2002 with her own funk-infused single "Work It Out" for the American film *Austin Powers in Goldmember*. Her solo studio albums featuring hip hop elements include *B-Day* (2005), *I Am . . . Sasha Fierce* (2008), *Beyoncé* (2013), and *Lemonade* (2016). In addition, her live-performance recordings and EPs sometimes include hip hop numbers, elements, or remixes. Beyoncé has collaborated with a long list of hip hop artists and producers, including American rapper Jay-Z, whom she married in 2008; Timbaland (1972–); and Missy Elliott (1971–).

In 2002, Beyoncé first appeared on the R&B, swing, and hip hop single "'03 Bonnie and Clyde" with Jay-Z. Beyoncé's first Billboard Hot 100 solo single, "Crazy in Love" (2003), also featured Jay-Z and contained hip hop elements. Her subsequent Billboard Hot 100 No. 1 and No. 2 hit singles that contain hip hop were "Check on It" (2005), "Single Ladies (Put a Ring on It)" (2008), and "Drunk in Love" (featuring Jay-Z, 2013).

Beyoncé's participation in hip hop songs usually entails her singing contrasting lyrical passages to the song's rap; however, since Destiny's Child, she has taken to

performing rap-singing within R&B songs. Perhaps the purest example of Beyoncé's rapping is on the single "Diva" (2009) from her album *I Am . . . Sasha Fierce*. Beyoncé has written, arranged, and choreographed songs in which she begins with a hip hop beat or drum loop, so hip hop has become a part of her creative process.

Melissa Ursula Dawn
Goldsmith

See also: Jay-Z; The United States

Further Reading

Barrett, Clara. 2016. "'Formation' of the Female Author in the Hip Hop Visual Album: Beyoncé and FKA Twigs." *Soundtrack* 9, nos. 1–2: 41–57.

Lee, Shayne. 2010. "Sultry Divas of Pop and Soul: Janet, Beyoncé, and Jill." In *Erotic Revolutionaries: Black Women, Sexuality, and Popular Culture*, chap. 2. Lanham, MD: Hamilton Books.

Further Listening

Beyoncé. 2008. *I Am . . . Sasha Fierce*. Music World Music/ Columbia.

American R&B and pop singer-songwriter Beyoncé poses at the 2014 MTV Video Music Awards in Los Angeles. Though she may rarely be caught rapping, Beyoncé has incorporated hip hop elements in her songwriting and has collaborated with other hip hop artists, including her husband, American rapper-songwriter and music producer Jay-Z. (Featureflash/Dreamstime.com)

Big Daddy Kane

(Antonio Hardy, 1968–, Brooklyn, New York)

Big Daddy Kane is an American rapper, record producer, actor, and model who has been in the music industry since he was 14 years old, starting out as a member of the rap collective the Juice Crew All Stars (aka Juice Crew, 1983–1991). Through the years, he has built a reputation of being one of the most skilled MCs in hip hop. Known for his ability to syncopate (stress unexpected beats through his use of words) over fast hip hop beats, he is considered a pioneer of fast rhyming. He has appeared on tracks with R&B legends such as Patti Labelle (Patricia Louise Holt, 1944–) and Quincy Jones (1933–). In 1990, he won the Grammy for Best Rap Performance by a Duo with Jones. He collaborated with Tupac Shakur (1971–1996) and toured with Jay-Z (1969–), whom he helped early in his career by bringing him out to freestyle while he made wardrobe changes. His style of rap is hard-edged and urban but with a touch of dry wit, including clever wordplay, brilliant satire, unexpected and highly literate similes, and good-natured boasting—in many ways foreshadowing the recent British chap hop style. More than any other rapper, Big Daddy Kane shows the influence of James Brown's (1933–2006) performance style, including the use of heavy funk rhythms (with liberal use of rhythm guitar), break-beats (he dances in most of his videos), and metatextual lines such as "Take it to the bridge." His hip hop dress style influenced a number of hip hop trends, such as high-top fades, velour suits, gold medallions, heavy chains, fedoras, and four-finger rings.

EARLY YEARS

In 1984, Big Daddy Kane became friends with rapper and beatboxer Biz Markie (Marcel Theo Hall, 1964–), and he started out collaborating with Biz Markie on his lyrics. The two eventually became members of the Queens-based Juice Crew, headed by producer Marley Marl (1962–). Big Daddy Kane went on to write for the Juice Crew, Roxanne Shanté (1969–), and Kurtis Blow (1959–). In 1987, Big Daddy Kane signed with Prism Records, which later was renamed Cold Chillin' Records (1986–1998), the label that produced Juice Crew, and debuted the underground hit single "Raw." He released his debut album *Long Live the Kane* (1988), which featured the hit "Ain't No Half Steppin.'" His second album and biggest hit was *It's a Big Daddy Thing* (1989), which included soul and chill hits such as "I Get the Job Done," "Rap Summary (Lean on Me)," and "Smooth Operator." *Long Live the Kane* reached No. 5 on Billboard's Top R&B albums and No. 116 on the Billboard 200, and *It's a Big Daddy Thing* peaked at Nos. 4 and 33 on those charts, respectively. Later albums, such as *Taste of Chocolate* (1990), *Prince of Darkness* (1991), *Looks Like a Job For . . .* (1993), *Daddy's Home* (1994), and *Veteranz Day* (1997), did not meet with the same commercial success, although all but the last charted in the Billboard 200. "Very Special," off *Looks Like a Job For . . .*, was his only Hot 100 hit, peaking at No. 31. In 1995, Kane recorded with Tupac Shakur and MC Hammer (1962–), and in the 2000s, he collaborated with A Tribe Called Quest (1985–1998, 2006–2013, 2015–), but this did little to revitalize his career; however, he did not give up touring.

ACTING

Big Daddy Kane took the idea of the hip hop persona into both acting and modeling. His acting debut was Mario Van Peebles's (1957–) revisionist American western, *Posse* (1993). That same year, he appeared in Robert Townsend's (1957–) superhero comedy *The Meteor Man*. His other film credits include *Dave Chappelle's Block Party* (2005), *Dead Heist* (2007), *Love for Sale* (2008), *Just Another Day* (2009), and *Exposed* (2016). He also posed for *Playgirl* in 1991 and for Madonna's (1958–) *Sex* book in 1992; later, in 2014, he discussed his upbringing, childhood, influences, relationships, sexual experiences, and decision to appear in Madonna's book on the *Dr. Zoe Today* radio show (2014–). In 2004, his music and name were used in the video game *Grand Theft Auto: San Andreas*, and in 2005, Big Daddy Kane was honored by VH1. Among his influences, Big Daddy Kane lists R&B singer Barry White (Barry Eugene Carter, 1944–2003), with whom he would collaborate on *Taste of Chocolate*.

Anthony J. Fonseca

See also: The United States

Further Reading

Bradley, Adam, and Andrew Dubois, eds. 2010. "Big Daddy Kane." Under "Part 2: 1985–92: The Golden Age" in *The Anthology of Rap*, pp. 136–44. New Haven, CT: Yale University Press.

Rausch, Andrew J. 2011. "Big Daddy Kane." In *I Am Hip Hop: Conversations on the Music and Culture*, chap. 3. Lanham, MD: Scarecrow.

Further Listening

Big Daddy Kane. 1988. *Long Live the Kane.* Cold Chillin'.

Big Daddy Kane. 1989. *It's a Big Daddy Thing.* Cold Chillin'.

Big Pun

(aka Big Punisher, Christopher Lee Rios, 1971–2000, Bronx, New York)

Big Pun was an American rapper known for his breathless delivery, as he needed only minimal pauses to breathe, resulting in longer lyrical lines and unexpected line breaks, as well as his songwriting. His lyrics emphasized alliteration, internal rhyming (of sometimes five or six words in a string of phrases), and the use of multisyllabic rhyme schemes—techniques that are trademarks of skilled rappers. His solo debut album features his rapping against salsa beats and heavy drum, piano, and electric guitar–based tunes, achieving a variety not often seen in 1990s rap. He died of a heart attack at age 29, having produced only two albums and appearing about a dozen times on other hip hop artists' recordings. Big Pun's biggest hit was a featured appearance on "From N.Y. to N.O." (1999), a song by New Orleans rapper Mr. Serv-On (Corey Smith, 1969–), which reached No. 20 on the Billboard Hot 100 and No. 3 on the Hot Rap Tracks chart. His biggest solo hit, "Still Not a Player," reached No. 13 on Billboard's Hot Rap chart and No. 24 on the Hot 100; his "I'm Not a Player" had reached No. 3 on the rap chart. With his debut album, Grammy-nominated *Capital Punishment* (1998), which reached No. 1 on the Top R&B/Hip-Hop Albums chart and No. 5 on the Billboard 200, Big Pun became the first Latino solo rapper to have an album certified multi-Platinum. His Platinum follow-up, *Yeeah Baby* (2000), reached the top spot on the R&B chart and hit No. 3 on the Billboard 200.

Big Pun had a turbulent childhood, became a homeless teenager, and struggled with depression. As a result, he developed an eating disorder, and by age 21 his weight had increased to 300 pounds. He began writing rap songs as a teen and formed an underground rap group. He then changed his stage name from Big Moon Dawg to Big Punisher and got his recording start with a guest appearance on the second album by the Bronx's Fat Joe (Joseph Antonio Cartagena, 1970–), *Jealous One's Envy* (1995). In 1997, Big Pun signed with New York City's Loud Records (1991–). He also became a member of Terror Squad (1998–2009), founded by Fat Joe, but Terror Squad released only one album. *Yeeeah Baby* had to be completed after his death. A posthumous compilation album, *Endangered Species* (2001), features both hits and previously unreleased material as well as remixes. It peaked at No. 7 on the Billboard 200. In 2000, Big Pun failed to make a scheduled performance on *Saturday Night Live* (1975–). Two days later, he suffered a fatal heart attack. At the time, he weighed 698 pounds. A tribute documentary film, *Big Pun: The Legacy*, was released in 2009*.

Anthony J. Fonseca

See also: Puerto Rico; The United States

Further Reading

Irizarry, Jason G. 2009. "Representin': Drawing from Hip Hop and Urban Youth Culture to Inform Education." *Education and Urban Society* 41, no. 4: 489–515.

Rivera, Raquel Z. 2003. "Remembering Big Pun." In *New York Ricans from the Hip Hop Zone*, chap. 9. New York: Palgrave Macmillan.

Further Listening

Big Pun. 1998. *Capital Punishment*. Loud Records.

Further Viewing

Yudin, Vlad, dir. 2008. *Big Pun: The Legacy.* New York: Vladar Company.

Birdman

(aka Baby, Bryan Williams, 1969–, New Orleans, Louisiana)

American rapper Birdman is a successful recording artist and co-owner, with his older brother Slim (aka Slim tha Don, Ronald Williams, 1967–), of Ca$h Money Records (1991–). Birdman also serves as company president. In the 2000s, Ca$h Money was a prominent southern rap, bounce, and Miami bass recording label, and Birdman used Ca$h Money as a home label to mentor and release up-and-coming rappers such as Juvenile (Terius Gray, 1975–) and Lil Wayne (1982–). Along with Slim, Birdman had a short-lived business venture that included an oil-and-gas exploration company, Bronald Oil and Gas, LLC (2010–2011). He also owns a clothing line called Respek (2016–) but has been sued for copyright infringement in a lawsuit that claims that the name was already in use. As of 2018, this lawsuit, and others involving Lil Wayne, have yet to be resolved.

RAGS TO RICHES

Birdman and his brother were born in the late 1960s in New Orleans. By the time he was five and Slim was seven, they were orphaned and homeless. The brothers eventually lived in the Magnolia Projects of the 3rd Ward, one of the most violent, crime-ridden housing units in the city. They sold drugs, which led to their arrests as teenagers. Birdman was sentenced, for drug possession, for three to five years at the Elayn Hunt Correctional Center, where after serving for almost two years he was acquitted.

When he was 21, Birdman decided to begin a recording label he named after the Cash Money Brothers in the American crime drama motion picture *New Jack*

City (1991). The Williams brothers signed several New Orleans–based rappers who became highly successful in their own right, including fellow Magnolia Projects inhabitant Juvenile. While offering Juvenile and Lil Wayne solo careers, Birdman also formed groups with them, including Hot Boy$ (1996–) and the B.G.z (1995–2001), with B.G. (aka Baby Gangsta, Christopher Dorsey, 1980–) and Lil Wayne. B.G.'s albums, especially *Solja Rags* (1997), which sold over 200,000 copies, helped Ca$h Money amass its initial revenue. Meanwhile, Birdman himself formed a duo with DJ Mannie Fresh (Byron O. Thomas, 1969–) called Big Tymer$ (1997–2005). Their first album, *How You Luv That* (1997), featured Hot Boy$ and other Ca$h Money rappers and sold over 100,000 copies. It managed to reach No. 168 on the Billboard 200 and No. 25 on Billboard's Top R&B/Hip Hop Albums despite no major radio or video airplay. The success of the album led to a 1998 distribution deal with Universal Music Group (then Universal Records, 1934–), a reissue of the album, and a subsequent release of *How You Luv That, Vol. 2* (1998).

In 1999, both Birdman and the Ca$h Money label saw an even greater wave of success. Lil Wayne's solo debut album, *Tha Block Is Hot* (1999), was certified Platinum, and was followed by *Lights Out* (2000) and *500 Degreez* (2002), which were certified Gold. In the meantime, the Big Tymer$'s *I Got Work* (2000) was also certified Platinum, followed by the duo's most successful and critically acclaimed album, *Hood Rich* (2002). The album debuted at No. 1 on the Billboard 200, and its hit, "Still Fly," peaked at No. 11 on the Billboard Hot 100, at No. 3 on Billboard's Hot Rap Tracks, and at No. 4 on Billboard's Hot R&B/Hip-Hop Songs. In 2003, "Still Fly" earned Big Tymer$ a Grammy nomination for Best Rap Performance by a Group or Duo.

CA$H MONEY AND BIRDMAN SINGLES

By 2001, Lil Wayne and Big Tymer$ were the largest contributors to Ca$h Money's rise to success. Birdman eventually rewarded Lil Wayne's accomplishments by giving him his own recording imprint, Young Money Entertainment (2005–). Birdman collaborated with Lil Wayne on *Like Father Like Son* (2006), which peaked at No. 3 on the Billboard 200 and No. 1 on both Billboard's Top R&B/Hip-Hop Albums and Top Rap Albums. Birdman worked on his own solo rap career throughout his development as a music producer.

Many years after his debut album as B-32, *I Need a Bag of Dope*, he released *Birdman* (2002), *Fast Money* (2005), *5*Stunna* (2007), and *Pricele$$* (2009). *Fast Money* peaked at No. 9 on the Billboard 200, and the others reached Nos. 24, 18, and 33. Exhibited on these albums is the same hard-hitting bass and, at times, the use of brass to counter it (heavy bass is a staple of Big Tymer$'s albums and Birdman's other productions). Producer Mannie Fresh (Byron O. Thomas, 1969–) played a significant role in recording *Fast Money*, while Lil Wayne contributed to the full string of studio album releases. *Pricele$$* also featured Canadian rapper Drake (1986–), who in 2009 signed on Lil Wayne's imprint, followed that year by Nicki Minaj (1982–).

FALL OF CA$H MONEY AND BUSINESS ISSUES

Since the 2010s, Birdman has successfully promoted hip hop artists, though his planned *Pricele$$2* album, later retitled *Bigga Than Life* (to be released in 2011), never came to fruition. Instead, Birdman collaborated with Lil Wayne to release "Fire Flame" and "I Get Money" (2011) and worked with Rick Ross (William Leonard Roberts II, 1976–) on "Born Stunna" (2012). A remix of the last featured Lil Wayne and Nicki Minaj. Though Nicki Minaj and other rappers on the label had huge success and developed significant careers in hip hop, Birdman's studio albums *Ms. Gladys* (2016), named in honor of his mother, and *From tha Briks* (2016) have not come close to enjoying the same success as his pre-2010 albums.

Trouble ensued when Lil Wayne's release of *Tha Carter V* was delayed; his subsequent statement revealed that he felt his creativity was being stifled. Lil Wayne's self-released *Sorry 4 the Wait 2* (2015) dissed Birdman, and he filed a $51 million lawsuit against him for the delay. Further lawsuits took place when Lil Wayne left Ca$h Money, claiming that the label failed to pay its artists and threatening that he would take Drake and Nicki Minaj with him. When Lil Wayne joined Jay-Z's (1969–) subscription-based music streaming service TIDAL (2014–) and released his *Free Weezy Album* (2015), Birdman filed a $50 million lawsuit against him.

Jacqueline M. DeMaio

See also: Bounce; Lil Wayne; Miami Bass; The United States

Further Reading

Baxter, Vern Kenneth, and Peter Marina. 2008. "Cultural Meaning and Hip Hop Fashion in the African American Male Youth Subculture of New Orleans." *Journal of Youth Studies* 11, no. 2: 93–113.

Pearson, David. 2016. "Bell Patterns, Polyrhythms, Propulsive Subdivisions, and Semitones: The Musical Poetics of Late-1990s Ca$h Money Records Style." *Journal of Popular Music Studies* 28, no. 3: 356–80.

Vozick-Levinson, Simon. 2015. "Lil Wayne Goes to War." *Rolling Stone* no. 1230, March 12, 11–12.

Further Listening

Birdman. 2005. *Fast Money.* Ca$h Money Records.

Birdman. 2009. *Pricele$$.* Universal Motown/Ca$h Money.

Black Eyed Peas

(Los Angeles, California, 1995–)

The Black Eyed Peas is a hip hop and electronica rap and dance (including breakdancing) quartet formed in 1995 by members apl.de.ap (Alan Pineda Lindo, 1974–), Taboo (Jamie Gomez, 1975–), and will.i.am (William James Adams, 1975–), along with guest vocalist Kim Hill (1962–). Hill left the band before it became successful and was replaced by singer Fergie (Stacey Ferguson, 1975–) in 2001, completing the four-person lineup that would make up the group to this day. Originally an alternative hip hop group that gained popularity by playing college campuses, the Black Eyed Peas evolved to become a hip hop, R&B, soul, funk, dance, and techno fusion band. In 2009, the group set the Billboard Hot 100 record for longest No. 1 chart run for a group when "I Gotta Feeling" (14 weeks at No. 1) assumed the Billboard No. 1 singles spot held by "Boom Boom Pow" (12 weeks at No. 1), making the group the top slot holder for a record 26 consecutive weeks. It also won various Grammy Awards, such as the 2004 award for Best Rap Performance by a Duo or Group, the 2005 awards for Favorite Pop/Rock Band and Favorite Rap/Hip Hop Band, Duo or Group, 2005, and the 2006 award for Best Pop Performance by a Duo or Group with Vocal. Overall, the band has won seven Grammy Awards, eight American Music Awards, and three World Music Awards.

DANCERS TURNED MUSICIANS

Group members will.i.am, who became a songwriter, rapper, and keyboardist, and apl.de.ap, who became a singer/rapper and drummer/programmer, first met as breakdancers in 1989 in East Los Angeles, where they danced with the Tribal Nation Crew (1990*). The two began creating their own beats and songs to dance to, creating the hip hop duo Atban Klann (A Tribe Beyond a Nation, 1991–1995). In 1992, the duo added three members and signed a recording contract with CEO Eazy-E's (1963–1995) Ruthless Records (1986–), but due to marketing problems caused by the band's eschewal of the violent gansta rap that defined Ruthless, a finished album (*Grass Roots*) was never released. Eazy-E's death resulted in their being dropped by the label.

The duo added Taboo, a Mexican American hip hop, electronica, and dance music rapper, DJ, guitarist, keyboardist, and songwriter, and reformed themselves as the Black Eyed Peas; with Taboo, a tenor who created spoken and chanted emphases to mark the ends of musical phrases and added vocalizations and crowd calls between lines and verses, the trio signed a contract with Interscope Records (1989–) in 1997. Vocalist Hill joined the crew for the 16-song debut in 1998, *Behind the Front*, which received positive reviews for its funky sound, and the four began a rigorous two-year tour that culminated in their second album, *Bridging the Gap* (2000). The Black Eyed Peas set itself apart from other rap groups by emphasizing not the gangster life—violence and materialism—in its lyrics, but social causes, romance/sex, and enjoying a community of human beings.

HOUSEHOLD FAME

The band's first album to feature Fergie and its third overall, *Elephunk* (2003), on A&M Records (1962–), made the Black Eyed Peas a household name, peaking at No. 14 on the Billboard 200, selling over 8.5 million copies worldwide, and spawning the group's first three Billboard Hot 100 hits: "Where Is the Love?," "Hey Mama," and "Let's Get It Started." Pop legend Justin Timberlake (1981–) produced the first, and the group joined Timberlake on his tour with Christina Aguilera (1980–). Its 2005 A&M album, *Monkey Business*, performed even better, reaching No. 2 on the Billboard 200 and selling over 10 million copies worldwide. It also gave the band its first Billboard Top 10 hits, "Don't Phunk with My Heart" and "My Humps."

The next album, *The E.N.D.* (2009), followed a hiatus wherein Fergie, Taboo, and will.i.am pursued solo careers and apl.de.ap worked on an English and Tagalog music project and video (apl.de.ap is Filipino and adopted by Americans). Returning to Interscope, the band debuted what was a harder, more energetic electronic sound that was influenced by will.i.am's trip to Australia at No. 1 on the Billboard 200. *The E.N.D.* sold 11 million copies worldwide; it spawned three Billboard No. 1 songs, "Boom Boom Pow," "I Gotta Feeling," and "Imma Be."

In 2004, will.i.am, who had produced most of the Black Eyed Peas songs, launched his record label, the will.i.am Music Group. In 2011, the Black Eyed Peas performed at the Super Bowl XLV halftime show. The other group remains philanthropically active, and rumors of a new group album exist as of 2018.

Anthony J. Fonseca

See also: Hip Hop Dance; The Philippines; The United States; will.i.am

Further Reading

Devitt, Rachel. 2008. "Lost in Translation: Filipino Diaspora(s), Postcolonial Hip Hop, and the Problems of Keeping It Real for the 'Contentless' Black Eyed Peas." *Asian Music* 39, no. 1: 108–34.

Norris, Chris. 2010. "The Black Eyed Peas." *Rolling Stone* no. 1103, April 29, 48–56.

Further Listening

Black Eyed Peas. 2003. *Elephunk.* AandM.

Black Eyed Peas. 2005. *Monkey Business.* AandM.

Black Eyed Peas. 2009. *The E.N.D.* Interscope.

Black Nationalism

Black Nationalism refers to a broad range of sociopolitical perspectives that imagine the global black population as part of one coherent nation. Specifically, Black Nationalism imagines black people of all nations as part of the African diaspora due to migration, colonial displacement, and the Atlantic slave trade. Black Nationalists generally believe that black people of African descent share fundamental common interests and should view their membership in the black global nation as their primary basis for cultural identification. The legacy of Black Nationalism is central to understanding the global character of hip hop.

INTELLECTUAL AND HISTORICAL FOUNDATIONS

Scholars often trace the origins of Black Nationalism to the African American abolitionist Martin Delany (1812–1885), whose encounters with racism convinced him that black-skinned people had no future in the United States and should seek to form their own nation. Similarly, Marcus Garvey (1887–1940), a Jamaican who founded the Universal Negro Improvement Association (UNIA) in 1914, first in Akron, Ohio, launched the "Back to Africa" movement, claiming that black people

The American group Public Enemy, pictured here in 2015, is just one of many hip hop acts to embrace and advocate for Black Nationalism. The group's advocacy includes performing free concerts at parks as a way to reach out to black communities facing gang activity, street violence, and poverty. (Christian Bertrand/Dreamstime.com)

of all nations should reclaim their rightful home on the African continent after years of colonization and racial oppression. Significantly, figures such as Delany and Garvey advocated the creation of a literal nation-state for the purpose of reunification; however, developing versions of Black Nationalism did not think strictly in terms of geographic boundaries—in these versions, a nation is more of an idea.

Many antiracist and anticolonial activists during the latter half of the 20th century adopted this perspective. Martinican author Frantz Fanon (1925–1961) was a trained psychiatrist who was interested in the psychological toll of colonialism and racism on black people. His books (both originally in French) *Black Skin, White Masks* (1952) and *The Wretched of the Earth* (1961) were widely read by black (and other) activists across the world. He argued that anticolonial struggles were essential not only to physically purge colonizers from native lands but also to allow colonized peoples to develop a collective, more ethnically pure, sense of self. Fanon's writing, the proliferation of anticolonial movements in Africa, the success of Maoism in China (1950s–1970s), and the struggle of the National Liberation Front (1960–1976) in Vietnam against French and U.S. intervention all had profound impacts on antiracist activists in the United States and Europe. Many key civil rights figures in the United States, such as Stokely Carmichael (1941–1998) and Malcolm X (1925–1965), explicitly drew connections between antiracist struggles at home and anticolonial movements abroad—African Americans were also a colonized people who needed to fight for self-determination.

Some activists have been critical of Black Nationalism. Many in the Marxist tradition see Black Nationalism as problematic because it encourages black workers to identify first along ethnic lines rather than on class lines. Many feminists and LGBTQ+ activists have noted that Black Nationalism tends to privilege the leadership of men. Others find the militant separatist rhetoric of individuals such as Malcolm X to be antithetical to the goal of unity. Furthermore, prominent Black Nationalists such as Louis Farrakhan (1933–) of the Nation of Islam (1930–) have been accused of anti-Semitism, misogyny, and homophobia. These activists question how and with whom black people should identify as they pursue social justice.

BLACK NATIONALISM AND GLOBAL HIP HOP

From its inception, Black Nationalism has had a strong influence on hip hop. Jamaican musical traditions such as reggae and dub followed migrants such as Kingston–born hip hop pioneer DJ Kool Herc (1955–) to the United States. Jamaica's own political climate was fraught with intense violence, and one of the nation's most influential modes of cultural resistance was the Rastafari movement (1930s–), which worshipped Ethiopian Emperor Haile Selassie I (Ras Tafari Makonnen Woldemikael, 1892–1975) as its deity. Rastafari was deeply Afrocentric and driven by the belief that Selassie would unify African nations and lead to the creation of a perfect world, or Zion. Reggae artists such as Jamaica's Bob Marley (Robert Nesta Marley, 1945–1981) were especially invested in the Rastafari tradition. Another early hip hop artist, Bronx, New York–born and—based Afrika Bambaataa (1957–), saw hip hop as a valuable tool for unifying black inner-city youth in ways that offered an alternative to joining street gangs. He formed the Universal Zulu Nation (1973–), now established in France, Japan, South Africa, Australia, and South Korea, drawing on the legacy of anticolonial struggles in Africa to give form to his distinctly nationalist movement. Members of the Zulu Nation employ Afrocentric garb and other markers of pan-African culture that reflect the nationalist politics of the movement.

Contemporary hip hop artists also invoke Black Nationalist themes. The influential and controversial rap group Public Enemy (1982–) emerged from the band members' shared interest in the black intellectual tradition. Public Enemy's politically charged music (and associated videos) contained many elements of Black Nationalism. For example, the music video for their track "Fight the Power," from their third album *Fear of a Black Planet* (1990), portrays a gathering of black people in New York City that is part concert and part political rally. The colors of the Black Nationalist flag (red, black, and green) are ubiquitous, and participants hold signs showing pictures of prominent black leaders and names of major cities across the United States. The activist rap duo dead prez's (1996–) motto, "Revolutionary but Gangsta," deliberately forms the acronym RBG, which can also stand for the colors of the Black Nationalist flag (its song "Read 'Bout Garvey" forms the same acronym and references the influential nationalist thinker and activist). The members of dead prez self-identify with the nationalist Uhuru Movement (1972–) of Africa and the International People's Democratic Uhuru Movement (1991–) of the

United States and frequently incorporate the Black Nationalist colors into their album artwork and music videos.

Bryan J. McCann

See also: Five Percent Nation; Nation of Islam; Political Hip Hop; Public Enemy; The Universal Zulu Nation

Further Reading

Fanon, Frantz. 1963. *The Wretched of the Earth*, translated by Constance Farrington. New York: Grove Press.

Hill Collins, Patricia. 2006. *From Black Power to Hip Hop: Racism, Nationalism, and Feminism*. Philadelphia: Temple University Press.

Further Listening

dead prez. 2004. *RBG: Revolutionary but Gangsta*. Sony Urban Music/Columbia.

Ice Cube. 1991. *Death Certificate*. Priority Records.

Public Enemy. 1990. *Fear of a Black Planet*. Def Jam Recordings/Columbia.

Blige, Mary J.

(Mary Jane Blige, 1971–, Bronx, New York)

Mary J. Blige, who has been nicknamed the Queen of Hip Hop Soul, is an American R&B, soul, and hip hop singer, songwriter, and music producer. She is best known for merging hip hop and neo soul in the early 1990s and for achieving commercial success in R&B. Her success and innovation earned her the honor of one of the Top 50 Most Influential R&B Artists in *Essence* magazine, and *Rolling Stone* listed her album *My Life* (1994) in its Top 500 Greatest Albums of All Time. Blige has also collaborated with a who's who of hip hop performers: R&B artists Faith Evans (1973–) and Case (Case Woodard, 1975–); rappers Method Man (Clifford Smith, 1971–), Jay-Z (1969–), and Ghostface Killah (Dennis Coles, 1970–); and the hip hop group Wu-Tang Clan (1992–). Blige also has acted in various television series and movies, most notably Tyler Perry's *I Can Do Bad All By Myself* (2009), *Rock of Ages* (2012), and the Lifetime film *Betty and Coretta* (2013), in which she portrays Dr. Betty Shabazz (Betty Dean Sanders, 1934–1997), wife of Malcolm X (1925–1965). Blige's vocal range is mezzo-soprano.

EARLY ALBUMS

Blige's father, jazz musician Thomas Blige (1951*–), left the family when she was four years old, but had taught her to appreciate jazz. Through her mother, Cora Blige (n.d.), she heard funk and soul artists such as Sam Cooke (1931–1964), Aretha Franklin (1942–), and Gladys Knight (1944–). In her formative years, Blige, her mother, and her sister sang gospel music at a Pentecostal church in Georgia. The family then moved to the Bronx, where she heard early hip hop DJs and was attracted to their various rhythms and sampling styles. Her breakthrough came in 1988 when she recorded a cover of Anita Baker's (1958–) "Caught Up in the Rapture" (1986) at a karaoke booth in White Plains, New York. After receiving the tape, Andre

Harrell (1960–), Uptown Records' (1986–1999) CEO, met with her in 1989 and signed her to the label, making her the label's first female and youngest artist.

Her debut album *What's the 411?* (1992) featured the hit singles "Real Love" and "You Remind Me," both of which topped the Hot R&B chart, with "Real Love" reaching the Billboard Top 10. Her use of vocals over a hip hop beat introduced the concept of hip hop soul, a subgenre of new jack swing (a music genre popular in the 1980s and 1990s that fuses jazz, hip hop soul, electronica, rap, and R&B). The album sold over three million copies and helped Blige reach a broader audience; it reached No. 6 on the Billboard 200. In 1993, *What's the 411? Remix* was released, featuring remixes of Blige's songs by producers such as Puff Daddy (1969–), K-Ci (Cedric Renard Hailey, 1969–), and the Notorious B.I.G. (1972–1997).

American singer-songwriter, record producer, and actress Mary J. Blige's musical style focuses on storytelling and incorporates hip hop and other genres like R&B, neo soul, new jack swing, and gospel music. Here the Grammy Award–winning musician attends the Critics' Choice Awards, held in 2018 in Santa Monica, California. (Starstock/Dreamstime.com)

Blige wrote or cowrote most of the songs on her second album, the certified triple-Platinum *My Life* (1994), with lyrics based on her experiences with drugs and alcohol, clinical depression, and abusive relationships. The songs "Be Happy," "Mary Jane (All Night Long)," and "I'm Goin' Down" reached the Top 40 and pushed the album to the No. 7 position on the Billboard 200 and to No. 1 on Billboard's Top R&B/Hip-Hop Albums chart. Her third album, *Share My World* (1997, MCA Records), contains more upbeat music, such as "Love Is All You Need" and "I Can Love You." *Share My World* hit No. 1 on the Billboard 200 and sold over three million copies in the United States, and Blige was nominated for Best Female R&B Vocal Performance and performed "Not Gon' Cry" at the 1997 Grammy Awards. In 1998, Blige won an American Music Award for *Share My World*.

LATER SUCCESS

Blige's later career began to adopt an adult contemporary sound, mixed with funk and soul from the 1970s and 1980s. Her album *Mary* (1999) went double

Platinum. In 2001, she released *No More Drama*, which features her best-selling single, "Family Affair," which ranked No. 1 on the Billboard Hot 100 for six weeks; it reintroduced Blige's signature hip hop soul sound from the early 1990s. *The Breakthrough* (2005) sold over seven million copies worldwide, reached No. 1 on the Billboard 200 and Top R&B/Hip-Hop Albums charts, and was nominated for eight Grammy Awards, winning three: Best R&B Album, Best R&B Song, and Best Female Vocal R&B Performance for "Be without You."

Celeste Roberts

See also: Neo Soul; New Jack Swing; The United States

Further Reading
Alexander, Danny. 2016. *Real Love, No Drama: The Music of Mary J. Blige.* American Music Series. Austin: University of Texas Press.
Lindsey, Treva B. 2013. "If You Look in *My Life*: Love, Hip Hop Soul, and Contemporary African American Womanhood." *African American Review* 46, no. 1: 87–99.

Further Listening
Blige, Mary J. 1994. *My Life.* Uptown Records.
Blige, Mary J. 2005. *The Breakthrough.* Geffen Records.

Bliss n' Eso

(BnE, Bliss n' Esoterikizm, 2000–, Sydney, Australia)

Bliss n' Eso is an Australian hip hop trio consisting of American rapper MC Bliss (Jonathan Notley, 1979–), Australian rapper MC Eso (aka Esoterik, Max Mac-Kinnon, 1979*–), and Australian DJ Izm (Tarik Ejjamai, n.d.). The trio is internationally known for live performances, extensive touring, collaborations, and albums. In 2004, Bliss n' Eso released their debut studio album, *Flowers in the Pavement*, which included "Hip Hop Blues," a track produced by Suffa (Matthew David Lambert, 1977–) from contemporary hip hop group Hilltop Hoods (1994–). Bliss n' Eso's five studio albums have charted on the ARIA Albums Chart: *Day of the Dog* (2006) peaked at No. 45; *Flying Colours* (2008) peaked at No. 10; and *Running on Air* (2010), *Circus in the Sky* (2013), and *Off the Grid* (2017) have all reached No. 1. *Flying Colours* won an ARIA Award for Best Urban Release in 2008, and *Running on Air* and *Circus in the Sky* were certified Platinum in Australia. From its fourth studio album (*Running on Air*) on, the trio has focused on uplifting messages—a result of members' becoming parents, touring Afghanistan in 2013, and getting sober, as in the song "Addicted," which is not about drugs but about being addicted to life. More positive messages exist in *Off the Grid* with "Moments" and "Friend Like You."

The three members formed Bliss n' Esoterikizm while in high school. In 1999, Bliss n' Esoterikizm issued an untitled promotional mixtape. In 2000, the trio released their first EP, *The Arrival*. That same year, the trio shortened its name to Bliss n' Eso and signed with Melbourne-based Obese Records (1995–2007). When the trio began in Sydney's small, underground hip hop scene, its recordings included sampling, looped beats, and turntablism and its lyrics resembled American hip hop artists such as Public Enemy (1982–) and various gangsta rappers. The trio focused on street life, sex, partying, and drugs—but it also began to introduce issues such as the evils of mass consumerism and preached music as salvation.

In 2004, the trio released its debut studio album *Flowers in the Pavement*. Meanwhile, it continued live concert shows, including a 2005 tour supporting 50 Cent's (1975–) debut major-label studio album *Get Rich or Die Tryin'* (2003). *Flying Colours*, which featured recordings in Australia, South Africa (with the Zulu Connection Choir, 1998–), and the United States, proved that the band's sound and storytelling rapping had matured. It was a product of the trio's 2006 signing on to the Illusive Sounds label (2003–), whose parent company was Mushroom Group (1972–) of Melbourne, the largest independent music and entertainment firm in Australia. As of 2018, all of Bliss n' Eso's albums have been recorded on this label.

Melissa Ursula Dawn Goldsmith

See also: Australia; Gangsta Rap; The United States

Further Reading

Hendrie, Doug. 2015. "African-Australian Hip Hop: Closer to the Real Thing?" Review essay in *Kill Your Darlings* 21 (April): [164]–81.

Maxwell, Ian. 2003. *Phat Beats, Dope Rhymes: Hip Hop Down Under Comin' Upper.* Middletown, CT: Wesleyan University Press.

O'Hanlon, Renae. 2006. "Australian Hip Hop: A Sociolinguistic Investigation." *Australian Journal of Linguistics* 26, no. 2: 193–209.

Further Listening

BnE. 2004. *Flowers in the Pavement.* Obese Records.

BnE. 2017. *Off the Grid.* Illusive Sounds.

Blondie

(1974–1982, 1997–, New York City, New York)

Blondie is an American punk, new wave, alternative, and experimental rock group from New York City that in 1981 released "Rapture," the first Billboard No. 1 hit featuring rap. The band had mainstream success in the late 1970s with Billboard Hot 100 No. 1 hits such as "Heart of Glass" (1979), "Call Me" (1980), and "The Tide Is High" (1981), among others, including additional No. 1 hits outside the United States, especially in the United Kingdom and Australia. Like other punk bands during their time, Blondie incorporated elements of reggae in its music, but what made it stand out was its use of disco, synth-pop, rock, musical references to or quotations of familiar tunes (from motion pictures to childhood nursery songs), funk, and rap.

"RAPTURE"

At the same time "Rapture" was a hit in the United States, it peaked at No. 4 and No. 5 on the Australian and U.K. charts, respectively. Two U.S. versions of "Rapture" and another version (targeted for the U.K. market) were released: the seven-inch single was included on Blondie's *Autoamerican* (1981), as was a slightly longer 12-inch version with an extra verse; another version was a special disco remix of the longer U.S. version with a different introduction and percussion section as well as a lengthier instrumental break that extended "Rapture" to 10 minutes. Through rapping, using hip hop music, and using musical references/quotations—the last resembles a live version of early sampling—Blondie incorporated elements that it used infrequently in its recorded output; the song nevertheless exemplifies efforts to help rap attain mainstream and worldwide attention. Rap, which is often associated with male performers and historical performance practice, is here performed by lead singer Debbie Harry (Deborah Ann Harry, b. Angela Tremble, 1945–), whose rapping voice is lower than her airy, muted soprano singing voice. "Rapture" was significant because it was rap's first Top 10 hit—and it was rapped by a woman.

Blondie is an all-white band, and the success of "Rapture" has been the focus of whether the song amounts to white appropriation of black music; however, "Rapture" also represents important collaboration between the early New York punk and hip hop scenes as well as between musicians such as Harry and guitarist/percussionist/songwriter Chris Stein (1950–) with hip hop pioneers and prominent graffiti artists such as Fab Five Freddy (1959–), Lee Quiñones (George Lee Quiñones, 1960–), and Jean-Michel Basquiat (1960–1988). The first hip hop video on MTV (1981–), "Rapture" is a one-shot take of Manhattan's Lower East Side, with Fab Five Freddy and Quiñones in the background spray-painting graffiti and Basquiat behind the turntables, replacing Grandmaster Flash (1958–), who did not appear for the video shooting. Harry and Blondie perform in the foreground.

The rap text of "Rapture" is an absurd story about the invasion of Earth by the Man from Mars, which involves his eating cars and people. Clean enough for radio, the text stresses end rhymes and uses the technique of namechecking—referencing several hip hop pioneers such as Fab Five Freddy and Grandmaster Flash. In the 1980s, Harry and Stein had visited underground hip hop clubs and block parties in New York. Both met Fab Five Freddy and later showed him their rap text before "Rapture" was recorded. In 1981, Blondie collaborated again with him, combining pop and rap, which resulted in an untitled U.K. EP and "Yuletide Throw Down," both issued by England's pop music magazine *Flexipop!* (1980–1983).

INFLUENCE

"Rapture" was the very first instance of rap heard on mainstream radio. Elements of the song were sampled and remixed right away. Blondie and Fab Five Freddy (as Blondie and Freddie) sampled multiple elements of "Rapture" in "Yuletown Throw Down." In 1981, Grandmaster Flash and the Furious Five (1976–1982, 1987–1988) released the hip hop classic "The Adventures of Grandmaster Flash on the Wheels of Steel," which showcased Grandmaster Flash's turntablism in a solo. The song sampled elements of "Rapture" in addition to other songs. In England, the new wave and disco project band Enigma (1981) also used multiple elements of "Rapture." Examples of artists' using "Rapture" in hip hop include the Jungle Brothers' (1987–) "In Dayz 2 Come" (1989), KRS-One's (1965–) "Step into a World ('Rapture's' Delight)" (1997), and Foxy Brown's (Inga DeCarlo Fung Marchand, 1978–) "I'll Be (Remix)" (1997), featuring Jay-Z's (1969–) and Destiny's Child's (1997–2006) "Independent Women Part 1" (2000).

Into the 2000s, "Rapture" is still being used in hip hop tracks, and Blondie has been involved in some of these efforts. In 2009, for the Rhythm video game *DJ Hero*, "Rapture" was remixed with the Beastie Boys' "Intergalactic" on *"Intergalactic" vs. "Rapture."* In 2014, Blondie rerecorded "Rapture" for their compilation album *Greatest Hits Deluxe Redux*, which celebrated the band's 40th anniversary. Covers also exist of the song, and as of 2018, the band still includes renditions of "Rapture" in its concert tours.

Melissa Ursula Dawn Goldsmith

See also: Fab Five Freddy; Graffiti Art; Turntablism; The United States

Further Reading

French, Kenneth. 2017. "Geography of American Rap: Rap Diffusion and Rap Centers." *GeoJournal* 82, no. 2: 259–72.

Stein, Chris. 2014. *Negative: Me, Blondie, and the Advent of Punk.* New York: Rizzoli.

Williams, Melvin L. 2017. "White Chicks with a Gangsta' Pitch: Gendered Whiteness in United States Rap Culture (1990–2017)." *Journal of Hip Hop Studies* 4, no. 1: 50–93.

Further Listening

Blondie. 1980. *Autoamerican.* Chrysalis.

Bolivia

Bolivia is a landlocked, mountainous South American nation with a multiethnic population of 11 million and a musical history of indigenous folk cultures, native and immigrant dance music (such as *kullawada*, *taquirari*, *carnavalito*, Afro-Bolivian *saya*, and *cueca*), and African music imported with slavery; its modern music scene can best be described as one that fuses these disparate traditional music styles with modern rhythms and beats. In Bolivian hip hop, this fusion can take various forms, including a blending of Andean folk styles and new hip hop beats with lyrics about revolution and social change. The hub of Bolivian hip hop is a major metropolis with the highest altitude in the world—at 13,615 feet, El Alto, an Andean urban center with a population of one million (over two million counting the metropolitan area), has become the sociopolitical rap geocenter since 2003.

Using radio media, specifically radio station Wayna Tambo (1995–), El Alto–based rappers such as Abraham Bojórquez (1981–2009), of the rap duo Ukamau y Ké (2003–2006); Grover Canaviri Huallpa (1982*–); and Dennis Quispe Issa (n.d.) rap in Aymara (an indigenous language), Spanish, English, and Portuguese about unity against poverty, political corruption, and social ills. Their urban and contemporary lyrics are juxtaposed against Andean flutes, guitars, trumpets, tubas, bongos, and traditional drums.

Women play a large part in Bolivian hip hop. La Paz–based Sdenka Suxo Cadena (1979*–) protests classism, materialism, and elitism, both as a solo artist and as part of the female rap group Nueva Flavah (2000–); with members also from La Paz, São Paulo–based sister rappers Santa Mala (2014–) rap about the condition of immigrants and Bolivian pride, sometimes juxtaposing sampling against traditional instruments and hip hop rhythms.

In addition, a movement called "Wayna Rap," which has spawned various anthology albums, has gained momentum in Bolivia. Wayna rap is retro 1970s and incorporates the sounds of original Bolivian music, eschewing North American elements in favor of Bolivian touches, such as highland wind instruments.

Anthony J. Fonseca

See also: Brazil; Peru

Further Reading

Ballivían, Rocio Ramírez, and Linda Herrera. 2012. "Schools of the Street: Hip Hop as Youth Pedagogy in Bolivia." *International Journal of Critical Pedagogy* 4, no. 1: 172–84.

Tarifa, Ariana. 2012. "Hip Hop as Empowerment: Voices in El Alto, Bolivia." *International Journal of Qualitative Studies in Education* 25, no. 4: 397–415.

Bolon and Bolon Player

(aka *Bolonfola*)

The *bolon* is a large West African harp (chordophone instrument) with three (traditional) or four (modern) strings on a wooden bow-shaped neck that are also strung to a goat skin–covered gourd (also called a *calabash*) that amplifies the resonant sound. A resonator is usually mounted at the top of the neck as well. A male musician usually plays the instrument by holding the gourd between his legs, with the strings facing him. The strings are plucked rather than strummed. The bolon is often confused with the *kora*, one of few major accompanying instruments that griots use in their performance practice. The bolon has a deeper, more resonant sound than the kora; in fact, it sounds like a string bass. Bolon players can create a beat—a form of beatmaking that serves as a rhythmic counterpoint to the melody that is simultaneously being played on the strings. Kora players may also beat on the calabash, but they do not do this as routinely as do bolon players. Unlike the kora players and griots, bolon players can use the beat in the foreground. The bolon is used in Afropop and modern music; however, the kora still overshadows it in hip hop music. Likewise, the griot remains more popular in hip hop than the bolon player.

In contrast to the griot, whose role supports the notion that hip hop is a continuation of African aesthetics, less attention has been given to the bolon's role or the player's role as social critic, which is ironic since the most important distinguishing feature of the bolon player is that he has the power to publicly express criticism of a leader, regime, or people, making him a precursor to the rapper who expresses political and social critique. Also unlike griots, the bolon player can be a free person or from a slave group known as the *jon*, and hereditary restrictions play no part in who becomes a bolon player. Because it is an instrument of the people, diverse West Africans play the bolon, and although the bolon is mostly associated with the Mandé or Fulani people, the Banbara, Senufo, Jola, and Kissi also play it. Bolon playing can be found in Mali, Guinea-Bissau, Ivory Coast, Burkina Faso, the Gambia, Senegal, and Sierra Leone, among other West African countries.

The bolon's history traces to a time before the Mali Empire (1235*–1670) and is often associated with hunting or war traditions. Bolon players took on the role of the bard, like griots, accompanying themselves with singing or other verbal arts. Unlike griots, who were often hired by nobility and wealthy patrons to praise them or to maintain historical information, bolon players expressed praise of a hunter's or warrior's strength, power, conquests, and accomplishments as well as encouraged hunters and warriors by predicting success.

Beyond the traditional use in hunting ceremonies, other bolon playing traditions emerged. For example, the bolon is used to accompany dance as a musical performance known as ballet tradition in Guinea-Bissau. The Jola use the bolon to accompany men's choruses in the Gambia and Senegal.

Melissa Ursula Dawn Goldsmith

See also: Burkina Faso; The Gambia; Griot; Guinea-Bissau; Ivory Coast; Mali; Senegal; Sierra Leone

Further Reading

Charry, Eric. 2000. "Hunter's Music." In *Mande Music: Traditional and Modern Music of the Maninka and Mandinka of Western Africa*, chap. 2. Chicago: University of Chicago Press.

Nomi, Dave. 2014. "The Politics of Silence: Music, Violence, and Protest in Guinea." *Ethnomusicology* 58, no. 1: 1–29.

Price, Tanya Y. 2013. "Rhythms of Culture: Djembe and African Memory in African-American Cultural Traditions." *Black Music Research Journal* 33, no. 2: 227–47.

Further Listening

Bassekou Kouyate and Ngoni Ba. 2007. *Segu blue* (*A Mixture of Blue*). With tracks 6 and 10 featuring Habib Sangare on bolon. Out Here Records.

Oumou Sangare. 2009. *Seya* (*Joy* in Mande). World Circuit.

The Bomb Squad

(1986–, Long Island, New York)

The Bomb Squad is an American hip hop production group from Long Island, New York, that has been active since 1986. It is best known for its work with another Long Island–based hip hop group, Public Enemy (1982–), but have also produced albums and singles for artists ranging from Paula Abdul (1962–) to Ziggy Marley (David Nesta Marley, 1968–). The Bomb Squad's original members included Hank Shocklee (James Henry Boxley III, 1967–), Keith Shocklee (Keith Matthew Boxley, 1962–), Chuck D (Carlton Douglas Ridenhour, 1960–), and Eric Sadler (aka Vietnam, 1960*–). Paul Shabazz (n.d.) joined the group by 1990, and in 1991, Gary G-Wiz (Gary Rinaldo, 1969–) came on board. The Bomb Squad's best-known productions were made in conjunction with Public Enemy, with lead rapper Chuck D being the common element. Public Enemy's first studio album, *Yo! Bum Rush the Show* (1987), was followed by critical and commercial successes *It Takes a Nation of Millions to Hold Us Back* (1988) and *Fear of a Black Planet* (1990); these albums, all produced by the Bomb Squad, helped define Public Enemy's sound.

Other artists sought the Bomb Squad's production for its albums or singles after hearing its work with Public Enemy. The Bomb Squad produced Ice Cube's (1969–) *AmeriKKKa's Most Wanted* (1990), which was his first solo album release after he left the West Coast hip hop group N.W.A. (1986–1991). *The Great Adventures of Slick Rick*, a 1988 album by the English-born American hip hop artist Slick Rick (1965–), contained several tracks produced by the Bomb Squad. The group also produced singles for New York–based hip hop artists, including Run-D.M.C. (1981–2002), Salt 'n' Pepa (1985–), Eric B and Rakim (1986–1993), and 3rd Bass (1987–2000). The Bomb Squad has also produced tracks for musicians, such as Vanessa Williams (1963–), in other musical genres.

The Bomb Squad's style of production is characterized by a dense sonic texture and often frenetic energy. Its earlier music contained sampled sounds from dozens of different source tracks; some of the tracks that the Bomb Squad produced for Public Enemy in the late 1980s and early 1990s contain well over 30 different sampled recordings per individual track. The members of the Bomb Squad drew samples from their enormous personal record collections that consisted of many different kinds of African American popular music, such as soul, funk, and R&B. In the early 1990s, due to legal issues and copyright restrictions, the Bomb Squad began sampling fewer source tracks, resulting in a notable change in its musical sound and style.

Amanda Sewell

See also: Chuck D; Public Enemy; The United States

Further Reading

Moon, Tom. 2013. "Public Enemy's Bomb Squad." In *The Rock History Reader*, edited by Theo Cateforis, chap. 48. New York: Routledge.

Sewell, Amanda. 2014. "How Copyright Affected the Musical Style and Critical Reception of Sample-Based Hip Hop." *Journal of Popular Music Studies* 26, nos. 2–3: 295–320.

Further Listening

Ice Cube. 1990. *AmeriKKKa's Most Wanted.* Priority.

Public Enemy. 1988. *It Takes a Nation of Millions to Hold Us Back.* Def Jam.

Public Enemy. 1990. *Fear of a Black Planet.* Def Jam.

Boogie Down Productions

(1985–1992, Bronx, New York)

Boogie Down Productions was a South Bronx, New York, hip hop band that served as a vehicle for KRS-One (Lawrence Krisna Parker, 1965–) during the early part of his rapping career. Its original lineup consisted of KRS-One, turntablist and producer DJ Scott La Rock (Scott Monroe Sterling, 1962–1987), and turntablist, beatboxer, and rapper D-Nice (Derrick Jones, 1970–). With the exception of KRS-One, the band's lineup changed often, with the first change occurring in 1987 after DJ Scott La Rock was murdered, the same year that the group's debut album, *Criminal Minded*, was released on B-Boy Records (1985–). The trio, along with producer Lee Smith (n.d.), is credited for pioneering a fusion of Jamaican dancehall reggae and hip hop and was an early example of urban rap—the band's lyrics contained frank and detailed descriptions of street life—which would soon be popularized as West Coast gangsta rap.

The band produced five more studio albums: *Man and His Music* (1988), *By All Means Necessary* (1988), *Ghetto Music: The Blueprint of Hip Hop* (1989), *Edutainment* (1990), and *Sex and Violence* (1992). Despite four certified-Gold albums, Boogie Down Productions ceased when KRS-One decided to pursue a solo career.

The band was also responsible for one of the first diss rap feuds, the Bridge Wars. This began when the Queensbridge-based Juice Crew (1983–1991) released a 1985 song, "The Bridge," which seemingly expresses local pride in the borough as the place where rap began and attacked Queens, New York, rapper LL Cool J (1968–), for alleged plagiarism. In response, Boogie Down Productions released its debut single, "South Bronx" (1986), which argued that the South Bronx was the birthplace of hip hop and contained lyrics that demeaned and threatened the Juice Crew, which responded with group member MC Shan's (Shawn Moltke, 1965–) "Kill That Noise" (1987). Boogie Down Productions, in turn, responded with the reggae-infused rap song "The Bridge Is Over" (1987). The feud, which has since been explained as KRS-One's jab at Juice Crew producer and DJ Mr. Magic (John Rivas, 1956–2009), who once dissed his music, expanded to other New York rappers. KRS-One lost interest after the death of DJ Scott La Rock. He began to call himself Teacha and started writing socially conscious lyrics; he also joined with other rappers in 1987 to create the Stop the Violence Movement.

Anthony J. Fonseca

See also: KRS-One; LL Cool J; The United States

Further Reading

Bradley, Adam, and Andrew Dubois, eds. 2010. "Boogie Down Productions." Under "Part 2: 1985–92: The Golden Age" in *The Anthology of Rap*, pp. 145–59. New Haven, CT: Yale University Press.

Coleman, Brian. 2007. "Boogie Down Productions: *Criminal Minded*." In *Check the Technique: Liner Notes for Hip Hop Junkies*, pp. 72–91. New York: Villard.

Further Listening

Boogie Down Productions. 1987. *Criminally Minded*. B-Boy Records.

Boogie Down Productions. 1990. *Edutainment*. Jive.

Bosnia and Herzegovina

Bosnia-Herzegovina is a Southeastern European country that borders Croatia, Serbia, and Montenegro. Hip hop's development there was constantly disrupted by political unrest, war, massacres, genocides, and ethnic cleansings through deportations. In the mid-1980s, there was limited access to American hip hop in Bosnia-Herzogovina, which was part of the dissipating Socialist Federative Republic of Yugoslavia (1945–1992). Bosnian Serbs initially took interest in break-dancing, and by the late 1980s, a pioneering rapper and anonymous graffiti artist from Bijeljina known as elvir reper (n.d.) had emerged. Tuzla became the main center for underground hip hop as rapping battles took place in artists' basements. Reper began rapping in American English, inspired by American hip hop groups such as Run-D.M.C. (1981–2002) and Public Enemy (1982–); however, he neither recorded nor resurfaced after the Bosnian War (1992–1995).

In 1990, the one-party communist power was replaced by a three-party national assembly representing the main populations: Bosniaks, Croats, and Serbs. Prompted by Slovenia and Croatia's 1991 independence from Yugoslavia, Bosniaks and Croats wanted independence as well, but were opposed by most Serbs. In 1991, members of the Serb Democratic Party (1990–), whose ideology included Serbian nationalism, conservatism, and anti-Islamic sentiment (most Bosniaks are Muslims who practice Sunni Islam), formed the First Assembly of the Serb People of Bosnia and Herzegovina (1991–1996), departing from the national assembly. That same year, the conservative Croatian Democratic Union (HDZ) established the Croatian Community of Herzeg-Bosnia (1991–1996). In 1992, the Serb Democratic Party created the Serbian Republic of Bosnia and Herzegovina, renaming it the Republika Srpska (1992–). Boycotted by Serbs, the Republic of Bosnia and Herzegovina nevertheless was admitted by the United Nations (UN). Serbian president Slobodan Milošević (1941–2006, in office 1989–2000) officially withdrew his Yugoslav People's Army (JNA) from Bosnia-Herzegovina; however, Bosnian Serbs belonging to JNA formed the Army of Republika Srpska and thus began the Bosnian War and the Siege of Sarajevo (1992–1996). The 1992 Bijeljina massacre resulted in the genocide of Bosniaks and dissenting Serbs, under the command of Milošević's JNA.

Using hip hop as a springboard for dissent, Bosniaks Edo Maajka (Edin Osmić, 1978–) and Crni Zvuk (Black Sound, 1990–2000)* rapped about the Bosnian War in Tuzla. Edo Maajka later fronted the successful Bosnian hip hop crew Disciplinska Komisija (DK, the Disciplinary Commission, 2000–), which fused old-school hip hop with reggae and rock. DK stood out for recording rap battle songs that protested against Bosnian political corruption and the right-wing politics of American president George W. Bush (1946–, in office 2001–2009). Despite the Bosnian War's end in 1996, musicians found no respite. The Kosovo War (1998–1999) affected hip hop by halting album production between 1998 and 2001. In 1999, the International Criminal Tribunal for the former Yugoslavia (ICTY) charged Milošević for war crimes, including genocide and crimes against humanity during the Croatian War of Independence (1991–1995), the Bosnian War, and the Kosovo War. Now freer, television, radio, and the Internet media introduced hip hop to more Bosnian-Herzegovinians. The first hip hop radio show that aired in Bosnia-Herzogovina was *FM JAM* (1999–), on Tuzla's 102.7 FM. *FM JAM* played local and global hip hop, remixes, demos, and freestyle battle recordings, providing rapper biographies. Other hip hop scenes emerged in Sarajevo and Mostar. Sarajevo Bosniak rappers include Jala Brat (Jasmin Fazlić, 1986–) and Buba Corelli (Amar

Hodžić, 1989–). Although female Bosnian rappers remain extremely rare, rapper and singer Sassja (Sanela Halilović, 1988–) has enjoyed success. From Tuzla, Sassja fuses hip hop with reggae and raga. In 2015, Sassja released her debut studio album, *Taktički praktično* (*Tactical Practical*).

The Yugoslav Wars were responsible for a Bosniak diaspora that eventually produced future rappers. Rapper Frenkie (Adnana Hamidović, 1982–) of DK escaped to Nuremberg, Germany, where he first engaged in hip hop through rapping and graffiti. Frenkie's earliest rap texts were in German, but after his return in 1998 to Tuzla, he started rapping in Bosnian, supporting Bosnian-Herzogovinian nationalism. Other acts remain outside the country. Hardcore rapper Genocide (Jusuf Dzilic, 1984–), from Zvornik, escaped the Bosnian War to Ireland and relocated to Hastings, New Zealand, where he raps in American vernacular about his homeland's struggles. Elvir Omerbegović (1979–) is a highly successful German rapper, hip hop producer, owner of the recording label Selfmade Records (2005–), and president of Rap at Universal Music Germany, part of Universal Music Group (1996–). Though Omerbegović was born and raised in Metmann, near Düsseldorf, he is of Bosnian-Serbian descent and grew up attending a supplementary Yugoslavian school.

Melissa Ursula Dawn Goldsmith

See also: Serbia

Further Reading

Kovač, Rok. 2013. "Hip Hop Ain't Dead—It Just Emigrated: Rap Music and Nationalism in Bosnia and Herzegovina." In *Hip Hop in Europe: Cultural Identities and Transnational Flows*, edited by Sina A. Nitzsche and Walter Grünzweig, chap. 14. Zürich, Switzerland: LIT Verlag.

Mujanović, Jasmin. 2017. "Nothing Left to Lose: Hip Hop in Bosnia-Herzogovina." In *Hip Hop at Europe's Edge: Music, Agency, and Social Change*, edited by Milosz Miszczynski and Adriana Helbig, chap. 2. Bloomington: Indiana University Press.

Further Listening

Frenkie. 2005. *Odličan* (*Excellent*). Menart/Fmjam Records.

Sassja. 2015. *Taktički praktično* (*Tactical Practical*). Menart.

Botswana

Botswana, a landlocked country in southern Africa, is one of the least populous African countries. Nonetheless, it has its own musical practices, which it often shares with South Africa, one of the countries that influences its popular music scene (others include the United States, India, and countries in Western Europe). American hip hop and South African *kwaito* reached Botswana through cultural interchange. Another influence was Motswana MC Mr T (aka Nomadic, Tebogo Mapine, n.d.), from Francistown, Botswana, whose music aired in Mafikeng (aka Mahikeng), South Africa, which is close to Botswana's border; he pioneered *motswako*, an influential subgenre of hip hop. Mr T belonged to P-Side Crew (1994–1999, 2007–) from Gaborone, which is often credited as one of Botswana's earliest hip hop crews. Botswana rapping texts vary, depending on whether the music is hip hop, motswako, or kwaito and depending on rappers' language preferences. Some hip hop artists prefer American vernacular English, whereas motswako tends to be rapped in Setswana—a language adopted as Botswana's common language—interwoven with American vernacular. Kwaito uses South African languages that may be known in Botswana, such as Afrikaans, Zulu, and American vernacular English. Rappers' opting for American vernacular English over British English is a result of American hip hop's influence on Botswana.

FROM TRADITIONAL MUSIC TO MOTSWAKO

The Batswana comprise descendants from the country's first inhabitants, the Tswana (Sotho tribal descendants and Basarwa Bushmen), but Botswana's population also includes the Kalanga, Basarwa, and Kgalagadi people. Botswana attained its independence in 1966. From 1885 until that time, it had been the United Kingdom's Bechuanaland Protectorate, with strong cultural influences from English and Irish colonization. Identity through music is important to the Batswana, and music is an integral part of early education and is offered as an elective throughout secondary and higher education. Dance is considered part of music.

Traditional Tswana music is mostly vocal and employs handclaps, stomping, whistles, and string instruments (chordophones)—including guitars—instead of drums. Call-and-response, in addition to singing in both unison and harmony, is used in a variety of traditional music, from *borankhana* to *setapa*. When the country was a British protectorate, performance of Tswana music was restricted, but since Botswana's independence, this traditional music is part of national identity, and its popularity remains strong. Also popular are genres such as American rock, jazz, and gospel; South African kwaito and motswako; and Botswana's own creations, *kwasa-kwasa* and *kwaito kwasa*. From Motswana kwaito emerged kwaito kwasa, a fusion of kwaito and kwasa-kwasa. The tempo is a compromise between fast kwaito and slow kwaso kwaso. The latter is Botswana's version of the Democratic Republic of Congo's *kwassa kwassa*, a kind of African rumba with sexually suggestive dance movements. Examples of Motswana kwaito kwasa musicians and Motswana kwaito artists are Vee (Odirile Vee Sento, 1983–) and Mapetla (Thabo Mapetla Ntirelang, n.d.), respectively. Although kwasa-kwasa dominates Botswana's music industry, some Motswana artists, such as the group Franco and Afro Musica (2001–) and rapper Jeff Matheatau (n.d.), as well as Franco (Frank Lesokwane, n.d.) as a soloist, are internationally famous.

Compared to other African countries, Botswana was an early adapter to hip hop, which first gained popularity in the country in the early 1980s. Early Motswana hip hop employed sampling, drum machine beats, beatboxing, turntablism, and hip hop instrumentation. Radio hosts known as DJ Sid (Ndala Baitsile, n.d.), D-Ski (David Molosiwa, n.d.), Draztik (Dave Balsher, 1973–), and Slim (aka Fat Free, Salim Mosidinyane, n.d.) initially popularized hip hop in Gaborone, Botswana's capital city. Draztik, originally from Francistown, was the scene's American West Coast rap connection, as he lived in Sacramento, California, between 1986 and

1993. The scene's American East Coast connection was Slim, who was born and raised in New York City before his 1990s move to Gaborone. Both rap in English and were members of the early hip hop group Cashless Society (1999–2006) and the project group Organik Interfaze (2000–2001).

Botswana's development of hip hop was influenced and interspersed with the development of kwaito and motswako. After the end of Apartheid (1948–1991) and when Nelson Mandela (1918–2013) came to power in South Africa in 1994, kwaito emerged there, but musicians from Botswana began performing it and engaging in kwaito culture, which shares characteristics with hip hop (despite its distinctness). Motswako became extremely popular in Botswana in the mid-1990s. Unlike kwaito, which has its own culture, motswako is a hip hop subgenre that may be politically or socioconsciously charged, as opposed to kwaito's lighter focus on gangster and street life.

Two examples of Motswana motswako rappers and singer-songwriters are Zeus (1986–) and Scar (Thato Matlhabaphiri, 1985–). Their rap lyrics emphasize partying, acquisition of wealth, and sex—but also have a sociopolitical side that protests capitalism. Elaborate storytelling videos have been essential to hip hop in Botswana, from its earlier days with Cashless Society in the 2000s to rappers such as Zeus and Scar in the 2010s.

Melissa Ursula Dawn Goldsmith

See also: Kwaito; Motswako; South Africa; The United States; Zeus

Further Reading

Rapoo, Connie. 2013. "Urbanized Soundtracks: Youth Popular Culture in the African City." *Social Dynamics: A Journal of African Studies* 39, no. 2: 368–83.

Rapoo, Connie. 2014. "Reconfiguring the City: Contemporary Youth Performance and Media Entertainment in Gaborone." *Botswana Notes and Records* 45: 66–76.

Further Listening

Cashless Society. 2003. *African Raw Material, Vol. 1.* Unreleased Records.

Zeus. 2015. *African Time.* Universal.

Bounce

Bounce is a hip hop subgenre that emerged in the early 1990s in New Orleans. Bounce uses rap but emphasizes its role as dance party and regional music; it also borrows elements from Mardi Gras parade culture. Bounce features call-and-response; Mardi Gras hollers, callouts, and chants (many of which are calls for dance party participation); brass ensembles; and hip hop beats. Some shouts, such as on the word "break" or the phrase "can I get an Amen," may be generic and are characteristic of other kinds of hip hop and hip hop–related global music genres, such as the shouted word "hai" used in Indian *bhangra-beat* music (hip hop music that accompanies dance linked to traditional *bhangra*'s agricultural-influenced movements); however, in bounce, shouts also reference specific neighborhoods, housing projects, and geographic areas of New Orleans. Whistling and the use of

Big Freedia performs in 2011 in her home city, New Orleans. She has brought national attention to bounce music, which incorporates elements found in hip hop like rapping, shouts, beats, and melodic hooks. Her lyrics celebrate being gay and include allusions to New Orleans and Southern black cultures, as well as braggadocio and insult humor. (Erika Goldring/WireImage/Getty Images)

vocalizations, including beatboxing, create beats. New Orleans LGBTQ+ communities have embraced bounce and favor it because of its flamboyant, lively, and participatory appeal, which seems reminiscent of glam rock and disco diva music. New Orleans is arguably the bounce capital of the world, though the subgenre was a national phenomenon by the early 2000s.

Some scholars cite bounce's earliest appearance at dance parties in New Orleans in 1991. MC T. Tucker (aka T.T. Tucker, Kevin Ventry, n.d.) and DJ Irv (Irvin Phillips, n.d.) performed raps that included Mardi Gras chants, hollers, and regional callouts, as exhibited in "Where Dey At." Hip hop elements such as rap that leads to calls and chanted refrains, melodic hooks over which chants may continue, rapid drum machine or synthesizer beats, and samples were also present in early bounce. Beats from earlier tracks, most notably the Showboys' (1985–2000) "Drag Rap (Trigger Man)" (1986), a narrative rap track over the beat from "Trigger Man," became part of the rhythmic structure for many bounce tracks. Its brass instrumentation is also used often. Another track that was used was Cameron Paul's (n.d.) "Brown Beats" (*Beats and Pieces*, 1987). Lyrics focused on sex rather than on politics, and less narrative was used in rap than that found in other recorded hip hop of the early to mid-1990s.

BOUNCE IN HIP HOP

Southern hip hop artists incorporated bounce elements in their music. By the late 1990s, a major New Orleans–based record label, Ca$h Money Records (1991–), owned and run by brothers Birdman (1969–) and Slim (Ronald Williams, 1967–), had access to this underground musical activity. The label became a prominent producer of bounce music. One of its producers, Mannie Fresh (Byron O. Thomas, 1969–), was also a New Orleans DJ, so airplay was inevitable. Nationally known New Orleans hip hop songs that have used bounce elements include Big Tymer$'s (1994–) "Get Your Roll On" (2000), Hot Boy$'s (1996–) "We on Fire" and "Tuesday and Thursday" (1999), Juvenile's "Solja Rags (1997), and Mystikal's (Michael Lawrence Tyler, 1970–) "Here I Go" (1995), "The Man Right Chea" (1997), and "Shake Ya Ass" (2000).

By 2000, bounce's popularity had spread to Mississippi and Texas. An early example is Brookhaven, Mississippi, native David Banner's (Lavell William Crump, 1974–) "Like a Pimp" (2003), which uses the beat from "Trigger Man." Bounce remixes have also gained popularity: Juvenile's "Nolia Clap Remix" (2004) peaked at No. 31 on the Billboard Hot 100 and No. 9 on Billboard's Hot Rap Tracks and Hot R&B/Hip-Hop Songs.

New Orleans hip hop artists continued to develop the subgenre, both underground and in the mainstream. Gay musician Big Freedia (Frederick Ross, 1978–) has helped the subgenre gain national attention. After Hurricane Katrina (2005), Big Freedia moved to and performed in Texas with other bounce artists before being able to return to New Orleans. In 2009, she performed with New Orleans transgender rappers Katey Red (anonymous, n.d.) and Sissy Nobby (anonymous, n.d.) at Voodoo Experience, and in 2010 she self-released the album *Big Freedia Hitz, Vol. 1*. This was the same year that the Ogden Museum of Southern Art in New Orleans featured the exhibit "Where They At: New Orleans Hip Hop and Bounce in Words and Pictures." In 2011, her album was nominated for a GLAAD (Gay and Lesbian Alliance Against Defamation, 1985–) Media Award for Outstanding Music Artist. In 2012, Big Freedia appeared on the television drama *Treme* (2010–2013). In 2016, Beyoncé's (1981–) "Formation" (with accompanying music video shot in New Orleans) sampled Big Freedia. Beyoncé's use of bounce in "Formation" was not her first, for she used elements of bounce in 2007 in "Get Me Bodied."

Jacqueline M. DeMaio

See also: Birdman; The United States

Further Reading

Cooper, Rich Paul. 2010. "Bouncin' Straight Out the Dirty Dirty: Community and Dance in New Orleans Rap." In *Hip Hop in America: A Regional Guide*, edited by Mickey Hess, vol. 2, chap. 20. Santa Barbara, CA: Greenwood.

Miller, Matt. 2012. *Bounce: Rap Music and Local Identity in New Orleans*. Amherst: University of Massachusetts Press.

Brand Nubian

(1989–1995, 1997–, New Rochelle, New York)

Brand Nubian is an American hip hop group featuring Grand Puba (Maxwell Dixon, 1966–), Sadat X (aka Derek X, Derek Murphy, 1968–), Lord Jamar (Lorenzo Dechalus, 1968–), and DJ Alamo (K. Jones, n.d.). From its debut album on, the group has been known for its alternative approach to hip hop and its concentration on socially conscious and politically charged raps associated with Islam and the Nation of Gods and Earths (the Five Percent Nation), an American organization founded in 1964 by former member of the Nation of Islam named Clarence 13X (1928–1969), a former student of Malcolm X (1925–1965). Clarence 13X believed that 5 percent of the people on Earth knew truth and could teach or enlighten the 85 percent who were kept in ignorance by the 10 percent who ruled.

In 1990, Elektra (1950–) released Brand Nubian's first album, *One for All*. It followed the success of the single "Brand Nubian." The album charted at No. 130 on the Billboard 200 and No. 34 on the R&B/Hip-Hop Albums chart, and it received positive reviews for its fusion of music, but caused some controversy (which improved sales, a total of 400,000 copies) because of its militant lyrics in songs such as "Drop the Bomb" and "Wake Up." The band's second and third albums,

Hailing from New Rochelle, New York, the East Coast alternative hip hop group Brand Nubian raps Afrocentric sociopolitical lyrics rooted in the teachings of the Nation of Gods and Earths. Pictured here are the group's three MCs: Grand Puba (left), Lord Jamar (far left), and Sadat X (right). Its best known lineup also included DJs Alamo (center) and Sincere (not pictured). (Johnny Nunez/WireImage/Getty Images)

In God We Trust (1993) and *Everything Is Everything* (1994), reached Nos. 12 and 54, respectively, on the Billboard 200, but experienced both mixed reviews and mediocre sales. Nonetheless, they both reached the Top 20 of the R&B/Hip-Hop Albums chart and produced two Hot Rap Tracks singles, "Word Is Bond" and "Hold On." The 1998 album *Foundation* (No. 59 on the Billboard 200, No. 12 on the R&B/Hip-Hop Albums chart) produced the group's highest-charting Billboard Hot 100 single at No. 54, "Don't Let It Go to Your Head." After various solo efforts, Brand Nubian's MCs reunited in 2004 for *Fire in the Hole*, released by Babygrande Records (2001–), but the album did not chart. Their 2007 album, *Time's Runnin' Out*, also did not chart. It contained no new material; rather, it was a remix of songs recorded during the *Foundation* sessions.

All Brand Nubian members have done solo albums on the side. Grand Puba began with a group called Masters of Ceremony (1985–1988), but when it disbanded, he became the lead MC for Brand Nubian for *One for All*. The album proved that although their music was hip hop, the group was comfortable with everything from reggae to new jack swing (Grand Puba left the group afterward, returning in 1997 in time for *Foundation*). Sadat X has also worked as an elementary school teacher and a firefighter in New Rochelle, where he also coaches youth basketball. Lord Jamar has done music production and television acting and is best known for his role as Supreme Allah on the TV series *Oz* (1997–2003); he has attracted some ire with controversial statements about homosexuality and race in hip hop, both as a member of Brand Nubian and as a solo act.

Anthony J. Fonseca

See also: Five Percent Nation; Political Hip Hop; The United States

Further Reading

Coleman, Brian. 2007. "Brand Nubian: *One for All*." In *Check the Technique: Liner Notes for Hip Hop Junkies*, pp. 92–104. New York: Villard.

Miyakawa, Felicia. 2005. *Five Percenter Rap: God Hop's Music, Message, and Black Muslim Mission*. Bloomington: Indiana University Press.

Further Listening

Brand Nubian. 1990. *One for All*. Elektra.

Brazil

Brazil saw an emergence of hip hop in the early 1980s, practiced primarily among working-class residents of urban peripheries. The music genre rose to prominence due to the activities of public b-boys and rappers who performed at nightclubs in the country's major urban centers. These individuals drew much of their inspiration from American hip hop culture, which was disseminated in Brazil by radio stations, touring artists and dancers from the United States, and American films such as *Wild Style* (1983) and *Beat Street* (1984). The cities of São Paulo (the country's largest city) and Brasília became especially well known as centers for hip hop, and remain so as of 2018. In São Paulo, the São Bento subway station became an early hotspot for b-boying, while open-air spaces such as Roosevelt Plaza and Galeria

24 de Março acted as important public locales for practitioners to meet up, exchange ideas, and perform.

During the 1990s, elements of hip hop culture began to work their way into the broader Brazilian popular music sphere. Rap and DJing in particular became increasingly commonplace creative practices in mainstream popular musicians' repertoires. In the country's sixth-largest metropolitan area, Recife, led by the pioneering artist Chico Science (Francisco de Assis França, 1966–1997), artists affiliated with the musical movement of *mangue* beat mixed rap and sampling practices with internationally circulated genres such as reggae and rock as well as regional northeastern Brazilian musical and performance styles such as *embolada* and *maracatu*.

EARLY HIP HOP AND THE EMERGENCE OF ACTIVISM

Most early Brazilian hip hop artists did not incorporate overtly political criticism in their performances. Beginning in the mid-1980s and continuing into the mid-1990s, however, antiracist commentary began to take a central place in Brazilian hip hop culture. Practitioners drew particular inspiration from U.S. cultural figures such as James Brown (1933–2006), Public Enemy (1982–), and Afrika Bambaataa (1957–) as well as earlier black Brazilian funk and soul musicians affiliated with the 1970s-era Black Soul movement, such as Rio de Janeiro's Tim Maia (Sebastião Rodrigues Maia, 1942–1998) and Banda Black Rio (1976–). These musical figures also provided raw sonic material for Brazilian DJs, who regularly sampled artists such as Brown in their own mixes. Brazilian hip hop figures were also influenced by existing racial ideologies and movements such as negritude, the Brazilian Movimento Negro Unificado (Unified Black Movement, 1978–), launched in Rio de Janeiro and São Paulo, and the U.S. Civil Rights Movement (1954–1968), especially the militant stance of the 1960s–1970s Black Power Movement.

Artists from São Paulo played central roles in this endeavor. By the late 1980s, the hip hop community centered in São Paulo's Roosevelt Plaza had developed an increasingly oppositional stance with regard to racial discrimination. In 1988, an affiliated group of São Paulo rappers formed the Sindicato Negro (Black Union), which fostered the growth of new rap groups throughout the city while promoting messages of black liberation, Afrocentricity, and racial consciousness. Prominent hip hop artists of this period addressed these issues front and center. Perhaps the best-known group of this era, Racionais MC's (1988–), from São Paulo, rose to national prominence in the late 1980s and became famous for frankly discussing the kind of entrenched exclusion, racism, and violence faced by the predominantly Afro-descendent residents of São Paulo's poorer outlying areas. This discourse, which was shared by contemporaries of the group, such as Posse Mente Zulu (Zulu Mind Posse, 1992–), also functioned as a criticism of broader national narratives with regard to race that constructed whiteness as ideal and downplayed the existence of racism in Brazilian society.

Over time, certain Brazilian hip hop artists who achieved mainstream popularity began to depart from the genre's initial social concerns. Rapper Gabriel O Pensador (Gabriel Contino, 1974–), who rose to prominence in 1993 with his controversial hit "Tô feliz (matei o presidente)" ("I'm Happy: I Killed the President"), from his self-titled debut album, became especially emblematic of this transformation. O Pensador, who hailed from a white, middle-class background in Rio de Janeiro, tended not to explicitly contextualize his music as a manifestation of traditional hip hop culture, preferring instead to place his raps within a broader hybrid cultural sphere that included such diverse music styles as samba and rock. The mid-1990s also saw the rise of evangelical Christian–themed gospel rap, which by the early 2000s had become a staple musical practice within hip hop communities and exerted increasing influence on mainstream hip hop discourse as a whole.

CONTEMPORARY HIP HOP

Since the late 1990s, Brazilian hip hop has seen a shift from being a predominantly racially focused discourse to commenting on the wider set of challenges faced by residents of the urban *periferia* (periphery), a concept that continues to be a central point of interest in contemporary Brazilian hip hop practice. New areas of focus include the problem of geographic distance between poorer neighborhoods and wealthier city centers and the broader experience of marginality felt by poor residents, who are routinely excluded from full participation in Brazilian society. Practitioners have sought to reinvent persistently negative media images of *periferia* residents—an endeavor that functions as part of a larger project of empowering a maligned and ignored section of the Brazilian population.

Brazilian hip hop culture continues to be grounded in these roots as of 2018, although contemporary practitioners address a variety of pressing issues. Some discuss the kinds of violence residents face on a daily basis, both from the Brazilian police, who are notorious for their indiscriminate use of force, and from gangs and drug traffickers. Many seek to highlight the day-to-day economic difficulties caused by endemic lack of access to professional opportunities and social services. Others continue to address racism and the country's broader legacy of racial discrimination, while others have expanded their critique to address other inequalities, such as prejudice faced as a result of sexism and homophobia. Despite the persistence of these negative forces in contemporary Brazilian society, hip hop culture continues to act as a key means and medium for marginalized citizens to build local communities and engage in constructive action for social change.

James McNally

See also: Political Hip Hop; Portugal

Further Reading

Burdick, John. 2013. "We Are All One in the *Periferia*: Blackness, Place, and Poverty in Gospel Rap." In *The Color of Sound: Race, Religion, and Music in Brazil*, chap. 2. New York: New York University Press.

Pardue, Derek. 2011. *Brazilian Hip Hoppers Speak from the Margins: We's on Tape*. New York: Palgrave Macmillan.

Further Listening

Gabriel O Pensador. 1993. *Gabriel O Pensador*. Chaos.

Racionais MC's. 1990. *Holocausto urbano* (*Urban Holocaust*). RDS Fonográfica.

Rappin' Hood. 2001. *Em sujeito homem* (*On the Subject of Man*). Trama.

Breakdancing

Breakdancing, sometimes called b-boying, b-girling, or break-boying, is an umbrella term that was adopted to include various dancing styles (funk styles that developed separately from breaking), including locking, popping, and electric boogaloo. The dance form as it is known today originated with the street dancing of African American and New York–based Puerto Rican youth, and it was originally called b-boying or breaking, though descriptions of similar street dance movements can be found as far back as 1877.

In the late 1960s and early 1970s, a Bronx, New York, street gang called the Black Spades (1968–) was influenced by the teachings of Malcolm X (1925–1965) and aspects of African American culture, including 1960s dance movements. Many of the gang's gatherings included dance, and an early form of b-boying emerged. In general, b-girling, which likely began in the early 1980s, is viewed as the female counterpart to b-boying, but some performers prefer the term hip hop dance or breaking, as b-girling implies a secondary presence. These female dancers view themselves as important and original contributors in both style creation and skill.

THE MOVES

Breakdancing consists of four kinds of movements: toprock, downrock, power moves, and freezes. Its accompanying music is hip hop and funk that uses breakbeats, where the music is paused and looped to give every performer a chance to solo. Changes in tempo also give performers time for power poses. B-boying is heavily influenced by choreography employed by James Brown (1933–2006) as well as martial arts moves popularized in various Kung Fu films. Uprock is a blend of all of these movements, resulting in an aggressive dance that looks like a mimicked Kung Fu martial arts fight with imaginary weapons.

Toprock includes steps performed in a standing position and introduces the audience to the role of facial expression. A lot of toprock has a bouncy nature to it; a dancer shifts weight frequently between feet, appearing to hop while moving the feet intricately. The dancer will then "drop" to downrock, involving floor work and footwork, where the dancer is supported by his or her hands on the floor, allowing legs and arms to move in different directions.

Power moves are more acrobatic, generally supported by the upper body; the legs are free to move. Such moves include the windmill, swipe, back spin, and head spin. Freezes are poses that the dancer strikes to emphasize certain beats in the music or signal the end of a solo. DJ Kool Herc (1955–) was known for taking rhythmic breakdown sections of dance records and prolonging them through looping.

STYLES AND SKILLS

The breakbeat provides a rhythmic basis that lets dancers display their improvisational skills within the duration of a break. This improvisation led to the first b-boy battle, where turn-based (a series of solos) dance competitions between two individuals or dance crews took place. The earliest b-boys were primarily New York

Puerto Rican Americans and African Americans; Bronx-based dance crews such as SalSoul (1974–1978) and Rockwell Association (1976–1978) consisted almost entirely of New York–based Puerto Ricans. Early b-boy styles were individualistic and depended on the region from which a dancer hailed, but video popularized and standardized moves and led to a blending of styles (through emulation). Some b-boys refer to this drifting sense and mixing of styles as the international or You-Tube style, terms coined by California breaker Kujo (Jacob Lyons, 1976–) in a 2012 issue of *B-Boy Magazine*. Breaking demands rigorous training and practice as well as honing of skills that rely on balance, endurance, body control, musicality, and physical strength. These dances are usually performed on very hard surfaces, which lends to a range of injuries over time, namely shin splints and joint deterioration.

INTERNATIONALIZATION

Crazy Legs (1966–), an original member of Rock Steady Crew (RSC, 1977–)—both from the Bronx, New York—became the breakdancing double for Jennifer Beals's (1963–) final dance audition in the American film *Flashdance* (1983). This appearance, as well as others in the American film *Wild Style* (1983) and the American documentary *Style Wars* (1983), brought international attention to breakdancing. He performed in Paris and London as part of the New York City Rap Tour (1982) with musicians Afrika Bambaataa (1957–), founder of Universal Zulu Nation (1973–), and GrandMixer DXT (aka Grand Mixer D.ST, 1960–).

By the early to mid-1980s, breakdancing was international. In Brazil, Ismael Toledo (n.d.), who in 1984 studied dance in the United States before returning to São Paulo, started to organize crews and opened a dance school called the Hip Hop Street College. In France, the Paris City Breakers (1984–) fashioned themselves after the Bronx-based New York City Breakers (NYCB, aka NYC Breakers, 1981–), who were rivals of Rock Steady Crew. NYCB appeared on *The Merv Griffin Show* (1962–1986) and, soon after that, many television shows and in films.

Though not a breaking crew, the Electric Boogaloos (1977–) from Fresno, California, are responsible for the spread of the popping- and toprock-inspired electric boogaloo, which was based on Brown's song "Do a Boogaloo" from his album *James Brown Plays New Breed (The Boo-Ga-Loo)* (1966) and his dance choreography. This dancing style, which is related to funk, is one of many West Coast styles. It makes use of popping and accentuating a body part with the beat of the music. It contains fluid motions, which inform moonwalks and head spins, rather than jerking movements. Locking, another West Coast hip hop dance style, is influenced by pantomime and is related to popping. Popping and locking are often performed together in what is called pop and lock. All breakdancing and popping/locking styles have achieved worldwide popularity.

Through its rise in the latter part of the 20th century, breakdancing, b-boying, and b-girling gained momentum, and into the 21st century, they are still developing as different international cultures embrace hip hop.

Paige A. Willson

See also: The Electric Boogaloos; Hip Hop Dance; New York City Breakers; Popping and Locking; Rock Steady Crew; Uprock

Further Reading

Anon. 2012. "Krazy Kujo Interview." Interview with Jacob Lyons (Kujo). *B-Boy Magazine*, February 15.

Price, Emmett G. III. 2006. *Hip Hop Culture*. Santa Barbara, CA: ABC-CLIO.

Schloss, Joseph G. 2009. *Foundation: B-Boys, B-Girls, and Hip Hop Culture in New York*. New York: Oxford University Press.

Brick City Club

(aka Jersey Club)

Brick City Club is a style of house music popular from 1995 to 2000; it is associated with DJ Tameil (Deshawn Paynes, 1978–), Tim Dolla (anonymous, n.d.), and DJ Lilman (Kevin Brown, 1989*–), club DJs in the Newark, New Jersey area. Brick City Club tracks, like most house music, consist of breakbeat music made of strung-together, repetitive sound bites (short looped vocal excerpts similar to trap and bounce) and musical phrases where dance rhythms and high energy are emphasized over lyrical content or musical complexity. Since it is a style of breakbeat, an electronic dance music technique, Brick City utilizes such sampled breakbeats for its main rhythm. These samples can range from jazz to funk and R&B, and likewise, breakbeat is usually associated with dance music. Despite its niche appeal, Brick City has a large cadre of followers, as attested to by the high number of hits on the YouTube sites maintained by house DJs such as Tameil and Lilman.

ELEMENTS OF SOUND

Although it is similar to other house music styles, Brick City has its own stable of beats, and its DJs use different mixing techniques. DJ Tameil began Brick City by bringing in music associated with Baltimore Club, which relies heavily on 4/4 (quadruple) meter, stays in the range of 130 to 140 beats per minute (bpm), and uses short, repetitive samples and syncopated kick patterns. Brick City uses a more pronounced kick in the programmed drum tracking, and samples are generally shorter; they are often referred to as *chopped*. Brick City also favors synthesizer sounds over brass, which is used more often in Baltimore Club.

The concept of breakbeat music derives from the need in some styles to create drum loops, sometimes sampled, during a break in certain styles of music. Breakbeat can be traced back to the late 1970s, when hip hop turntablists such as DJ Kool Herc (1955–) began linking several irregular funk breaks in a row (in his case, on two turntables used alternatively) to form the rhythmic base for hip hop songs. Breakbeat became very popular in clubs because the extended breakbeat provided breakers with more time to showcase their floor skills and acrobatic moves. In time, breakbeat music began to subdivide into styles such as jungle, drum and bass, big beat, electro-funk, and Miami bass.

Computerized sampling and music editing have made breakbeats easier to create and cut, paste, and loop, and audio production software allows for the addition of transformative effects such as filters, reverb, reversing, slowing/speeding of the tempo, and pitch shifting. More sophisticated software allows for individual instruments to be isolated, sampled, and transformed as well, leading to an endless possibility of breakbeat patterns from a limited number of samples.

Brick City caught on because of its energy; Newark's urban crowds liked the fast and aggressive dance music with a hip hop feel. The style was renamed Jersey Club when DJs outside Newark became more involved with its production and popularity. The style has made its way into hip hop with artists such as Missy Elliott (1971–), who used it on her album *Miss E . . . So Addictive* (2001), and it has influenced EDM (electronic dance music) performers.

Anthony J. Fonseca

See also: Hip House; The United States

Further Reading

Frane, Andrew V. 2017. "Swing Rhythm in Classic Drum Breaks from Hip Hop's Breakbeat Canon." *Music Perception* 34, no. 3: 291–302.

French, Kenneth. 2017. "Geography of American Rap: Rap Diffusion and Rap Centers." *GeoJournal* 82, no. 2: 259–72.

Roberts, Andrea. 2010. "The Bricks and Beyond: Hip Hop in Newark and Northern New Jersey." In *Hip Hop in America: A Regional Guide*, edited by Mickey Hess, vol. 1, chap 8. Santa Barbara, CA: Greenwood.

Further Listening

Various Artists. 2008. *The Brick Bandits EP.* Ol' Head Records.

Briggs

(Adam Briggs, 1986–, Shepparton, Victoria, Australia)

Briggs is an indigenous (of the Yorta Yorta people) Australian rapper, record label owner, comedy writer, and actor. He is famous both as a soloist and as founder of the hip hop duo A.B. Original (2014–). As a solo rap act, he has two albums and one EP to his credit: *Homemade Bombs* (EP, 2009), *The Blacklist* (2010), and *Sheplife* (2014); he also released a mixtape, *Briggs and Friends, Vol. 1*, in 2013. As a member of A.B. Original, he has released one album, *Reclaim Australia* (2016). In 2015, he founded the Bad Apples Music record label, which he uses to give exposure to indigenous hip hop artists. Briggs started out in music as a high school student, playing guitar in a punk band, but he soon found that he had a talent for rapping. He formed an early band called 912 (aka Misdemeanour, 2005–2006), but rapper Reason (Jason Shulman, n.d.) soon afterward discovered him and took him on tour as his hype man.

In 2009, internationally famous Adelaide, Australia–based hip hop band Hilltop Hoods (1994–) took Briggs on their European tour. In 2010, *The Blacklist* was released on the Hilltop Hoods' Golden Era Records (2009–). His musical themes include racism and economic inequality, and he has been a prominent activist against blackface. His raps are aggressive and fast-paced, involving lots of stream-of-consciousness lyricism and wordplay, and he uses vocalizations such as trills and stutters for effect; musically, he has a penchant for metal-style guitars set against an intricate interplay of samples and beats, making his songs diverse and complex. As a writer and actor, he has worked with several series: *Black Comedy* (2014–), *The Weekly with Charlie Pickering* (2015–), and *Cleverman* (2016–). In addition, he is slated to write for a new Matt Groening (Matthew Abraham Groening, 1954–) cartoon series, *Disenchantment*, scheduled for 2018.

Anthony J. Fonseca

See also: Australia; Political Hip Hop

Further Reading

Gooding, Frederick W. Jr., Matthew Brandel, Corbin Jountti, Andrew Shadwick, and Bryantee Williams-Bailey. 2016. "Think Global, Act Local." *Alternative: An International Journal of Indigenous Peoples* 12, no. 5: 466–79.

Morgan, George, and Andrew Warren. 2011. "Aboriginal Youth, Hip Hop and the Politics of Identification." *Ethnic and Racial Studies* 34, no. 6: 925–47.

Further Listening

Briggs. 2010. *The Blacklist.* Golden Era Records.

Briggs. 2014. *Sheplife.* Golden Era.

Brotha Lynch Hung

(Kevin Danell Mann, 1969–, Sacramento, California)

Brotha Lynch Hung is an American West Coast hip hop, gangsta rapper, and record producer whose debut nine-track EP, *24 Deep* (1993), is considered an early version of horrorcore, a gory and gratuitously violent style of gangsta rap. The EP, on Sacramento-based Black Market Records (1989–), reached No. 91 on the Top R&B/Hip-Hop Albums chart.

Even though he is more involved with the second wave of horrorcore artists—the first having occurred between 1982 and 1989 with Houston-based Ganksta N-I-P's (Lewayne Williams, 1969–) debut album *The South Park Psycho* and Detroit-based Esham's (Rashaam Smith, 1973–) self-described acid rap debut album *Boomin' "Words from Hell 1990"* (1989)—Brotha Lynch Hung is considered an innovator of horrorcore. He has released nine studio albums and two mixtapes. His albums are *Season of da Siccness: The Resurrection* (1995), *Loaded* (1997), *EBK4* (2000), *The Virus* (2001), *Lynch by Inch: Suicide Note* (2003), *Snuff Tapes* (2008), *Dinner and a Movie* (2010), *Coathanga Strangla* (2011), and *Mannibalector* (2013). His highest-ranking album on the Billboard 200 was *Loaded*, which peaked at No. 28 and also holds the distinction of being his only album to reach the Top 10 on the Top R&B/Hip-Hop Albums chart. He did not chart on the Top Rap Albums chart until *Dinner and a Movie*, but it, *Coathanga Strangla*, and *Mannibalector*, three albums in his Strange Music Trilogy about a murderous cannibal, all reached the Top 10 on that chart.

DEBUT ALBUM

As a teen, Brotha Lynch Hung was a member of the 24th St. Garden Blocc subset of the Crips (1969–), but after being shot at a party when he attempted to break up a confrontation between a fellow Crip and a Bloods (1972–) member, he decided to leave the gang. He had been rapping since 1982, but his break came in 1992 when he appeared on and produced many of the tracks on X-Raided's (Anarae Brown, 1974–) debut album *Psycho Active*, released just before X-Raided was arrested for murder.

Psycho Active serves as an excellent chronicle of the relationship between gangsta rap and horrorcore, as its two sections are titled *N—a S—t* and *Psycho S—t*, the latter being an excellent descriptor for horrorcore. In 1991, having previously worked with X-Raided, Brotha Lynch Hung released the mixtape *N—z in Black* (aka *N—s in Blacc*).

SEASON OF THE SICCNESS AND LOADED

Brotha Lynch Hung was at the center of a 1996 controversy when one of his songs, "Locc 2 da Brain" from *Season of the Siccness*, supposedly influenced an 18-year-old Colorado man to fatally shoot three acquaintances. The album begins with a reference to the drug-tripping culture of horrorcore when a voice is heard saying that listeners need to be high to listen to this new style of music (which is at odds with the following narration that the rapper needs to kill because his brain is "sick," a sickness caused by living with "the devil," the "triple six," in an urban neighborhood). In *Loaded*, Brotha Lynch Hung raps of himself as the man for whom the government needed to reopen Alcatraz because he grew up in violence, so it is all he knows.

After the 2000s, Brotha Lynch Hung also made some collaborative recordings, including *Blocc Movement* (2001) with Sacramento-based rapper C-Bo (Shawn Thomas, 1971–), *The Plague* (2002) with the North Las Vegas, Nevada, hip hop trio Doomsday Productions (1994–2004)*, *Uthanizm* (2003) with Sacramento-based rapper Tall Cann G (Ramon Ross, 1977), *The New Season* (2006) with Compton, California–based rapper MC Eiht (Aaron Tyler, 1967–), and *The Fixx* (2007) with Sacramento-based rapper Cos (Chris Mathias, n.d.).

Anthony J. Fonseca

See also: Gangsta Rap; Hardcore Hip Hop; Horrorcore; The United States

Further Reading

Edwards, Paul. 2013. *How to Rap 2: Advanced Flow and Delivery Techniques.* Chicago: Chicago Review Press.

Forman, Murray. 2002. *The 'Hood Comes First: Race, Space, and Place in Rap and Hip Hop.* Middletown, CT: Wesleyan University Press.

Libman, Kristian C. 2013. "Brotha Lynch Hung Isn't Recognized as a Rap Pioneer, but He Should Be." *Phoenix New Times*, April 2.

Further Listening

Brotha Lynch Hung. 1995. *Season of da Siccness (The Resurrection).* Black Market Records.

Brotha Lynch Hung. 1997. *Loaded.* Black Market Records.

Brothablack

(Shannon Narrun Williams, 1978–, Sydney, Australia)

Brothablack of the Yiman Tribe is a Sydney-based indigenous hip hop performer, rapper, breakdancer, beatboxer, and actor. At age 14, Brothablack became a founding member of the hip hop group South West Syndicate (1992–2003) and eventually became a solo musician with over 100 stage performances, including Urban Theatre Projects' *The Longest Night* (Adelaide Festival, 2002). Also an educator of and activist for indigenous youth, he appeared at the 2006 Sydney Festival and in 2007 toured Canada. He worked with the 1998 and 2000 Sydney Writers' Festivals and served as MC for the National Indigenous 3on3 Basketball and Hip Hop Challenge. In addition, he cohosted the television program *Move It Mob Style* with Naomi Wenitong (1982–), an indigenous singer-songwriter based in Newcastle. His solo album, *More Than a Feeling* (2006) received positive reviews. His music is best described as old-school rap, with heavy guitars, scratching, and highly energized vocal deliveries; in his videos, he often positions himself as a teacher or mentor, lecturing via rapping.

When he was a preteen, Brothablack began playing drums and singing. He began his music career in 1992 with South West Syndicate. The multinational band won a 2003 Deadly Award (Australian Aboriginal and Torres Strait Islander achievement in music and other entertainment areas) for Most Promising New Talent in Music. In 2007, he teamed up with the Australian hip hop group Hilltop Hoods (1994–) to draw attention to indigenous mortality rates through song. Brothablack has received extensive airplay on government-funded Triple J radio. He was also involved in a video for the Australian Human Rights Commission. As of 2018, he doubles as an Aboriginal Education Officer at James Meehan High School, Macquarie Fields, Sydney.

Anthony J. Fonseca

See also: Australia; Political Hip Hop

Further Reading

Anon. "Brothablack." 2005. *Deadly Vibe* 101 (July).

Fernandes, Sujatha. 2011. "Blackfulla Blackfulla." In *The Edge: In Search of the Global Hip Hop Generation*, chap. 3. New York: Verso.

Morgan, George, and Andrew Warren. 2011. "Aboriginal Youth, Hip Hop and the Politics of Identification." *Ethnic and Racial Studies* 34, no. 6: 925–47.

Further Listening

Brothablack. 2006. *More Than a Feeling*. Self-released.

Brown, James

(aka James Joseph Brown Jr., James Joseph Brown, 1933–2006, Barnwell, South Carolina)

James Brown, often referred to as the Godfather of Soul, was an American funk, R&B, and soul singer, songwriter, record producer, and dancer who began recording in 1953 and was still active as a touring act when he died in 2006. During his lengthy career, he had 44 records certified Gold and influenced many music styles, including hip hop. As far back as 1970, he introduced the idea of a funk-based MC and used the call-and-response structure. In performance versions of the song "Get Up (I Feel Like Being a) Sex Machine," he uses audience calls and calls to his band, the J.B.s (1970–2006), to give him a beat. He also recorded some of the earliest funk-based social consciousness hits, such as "Say It Loud: I'm Black and I'm Proud" (1969), throughout which he uses what would become his vocal trademark, vocalizations that bridged the gap between talking and singing, with a liberal use of grunts, squeals, and screams—this style becoming a precursor to rapping. In addition, his 1967 funk hit with the Famous Flames (1953–1968), "Cold Sweat," made popular the idea of the extended drum break. His drum break from the second version of "Give It Up or Turnit a Loose" (1968) was the most popular 1980s break used for breakdancing.

Brown continued to perform and record until his death in 2006. He was inducted as a solo performer into the Rock and Roll Hall of Fame in 1986 (the Famous Flames were inducted in 2012) and the Songwriters Hall of Fame in 2000. Brown was awarded a Lifetime Achievement Award at the 34th annual Grammy Awards, and in 1997 he was honored with a star on the Hollywood Walk of Fame. In 2003, Brown was also a recipient of Kennedy Center Honors.

EARLY YEARS

Brown grew up in extreme poverty in rural South Carolina until his parents moved to Augusta, Georgia when he was four or five years old. After his mother left for New York City, he raised himself on the streets through his singing and hustling, and he won a talent show at age 11. He also performed at dances to entertain troops from Camp Gordon at the start of World War II (1939–1945), learning piano, guitar, and harmonica, but at 16 Brown was convicted of armed robbery and sent to a juvenile detention center in Toccoa, Georgia. After being parolled in 1952, he straightened up and joined a gospel group in Toccoa, which led to the Gospel Starlighters (aka The Avons and the Five Royals, 1952–1955), an R&B vocal group led by Bobby Byrd (1934–2007). Eventually, the group would change its name to the Flames and then the Famous Flames, with Byrd as its leader and Brown as lead singer.

The band's big break came after Brown contacted Georgia native Little Richard (Richard Wayne Penniman, 1932–), who helped them find new management and get a demo recording. The band's 1958 song "Try Me" went to No. 2 on the R&B chart and reached the Top 50 of the pop charts. Early on, Brown was known as an over-the-top live performer, and he quickly became the band's main attraction. When new management wanted to change the band name to James Brown and the Famous Flames, the band broke up; Brown would later reunite with Byrd for various projects.

Brown saw his first real success in the 1960s. His album with the Famous Flames, *Live at the Apollo* (1963), became a hit and reached No. 2 on the Billboard 200, as did his albums *Papa's Got a Brand New Bag* (1965, with the Famous Flames), *I Got You (I Feel Good)* (1966), and *It's a Man's Man's Man's World* (1966), all charting in the Billboard 200 and spawning titular Top 10 hit singles in the Bill-board Hot 100 chart, earning him his first Grammy Award. Beginning with "Papa's Got a Brand New Bag," Brown had 16 No. 1 hits on the R&B charts; however, he never managed a No. 1 song on the Hot 100, his highest-ranking song being "I Feel Good," which reached No. 3. By the mid-1970s, Brown was introducing world beats into his brand of funk. Some versions of "Bring It Up" make use of Cuban bongos. He also acquired a new nickname, Soul Brother No. 1.

BOOM AND BUST

Besides recording, Brown got into the music business during the late 1960s, buying various radio stations in markets such as Augusta, Georgia; Baltimore, Maryland and Knoxville, Tennessee. Brown renamed the Knoxville station as WJBE, and it began airing a rhythm-and-blues format in January 1968. Brown also branched out musically, recording with various musicians, including predominantly white jazz bands such as the Dee Felice Trio (1963–1969) and Louie Bellson (Luigi Paulino Alfredo Francesco Antonio Balassoni, 1924–2009) and his orchestra. In 1971, Brown began recording for Polydor Records (1913–), which purchased his label, People (1971–1976), as an imprint. His domestic sales took a nose dive after he proclaimed support for Richard Nixon (1913–1994) in the 1972 presidential election, but his international tours remained sold out. He also ran into tax problems with the IRS for back taxes. By 1973, he was working on film scores and movie soundtracks, and by 1974, his domestic boycott was having little effect, and he returned to the top of the R&B charts with "The Payback," "My Thang," and "Papa Don't Take No Mess." Brown also completed his second African tour, and in 1975, he produced, directed, and hosted the television show *Future Shock* (1976–1978).

Between 1975 and 1991, Brown's sales and R&B chart success declined, resulting in lower concert attendance. His disputes with the IRS ruined his businesses. His ex–band members moved on. Brown left Polydor in 1981 and released his final Top 10 Billboard Hot 100 hit, "Living in America," which won a Grammy. In 1988, his album *I'm Real* spawned his final two Top 10 R&B hits. Brown was imprisoned again in late 1988 for aggravated assault and other felonies but served only two and a half years.

Brown's final studio albums, *I'm Back* (1998) and *The Next Step* (2002), did not chart; however, he continued to tour. One of Brown's legacies was a touring show that was nothing short of extravagant, ideal for a musician who styled himself as the hardest-working man in show business. He employed about 50 people for the James Brown Revue, which performed over 330 shows a year.

At the time of his death, Brown's shows included three guitarists, two bass guitar players, two drummers, three horns, and a percussionist. Brown died on Christmas Day in 2006. Public ceremonies were held for him at the Apollo Theater in New York City and at the James Brown Arena in Augusta, where a statue serves as his memorial.

Anthony J. Fonseca

See also: Black Nationalism; The United States

Further Reading

Brackett, David. 1992. "James Brown's 'Superbad' and the Double-Voiced Utterance."
     Popular Music 11, no. 3: 309–24.

Bua, Justin. 2011. "James Brown." *The Legends of Hip Hop.* New York: Harper Design.

Further Listening

Brown, James. 1963. *James Brown: Live at the Apollo.* King Records.

Brown, James. 1969. *James Brown: Say It Loud: I'm Black and I'm Proud.* King Records.

Brown, James. 1970. *Sex Machine.* King Records.

Brown, James. 1972. *There It Is.* Polydor.

Brown, James. 1973. *James Brown: The Payback.* Polydor.

Brunei

Brunei is a sovereign Southeast Asian Sunni country located on the north coast of the island of Borneo. It is roughly the size of the state of Delaware, with approximately half a million residents living mainly in urban areas, predominantly in its largest city and capital, Bandar Seri Begawan. Most citizens are Islamic (following Sharia law), and the government is an absolute monarchy, headed by a sultan—its legislative assembly has only consultation power. Because of Sharia law and the government's control of the media, combined with a small population of youth and therefore a small buyer's market, the hip hop scene was quiet until recently, when businesses globalized and started hiring from other countries. These new workers brought their children, and these new youth introduced hip hop. The genre's first well known hip hop artist, Jazz Hassan (Jasmin Hassan, 1987–), emerged and became known for collaborations with other artists, such as fellow Brunei award-winning producer and musician Udi (Udi Luqman, n.d.).

A former British protectorate (under Australian officers and servicemen) that gained its independence in 1984, Brunei is governed by its constitution and the national tradition of the Malay Islamic Monarchy, using the concept of Melayu Islam Beraja (MIB). Its official language is Malay, although British English and Cantonese are also prominent. A youth movement, the Barisan Pemuda (BARIP, 1946–1948) was the country's first political party. A nationalist identity movement, BARIP contributed to the composition of the country's national anthem.

As CEO of the Jazz My Way line of clothing and of FlowRockzMusic, Jazz Hassan worked with Udi and Erhyme on the song "Mind Game" (2011), which peaked at No. 1 in Malaysia. Jazz Hassan influenced R.V.Boyz (2008–), a four-man rap crew from the Rimba suburb of Bandar Seri Begawan, introducing *crunk* and *snap* styles to Brunei's youth. Hip hop dance has also taken a small hold, with the Brunei Darussalam (n.d.) team winning seven gold medals at the World Championship of Performing Arts in 2015.

Anthony J. Fonseca

See also: Australia; Fashion

Further Reading

Künzler, Daniel. 2007. "The 'Lost Generation': African Hip Hop Movements and the Protest of the Young (Male) Urban." In *Civil Society: Local and Regional Responses to Global Challenges*, edited by Mark Herkenrath, chap. 3. Zürich, Switzerland: LIT Verlag.

Perchard, Tom, Devon Powers, and Nabeel Zuberi. 2017. "Listening While Muslim." *Popular Music* 36, no. 1: 33–42.

Wright, Robin B. 2011. "Hip Hop Islam." In *Rock the Casbah: Rage and Rebellion across the Islamic World*, chap. 5. New York: Simon & Schuster.

Bubba Sparxxx

(Warren Anderson Mathis, 1977–, LaGrange, Georgia)

Bubba Sparxxx is an American southern rapper and producer who is considered the best of the so-called hick hop rappers, a term used to describe country rappers whose lyrics are about American country life and whose music features country and folk instrumentation. His raps include references to growing up in the country, such as his being "baptized in gravy" and being a "bullet hole in the stop sign kind." He came onto the hip hop scene with his song "Ugly," from *Dark Days, Bright Nights* (2000), which features beats created by Timbaland (1972–) and samples from Missy Elliott's (1971–) "Get Ur Freak On" (2000), which Bubba Sparxxx emulates rhythmically in his rap delivery. The song's music video concludes with a comical moment where he and Elliott have a tongue-in-cheek visual exchange about violations of copyright (the line "copywritten, so don't copy me" being an actual line in "Get Ur Freak On"); however, his breakout hit was the more mainstream hip hop "Ms. New Booty," from *The Charm* (2005), which was certified Gold and got as high as No. 7 on the Billboard Hot 100 charts. It was from his first album with Virgin Records (1972–2013), with whom he had signed in 2004. His rapping style is low-key, measured, and articulated, with emphasis on clever near-rhymes.

Bubba Sparxxx's upbringing was a typical country one: his closest neighbor and best friend lived half a mile away from his family. He was nevertheless able to acquire rap mixtapes from New York City through the mail, and he became an early fan of 2 Live Crew (1982–1991, 1994–1998), whose Miami bass sound and sexualized lyrics influenced his songs and videos. Bubba Sparxxx became a rapper after moving to Athens, Georgia, in 1999. That city's huge music scene allowed him to meet Bobby Stamps (n.d.) of New South Entertainment (1995–), who became his manager and arranged various collaborations so that he could work on his first album. He signed to Interscope Records (aka Interscope Geffen, 1989–) and began working with Timbaland, who released Bubba Sparxxx's debut album via his (Timbaland's) Beatclub Records (2001–2004) imprint. He also became a part of Big Boi's (Atwan André Patton, 1975–) Purple Ribbon Records (aka Aquemini Records, 2001–) crew. *Dark Days, Bright Nights* rose to No. 3 on the Billboard 200.

But success took its toll on the rapper, and he eventually succumbed to an opiate addiction around 2006 and had to check himself into rehab. A 2008 arrest for drug possession (the charges were ultimately dropped) marked the low point in his career and acted as a wake-up call—he returned to treatment and semiretired to farm life in Georgia. Three years later, he returned to recording, and in 2013 he released the album *Pain Management*, which he followed with *Made on McCosh Mill Road* (2014), both on country rap label Backroad Records (2001–). Neither album charted.

Anthony J. Fonseca

See also: Timbaland; The United States

Further Reading

Dreisinger, Baz. 2008. "Contagious Beats: Passing, Autobiography, and Discourses of American Music." *Near Black: White-to-Black Passing in American Culture.* Amherst: University of Massachusetts Press.

Grem, Darren E. 2006. "'The South Got Something to Say': Atlanta's Dirty South and the Southernization of Hip Hop America." *Southern Cultures* 12, no. 4: 55–73.

Hendrickson, Matt. 2001. "Bubba Sparxxx: Hillbilly Hip Hop." *Rolling Stone* no. 879, October 11, 45.

Further Listening

Bubba Sparxxx. 2001. *Dark Days, Bright Nights.* Interscope Records.

Bubbles

(aka Hanifa, Hanifa McQueen-Hudson, 1969–, Wolverhampton, England)

Bubbles is the stage name for Hanifa McQueen-Hudson, an English breakdancer or b-girl who combines hip hop dance with painting. A groundbreaking artist on many levels, she was always thought to be male by her early audiences. Though she challenges gender identification even as an adult, by the early 1990s she chose to focus on her education and on raising a family. She also stopped using the moniker *b-girl* and her stage name Bubbles and began calling herself a breakdancer; she changed her stage name to Hanifa, her given first name. In 2006, she began exploring painting as an art after noticing patterns in scuff marks on the floor that she had made with her trainers while breakdancing. Her son, who would come home with painted footprint and handprint cutouts from nursery school, also served as inspiration. She then developed her version of performance art, which she calls Artbreaker. Recorded on video, she breakdances over a canvas with various paints on her shoes, hands, and clothes. Having years of graffiti experience with painting, she finishes her artwork by adding foreground objects, such as musical instruments and abstract figures.

In 1982, when she was 12, as Bubbles she started breakdancing and battling with her brothers and quickly excelled at spinning and windmills. By 14, she had joined her brothers' dance troupe, the B-Boys (n.d.), and was featured as the U.K.'s first b-girl in an English music video–based documentary, *Electro Rock* (1985). Dressed in a red tracksuit and singled out in the documentary as being the only female, her appearance led to notoriety and offers to dance professionally on several U.K. television shows. Soon afterward, the German sports footwear and clothing company

Puma sponsored both Bubbles and the B-Boys. Though she is from England, McQueen-Hudson identifies with her parents' Jamaican roots.

Melissa Ursula Dawn Goldsmith

See also: Breakdancing; Fashion; Filmmaking (Documentaries); Graffiti Art; The United Kingdom

Further Reading

García, Ana "Rokafella." 2005. Introduction to *We B*Girlz* by Nika Kramer and Martha Cooper. New York: powerHouse Books.

Lockley, Mike. 2015. "Hanifa's Getting Big Kick Out of Her Art." *Sunday Mercury* (Birmingham, England), September 6, 13.

Schloss, Joseph G. 2009. *Foundation: B-Boys, B-Girls, and Hip Hop Culture in New York.* New York: Oxford University Press.

Bulgaria

Bulgaria is a Southeastern European nation that, in 1946, became part of the Soviet-led Eastern Bloc. By 1989, it had evolved into a limited democracy, and a constitution was adopted in 1991. Its capital, Sofia, is also its largest city. Bulgarian folk music is known for its asymmetrical rhythms and microtonal shadings. Hip hop had to compete with a strong traditional folk and pop music scene, so it was slow to take hold in Bulgaria. It first reached Bulgaria in the mid-1980s, when underground rap and amateur breakdancing crews emerged. The first Bulgarian rap song was "This Is a Fake Love" (1986) by MC Guinness (Ivo Trombona, n.d.). Early hip hop acts included the band Gumeni Glavi (Rubber Heads, 1994–), whose debut album sold over 100,000 copies.

Bulgaria's traditional music features instruments such as the accordion, *gaida* (a bagpipe), *kaval* (a flute), *gadulka* and *tambora* (a bowed lutelike fiddle that uses sympathetic tuning and a fretted lute), *tarabuka* or *dumbek* (a finger drum), and *tupan* (a large drum similar to the Indian *dhol* and played with mallets).

In 1999, Bulgarian hip hop took serious hold when Big Talk (Henry Orhan Sami Beggin, n.d.) emerged. In addition, notable pop musicians such as Lili Ivanova (Lilyana Ivanova Petrova, 1939–), Philipp Kirkorov (Philipp Bedrosovich Kirkorov, 1967–), and Mira Aroyo (1977–) of the Liverpool, England–based electronica band Ladytron (1999–) began to incorporate hip hop beats into their music. Also, around the turn of the 21st century, rapper and clothing entrepreneur and label owner Big Sha (aka Misho Shamara, Mihail Stanislavov Mihaylov, 1972–) began to invest in hip hop clubs and festivals, and underground mainstay Gumeni Glavi began to produce mainstream hip hop, highly influenced by the American hip hop scene.

Big Sha, from Varna, was known for prosocialist political messages and is today considered among the country's most popular mainstream rap acts, as are Varna-born rapper 100 Kila (Yavor Yanakiev, 1985–) and Sofia-based band Upsurt (1996–). Big Sha became the first Bulgarian rapper to be featured with an American rapper in Bulgarian pop star LiLana's (Lilana Hristova Deyanova, 1985–) song "Dime Piece" (1999), which also featured Snoop Dogg (1971–).

Upsurt performs both party and sociopolitical rap in Bulgarian. The most popular underground early rap act was Pleven-born and Sofia-based rapper and label owner Spens (Stanislav Naydenov, 1975–).

Recent acts include Sofia-based freestyle rapper, producer, and label owner Krisko (Kristian Talev, 1988–) and hip hop and R&B singer DENA (Denitza Todorova, 1984–), who performs old-school hip hop.

Anthony J. Fonseca

See also: Russia

Further Reading
Levy, Claire. 2001. "Rap in Bulgaria: Between Fashion and Reality." In *Global Noise: Rap and Hip Hop outside the U.S.A.*, edited by Tony Mitchell, chap. 5. Middletown, CT: Wesleyan University Press.

Levy, Claire. 2004. "Who Is the 'Other' in the Balkans? Local Ethnic Music as a Different Source of Identities in Bulgaria." In *Music, Space and Place: Popular Music and Cultural Identity*, edited by Sheila Whiteley, Andy Bennett, and Stan Hawkins, chap. 2. Aldershot, England: Ashgate.

Further Listening
Spens. 2001 and 2003. *Prekaleno lichno* (*Too Personal*), Parts 1 and 2. Sniper Records.

Burkina Faso

Burkina Faso, a French-speaking country in West Africa, has since the late 1990s seen hip hop become an important aspect of musical culture that focuses on percussion ensembles, *balafon* (a wooden xylophone or percussion idiophone) bands, and the traditional music of over 70 ethnic groups. The entire country has lively hip hop and urban arts scenes. Since 2001, Burkina Faso's capital, Ouagadougou, has hosted the Ouago/Waga Hip Hop Festival. The event features Burkina Faso and other African urban cultures' music and art.

Burkina Faso hip hop acts have included Ouagadougou-based artists such as Awa Sissao (n.d.), Afrik'slam (n.d.), Faso Kombat (1998*–2013), OBC (2004–), Onasis (Onasis Wendker, n.d.), producer and actor Smockey (Serge Bembara, 1971–), Wem-Teng Clan (2000*–), and Yeleen (1998*–) in addition to Lankoué-born traditional/hip hop fusion musician Tim Winsey (Tim Winsé, 1973–). The programs have also included artists from other African nations: Negrissim' (1995–) from Yaounde, Cameroon; Fredy Massamba (1971–) from Pointe-Noire, Democratic Republic of Congo; and King Ayisoba (Albert Apoozore, 1974*–), from Bongo Soe, Ghana, among others.

In addition to concerts and emcee battles, the Ouago/Waga Hip Hop Festival hosts residencies for musicians who lead workshops on rap, beatboxing, and sampling. Francophonia International Organisation, Africalia (Belgium), Culture France, and the Paris arts collective Staycalm! sponsor the activities. The festival's intention is to promote hip hop activity and engagement in the arts among Burkina Faso youth. By the mid-2000s, related mini-festivals were taking place in smaller cities, such as Bobo Dioulasso, Koudougou, and Pô.

Music producer, actor, and Sankarist political activist Smockey holds his award for his hip hop music work at the 8th presentation of the Kora Awards in 2010 in his home city, Ouagadougou. One of the most successful acts from Burkina Faso, Smockey has given back to his community by establishing a studio that supports and records Burkinabé artists in the capital city. (AHMED OUOBA/AFP/Getty Images)

Burkinabé hip hop is exceptionally diverse. Some is influenced by French, Belgian, and other prominent West African styles and stresses rap, jazz, R&B, and soul with Western instruments such as guitar and synthesizer, whereas other types incorporate reggae as well as local village singing styles and indigenous instruments such as the *kora* (a string instrument associated with the country's griot song tradition) and *lolo* (similar to a mouth bow). Song texts are also diverse, ranging from Art Melody's (1978–) rap that criticizes current civilian conditions in Burkina Faso and Onasis's reggae-rap to Faso Kombat's chanting with Quran-inspired texts and Winsey's fusion with traditional instruments. Other notable hip hop activity includes busking and recording in privately owned studios.

Burkina Faso borders Benin, Ghana, Ivory Coast, Mali, Niger, and Togo. British, French, and German colonization combined with wars, slave trade, and diaspora have affected Burkina Faso's cultural interactions. Over half of its population is Voltaic Mossi. The country is secular, though the main religions are Islam, Christianity, and Animism. Since the 1980s, Burkina Faso has experienced periods of progress and political unrest. In 1983, Thomas Sankara (1949–1987) led a coup d'état that put his leftist government in power. His programs included education, vaccination, and building infrastructure within a Marxist framework, but in 1987, Sankara's colleague Blaise Compaoré (1951–) led a coupe, murdering Sankara and then reversing all Sankarist policies. Prior to Campaoré's reelection, his government revised the country's constitution. Burkina Faso remains one of Africa's least developed countries.

In 2014, demonstrations used hip hop to overthrow the Compaoré government. In 2015, Compaoré resigned. Smockey, a Sankarist and prominent leader in the 2014 uprising against Compaoré, has recorded many Burkinabé hip hop performers at his studio. Just after the 2015 coup d'état, General Gilbert Diendéré's (1960*–) army, which led the military junta that temporarily seized power in Burkina Faso, bombed Smockey's studio in Ouagadougou. Diendéré served for many years as the aide to Compaoré and likely took a major role in the coup d'état that led to Sankara's assassination. Ultimately, Burkina Faso elected left-center social democracy progressive Roch Marc Christian Kaboré (1957–, in office 2015–), the first noninterim president in nearly 50 years without a military past.

Melissa Ursula Dawn Goldsmith

See also: France; Ghana; Griot; Senegal

Further Reading

Amuzu, Evershed K., and John Victor Singler. 2014. "Codeswitching in West Africa." *International Journal of Bilingualism* 18, no. 4: 329–45.

Künzler, Daniel. 2007. "The 'Lost Generation': African Hip Hop Movements and the Protest of the Young (Male) Urban." In *Civil Society: Local and Regional Responses to Global Challenges*, edited by Mark Herkenrath, chap. 3. Zürich, Switzerland: LIT Verlag.

Further Listening

Smockey. 1999. *Tout le monde sur la steupi!* (*Everyone on the Steupi!*). Odeon.

Various Artists. 2008. *Fangafrika: La voix des sans-voix* (*Fangafrika: The Voice of the Voiceless*). Mondomix.

Winsey, Tim. 2004. *Zèssa.* Kaba Networks.

Busta Rhymes

(aka Busta Rhymez, Trevor Smith Jr., 1972–, Brooklyn, New York)

Busta Rhymes is an American rapper, record producer, and executive, having founded the record label Conglomerate (aka Flipmode Entertainment, 1994–), featuring the production crew the Conglomerate (aka The Flipmode Squad, 1996–). As an MC, he is best known for his rhyming technique, wherein he breathlessly raps quickly while using internal rhyme and half rhyme, as well as for his outspokenness, his lavish fashion sense, and his appearance in innovative music videos. He has been a guest performer for acts such as A Tribe Called Quest (1985–1998, 2006–2013, 2015–), Boyz II Men (1988–), and Missy Elliott (1971–). He has appeared in minor film roles in *Who's the Man* (1993) and *Higher Learning* (1995) and has lent his voice to animated television series such as *Rugrats* (1991–2004) and *The Boondocks* (2005–2014).

As a teen, he cofounded the rap group Leaders of the New School (1989–1994), which charted twice on the Billboard 200. His first five solo albums, mostly on Elektra Records (1950–), were *The Coming* (1996), *When Disaster Strikes* (1997), *Extinction Level Event: The Final World Front* (1998), *Anarchy* (2000), and *Genesis* (2001), all of which have been certified Platinum, four hitting the Top 10 of the Billboard 200; his 2006 album, *The Big Bang*, went to No. 1. He has had four No. 1 albums on Billboard's Top R&B/Hip-Hop Albums chart. He has been nominated for 11 Grammy Awards.

East Coast rapper, singer-songwriter, and music producer Busta Rhymes's rapping style involves a complex and high-speed delivery that is full of internal and half rhymes. In 1994 he founded Flipmode Entertainment, which became The Conglomerate Entertainment in 2011. Conglomerate produced his Platinum- and Gold-certified albums, among others. (Sbukley /Dreamstime.com)

EARLY YEARS

Busta Rhymes was born in a two-parent family with a Jamaican American ethnic background. He was born in Brooklyn, New York, but his family moved to the suburbs of Long Island, New York, when he was 12 years old. This move meant that as an adolescent, Busta Rhymes had a middle-class childhood, but he grew up idolizing Public Enemy (1982–) and benefiting from the strong rap scene for which the borough was known. He began to see he might have a future in music, and he was able to parley his Brooklyn background into respect from other rappers. While in junior high, he met rapper Charlie Brown (Bryan Higgins, n.d.), and their early act was received positively by Public Enemy's Chuck D (1960–) and the Public Enemy production team, the Bomb Squad (1986–), so they decided to mentor the young duo.

Busta Rhymes and Charlie Brown began honing their skills on harmonies and unison rap, and they started working on choreography, later adding a third MC and a turntablist, respectively Dinco D (James Jackson, 1971*–) and Cut Monitor Milo (Sheldon Scott, 1970*–), to create Leaders of the New School, which was given a record contract with Elektra due to Chuck D's contacts. The group opened for Public Enemy and recorded two albums, *A Future without a Past* (1991) and *T.I.M.E.: The Inner Mind's Eye* (1993), both of which were considered successes, especially for the group's introduction of unison raps and stomping. In 1992, the group appeared on A Tribe Called Quest's EP *Scenario*, and reviews of this and Leaders of the New School albums noted that Busta Rhymes was a standout; he soon developed a reputation for being outlandish, somewhat of a budding auteur, but a highly marketable and therefore sought-after one.

AS A SOLO ACT

Leaders of the New School took a hiatus, at which time Busta Rhymes concentrated on his home life and Muslim spirituality. It was during this three-year period that he worked on his solo act. He enjoyed immediate success, as his first single, "Woo hah!! Got You All in Check" (1996) from *The Coming*, broke into the Hot 100, peaking at No. 8. The album's tour was part of a rap omnibus that featured a who's who of hip hop: Fugees (1992–1997), Cypress Hill (1987–), and A Tribe Called Quest. His sophomore album, *When Disaster Strikes*, reached No. 3 on the Billboard 200 and No. 1 on Billboard's Top R&B/Hip-Hop Albums chart. The album spawned the hit singles "Put Your Hands Where My Eyes Can See," "Turn It Up/Fire It Up," and "Dangerous," the latter two reaching the Hot 100 Top 10. The album featured Puff Daddy (1969–) and Erykah Badu (1971–).

Able to experiment more as a successful soloist, on his next album, *Extinction Level Event*, he worked with heavy metal singer/songwriter Ozzy Osbourne (John Michael Osbourne, 1948–) and sampled composer Bernard Hermann's (1911–1975) music from the horror film *Psycho* (1960). His next two albums underperformed on the charts (despite brisk sales), so Busta Rhymes switched labels and went with Interscope Records (1989–), resulting in his 2006 No. 1 effort, *The Big Bang*. His eighth studio album, *Back on My B. S.* (2009), debuted at No. 5 on the Billboard 200. He then spent a brief stint on Ca$h Money Records (1991–).

Anthony J. Fonseca

See also: Nation of Islam; The United States

Further Reading

Bradley, Adam, and Andrew Dubois, eds. 2010. "Busta Rhymes." Under "Part 3: 1993–99: Rap Goes Mainstream" in *The Anthology of Rap*, pp. 347–49. New Haven, CT: Yale University Press.

McMurray, Anaya. 2008. "Hotep and Hip Hop: Can Black Muslim Women Be Down with Hip Hop?" *Meridians* 8, no. 1: 74–92.

Young, Jennifer R. 2010. "Brooklyn Beats: Hip Hop's Home to Everyone from Everywhere." In *Hip Hop in America: A Regional Guide*, edited by Mickey Hess, vol. 1, chap. 4. Santa Barbara, CA: Greenwood.

Further Listening

Busta Rhymes. 1996. *The Coming*. Elektra.

Busta Rhymes. 1997. *When Disaster Strikes*. Elektra.

Busta Rhymes. 2009. *Back on My B. S.* Universal Motown.

Cambodia

Cambodia, an Indochina Peninsula country, has a history marred by the Vietnam War–related U.S. bombing of Cambodia (1970–1973), the Khmer Rouge Genocide (1975–1979), and the Cambodian–Vietnamese War (1979–1991). All events stifled the country's musical growth, and hip hop did not emerge in the country until the late 1990s through returning Cambodian diaspora, such as radio disc jockey and hip hop producer DJ Sope (Sophoann Sope Hul, 1965*–). He has faced an uphill battle as the current sociopolitical climate is grim: widespread poverty and hunger, pervasive corruption, and lack of political freedom—although its economy is one of the fastest growing in Southeast Asia. Phnom Penh, its capital city, is home to almost two million citizens, who mainly speak the country's official language, Khmer.

Cambodian music is a hybridization of cultural traditions and Westernized popular music, especially slow-paced crooner music and dance music. In the 1960s and 1970s, rock music influenced Cambodian musicians, who created a unique sound by mixing it with traditional melodies; however, virtually all of these musicians were killed during the Khmer Rouge Genocide, which targeted the arts. Western-influenced music nevertheless returned by the late 1990s. Cambodian millennials generally have had little firsthand knowledge of the war, reconstruction, and instability that have made Cambodia what it is today; in fact, they have experienced economic progress, rapid social change, and globalism—and they have been eager to adopt and reinterpret trends from the United States.

Cambodia's first alternative music label, Yab Moung Records (2012–), specialized in death metal, Khmer blues, rock, alternative music, and hip hop, but Cambodian hip hop acts have yet to make their mark internationally. Currently, the most popular Cambodian hip hop artist is rapper Lisha (Jessica Srin, 1981–), who raps in English and Khmer and sees hip hop as the ultimate freedom of speech to address issues such as gender inequality and gender role conformity.

Among the current Cambodian hip hop diaspora are CS (Chanthy Sok, 1978–), a Long Beach, California, rapper whose songs, infused with traditional Cambodian music, tell of the struggle of Cambodians who fled the Khmer Rouge and found themselves impoverished and bullied in urban cities, then turning to crime, something he and Tee Cambo (Yung Tee, 1990*–) explore in the G-funk–style song "Cambo" (2014). Bross La (Dara La Paul, 1988–) is a rapper and singer-songwriter who lives in Minnesota and has traveled back to Cambodia to help develop an authentic Cambodian hip hop sound. His single "Sork Kley" ("Short Hair," 2016), which challenges traditional expectations of women while combining traditional music with hip hop beats, has become a hit. Tony Keo (Anthony Keo, 1989–) is a Montreal-based rapper who writes, produces, and sings hip hop music in English,

French, and Khmer; and Honey Cocaine (aka Honey C, Sochitta Sal, 1992–) is a Toronto-based rapper-songwriter who raps about being an assertive and aggressive gangsta-style woman against synthesizer heavy beats and 808 drums.

Anthony J. Fonseca

See also: Vietnam

Further Reading

Grossberg, Romi. 2013. "Healing through Hip Hop in the Slums of Phnom Penh Cambodia." *Rupkatha Journal on Interdisciplinary Studies in the Humanities* 5, no. 2: 107–18.

Schlund-Vials, Cathy J. 2008. "A Transnational Hip Hop Nation: PraCh, Cambodia, and Memorializing the Killing Fields." *Life Writing* 5 (June): 11–27.

Further Listening

Honey Cocaine. 2013. *Thug Love.* Self-released.

Cameroon

Cameroon is a Central African country whose history is one of occupation. It was a German colony from 1884 to 1918 and after World War I (1914–1918) was made into a French colony until the 1950s, when its citizens began a war for independence, which lasted until 1971. French and English are the official languages of Cameroon, known for its native styles of music, particularly the laid-back *urban makossa* and the 6/8-rhythm *bikutsi*, a balafon- and drum-based dance music associated with various moves that prefigure hip hop's twerking. Bikutsi became more mainstream in the 1950s, and as guitars, drum kits, and horns became accessible, the sound became internationally famous through artists such as guitarist and singer Messi Martin (Messi Me Nkonda Martin, 1946*–) and singer Anne-Marie Nzie (1932–2016). In the 1960s and 1970s, both makossa and bikutsi were modernized, creating funky dance music that became the most popular sound in Cameroon. With their 1988 debut album, the band Les Têtes Brulées (1980–2000)*, led by guitarist Zanzibar (Théodore Epeme, n.d.), created an extremely popular form of bikutsi that was both more Western guitar oriented and tied to traditional forms.

While makossa and bikutsi are about everyday life and are generally celebratory music styles, hip hop offered musicians opportunity to be more socially conscious, but in the 1980s, it was marginalized. It took pioneering record labels such as Mapane Records (1998–2006) and Zomloa Records (aka Zomba Music Group, 1975–) to make hip hop more viable. Early hip hop artists included rapper Krotal (Paul Edouard Etoundi Onambélé, 1975–) and rap crews Negrissim (1995–), Feu Rouge (1999–), and Ultimatum (1993–1997). Krotal opened for Senegalese group Positive Black Soul (aka PBS, 1989–) during their Cameroon and Senegal tours. Negrissim was famous for songs about the joys and struggles of contemporary rural and urban life in Dakar, Senegal.

These gave rise to the second wave of Cameroon hip hop artists, Koppo (Patrice Minko'o, 1976*–), who experimented with spoken-word poetry and hip hop, and Lady B (Rosine Mireille Obounou, 1984*–), who came from a dance background. Current artists include rapper Stanley Enow (1986–), who had a huge hit in "Hein pére" ("Hey/All right, Father," 2013) and won the MTV Africa Music Award for the best newcomer in 2014, and the most famous Cameroon rapper, Jovi (aka Le Monstre, Ndukong Godlove Nfor, 1983–), who raps in English, French, local languages, and slang about everyday life in Cameroon and runs his own label, New Bell Music (n.d.). His 2014 hit "Et P8 Koi?" ("And Then What?") led to a nomination for an MTV Africa Music Award.

Anthony J. Fonseca

See also: Enow, Stanley; France; Germany; Senegal

Further Reading

Anyefru, Emmanuel. 2011. "The Refusal to Belong: Limits of the Discourse on Anglophone Nationalism in Cameroon." *Journal of Third World Studies* 28, no. 2: 277–306.

Künzler, Daniel. 2007. "The 'Lost Generation': African Hip Hop Movements and the Protest of the Young (Male) Urban." In *Civil Society: Local and Regional Responses to Global Challenges*, edited by Mark Herkenrath, chap. 3. Zürich, Switzerland: LIT Verlag.

Further Listening

Jovi. 2015. *Mboko God.* New Bell Music.

Campbell, Don

(aka Campbellock, 1951–, St. Louis, Missouri)

Don Campbell is an American funk and hip hop dancer and choreographer best known for creating a dance called the Campbellock, which he popularized in the 1970s. His stop-and-go style of dancing influenced others, who created their own moves until ultimately the technique of locking became a phenomenon. Originally performed to and intended for funk music, locking was eventually adopted into hip hop dance routines; hence, Campbell is credited with being the inventor of locking. He is also famous for his featured dancing on the dance variety show *Soul Train* (1971–2006) and his formation, along with choreographer Toni Basil (Antonia Christina Basilotta, 1943–), of the Lockers (1971–1976), originally called the Campbellock Dancers, which became a huge influence on future locking dancers, for both dance moves and clothing.

In the 1960s, Campbell moved to California and studied commercial art at the Los Angeles Trade–Technical College, where he discovered his love for dance. In 1972, he recorded, as Don "Soul Train" Campbell, "Campbell Lock" (Stanson Records), a funk instrumental designed to background his new dance. As leader of the Lockers, he appeared on shows for the Grammys and the Oscars.

Campbell is now an instructor and has taught classes in many cities in the United States as well as countries such as Japan, Canada, Portugal, England, the Netherlands, and Germany, and he serves as one of hip hop's ambassadors for b-boy summits, breakdance championships, and hip hop dance championships. He has been honored at the Rock and Roll Hall of Fame, which displays some of his costumes.

Anthony J. Fonseca

See also: Hip Hop Dance; Popping and Locking; The United States

Further Reading

Fuhrer, Margaret. 2014. "Urban and Commercial Dance." In *American Dance: The Complete Illustrated History*, chap. 10. Minneapolis, MN: Voyageur Press.

Guzman-Sanchez, Thomas. 2012. "South Central Los Angeles." In *Underground Dance Masters: Final History of a Forgotten Era*, chap. 5. Santa Barbara, CA: Praeger.

Canada

Canada is a North American parliamentary democracy composed of 10 sparsely populated provinces and three territories. The world's fourth-largest country by landmass, Canada borders the United States and is more highly urbanized, with over 80 percent of its 35 million people living in large cities such as Ottawa, Toronto, Montreal, Vancouver, and Calgary. Canada's population is a combination of descendants of French, English, Irish, Scottish, Portuguese, and post–American Revolutionary War (1775–1783) loyalist immigrants as well as indigenous peoples. Canada is officially bilingual; since 1969, French and English have been its two nationally recognized languages. Canada has one of the world's most ethnically

Maestro Fresh-Wes performs at a 2015 concert in Toronto. Canada's first commercially successful rapper, Maestro Fresh-Wes's old-school rapping approach was similar to Big Daddy Kane: Both employed intricate, clever rhymes, and fast-paced rapping against steady beats, turntables, and samples. (George Pimentel/WireImage/Getty Images)

diverse populations. Its indigenous peoples include the First Nations, Inuit, and Métis. Hip hop first emerged in Canada in the 1980s, but it remained an underground music scene for 20 years. The first Canadian rap single was by the Ottawa duo Singing Fools (1982–1990), whose 1982 English sociopolitical protest song "The Bum Rap" became a minor hit; the next year, Montreal's Lucien Francœur (1948–) released the French funk rap song "Rap-à-Billy."

Canada's music reflects its own diverse influences as well as American influence, and its music industry is the sixth largest in the world, its first commercial recordings having been released in 1900 on the American E. Berliner Gramophone Company (1887–1829; later purchased by RCA, 1919–) label that became established in 1899 in Montreal. Canada's first independent label, related to Berliner, was the Compo Company (1918–1970). The country's first radio stations emerged in the 1920s, with its first performing rights society being created in 1925 (the Canadian Performing Rights Society, aka the Composers, Authors and Publishers Association of Canada or CAPAC, 1925–). Each of its indigenous communities has introduced musical traditions into the national consciousness, including styles such as chanting or using instruments made from natural materials, whereas its immigrants from France introduced the fiddle, violins, guitars, flutes, drums, fifes, and trumpets and the Irish introduced Celtic music.

Musical tastes in the 20th century reflected those in the neighboring United States, as fans listened to swing, jazz, and popular standards. Big-band leader Guy Lombardo (Gaetano Alberto Lombardo, 1902–1977) and his band the Royal Canadians (1924–1979, 1989–) became internationally famous in the 1920s, selling over 250 million records. In the jazz arena, Montreal native Oscar Peterson (1925–2007) became known as a virtuoso jazz pianist, and in popular music, country singer Hank Snow (Clarence Eugene Snow, 1914–1999) became a hit in America. In the 1950s, rock music became popular with the emergence of Paul Anka (1941–), whose 1958 song "Diana" reached No. 1 on the U.S. Billboard Hot 100. This continued into the 1960s with the international popularity of singer-songwriters Neil Young (1945–), Leonard Cohen (1934–2016), and Joni Mitchell (Roberta Joan Anderson, 1943–) and bands such as Rush (1968) as well as more recent multi-Platinum sellers such as Alanis Morissette (1974–), Avril Lavigne (1984–), Michael Bublé (1975–), and Céline Dion (1968–).

EARLIEST HIP HOP AND THE FIRST WAVE

The first commercially successful rapper was Maestro Fresh-Wes (Wesley Williams, 1968–), an old-school rapper comparable to the American rapper Big Daddy Kane (1968–). Like Kane, Maestro Fresh-Wes used intricate rhymes and fast-paced rapping against steady beats, turntables, and samples, including classical pieces. Also popular among Toronto-based hip hop acts in the early 1990s were the short-lived group Main Source (1989–1994); the jazz rap duo Dream Warriors (1988–2002); rapper Dan-e-o (Daniel Faraldo, 1977–), an actor and singer of Jamaican and Spanish descent; rapper Devon (Devon Martin, n.d.), whose "Mr. Metro" (1990) questioned police racism; and rapper and actor Michie Mee (Michelle McCullock, 1970–), Canada's first notable female MC.

Toronto-based, Jamaican-born radio DJ Ron Nelson (1962–) helped to popularize hip hop music in Canada by promoting early acts such as Maestro Fresh-Wes and Michee Mee. "Northern Touch," a collective song that served as the Canadian hip hopper mission statement, was released as a single in 1998, and this galvanized hip hop artists and brought Vancouver-based rap group Rascalz (1989–) into the public eye; the group became even more popular when it refused a 1998 Juno Award for Best Rap Recording because the presentation was done off-camera, along with technical awards, and the result was that the following year, the Junos moved the Rap award to the main ceremony. Hip hop found its way into the mainstream in 2001 when radio station CFXJ (93.5) became the country's first urban music station.

THE SECOND WAVE

A second generation of Canadian hip hop artists, including Kardinal Offishall (Jason D. Harrow, 1976–), Drake (Aubrey Drake Graham, 1986–), and Somali Canadian K'naan (Keinan Abdi Warsame, 1978–), emerged. In 2008, Kardinal Offishall reached the Billboard Hot 100 Top 10 with the song "Dangerous." In 2009, K'naan's single "Wavin' Flag" was named the official Coca-Cola theme song of the 2010 FIFA World Cup. Drake went on to rewrite the Billboard Hot 100 record books in various categories. These successes paved the way for rappers such as PARTYNEXTDOOR (Jahron Anthony Brathwaite, 1985–), Nav (Navraj Singh Goraya, 1989–), the Weeknd (Abel Makkonen Tesfaye, 1990–), Tory Lanez (Daystar Peterson, 1992–), and Roy Wood$ (Denzel Spencer, 1996–) as well as rap duo Majid Jordan (2011–). Crossover artists include singer-songwriter Nelly Kim Furtado (1978–), who sings hip hop in addition to dance-pop, folk, R&B, and Latin music, and the electronic music and hip hop band Keys N Krates (2008–), which employs turntablism.

QUEBECOISE HIP HOP

Though "Rap-à-Billy" was the first French Canadian hip hop single, French Canadian–language hip hop (aka Quebecoise or French Canadian hip hop) did not emerge fully until the early 1990s in Montreal. It spread quickly to Quebec City with groups such as Dubmatique (1992–), Loco Locass (1995–), Muzion (1996–2014), Sans Pression (SP, 1997–), and Atach Tatuq (aka Traumaturges, 1998–), as well as rappers such as Anodajay (Steve Jolin, 1977–) and Haitian Canadian Yvon Krevé (Henry Green-Dupré, n.d.). Dubmatique, the first Quebec hip hop band to have commercial success, had members from Senegal and Canada who were inspired by French hip hop. The band's first album, *La force de compendre* (*The Strength to Understand*, 1997), had singles that topped Canadian francophone popular music charts and was certified Platinum in Canada. Like its English-language Canadian contemporaries, French Canadian hip hop is at times fused with R&B, funk, pop, jazz, and other kinds of music. Acts such as Loco Locass have focused on political rap, focusing especially on the nationalist message of Quebec sovereignty.

Later Quebecoise acts included Sir Pathétik (Raphaël Bérubé (n.d.) and Ale Dee (Alexandre Duhaime, n.d.), both members of Mine de rien (Casual, aka Chosen One, 2000–2010)*; Manu Militari (aka M-A-N-U, 1979–) of the group Rime Organisé (2000–); Muzion's Imposs (Stanley Rimsky Salgado, n.d.); KNLO Craqnuques (aka KenLo, Akena Lohamba Okoko, 1984–); Souldia (Kevin Saint-Laurent, 1985–); and the group Loud Lary Ajust (2011–2016). Some acts, such as the experimental hip hop band Dead Obies (2011–), combine English and French—known as *Franglais*—in their hip hop songs. Others, such as Alaclair Ensemble (2010–), rap in both French and English, reflecting the Bas-Canada mythology it employs, in which English and French coexist without any issues. Criollo (2003–), from Montreal, is a band that combines hip hop with a Latin musical style that it created, *bahire*, a fusion of the Dominican Republic's bachata, reggae, reggaetón, and R&B. It stands out for rapping and singing in Spanish.

FIRST NATIONS, MÉTIS, AND CANADIAN HIP HOP

Starting in the 1990s, Canadian indigenous-themed hip hop has become popular among many First Nations descendants, who live from Canada's Northwest Coast to its Atlantic coastal region and the St. Lawrence River Valley. In addition, hip hop has been especially popular with the Métis in Canada, who can trace their heritage to European settlers and First Nations peoples (often Algonquin, Cree, Maliseet, Mi'kmaq, Ojibwe, Saulteaux, and Wabanaki).

Early acts include Alida Kinnie Starr (1970–), a part Mohawk singer-songwriter from Calgary who fuses hip hop with laid-back alternative rock. Also from Alberta, War Party (1995–2004) is a Cree hip hop crew from Hobbema that fuses hip hop with chants that focus on Cree themes and stories. War Party eventually founded and was absorbed with additional musicians into Team RezOfficial (2003–), a mostly Cree group. Team RezOfficial's "Lonely," from its album *The World (And Everything in It)* (2009), became the first aboriginal No. 1 single on MuchMusic's (aka Much, 1984–, a Canadian English language specialty channel comparable to MTV, 1981–) music video show *RapCity* (1995–). War Party was the first aboriginal group to host this show. Active since 1998 and a contemporary of Kinnie Starr and War Party is Muskoday First Nations (Cree) rapper Eekwol (Lindsay Knight, n.d.), who is an activist and scholar and raps against stereotypes of native women.

Some later acts include Inez (Inez Jasper, b. Inez Point, 1981–), of Métis and Ojibway heritage; Joey Stylez (Joseph Dale Marlin LaPlante, 1981–), of Métis heritage; Lil Pappie (Nicholaus Gordon, 1991–), of Dakota descent; Young Kidd (Frankie Fontaine, 1988–), of Jamaican and Sagkeeng First Nations heritage; and Samian (Samuel Tremblay, 1983–), of Abitibiwinni First Nations (Algonquian) heritage. The last is a rapper for the Quebecoise hip hop group Loco Locass, though he also raps in English. Many are Native activists and have been active in politics; however, artists such as Inez balance indigenous themes such as struggling with being different with lighter dance-oriented songs. Inez also fuses hip hop with pop and R&B. Her album *Burn Me Down* (2013) also includes traditional Sto:lo (aka Staulo or Stahlo—a First Nations people from the Fraser Valley and Canyon in British Columbia) singing.

Other groups include Reddnation (2000–), from Alberta and of Cree descent; A Tribe Called Red (2007–), with members of Mohawk descent and Nipissing First Nations heritage; and Winnipeg's Most (2010–2012), a partly aboriginal group. Both Reddnation and A Tribe Called Red fuse electronica with hip hop; the latter also fuses reggae, dubstep, and *moombahton* (a combination of house music and Puerto Rican reggaetón) with First Nations–inspired heavy drumming and vocal chants. A Tribe Called Red's sound is often called "powwow-step," and the crew raps mostly in English. Its name is inspired by the American East Coast alternative hip hop group A Tribe Called Quest (ATCQ, 1985–1998, 2006–2013, 2015–). Winnipeg's Most raps in English and has focused on themes such as street violence, ancestral memory, facing discrimination and inequality, and everyday urban life.

In the 2010s, as acts such as Inez and Reddnation have received critical acclaim, more people have become interested in Canadian indigenous hip hop. In 2013, the Nativehiphop Festival was established in Vancouver. The three-day festival focuses on all aspects of First Nations and Native American hip hop. The most famous Inuit hip hop crew, Nuuk Posse (1985–), is not Canadian but from Greenland; however, it has performed in Canada, rapping in Danish, English, and Kalaallisut—a Greenlandic language closely related to the Canadian Inuit language Inuktitut. However, more research on hip hop and Canadian Inuits is needed.

Anthony J. Fonseca and Melissa Ursula Dawn Goldsmith

See also: Drake; France; K'Naan; Political Hip Hop; The United States

Further Reading

Jones, Christopher M. 2011. "Hip Hop Quebec: Self and Synthesis." *Popular Music and Society* 34, no. 2: 177–202.

Ransom, Amy J. 2013. "'Québec History X': Re-visioning the Past through Rap." *American Review of Canadian Studies* 43, no. 1: 12–29.

Further Listening

Dead Obies. 2016. *Gesamtkunstwerk* (*Total Art Work*). Bonsound.

Loco Locass. 2012. *Le Québec est mort, vive le Québec!* (*Quebec Is Dead, Long Live Quebec!*). Audiogram.

A Tribe Called Red. 2016. *We Are the Halluci Nation.* Radicalized Records.

Winnipeg's Most. 2010. *Winnipeg's Most.* Heatbag Records.

Cape Verde

Cape Verde, an Atlantic archipelago island nation, has since the 1990s differentiated itself from other African countries by having an extremely stable democracy and robust economic growth—after gaining its independence from Portugal in 1975. Before and during this time, Cape Verde experienced political unrest in transitioning to a multiparty democracy, and this unrest resulted in a growing Cape Verdean diaspora. As of 2018, most Cape Verdean hip hop acts reside and record in other countries, notably in the United States (Providence, Rhode Island, and the Greater Boston area), the Netherlands (Rotterdam), and Portugal (Lisbon).

It is difficult to pinpoint exactly when Cape Verdeans first had access to hip hop. By the late 1980s, tourists and travelers, especially from neighboring Senegal, brought CDs and videotapes to Cape Verde, but the rise of Cape Verdean hip hop began in the early 1990s with citizens' access to American television stations MTV (1981–) and BET (1980–). Cape Verdean musical preferences include the country's native *morna*, *coladeira*, and music for *batuque* and *funaná*; its *cabo love*, a version of Guadeloupean *zouk*; Jamaican reggae and ragga; Senegalese *mbalax*; and American R&B and jazz—and its hip hop is often fused with these genres. Rapping texts are usually in Cape Verdean Creole (aka Kabuverdianu and sometimes spelled "Kriol"), but English, Dutch, and Portugese are also used. Lyrics usually localize gangsta rap and/or protest economic disparity and corruption. In time, rap topics expanded to include embracing change and ethnic pride as well as protesting against Cape Verde's activities as a Banana Republic (often a third-world country that is politically and economically unstable that has limited resources for export and must rely on either tourism or some other kind of limited resource, such as bananas).

One early popular pioneering Cape Verdean rapper was Eddy Fort Moda Grog (aka Eddy (FMG), Eddy Fortes, 1950–) from Mindelo, São Vicente, Cape Verde. In the 1990s, Eddy (FMG) fused hardcore hip hop with R&B as a soloist and as part of the Dutch Cape Verdean crew Cabo Funk Alliance (1992–). Notable hip hop acts after the 2000s have included Praia-based rapper Hélio Batalha (1989*–) and Batchart (Edison Silva, n.d.). What connects Cape Verdean hip hop artists active outside the islands is the fact that they rap in Cape Verdean Creole, focus on Cape Verdean–related topics, and/or employ Cape Verdean music. First-generation rapper, writer, promoter, and entertainment company and recording label owner Chachi (Charles Carvalho, n.d.) fuses hip hop with jazz. Active in Providence, Chachi was the opening act for American hip hop artists such as Talib Kweli (1975–) and Wu-Tang Clan (1992–). Three notable DutchCape Verdean acts are MC Alee (Elidio Gomes, n.d.), GMB (Gery Mendes Borges, 1984–), and Nelson Freitas (Nelson De Freitas, 1975–), the last being from Rotterdam. MC Alee performs hardcore rap and electronica, whereas GMB fuses hip hop with electronica, jazz, retro hi-NRG, funk, and traditional Cape Verdean music such as *cabo love* (based on the *coladeira*, which was originally moderately slow, joyful or satirical dance music, and the Haitian *compass*, also dance music); Freitas fuses hip hop with R&B, zouk, Angolan *kizomba*, and traditional Cape Verdean music. Boss AC (Ângelo César do Rosário Firmino, 1975–), born in Cape Verde and raised in Lisbon, was one of the pioneering rappers of Portugese hip hop, commonly called hip hop Tuga.

Melissa Ursula Dawn Goldsmith

See also: Portugal

Further Reading

Pardue, Derek. 2015. *Cape Verde, Let's Go: Creole Rappers and Citizenship in Portugal.* Urbana-Champaign: University of Illinois Press.

Saucier, P. Khalil. 2015. *Necessarily Black: Cape Verdean Youth, Hip Hop Culture, and a Critique of Identity.* East Lansing: Michigan State University Press.

Further Listening
Chachi Carvalho. 2013. *Cape Verdean in America.* Chachihiphop.

Celtic Hip Hop

Celtic hip hop focuses on Celtic subject matter such as the immigrant experience; folklore, culture, and folksongs; sports and historical events; and nationalist, anti-war, anticapitalist, or anarchist sentiments. Though it is mostly American or Irish American, Celtic hip hop is often Scottish, English, or French, much like Celtic rock. Celtic hip hop may also be, regardless of lyrical content, a fusion of Celtic instruments and music (such as jigs or reels) with elements of hip hop such as rap and beats.

Though Irish hip hop acts such as Rob Kelly (1978–), the Rubberbandits (2000–), and GMC (Garry McCarthy, n.d.) use Irish (thus Celtic) lyrical content, American Celtic hip hop bands such as Los Angeles–based House of Pain (1991–1996, 2017–); Vallejo, California–based Emcee Lynx (aka Lynx T'chass, Jedediah, anonymous, 1980–); and New York City–based Black 47 (1989–2014) have gained strong cult popularity. House of Pain focuses on hardcore rap lyrics about the Irish American experience. The band Beltaine's Fire (2005–2011) backed Emcee Lynx before he began his solo career. In addition to Celtic subject matter, the band plays Irish, Scottish, and Celtic music as well as funk, jazz, and rock. Black 47 is a Celtic punk and alternative rock band that has employed rap. With members from the United States and Ireland, Black 47's early album *Fire of Freedom* (1993) included rap about English colonialism, the immigrant experience, and Irish identity, as in the self-referential "Rockin' the Bronx." The band also used Jamaican toasting and nationalist lyrical content in "Fire of Freedom." Bagpipes were also often employed with Black 47's hip hop beats as well as in alternative rock ballads such as "Forty Shades of Blue" (which parodies "Down by the Salley Gardens" to the traditional Irish air "The Maids of Mourne Shore").

With its prehistory in Dublin, Ireland, and Bristol, England, the band Marxman (1989–1996) formed in London. It fused hardcore rap, political hip hop, and ambient electronica with traditional Irish music. As its name suggests, Marxman's lyrical content focused on strong, militant, socialist messages as well as protests against England's control over Ireland, economic disparity, and domestic violence. The French group Manau (1998–), based in Paris, fuses French rap with Breton traditional melodies and instruments such as bagpipes, bombard, harp, and fiddle with hip hop beats. Its members are French, but all trace their roots to Brittany. Manau's single "La tribu de Dana" ("The Tribe of Dana," 1998) became a hit in France. The vast majority of Celtic hip hop songs are in English, but they often include texts in living Celtic languages such as Irish and Scottish Gaelic.

Melissa Ursula Dawn Goldsmith

See also: France; Ireland; Marxman; The United Kingdom; The United States

Further Reading
Batson, Charles R. 2009. "Panique Celtique: Manau's Celtic Rap, Breton Cultural Expression, and Contestatory Performance in Contemporary France." *French Politics, Culture, & Society* 27, no. 2: 63–83, 155.

Moriarty, Máiréad. 2015. "Hip Hop, LPP, and Globalization." In *Globalizing Language Policy and Planning: An Irish Language Perspective*, chap. 6. New York: Palgrave Macmillan.

Further Listening

Black 47. 1993. *Fire of Freedom*. SBK Records.

Kelly, Rob. 2016. *Kel jefe* (*Celtic Boss*). Soulspazm.

Manau. 2015. *Celtique d'aujourd'hui* (*Celtic Today*). Atypik Productions.

Chance the Rapper

(Chancelor Jonathan Bennett, 1993–, Chicago, Illinois)

Chance the Rapper is an American hip hop singer-songwriter, recording artist, producer, and philanthropist. His solo output includes three self-released mixtapes: *10 Day* (2012), *Acid Rap* (2013), and *Coloring Book* (2016). All were distributed on the Internet through streaming services. Chance the Rapper's global significance is that he became successful as an independent artist through free streams of his mixtapes. *10 Day* and *Acid Rap* received critical acclaim, and in 2017, *Coloring Book* was the first Grammy Award–winning streaming-only album, earning three awards—Best Rap Album, Best New Artist, and Best Rap Performance. Based on number of streams alone, *Coloring Book* was also the first album to chart on the Billboard 200, peaking at No. 8.

Chance the Rapper is a tenor, and both his singing and rapping voices are smooth and soft. His texts are informed by intelligent metaphors, internal rhymes, and humor. He combines hip hop, gospel, and R&B and plays piano and other instruments; he also employs samples. His themes include relationships, love, dance, and pride for his home city, Chicago.

His notoriety began after *Acid Rap*, when he began touring with the rapper-production duo Macklemore and Ryan Lewis (2008–). Meanwhile, he was a member of Savemoney (2014–), a Chicago hip hop collective, as well as a lead vocalist for the band the Social Experiment (2014–), who in 2015 released their own critically acclaimed hip hop, R&B, and neo soul album, *Surf*.

Between 2013 and 2018, Chance the Rapper collaborated on singles and EPs with hip hop, electronic, R&B, soul, and dubstep singer-songwriter-producers such as James Blake (James Blake Litherland, 1988–) and John Legend (John Roger Stephens, 1978–) as well as MCs such as rapper Action Bronson (Arian Asllani, 1983–) and rapper-turntablist-producer DJ Khaled (Khaled Mohamed Khaled, 1975–).

Melissa Ursula Dawn Goldsmith

See also: The United States

Further Reading

Best, Cassidy, Katie Braile, Emily Falvey, Samantha Ross, Julia Rotunno, and David Schreiber. 2017. "A 'Chance' of Success: The Influence of Subcultural Capital on the Commercial Success of Chance the Rapper." *MEIEA Journal* 17, no. 1: 31–58.

Chance the Rapper. 2017. Foreword to *A People's History of Chicago* by Kevin Coval. Breakbeat Poets Series. Chicago: Haymarket Books.

Further Listening
Chance the Rapper. 2012. *10 Day*. Self-released.
Chance the Rapper. 2013. *Acid Rap*. Self-released.
Chance the Rapper. 2016. *Coloring Book*. Self-released.

Chap Hop

Chap hop, a subgenre of hip hop that takes the language of hip hop and pairs it with the music, values, and aesthetics of the Chappist Movement, which emerged in the late 1990s and is epitomized in publications such as *The Chap* magazine. Chap hop originated in the 2000s in parts of England. The Chappist Movement is a tongue-in-cheek approach to men's fashion and attitudes, suggesting that men return to the styles and attitudes of the British chap, such as tweed clothing, omnipresent deerstalker, bowler, and boater hats, and proper British manners. Typically, chap hop artists rap using Received Pronunciation English (RP, also known as BBC English), which is the Standard English accent of the United Kingdom, and they employ the grammar and vocabulary of the Queen's English. The style of delivery is intended to evoke stereotypes of British English; the topics of most chap hop tracks also emphasize English cultural stereotypes, such as cricket players, pipe smokers, and tea drinkers. The artists themselves dress in Victorian- or Edwardian-era-style clothing and many sport highly cultivated facial hair styles, such as handlebar mustaches. In 2014, chap hop made headlines in England's *Daily Mail* newspaper when the country's education secretary, Michael Gove, told a reporter that chap hop artists Professor Elemental (Paul Alborough, 1975–) and Mr. B The Gentleman Rhymer (Jim Burke, 1970–), who recorded on the labels Tea Sea Records (2007*–), Grot Business (n.d.), and the Chap-Hop Business Concern (2011*–), were among his favorite musicians.

ARTISTS

Chap hop first drew widespread attention in 2010, when Mr. B The Gentleman Rhymer released his "Chap Hop History" music video on YouTube. The track is a medley of several classic hip hop tracks, including the Sugarhill Gang's (1979–1985, 1994–) "Rapper's Delight" (1979), Run-D.M.C.'s (1981–2002) "King of Rock" (1985), and LL Cool J's (1968–) "Mama Said Knock You Out" (1990). Each stanza of the track features lyrics in RP rapped against samples played on a banjolele, a four-stringed instrument with the size and tuning system of a ukulele and the tone and construction of a banjo. Mr. B has provided musical anthems for the Chap Olympiad, an annual summer event held in Bedford Square Gardens in London in which competitors sport cravats and smoke pipes and prizes are awarded for the best-creased trousers and the most rakish hairstyles.

Professor Elemental is a steampunk character who evokes the science fiction of Jules Verne (1828–1905) through his raps, as he frequently sports a pith helmet and refers to himself as a mad scientist. Professor Elemental is accompanied by an orangutan butler named Geoffrey, with whom he conducts scientific experiments. He first came to prominence with the track "Cup of Brown Joy" (2010), an ode to tea.

Other chap hop artists include Poplock Holmes (anonymous, 1976–) and Sir Reginald Pikedevant, Esquire (anonymous, n.d.). Most of Poplock Holmes's tracks pay homage to Sherlock Holmes stories, such as the song "The Pound of the Basskervilles." In 2011, Sir Reginald Pikedevant, Esquire released a single called "Just Glue Some Gears on It (And Call It Steampunk)," and after the track was repeatedly misattributed to both Professor Elemental and to Mr. B, Sir Reginald recorded "A Belated Introduction," in which he set himself apart from the two other artists.

ASSOCIATIONS WITH STEAMPUNK

Because of its close affiliation with and use of elements of the Victorian era, chap hop is often associated with the steampunk movement. Steampunk is a 21st-century pop culture fad in which the sensibilities of the Victorian age are combined with the interests of science fiction writers of the era, such as Verne and H. G. Wells (1866–1946). Steampunk also shows a great interest in technology, especially the role of gears, cogs, and eyepieces. Professor Elemental regularly appears at steampunk events and has been the headlining act at the Steampunk World's Fair, a convention held in the United States annually since 2010, as well as Waltz on the Wye, a steampunk festival held since 2011 in Chepstow, a town on the border of England and Wales.

Poplock Holmes identifies as a steampunk artist more than as a chap hop artist, although he has accepted his placement within the chap hop genre. Sir Reginald Pikedevant's "Just Glue Some Gears on It (And Call It Steampunk)" mocks those who misunderstand the aesthetics and values of steampunk culture and misattribute cultural phenomena to steampunk. Not all chap hop musicians consider themselves part of the steampunk movement, however. For example, Mr. B has kept his distance from such associations, preferring to remain unaffiliated with any particular artistic or cultural phenomenon.

FEUD BETWEEN MR. B AND PROFESSOR ELEMENTAL

Professor Elemental, who initially identified himself as a steampunk artist and not as a chap hop artist, became irritated when people began mistaking him for Mr. B. In 2010, Professor Elemental released the song and video "Fighting Trousers," in which he attacked Mr. B's signature tweed and his signature instrument, the banjolele, suggesting that Mr. B should perhaps find another profession; in the music video, Professor Elemental appears in a boxing ring, as if preparing for a fight. In response to Professor Elemental's track, Mr. B released "Like a Chap," in which he articulates all of his superior attributes—his pipe, his facial hair, his silk-lined wool clothes, and his hats.

The feud was all in good fun. Professor Elemental briefly appeared in the music video of "Like a Chap" as the two struggled to take a British flag away from each other. Afterward, Professor Elemental tweeted that he loved the video and was grateful that Mr. B let him make an appearance. They have appeared together both live and in recordings since the feud. During a 2011 performance, they engaged in a "chap-off," in which they had a rhyme battle over who was the superior RP rapper. In 2012, Mr. B was a guest artist on "The Duel," a track on Professor Elemental's album *Father of Invention*.

Amanda Sewell

See also: Mr. B The Gentleman Rhymer; Nerdcore; Professor Elemental; The United Kingdom

Further Reading

Robinson, Frances. 2011. "In 'Chap Hop,' Gentleman Rappers Bust Rhymes about Tea, Cricket." *Wall Street Journal*, April 4, A1, A14.

Walters, Simon. 2014. "Gove's Favorite Rapper Revealed: Minister Professes Love for 'Chap Hop' Star Who Calls Boris Simple, Cameron an 'Airy-Fairy Dud,' and Osborne Tight-Fisted." *Daily Mail*, March 22.

Further Listening

Mr. B The Gentleman Rhymer. 2013. *Can't Stop, Shan't Stop.* Chap Hop Business Concern.

Professor Elemental. 2012. *The Indifference Engine.* Tea Sea Records.

The Chemical Brothers

(1995–, Manchester, England)

The Chemical Brothers is a London- and Manchester-based drum and bass duo of Ed Simons (1970–) and Tom Rowlands (1971–). For over 20 years, the duo has been ranked among the world's top electronic dance music groups. The Chemical Brothers has been especially popular in the United Kingdom, with a half dozen No. 1 albums and 13 Top 20 singles, including two No. 1 singles. The duo's characteristic loud, full, high-energy sound has been described as dance music for rock fans (and vice versa), with musical elements ranging from hip hop and related pop genres to the minimalist-style composer Philip Glass (1937–). The Chemical Brothers are important both for establishing the sound of *big beat* and for making dance music a genre for listening, using a variety of sonic effects within the limits of a 4/4 (quadruple) meter and exceptionally regular phrasing. Its frequent use of guest vocalists is also significant. The duo's concerts of intricate tracks mixed live and coordinated with visual effects are an example of its exceptional musicianship in a genre that often relies on routine.

EARLY INTERESTS AND FORMATIVE YEARS

Simons grew up in London, where he attended public school. He had strong interests in hip hop and frequented dance clubs at age 14 before studying history at the University of Manchester. Rowlands was raised in Henley-on-Thames and attended school in Reading, where his chief interest was anything Scottish, including learning the bagpipes. His musical interests were eclectic, but he was especially drawn to Public Enemy (1982–), Kraftwerk (1970–), and other pioneer electronic groups.

Rowlands enrolled at the University of Manchester, where he met Simons in the local music scene. In 1992, the pair began working as DJs, playing hip hop, techno, and house. They called themselves the Dust Brothers, after the Los Angeles–based producing duo best known for their work on the Beastie Boys' (1981–2012) *Paul's Boutique* (1989). In need of instrumental hip hop tracks to play, Simons and Rowlands began to make their own with a basic computer, sampler, and keyboard setup. Their first effort sampled the goth-pop collective This Mortal Coil's (1983–1991) "Song to the Siren" (1983). Within a year they were doing their own remixes, which led to the EP *Fourteenth Century Sky* (1994), whose first track, "Chemical Beats," established the duo's sound. About that time, the Los Angeles–based Dust Brothers became aware of their U.K. namesakes and sued. Simons and Rowlands then took the name the Chemical Brothers, under which they made their first international tour in 1995.

ALBUMS AND AWARDS

The duo's first album, *Exit Planet Dust*—in obvious reference to its former name—was released in 1995 and was certified Platinum and considered one of the best releases of the 1990s. That same year, The Chemical Brothers released their first mix album, *Live at the Social, Vol. 1* (1996), and also received its first Grammy Award for the single "Block Rockin' Beats." *Dig Your Own Hole* (1997), the group's second studio album, would be the first of six albums to reach No. 1 on the U.K. charts and the first to appear on the Billboard 200. The duo also toured extensively at that time and made well received appearances in the United States. With *Surrender* (1999), the Chemical Brothers expanded its work to include a growing number of guest performers, mostly vocalists. The video for "Let Forever Be," its first collaboration with French director Michel Gondry (1963–), attracted attention for its exceptional film effects. Over the next two years the duo was quite active performing, and it also released several singles and EPs on the way to their fourth album, *Come with Us* (2002). That album featured another track, "Star Guitar," with a Gondry video. Both *Push the Button* (2005) and its single "Galvanize" won Grammys.

Further (2010) is notable for having videos for each of its eight tracks. That same year, the Chemical Brothers provided several tracks for the American motion picture *Black Swan* (2010), and a year later it created their first full score for the multinationally produced motion picture *Hanna* (2011). Additionally, its music has been used (often uncredited) in over 100 different television shows, motion pictures, and video games since 1995. Its most recent album, *Born in the Echoes* (2015), debuted at the No. 1 position on the U.K. chart, which confirms the duo's status as the leading dance music composers in the United Kingdom.

Scott Warfield

See also: The United Kingdom

Further Reading

Reynolds, Simon. 1999. "Back to the Lab." *Spin* 15, no. 7: 94–98.

Zeiner-Henriksen, Hans. 2014. "Old Instruments, New Agendas: The Chemical Brothers and the ARP 2600." *Dancecult: Journal of Electronic Dance Music Culture* 6, no. 1: 26–40.

Further Listening

The Chemical Brothers. 1995. *Exit Planet Dust*. Freestyle Dust/Junior Boy's Own/Virgin
    Records.

Chicano Rap

Chicano rap is a style of hip hop that combines Latin rhythms, hip hop beats, and
dance or gangsta rap lyrics. It is popular among southwestern and midwestern Mexican Americans, who often self-identify as *Chicano* (aka Chicana, Xicano, or
Xicana), a term that emerged during the 1960s Chicano Civil Rights Movement
(aka El Movimiento). Although the term *Chicano* is sometimes used interchange-
ably with the label *Mexican American*, they signal noticeable differences. In Mexican American cultures, especially in the Southwest and in Southern California, a
Chicano identity is closely tied to cultural pride. Chicano music can be traced back
to Tuscon, Arizona, native Lalo Guerrero (Eduardo Guerrero, 1916–2005), who
wrote big band and swing songs in the 1930s. In the 1950s and 1960s, Chicano rock
music emerged with musicians such as Los Angeles–based Ritchie Valens (Richard
Steven Valenzuela, 1941–1959); Autlán de Navarro, Mexico–based Carlos Santana
(1947–); and Tucson, Arizona–based Linda Ronstadt (1946–).

In the pop music genre, Houston-based singer Selena (Selena Quintanilla, 1971–
1995) became an icon, recording songs that mixed Mexican, Tejano, and American elements, and Zack de la Rocha (Zacharias Manuel de la Rocha, 1970–) and
his Los Angeles–based rap metal band Rage against the Machine (1991–2000,
2007–2011) performed songs with socially conscious messages. All four of Rage
against the Machine's studio albums charted, and most went multi-Platinum. Its
recordings include its eponymous album (1992), *Evil Empire* (1996), *The Battle of
Los Angeles* (1999), and *Renegades* (2000). Both *Evil Empire* and *The Battle of Los
Angeles* peaked at No. 1 on the Billboard 200.

Cuban American rapper Mellow Man Ace (Ulpiano Sergio Reyes, 1967–) had a
1990 bilingual hit with "Mentirosa," but Chicano rap's first popular artist was Los
Angeles breakdancer, electro-hop rapper, songwriter, and record producer Kid Frost
(aka Frost, Arturo Molina Jr., 1962–). In 1990, he released his debut album, *Hispanic Causing Panic*, on Virgin Records America (aka Virgin Records, 1972–), and
it included his Spanglish G-funk–style single, "La Raza," which peaked at No. 42
on the Billboard Hot 100 chart. "La Raza" challenged Chicano stereotypes, called
for unity and pride with references to Aztec warriors and rapped phrases such as
"Chicano, and I'm brown and proud," and made boasts about Chicano abilities to
fight back if engaged.

In 1991, Kid Frost and Mellow Man Ace, along with Mexican American rapper
A.L.T. (Alvin Lowell Trivette, 1989–), formed the project band Latin Alliance
(1991), which released one album. A.L.T. had a 1992 hit with "Tequila." Mellow
Man Ace's brother Sen Dog (Senen Reyes, 1965–) went on to cofound rap trio
Cypress Hill (1988–), which also featured Mexican American rapper B-Real (Louis
Freese, 1970–). Cypress Hill went on to have three Top 10 albums on the Billboard
200, four Platinum-certified studio albums, and a Top 20 hit with "Insane in the
Brain" (1993). A Chicano version of N.W.A. (1986–1991) named Brownside (1993–)

was created by Eazy-E (Eric Lynn Wright, 1964–1995). Although Brownside did not chart and was dropped from Ruthless Records (1986–) after Eazy-E's death, it did introduce gang-based Sureño slang into rap. Around the same time, San Diego rapper Jonny Z (John Zazueta, n.d.) had a hit with "Shake Shake (Shake That Culo)." Current Chicano rap musicians include San Diego, California, rapper, producer, and actor Lil Rob (Roberto L. Flores, 1975–) and Los Angeles rapper Serio (Jonathán Pérez, n.d.).

Anthony J. Fonseca

See also: Cypress Hill; Mexico; Political Hip Hop; The United States

Further Reading

McFarland, Pancho. 2006. "Chicano Rap Roots: Black–Brown Cultural Exchange and the Making of a Genre." *Callaloo* 29, no. 3: 939–55.

McFarland, Pancho. 2008. *Chicano Rap: Gender and Violence in the Postindustrial Barrio.* Austin: University of Texas Press.

Further Listening

Brownside. 2016. *Bangin Story'z.* East Town Records.

Kid Frost. 1990. *Hispanic Causing Pain.* Virgin America.

Chile

Chile is a relatively isolated Spanish-speaking South American country located between the Andes mountain range and the Pacific Ocean. Despite a population of 18 million, the country has seen comparatively little development of a hip hop scene, and this has been present primarily in its largest urban area, Santiago. Hip hop's slow growth may be attributed in part to societal homogeneity, as Chile lacks many social intersections that have inspired hip hop aesthetics elsewhere. The repressive censorship policies of the Augusto Pinochet (1915–2006) dictatorship (1973–1990) and its aftermath also presented significant obstacles to the oppositional rhetoric common to hip hop discourse. Although only a few Chilean hip hop acts have achieved noteworthy success, the genre has become increasingly popular in recent years.

EARLY HIP HOP

In the 1980s, breakdancing, impromptu rap battles, graffiti markings, and the clandestine exchange of foreign cassettes could be seen on street corners in Santiago. Underground hip hop music became more popular in the 1990s, spurred in part by the return of Chilean youth raised in exile after Pinochet's reign of terror. Among the early pioneers, La Pozze Latina (1991–2000) incorporated drum machines and samplers to create infectious grooves that introduced rap. Notably, the band's video for "Con el color de mi aliento" ("With the Color of My Breath"), from the album *Pozzeidos x "La ilusión"* (*Possessed by "The Illusion,"* a wordplay on *posse* and *possessed*), was one of the first Latin American–produced hip hop tracks to appear on *MTV en español* (1998–2010). In 1993, the similarly influential group

Panteras Negras (Black Panthers, 1989–2004, 2011–) also recorded their second album, *Reyes de la jungle* (*Kings of the Jungle*), on the Santiago-based Alerce label (1976–).

Chilean hip hop took a turn toward the mainstream in the late 1990s as the group Tiro de Gracia (Coup de grâce, 1993–2007, 2013–) signed with a Latin subsidiary of EMI (1931–2012) to release their debut album, *Ser hümano!* (*Human Being!*, 1997), which offered a funk-infused rap style that included contributions from several prominent Chilean musicians, DJs, and producers. The band's success paved the way for other popular Chilean hip hop ensembles, such as Los Tetas (The T— or The Breasts, 1994–2004, 2011–) and De Kiruza (1987–1999, 2007–).

INTO THE 21st CENTURY

Though the turn of the century saw the withdrawal of major-label support and a lull in hip hop production, the genre has experienced rejuvenation in recent years. One of Latin America's most successful female rap artists, Ana Tijoux (Anamaria Merino Tijoux, 1977–), was raised in exile in France but returned to Chile, where she fronted Makiza (Maqui Warrior, 1997–2006). Her 2014 collaboration with Uruguayan Jorge Drexler (Jorge Abner Drexler Prada, 1964–), "Universos paralelos" ("Parallel Universes"), earned a Latin Grammy nomination for Song of the Year, and her 2014 album *Vengo* (*I Come . . .*) garnered a Grammy nomination for Best Latin Pop, Rock, or Urban Album. The newest generation of Chilean hip hop has also generated a strong undercurrent of explicitly political, independent acts, best demonstrated by underground rappers such as SubVerso (Vicente Durán, 1975*–) and the up-tempo fusion of bands such as Sinergia (1994–) and Juana Fe (2004–).

J. Ryan Bodiford

See also: Argentina; France; Tijoux, Ana

Further Reading
Istodor, Luca. 2017. "Ana Tijoux's Radical Crossing of Borders." *Revista: Harvard Review of Latin America* 16, no. 2: 65–66.
Lindholm, Susan. 2017. "Hip Hop Practice as Identity and Memory Work in and in-between Chile and Sweden." *Suomen antropologi: Journal of the Finnish Anthropological Society* 42, no. 2: 60–74.

Further Listening
Panteras Negras. 1993. *Reyes de la jungle* (*Kings of the Jungle*). Alerce.
Tijoux, Ana. 2014. *Vengo* (*I Come*). Nacional Records.
Tiro de Gracia. 1997. *Ser hümano!* (*Human Being!*). EMI Latin.

China

China's hip hop scene, like its C-pop, Cantopop, Mandopop, and Hokkien pop scenes, is relatively recent, having emerged around 1990, when U.K., Filipino, and Congolese DJs started playing hip hop music. In addition, nightclubs such as

Juliana's in Beijing started playing the music, and American films such as *Beat Street* (1984) made their way into the country. Juliana's introduced Chinese clubbers to U.S. labels such as Sugar Hill Records (1978–1998) and Tommy Boy Entertainment (aka Tommy Boy Records, 1981–), and the United Kingdom's Streetsounds (1982–) label. By 1994, a nightly hip hop club had opened in Shanghai. The first recorded Chinese-language rapping was performed in the song "Caged Bird" from the album *The Power of the Powerless* (1998) by Beijing psychedelic rock singer, trumpeter, and guitarist Cui Jian (1961–).

Early hip hop–influenced artists included Taiwanese rapper MC HotDog (Yáo Zhōngrén, 1978–), Hong Kong R&B ballad singers Sandy Lam (Lín Yìlián, 1966–) and Shirley Kwan (Guān Shúyí, 1966–), and Hong Kong rap bands such as the duo Softhard (1988–1995, 2006–) and the rap group LMF (aka Lazy Mutha F—a, 1993–2003, 2009–), the latter being the first signed by a major record label, the Warner Music Group (1958–). Multinational Beijing hip hop group Yin Ts'ang (2001–) was the first mainland Chinese hip hop band to release an album to critical acclaim. It won back-to-back Best Group and Most Dedicated to the Art awards at the first and second annual Chinese hip hop awards and best rap group in China at the 2009 Kappa-YoHo Pop Music Awards.

POST-1989 CHINESE HIP HOP

Generally, the spread of hip hop was made more difficult by the government after the Tiananmen Square protests of 1989, student-led demonstrations in Beijing that were part of the popular national movement called the '89 Democracy Movement. The protests were forcibly suppressed after the government declared martial law and several hundred demonstrators were killed in the Tiananmen Square Massacre. The government promoted traditional Chinese culture, but music and video smuggled into China had allowed for the underground interaction of Western hip hop and Chinese youth, the biggest audience for rap music. Many rappers chose English as their lyric language, although there was some push to rap in one of the Chinese dialects, and some arguing over which dialect should be used.

Chinese youth flocked to the messages and hardcore style of LMF, with lyrics that expressed discontent toward the political and economic turmoil of Hong Kong in songs such as "WTF" (2003), from *Finalazy* (2003), as well as songs that emphasized cultural identity, such as "1127" from *Xī wū mén* (*Heiwumen*, aka *CrazyChildren*, 2002). In songs that incorporated elements of hip hop, bounce, metal, hardcore punk, and rock, LMF also criticized Hong Kong's pop music culture as being commercial, stale, and uncreative. Recent Chinese rap artists include Hong Kong hip hop duo FAMA (Farmer, 2000–) and onetime Hong Kong resident, Chinese American rapper MC Jin (Jin Au-Yeung, 1982–). MC Jin was born in Miami, then lived in Hong Kong and finally New York City, where he performs as a rapper-songwriter. He raps in English and Cantonese and had his first two albums put out on the Ruff Ryders (1988–) record label.

Because of Western influence, hip hop culture continues to grow in China as Americans such as Dana Burton (n.d.) immigrate. Burton, who arrived in China in 1999, started the Iron Mic annual freestyle competition in 2001 to encourage Chinese youth to find their own rap voices. The new generation of Chinese rappers use trip hop's (downtempo) funky beats in their music. Of the new Chinese rappers, the Higher Brothers (2016–), part of the Sichuan-based rap collective Chengdu Rap House (2012–), are the most popular. The group finished a China tour in 2017 and are scheduled for a U.S. tour in 2018.

Anthony J. Fonseca

See also: Malaysia; Taiwan

Further Reading

Khan, Katy. 2009. "Chinese Hip Hop Music: Negotiating for Cultural Freedoms in the Twenty-First Century." *Muziki: Journal of Music Research in Africa* 6, no. 2: 232–40.

Liu, Jin. 2014. "Alternative Voice and Local Youth Identity in Chinese Local-Language Rap Music." *Positions: Asia Critique* 22, no. 1: 263–92.

Further Listening

LMF. 2003. *Finalazy.* Warner Music Hong Kong.

Chopper

Chopper is an American Midwest style of rapping defined by the fast-paced delivery of rap vocals. It began in the 1980s in urban areas such as Cleveland, Chicago, and Kansas City, Missouri. By the early 1990s, it had spread to Los Angeles with the Project Blowed (1994–) movement, led by Aceyalone (1970–) and Abstract Rude (Aaron Pointer, n.d.), as well as groups such as Aceyalone's Freestyle Fellowship (1991–1993, 1998–) and Riddlore? (Henry Lee Owens, n.d.) and his group C.V.E. (n.d.). Other early practitioners included Flint, Michigan's the Dayton Family (1993–) and Chicago's Twista (aka Tung Twista, Carl Terrell Mitchell, 1973–), although Cleveland's Bone Thugs-n-Harmony (1991–) were by far the best known of the early practitioners of chopper. The style became even more popular when Kansas City underground rapper/songwriter Tech N9ne (1971–) released a number of chopper-heavy collaborative singles. Tech N9ne went on to sell over two million albums and has licensed his music in film, television, and video games, in addition to achieving fame as a record producer, actor, and entrepreneur as well as cofounder of Strange Music (1999–). His single "Midwest Choppers 2" (2009) from *Sickology 101* actually explains his goal of spreading the word on chopper rap, through what he calls "elite" and "intricate" tongues, around the world, including California, New York, Denmark, and Australia, but he goes on to note that the most accurate choppers are from the Midwest.

THE SOUND

Generally, like its namesake, the AK-47 semiautomatic rifle (Tech N9ne is named after the related TEC-9 semiautomatic pistol), chopper style places an emphasis on speed. Some rappers also liken chopper to a helicopter (also nicknamed a chopper) because of the speed of its blades and its staccato rhythm, which influenced some chopper rap; however, what makes an expert chopper is the combination of speed, enunciation, and clarity.

Arguably, the first artist to use this style was Kool Moe Dee (1963–) of the Treacherous Three (1978–1984), who used speed rapping on "The New Rap Language" (1980). Jamaican and Jamaican American rappers Daddy Freddy (S. Frederick Small, 1965–) and Shinehead (Edmund Carl Aiken, 1962–) took up the speed rap torch in the 1980s. California-based JJ Fad (1985–1992, 2009–) helped speed rapping go mainstream, as its single "Supersonic" (1987) led to its becoming the first female rap group to earn a Grammy nomination. "Supersonic" featured innovative, fast, double-time rapping, which would later influence the extended block rhymes of Eminem (1972–).

Chopper's stars include some of the fastest rappers in the world, such as Krayzie Bone (Anthony Henderson, 1973–) and Bizzy Bone (Bryon Anthony McCane II, 1976–) of Bone Thugs-n-Harmony, as well as Busta Rhymes (1972–), Krizz Kaliko (Samuel William Christopher Watson IV, 1974–), and Snow tha Product (Claudia Alexandra Feliciano, 1987–). Tech N9ne has helped the style to spread by purposefully working with rappers from the Midwest, the South, and both the West and East Coasts as well as from Denmark and Turkey. As of 2018, the chopper style is being used by many rappers, even alternated with slow-paced raps by artists such as Kendrick Lamar (1987–).

Anthony J. Fonseca

See also: Busta Rhymes; Kool Moe Dee; MC; Tech N9ne; The United States

Further Reading

Cramer, Jennifer, and Jill Hallett. 2010. "From Chi-Town to the Dirty-Dirty: Regional Identity Markers in U.S. Hip Hop." In *The Languages of Global Hip Hop*, edited by Marina Terkourafi, chap. 10. New York: Continuum.

French, Kenneth. 2017. "Geography of American Rap: Rap Diffusion and Rap Centers." *GeoJournal* 82, no. 2: 259–72.

Further Listening

JJ Fad. 1987. *Supersonic.* Dream Team Records.

Tech N9ne Collabos. 2009. *Sickology 101.* Strange Music.

Christian Hip Hop

(aka CHH, gospel hip hop, gospel rap, Christian rap, holy hip hop)

Christian hip hop is a subgenre of hip hop music in which the genre's thematic concerns and lyrical content have been modified to express Christian values and goals. Though it has global reach, it is by far more prevalent in the United States, where CHH artists and their audiences have created performance spaces as part of established Christian ministries and in independent neighborhood or dance club communities. The boundary between hip hop and CHH is porous. In fact, many rappers reference Christian values and biblical verses, and many Christian rappers self-identify simply as rappers who happen to be Christian, usually performing

San Francisco born rapper-songwriter, beatboxer, and actor T-Bone started his career as a gangsta rapper, but shifted his focus to combine gangsta rap themes with Christian Hip Hop by the early 1990s. (Paul Mounce/Corbis via Getty Images)

outside (or tangentially to) the contemporary Christian music industry. CHH rappers and musicians thus inhabit a marginal space.

CHH emerged in 1985 with Stephen Wiley's (1956–) four-song EP *Bible Break*, released a full six years after "Rapper's Delight" by the Sugarhill Gang (1979–1985, 1994–). Like many of his contemporaries in the early CHH scene, Wiley was an African American youth minister who used rap to teach his students. *Bible Break* outlined some basics of the salvation doctrine and included a verse meant to help children memorize the books of the Bible. In 1987, Michael Peace (1969–) released his highly influential *RRRock it Right*, widely recognized as the first full-length commercially released CHH album. Other early CHH MCs and groups include D-Boy Rodriguez (Danny Rodriguez, 1967–1990), Dynamic Twins (1989–), LPG (aka Living Proof of Grace, 1984–), P.I.D. (aka Preachers in Disguise or Preachas, 1988–), and S.F.C. (aka Soldiers for Christ, 1987–).

CHRISTIAN HIP HOP SINCE THE 1990s

As CHH matured, it began to sound more and more like hip hop as it began to incorporate hip hop aesthetics and musical practices. Peace's vocal performances, for instance, were audibly influenced by early LL Cool J (1968–); gangsta rap hit the CHH scene in the early 1990s with Christian groups such as Gospel Gangstaz (1994–). Other prominent CHH groups include the Cross Movement (1996–2008), KJ-52 (Jonah Kirsten Sorrentino, 1975–), Lecrae (Lecrae Devaughn Moore, 1979–), MA$E (Mason Durell Betha, 1977–), the New Breed (aka Israel Houghton and the New Breed, 1998–2005), and T-Bone (Rene Francisco Sotomayor, 1973–).

Though CHH, like its hip hop counterpart, is largely dominated by African American male performers, female rappers such as Elle R.O.C. (Lanette Chambers, n.d.) and Sister Souljah (Lisa Williamson, 1964–) emerged after 1992. The success of RedCloud (Henry Andrade, 1978–) ushered in the representation of

Native Americans and Hispanic Americans in CHH. Since the 1990s, several labels have been devoted solely to CHH, including Reach Records (2004–) and Cross Movement Records (1997–). CHH festivals and awards have also proliferated. Until 2014, the annual New York–based Christian music festival, Rap Fest, provided the community with a central performance venue (for over 20 years). The Kingdom Choice Awards, an annual CHH and urban gospel music awards show, was founded in 2009, and the online CHH magazine *Rapzilla* has been providing news, music reviews, and online media for the community since 2003.

GLOBAL CHRISTIAN HIP HOP

Though the CHH scene is centralized in the United States, Christian rappers span the globe. Double M (Maged Medhat*, n.d.), for instance, is a rapper from Egypt who found inspiration in Lecrae and KJ-52. A number of artists have come out of the African continent, including Zimbabwe's Ill Ceey (Courtney Antipas, n.d.), Malawi's David Kalilani (1982*–), and South Africa's Blaque Nubon (Mlungisi Ngubane, 1988*–).

Other notable CHH artists found worldwide include Indonesia's Disciples (2006*–) and Ekaterinburg, Russia's Nastoyatel (Maxim Kurlenko, 1974*–), formerly of the hip hop band Ek Playaz (2003–2009). The "Hip Hop Church" Krosswerdz, which was formed in 2006 by an Australian national network of CHH artists, leads church services in Sydney and across the nation. In addition, Belgian-born Chad Horton (1988–) was a cocreator of CHH e-zine *Rapzilla* (2003–). Further, amateur Christian rap groups have a strong presence in places such as São Paulo and London.

RECEPTION AND ONGOING DIALOGUE

CHH has prompted several key conversations within the Christian community and among scholars. The primary discussion has centered on the anxieties the subgenre incites within both the black church and the Christian community as a whole. Several key figures in the black church community, including Rev. Calvin O. Butts III (1949–) and G. Craige Lewis (George Craige Lewis, 1969–) of EX Ministries, have openly condemned CHH for drawing upon the aesthetics of a genre they consider to be fundamentally promiscuous, misogynistic, and violent. A growing segment of the Christian community, however, has embraced CHH as both a style of worship and a community ministry, capitalizing on hip hop's ability to more deeply name and address the needs of current generations and recognizing the liberating power of this genre as an African American musical form that challenges deeply entrenched and damaging social hierarchies.

Mainstream hip hop has often been considered religious in its own right, certainly in terms of its Islamic influences, but also with openly religious rappers such as Tupac Shakur (1971–1996), MC Hammer (1962–), and Kanye West (1977–), who have woven Christian symbolism and biblical verse into their songs. Rappers have been accepted as modern-day and streetwise preachers and theologians by younger generations whose relationship to the Christian church has dissolved; in this role, Shakur crafted a portrait of Jesus as "Black Jesuz"—not white but multiracial, in tune with the pain of inner-city life, and sharing in the experiences of the poor and the oppressed. Black Jesuz both transcends current theological thought and gives access to a theology that continues to resonate strongly in CHH to the disenfranchised.

Scholars usually describe CHH as a highly marginal practice, a subgenre that exists at the edges of both hip hop and Christian culture. CHH artists curate this status to avoid being pigeonholed in either community; they reject what they view as the negative values of hip hop as well as the mainstream stigma of the contemporary Christian music industry. CHH is further characterized by a preoccupation with authenticity. By emphasizing their theological mastery and their marginality, artists generate a sense of authenticity and integrity that makes their lyrics relevant to the lived experiences of their audiences.

Jessica Leah Getman

See also: MC Hammer; Political Hip Hop

Further Reading

Pinn, Anthony B., ed. 2003. *Noise and Spirit: The Religious and Spiritual Sensibilities of Rap Music.* New York: New York University Press.

Zanfagna, Christina. 2012. "Kingdom Business: Holy Hip Hop's Evangelical Hustle." *Journal of Popular Music Studies* 24, no. 2: 196–216.

Further Listening

Gospel Gangstas. 1994. *Gang Affiliated.* Holy Terra Records.

Wiley, Stephen. 1985. *Bible Break.* Brentwood Music.

Christie Z-Pabon

(1969*–, Pennsylvania*)

Christie Z-Pabon is a DJ battle promoter, publicist, and organizer as well as a hip hop activist. In the mid-1980s, she became interested in hip hop music, particularly its turntablism and dance aspects. She tuned in to and taped Sly Jock (Clifford Charlton, n.d.) on WAMO (formerly WHOD, 1948–), the first radio station in Pittsburgh, Pennsylvania, to broadcast hip hop. Her early hip hop exposure included purchasing 12-inch albums at a local record store and seeing b-boys perform live at school functions. Her earliest experience promoting hip hop was in college in the early 1990s, when she organized Pittsburgh's earliest hip hop parties. Christie Z-Pabon organizes b-boy/b-girl battle scenes, listening to artists' issues and providing a fair environment in which their expression of art can be judged. As one of very few women on the DJ battle scene, Christie Z-Pabon advocates for women's involvement. She is a strong proponent of the DJ battle as a space for innovation, creation, and preservation of hip hop. Starting in the 2000s, Christie Z-Pabon was involved in hip hop scholarship through offering historical information about DJ battles and the art of the battle, proofreading and providing editorial suggestions to researchers, and compiling lists of DJ battle champions, outcomes, and statistics.

FROM ENTHUSIAST TO PROMOTER AND CEO

In 1996, Christie Z-Pabon moved from Perryopolis, Pennsylvania, to New York City and briefly worked as a mental health specialist in the Bronx; however, her main goal was to attend many DJ battles. While attending Universal Zulu Nation's (1973–) anniversary in Harlem, she met hip hop dance pioneer and choreographer Popmaster Fabel (Jorge Pabon, 1965*–), whom she married in 1997. A year later, she began working in sales at DMC U.S.A., home of the New York City Regional DJ Battle and affiliated with the DMC World DJ Championships (1985–). DMC, or Disco Mix Club, 1983–, is a London-based remix label. At DMC U.S.A., Christie Z-Pabon learned more about turntablism and creating DJ battle routines. By 1999, she was organizing DJ battles, including the United States' sole hosting of the DMC World Finals.

In 2000, she left DMC to organize her own DJ battles nationwide. With her husband, Christie Z-Pabon established Tools of War Park Jams in 2003, a New York City grassroots hip hop promotion organization and battling event series that brings hip hop artists and culture back to New York City parks—hip hop's initial venue. In 2008, she became CEO of DMC U.S.A.

Melissa Ursula Dawn Goldsmith

See also: Battling; Breakdancing; Hip Hop Dance; MC; Turntablism; The United States

Further Reading

Katz, Mark. 2010. "The Turntable as Weapon: Understanding the Hip Hop DJ Battle." In *Capturing Sound: How Technology Has Changed Music*, rev. ed, chap. 6. Berkeley: University of California Press.

Katz, Mark. 2012. *Groove Music: The Art and Culture of the Hip Hop DJ.* New York: Oxford University Press, 2012.

Chuck D

(Carlton Douglas Ridenhour, 1960–, Queens, New York)

Chuck D is an American rapper and producer, best known for his role as the leader of Public Enemy (1982–), established in Long Island, New York, and as a part of the Long Island production team the Bomb Squad (1986–). He is widely considered one of the progenitors of socially conscious and political hip hop, and many critics rank him as one of the most talented rappers of all time. Along with the multilayered sound of the Bomb Squad's production style, Chuck D's explosive delivery and historically-informed, socially conscious lyrics are among the most defining features of Public Enemy's style. His lyrics often feature complex poetic meters that vary in style, both within individual tracks and across entire albums. "Fight the Power," a single from the 1990 album *Fear of a Black Planet*, is regarded as one of Chuck D's—and, by extension, Public Enemy's—most influential tracks and is considered a hip hop classic. In its lyrics, Chuck D alludes to various funk and soul artists and songs, including Bobby Byrd's (Robert Howard Byrd, 1934–2007) "I Know You Got Soul" (1971) and James Brown's (1933–2006) "Funky Drummer" (1970). He also accuses individuals and institutions, most notably Elvis Presley (1935–1977), of being racist. The song also encourages black listeners to educate themselves and find their own heroes, even if those heroes are not necessarily recognized by the white mainstream.

In the early 1980s, Chuck D was a student at Adelphi College in New York, where he met rapper Flavor Flav (1959–), journalist and critic Harry Allen (1964–), and other people who became key figures in Public Enemy's formative years. Rick Rubin (Frederick Jay Rubin, 1963–) signed Chuck D (and the group) to the new Def Jam Records (1983–) label. In 1987, Public Enemy released its first album, *Yo! Bum Rush the Show*. In his dual role as rapper and producer for Public Enemy, Chuck D frequently samples snippets of his own rapped lyrics for new tracks. For instance, samples of his voice from the 1987 single "Bring the Noise" have appeared in several other Public Enemy tracks, such as "Black Steel in the Hour of Chaos" (1988) and "Night of the Living Baseheads" (1988). In the late 1990s, he sued for defamation and copyright infringement over the unauthorized sample of his voice that can be heard in the Notorious B.I.G.'s (1972–1997) "Ten Crack Commandments" (1997).

Chuck D has also recorded separately from Public Enemy. His solo albums include *Autobiography of Mistachuck* (1996) and *The Black in Man* (2014). He has collaborated with artists including Confrontation Camp (2000), hard rock and pop singer Meat Loaf (1947–), and hardcore, punk, and spoken-word artist Henry Rollins (1961). In 2016, Chuck D and Public Enemy's DJ Lord (Lord Aswod, 1975–) joined forces with three members of Rage against the Machine (1991–) and Cypress Hill's (1988–) B-Real (Louis Freese, 1970–) to form the rap-rock supergroup Prophets of Rage. In 2016, Prophets of Rage released its first EP, *The Party's Over*, which featured live covers of Rage against the Machine and Public Enemy songs. Its eponymous debut studio album was released in 2017.

Amanda Sewell

See also: Allen, Harry; The Bomb Squad; Flavor Flav; Political Hip Hop; Public Enemy; The United States

Further Reading

Chuck D [Carlton Ridenhour]. 2008. "Three Pieces." In *Sound Unbound: Sampling Digital Music and Culture*, edited by Paul Miller (DJ Spooky), chap. 29. Cambridge, MA: MIT Press.

Jah, Yusef, and Chuck D. 2006. *Lyrics of a Rap Revolutionary: Times, Rhymes, and Mind of Chuck D.* Beverly Hills, CA: Off da Books.

Rausch, Andrew J. 2011. "Chuck D." In *I Am Hip Hop: Conversations on the Music and Culture*, chap. 6. Lanham, MD: Scarecrow.

Further Listening

Prophets of Rage. 2017. *Prophets of Rage.* Fantasy Records.

Public Enemy. 1988. *It Takes a Nation of Millions to Hold Us Back.* Def Jam.

Public Enemy. 1990. *Fear of a Black Planet.* Def Jam.

Clowning

Clowning is a style of hip hop dance that originated in 1992 in Compton, California, with Tommy the Clown (Thomas Johnson, n.d.), a dancer and entertainer also known as a spokesperson for Governor Gray Davis (1942–). Growing up in Compton, Johnson was involved in several crimes and spent five years in jail. By 1992, he had opted to create a better life for himself through hip hop dance. Interested in motivating youth living in gang-infested communities to use hip hop dance to stay away from crime and violence, he promoted his Compton-based dance crew, the Hip Hop Clowns (1992–), for area parties. His strategy for appealing to audiences and for getting his message across to them was to have his dancers wear clown paint and costuming (capturing the attention of children who were theoretically too young to be influenced by gangs) while their act consisted of hip hop dancing (showing preteens that there are more constructive options than gangs and drugs). Part of the act was to invite youth to dance with them.

Clowning included early breakdancing movements such as popping and locking. Johnson also included movements from other black popular and street dance styles, including the butterfly and the rode, both from Jamaican dancehall and gangsta boogie walks. In time, clowning also adapted movements such as booty popping, freaking, snaking and winding, and twerking (originally performed by female strippers, but male clown dancers perform these moves). By the mid-1990s, about 50 clowning crews existed in Los Angeles, and by the late 1990s, the Hip Hop Clowns were touring worldwide. Clowning became so popular among South Central Los Angeles–area youth that Johnson shifted his focus to teaching at his dance school, the Tommy the Clown Academy. From Johnson's Hip Hop Clowns, another dance style emerged: krumping.

CLOWNING VS. KRUMPING

First-generation krumping was more energetic, aggressive, and menacing than clowning. Dancers eschewed circus clown makeup and costuming in favor of street fashion, usually dark clothing, sometimes accentuated by gothic face paint that resembled African ceremonial war paint. All from Los Angeles, former Hip Hop Clowns members, Big Mijo (Jo' Artis Ratti, 1985–) and Tight Eyez (Ceasare Willis, 1985–), followed by Los Angeles–based krumping innovator and choreographer Lil'C (Christopher Toler, 1983–), rooted krumping in raw, pent-up emotion that was expressed in jerking movements ("the krump"). These usually involved spine flexing and chest pops, accentuated by quick, jerky, sometimes violent arm and hand movements that mimicked fighting. In time, erotic dance–inspired moves were eliminated. Johnson's school eventually taught both clowning and krumping.

In 2004, to help resolve rivalry issues between different clowning and krumping crews, Johnson began the Battle Zone Event at the Great Western Forum in Inglewood, California. During the 2000s, Johnson partnered with the Los Angeles Unified School District and taught in-school clowning and krumping workshops. Because of the two dance styles' appearances in videos by Madonna (1958–), Missy Elliott (1971–), the Chemical Brothers (1995–), and others, the popularity of krumping has surpassed clowning. Today, clowning and krumping exist separately and together, the latter in krump clowning, a dance style that combines movements from both.

Melissa Ursula Dawn Goldsmith

See also: Hip Hop Dance; Krumping; Popping and Locking; The United States

Further Reading

Fuhrer, Margaret. 2014. "Urban and Commercial Dance." In *American Dance: The Complete Illustrated History*, chap. 10. Minneapolis, MN: Voyageur Press.

Kuehn, Kathleen M. 2010. "The Commodification of Blackness in David LaChapelle's *Rize*." *Journal of Information Ethics* 19, no. 2: 52–66.

Further Viewing

LaChapelle, David. 2005. *Rize.* Lionsgate.

C-Murder

(Corey Miller, 1971–, New Orleans, Louisiana)

C-Murder is an American rapper and hip hop musician, songwriter, producer, record label creator/owner, author, and actor from New Orleans. He is also the brother of rapper and producer Master P (Percy Robert Miller, 1970–) and rapper Silkk the Shocker (Vyshonne King Miller, 1975–) and uncle of rapper-actor Lil Romeo (Percy Romeo Miller Jr., 1989–). C-Murder founded and owns the hip hop record labels TRU and Bossalinie Records (both 2000–). He took his stage name from his childhood in New Orleans's Calliope Projects, where he witnessed various crimes. Under the name C-Murder, he has authored the novel *Death around the Corner* (2007) and three self-published books, including a collection of poetry, *Red Beans and Dirty Rice for the Soul* (2014). As of 2018, he continues to serve jail time for a 2009 nightclub murder.

EARLY SUCCESS

While in New Orleans, C-Murder achieved musical success early with the No Limit Records (1990–2003) trio TRU (The Real Untouchables, 1992–2005). In 1998, C-Murder went solo. His first two albums, *Life or Death* (1998) and *Bossaline* (1999), were certified Platinum and Gold and peaked at Nos. 3 and 2, respectively, on the Billboard 200. His breakthrough album, *Trapped in Crime* (2000), peaked at No. 8 but topped the Hot R&B/Hip-Hop Songs chart and contained his biggest hit, "Down for My N's," which featured Snoop Dogg (1971–). His lyrics are informed by scenes of urban poverty and violence juxtaposed against lavish production values that show a willingness to experiment with mixing, sampling, rhythm (the use of bounce techniques), and intricate vocal overlays. His albums often include humorous interludes and melodic piano intros. His fourth album, *C-P-3.com* (2001), reached no higher than No. 45. By the time of his fifth and sixth albums, *The Truest S#!@ I Ever Said* (2005) and *The TRU Story . . . Continued* (2006), he had been incarcerated for murder and was appealing his conviction. While in prison, he has released *Screamin' 4 Vengeance* (2008), *Community Service* (2009), *Calliope*

Click, Vol. 1 (2009), *Tomorrow* (2010), *Ricochet* (2013), and *Ain't No Heaven in the Pen* (2015).

MURDER TRIAL

In August 2009, C-Murder went to trial, accused of killing a 16-year-old fan after a fight. After five days, the jury came to a deadlock, but the judge instructed the jury to resolve the deadlock, which resulted that same day in a guilty verdict. Miller was convicted of second-degree murder, but his defense argued that one of the jurors was intimidated and that judicial pressure had led to the vote change. In 2011, his conviction was upheld, and in 2013 the Supreme Court rejected his final appeal. Many activist groups have since conducted a "Free C-Murder" campaign.

Anthony J. Fonseca

See also: Bounce; Gangsta Rap; Master P; The United States

Further Reading

Dreisinger, Baz. 2005. "Pop Music; Hard Rhymes; Their Albums Are Being Released Even If Many of the Artists Who Recorded Them Aren't: In the Subgenre of Prison Rap, There's an Underlying Message That You Can't Excape." *Los Angeles Times*, April 3, E1.

George, Courtney. 2016. "From Bounce to the Mainstream: Hip Hop Representations of Post-Katrina New Orleans in Music, Film and Television." *European Journal of American Culture* 35, no. 1: 17–32.

Kubrin, Charis E. 2005. "Gangstas, Thugs, and Hustlas: Identity and the Code of the Street in Rap Music." *Social Problems* 52, no. 3: 360–78.

Further Listening

C-Murder. 1995. *True.* No Limit.

C-Murder. 1999. *Bossalinie.* No Limit.

C-Murder. 2013. *Ricochet.* TRU Records.

Coldcut

(1986–, London, England)

Coldcut is an English electronic music duo comprised of DJs Jonathan More (Jonathan Richard More, n.d.) and Matt Black (Matthew Cohen, 1961–). Best known for its contributions to the acid house, club, dance, and ambient genres, Coldcut became a pioneer of the mid-1980s experimental/electronic hip hop scene.

In 1988, Coldcut released the single "Doctorin' the House," featuring English dance and funk singer Yazz (Yasmin Evans, 1960–). The single reached No. 6 on the charts. In the same year, it released a cover of M People's (1990–) "The Only Way Is Up" (originally composed in 1980 by George Jackson, 1945–2013, and Johnny Henderson, n.d.) under the name Yazz and the Plastic Population. The song climbed to No. 1 on the U.K. Singles Chart and held this position for five weeks. Coldcut reached commercial success with its debut album *What's That Noise?* (1989), which peaked at No. 20 on the United Kingdom's Official Albums Chart and was certified Silver.

HEX

Meeting in 1986 at Reckless Records, More and Black began working together at the pirate radio station Network 21 in London. Their first single was "Say Kids What Time Is It," which samples the children's television show *Howdy Doody* (1947–1960) in addition to various soul, hip hop, and funk songs. It is recognized as the United Kingdom's first record to be made entirely of samples from other artists and media. In 1987, More and Black worked together on the underground electronic music show *Solid Steel* (1988–), which allows experimental DJs to showcase their live or recorded mixes. In the same year, Coldcut formed the record label Ahead of Our Time and released the single "Beats + Pieces," sometimes credited as the first record to showcase big beat music. In October 1987, Coldcut released its remix of Eric B. and Rakim's (1986–1993) hip hop song "Paid in Full" for Island Records (1959–), which helped to usher hip hop into the United Kingdom's mainstream culture.

In 1988, More and Black formed Hex (1988–1997), a multimedia pop group that created music videos for electronic music producer Kevin Saunderson (1964–), singer Queen Latifah (1970–), and the English neo-psychedelic experimental rock band Spiritualized (1990–) while integrating the contemporary media technology of video sampling, CD-ROMs, and interactive computing. Using a variety of media, such as art exhibits and video games, Hex introduced media amalgams such as computer-generated audio performances and interactive collaborative instruments. Continuing their work with Hex, More, Black, and their team released the video game *Top Banana* (1991) for the Commodore CDTV machine. In 1992, Hex's first single, "Global Chaos Digital Love Opus 1," used video clips from raves combined with techno and ambient interactive visuals. Hex also released the Global Chaos CDTV, a predecessor to the "CD+" concept. This disc combined music, graphics, and game play into one medium. National media gave Hex's innovative creation extensive coverage. Hex began to create visuals for Coldcut's live shows throughout the 1990s and also included music videos and interactive playful art/music programs on the duo's CD-ROMs, an advanced practice that earned the group admiration for its entry into the computer age. By 1996, More and Black had reclaimed the Coldcut name and its reputation for interactive live shows and content.

NINJA TUNE

In 1990, Coldcut formed its second record label, Ninja Tune, which permitted the duo (under different aliases, such as Bogus Order and DJ Food) to release music that reflects their creativity without the constraints of major record labels. Because Coldcut had previously signed with major record label Arista, the group did not release any official Coldcut singles or albums for three years as More and Black focused on their independent label. In 1997, Coldcut's album *Let Us Play!* was the first Ninja Tune label release. Tracks featured their iconic "cut-and-paste" experimental sound, including guest performances from Grandmaster Flash (1958–), the Herbaliser (1995–), and Daniel Pemberton (1977–). That same year,

Black worked with Cambridge-based developers Camart to create VJAMM, a real-time video manipulation software that revolutionized the audiovisual field by allowing users to remix and combine sound and images, a major part of the club scene. In 1998, the American Museum of the Moving Image gave VJAMM a permanent spot in its collection. Black created DJamm with Camart; this program allowed users to split loops into as many segments as they wished.

In 2010, Ninja Tune released *Ninja Tune: 20 Years of Beats and Pieces*, a book celebrating 20 years of successful contributions to dance, hip hop, and electronic music. Coldcut also released a music-making app called Ninja Jamm for Android and iOS cellular phones.

Celeste Roberts

See also: The United Kingdom

Further Reading

Bogdanov, Vladimir. 2001. *All Music Guide to Electronica: The Definitive Guide to Electronic Music.* Milwaukee, WI: Backbeat Books.

Bogdanov, Vladimir. 2003. *All Music Guide to Hip Hop: The Definitive Guide to Rap and Hip Hop.* Milwaukee, WI: Backbeat Books.

Further Listening

Coldcut. 1989. *What's That Noise?* Ahead of Our Time.

Colombia

Colombia, nicknamed the land of a thousand rhythms, is a South American nation with a diverse culture that contains a variety of both traditional and modern music as a result of the mixture of African, native indigenous, and European (especially Spanish) influences. When it comes to Colombia's contemporary popular music scene, the influence of bands from the United States is extremely important. Hip hop came to Colombia in the late 1980s with the popularity of breakdancing and the music of American rap artists N.W.A. (1986–1991) and MC Hammer (1962–) in the major urban areas of Medellín, Cali, and Bogotá. In the 1990s, two Colombian hip hop groups, La Etnnia (Ethnicity, 1994–2014) and Bogotá-based Gotas de Rap (Rap Beats, 1994–1995), became popular, becoming the pioneers of Colombian rap, known for its extreme political and social views, including protests against violence, corruption, inequality, and marginalization. Le Etnnia cultivated a West Coast gangsta rap sound, with lots of emphasis on rolling basslines and drums against a synthesizer background. Gotas de Rap was a bit more eclectic in its approach, using various American styles.

DEVELOPING THEMES

Near the turn of the century, Cali-based Asilo 38 (Asylum 38, 2000–) made hip hop more polished, adding a reggae backdrop, counterrhythms, and new instrumentation, such as rock-based keyboards or classical and traditional strings. Thematically, Colombian hip hop is informed by cultural struggle, and its style is generally based on the urban music of U.S. West Coast acts such as N.W.A. Colombia's rappers include a large number of rural poor who were forced into the cities by a civil war between the state and the Revolutionary Armed Forces of Colombia (FARC, 1964–2017) that has been devastating rural communities for decades. Jobless and surrounded by drug traffickers and citywide corruption, they use rap to express their anger and call for unity and self-respect.

INFLUENCES AND POPULAR COLOMBIAN ACTS

Much contemporary Colombian music is influenced by traditional Colombian music, which includes *cumbia*, a social issue–based dance music that owes its origins to Spanish, indigenous, and African music (brought over by slaves) and is highly dependent on percussion rhythms (a Colombian version, the *cumbia cienaguera*, is considered the unofficial music of the nation); *champeta* music, which is influenced by *soukous*, *compas*, *zouk*, and reggae as well as Jamaican ragamuffin; and *currulao*, which has its roots among Afro-Colombians and uses a *cununo* (a special drum for creating a unique rhythm), percussive shakers, and marimba. As in most countries, bands are promoted through large record labels such as Medellín-based Discos Fuentes (1934–) and independent music studios, but the government, through the Ministry of Culture, also plays a huge role; rumors exist that at least one rapper a year is assassinated by the government, and some rappers live in exile. Hip hop and rap began as an underground economy run by do-it-yourself artists and independent labels, but as the music became popular and marketable, the larger labels started to become interested.

Rock music came to Colombia by way of Mexico in the late 1950s with the importation of music by Enrique Guzmán (Enrique Alejandro Guzmán Vargas, 1943–) and César Costa (César Roel Schreurs, 1941–), which quickly led to native rock music. By the 1990s, punk and metal bands had appeared in Bogotá, Medellín, and Cali, with bands such as Aterciopelados (Velvety or Peachy Ones, 1992–) and Kraken (1984–) giving Colombian punk a voice. Rock al Parque, the largest free rock festival in Latin America, is an annual three-day celebration hosted by Bogotá and features artists such as Colombian American the Monas (2005–) and Shakira (1977–), who are both popular in the United States.

Around 2000, Puerto Rican reggaetón became popular, battling with and cross-pollenating hip hop. By 2006, an Afro-Colombian group called ChocQuibTown (aka Choc Quib Town, 2000–) began to emerge as the most popular hip hop band in the nation. ChocQuibTown uses local sounds and dance rhythms to rap about marginalization, fairness, and community, producing positive messages of self-realization. At about the same time, San Andres–based Jiggy Drama (Heartan Lever Criado, 1983–) became very popular despite the controversial nature of his raps. Although based in New York City, Tres Coronas (2001–2006) had become one of the best-known Colombian hip hop crews. Other popular hip hop acts include La Mambanegra (The Black Mamba, 2014–), Profetas (Prophets, 1997–), Nelda Piña y la BOA (Nelda Piña and the Boa Constrictor, 2014–), Pedrina y Río (2012–), and Elkin Robinson (2014–). Most of these more recent music acts favor R&B–flavored hip hop fused with reggae. The ability of a song to inspire dance is emphasized. In addition to music, hip hop culture, including baggy fashions and oversized jewelry, has become a party favorite; major radio stations are offering hip hop shows.

Anthony J. Fonseca

See also: Cumbia Rap; Gangsta Rap; Mexico; Political Hip Hop; Venezuela

Further Reading

Dennis, Christopher. 2012. *Afro-Colombian Hip Hop: Globalization, Transcultural Music, and Ethnic Identities.* Lanham, MD: Lexington Books.

Tickner, Arlene. 2008. "Aquí en el Ghetto: Hip Hop in Colombia, Cuba, and Mexico" (*Here in the Ghetto*). *Latin American Politics and Society* 50, no. 3: 121–46.

Further Listening

Asilo 38. 2016. *Anarkolombia.* Self-released on iTunes and Spotify.

Common

(aka Common Sense, Lonnie Rashid Lynn Jr., 1972–, Chicago, Illinois)

Common is an American rapper and actor known for his verbose and socially conscious lyricism. He is best known for his breakout hit "Take It EZ" (1992). His notable albums include *Can I Borrow a Dollar?* (1992), *Resurrection* (1994), *One Day It'll All Make Sense* (1997), *Like Water for Chocolate* (2000), *Electric Circus* (2002), *Be* (2005), *Finding Forever* (2007), and *Universal Mind Control* (2008). The latter three were released on Kanye West's (1977–) New York City–based GOOD Music label (aka Getting Out Our Dreams, 2004–). Common's subsequent albums were *The Dreamer/The Believer* (2011) on the Warner Bros. label (1958–), *Nobody Smiling* (2014) on Def Jam Recordings (1983–), and *Black America Again* (2016) on producer Immenslope's (aka No I.D., Ernest Dion Wilson, 1971–) ARTium Recordings (2011–), an imprint of Def Jam.

Common's first big break was appearing as the featured artist in *The Source*'s new artist column, *Unsigned Hype.* Following this media attention in an influential hip hop magazine, Common (as Common Sense) signed with Relativity Records and made his musical debut with the release of "Take It EZ" and his first full-length album, *Can I Borrow a Dollar?.* The album, produced by Immenslope and Twilite Tone (Anthony Khan, 1971–), features jazzy, laid-back instrumentation, which includes samples from earlier hip hop and R&B songs. These are accompanied by Common's melodic, lyrical vocals. Three singles from the album, "Take It EZ," "Breaker 1/9," and "Soul by the Pound," each charted on Billboard's Hot Rap Singles, but the album failed to garner much attention outside the local Chicago scene.

Resurrection, also produced by No I.D., performed poorly on the Billboard charts; however, it helped garner the rapper a strong following in the alternative and underground hip hop scene and cemented his reputation as a verbose and eloquent lyricist. Many tracks on the album, such as "Nuthin' to Do," reflect the deteriorated conditions of many black neighborhoods in Chicago's South Side. The album closes with "Pop's Rap," which features Common's father, Lonnie Lynn

Beginning as an underground rapper in Chicago and then becoming associated with East Coast hip hop acts, Common's lyrical content focused on socially conscious, Afrocentric themes. His disdain for gangsta rap placed him in the center of a lengthy East Coast–West Coast hip hop feud with Westside Connection, a group that featured Ice Cube. (Starstock/Dreamstime.com)

(1943–2014), reciting his own spoken-word poetry. Lynn would appear on three more Common albums. The breakout track from *Resurrection* was "I Used to Love H.E.R.," whose lyrics describe the moral decline of a woman—but in this the case woman serves as a symbol for hip hop. Common expresses disdain at the contemporary shift in the content and sound of hip hop away from socially conscious, Afrocentric rap and toward the increasingly popular gangsta rap, which had emerged primarily from the West Coast. Having been released during the height of the East Coast–West Coast hip hop rivalry (with Common, a midwestern rapper, being more closely associated with the East Coast), the song inspired many responses, including one from the West Coast group Westside Connection (1994–2005), a gangsta rap group featuring Ice Cube (1969–), who felt that references to "the boys in the hood" in one of Common's songs were a direct attack on him personally and on N.W.A.'s (1986–1991) well known 1987 single "Boyz-n-the-Hood."

Westside Connection's 1995 song, "Westside Slaughterhouse," was the band's diss track response. The lyrics mention Common by name in addition to other East Coast rappers. In turn, Common released the diss track "The B— in Yoo" in 1996, in which he attacked Ice Cube and suggested that the West Coast rapper took his (Common's) lyrics out of context. The feud continued for years until both sides were able to meet and resolve their differences.

One Day It'll All Make Sense featured collaborations with Lauryn Hill (1975–), De La Soul (1987–), Q-Tip (Jonathan William Davis, 1970–), and Erykah Badu (1971–), among others. Released just before the birth of Common's first child, the album features tracks addressing personal and family issues such as abortion, as in "Retrospect for Life," and transitioning into parenthood, as in "G.O.D. (Gaining One's Definition)." *One Day* ends with a spoken-word piece by Lynn, "Pop's Rap, Pt. 2/ Fatherhood." Common then joined the neo soul/hip hop collective Soulquarians

(1990s–2000s*). Soulquarians members D'Angelo (Michael Eugene Archer, 1974–), James Poyser (1967–), and J Dilla (James Dewitt Yancey, 1974–2006) collaborated on Common's fourth studio album, *Like Water for Chocolate*. This was his first of two albums recorded for MCA Records (1934–2003). The second, *Electric Circus*, was hailed as an eclectic mix of musical influences including hip hop, pop, electronica, and rock but was not as commercially successful as *Like Water for Chocolate*.

Subsequent albums have had a similar eclecticism and have received critical acclaim and success. Common followed with *Be* and *Finding Forever*, which combine hip hop and neo soul. *Universal Mind Control*, produced by Pharell (1973–), once more fuses hip hop with electronic, this time adding techno. *The Dreamer/The Believer* returns to alternative hip hop, featuring poet Maya Angelou (Marguerite Annie Johnson, 1928–2014) on the first track, "The Dreamer." In contrast to the mostly positive tone of *The Dreamer/The Believer*, *Nobody's Smiling* focuses on Chicago's urban violence and crime. Common's most recent album, *Black America Again*, has received strong critical acclaim, particularly for its sociopolitical lyrical content focused on being black in the United States in 2016 and on the country's future potential. The album peaked at No. 25 on the Billboard 200. It features Stevie Wonder (1950–) on its title track.

In addition to recording, Common has also maintained an acting career, having appeared on television shows, most notably *Girlfriends* (2000–2008) in 2003 and *The Mindy Project* (2012–) in 2013, and costarring in American film dramas such as *Selma* (2014) and *John Wick: Chapter 2* (2017).

Lauron Jockwig Kehrer

See also: J Dilla; Neo Soul; Political Hip Hop; The United States

Further Reading

Bradley, Adam, and Andrew Dubois, eds. 2010. "Common." Under "Part 3: 1993–99: Rap Goes Mainstream" in *The Anthology of Rap*, pp. 363–72. New Haven, CT: Yale University Press.

Cramer, Jennifer, and Jill Hallett. 2010. "From Chi-Town to the Dirty-Dirty: Regional Identity Markers in U.S. Hip Hop." In *The Languages of Global Hip Hop*, edited by Marina Terkourafi, chap. 10. New York: Continuum.

Kot, Greg. 2005. "Common Ground: How Hip Hop's Kanye West and Common Are Recapturing Their Chicago Roots." *Chicago Tribune*, April 17, 7.1.

Further Listening

Common. 1994. *Resurrection*. Relativity.

Company Flow

(1995–1999, Queens, New York)

Company Flow was a short-lived but highly respected avant-garde/experimental and iconoclastic underground American hip hop trio associated with the independent record label Rawkus Records (1995–2001). Rapper and producer El-P (Jaime Meline, 1975–) joined with DJ and producer Mr. Len (Leonard Smythe, 1975–) to found the group in 1993 in Queens. A second rapper and grafitti artist, Bigg Jus

(Justin Ingleton, n.d.) was added to the duo after El-P met him through New York–based underground rapper and indie label owner ANTTEX (Darren E. Johnson, 1966–). The trio's first EP, *Funcrusher* (1995), led to a deal with Rawkus Records and the release of the band's debut album, *Funcrusher Plus* (1997), which has become a cult classic among hip hop fans because of the complexity of its music, which combines trance, chillout, experimental alternative, hip hop, and rap to create a filtered sound where everything is placed in the background. Music and lyrics take on an ethereal, dreamscape quality, and texts are informed by not only the urban experience but also dystopian literature and science fiction imagery as well as references to anime films. Company Flow released only one other album, a series of experimental instrumentals called *Little Johnny from the Hospitul: Breaks and Instrumentals, Vol.1* (1999).

Company Flow was created when El-P met Mr. Len, who was hired to DJ his birthday party in 1993. The two formed Company Flow and released a vinyl single, "Juvenile Technique" (1992), on a now defunct Long Island indie label called Libra Records (1991–1997), with which ANTTEX was involved. ANTTEX also introduced El-P to two DJs at WKCR, broadcast from Columbia University in New York City, who were so impressed with El-P's freestyling that they began playing Company Flow (now a trio) singles, which quickly built a college-based and community fan following.

After Bigg Jus was added to the band, it released *Funcrusher* as well as three singles, including the popular "8 Steps to Perfection" (credited to El-P and Big Juss, 1996), which was produced by El-P. The trio then signed with Rawkus, the same label that would release works by Mos Def (1973–) in 1997 and Talib Kweli (1975–) in 1998. After the release of *Funcrusher Plus*, Bigg Jus wanted to start a solo career, so the band dissolved, although El-P and Mr. Len worked together to release *Little Johnny from the Hospitul*. El-P went on to create his own record label, Definitive Jux Music (1997–), which has released albums by El-P's most current band and cult favorite *Run the Jewels* (2013–), which charted at No. 27 on Billboard's Top R&B and Hip-Hop Albums, followed by *Run the Jewels 2* (2014) and *Run the Jewels 3* (2016), which charted on the Billboard 200 at Nos. 50 and 13, respectively.

El-P also pursued a solo career, releasing three albums that charted on the Billboard 200: *Fantastic Damage* (2002), *I'll Sleep When You're Dead* (2007), and *Cancer 4 Cure* (2012). Mr. Len went on to release the fan favorite *Pity the Fool: Experiments in Therapy behind the Mask of Music While Handing Out Dummysmacks* (2001) with Matador Records (1989–) and to create Smacks Records (2003–). He also released *Beats and Things, Vol. 1* (2004) and *Smacks Records: For Those of You Just Joining Us* (2005). Bigg Jus released three albums, *Black Mamba Serums* (2004), *Poor People's Day* (2005), and *Machines That Make Civilization Fun* (2012). Company Flow reunited in 2007 and 2011 for performances in Brooklyn and New York City; the trio performed its final show at the Coachella Valley Music and Arts Festival in 2012.

Anthony J. Fonseca

See also: The United States

Further Reading

Kot, Greg. 2002. "The Hip Hop Underground Mixes It Up." *Chicago Tribune*, April 28, 7.1.

Kot, Greg. 2002. "Pushing the Limits: Fresh Rap from the Hip Hop Underground." *The Record* (Bergen County, New Jersey), May 9, F07.

Murphy, Bill. 2004. "El-P." Interview with El-P. *Remix* 6, no. 4: 18.

Further Listening

Company Flow. 1997. *Funcrusher Plus*. Rawkus Records.

Compton's Most Wanted

(aka C.M.W., 1987–1993, 2015–, Compton, California)

Compton's Most Wanted (aka C.M.W.) is an American West Coast gangsta rap, hip hop, and G-funk band whose consistent lineup has been three Compton, California–born MCs, Boom Bam (Gene Heisser, 1971–), MC Eiht (Aaron Tyler, 1967*–), and Tha Chill (aka Chill MC, Vernon Johnson, 1970–), as well as Inglewood, California, producer DJ Slip (Terry K. Allen, 1972–). A fourth member, known as DJ Ant Capone (anonymous, n.d.), also from Compton, was in the band originally but left in 1989 and was immediately replaced by scratcher and turntablist DJ Mike T (Michael Bryant, n.d.). The group's third album, *Music to Driveby* (1992), is considered a gangsta rap classic, peaking at No. 66 on the Billboard 200 but producing "Hood Took Me Under," a Top 10 Hot Rap single. Its music is defined by its slow pacing, with heavy doses of funk instrumentation, such as bass and rhythm guitar loops, usually processed through delay pedals. Both the rap and the vocals tend to be pensive and measured, with an understated sense of frustration and anger behind the lyrics; in many cases, the songs are melancholic. C.M.W. is also known for its liberal use of samples from 1970s soul and funk records. The band's best-known vocalist, MC Eiht, keeps his rap tense but measured, with heavy emphasis on rhymed couplets; he often plays up the final rhyme in each couplet by vocal emphasis, pacing, or well-timed pausing.

The band began to form in the mid-1980s, when Tha Chill and Ant Capone began penning raps and creating demo tapes with MC Ren (Lorenzo Jerald Patterson, 1969–) of N.W.A. (1986–1991). MC Eiht, a corner boy who also wrote street raps as a way to escape drug addiction and street life, joined the duo. One of the group's tapes found its way into the hands of the Unknown DJ (Andre Manuel, n.d.) of the label Techno-Hop (1984–) in 1987, and he took it to DJ Slip, owner of Music People—DJ4HIRE, Los Angeles County's largest DJ rental business. Slip added the group to his Sound Control Mob (1988*–), a coalition of DJs and MCs from various groups in the Los Angeles area who would soon get a record deal with World Class Wreckin' Cru (1984–1986) label Kru-Cut (1984–1989).

C.M.W.'s first single, "This Is Compton" (1989), on the Kru-Cut and Techno-Kut (1989–1990)* labels, got it a contract with Orpheus Records (1967*–) and led to its first album, *It's a Compton Thang* (1990), which reached No. 132 on the Billboard 200. A second album, *Straight Checkn 'Em* (1991), which featured DJ Slip and the Unknown DJ, peaked at No. 92 and produced "Growin' Up in the Hood," which made the soundtrack of *Boyz in the Hood* (1991). Following the release of

Music to Driveby, the band went on hiatus due to Tha Chill's legal problems and the band's artistic issues; MC Eiht went solo. During this time, C.M.W. got into a minor feud with Bronx, New York, rapper Tim Dog (Timothy Blair, 1967–2013) over what they considered to be his selling out and produced a popular parody song, "Who's Xxxing Who?" (1992). The band's fourth and fifth albums, *Represent* (2000) and *Music to Gang Bang* (2006), were not commercially successful.

In 1993, MC Eiht, who gained popularity after acting roles in *Boyz n the Hood* and *Menace II Society* (1993), signed with DJ Mike T for three solo albums (the albums are often credited to C.M.W. but were in actuality solo performances with guests from the band), including his certified-Gold debut, *We Come Strapped* (1994), which sold over 600,000 copies and reached the top spot on the R&B album chart and No. 5 on the Billboard 200. He followed these with *Death Threatz* (1995) and *Last Man Standing* (1996, sometimes credited as his first solo album), all on Epic Street Records (1993–1998), then moved on to the independent Los Angeles–based label Hoo Bangin' (1996–), distributed by Priority Records (1985–), to record *Section 8* (1999) and *N' My Neighborhood* (2000). MC Eiht continued a solo and guest musician career with various labels.

Anthony J. Fonseca

See also: Gangsta Rap; N.W.A.; The United States

Further Reading

Forman, Murray. 2002. "Boyz n Girlz in the 'Hood: From Space to Place." In *The 'Hood Comes First: Race, Space, and Place in Rap and Hip Hop*, chap. 6. Middletown, CT: Wesleyan University Press.

Woodstra, Chris, John Bush, and Stephen Thomas Erlewine. 2008. *Old School Rap and Hip Hop*. New York: Backbeat Books.

Further Listening

Compton's Most Wanted. 2001. *When We Wuz Bangin' 1989–99: The Hitz*. Right Stuff.

Congo

The Congo comprises two Central African countries that use the Congo River as their border: the Democratic Republic of the Congo (aka DRC, Congo-Kinshasa), which from 1971 to 1997 was known as Zaire and was a Belgian colony; and the Republic of the Congo (aka ROC, Congo-Brazzaville), which was a French colony and is sometimes considered part of West Africa. The DRC is one of the most dangerous countries in the world and one of the poorest. It has recently been plagued by the First (1996–1997) and Second (1998–2003) Congo Wars, which followed its involvement in the neighboring Rwandan Civil War (1990–1994), leading to the Rwandan genocide (1994). In addition, corruption, further conflicts, and resulting media blackouts and protests took place in the 2000s to 2010s. Limited media delayed access to hip hop in both countries. By the late 1990s, however, Congolese hip hop activity was present in Kinshasa and Brazzaville, DRC, and the Republic of the Congo's capital cities as well as in other urban cities. Successful Congolese hip hop acts have resulted mostly from diaspora as Congolese performers have settled and recorded outside both countries.

Although over 250 different ethnic populations reside in the Congo, the official language of both countries is French. Likewise, Congolese rapping texts favor French, but also Lingala, a Bantu language spoken by black Africans (including Kongo, Luba, Mongo, Sangha, Teke, and M'Bochi peoples), who are the majority population. Bridging languages such as Swahili and the creole language Kituba (a lingua franca in Central Africa) are less used. Generally, Congolese rappers prefer Lingala, but many will interweave Swahili and French. Other languages used include American vernacular and Portuguese. Other popular music in both countries consists of traditional Congolese rumba as well as *soukous kwassa kwassa*, Guadeloupean *zouk*, and American R&B and jazz. As of 2018, hip hop is also popular but remains an alternative to other popular tastes.

DEMOCRATIC REPUBLIC OF THE CONGO

As of 2018, concern about freedom of speech and threats of violence have driven hip hop activity indoors. For example, at the Yolé!Africa youth cultural center in Goma, male teens discuss politics and work on rapping lyrics, often focusing on exposing corruption, facing extreme adversity during wars and conflicts (including displacement), and desiring change. Nonetheless, most DRC hip hop is performed by artists in exile. One exception to the rule is R&B, rumba, soukous, and *ndombolo* singer-songwriter and guitarist Fally Ipupa (Fally Ipupa N'simba, 1977–), whose solo recording career fuses these music genres with hip hop. He raps and sings in Lingala, French, and American vernacular.

Perhaps the most famous DRC hip hop artist living in exile is Ya Kid K (Manuela Barbara Kamosi Moaso Djogi, 1972–), a Kinshasa-born female rapper and singer-songwriter of Congolese Belgian descent who has lived in Belgium, Chicago, and Dallas. Ya Kid K is best known for singing and writing the lyrics to Belgian hip hop, hip house, tech house, and electronica project group Technotronic's (1988–2000) "Pump Up the Jam" (1989), a hit that took place before the emergence of Congolese hip hop. The song peaked at No. 2 on the U.K. Singles Chart and on the Billboard Hot 100. Ya Kid K's sister, R&B, pop, and soul singer Leki (Karoline Kamosi, 1978–), also born in Kinshasa, was involved with Technotronic as well. There is a long list of successful DRC rappers living elsewhere: Frank T (Tshimini Nsombolay, 1973–), raised and residing in Madrid and a pioneer of the 1980s hip hop scene there, raps in Spanish and fuses hip hop with electronica; Kaysha (Edward Mokolo Jr., 1974–), born in Kinshasa and raised in France, fuses hip hop with Afropop, *kizomba*, zouk, and *zouk R&B*; and Gracias (Deogracias Masomi, 1987–), currently residing in Helsinki, raps mostly in English.

Though many DRC hip hop artists have taken their music in a different direction from addressing their roots, several focus a great deal on DRC issues. Rapper and singer-songwriter Apkass (Alain Kasanda, n.d.), born in Kinshasa but living in Paris since he was 11 years old, raps in French and fuses hip hop with jazz that emphasizes heavy bass. Apkass's interest in hip hop emerged in 1991 when he was already in France. Since 1997, Apkass has rapped about his homeland and supporting African unity, among other topics. The rap group Lopango ya Banka (Land of the Ancestors, 1997–) consists of DRC Congolese rappers living in Germany. Its members first intended only to teach African diaspora youth in Germany about their heritage and preserving Lingala as a language. By 2003, the group had begun rapping, opting for Lingala. Its music videos include subtitles in German, French, and English. Rapping texts focus on social issues, unity, positive aspects of being Congolese and African, aspirations, and spirituality—and these messages are addressed to Congolese at home and abroad.

REPUBLIC OF THE CONGO

Though conditions in Congo are considerably better than they have been, many musicians record elsewhere; hip hop artists are no different. The Parisian collective Bisso Na Bisso (1999–) consists of members who are Congolese-Brazzaville-born and fuse hip hop with traditional Congolese rumba, soukous, and zouk. Members include the French hip hop duo Ärsenik (1992–), Congolese-Brazzaville-born French rapper Passi (Passi Ballende, 1972–), and French rappers Calbo (Calboni M'Bani, n.d.) and Lino (Gaëlino M'Bani, n.d.). The latter's family is Congolese. All rap in Lingala and French. Rapper and spoken-word artist Abd al Malik (Régis Fayette-Mikano, 1975–) was born in Paris, but from age two to five, he grew up in Congo-Brassaville before relocating to Strasbourg, France. Abd al Malik has a concurrent solo rap career while being a member of the Strasbourg hip hop group New African Poets (NAP, 1988–). His own style fuses hip hop with jazz and slam poetry, with inspiration from Sufism as well as singer-songwriters and chansonnier Jacques Brel (1929–1978) and Claude Nougaro (1929–2004).

Both ROC and DRC hip hop acts, whether living inside these countries or in exile, share a common past, so when Congolese history or other connections to Congo are the focus of the music, the artists themselves make virtually no cultural distinction between being from the DRC or the ROC. This practice suggests how colonialism divided the same people into two countries without considering the Congolese as people, creating a purely artificial yet political border. Musicians from the DRC, for example, do not protest against people who have more rights or material access by living in the ROC, but rather about their country's own socioeconomic inequality. Both Congolese hip hop and jazz musicians employ a lot of improvisation, which is perceived as a musical connection to their homeland.

Melissa Ursula Dawn Goldsmith

See also: Belgium; France

Further Reading

Mertens, Jamina, Wouter Goedertier, Idesbald Goddeeris, and Dominique De Brabanter. 2013. "A New Floor for the Silenced? Congolese Hip Hop in Belgium." *Social Transformations: Journal of the Global South* 1, no. 1: 87–113.

Stewart, Gary. 2000. *Rumba on the River: A Popular History of the Two Congos.* London: Verso.

Further Listening

Apkass. 2008. *En merchant vers le soleil (Walking toward the Sun).* MVS Records.

Bisso Na Bisso. 1999. *Racines (Roots).* V2 Music.

Coolio

(Artis Leon Ivey Jr., 1963–, Compton, California)

Coolio is a hip hop, gangsta rap, G-funk, and West Coast singer and rapper who began recording in 1987; he went on to become a record producer, actor, and professional chef. His albums *It Takes a Thief* (1994), *Gangsta's Paradise* (1995), and *My Soul* (1997) helped him to become a mainstream star, as did his 1996 Grammy Award–winning hit single "Gangsta's Paradise," which sold five million copies in the United States and went to No. 1 in the United States, Australia, Austria, Denmark, France, Germany, Ireland, Italy, the Netherlands, Norway, New Zealand, Sweden, Switzerland, and the United Kingdom.

A studious child, Coolio soon found his life changed when he became a victim of bullying, his parents divorced, and his mother became an alcoholic. As a young adult, he was incarcerated for possession of a stolen check, and by 1985 he was a cocaine addict. It was then that he moved to San José, California, to live with his father and turn his life around.

Coolio started out as a fixture in the South Central Los Angeles, California rap scene in the early 1980s. He turned to rapping and recorded some demo singles in 1987 that gained him a positive reputation with the Los Angeles rap scene and led to his stint with WC and the MAAD Circle (1990–1996, 2007–2014), which was produced by Ice Cube (1969–), appearing on the band's debut album *Ain't a Damn Thing Changed* (1991), which sold over 150,000 copies. He was then signed in 1993 as a solo act by Tommy Boy Records (1981–), for whom he worked on his debut album, *It Takes a Thief*, which was certified Platinum and produced the hit "Fantastic Voyage," a song that went to No. 3 on the Billboard Hot 100, as well as other hits "County Line," and "I Remember." His follow-up, "Gangsta's Paradise," reached the top spot on the Billboard Hot 100 for three weeks. The follow-up album, *Gangsta's Paradise*, was certified double Platinum and produced the Top 10 hit "1, 2, 3, 4 (Sumpin' New)." *My Soul* also went Platinum, but he was dropped from Tommy Boy Records.

Coolio differed from most gangsta rappers in that he emphasized positive messages and the ability to change one's life, lessons he himself lived out. He is known for his raspy baritone and an overarticulated delivery as well as his unique hairstyles.

After his first few albums, he began independently releasing albums on various international labels and created a web-based cooking show, *Cookin' with Coolio* (2014–), which followed from his writing a popular soul food and special diet cookbook, *Cookin' with Coolio: 5 Star Meals at a 1 Star Price* (2009). Part of his purpose is to help people who grew up in poverty, as he did, to eat healthily.

Anthony J. Fonseca

See also: Gangsta Rap; G-Funk; The United States

Further Reading

Forman, Murray. 2002. "Boyz n Girlz in the 'Hood: From Space to Place." In *The 'Hood Comes First: Race, Space, and Place in Rap and Hip Hop*, chap. 6. Middletown, CT: Wesleyan University Press.

Kemp, Mark. 1995. "Paradise Found." *Rolling Stone* no. 723, December 14, 33–34.

Quinn, Eithne. 2005. "Alwayz into Somethin': Gangsta's Emergence in 1980s Los Angeles." In *Nuthin' but a "G" Thang: The Culture and Commerce of Gangsta Rap*, chap. 3. New York: Columbia University Press.

Further Listening
Coolio. 1994. *It Takes a Thief.* Tommy Boy Records.

Costa Rica

The Republic of Costa Rica is a Central American sovereign country (since 1847) with a population of around five million. Nearly a quarter of its people live in the metropolitan area of the capital and largest city, San José. It is home to *cumbia*—a dance music that originated along Colombia's Caribbean coast. Many kinds of music are also popular: pan-Caribbean calypso and rumba; American, British, and Latin hip hop, disco, metal, rock, and pop; Puerto Rican reggaetón; Cuban salsa; Trinbagonian soca; and indigenous traditional music. American, British, and Latin rock and pop have been popular among Costa Rican youth, especially urban youth, for decades, and these same youth became the audience for hip hop, a natural progression from Afro-Caribbean rhythmic percussion sounds that had taken hold along the country's Caribbean coast, where rumba, calypso, and reggae are popular, with bands such as Limón-based Mekatelyu (1998–). Starting in the mid-1990s, hip hop culture has grown, beginning with artists such as Tapon (Cristian Gómez Vargas, 1979–) and songs such as "Creada a mi manera" ("Created in My Own Way," 2007).

Currently, Costa Rica boasts a double-Platinum Afro–Costa Rican rapper-songwriter, San José native and ex–Ragga By Roots (1990–97*) rapper Huba (Huba Antonio Watson Webley, 1971*–). He began by showcasing his breakdancing skills during visits to Limón, writing his first rap at age 18. Current rappers include OchoSeis (Daniel Smith, n.d.), 3SCRIVAS (2014–), Wako Guerrilla Callejera (Daniel Chaverri, n.d.), DJP (Pietro Wolbrom Prescod, n.d.) and his brother Toledo (Toledo Wolbrom Prescod, 1981*–), Jahricio (Mauricio Alvarado, 1971*–), and Crypy 626 (Gerson Rodriguez, 1986*–). Their songs can be heard on Urban Radio (an FM station) and on the Internet, where they are shared for free. Generally, Costa Rican rap is concerned with social issues, self-improvement and empowerment, and recently, women's rights.

Anthony J. Fonseca

See also: Colombia; Cumbia Rap; Reggaetón

Further Reading
Morales, Ed. 2003. *The Latin Beat: The Rhythms and Roots of Latin Music from Bossa Nova to Salsa and Beyond.* Cambridge, MA: Da Capo Press.

Pabón, Jessica N. 2016. "Daring to Be 'Mujeres Libres, Lindas, Locas': An Interview with the Ladies Destroying Crew of Nicaragua and Costa Rica." In *La Verdad: An International Dialogue on Hip Hop Latinidades*, edited by Melissa Castillo-Garsow and Jason Nicholls, chap. 13. Columbus: Ohio State University Press.

Crazy Legs

(Richard Colón, 1966–, Bronx, New York)

Crazy Legs is the stage name for Richard Colón, a Puerto Rican American b-boy and founding member of the Manhattan, New York, branch of Rock Steady Crew (RSC, 1977–); he is current president of the RSC organization. His showmanship and competitiveness drew a wider, worldwide audience to the dance form. He created and popularized the "W" move, in which the dancer's legs sit behind him or her in a W shape, and the continuous backspin, also known as the windmill, in which the dancer repeatedly spins on his or her back with legs in a wide V shape. Both became standard downrock (floor) moves. He has toured extensively throughout the United States, Japan, Australia, South America, and Europe. Colón danced as Jennifer Beals's (1963–) body double in her final breakdancing scene in the American motion picture *Flashdance* (1983) and performed as himself in the American films *Wild Style* (1983), *Style Wars* (1983), and *Beat Street* (1984). Though interest in b-boying and b-girling waned in the late 1980s, Colón played a significant role in preserving and reviving the art form.

THE BRONX HIP HOP DANCE CREWS

Colón was involved with the original Rock Steady Crew in the Bronx as well as being a member of the Bronx Boys crew (1975–1979). He was briefly a member of the Manhattan-based Rockwell Association before starting a Manhattan branch of the RSC in 1979. Colón battled and recruited well known b-boys, such as Frosty Freeze (1963–2008) and Ken Swift (1966–), to the Manhattan branch of the RSC. Crazy Legs and Rock Steady Crew popularized b-boying and b-girling outside the original audience, performing in downtown nightclubs and touring London and Paris in 1983 on the Roxy Tour, the first international hip hop tour, with other hip hop pioneers, such as Afrika Bambaataa (1957–) and Fab Five Freddy (1959–).

CHOREOGRAPHY AND DANCE APPEARANCES

Colón choreographed and/or performed in multiple theatrical productions in the United States, including *So! What Happens Now?* (1991), *Concrete Jungle* (1992), and *Jam on the Groove* (1995). He was nominated for a 1998 MTV award for Best Choreography in a Video for *Wyclef Jean Featuring Refugee Allstars*'s (1997) track "We Trying to Stay Alive." In 1999, he choreographed and performed in the American-released music video for Moby's (Richard Melville Hall, 1965–) "Bodyrock."

Colón has been featured in multiple films about hip hop and b-boying, and coproduced and starred in the 2002 American documentary *The Freshest Kids: A History of the B-Boy*. In 1994, Colón received a Hip Hop Pioneer Award from *The Source* magazine at their inaugural awards show. The film *Bouncing Cats* (2010) documents his work with young dancers and Breakdance Project Uganda in northern Uganda (2006–).

Katy E. Leonard

See also: Breakdancing; Hip Hop Dance; Frosty Freeze; Ken Swift; Puerto Rico; Rock Steady Crew; The United States

Further Reading

Fuhrer, Margaret. 2014. "Urban and Commercial Dance." In *American Dance: The Complete Illustrated History*, chap. 10. Minneapolis, MN: Voyageur Press.

Rajakumar, Mohanalakshmi. 2012. "The Breaks' in Break Dancing." In *Hip Hop Dance*, chap. 1. *The American Dance Floor*. Santa Barbara, CA: Greenwood.

Further Viewing

Elderkin, Nabil, dir. 2010. *Bouncing Cats*. Vienna, Austria: Red Bull Media House.

Israel, dir. 2002. *The Freshest Kids: A History of the B-Boy*. Chatsworth, CA: QD3 Entertainment.

Silver, Tony, dir. 1983. *Style Wars*. Los Angeles, CA: Public Art Films.

C-Real

(Cyril-Alex Gockel, 1984–, Hohoe, Ghana)

C-Real is a Ghanaian hip hop musician and rapper, poet, entrepreneur, record producer, and creator/CEO of MixDown Studios and Pulse Communications (2011–), which specializes in radio commercials, TV voice-overs and music overlays, music and beat production, mixing and mastering, and video production. He records out of Accra, the urban capital and most populous city of Ghana, and often includes other Ghanaian musicians on his projects.

A graduate of the University of Ghana, C-Real started writing poetry and rap verses in 2009, and that same year he won the Ghanaian edition of the Emcee Africa talent show, finishing second in the finals. Also in 2009, he released a seven-track mixtape, *Multiples of C*, and in 2012, he collaborated on a second, nine-track mixtape, *Project Hip Hop*. In 2012, he was featured on the song "Next Up," from the compilation *The Rising Stars of Gh Vol 1*. That year, C-Real released his debut studio album, *Em C.E.O.*, containing the lead single "I Be the Swag," accompanied by a boxing ring–inspired MC battle music video that was nominated for Best Hip Hop Video at the 2011 4Syte Music Video Awards. The videos for the second and third singles, "Em.CEO" and "Opeimu," were nominated for the same award in 2012 and 2013, respectively.

In 2014, C-Real released a 10-track mixtape, *The Reigning Season*, with vocals in pidgin English, Twi, Ewe, and Ga. C-Real lists as his influences American rappers such as the Notorious B.I.G. (1972–1997), Jay-Z (1969–), Method Man (Clifford Smith, 1971–), and Nas (1973–), to whom he pays homage in his 2014 song "One Mic." After his subsequent recording project, the mixtape *Project Hip Hop 2*, he began working on his second studio album and a spoken-word album.

Anthony J. Fonseca

See also: Ghana

Further Reading

Collins, John. 2012. "Contemporary Ghanaian Popular Music Since the 1980s." In *Hip Hop Africa: New African Music in a Globalizing World*, edited by Eric Charry, chap. 10. Bloomington: Indiana University Press.

Shipley, Jesse Weaver. 2013. "Transnational Circulation and Digital Fatigue in Ghana's Azonto Dance Craze." *American Ethnologist* 40, no. 2: 362–81.

Crip Walk

(aka C-walk)

A Crip walk, a subset of what is called gangsta walk dance, is a West Coast hip hop dance move that emphasizes footwork. In its contemporary versions, moves such as the moonwalk, foot crossovers, slides, hops, shuffles, and heel-to-toe rolls (where the dancer alternates between moving on just the balls of the feet with moving flat-footed, as in dubstepping) make up a good portion of the dance's moves. In early versions, the feet were moved much more simply, often to spell out words such as C-R-I-P or B-L-O-O-D, the latter then being crossed out by foot movement. As the dance developed over time, leg movements such as bending at the knees and then straightening to create a pumping action or pointing the feet outward from the knees and then sliding the feet in unison also became common. Arm movements are usually either restricted or are deemphasized, although in gang-based versions, gang signs can be signaled with the hands.

The Crip walk can be traced back to the early 1970s in California, when members of the Los Angeles–based Crips (1969–), a gang associated with the South Central (Compton) area, began hip hop dancing with a style that used quick and intricate footwork. Members used it typically while at parties, ostensibly to display gang affiliation. Reports indicate that the Crip walk was also used after a gang execution, as a means of leaving the Crips' signature, and could be used by a robbery lookout to indicate that a potential robbery location was clear. As the gang dance was adopted by rappers on the U.S. West Coast, it came to be called the Crip walk, although at one point music videos showing the dance were censored because of its alleged link to criminal activity, and some schools censored it out of fear of rival gang reprisal.

Nonetheless, references to the Crip walk found their way into rap songs, such as Xzibit's (Alvin Nathaniel Joiner, 1974–) "Get Your Walk On" (2001) and J-kwon's (Jerrell C. Jones, 1986–) "Hood Hop" (2004). The dance itself found its way into hip hop music videos, as in Snoop Dogg (1971–) and Pharrell's (1973–) "Drop It Like It's Hot" (2004), where Snoop Dogg can be seen clearly Crip-walking at the beginning and end of the video, and versions of dances that incorporate crip walk moves into a more bouncy dance style can be seen in Compton-born Kendrick Lamar's (1987–) recent video for "I" (2014).

Unfortunately, anything resembling the Crip walk can be mislabeled as such, as was the case in the 2012 Summer Olympics when internationally renowned tennis player Serena Williams (1981–) danced after defeating Maria Sharapova (1987–) in the gold-medal match; a simple shuffling of her feet was immediately (and likely incorrectly) decried as a Crip walk moment. Non-gang-related variations of the Crip walk include the clown walk, the crown walk, and the Kilwaukee walk. The Bloods, the Crips' rival gang, responded with its own dance version, the Blood bounce, which added more bounce to the C-walk as well as visible swaggering.

Anthony J. Fonseca

See also: Gangs (United States); Gangsta Rap; Hip Hop Dance; Snoop Dogg; The United States

Further Reading

Phillips, Susan A. 2009. "Crip Walk, Villain Dance, Pueblo Stroll: The Embodiment of Writing in African American Gang Dance." *Anthropological Quarterly* 82, no. 1: 69–97.

Thomas, R. Murray. 2008. "Ceremonies and Performances." In *What Schools Ban and Why*, chap. 14. Westport, CT: Praeger.

Croatia

Croatia, a Southeast European country, shares borders with musically influential nations such as Bosnia-Herzogovina, Montenegro, Serbia, Slovenia, and Hungary as well as a maritime border with Italy, which is also musically influential. Music found its way in because for centuries, Dubrovnik, a Mediterranean Sea port city located in the south, has been a popular tourist destination, though tourism decreased while the country was the Socialist Republic of Croatia (1943–1991) and under communist rule within the Socialist Federative Republic of Yugoslavia (1945–1992). Croatia was one of the first countries to seek independence from the Soviet Union in 1991, and in 1992 Croatia attained recognition by the United Nations (UN). Political unrest, the Yugoslav Wars (1991–2001), and dominant popular musical tastes favoring rock and new wave were all factors that kept Croatian hip hop an alternative music into the late 1990s.

Hip hop first came to Croatia in the 1980s through travelers bringing American, Italian, and other European rap recordings to coastal destinations such as Dubrovnik and Split. Though tourist-oriented nightclubs played hip hop, Rijeka and Zagreb developed the earliest Croatian hip hop scenes. Pioneering rapper MC Buffalo (Dejan Bubalo, 1971–2012), from Rijeka, was first to record a rap audiocassette in Croatia, *MC Buffalo's 1st Cut* (1991), just at the beginning of the Yugoslav Wars. In 1992, his rap-rock band MC Buffalo and Maderfa'N'kerz (1991–1996) recorded the album *Rijeka* (alluding to the city Rijeka, which also means "river"), which featured the song "Moja domovnica" ("My Citizenship Document"), a parody of the Croatian patriotic song "Moja domovina" ("My Homeland," 1991). It became the first banned Croatian rap song. In 1992, the hardcore rap group Ugly Leaders (1988–2001), also from Rijeka, released *Channel Is Deep and Beech*, an album in Croatian and American vernacular that had tracks banned for their vulgarity. Texts not only protested political corruption, oppression, and the Yugoslav Wars but also emphasized the pleasures of sex, drinking, drugs, and partying. Early Croatian hip hop featured programmed beats and sometimes bass guitar, but soon musicians added synthesizers, original beats, turntablism, and other instruments.

In the late 1990s and into the 2000s, groups from Zagreb and Split emerged as hip hop received more radio airplay. Songs after the war continued to protest corruption and economic disparity. Thug and gangsta rap topics were also covered. In 1999, the hip hop band Tram 11 (1996–2003), from Zagreb, had the first No. 1 rap hit on the Croatian singles charts with "Hrvatski velikani" ("Croatian Greats"). Other Croatian hip hop artists emerging between the 1990s and the 2000s included Tram 11's General Woo (Srđan Ćuk, 1977–). Others include Target (Nenad Šimun, n.d.), El Bahatee (Stiv Kahlina, 1979–), Stoka (Livestock, Marin Ivanović, 1981–), and Elemental (1998–), all from Zagreb. Split bands included the rap-rock band Beat Fleet (TBF, 1997–), Aleksandar Antić (1973–), and Dječaci (Boys, 2005–). Elemental fuses hip hop with reggae, rock, funk, and soul and is the only Croatian hip hop band fronted by a female MC, Remi (Mirela Priselac Remi, 1979–).

Melissa Ursula Dawn Goldsmith

See also: Bosnia and Herzegovina; Hungary; Montenegro; Serbia; Slovenia

Further Reading

Baker, Catherine. 2009. "War Memory and Musical Tradition: Commemorating Croatia's Homeland War through Popular Music and Rap in Eastern Slavonia." *Journal of Contemporary European Studies* 17, no. 1: 35–45.

Greenwalt, Alexander. 1996. "RijeKKKa's Most Psycho: Ugly Rappers after the War." *The Village Voice*, September 3, p. 31.

Further Listening

Elemental. 2016. *Tijelo* (*Body*). 383.

Ugly Leaders. 1993. *Channel Is Deep and Beech.* Channel/Damn Good Records/Superfreak Productions.

Crunkcore

Crunkcore is an American hybrid subgenre of electronica/dance-pop, screamo, and crunk, and because of the last, it sometimes contains recognizable elements of hip hop. At its most basic, crunkcore is "scream meets crunk," the latter being a hybrization of electronica/dance-pop and rap. Crunk emerged in the South in the early 1990s and by 2000 was being played on mainstream radio. Defined by its up-tempo, danceable sound, which makes it perfect for clubbing, generally speaking crunk is informed by a consistent groove, but as electronica it incorporates multitracked synthesized melodic riffs and the use of drum machines. Like rap, it also contains pronounced bass, as well as frenetic calls and shouts to accompany vocals (sometimes using call-and-response). *Crunkcore* likely derives from the phrase *crank up*, as in cranking up both energy and volume in song. Critics consider the subgenre another example of white appropriation of African American music, especially since all of the major crunkcore bands are white.

SCREAMO

The other major element of crunkcore, screamo, also began in the 1990s. Screamo can best be described as grindcore (power-chord hardcore metal) meets emo (a highly emotional style of music featuring melodramatic and confessional lyrics).

Screamo, however, is so overly aggressive that, although emotional, its vocal lines degenerate into screams and growls. Early screamo tended to be highly experimental and nonmelodic, even dissonant. Crunkcore, therefore, usually contains more synthesizer than hip hop and is oriented toward high-energy, dance club–style dancing rather than breakdancing or swaggering. Its main vocals can be screamed or sung (usually with a lot of autotuning), and, when sung, are accompanied by screamo screaming or growling in backing vocals. More metal-based crunkcore bands eschew keyboard for heavy power-chord guitar, loud bass, and intricate drum kit work. Like many styles of rap, crunkcore is often accused of being sexist, misogynistic, and vulgar. The crunkcore scene has more in common with the emo and punk scenes than with hip hop, as far as fashion an aesthetics are concerned.

BANDS AND THEIR (UN)POPULARITY

Some of the more popular crunkcore bands include 3OH!3 (2004–), Millionaries (2007–), Family Force Five (aka Family Force 5 or FF5, 2004–), Blood on the Dance Floor (2007–), Breathe Carolina (2007–), and Hollywood Undead (2005–)—these bands all owe their success to brokeNCYDE (aka Brokencyde, 2006–), the band most responsible for crunkcore's rise, as well as most of its negative publicity. The duo 3OH!3 (2004–) is best known for "Don't Trust Me," which peaked in the Hot 100 Top 10. The duo has collaborated with Katy Perry (1984–) and Ke$ha (Kesha Rose Sebert, 1987–) and is considered a pioneer in using pre-programmed beats in emo music.

Millionaires is the most famous of the female crunkcore bands—although it uses little screamo or hip hop elements. Like Breathe Carolina, Millionaires is an electronica duo, but because of Millionaire's electro-pop sound and explicit lyrics that aggrandize sexual and illegal activity, it is usually included in any crunkcore discussion. FF5 combines the hard-edged sound of crunkcore with Christian rock messages. Along with Blood on the Dance Floor, an electronica duo that has released eight studio albums, FF5, with five studio albums and nine EPs, is one of the most prolific crunkcore bands.

Hollywood Undead, hailing from Los Angeles, is considered a rap band, and of all the crunkcore bands, it most embraces the rap ethos; all its members use pseudonyms and wear masks. Albuquerque, New Mexico's brokeNCYDE combines crunk with both autotuned and screamed vocals. Its July 2008 MTV performance was a benchmark event for crunkcore. The band's lyrics have been attacked as misogynistic and puerile, which has done little to dissuade its fan base.

Anthony J. Fonseca

See also: Hardcore Hip Hop; The United States

Further Reading

Grem, Darren E. 2006. "'The South Got Something to Say': Atlanta's Dirty South and the Southernization of Hip Hop America." *Southern Cultures* 12, no. 4: 55–73.

Ryan Force, William. 2009. "Consumption Styles and the Fluid Complexity of Punk Authenticity." *Symbolic Interaction* 32, no. 4: 289–309.

Further Listening
brokeNCYDE. 2007. *The Broken!* Seven Sound Entertainment.
FF5. 2015. *Time Still Stands.* Word.
3OH!3. *3OH!3.* 2007. Self-released.

Cuba

Cuba, the largest island of the Caribbean, has a rich and vibrant hip hop culture. Hip hop appeared in this Spanish-speaking nation in the mid-1980s—the makeshift radio and television antennas of residents living in the northeasternmost areas of the island (about 90 miles from the southern tip of Florida) allowed Cubans to receive broadcasts from Miami. The residents of the suburbs of Cuba's capital, Havana, were predominantly poor and black (often referred to as moreno, negro, or Afro-Cuban). Along with the distinct and novel sound of the music, they liked the fact that hip hop came from the voices of people in the United States who were similar to them in that they were economically disadvantaged and socially marginalized black youth. These commonalities made hip hop a music genre and culture that was quickly embraced and adapted. Additionally, athletes who traveled or lived abroad either mailed or carried in vinyl records, audiocassettes, and VHS tapes to the island, despite the fact that Cuba and the United States have not had a political or economic relationship since America's 1960 financial and economic embargo against the island that began because of opposing political views. The introduction and subsequent adaptation of hip hop in Cuba is an example of how Cubans cleverly circumvented the blockade between countries. By the 1990s, hip hop had a large Cuban following and a significant number of Havana-based producers of the music.

ELEMENTS AND IMPORTANCE TO CUBAN CULTURE

Cuban hip hop, also referred to as rap Cubano, incorporates strong bass riffs, multilayered percussions, jazz piano riffs, and brass instrument melodies. The beats of congas and bongos used in Afro-Cuban folkloric music such as rumba, *guaguancó*, and *son* (pronounced "sown") are also present. The highly synthesized sounds produced from synthesizers and computers that characterize hip hop more broadly are also common components. Notable elements of Cuban hip hop's lyrical content are its focus on Cuban nationalism and pride; the living conditions of poor urban areas; local and international political, economic, and social realities; and racial disparities on the socialist island. In this way, Cuban hip hop maintains the genre's tradition of being a tool to voice the concerns of disenfranchised people by providing a forum for social critique. Rap Cubano, however, does not generally criticize the government or its policies but rather focuses on other topics, such as respect and adoration of the Orishas, divine figures that are a part of a pantheon of West African–originated divinities and were carried to areas such as Brazil, Puerto Rico, Haiti, Trinidad, and Cuba during the transatlantic slave trade of the 15th to

19th centuries. These divinities are still honored today as divine saints (or *santos*) and are also a distinct part of Cuban hip hop culture.

All of the distinct elements that compose hip hop culture are visible in Cuba, including MCing (rapping), breakdancing (b-boying/b-girling), other styles of hip hop dance, graffiti art, and DJing techniques. Hip hop is so deeply rooted and widespread that it is formally recognized by the government as being an important part of Cuba's national culture. In 2002, the country's Ministry of Culture established the Cuban Rap Agency (Agencia de Rap Cubano, ARC) to further develop and promote hip hop locally and internationally. The ARC ran and financed the country's first national hip hop magazine, *Movimiento* (*Movement*, 2002–) and began its own record label, Asere Records (2002–), to produce hip hop albums. Government support of Cuban hip hop demonstrates that the music and its surrounding culture are being validated and valued as important artistic expression, although it also allows for potential control of or influence over the music's lyrical content, which can curtail social critique or make the music too commercial—so much so that its rich social content could be compromised.

NOTABLE ARTISTS

Notable Cuban hip hop artists include the rap duo Anónimo Consejo (2002–2011), which incorporates creative instrumentation (woodwinds, strings) into its raps and fuses rap with reggae and other genres; the band Doble Filo (Double Edge, 1995–); the band Obsesión (1996–), which incorporates R&B and boy band vocals into its melodic sound; and the group Orishas (aka Amenaza, 1999–), which uses West Coast beats and Latino rhythms, as well as keyboards played against traditional percussions and brass, to create a laid-back and measured rap sound.

Sabia McCoy-Torres

See also: Graffiti Art; The United States

Further Reading

Baker, Geoffrey. 2011. *Buena Vista in the Club: Rap, Reggaetón, and Revolution in Havana.* Durham, NC: Duke University Press.

Fernandes, Sujatha. 2015. "Cuban Hip Hop." In *The Cambridge Companion to Hip Hop*, edited by Justin Williams, chap. 20. Cambridge, England: Cambridge University Press.

West-Durán, Alan. 2004. "Rap's Diasporic Dialogues: Cuba's Redefinition of Blackness." *Journal of Popular Music Studies* 16, no. 1: 4–39.

Further Listening

Orishas. 1999. *A lo Cubano.* Universal Music Latino/Surco Records.

Various Artists. 2002. *Cuban Hip Hop All Stars, Vol. 1.* Flavor Records.

Cumbia Rap

Cumbia rap is a style of hip hop music that combines hip hop beats, reggae, rapping, and *cumbia* music, which stems from the traditional Colombian rhythm. Like

The duo Crooked Stilo was formed by brothers Victor and Johnny Lopez (pictured in 2008 in Los Angeles), who grew up in El Salvador and then immigrated to East Los Angeles. Crooked Stilo performs cumbia rap—a fusion of cumbia and American hip hop with Spanish lyrics. (Timothy Norris/Getty Images)

many styles of hip hop, cumbia rap is dance oriented and infused with Latin rhythm and instrumentation. Cumbia traces back to African Colombians, where it began as a courtship dance in Caribbean coastal areas. Influences from indigenous populations and European (especially Spanish) colonialists led to a modification in instrumentation and styles, and as cumbia spread throughout Latin America, it evolved to fit local populations. Typical traditional cumbia instrumentation includes African drums, maracas, *guache* (large cylindrical shakers made of bamboo and played with two hands in a method similar to that used with a rain stick), wood blocks or bells, and whistles. Cumbia was introduced in the United States during the 1980s by Colombian immigrants fleeing political persecution and began to thrive in cities such as Los Angeles, New York, Chicago, and Corpus Christi, Texas, and in more urban areas became fused with Afrobeat, punk, and brass-based maria-chi pop.

Cumbia made its way into rap when Tex-Mex and Chicana acts such as Houston-based, Grammy Award–winning rap band La Mafia (1980–); Chicago- and Corpus Christi, Texas–based La Sombra (The Shadow, 1980–1995), which has released over 20 albums in Spanish and English; and Selena y los Dinos (Selena and the Dinos, 1982–1995), which featured iconic singer Selena (Selena Quintanilla-Pérez, 1971–1995), began rapping against cumbia beats. Other pioneers of cumbia rap include Crooked Stilo (1991–) from Los Angeles, Los Kumbia Kings (1997–2006) from Corpus Christi, and Chicos de Barrio (Guys from the Neighborhood, 1995–), from

Torreon, Mexico. Rap duo Crooked Stilo was formed by brothers who grew up in El Salvador but immigrated to East Los Angeles, where gang warfare, drugs, and alcohol were prevalent—the fusion of cumbia and rap music they created was their way of addressing these issues. Los Kumbia Kings combines cumbia, hip hop, and R&B to create songs in Spanish and English and was cofounded by A. B. Quintanilla (Abraham Isaac Quintanilla III, 1963–), the brother of Selena. Chicos de Barrio are a cumbia rap group that combines urban, hip hop, salsa, reggae, and *vallenato* (popular folk music from Colombia's Caribbean region that originated with farmers and has its roots in the musical practices of West African griots and Spanish minstrels).

Anthony J. Fonseca

See also: Colombia

Further Reading
Medina, Cruz. 2014. "(Who Discovered) America: Ozomatli and the Mestiz@ Rhetoric of Hip Hop." *Alter/Nativas, Latin American Cultural Studies Journal* 1, no. 2: 24.

Rekedal, Jacob. 2014. "Hip Hop Mapuche on the Araucanian Frontera." *Alter/Nativas, Latin American Cultural Studies Journal* 1, no. 2: 35.

Further Listening
Chicos de Barrio. 1997. *En tu corazon* (*In Your Heart*). Wea Latina.

La Mafia. 1997. *En tus manos* (*In Your Hands*). Epic.

Cut Chemist

(Lucas MacFadden, 1972–, Los Angeles, California)

Cut Chemist is a West Los Angeles–based turntablist, DJ, keyboardist, and producer best known for his sample-based turntablism and his collaborations with turntablist DJ Shadow (1972–). He is also a member of the American alternative hip hop group Jurassic 5 (aka J5, 1993–2007, 2013–) and the Latin, hip hop, funk, jazz, and rock fusion band Ozomatli (1995–). He has an eclectic range of musical styles, primarily recording alternative and instrumental hip hop and fusing it with jazz, funk, soul, ambient electronica, dance, and world music.

He grew up in a musical home in Hollywood, where both parents were amateur musicians. Listening to KDAY AM 1580 (1961–), the first ever 24-hour hip hop radio station, he became especially inspired by East Coast hip hop and began DJing in 1984, and by age 18 he was recording with friends. Near the time of the Los Angeles–based rap crew Unity Committee's (1987–1993) formation, as Cut Chemist, he became its DJ and had his recording debut on Unity Committee's B side of the single "Unified Rebelution," titled "Lesson 4: The Radio" (1993). In 1995, Unity Committee members joined Los Angeles–based rapping crew the Rebels of Rhythm (1987*–1993) to form the alternative hip hop group Jurassic 5, in which Cut Chemist worked with another turntablist, DJ Nu-Mark (Mark Potsic, 1971–).

In 1995, Cut Chemist began recording his own DJ mixes on mixtapes for the independent Los Angeles label Hip Hop Vibes (1980s–1990s*). These included *Sick Experiment* (1995), *Rare Equations* (1995), *The Diabolical* (1996), and *Theories Not Yet Proven* (1997). He later recorded another DJ mix, *Live at the Future*

Primitive Soundsession Version 1.1 (1998), with turntablist crew Invisibl Skratch Piklz's (1989–) member Shortkut (Jonathan Cruz, 1975–) on the San Francisco–based label Future Primitive Sound (1998*–2006). Cut Chemist also joined the Latin and Chicano rock, hip hop, world music, and funk fusion band Ozomatli, appearing on its eponymous debut studio album (1998) and *Embrace the Chaos* (2001). In the meantime, he began collaborating with DJ Shadow on the mixtape *Brainfreeze* (1999), which fused instrumental hip hop with funk and soul. Their subsequent albums included *Product Placement* (2001), *Product Placement on Tour* (2004), *The Litmus Test* (2004), *The Hard Sell* (2007), and *The Hard Sell (Encore)* (2008). In 2004, he departed from Jurassic 5 and Ozomatli to finish his debut solo album, *The Audience's Listening* (2006).

At times appearing in a white chemistry lab coat, Cut Chemist performs at concerts and parties using turntables, a controller, and a laptop. As his name suggests, Cut Chemist's music focuses on the turntablist technique of cutting—isolating instrumental breaks—combined with mixing. He uses mostly the right turntable deck, scratching regular style (forward hand movement) with some hamster style (backward hand movement) while cutting breaks. He takes his samples from albums and, as of the 2010s, layers live turntablism over his use of the digital audio workstation ProTools (1989–), on which he creates samples and adds synthesizer and other recorded sounds. In addition to releasing numerous EPs as a solo artist since his debut studio album, Cut Chemist self-released *The Audience's Following* in 2016.

Cut Chemist has toured worldwide. An avid album collector (known in hip hop culture as a crate digger), he searches to expand his collection while at home and on tour. His collection of vintage albums, particularly hard-to-find classic and global hip hop as well as electronica recordings, contribute to his sound.

Melissa Ursula Dawn Goldsmith

See also: DJ Shadow; Turntablism; The United States

Further Reading

Hutton, Erin. 2005. "Cut Chemist." Interview with Cut Chemist. *Remix* 7, no. 5: 24.

Katz, Mark. 2012. *Groove Music: The Art and Culture of the Hip Hop DJ.* Oxford and New York: Oxford University Press.

Wang, Oliver. 2010. "On the Record: Cut Chemist Mines the Depths of Africa: 'Sound of the Police' Mixes Up and Revels in the Continent's '60s and '70s Music Scenes." *Los Angeles Times*, August 8, E10.

Further Listening

Cut Chemist. 2006. *The Audience's Listening.* Warner Bros. Records/A Stable Sound.

Cut Chemist. 2016. *The Audience's Following.* Self-released.

DJ Shadow and Cut Chemist. 1999. *Brainfreeze.* Sixty 7 Recordings.

Cypress Hill

(1988–, Los Angeles, California)

Cypress Hill is an American hip hop trio from South Gate, California. The group consists of Cuban rapper Sen Dog (Senen Reyes, 1965–), American turntablist DJ

From South Gate, California, Cypress Hill was the first Latin-American hip hop group to release multi-Platinum studio albums. Since their height of fame in the 1990s, the group, which consisted of lead rapper B-Real, rapper Sen Dog, DJ Muggs, and percussionist Bobo, excelled at performing live. (Neilson Barnard/Getty Images)

Muggs (Lawrence Muggerud, 1968–), and Mexican American rapper B-Real (Louis Freese, 1970–). Its original incarnation, DVX (Devastating Vocal Excellence, 1988), also featured Sen Dog's brother, Mellow Man Ace (Ulpiano Sergio Reyes, 1967–), who left to go solo. Cypress Hill became the first certified Platinum and multi-Platinum Latino American hip hop recording artist (the Reyes brothers were born in Pinar del Rio, Cuba, and immigrated with their families to the United States as children). The band has sold 18 million albums internationally and is important for its popularization of West Coast hip hop.

Cypress Hill's lyrical content focuses on drugs, insanity, police brutality, and absurdity. Cypress Hill's sound, which was partially created by record executive/producer Joe Nicolo (1956–), is defined by its use of funk, hardcore rock, and metal conventions; offbeat sampling; use of childlike, playfully melodic motifs; and idiosyncratic vocals. B-Real is known specifically for his exaggerated, high-pitched, nasally but smooth vocal delivery, a technique he borrowed and evolved from the Beastie Boys (1981–2012) and perfected at the request of DJ Muggs and Sen Dog; it made the band's sound unique, allowing it to stand apart from other rap and hip hop bands. This set up a contrast to Sen Dog's deep, gravelly (and sometimes processed with harmonizing) vocals, which are generally shouted at the end of phrases. The band is also unique for its bilingual approach to lyrics. The music is defined by heavy bass and unusual sound effects (digital and analog, including animal sounds), which are looped throughout each song.

FIRST RECORDING DEAL

After DJ Muggs's first band, a clean-cut early rap band called 7A3, produced an unsuccessful debut album (*Coolin' in Cali*, 1988), he worked with Sen Dog and B-Real on a thug rap–influenced successful 1989 demo. This got the trio its first record deal, as Cypress Hill signed with Ruffhouse Records, a subsidiary of Columbia Records, and its records were distributed internationally by Columbia. They released their first album, *Cypress Hill* (1991), which went double Platinum, peaking at No. 31 on the Billboard 200 and No. 4 on the Top R&B/Hip-Hop Albums chart. Two singles, "The Phuncky Feel One" and "Hand on the Pump," reached the Top 10 of Hot Rap Singles. A third single, "Latin Lingo," introduced Spanish into rap and hip hop. The trio was so successful that it was invited to play at Lollapalooza in 1992. Its second album, *Black Sunday* (1993), debuted at No. 1 on the Billboard 200 in 1993, reached the top spot on the Top R&B/Hip-Hop Albums chart, and was certified triple Platinum; because their debut album was still in the Top 10, Cypress Hill became the first rap group to have two albums simultaneously in the Top 10. *Black Sunday*'s lead single, "Insane in the Brain," peaked at No. 19 on the Billboard Hot 100 and became their second No. 1 on the Hot Rap chart. The trio also became a hot property on the touring circuit as they began their Soul Assassins tour, toured with Rage against the Machine (1991–2000, 2007–2011), played at Woodstock '94, and headlined at Lollapalooza (1995). A new band member, percussionist Eric Bobo (Eric Correa, 1968–), was added. During this time, *Rolling Stone* named them the best rap group in the country. Their third album, *III: Temples of Boom* (1995), also went Platinum and was their first release to appear on every major international chart.

In the late 1990s, Sen Dog decided to pursue a different sound, so he formed a funk, metal, and Latin fusion rap band, SX-10 (1996–), and DJ Muggs released *Soul Assassins: Chapter I* (1997; followed by *Soul Assassins II*, 2000). Cypress Hill's fourth album, *IV* (1998), was also released, and it reached Platinum status, peaking at No. 11 on both the Billboard 200 and the Top R&B/Hip-Hop Albums chart. The band continued to tour and in 1996 joined the Smokin' Grooves tour (Cypress Hill was known as an ardent champion for marijuana culture). In 1999, the band ventured into new territory: it licensed three songs; B-Real did voice work for the first-person-shooter video game *Kingpin: Life of Crime* (Xatrix Entertainment, released in 1999); and the band released a greatest-hits album in Spanish, *Los Grandes éxitos en español*, also on Ruffhouse Records.

In 2000, SX-10 released its first album, *Mad Dog American*, on Sen Dog's newly created Latin Thug Records (2000*–), distributed by Koch Entertainment (1987–2005), which also distributed later No Limit's recordings; Sen Dog's forays into metal rap influenced the next Cypress Hill album, *Skull and Bones*, a two-disc half rap, half metal and rock album released on the Columbia label. *Skull and Bones* peaked at No. 5 on the Billboard 200 and No. 4 on the Top R&B/Hip-Hop Albums chart; it also reached No. 6 in the United Kingdom, becoming their best-charting album there. All of this was accomplished without a hit single. The band also released *Live at the Fillmore*, recorded in San Francisco in 2000. It was distributed internationally by Columbia Records (1887–) but had only moderate success.

DECLINE AND FINAL ALBUMS

The band's popularity began to wane around the turn of the 21st century, and its final three albums, *Stoned Raiders* (2001), *Till Death Do Us Part* (2004), and *Rise Up* (2010), all had disappointing sales. The band took on Snoop Dogg (1971–) as creative chairman in 2010 and moved from Columbia and Sony (1929–) to Priority Records (1985–), the distributor partially responsible for the success of the Death Row (1991–2008) and No Limit (1990–) labels and their artists. It also gave away free downloads of *Rise Up*'s lead single, "It Ain't Nothin'." Meanwhile, B-Real began working on solo mixtapes and albums, *The Gunslinger, vols. I, II, and III* (2005, 2006, 2007) and *Smoke n Mirrors* (2009), the last with Duck Down Music (1995–). In 2012, Cypress Hill teamed up with English dubstep artist Rusko (Christopher William Mercer, 1985–) on V2 Records (1996–) out of London to produce *Cypress X Rusko*, an EP of five songs that bridged electronica (dubstep) with hip hop. Over the course of its career, the band garnered three Grammy nominations, and it was named Billboard's best rap artist in 1991. The band has also been the official spokesperson for NORML (the National Organization for the Reform of Marijuana Laws).

Anthony J. Fonseca

See also: Chicano Rap; Cuba; Political Hip Hop; Turntablism; The United States

Further Reading

Coleman, Brian. 2007. "Cypress Hill: *Cypress Hill.*" In *Check the Technique: Liner Notes for Hip Hop Junkies*, pp. 120–31. New York: Villard.

McFarland, Pancho. 2006. "Chicano Rap Roots: Black–Brown Cultural Exchange and the Making of a Genre." *Callaloo* 29, no. 3: 939–55.

Further Listening

Cypress Hill. 1988. *IV.* Ruffhouse.

Cyprus

The Republic of Cyprus, located in the Eastern Mediterranean, has a population that contains a large majority of Greek Cypriots, as well as a small minority of Turkish Cypriots. Since Cypriot independence from the United Kingdom in 1960, intercommunal violence has intensified. Turkish Cypriots have controlled the North since 1974. When the Turkish Republic of Northern Cyprus was established in 1983 with only Turkey recognizing this new state, political unrest and Cypriot diaspora ensued. Nicosia, divided by a United Nations (UN) buffer, is a major hip hop center. The first use of the Greek Cypriot dialect in hip hop was in the late 1980s in London, where rapper, dub poet, and DJ Haji Mike (Mike Hajimichael) performed. Haji Mike fused hip hop with reggae, ragga, dub, dancehall, and Cypriot traditional music. His studio albums *Haji Mike on the Mike* (1994), *Aphrodite's Dream* (1997), and *Midnight Stories at 3 A.M.* (2015) were released in Cyprus; a reggae album, *Virtual Oasis* (2010), was released in the United Kingdom. Haji Mike's texts also included some English, a Greek Cypriot English dialect called Gringlish, and Turkish. As of 2018, he is a professor in the Department of Communications at the University of Nicosia.

GREEK CYPRIOT HIP HOP

By the early 1990s, American hip hop had arrived in Cyprus via tourism, which led to discotheques becoming the first hip hop venues. In addition to American hip hop, Greek hip hop influenced (and motivated) Greek Cypriot hip hop. In 1992, the first Greek Cypriot rapping crew, Vaomenoi Esso (Locked Doors, 1992–), from Nicosia, self-released the earliest Cypriot hip hop recordings, rapping in Greek Cypriot. One of Vaomenoi Esso's founding members, Mastermind (aka John Wu, Giannos Wu, 1976–), of Greek Cypriot–Chinese descent, pursued a solo career and was the first Cypriot to own his own label, Narrow Path Entertainment (2003*–). In 1997, he started rapping only in Greek. Mastermind's *Apaghorevménes gnósis* (*Forbidden Knowledge*, 1999) was the first Cypriot hip hop album released in Greece. Pioneering hip hop acts included fellow Vaomenoi Esso founder Ponokéfalos (Headache, Mike Wildcut, n.d.) and IUT (Invisible Underground Threat, 1990s*).

Since the 2000s, Greek Cypriot hip hop has been mainstream popular music in Cyprus. The Ayia Napa Youth Festival (2010–), featuring hip hop, takes place in the South. Recent Greek Cypriot hip hop artists have included Diam's (Mélanie Georgiades, 1980–), DJ Sparky T (Thodoris Sartzetakis, n.d.), HCH (Hardcore Heads, 2001–), D.R.I.G. (2002–), POTS (Part of the Soul, 2003–), and A.M. SNiPER (Anthony Melas, 1982–), among many others. The last belonged to the hip hop, grime, and garage group So Solid Crew (1998–) in London, the current home of many rappers and producers of Greek and Turkish Cypriot descent.

TURKISH CYPRIOT HIP HOP

Turkish Cypriot hip hop emerged close to the same time as Greek Cypriot hip hop; however, isolation has limited its reach beyond Turkey. Analogous to Greek hip hop's influence on the development of Greek Cypriot hip hop, Turkish hip hop has influenced the development of Turkish Cypriot hip hop. Like Greek Cypriot hip hop, Nicosia is also a major center for Turkish Cypriot hip hop. MC X-Force (anonymous, n.d.) is a Turkish Cypriot rapper from North Nicosia who has collaborated with Greek Cypriot hip hop artists. Common themes in Greek and Turkish Cypriot hip hop include unifying Cyprus as well as protesting against violence and capitalism.

Melissa Ursula Dawn Goldsmith

See also: Greece; Turkey; The United Kingdom

Further Reading

Hajimichael, Mike. 2013. "Hip Hop and Cyprus: Language, Motivation, Unity, and Division." In *Hip Hop in Europe: Cultural Identities and Transnational Flows*, edited by Sina A. Nitzsche and Walter Grünzweig, chap. 1. Zürich, Switzerland: LIT Verlag.

Stylianou, Evros. 2010. "Keeping It Native(?): The Conflicts and Contradictions of Cypriot Hip Hop." In *The Languages of Global Hip Hop*, edited by Marina Terkourafi, chap. 8. New York: Continuum.

Further Listening

Various Artists. 2007. *The Rise of Cyprus Hip Hop: The Beginning.* Tricky Productions.

Czech Republic

The Czech Republic, formerly known as Czechoslovakia, saw its hip hop scene emerge in 1989 after the nonviolent Velvet Revolution against the one-party rule of the Communist Party took place. The result was the dissolution of Czechoslovakia and the formation of the Czech Republic and the Slovak Republic (both ruled by a parliamentary system with democratic elections since 1990). Despite tensions between Czechs and Slovaks, both countries have peacefully coexisted since their formation. Czech hip hop artists often collaborate with Slovak hip hop artists, and songs have become hits in both countries. Since 2002, the Czech Republic has hosted the international festival Hip Hop Kemp in Hradec Králové in eastern Bohemia, home to Prague, the Czech Republic's main hip hop center and capital city. Lyrics are mostly in the Czech language; however, American vernacular English is often interwoven, and other languages such as Romani have been used. Early lyrical content focused on gangsta rap themes such as enjoying parties and drugs and attaining wealth and sex. But the underground scene in Prague also encouraged communal rapping as sociopolitical venting. One pioneering rap crew was Peneři Strýča Homeboye (PSH, 1992–) from Prague, formed by rapper Orion (Michal Opletal, 1976–) and backed by turntablist DJ Richard (Richard Hlaváček, 1977–).

Chaozz (1995–2002), from Prague, was the first commercially and internationally successful Czech hip hop group. Its debut album . . . *a nastal chaos* (. . . *and There Was Chaos*, 1996) was certified Platinum in the Czech Republic and Gold in Slovakia, followed by *Zprdeleklika* (1997), which was certified Gold in both countries. The group Prago Union (2002–) was partly formed by members of Chaozz. In 2005, it released its debut album *HDP* (*Hrubý domáci produkt*, *Gross Domestic Product*), which features collaborations with American producer Kut Masta Kurt (aka The Funky Red Neck, Kurt Matlin, n.d.) and appearances by American rappers Masta Ace (Duval Clear, 1966–) and Planet Asia (Jason Green, 1976–).

Twenty-first-century rapping topics have expanded to address more localized issues such as race. Prague was historically built to segregate minority populations such as Romani people. The internationally renowned Prague-based group Gipsy.cz (2004–), with members of Czech, Romani, and Indian descent, raps in the Romani language with some Czech and English. Songs deal with discrimination against the Romani people (who self-identify with blacks) among other topics. Gipsy.cz stands out not only for its rapping in Romani but also for its fusion of hip hop with traditional gypsy music and instrumentation (violin, guitar, accordion, and double bass).

From the mid-1990s into the 2000s, hip hop scenes have emerged in other major cities. Formed in Brno, Naše Věc (Our Thing, 1997–2006) was a rapping crew that became nationally popular and was a leading act at Hip Hop Kemp. Personnel changes led to the group's split, but Naše Věc was known for its hardcore sound and rowdy concerts.

Melissa Ursula Dawn Goldsmith

See also: Slovakia

Further Reading

Oravcová, Anna. 2016. "'Rap on Rap Is Sacred': The Appropriation of Hip Hop in the Czech Republic." In *Eastern European Youth Cultures in a Global Context*, edited by Matthias Schwartz and Heike Winkel, chap. 6. Basingstoke, England: Palgrave Macmillan.

Oravcová, Anna. 2017. "The Power of the Words: Discourses of Authenticity in Czech Rap Music." In *Hip Hop at Europe's Edge: Music, Agency, and Social Change*, edited by Milosz Miszczynski and Adriana Helbig, chap. 15. Bloomington: Indiana University Press.

Further Listening

Gypsy.cz. 2013. *Upgrade.* Bangatone Records.

Prago Union. 2010. *HDP.* Strojovna/BBRekordy/Universal.

D

Da Brat

(Shawntae Harris, 1974–, Chicago, Illinois)

Da Brat is an American rapper whose debut album, *Funkdafied* (1994), and single "Funkdafied" made her the first solo female rap artist to have a certified-Platinum album and single by the Recording Industry Association of America (RIAA). Her style blends musical aspects of reality rap, funk, and pop and some elements of gangsta rap, giving her work a wide appeal. She has also made numerous television and movie appearances, most notably in the American films *Kazaam* (1996) and *Glitter* (2001) as well as the television shows *The Parent 'Hood* (1997–1998), *Sabrina, the Teenage Witch* (2002), and *Empire* (2015). She has appeared on the reality television series *The Surreal Life* (2005) and *Celebrity Fit Club* (2007).

She grew up in two households on Chicago's West Side, where she played drums and sang in a church choir. In 1992, her hip hop career got its jump start when she won a local rap competition sponsored by *Yo! MTV Raps* (1988–1995), a television program that featured videos, interviews, and performances by hip hop artists. As part of the grand prize for the competition, she met Kris Kross (1991–2001), whose single "Jump" (1992) from the album *Totally Krossed Out* on Ruffhouse Records (1989–) had put them at the top of the charts. Kriss Kross then introduced her to Jermaine Dupri (Jermaine Dupri Mauldin, 1972–), an influential record producer and songwriter. Dupri signed her to his Atlanta label, So So Def Recordings (1993–), and produced her highly successful debut album, *Funkdafied*, which produced three hit singles. "Funkdafied" reached No. 1 on the rap singles chart and No. 6 on the Billboard Hot 100. The follow-up single, "Fa All Y'all," spent 12 weeks at No. 37 on the Billboard Hot 100, making it her second Top 40 hit. The album's third single, "Give It 2 You," reached No. 26.

Da Brat has subsequently released three studio albums, *Anuthatantrum* (1996), *Unrestricted* (2000), and *Limelite, Luv and Niteclubz* (2003), none of which achieved the same level of success or recognition as *Funkdafied*, although *Unrestricted* peaked at No. 5 on the Billboard 200. She is also well known for her collaborations with and appearances on albums of high-profile artists, including the Notorious B.I.G. (1972–1997), Mariah Carey (1970–), Missy Elliott (1971–), Lil' Kim (1975–), Lisa Lopes (aka Left Eye, 1971–2002), Ludacris (1977–), and the group Dru Hill (1992–). In the early years of her career, Da Brat positioned herself as a female version of Snoop Doggy Dogg (1971–), not only emulating the rapper's relaxed rhyming tempo and G-funk musical style but also appearing in baggy clothes. Her look and performance style were distinct from those of other female rappers at the time, especially Lil' Kim and Foxy Brown (Inga DeCarlo Fung

Marchand, 1978–), who presented themselves as hyperfeminine, wore tight-fitting and revealing clothing, and often emphasized explicitly sexual lyrics.

Lauron Jockwig Kehrer

See also: Gangsta Rap; Lil' Kim; The United States

Further Reading

Bost, Suzanne. 2001. "'Be Deceived If Ya Wanna Be Foolish': (Re)constructing Body, Genre, and Gender in Feminist Rap." *Postmodern Culture* 12, no. 1: 1–31.

Cheney, Warren Scott. 2010. "The Evolution of the Second City Lyric: Hip Hop in Chicago and Gary, Indiana." In *Hip Hop in America: A Regional Guide*, edited by Mickey Hess, vol. 2, chap. 13. Santa Barbara, CA: Greenwood.

Further Listening

Da Brat. 1994. *Funkdafied.* So So Def Recordings.

Daara J

(1997–, Dakar, Senegal)

Daara J is arguably Africa's best-known hip hop group of the early 21st century, having consistently received high praise for its international chart-topping albums and for its sold-out concerts in venues in major cities such as Paris, London, and New York. The band is proof that Africa is capable of producing original, complex hip hop music with global appeal.

Daara J (roughly translated as "the school") began with humble roots, the group's members hailing from the modest Allées du Centenaire quarter of the Colobane district of Dakar, which its founders, Faada (Faada Freddy, 1975–) and Ndongo D (anonymous, n.d.), call home. In Ndongo's home, the duo, joined by Lord Aladji Man (aka Lord Aladjiman, El Hadj Mansour Jacques Sagna, 1975–), created many of its melodic hooks and song texts. The trio's first two albums, *Daara J* (1998) and *Xalima* (1999), produced by reggae legend Mad Professor (Neil Joseph Stephen Fraser, 1955–), were immediate successes and paved the way for the group's third work, a mixtape cassette titled *Exodus* (2000), locally produced by Dakar's Studio 2000 (1998*–), and the debut album *Boomerang* (2003), released by the U.K. label Wrasse Records (1998–2005), which catapulted the band internationally.

Daara J's original members worked together until 2008, when Aladji Man split from the group. Since 2008, Faada Freddy and Ndongo have carried the mantle of the group with other successful albums such as *School of Life* (2010) and *Foundation* (as Daara J Family, 2016), the latter under a variant loose translation of the band's name. Since 2010, Daara J has ranked among the world's top hip hop rappers in the charts and locally has had a strong influence among the Senegalese youth, who draw on its social, political, and cultural messages, emphasizing the importance of melding tradition with modernity while denouncing greed, corruption, despotism, and violence.

Musically, the band draws heavily on Senegalese musical traditions, including traditional Wolof *bakk* and *tassou* (two forms of praise poetry) and the use of various melodies taken from the tunes of griots (traditional historians, poets, and diplomats), as well as Islamic Sufi chants; these appeal to the band's larger fan base, especially Senegalese immigrants living abroad, as it speaks of their cultural origin and responsibilities. It sometimes combines these with R&B-style choruses and reggae beats. For example, the song "Temps Boy" contains Faada Freddy's rap in Wolof about the importance of childhood memories: "So guissatoul noay teggui yoon / fattalikoul temps boy," which translates to "If you do not know where you are going / remember the time of your childhood." For the Senegalese, childhood memories are vital, since they lead the individual along the most righteous path. In Daara J's worldview, one must tread this path with fit (courage). As the song "Tomorrow" from *School of Life* (2010) remarks, one must begin to work early (as in now), knowing that the road to success takes time (expressed as "yoonu ndam dou gaaw").

Babacar M'Baye

See also: Political Hip Hop; Senegal

Further Reading

Tang, Patricia. 2012. "The Rapper as Modern Griot: Reclaiming Ancient Traditions." In *Hip Hop Africa: New African Music in a Globalizing World*, edited by Eric Charry, chap. 5. Bloomington: Indiana University Press.

Veit-Wild, Flora, and Alain Ricard, eds. 2005. *Interfaces between the Oral and the Written*. Amsterdam: Rodopi.

Further Listening

Daara J. 2003. *Boomerang*. Wrasse Records.

dälek

(1997–, Newark, New Jersey)

Dälek (stylized as dälek) is an American experimental hip hop group that was until recently mainly composed of MC dälek (Will Brooks, 1975–) and Oktopus (aka Deadverse, Alap Momin, 1974*–) along with off-and-on producer and electronics expert Mike Manteca (n.d.) and, at various times, producers and turntablists DJ rEk (Rudy Chicata, n.d.), Still (His-Chang Linaka, n.d.), DJ Motiv (anonymous, n.d.), and Joshua Booth (n.d.). Musically, dälek differs from most hip hop bands because it infuses its hip hop beats with industrial music, guitar feedback, layers of synthesized and sampled noise, and a "wall of sound" philosophy as well as atypical spoken-word sampling. MC dälek's raps are usually sociopolitical and often backgrounded and filtered, sometimes becoming part of the instrumental soundscape along with chants and spoken-word samples.

The original studio lineup consisted of MC dälek, Oktopus, and Booth, with DJ rEk (1998–2002), Still (2002–2005), and Motiv (2006–2009) standing in for tours. Its sound has evolved over time but has always been cutting-edge. Its debut five-track EP, *Negro Necro Nekros* (1998), was notable for its instrumentation and use of industrial sounds, and its debut album, *From Filthy Tongue of Gods and Griots* (2002), included turntables as well as electric and acoustic guitars.

Dälek has shared the stage with hip hop artists such as Prince Paul (Paul Edward Huston, 1967–), De La Soul (1987–), the Pharcyde (1989–), Grandmaster Flash (1958–), and KRS-One (1965–). The band went on hiatus in 2009 when MC dälek completed his doctorate in 2009. Oktopus left the band in 2010 to move to Germany.

The group reunited in 2015, and guitarist Mike Mare (n.d.) joined that year. It has since released the seven-track EP *Asphalt for Eden* (2016) and a full-length album, *Endangered Philosophies* (2017). As of 2018, dälek has released six full-length albums and a number of solo and collaborative remix EPs (usually titled "X vs. dälek," where X stands for the other collaborative artist), mainly on indie label Ipecac Recordings (1999–).

Anthony J. Fonseca

See also: Nerdcore; Political Hip Hop; The United States

Further Reading

Chuter, Jack. 2016. "Interview: dälek." *ATTN: Magazine*, April 1.

D'Errico, Mike. 2015. "Off the Grid: Instrumental Hip Hop and Experimentation after the Golden Age." In *The Cambridge Companion to Hip Hop*, edited by Justin Williams, chap. 22. Cambridge: Cambridge University Press.

Mu'id, Niamo. 2004. "Live, From Newark: The National Hip Hop Political Convention." *Socialism and Democracy* 18, no. 2: 221–29.

Further Listening

dälek. 2002. *From Filthy Tongue of Gods and Griots.* Ipecac Recordings.

dälek. 2007. *Abandoned Language.* Ipecac Recordings.

Danger Mouse

(Brian Joseph Burton, 1977–, White Plains, New York)

Danger Mouse is an American music producer and multi-instrumentalist who first came to prominence for *The Grey Album* (2004), a self-released digital download in which he mixed the Beatles' (1960–1970) album *The Beatles* (aka *The White Album*, 1968) and Jay-Z's (1969–) *The Black Album* (2003). Since then, he has been a member of Gnarls Barkley (1999–) and released the project album *The Mouse and the Mask* (2005) as half of the project band DANGERDOOM (2005–2006). In addition, he has produced albums for dozens of different artists and won several Grammy Awards.

THE GREY ALBUM

The Grey Album is a noncommercial project in which Danger Mouse combined hundreds of samples from *The White Album* with an a cappella copy of *The Black Album*, which was released by Jay-Z to encourage remixes. Rather than creating a mashup, in which the intact instrumentation of the Beatles' songs is juxtaposed against Jay-Z's rapping, Danger Mouse sampled minute fragments from songs off *The White Album*. He combined these with hip hop beats and Jay-Z's rapped lyrics. His remix of Jay-Z's "Encore," for example, features fragments of the Beatles' "Glass Onion" and "Savoy Truffle." Danger Mouse received a cease-and-desist letter from EMI (1931–2012), the copyright holder of the Beatles' music. EMI's actions sparked an online protest, leading to the Grey Tuesday protest (February 24, 2004), when dozens of participating websites made the album available, and estimates of 100,000 to one million copies were downloaded (the exact number is still debatable; as of 2018, the album has been made available by distributors in European countries with less restrictive copyright laws). The album sparked conversations about the relationship of copyright and creative expression, and a number of critics named *The Grey Album* as one of the best albums of the year.

DANGERDOOM AND GNARLS BARKLEY

Danger Mouse went on to serve as the production half of two groups with different musical styles. Along with English rapper MF DOOM (Daniel Dumile, 1971–), Danger Mouse formed DANGERDOOM and recorded *The Mouse and the Mask*. The album featured audio samples from several Cartoon Network television programs featured in the Adult Swim (2001–) programming block, and it was made available for free on Adult Swim's website. Several tracks featured guest verses by rappers including Ghostface Killah (Dennis Coles, 1970–), Talib Kweli (1975–), and CeeLo Green (Thomas DeCarlo Callaway, 1974–). Danger Mouse paired up with Green to form Gnarls Barkley, a neo soul group. The two met in the late 1990s when Danger Mouse opened for the Atlanta hip hop quartet Goodie Mob (1991–), of which Green was a member. Gnarls Barkley's debut album, *St. Elsewhere* (2006), featured the single "Crazy." The album peaked at No. 4 on the Billboard 200, and the song got as high as No. 2 on the Hot 100 and won a Grammy for Song of the Year. The duo's follow-up album, *The Odd Couple* (2008), was not nearly as critically or commercially successful as *St. Elsewhere*.

COLLABORATIONS SINCE 2007

English hip hop, alternative rock, electronic world, and Britpop musician Damon Albarn (1968–) enlisted Danger Mouse to produce an album for his virtual band Gorillaz (1998–). Gorillaz's *Demon Days*, released in 2005, is a hybrid of musical and stylistic genres that earned Danger Mouse his first Grammy Award nomination as producer. Danger Mouse has since produced albums for dozens of different artists of varying styles, genres, ages, and nationalities. With the exception of A$AP Rocky's (Rakim Mayer, 1988–) album *At.Long.Last.A$AP* (2015), most of Danger Mouse's post-2007 collaborations have been with rock, alternative, and pop artists rather than hip hop artists. Among these collaborations are Beck's (Bek David Campbell, 1970–) *Guilt* (2008); the Black Keys' (2001–) *Brothers* (2010), *El Camino* (2011), and *Turn Blue* (2013); Norah Jones's (Geetali Norah Shankar, 1979–) *Little Broken Hearts* (2012); U2's (1976–) *Songs of Innocence* (2014); and Adele's (Adele Laurie Blue Adkins, 1988–) *25* (2015). As of 2018, Danger Mouse is producing the latest album for the Red Hot Chili Peppers (1983–), its first album since 1989 not to be produced by Rick Rubin (Frederick J. Rubin, 1963–). In 2008, Danger Mouse cofounded the Los Angeles duo Broken Bells with James Mercer (1970–), the vocalist and guitarist of alternative indie rock band the Shins (1996–). As of 2018, Broken Bells has produced two Top 10 studio albums.

Amanda Sewell

See also: Jay-Z; Neo Soul; The United States

Further Reading

Adams, Kyle. 2015. "What Did Danger Mouse Do? *The Grey Album* and Musical Composition in Configurable Culture." *Music Theory Spectrum* 37, no. 1: 7–24.

McLeod, Kembrew. 2005. "Confessions of an Intellectual (Property): Danger Mouse, Mickey Mouse, Sonny Bono, and My Long and Winding Path as a Copyright Activist-Academic." *Popular Music and Society* 28, no. 1: 79–93.

Further Listening

Danger Mouse. 2004. *The Grey Album.* Self-released.

DANGERDOOM. 2005. *The Mouse and the Mask.* Epitaph.

Further Viewing

Cronin, Shaun, and Twila Raftu, dirs. 2006. *Alternative Freedom.* N.p.: Project Free Zarathustra.

Johnson, Andreas, Ralf Christensen, and Henrik Moltke, dirs. 2007. *Good Copy Bad Copy.* Copenhagen, Denmark: Danish National Television Broadcasting Network.

Das EFX

(1988–, Brooklyn, New York)

Das EFX is a 1990s American hip hop duo whose name comes from the names of its members, Dray (aka Krazy Drayz, Andre Weston, 1970–) and Skoob (aka Books, William Hines, 1970–), which became "DAS" (for Dray and Scoob), and "EFX" (for their love of production effects). The two MCs, who were affiliated with EPMD (1986–1993, 2006–), are known for a stream-of-consciousness lyricism and intricate rhyme schemes informed by an idiosyncratic stammering pattern—elongated syllables and nonsense sounds tacked onto the beginnings and ends of words (referred to as their "diggity" sound). The duo also popularized a fast-paced rap delivery and the use of clever satire in lyrics, and this was juxtaposed against a repetitive but smooth funk and R&B melody, with a jazz-influenced, bass-heavy rhythm section that sometimes paused unpredictably.

Das EFX's debut album, *Dead Serious* (1992), was certified Platinum, but by its second album, *Straight Up Sewaside* (1993), Das EFX had to reinvent itself because its style was being imitated and had become common. By its third album, *Hold It Down* (1995), which produced two songs that charted on the Hot Rap Songs chart, the band had dropped its idiosyncratic stuttering and found itself caught in the middle of the EPMD breakup, which caused a three-year hiatus. Two albums followed, *Generation EFX* (1998) and *How We Do* (2003), but the duo's impetus had been halted. Das EFX would not chart again.

RAPPING CAREER AND UNUSUAL STYLE

Brooklyn, New York–based Skoob and Teaneck, New Jersey native Dray met in 1988 English courses at Virginia State University in Petersburg, Virginia, where they began rapping together. Their bouncy, quick-paced style caught the eye of EPMD in a contest. EPMD helped get them signed to a recording contract. The duo's debut single, "They Want EFX," peaked at No. 25 on the Billboard Hot 100, reaching the top spot on the Hot Rap Songs chart. The duo's next three singles, "Mic Checka" (1992), "Straight out the Sewer" (1992), and "Freakit" (1993), all reached the Hot Raps Top 10. After the success of its first album, Das EFX moved out to Long Island, New York, and created a production studio. But by 1995, Das EFX was no longer seeing commercial album success. The duo continued to record for two more albums only and afterward began touring worldwide from 2007 to 2010. Das EFX continues to tour as of 2018.

Though its influence on other rap musicians was short-lived, Das EFX is referenced still, in the form of parody, such as comedian Dave Chappelle's (David Khari Webber Chappelle, 1973–) use of the "diggity" speech pattern in several of his skits. Nonetheless, the duo has left a legacy that is uniquely its own: recreating the English language with a seamless stuttering style and creating rap music that eschewed gangsta rap's harshness in tone and lyricism.

Anthony J. Fonseca

See also: EPMD; The United States

Further Reading

Coleman, Brian. 2007. "Das EFX: *Dead Serious.*" In *Check the Technique: Liner Notes for Hip Hop Junkies*, pp. 132–42. New York: Villard.

Edwards, Paul. 2013. *How to Rap 2: Advanced Flow and Delivery Techniques.* Chicago: Chicago Review Press.

Further Listening

Das EFX. 1992. *Dead Serious.* Eastwest Records America.

Das Racist

(2008–2012, Brooklyn, New York)

Das Racist, a vernacular version of the phrase "That's racist," was an American absurdist alternative hip hop group composed of Indian American and Afro-Cuban rappers Heems (Himanshu Kumar Suri, 1985–) and Kool A.D. (Victor Vazquez, 1983–), respectively, and Indian American hype man Dapwell (Ashok Kondabolu, 1985–). Despite having only one studio album, the group is famous for its humor, erudite allusions, and unconventional style, exemplified by its first minor hit, "Combination Pizza Hut and Taco Bell" (2008), a guitar- and synth-based B-52's (1976–) style song that begins with a chant of what sounds like a combination of "ha" or "high," immediately establishing the song as drug humor. Other songs such as "Michael Jackson" (2011) and "Girl" (2011) showcase the band's versatility with *bhangra-beat* and Pet Shop Boys (1981–) or New Order (1980–1993, 1998–2007,

Das Racist performs in 2012 at Bonnaroo in Manchester, Tennessee. The Brooklyn alternative hip hop act had a strong college-based cult following for its incorporation of absurdist humor and academic subject matter in its lyrics, unconventional vocals and instruments, as well as modern and postmodern techniques like dadaism and cognitive dissonance. (FilmMagic/Getty Images)

2011–) style electronic dance music backgrounds (e.g., synth-pop and new wave). The band's lyrics are full of metatextuality, with phrases such as "inside jokes in all of my rhymes."

Das Racist established itself not through albums but through mixtapes: *Shut Up, Dude* (2010) and *Sit Down, Man* (2010) established the group's cultural-, racial-, and music industry–based satire and wordplay—the latter bordering on free word association and non sequiturs but containing cleverly associated references. Its idiosyncratic rapping style can best be described as an alternation between a monotone, chantlike laid-back rap or monotone chopper-style speed free association (depending on the song) juxtaposed against comic pitch-altered vocalizations.

The band's commercial album, *Relax* (2011), released on Heems's Greedhead Music (2008–2015) label, charted in the Billboard 200, peaking at No. 103, and got the band onto the cover of *Spin* (1985–). The band broke up before it could produce a contracted second album with major label Sony Music (1929–). Heems released two solo mixtapes and Kool A.D. went on to release three; Dapwell, as Ashok Kond-abolu, went on to perform comedy.

Anthony J. Fonseca

See also: Chopper; India; Nerdcore; Political Hip Hop; The United States

Further Reading

Burton, Juston D., and Ali Colleen Neff. 2015. "Sounding Global Southerness." *Journal of Popular Music Studies* 27, no. 4: 381–86.

Helaluddin, Shareeka. 2014. "Talking Race, Claiming Space: Interrogating the Political Practice of Desi Hip Hop." *Sydney Undergraduate Journal of Musicology* 4 (December): 17–25.

Mitter, Siddhartha. 2011. "Das Racist Is Not Your Typical Rap Story: Trio Left Corporate Lifestyle to Stretch Society's Boundaries." *The Boston Globe*, September 23, G24.

Further Listening

Das Racist. 2010. *Sit Down, Man.* Greedhead Music.

Davenport, N'Dea

(1966–, Atlanta, Georgia)

N'Dea Davenport is an American singer-songwriter, percussionist, dancer, and pro-ducer best known as the lead singer of the Brand New Heavies (TBNH, aka The Heavies, 1985–), a retro acid jazz, funk, and soul band hailing from Ealing in West London. Davenport is a mezzo-soprano. Her voice's range, amplitude, drama, and flexibility sound reminiscent of early Donna Summer (LaDonna Adrian Gaines, 1948–2012) or Irene Cara (Irene Cara Escalera, 1962–).

Davenport was an only child whose parents were a headmaster and a school counselor in Atlanta, so she entertained herself by singing and playing piano in church, acting in theatrical productions, and earning dance scholarships. After col-lege, she moved to Los Angeles, where she became involved in the city's 1990s underground club and rave scenes. After finding work as a studio session backup singer, Davenport eventually met Fab Five Freddy (1959–), who recommended her to work for the new independent label Delicious Vinyl (1987–), which wanted to expand the label beyond hip hop recordings despite successful releases by acts such as Tone Lōc (Anthony Terrell Smith, 1966–), with "Funky Cold Medina" and "Wild Thing" (1989). After Delicious Vinyl executives auditioned and introduced Dav-enport to the Brand New Heavies, she relocated to London from 1990 to 1998, though ultimately TBNH toured extensively worldwide.

TBNH's second lead singer, Davenport saw success not only in England but also worldwide: TBNH's eponymous debut album (1990), which was certified Silver by the British Phonographic Industry (BPI), peaked at No. 17 on Billboard's Top R&B Albums chart, and *Brother and Sister* (1994) was an international hit beyond the United Kingdom and United States and was BPI-certified Platinum. Davenport's own eponymous solo debut album (1998) combined hip hop with acid jazz, bayou funk, neo soul, and electronic music.

By 1995, Davenport had left TBNH and moved to New Orleans while conducting professional business in New York City. In 1998, she began her solo career when she released *N'Dea Davenport*. By the 2000s, she was working as a New York club DJ. She reunited with TBNH on their studio albums *Get Used to It* (2006) and *Forward!* (2013) as well as their homecoming concert album *Live in London* (2009). Since 2016, Davenport has rejoined TBNH.

Concurrently with Davenport's fronting TBNH and her own solo career, she has recorded on several hip hop albums and collaborated with rappers and producers. Her most notable appearance was on Guru's (Keith Edward Elam, 1961–2010) *Jazzmatazz, Vol. 2* (1993), an album that combines hip hop and acid jazz. In 1998, she worked with J Dilla (1974–2006), who remixed and produced two tracks off her solo album: "Whatever You Want" and "Bulls—tin'." The latter featured American rapper Mos Def (1973–).

Melissa Ursula Dawn Goldsmith

See also: The United Kingdom; The United States

Further Reading

Dunlevy, T'cha. 1998. "Things Got Too Heavy: N'Dea Davenport Left Acid-Jazz Darlings to Evolve on Her Own." Interview with N'Dea Davenport. *The Gazette* (Montreal). October 22, E1.

Stewart, Jess. 2014. "Retaining a New Format: Jazz-Rap, Cultural Memory, and the New Cultural Politics of Difference." *Critical Studies in Improvisation/Études critiques en improvisation* 10, no. 1: 13.

Further Listening

N'Dea Davenport. 1998. *N'Dea Davenport*. V2.

Davey D

(David Cook, n.d., n.p.)

Davey D is a hip hop activist, nationally syndicated radio host and radio show producer, rapper, journalist, scholar, and educator. His interests in hip hop first unfolded in 1977, when he was an MC for two rapping crews, TDK (Total Def Krew, n.d.) and the Avengers (n.d.). In the early 1980s, he moved from the Bronx, New York, to the San Francisco Bay Area to major in journalism at the University of California, Berkeley. His senior thesis was on rap music, and he owned a mobile DJ company, wrote for magazines such as *BAM* (*Bay Area Music*, 1976–1999) and local newspapers, including the *San Francisco Bay Guardian* (1966–2014, 2016–), and worked as a radio DJ for Berkeley's KALX (1962–). He led the first rap radio DJ collective, the Oakland-based Hip Hop Coalition (1997–), which promoted hip hop, including local hip hop groups. The coalition also demanded social justice for minorities, provided hip hop news, supported causes that promised positive community change, and created hip hop diplomacy shows. From 1990 to 2001, Davey D was the community affairs manager at KMEL (1946–) in San Francisco, on which he created radio shows such as *Street Knowledge* (1995–) and *The Local Flava Hip Hop Hour* (2000*–). He also founded *D's Street Soldier Program* (1992–) to help the Bay Area's young people gain college skills, avoid violence and crime, and give back to their community. On KPFA, he hosted *Friday Night Vibe* (*FNV*, 1995*–) and cofounded *Hard Knock Radio* (1999–). He also started several Internet blogs and projects, most importantly *Davey D's HipHop Corner* (1992–), one of the first and largest hip hop sites on the Internet.

In 2001, KMEL fired Davey D, claiming it was because of budget cuts; however, the firing coincided with his interview with Congresswoman Barbara Lee (1946–) on opposing the U.S. war in Afghanistan (2001–). He criticized U.S. militarism and Clear Channel Radio's (now iHeartMediaInc, 1972–2008, 2008–) questionable business decisions. Protest rallies ensued to rehire him; though these efforts failed, they were nevertheless successful in bringing shows such as *Hard Knock Radio* back on the air. In 2003, Davey D, Universal Zulu Nation (1973–), and rapper Chuck D (1960–), among others, condemned companies such as Clear Channel for removing community shows, leading to a lack of representation of black music with positive messages. As of 2018, *Hard Knock Radio* is still running, now on KPFA, reaching one million listeners per day. Davey D's books include *How to Get Stupid White Men Out of Office* (Soft Skull, 2004) and *BAF—Be a Father to Your Child* (Seven Stories Press, 2008). Among many other journalistic efforts, Davey D started *HHPN* (*Hip Hop Political Newsletter*, 2002–) and was managing editor of *The Southern Shift News* (2008–2010), which aimed to encourage new voters to flip the third-largest county in the nation, Harris County (Texas), from Republican to Democrat. As of 2018, he is a lecturer at San Francisco State University, where he coteaches the course Hip Hop, Globalization, and the Politics of Identity.

Melissa Ursula Dawn Goldsmith

See also: Hip Hop Diplomacy; The United States

Further Reading

Blanchard, Becky. 1999. "The Social Significance of Rap and Hip Hop Culture." *Journal of Poverty and Prejudice* (Spring).

Klinenberg, Eric. 2007. "Clear Channel Comes to Town." In *Fighting for Air: The Battle to Control America's Media*, chap. 3. New York: Metropolitan Books.

McLeod, Kembrew. 2002. "The Politics and History of Hip Hop Journalism." In *Pop Music and the Press*, edited by Steve Jones, chap. 9. Philadelphia: Temple University Press.

Davy D

(aka Davy DMX, David Reeves, 1960–, Beckley, West Virginia)

Davy D is an American multi-instrumentalist, DJ, songwriter, beats programmer, and music producer whose is best known for his collaboration with Kurtis Blow (1959–), Run-D.M.C. (1981–2002), the Fat Boys (1982–1991, 2008–), Jam Master Jay (Jason William Mizell, 1965–2002), and Public Enemy (1982–). He is also known as Davy DMX, named after the Oberheim DMX (manufactured from 1981 into the mid-1980s), a programmable digital drum machine that he favored in his early work.

When he was 10 years old, his family moved to Queens, New York, where, inspired by the Jackson 5 (1964–1989), he taught himself guitar and later bass, drums, and keyboards. He became a musician and DJ during hip hop's formative years and by 1979 had become a DJ, turntablist, and backing vocalist for Kurtis Blow, who produced songs that Davy D cowrote in the early 1980s, including the Fat Boys' "Jail House Rap" (1984) and "Hard Core Reggae" (1985). In 1982, he played guitar in the pioneering hip hop band Orange Krush (1981–1983*) in Queens, New York. That same year, Orange Krush released the influential single "Action," a combination of hip hop and rock music. "Action" has been sampled over 50 times and continues to be sampled as of 2018.

In 1983, Davy D turned his attention to music production, though he continued as a session musician and songwriter, produced for fellow Tuff City Records (1981–) artists such as Spoonie Gee (1963–), among others, and worked on Run-D.M.C.'s *Tougher Than Leather* (1988) for Profile Records (1980–). In 1987, he released his only solo album, *Davy's Ride*, a mostly instrumental hip hop recording, for Def Jam Recordings (1983–), and it peaked at No. 34 on Billboard's R&B albums chart.

Melissa Ursula Dawn Goldsmith

See also: Jam Master Jay; Kurtis Blow; Public Enemy; Run-D.M.C.; The United States

Further Reading
Leslie, Jimmy. 2011. "Davy DMX: Heavy Hooks with Public Enemy." *Bass Player* 22, no. 6: 17.

Mansfield, Joe, and Dave Tompkins. 2014. *Beat Box: A Drum Machine Obsession*. Berkeley, CA: Gingko Press.

Further Listening
Davy D. 1987. *Davy's Ride*. Def Jam Recordings.

Day, Wendy

(anonymous, 1962–)

Wendy Day is an Atlanta-based entrepreneur, manager, mentor, and advocate for hip hop sound recording artists. Day has negotiated sound recording deals for some of the best-known rappers and hip hop artists in the United States, including David Banner (Lavell William Crump, 1974–), Eminem (1972–), and Slick Rick (1965–). She has also negotiated recording deals with large music industry companies for independent labels such as Ca$h Money Records (1991–) and No Limit Records (1990–).

Day's advocacy began during the Golden Age of Hip Hop (1986–1994) in the early 1990s when hip hop artists, often without executive representation, were signing recording contracts that prevented them from earning money or made them lose money; in some cases, artists were billed for sound engineering or studio time. In 1992, she founded Rap Coalition, which aimed to educate hip hop artists on the music industry, maximize record deals to their benefit, build independent labels, and break unreasonable contracts. Rap Coalition's Board of Advisors included Banner, Chuck D (1960–), Killah Priest (Walter Reed, 1970–), Sticky Fingaz (Kirk Jones, 1973–), and Tupac Shakur (1971–1996).

As of 2018, Wendy Day no longer manages hip hop artists; however, her eponymous website helps hip hop artists find funding for their own recording labels. She has also written an instructional book, *How to Get a Record Deal* (Atlanta: Finders Keepers, 2011).

Melissa Ursula Dawn Goldsmith

See also: Chuck D; Eminem; Hip Hop Diplomacy; Slick Rick; Tupac Shakur; The United States

Further Reading

Balaji, Murali. 2012. "The Construction of 'Street Credibility' in Atlanta's Hip Hop Music Scene: Analyzing the Role of Cultural Gatekeepers." *Critical Studies in Media Communication* 29, no. 4: 313–30.

Kelley, Norman. 2004. "Wendy Day, Advocate for Rappers." In *That's the Joint! The Hip Hop Studies Reader*, edited by Murray Forman and Mark Anthony Neal, chap. 39. New York: Routledge.

De La Soul

(1987–, Long Island, New York)

De La Soul is an American hip hop trio whose debut album, *3 Feet High and Rising* (1989), on the Tommy Boy label (1981–), is generally regarded by critics as one of the greatest hip hop albums of the 1980s, if not of all time. Brooklyn-based members Trugoy the Dove (aka Dave, David Jolicoeur, 1968–) and Maseo (Vincent Mason Jr., 1970–), along with Bronx-based Posdnous (aka Pos, Kelvin Mercer, 1969–), have been the only members of the group since its founding.

3 FEET HIGH AND RISING

The album *3 Feet High and Rising* was produced by DJ and producer Prince Paul (Paul Edward Huston, 1967–) and featured the hallmarks of De La Soul's style, including quirky lyrics, eclectic sampling, and skits. The album samples sounds from not only funk and soul but also French-language instruction records, American blue-eyed soul artists such as Hall and Oates (1970–), and American rock groups such as the Turtles (1965–1970, 2010–). For example, the album's title is an adaptation of Johnny Cash's (1932–2003) song "Five Feet High and Rising" (1974), and a sample of Cash's asking the song's repeated line "How high's the water, mama?" appears in the single "The Magic Number." The track "Cool Breeze on the Rocks" is a collage of dozens of different sung and spoken samples from artists, including musicians Michael Jackson (1958–2009), Flavor Flav (1959–), MC Lyte (1970–), and actor and stand-up comedian Richard Pryor (1940–2005). Individual tracks on the album were linked with an abstract game show in which each member of the group was asked for the answer to a question that was never asked. Song lyrics espoused De La Soul's concept of the D.A.I.S.Y. Age (an acronym for "da inner sound, y'all" and a catchall term for harmony and peace).

With the release of *3 Feet High and Rising*, De La Soul came to be associated with the New York–based Native Tongues (1988–1996) collective. Other Native Tongues artists included the Jungle Brothers (1987–2008) as well as Queens-based groups Black Sheep (1989–1995) and A Tribe Called Quest (1985–1998, 2006–2013, 2015–). The music of Native Tongues groups generally promoted Afrocentric lyrics and featured jazz-based samples, quirky or unusual sampling, and a general sense of positivity.

SUBSEQUENT ALBUMS

The group had to change its approach to production in sampling for all of its subsequent albums after the Turtles sued De La Soul for its sampling of "You Showed Me" (1969) in the interlude track "Transmitting Live from Mars" on *3 Feet High and Rising*. The case was settled out of court for an undisclosed sum, but the members of De La Soul became cautious about sample clearance and choices of material to sample on its subsequent albums. For example, 1993's *Buhloone Mindstate* featured new performances by legendary funk musicians, such as trombonist Fred Wesley (1943–) and saxophonist Maceo Parker (1943–), as opposed to samples of existing funk music recordings.

De La Soul's lyrics began to take on darker subjects as well. For example, its second album, *De La Soul Is Dead* (1991), included tracks such as "Millie Pulled a Pistol on Santa" (in which a child violently confronts her abuser) and "My Brother's a Basehead" (a tale of crack addiction). *Buhloone Mindstate* included the track "Patti Dooke," in which the members of De La Soul railed against what they perceived as mainstream efforts to control the messages and style of black music.

INTO THE 21ST CENTURY

De La Soul released albums every three or four years until 2004, after which it did not release another album until 2012's *Plug 1 and Plug 2 Present . . . First Serve*. De La Soul remained active in the interim, however, collaborating with groups such as Gorillaz (1998–), Yo La Tengo (1984–), and LA Symphony (1997–2009, 2012–). The group won its first Grammy Award in 2006 for its collaboration with Gorillaz on the single "Feel Good Inc." In 2015, the members of De La Soul launched a Kickstarter campaign to help fund their ninth studio album, *And the Anonymous Nobody* (2016) released on the band's label, AOI Records (2003–).

Amanda Sewell

See also: Native Tongues; Neo Soul; The United States

Further Reading

Coleman, Brian. 2007. "De La Soul: *3 Feet High and Rising.*" In *Check the Technique: Liner Notes for Hip Hop Junkies*, pp. 143–58. New York: Villard.

Sewell, Amanda. 2014. "How Copyright Affected the Musical Style and Critical Reception of Sample-Based Hip Hop." *Journal of Popular Music Studies* 26, nos. 2–3: 295–320.

Further Listening

De La Soul. 1989. *3 Feet High and Rising.* Tommy Boy.

De La Soul. 1993. *Buhloone Mindstate.* Tommy Boy.

Denmark

Denmark has been the site of art events since the early 1970s, in both shanty towns such as Christiania and urban areas such as Copenhagen, its capital city, whose nearby suburbs have offered fertile ground for cultivating hip hop activity. Since the early 1980s, Danish media and music journals have given increased attention to the growth of underground art, dance, and music as well as to hip hop, especially in the form of concert appearances by American music groups such as Fugees (1992–1997). Eventually, Danish hip hop found inspiration and motivation to develop its own particular stylistic features.

Danish interest in hip hop has been shared by white middle-class Danish youth and youth who are representative of various economic classes and ethnicities. As an aspect of Danish modernism, hip hop is part of a fascinating counterculture, one that runs counter to the Danish government, particularly its emphasis on regal or royal culture—sometimes rivaling the traditional placement of Hans Christian Anderson (1805–1875) and the amusement park Tivoli Gardens as the centerpieces of Danish tourism. Hip hop's start was auspicious, however. From the 1980s into the early 2000s, Danish hip hop rarely received global attention. By the 2010s, Danish rappers—many born in other countries, arriving from the African and Middle Eastern diasporas (first-generation Danes)—had found mainstream national success and fame abroad. Today, hip hop in Copenhagen is accepted as part of the city's cultural life, and hip hop activity is now found in other Danish cities, though as in most cultures, the capital remains the epicenter. Conservative efforts to limit hip hop activity, as well as to criticize the music, have failed.

ESTABLISHING HIP HOP

By the early 1980s, breakdancing, graffiti, and rap existed in Denmark. Concerts by American rappers and rap groups such as Ice Cube (1969–), LL Cool J (1968–), Public Enemy (1982–), and Run-D.M.C. (1981–2002) were early influences for Copenhagen rap acts, such as the group MC Einar (1987–1990) and the duo Rockers by Choice (1986–) as well as Clemens (Clemens Legolas Telling, 1979–), from Roskilde, Denmark, and Jonny Hefty (Jakob Ørom, 1969–) of the rap-metal band Geronimo (1980–1996), from Aalborg, Denmark. In 1988, MC Einar released *Den nye stil* (*The New Style*), the first successful rap album in Danish; by the 1990s, rap in the Danish language had grown in popularity.

In comparison to other European countries, Denmark's hip hop has taken longer to emerge from the underground and into the mainstream. The sound of early Danish hip hop was influenced by American old-school hip hop and R&B—fusion with other genres such as heavy metal and reggae were soon to follow. By the mid-1990s, Danish song texts from rap groups such as Østkyst Hustlers (1993–), from Roskilde/Copenhagen, and Den Gale Pose (DGP, the Mad Posse, aka Madness 4 Real, 1990*–2002, 2011–), from Hillerød, often focused on the cultural situation in Denmark, which partly explains why the initial success of Danish hip hop was insular. In the mid-1990s, groups began to explore innovative directions, such as using acoustic instruments. For example, on their album *Mod Rov* (aka *Towards*

Prey, 1996), Jokeren (Jesper Dahl, 1973–), also from Hillerød, and his group DGP use trumpets and piano. The Copenhagen rap group Malk de Koijn (1994–) invented the fictional Aberdeen—a set of imaginary universes that serve as the setting for the songs from their album *Smash Hits in Aberdeen* (1998), which incorporated some English language, absurd humor, trumpets and saxophones, and swing-influenced music in addition to multiple synthesizers and turntables.

NEW WAVE AND COMMERCIAL SUCCESS

By the 2000s, a new wave of Danish hip hop artists and groups had emerged, with a few achieving international success. These groups include Brøndby Strand–based Outlandish (1997–), which combined hip hop with folk, pop, soul, and world music, reflecting the group members' ethnic backgrounds (Moroccan, Pakistani, and Cuban Honduran descent); Copenhagen's Gypsies (2000–), an R&B and hip hop band that eschewed the use of turntables and backing tracks; and Copenhagen horrorcore group Suspekt (1997–). Je m'appelle Mads (2003–), a comedy music duo from Copenhagen, have also incorporated hip hop, including rap and electronic music, into their songs, with international commercial success. In addition, earlier Danish hip hop artists such as Jokeren became prolific producers, working on albums by American rappers such as Ice Cube. Since 2004, Jokeren has had several hits on the Danish Tracklisten, including "Jeg vil altid (Elske dig for evig)" ("I Want to Hide [Love You Forever]," 2011), which reached No. 1. Originally from Aarhus, Danish rapper-songwriter L.O.C. (Liam Nygaard O'Connor, 1979–), has been involved in Danish hip hop since the 1990s. In 2003, L.O.C. released *Inkarneret* (*Incarnate*), which went Platinum, followed by the certified-Platinum albums *Cassiopeia* (2005), *Melankolia/XxxCouture* (2008), and *Libertiner* (*Libertine*, 2011), as well as the Gold album *Prestige, Paranoia, Persona, Vols. 1 and 2* (2012); he is, as of 2018, the best-selling rap recording artist from Denmark. He has collaborated with Jokeren and Suspekt, forming the group Selvmord (Suicide), whose self-titled album (2009) was certified Gold.

Sense of humor and metatextuality remain important elements of Danish hip hop. Much of the sense of humor is based on wordplay that includes an awareness of similarities and differences between the Danish and English languages. Unlike Scandinavian hip hop or other kinds of popular musical genre-related scenes, Danish hip hop has always been extremely male-dominated.

Melissa Ursula Dawn Goldsmith

See also: Breakdancing; Graffiti Art; Hardcore Hip Hop; Horrorcore; Nerdcore

Further Reading

Krogh, Mads. 2011. "On Hip Hop Criticism and the Constitution of Hip Hop Culture in Denmark." *Popular Musicology Online*, no. 5.

Preisler, Bent. 2003. "English in Danish and the Danes' English." *International Journal of the Sociology of Language* 2003, no. 159: 109–26.

Stær, Andreas. 2017. "'Ghetto Language' in Danish Mainstream Rap." *Language and Communication* 52 (January): 60–73.

Further Listening

Gypsies. 2009. *For the Feeble Hearted.* Superstar Records.

L.O.C. 2003. *Inkarneret (Incarnate).* Virgin.

Malk de Koijn. 1998. *Smash Hit in Aberdeen.* RCA.

MC Einar. 1988. *Den nye stil (The New Style).* CBS.

Outlandish. 2002. *Bread and Barrels of Water.* RCA.

Specktors. 2012. *Kadavermarch (Cadaver March).* EMI Music Denmark.

Suspekt. 2014. *V.* Universal Music (Denmark).

Die Antwoord

(2008–, Cape Town, South Africa)

Die Antwoord, a name that means "the answer" in Afrikaans, embodies South Africa's counterculture of *zef* (an Afrikaans word used as a derogatory slang term for describing the common working class of Cape Town suburbs). The band's members embrace the term and take ownership of what it means to be *zef*, establishing its own *zef* subculture. Die Antwoord's music is informed by a technique that combines rave and hip hop. The band's carefully curated visual image is intentionally shocking and edgy, and its songs consist of foul-mouthed lyrics rapped over catchy musical motifs and infectious beats. Rappers Ninja (Watkin Tudor Jones, 1974–), from Johannesburg, and ¥o-landi Vi$$er (Anri du Toit, 1984–), from Port Alfred, along with DJ Hi-Tek (aka God, Justin de Nobrega, n.d.), of Cape Town, make up the group. Previously, all three were part of the hip hop group Max-Normal.TV (aka Max Normal, 2001–2002, 2005–2008).

The signature Die Antwoord sound consists of Ninja's rough, coarse rap style mixed with ¥o-landi Vi$$er's eerie, shrill, childlike voice, layered over DJ Hi-Tek's rap rave beats, with lyrics sung in both Afrikaans and English. Their performances are frenetic and usually feature costumes and odd contact lenses (including yellow ones with dollar signs for pupils). Ninja and ¥o-landi Vi$$er have consistently maintained public personas as wild, savage, and absurd parodies of South African *zef* stereotypes. With surreal, exaggerated, and overtly sexual portrayals of *zef* characters, Die Antwoord's provocative music videos have earned them an extensive cult following.

Their debut album *O* (2009) was originally an Internet-only release that led to a record contract with the American label Interscope Records (1989–). Their first release under Interscope was the EP *5* (2010), soon followed by the physical release of *O* (2010), which had a track listing slightly altered from the original. The *O* track "Evil Boy" was produced by Mississippi-born, Los Angeles–based rapper, songwriter, and turntablist DJ Diplo (Thomas Wesley Pentz, 1978–). With rap lyrics drawing attention to a Xhosa rite of passage, the collaboration gained notoriety (and later accusations of exploitation) for the song's subject matter.

After leaving Interscope records, Die Antwoord formed the label Zef Recordz (2011–) and released their second studio album, *Ten$ion* (2012). There were four videos released for the album, and "Fatty Boom Boom" was the most controversial.

Some of its scenes show ¥o-landi Vi$$er covered in charcoal-black body paint (including blackface); the song and video mock Lady Gaga (1986–) for offering to take them on tour with her. The hype for their third album, *Donker Mag* (2014), started a year before its release with the highly controversial single and video "Cookie Thumper." Videos for *Donker Mag* tracks "Pitbull Terrier" and "Ugly Boy" were later released.

In addition to its own projects, Die Antwoord has appeared in a few films, including the two South African short films *Straight from the Horse's Piel* (2010) and *Umshini Wam* (*My Machine*, named after a Zulu language struggle song, 2011). Ninja and ¥o-landi Vi$$er also appeared in the full-length American feature science fiction film *CHAPPiE* (2015).

Lindsey E. Hartman

See also: South Africa

Further Reading

Marx, Hannelie, and Viola Candice Milton. 2011. "Bastardized Whiteness: 'Zef'-Culture, Die Antwoord and the Reconfiguration of Contemporary Afrikaans Identities." *Social Identities* 17, no. 6: 723–45.

Schmidt, Bryan. 2014. "'Fatty Boom Boom' and the Transnationality of Blackface in Die Antwoord's Racial Project." *TDR: The Drama Review* 58, no. 2: 132–48.

Further Listening

Die Antwoord. 2014. *Donker Mag.* Zef Recordz/Just Music.

Dilated Peoples

(1992–, Los Angeles, California)

Dilated Peoples is an American alternative hip hop trio consisting of rapper and actor Rakaa (aka Rakaa Iriscience, Rakaa Taylor, n.d.), rapper and producer Evidence (Michael Taylor Perretta, 1976–), and turntablist and producer DJ Babu (aka Babu, The Turntablist or Melvin Babu, Chris Oroc, 1974–) from World Famous Beat Junkies (aka Beat Junkies, 1992–). The trio's discography includes six studio albums: *Imagery, Battlehymns, and Political Poetry* (completed in 1995 but never officially released); *The Platform* (2000); *Expansion Team* (2002); *Neighborhood Watch* (2004); *20/20* (2006); and *Directors of Photography* (2014). With the exception of Dilated Peoples' first album, all of its albums have charted on the Billboard 200; most notably, *Expansion Team* peaked at No. 36. It also peaked at No. 55 on the U.K. Albums Chart and, along with *Directors of Photography*, which peaked at No. 9, peaked at No. 8 on Billboard's Top R&B/Hip-Hop Albums chart. Dilated Peoples is best known for its song "This Way" (2004) and the song's video, which featured American hip hop artists Kanye West (1977–), John Legend (1978–), and Xzibit (Alvin Nathaniel Joiner, 1974–). The trio is also well known for its combination of West Coast freestyle sound and East Coast old-school sound and its metatextual rapping as well as its live performances and collaborations with notable artists such as West, American DJ and record producer the Alchemist (1977–),

Gang Starr's (1986–2003) DJ Premier (Christopher Edwin Martin, 1966–), and the hardcore West Coast trio Tha Alkaholiks (aka Tha Liks, 1992–2006, 2011–).

Dilated Peoples began when rappers Evidence and Iriscience recruited DJ Babu. The trio worked on *Imagery, Battlehymns, and Political Poetry* as well as its first 12-inch singles on vinyl. The singles "Third Degree," "Confidence," and "Global Dynamics" were released in 1997, and "Work the Angles," "Main Event," and "Triple Optics" followed in 1998 on the Oakland, California, ABB Records (Always Bigger and Better, 1997–) hip hop label. By 1998, Dilated Peoples had signed on with Capitol Records (1942–). Though *The Platform* was its first album that charted in both the United States and the United Kingdom, Dilated Peoples hit its stride with *Expansion Team*, a combination of jazz-fused hip hop, electronica, trip hop, samples ranging from Hitchcock film stingers to 1970s television shows, and DJ Babu's turntablism (especially on the track "Dilated Junkies"). Dilated Peoples' next best known album, *Neighborhood Watch*, gained extra exposure through having some of its tracks on popular video games. *Directors of Photography* came after the slightly less well received *20/20*. The album explores boombap production as a retro sound. Evidence released his debut solo album with *Another Sound Mission, Vol. 1* (2005), followed by three charting albums—*The Weatherman LP* (2007), *Cats & Dogs* (2011), and *Lord Steppington* (with the Alchemist, 2014)—and Rakaa's debut solo album was *Crown of Thorns* (2010). As of 2018, DJ Babu continues producing and remains an active member of World Famous Beat Junkies.

Melissa Ursula Dawn Goldsmith

See also: DJ Babu; Turntablism; The United States; World Famous Beat Junkies

Further Reading

Harrington, Richard. 2002. "Up to *Scratch* with Dilated Peoples." *The Washington Post*, March 15, WW08.

Katz, Mark. 2012. "Turntablism: 1989–96." In *Groove Music: The Art and Culture of the Hip Hop DJ*, chap. 5. New York: Oxford University Press.

Palmer, Tamara. 2003. "Babu." Interview with DJ Babu. *Remix* 5, no. 12: 20.

Further Listening

Dilated Peoples. 2001. *Expansion Team*. Capitol.

Dilated Peoples. 2014. *Directors of Photography*. Rhymesayers Entertainment.

Dirty Rap

(aka Pornocore)

Dirty rap is a subgenre of hip hop that specifically involves lyrics that emphasize sex and explicit descriptions of sex professionals. Although most rappers and hip hop artists have released at least one song that has explicit sexual language, dirty rap stands apart for its exaggerations—rappers, male and/or female, will emphasize a sexual superiority, making themselves the sexual superhero or menace, possessing, among other skills, the ability to destroy their sexual partner(s), with exploits lasting for hours and even days. This is accompanied by the demeaning of the partner. In cases of rape lyrics, the partner is described as someone who wanted the encounter, playing to the psychology of sexual predators, who often blame their victims. If the rapper is female, men, as objects, are equally demeaned, with implications that they are bums, are stupid, and/or possess no redeeming qualities except the ability to be used for sexual gratification. If there are positive messages in dirty rap, it is that the sexual objects are usually revered for their amazing physical attributes and sexual prowess.

Dirty rap originated in the mid-1980s with groups such as 2 Live Crew (1982–1998, 2010–) and N.W.A. (1986–1991), who rapped about crime and hatred of the police, about making more money than everyone else, and about sexual exploits. In 1988, Eazy-E's song "Still Talkin'" explicitly describes the way he selects some women with whom to have intercourse; he also raps about his sexual prowess, his longevity, the number of women he can handle, and how he needs to choose between two women who want to please him in different ways—he decides to use one for sex and save the other one for a rainy day, based on their bodies. Rap band 2 Live Crew has a song on its 1990 album *Banned in the U.S.A.* called "Face Down A— Up," in which each of the band's rappers' sexual exploits and what each prefers is described in explicit, rhyming detail. In 1992, in one of Ice Cube's (1969–) songs, "It Was a Good Day," he brags about the size of his genitalia and his ability to put women to sleep through great sex.

Over the next decade, the content of dirty rap's lyrics did not vary much, yet instrumentation and musical choices were adjusted to fit the mainstream rap aesthetic. Some of these adjustments included more intense bass thumps, set under sampled portions of previous rock or funk tunes. In the late 1990s and early 2000s, producer and rapper Dr. Dre's (1965–) signature slow, consistent beat with time-adjusted sampling (G-funk) was utilized by various dirty rap acts, for example, Ludacris's (1977–) "What's Your Fantasy" (2000) and "Move B—" (2002) as well as Lil' Troy's (Troy Lane Birklett, 1966–) "Wanna Be a Baller" (1999) and "Where's the Love" (1999). In addition, Juicy J (Jordan Michael Houston, 1975–) uses pornographic lyrics, integrating them into his mainstream rap and hip hop in "Bandz a Make Her Dance" (2012).

Expanding on the use of sampling, mash-up artist Girl Talk (Greg Michael Gillis, 1981–) became quite famous with wholly sampled albums such as *Night Ripper* (2006) and *Feed the Animals* (2008). These albums consisted of not only sampled backgrounds featuring up to 15 different song riffs but also the dirty rap lyrics and beats of other rap artists. One of Girl Talk's most famous songs, "Play Your Part Pt.1" (2008), features the samples of bands UGK (1987–2007) and OutKast (1991–) and solo rappers Ludacris, DJ Funk (Charles Chambers, n.d.), Unk (Anthony Platt, 1982–), Shawnna (Rashawnna Guy, 1978–), Birdman (1969–), Lil Wayne (1982–), T.I. (Clifford Joseph Harris Jr., 1980–), Jay-Z (1969–), Kelis (Kelis Rogers, 1979–), and Too $hort (Todd Anthony Shaw, 1964–).

As of 2018, artists such as Foxy Brown (Inga DeCarlo Fung Marchand, 1978–), Lil' Kim (1975–), Akinyele (Akinyele Adams, 1970–), and Nicki Minaj (1982–) are integrating pornographic lyrics into mainstream rap and hip hop. Minaj's 2014 song "Anaconda" is an excellent example of a female rapper's using dirty rap. Even comedian, actor, DJ, and rapper Childish Gambino (Donald McKinley Glover, 1983–)

features dirty rap lyrics in a few of his songs, as in "The Worst Guys," where he brags about a ménage a trois where he destroyed his female sex partner. Explicit sexual lyrics have been used in many genres of music over the past five decades (each generation defining what is considered too explicit). Dirty rap is no different.

Matthew Schlief

See also: Lil' Kim; Nicki Minaj; 2 Live Crew; The United States

Further Reading

Herd, Denise. 2015. "Conflicting Paradigms on Gender and Sexuality in Rap Music: A Systematic Review." *Sexuality and Culture* 19, no. 3: 577–89.

Westhoff, Ben. 2011. *Dirty South: OutKast, Lil Wayne, Soulja Boy, and the Southern Rappers Who Reinvented Hip Hop.* Chicago: Chicago Review Press.

Further Listening

Lil' Kim. 1996. *Hard Core.* Big Beat.

Nicki Minaj. 2014. *The Pinkprint.* Young Money Entertainment/Ca$h Money Records/ Republic Records.

Dirty South

(aka Southern Hip Hop, South Coast, Third Coast)

Dirty South emerged around 1995 in the southern United States, initially as a small-scale region of hip hop production (after New York City and Los Angeles). In recent years, the American South, particularly Atlanta, has become a major hub for the genre. Dirty South rap is associated with regional slang and speech patterns, place references, danceable beats, pronounced bass influenced by the Jamaican sound system culture (using technology, sometimes DIY, to create a better sound), and lyrics reminiscent of signifying and toasting traditions. Major southern cities of hip hop production include Atlanta, New Orleans, Houston, Memphis, and Miami. Some artists, such as Luke (aka Luke Skyywalker, Luther Roderick Campbell, 1960–), who is from Miami, have argued that Dirty South refers only to Atlanta rap, but the term is more generally accepted as pertaining to the region as a whole. Part of local slang since the 1980s, Dirty South was popularized in the Atlanta-based Goodie Mob (1991–) song of the same name on the album *Soul Food* (1995).

Though it has been dismissed as raunchy, overly simple club or car music, Dirty South also addresses lyrical themes of economic and social exclusion, imagined homeland, racism, political corruption, rurality, and criminality. The southern drawl appeared in rapped vocal style before the popularization of southern rap, most notably in West Coast rapper Snoop Dogg's (1971–) inflected speech. Dirty South speech patterns continue to be distinct and identifiable, somewhat controversially mimicked by artists from outside the region, such as Australian rapper Iggy Azalea (1990–).

EARLY SOUTHERN ARTISTS

The Geto Boys (1986–), from Houston, were among the earliest southern rappers to gain mainstream attention, releasing their first album with local label

Rap-A-Lot Records in 1988. The growing popularity of the Geto Boys and U.G.K. (1987–2007, Port Arthur, Texas), who popularized the vernacular term *trill* (true + real) and emphasized southern enunciation and bluesy beats, marked Texas as an early home of southern rap, though the style remained thematically similar to West Coast gangsta rap. Other Dirty South precursors include the Miami bass sound, heard in dance songs such as Atlanta-based Tag Team's (1993–1995) "Whoomp! (There It Is)" (1993) and 69 Boyz's (1992–, Jacksonville, Florida) "Tootsie Roll" (1994). The Miami group 2 Live Crew (1982–) created extreme examples of the sexual lyrical themes that came to be associated with the Dirty South. Their controversial 1989 album *As Nasty as They Wanna Be* was the first album ruled to be obscene by U.S. courts. A key figure in Miami bass, Luke Records (formerly Luke Skyywalker Records, 1985–), produced tracks for MC Shy-D (Peter Jones, 1967*–), a Bronx-raised, Miami bass–influenced artist who claimed Atlanta as his home. Luke was known for his shouted call-and-response outbursts over tracks, predating the techniques of Atlanta-based crunk producer Lil Jon (Jonathan Smith, 1971–).

Master P (1970–) founded No Limit Records (1990–2003) in New Orleans, and, like Rap-A-Lot Records in Houston, he produced songs that extended the geographic range of West Coast gangsta rap, which commonly focused on drugs, crime, and sex. His album *Ice Cream Man* (1996) added southern influences to the vocal style and beats and was successful beyond the southern United States. Jermaine Dupri (1972–), a former b-boy, founded So So Def Records (1993–) in Atlanta in 1993, promoting acts such as 13-year-old Kris Kross (1991–2001). Like Dupri's So So Def, Antonio Marquis Reid (aka L.A. Reid, 1956–) and Babyface's (1959–) Atlanta-based LaFace Records (1989–2001, 2004–2011) focused mostly on R&B groups, but both labels were key in situating Atlanta's status in the music industry.

The commercial and critical success of OutKast's (1992–) *Southernplayalisticadillacmuzik* in 1994, produced by Organized Noize (1992–) in Atlanta, and their contentious win of the Best New Rap Group award at the 1995 Source Awards predicted a shift in the geographic focus of hip hop. Though other groups, such as Afrocentric Atlanta transplants Arrested Development (1988–1996, 2000–), addressed regional themes of homeland, family, and country life, OutKast was one of the first mainstream groups to have a distinctly identifiable southern sound and address explicitly local, southern themes. Rather than mimicking the sounds of the East and West Coast, OutKast's albums, particularly *ATLiens* (1996), drew attention to and reveled in their outsider status. Other groups with less mainstream airplay, such as Memphis artists Eightball and MJG (aka 8Ball and MJG, 1991–), also demonstrated these themes and sounds on albums such as *On the Outside Looking In* (1994). Other Atlanta artists of the mid-1990s, particularly Ludacris (1977–) and Goodie Mob, demonstrated a clear Dirty South aesthetic.

RISE OF SOUTHERN RAP IN THE 2000s

New Orleans's Ca$h Money Records (1991–), founded by brothers Birdman (1969–), a rapper, and Slim (Ronald Williams 1967–), a producer, added the bounce sound to the Dirty South mix. Bounce-influenced southern rap may be heard in 1999 commercially successful singles by two members of Ca$h Money's the Hot Boys (aka the Hot Boy$ or the Hot Boyz, 1997–). Juvenile's (Terius Gray, 1975–) "Back That Azz Up" (aka "Back That Thang Up") and Lil Wayne's (1982–) "Tha Block Is Hot" both charted on the Hot Rap Singles chart, with Juvenile's song going to No. 1.

The Dirty South sound dominated American pop and hip hop/R&B airwaves in the early 2000s. This usurpation of hip hop preeminence was bemoaned by many East and West Coast artists, many of whom characterized southern rap as merely "booty shake" music. The rise of southern rap opened the door for other regions around the world, proving that hip hop outside New York and California could be both meaningful and marketable. Subgenres that may fall under the Dirty South designation include crunk, bounce, screw, trap, buck, and snap.

Katy E. Leonard

See also: Birdman; Bounce; Geto Boys; Master P; Miami Bass; OutKast; The United States

Further Reading

Grem, Darren E. 2006. "'The South Got Something to Say': Atlanta's Dirty South and the Southernization of Hip Hop America." *Southern Cultures* 12, no. 4: 55–73.

Miller, Matt. 2004. "Rap's Dirty South: From Subculture to Pop Culture." *Journal of Popular Music Studies* 16, no. 2: 175–212.

Sarig, Roni. 2007. *Third Coast: OutKast, Timbaland, and How Hip Hop Became a Southern Thing.* Cambridge, MA: Da Capo Press.

Further Listening

Geto Boys. 1991. *We Can't Be Stopped.* Rap-A-Lot Records.

Goodie Mob. 1995. *Soul Food.* LaFace Records.

Lil Jon and the East Side Boyz. 2002. *Kings of Crunk.* TVT Records.

Lil Wayne. 2008. *Tha Carter III.* Ca$h Money Records.

Ludacris. 2001. *Word of Mouf.* Def Jam South.

Disability Hip Hop

(aka Dis Hop, Krip Hop, Dip Hop)

Disability hip hop is music that incorporates a variety of hip hop styles with lyrical content that addresses disability and the disabled experience. The many purposes of disability hip hop include activism, consciousness raising, education, and protesting against social and political conditions such as lack of access, care, and socialization as well as discrimination. Disability hip hop is highly inclusive: the disability hip hop community also includes artists who have disabilities because of diseases, disorders, syndromes, and malaises. More research is needed on disability hip hop as a global phenomenon.

One organized community of disability hip hop is Krip Hop, a movement founded in the 1990s by African American poet, writer, and activist Leroy F. Moore Jr. (1967–). The son of parents who belonged to the Black Panthers and having been diagnosed with cerebral palsy, Moore became the voice of Krip Hop in Berkeley,

California. Through his movement, hip hop was first used at gatherings for disabled artists to express themselves. By the 2000s, Moore's Krip Hop series was appearing on the progressive radio station KPFA's (1949–) show *Pushing Limits*. The show was geared toward Berkeley's disabled community and provided information on news, culture, and the arts.

What began as a local effort has become a global one: in 2007, Moore created Krip Hop Nation, which invites various disabled hip hop artists from around the world to share their music and to use it for disability advocacy and awareness. Krip Hop Nation has also addressed the problem of disability hip hop's being performed mostly in first-world countries such as the United States, Canada, England, and Germany. It has worked toward establishing the names of disabled artists through recording. Its 10th-year anniversary studio album, *The Best of Krip Hop Nation* (2017), features various disabled artists, such as Denver-based Kalyn Heffernan (1989–) of Wheelchair Sports Camp (1997–), who fuses at times humorous and satirical old-school hip hop with funk and jazz, as well as the Real Toni Hickman (n.d.), DJ Ann Jewelz (Julie Ann Jewelz Haneyj, n.d.), and Seattle-based King Khazm (anonymous, n.d.) of the jazz-rock–inspired hip hop group 206 Zulu (2004–).

Another kind of disability hip hop is Dip Hop, which is Deaf hip hop performed by deaf artists. Dip Hop began in the early 2000s and, like Krip Hop, continues strongly today. Dip Hop artists have also worked with Krip Hop artists, showing mutual support for their art. One of the most famous deaf rappers is Wawa (Wawa Snipes, n.d.), who has been active since 2000. Wawa uses sign language as a way to bridge hearing audience members into the deaf world. In addition to focusing on being deaf and encountering a hearing world, Wawa's lyrical content includes romance, humor, and positive messages. His music fuses hip hop with pop.

Melissa Ursula Dawn Goldsmith

See also: Political Hip Hop; The United States

Further Reading

Bailey, Moya. 2011. "'The Illest': Disability as Metaphor in Hip Hop Music." In *Blackness and Disability: Critical Examinations and Cultural Interventions*, edited by Christopher M. Bell, pp. 141–48. East Lansing: Michigan State University Press.

Howe, Blake, Stephanie Jensen-Moulton, Neil Lerner, and Joseph Straus, eds. 2016. *The Oxford Handbook of Music and Disability Studies.* New York: Oxford University Press.

Further Listening

Various Artists. 2017. *The Best of Krip Hop Nation.* Krip Hop Nation.

DJ Babu

(aka Babu, The Turntablist or Melvin Babu, Chris Oroc, 1974–, Washington, DC)

DJ Babu is a Filipino American turntablist and producer. He is best known as a member of Dilated Peoples (1992–), a hip hop trio he joined in 1997, and Beat

DJ Babu mastered playing the turntable using regular style, scratching a record album forward first. He is a member of the accomplished and award-winning Long Beach and West Los Angeles turntablist crew World Famous Beat Junkies and the Los Angeles alternative hip hop trio Dilated Peoples. (Chelsea Lauren/WireImage/Getty Images)

Junkies (aka, World Famous Beat Junkies, 1992–), an American hip hop crew of turntablists, both from California. The latter goes beyond beat production, boasting its own record pool (to provide to members exclusive cuts and edits); clothing line; radio station, Beat Junkie Radio (2015–); and DJ school, the Beat Junkie Institute of Sound (2017). Beat Junkies has won prestigious international DJ battles and competitions. DJ Babu was also part of the duo the Likwit Junkies (2003–2005).

Individually, DJ Babu has won multiple competition titles and is famous for his 1997 beat juggling routine, called "Blind Alley," which involves constant alternation between two turntables, quick stops/breaks and melodic shifts, and constant hiccups and reversals. As a recording artist, under the pseudonym the Turntablist, he is responsible for *Super Duck Breaks* (1996), a popular DJ battle album on the Stones Throw Records (1996–) label. Also a photographer, he has chronicled turntablism through shots taken from behind the instrument; he has been credited as producer on over 100 recordings, and some credit him for coining the term *turntablist*.

Though born in Washington, DC, he grew up in Southern California, near Los Angeles.

In 2001, along with Beat Junkie artists J Rocc (Jason Jackson, n.d.) and Rhettmatic (Nazareth Nirza, n.d.), he went on the 45-city Word-of-Mouth U.S. tour to showcase turntable expertise. As a member of Dilated Peoples, he is part of what is considered the Los Angeles underground's most cutting-edge act, which has been compared to legendary acts such as EPMD (1986–1993, 2006–) and Run-D.M.C. (1981–2002). Dilated Peoples is known for pushing the limits of the musical genre through experimentation and crossover sampling.

Anthony J. Fonseca

See also: Dilated Peoples; The Philippines; Turntablism; The United States; World Famous Beat Junkies

Further Reading

Harrison, Anthony Kwame. 2012. "Post-colonial Consciousness, Knowledge Production, and Identity Inscription within Filipino American Hip Hop Music." *Perfect Beat* 13, no. 1: 29–48.

Katz, Mark. 2012. "Turntablism: 1989–96." In *Groove Music: The Art and Culture of the Hip Hop DJ*, chap. 5. New York: Oxford University Press.

Palmer, Tamara. 2003. "Babu." Interview with DJ Babu. *Remix* 5, no. 12: 20.

DJ Bobcat

(aka Bobcat, Bobby Ervin, 1967–, Los Angeles, California)

DJ Bobcat is an American hip hop producer, DJ, and entrepreneur best known for his work with LL Cool J (1968–) and Ice Cube (1969–). DJ Bobcat began his career as a DJ and turntablist in Los Angeles. He was a member of the hip hop crew Uncle Jamm's Army (1977–1988), founded by Uncle Jamm (Rodger Clayton, 1959*–2010). Key members of Uncle Jamm's Army in the 1980s included DJ Pooh (Mark Jordan, 1969–) and Ice-T (1958–). DJ Bobcat's record scratching is featured in the group's single "The Roach Is on the Wall" (1985). Several members of Uncle Jamm's Army, including DJ Bobcat and DJ Pooh, went on to form the L.A. Posse (1987–1991) production team. In 1987, Russell Simmons (1957–) signed the L.A. Posse to Def Jam Recordings (1983–) to produce LL Cool J's second studio album, *Bigger and Deffer (BAD)* (1987). DJ Bobcat was involved in the production of some of the album's most iconic singles, including "I Need Love" and "Go Cut Creator Go."

The next year, DJ Bobcat released his first solo album, *Cat Got Ya Tongue* (1988). Throughout the late 1980s and into the 1990s, DJ Bobcat produced a veritable who's who of hip hop tracks and albums, including LL Cool J's Grammy Award–winning single "Mama Said Knock You Out" (1990), MC Ren's (Lorenzo Patterson, 1969–) EP *Kizz My Black Azz* (1992), three singles on Tupac Shakur's (1971–1996) album *Strictly 4 My N.—A.Z.* (1993), two singles on Eazy-E's (1963–1995) final solo album *Str8 off tha Streetz of Muthaphukkin Compton* (1996), and the single "Holla at Me" from Shakur's album *All Eyez on Me* (1996).

Since the late 1990s, DJ Bobcat has worked with a variety of hip hop artists, continuing to produce singles and albums. He produced "Comin' after You" (1998), a single from MC Ren's album *Ruthless for Life*. The single was a tribute to the recently deceased Eazy-E and featured a guest appearance by Ice Cube, marking the first time MC Ren and Ice Cube had recorded together since 1989, when Ice Cube left N.W.A. (1986–1991). DJ Bobcat continues to perform DJ sets as a solo and a guest artist, but he has not produced new material since the late 1990s. In the 2000s, he began focusing on the entrepreneurial dimension of hip hop. He and his wife established the Foundation Entertainment Agency, a marketing firm and DJ network dedicated to connecting DJs with projects, promotions, and gigs on a global scale.

Amanda Sewell

See also: Ice Cube; LL Cool J; Turntablism; The United States

Further Reading

Sanchez, Tim. 2013. "Lessons from a Legend: DJ Bobcat." Interview with DJ Bobcat. *All-HipHop* 17 (January 2013).

Sewell, Amanda. 2014. "How Copyright Affected the Musical Style and Critical Reception of Sample-Based Hip Hop." *Journal of Popular Music Studies* 26, nos. 2–3: 295–320.

Further Listening

DJ Bobcat. 1988. *Cat Got Ya Tongue.* Arista.

LL Cool J. 1987. *Bigger and Deffer.* Def Jam.

Tupac Shakur. 1993. *Strictly 4 My N.—.A.Z.* Interscope.

DJ Jazzy Jeff

(Jeffrey Allen Townes, 1965–, Philadelphia, Pennsylvania)

DJ Jazzy Jeff is an American hip hop and R&B DJ, record producer, actor, and former world DJ champion (Battle of the Deejays, New Music Seminar, 1986) but is best known as the turntablist for the hip hop and rap duo DJ Jazzy Jeff and the Fresh Prince (1985–1994) with American actor and hip hop performer Will Smith (1968–) in Philadelphia. As part of the duo, Jazzy Jeff won two Grammy Awards, the first for "Parents Just Don't Understand," an MTV favorite that launched Smith's acting career, and the second for "Summertime," the duo's only Top 10 hit, which peaked at No. 4 on the Billboard Hot 100 and made it to No. 1 in the United Kingdom. Overall, the duo had five Top 40 hits as well as two certified-Platinum and three Gold albums, the album *He's the DJ, I'm the Rapper* (1988) going triple Platinum. In his home city, Jazzy Jeff also founded A Touch of Jazz, Inc. (1990–), creating a stable of producers working on rap and R&B projects. He also played the character Jazz on *The Fresh Prince of Bel-Air* (1990–1996), which starred Smith. He is known for the diversity of his sampling and is cocredited with unique turntable techniques called "transformer" and "chirp" scratches. As a member of DJ Jazzy Jeff and the Fresh Prince, he is known for producing humorous party anthems and lighthearted lyrics and music.

Jazzy Jeff became a block party DJ while still in high school (having DJed since the age of 10), releasing his first song, "Jazzy Jeff Scratch," (1985, Renaissance Recording) as the B side of the short-lived Korner Boyz's (1985–) "The Saga of Roxanne" (1985). He met Smith at a house party, where Smith filled in for his hype man. Along with beatboxer Ready Rock C (Clarence Holmes, 1968–), they formed a trio. As Jazzy Jeff and the Fresh Prince, the group signed with Word Records (soon renamed Word Up), culminating in the single "Girls Ain't Nothing but Trouble" (1987). The band became DJ Jazzy Jeff and the Fresh Prince by the first album, *Rock the House*, which was released on both Word Up in 1986 and Jive/RCA in 1987.

The band moved over to Jive Records (1981–), and *He's the DJ, I'm the Rapper* followed; "Parents Just Don't Understand" won the first ever Grammy for a hip hop or rap song. By its third album, *And in This Corner* (1989), the duo's popularity was waning. Rock C officially left the group before the release of *Homebase* (1991), which went Platinum, and *Code Red* (1993), its final album.

As a solo act, Jazzy Jeff has released two albums, *The Magnificent* (2002) and *The Return of the Magnificent* (2007), as well as two albums with Ayah (Merna Bishouty, n.d.), *This Way* (2010) and *Back for More* (2011). He also collaborated with Smith on his solo album *Willennium* (1999). *The Return of the Magnificent* featured collaborations with Big Daddy Kane (1968–) and Method Man (Clifford Smith, 1970–). In 2000, he produced the critically acclaimed and Grammy-nominated *Who Is Jill Scott? Words and Sounds, Vol. 1*.

Anthony J. Fonseca

See also: Battling; Turntablism; The United States; Smith, Will

Further Reading

Katz, Mark. 2012. *Groove Music: The Art and Culture of the Hip Hop DJ.* New York: Oxford University Press.

Webber, Stephen. 2008. *DJ Skills: The Essential Guide to Mixing and Scratching.* Burlington, MA: Focal Press.

DJ QBert

(Richard Quitevis, 1969–, San Francisco, California)

DJ QBert is a renowned Filipino American turntablist who performed regularly with San Francisco–based childhood friends Mix Master Mike (1970–) and DJ Apollo (Apollo Novicio, n.d.) in the late 1980s and early 1990s. The trio, using the names Shadow DJs, Rock Steady DJs, Shadow of the Prophet, and Invisibl Skratch Piklz (1995–2000, 2014–), won the international Disco Mix Club World DJ Championships three years in a row before being asked to retire from competition in 1994. The trio laid the foundation for applying the band concept to turntablism, treating the turntable as a musical instrument and giving each DJ a specialized sonic role within the larger ensemble. In fact, Invisibl Skratch Piklz were at the forefront of turntablist-oriented videos and websites; this made it easier for other DJs to learn scratch techniques and expand the turntablist community. DJ QBert scratches albums hamster style (moving backward to forward), a technique that many turntablists believe originated with him. In 2009, QBert launched the QBert Skratch University, an interactive online school and community for DJs that features a video exchange learning platform where students can submit practice videos and receive helpful tips and techniques in response.

DJ QBert's solo endeavors include a mixtape, *Demolition Pumpkin Squeeze Musik* (1994), and a critically acclaimed first album, *Wave Twisters: Episode 7*

Million: Sonic Wars within the Protons (1998). Working with animators and digital artists, QBert transformed *Wave Twisters* into an animated hip hop film that was released in 2001. In 2014, he released his double-album *Extraterrestria/GalaXXX-ian* as digital media on the Thud Rumble (1996–) label. Funded by a Kickstarter campaign that raised $128,378, the album features a cover that can be transformed into a Bluetooth-enabled DJ controller that functions like a tactile soundboard. By using the DJay app on an iPad or iPhone, fans can run tracks from QBert's album (or any MP3) and manipulate them with the use of the built-in controller.

With his Invisibl Skratch Piklz partner Yogafrog (Ritchie Desuasido, 1974–) and through Thud Rumble, DJ QBert designs and releases innovative DJ products, such as an all-in-one turntable and mixer combination called the QFO. In 2016, Invisibl Skratch Piklz—now consisting of DJ QBert, Philippines-born D-Styles (Dave Cuasito, 1972–), and San Francisco–born Shortkut (Jonathan Cruz, 1975–)—released an album, *The 13th Floor*, on the Los Angeles Alpha Pup Records (2004–) label. DJ QBert has been featured in two American documentaries: *Hang the DJ* (1998, Aska Film Distribution) and *Scratch* (2001, Warner Brothers Distribution). He has collaborated on several video games, including *Tony Hawk Underground* (2003), *Street Fighter 4* (2008), and *DJ Hero 2* (2010).

In 2000, he was knighted as a grandmixer by GrandMixer DXT (aka Grand Mixer D.ST, Derek Showard, 1960–). In 2010, audio products manufacturer Pioneer DJ and *DJ Times* magazine awarded him the title of America's Best DJ.

Antonette Adiova

See also: Invisibl Skratch Piklz; The Philippines; Turntablism; The United States

Further Reading

Bua, Justin. 2011. "QBert." *The Legends of Hip Hop.* New York: Harper Design.

Katz, Mark. 2006. "Men, Women, and Turntables: Gender and the DJ Battle." *The Musical Quarterly* 89, no. 4: 580–99.

Wang, Oliver. 2015. *Legions of Boom: Filipino American Mobile DJ Crews in the San Francisco Bay Area.* Durham, NC: Duke University Press.

Further Listening

DJ QBert. 1998. *Wave Twisters: Episode 7 Million: Sonic Wars within the Protons.* Galactic Butt Hair Records.

DJ Rap

(formerly Ambience, Charissa Saverio, 1969–, Singapore)

DJ Rap is an English dance DJ, composer, music engineer, music producer, turntablist, singer, and former topless model. She combines drum and bass (jungle style), house music, EDM (electronic dance music), and, later, trip hop in her work. She was born in Singapore but spent her teen and adult years in Southampton and East London. In the late 1980s, she became a dance DJ and mixer on the London rave scene, but quickly moved on to music production.

Using the alias Ambience, in 1989 she released her underground breakbeat single "The Adored" on the London-based label Raw Bass (1989–1992). Soon she was producing old-school jungle music fused with electronica, as on her albums *Intelligence* with Voyager (Pete Parsons, n.d.) and *Journeys through the Land of Drum 'n' Bass* (both 1995). Meanwhile, she continued producing other recordings for project bands such as Engineers without Fears (1993–2001)* and singles such as "Spiritual Aura" (1994), which sampled rapper Big Daddy Kane's (1968–) song "Raw" (1987). She also began her own independent London-based record labels, Proper Talent, Improper Talent, and Propa Talent, among others (1994–).

In 1997, DJ Rap signed with Sony's subsidiary Higher Ground, which released *Learning Curve* (1999), her most successful and critically acclaimed album. DJ Rap both raps and sings on her albums, and her singing voice resembles the thin mezzo-soprano of Madonna (1958–). Though it is not a drum-and- bass album, *Learning Curve* exemplifies DJ Rap's musical style, combining electronica grooves with hip hop as well as focusing on lyrical content that ranges from uplifting messages, such as having to be a strong woman in this world, to light dancing and clubbing topics. In 2006, *Shejay* ranked DJ Rap as the No. 1 female DJ in the world.

Melissa Ursula Dawn Goldsmith

See also: Hip House; Singapore; The United Kingdom

Further Reading

Craig, Todd, and Carmen Kynard. 2017. "Sista Girl Rock: Women of Colour and Hip Hop Deejaying as Raced/Gendered Knowledge and Language." *Changing English: Studies in Culture and Education* 24, no. 2: 143–58.

Farrugia, Rebekah. 2012. "Sex Kittens, T-Shirt DJs and Dykes: Negotiating Identities in an Era of DJ Commodification." In *Beyond the Dance Floor: Female DJs, Technology, and Electronic Dance Music Culture*, chap. 2. Chicago: Intellect.

Hsieh, Christine. 2005. "DJ Rap." Interview with DJ Rap. *Remix* 7, no. 7: 20.

Pabón-Colón, Jessica Nydia. 2017. "Writin', Breakin', Beatboxin': Strategically Performing 'Women' in Hip Hop." *Signs: Journal of Women in Culture and Society* 43, no. 1: 175–200.

Further Listening

DJ Rap. 1999. *Learning Curve.* Higher Ground HIGH 7CD/Columbia.

DJ Rap. 2010. *Synthesis.* Ministry of Sound America.

DJ Shadow

(Joshua Paul Davis, 1972–, San José, California)

DJ Shadow is a turntablist and producer known for his experimental instrumental style and distinctive usage of sampling. His innovative and critically acclaimed album, *Endtroducing . . . . .* (1996), released on the British trip hop label Mo' Wax, helped pave the way for other experimental DJs. Consisting almost entirely of sampled content from his vast vinyl collection, *Endtroducing . . . . .* became a critically acclaimed success in the United Kingdom and United States. DJ Shadow began experimenting with sampling using a four-track recorder while in high school. Later, while working at the University of California, Davis, radio station KDVS, he met and collaborated with the American duo Blackalicious (1992–) and Japanese rapper and producer Asia Born (aka Lyrics Born, Tsutomo Shimura, 1972–). In 1991, DJ Shadow self-released his first mixtape, *Hip Hop Reconstruction from the Ground Up*. With his connections at the radio station, DJ Shadow helped form the record label Solesides (1991–1996). The label's first release was a two-sided EP, *Send Them/ Entropy* (1993), featuring his track "Entropy" and Asia Born's "Send Them." Divided into seven parts, "Entropy" is an 18-minute sound collage made up of DJ Shadow's distinctive sampling style.

After the release of "Entropy," Shadow was signed to the London label Mo' Wax (1992–). His first releases were the singles "In/Flux" (1993) and "Lost and Found" (1994). He went on to produce the album *Psyence Fiction* (1998) for the Mo' Wax recording group U.N.K.L.E. (1994–). The album featured guest musicians Thom Yorke (Thomas Edward Yorke, 1968–), Mike D. (Michael Diamond, 1965–), and Kool G. Rap (Nathaniel Thomas Wilson, 1968–). *The Outsider* featured a new music style that included elements of hyphy, blues, punk rock, and pop rap, which was a striking departure from his earlier work.

DJ Shadow has released four more full-length studio albums: *The Private Press* (2002), *The Outsider* (2006), *The Less You Know, The Better* (2011), and *The Mountain Will Fall* (2016). Just before the release of *The Less You Know, The Better*, the song "I'm Excited," featuring Nigerian rapper Afrikan Boy (Olushola Ajose, 1989–), was briefly released with an accompanying music video. Because he was unable to secure rights to sampled material, he had to pull the single and video, so neither made it onto *The Less You Know* album, and as of 2018, remain officially unreleased. After establishing the record label Liquid Amber (2014–), DJ Shadow released a three-track EP of his own titled *Liquid Amber* (2014). Artists that have signed to Shadow's label include Bleep Bloop (Aaron Triggs, 1992*–), MOPHONO (aka DJ Centipede, Benji Illgen, 1976–), and the Ruckazoid (Ricci Rucker, n.d.). Under the alias Nite School Klik (2015–), DJ Shadow and grime artist G Jones (Greg Jones, n.d.) have released a self-titled EP for Liquid Amber, *Nite School Klik EP* (2015).

Lindsey E. Hartman

See also: Cut Chemist; Trip Hop; The United States

Further Reading

Brewster, Bill, and Frank Broughton. 2010. "DJ Shadow: Vinyl Resurrectionist." In *The Record Players: DJ Revolutionaries*, pp. 225–31. New York: Black Cat.

Katz, Mark. 2012. *Groove Music: The Art and Culture of the Hip Hop DJ.* New York: Oxford University Press.

Further Listening

DJ Shadow. 1996. *Endtroducing . . . . .* Mo' Wax.

DJ Spinderella

(Deidra Muriel Roper, 1971–, Brooklyn, New York)

DJ Spinderella is a hip hop, dance, and rap music turntablist, vocalist, and sometime actor known for her role as part of the 1994 Grammy Award–winning trio Salt-N-Pepa (1986–2002, 2007–), from Queens, New York. The band has sold over 15 million records internationally and formed the short-lived record label Red Ant.

DJ Spinderella's career began when she was just 16. In 1986, Salt-N-Pepa (Cheryl James, 1966–; Sandy Denton, 1969–) was scheduled to perform at the Westchester Music Festival in New York. The duo's original DJ/turntablist had recently married and needed to be replaced, so the duo selected Roper after an audition. She took her stage name DJ Spinderella from producer Hurby Azor (Herby Azor, 1965–), who formed the group and produced most of their songs. As a member of the band, Spinderella serves as DJ and MC during live performances, engages the audience with banter, plays turntables, dances, and sings backing vocals; she has produced a handful of Salt-N-Pepa's songs. The band's biggest hits were "Push It" (1986), "Shoop" (1993), and "None of Your Business" (1993), and the band's biggest album is *Very Necessary* (1993), which reached quintuple Platinum.

In 2003, Spinderella became a radio disc jockey at KKBT 100.3 in Los Angeles, where she cohosted *The BackSpin*, a nationally syndicated weekly show that sought to highlight old-school hip hop. In 2010, she moved to Dallas to do spinning for a midday shift at KSOC–94.5 (K-Soul). As of 2018, she continues to perform with Salt-N-Pepa, which reunited in 2007. She created the Spinderella DJ Academy to teach turntablism to teens and children.

Anthony J. Fonseca

See also: Salt-N-Pepa; Turntablism; The United States

Further Reading

Chappell, Kevin. 1998. "The Salt-N-Pepa Nobody Knows." *Ebony* 53, no. 4: 176, 178, 180.

Rausch, Andrew J. 2011. "Spinderella." In *I Am Hip Hop: Conversations on the Music and Culture*, chap. 22. Lanham, MD: Scarecrow.

DJ Vadim

(aka Daddy Vad, Andre Gurov, One Self, Vadim Alexsandrovich Peare, Leningrad, U.S.S.R., now Saint Petersburg, Russia, n.d.)

DJ Vadim is a Russian-born English DJ, record label owner, writer, radio host, and music promoter whose family moved to London when he was three years old. He is best known as a producer, remixer, and turntablist who has collaborated with a long list of internationally known artists, from Stevie Wonder (1950–) and Kraftwerk (1969–) to Public Enemy (1982–), the Roots (1987–), Dilated Peoples (1992–), and Antipop Consortium (1997–2002, 2007–). DJ Vadim has produced recordings for—among others—Canadian horrorcore hip hop group Swollen Members (1992–), the American electronic group the Glitch Mob (2006–), the French hip hop trio TTC (1998–), and Swedish-born rapper, singer-songwriter, and producer Yarah Bravo (n.d.), DJ Vadim's future wife, who collaborated with him as a member of his project group One Self (2005–2006). DJ Vadim is notable for his expert turntablism, as seen in concert. Though his own albums have not charted, they have earned critical acclaim.

EMERGENCE

DJ Vadim was performing at clubs and concerts in London's hip hop scene by 1994 and began the independent record label Jazz Fudge (1994–2004). The Jazz Fudge recordings included alternative hip hop, trip hop (downtempo), electronica, jazz, funk, reggae, blues, and neo soul. DJ Vadim's sound also incorporates world music instruments, synthesizers, bass-heavy programmed loops, scratching, and frequent breaks. He self-released his recordings and remixes under several monikers, collaborated with DJ colleagues and rappers, and recorded unsigned artists. His earliest compilation album, *Organised Sound* (1996), credits him as DJ Vadim (artist) and Pierre Vadim (composer and producer) and features hip hop artists such as London-born Barbadian producer and rapper Lewis Parker (1977–), English DJ and producer Mark B (Mark Barnes, 1970–2016), English rapper and radio presenter M.C.M. (Mark Layman, n.d.), and English electro-dance and techno musician, producer, and artist Trevor Jackson (aka Skull, Underdog, n.d.). All moved on to successful careers in hip hop and producing.

NINJA TUNE AND BBE

In 1995, DJ Vadim signed with the larger independent label Ninja Tune (1990–), which was owned by the English electronic duo Coldcut (1986–) and based in London, with offices in Los Angeles and Montreal. Ninja Tune released DJ Vadim's albums *U.S.S.R.: Repertoire (The Theory of Verticality)* (1996), *U.S.S.R.: Reconstruction (Theories Explained)* (1997), *U.S.S.R.: Life from the Other Side* (1999), and *U.S.S.R.: The Art of Listening* (2002). These albums fuse alternative and instrumental hip hop with abstract electronica art music. In the 2000s, DJ Vadim toured worldwide by putting together live project groups. In 2007, he signed to BBE (Barely Breaking Even, 1996–) and released albums that demonstrated his more developed fusion of hip hop, electronica, reggae, ragga, dubstep, dancehall, and neo soul: *The Soundcatcher Extras* (2007); *U Can't Lurn Imaginashun* (2009); *Don't Be Scared* (2012); *Dubcatcher* (2014); and, with Ghana-born hip hop, R&B, and reggae singer-songwriter and rapper Sena (Veronika Dagadu, n.d.), *Go Slow* (2015).

Melissa Ursula Dawn Goldsmith

See also: Russia; Turntablism; The United Kingdom

Further Reading

Curry, Ben. 2015. "Hip Hop Turntablism, Creativity and Collaboration." *Popular Music* 34, no. 1: 137–40.

Harrington, Richard. 2002. "DJ Vadim's Minimalist Approach." *The Washington Post*, April 26, WW08.

Snapper, Juliana. 2004. "Scratching the Surface: Spinning Time and Identity in Hip Hop Turntablism." *European Journal of Cultural Studies* 7, no. 1: 9–25.

Further Listening

DJ Vadim. 2009. *U Can't Lurn Imaginashun.* BBE.

DMX

(Earl Simmons, 1970–, Mount Vernon, New York)

DMX, sometimes known as Dark Man X, is an American rapper, hip hop musician, and actor who, like his old-school contemporary Davy D (aka Davy DMX, 1960–), took his stage name from the Oberheim DMX drum machine (1981–1985*) he played early in his career. DMX was raised in Yonkers, New York. In 1986, he began beat-boxing, and in 1991, he began recording demos. By 1992, he had released a single on Atlantic's Ruff Ryders (1988–) label, followed by a string of singles on other labels, including Columbia-Ruffhouse (1989–) and Def Jam Recordings (1983–). He also made guest appearances on various songs before releasing his first album, *Flesh of My Flesh, Blood of My Blood*, on Def Jam in 1998. He is best known for his Grammy–nominated third album . . . *And Then There Was X* (1999), which included the hit single "Party Up," which reached No. 27 on the Billboard Hot 100.

Still using his "Dark Man X" persona, as exemplified in 2017 at a concert in East Rutherford, New Jersey, American rapper DMX focuses on gangsta rap themes that include street violence, acquiring wealth, partying, and womanizing. With a gruff-voiced delivery, DMX's rapping style ranges from angry and confrontational, to motivational, to preachy. (Taylor Hill/WireImage/Getty Images)

DMX has released eight solo studio albums, six going to No. 1 on the R&B chart and five reaching No. 1 on the Billboard 200 chart. He has had roles in 16 films, including *Romeo Must Die* (2000), *Exit Wounds* (2001), and *Cradle 2 the Grave* (2003), and was the star of the six-part reality television series *DMX: Soul of a Man* (BET, 2006). DMX also founded a short-lived label, Bloodline Records, and the related movie company, Bloodline Films (both 2000–2007*). In 2003, he published his memoirs, *E.A.R.L.: The Autobiography of DMX* (HarperEntertainment). DMX has been incarcerated numerous times for various crimes, mostly misdemeanors. He has been arrested for animal cruelty, possession of illegal weapons, drug possession (marijuana and cocaine), resisting arrest, violations of parole, reckless driving, driving under the influence, driving without a license, outstanding child support, and impersonating a federal agent (in an attempt to escape a drug arrest at an airport). These negative experiences, as well as his suffering from an abusive childhood himself, were used to create his rapping persona as "Dark Man X," as was his lyrical content that often focused on confrontational gangsta rap, partying, and womanizing. In 2009, DMX went into semiretirement to study the Bible and prepare to become a preacher, with plans to release a gospel album.

In 1992, DMX first started recording on the Columbia Records, but his single, "Born Loser," was not marketed and went unnoticed; his protest allowed him to get out of his contract. He took some time to perfect his style and appeared on records by notable rappers such as LL Cool J (1968–) and Ice Cube (1969–). In 1998, he began releasing albums—two in the same year, in fact. Both *It's Dark and Hell Is Hot* and *Flesh of My Flesh, Blood of My Blood* debuted at No. 1 on the Hot 100, a Billboard record. The former produced the hit song "Get at Me Dog," which reached No. 39 on the Hot 100 and No. 6 on the Hot Rap Singles chart and was certified Gold. The album, which also contained the popular "Ruff Ryders' Anthem" (whose video was nominated for Best Rap Video at MTV's 1999 Video Music Awards and became a popular ringtone), was the first of five consecutive DMX albums to debut at No. 1 on the Billboard 200 chart. It sold five million copies; it also was the first of six albums to reach No. 1 on the R&B chart. *Flesh of My Flesh* sold 670,000 copies sold in a week—it was ultimately certified four-times Platinum. His next two albums, . . . *And Then There Was X* and *The Great Depression* (2001), were certified six-times Platinum and triple Platinum, respectively.

His fifth album, *Grand Champ* (2003), made history, as DMX became the only musical artist to release five consecutive albums that debuted at No. 1. Two of its singles, "Where the Hood At?" and "Get It on the Floor," reached the Hot 100 but did not make it into the Top 40. DMX announced retirement after its release but came back in 2006 to release *Year of the Dog . . . Again* on Columbia, Sony Urban Music (2004–2006), and Ruff Ryders Entertainment (1988–), spawning two singles, "Lord Give Me a Sign" and "We in Here," but neither charted well. *Undisputed* (2012) reached only No. 19 on the Billboard 200, although it did reach the Top Three on both the R&B and rap charts; *Redemption of the Beast* (2015), a double album, did not chart. Both were released on his independent label Seven Arts Music (2012–) after he won a 2010 copyright lawsuit against BMI (Broadcast Music, Inc., 1939–).

His music is informed by a lyrical content that is blunt, angry, and aggressive, and his songs preach strength as a method of surviving life on the streets—a marked difference from the emphasis on bling and glamor seen in much of the rap music with which he was in dialogue. Musically, DMX's songs emphasize simple beats, usually accompanied by a keyboard voice to create an atmospheric feel, with a typically slow-paced, funk-inspired rhythm juxtaposed against his gruff, gravelly delivery of rhymed quartets, which features vocal doubling to accentuate lines or choruses. Conversely, DMX is just as comfortable with fast-paced, more synth-oriented angry raps, as in "Where the Hood At?"

Anthony J. Fonseca

See also: Gangsta Rap; The United States

Further Reading

Belle, Crystal. 2014. "From Jay-Z to Dead Prez: Examining Representations of Black Masculinity in Mainstream Versus Underground Hip Hop Music." *Journal of Black Studies* 45, no. 4: 287–300.

Bradley, Adam, and Andrew Dubois, eds. 2010. "DMX." Under "Part 3: 1993–99: Rap Goes Mainstream" in *The Anthology of Rap*, pp. 375–80. New Haven, CT: Yale University Press.

Further Listening

DMX. 1998. *Flesh of My Flesh, Blood of My Blood.* Def Jam.
DMX. 1999. . . . *And Then There Was X.* Def Jam.

The Dominican Republic

The Dominican Republic is a sovereign state of 10 million people on Hispaniola, a Caribbean island (Haiti takes up the rest of the island). Santo Domingo, its capital city, is home to three million people. Despite political unrest, the country has recently enjoyed one of the fastest-growing economies in the Americas, which has had the side effect of strong international migration, especially illegal Haitian immigration—and because of income inequality, a large Dominican diaspora exists, especially in the United States. The country's music is primarily influenced by West African traditions, and it is famous for its merengue and bachata music. Dominican rock, influenced by U.K. and American rock, emerged in the early 1980s, when Transporte Urbano (1982–2004) pioneered the sound. Hip hop spread to the Dominican Republic in the mid-1980s, soon to be followed by reggaetón in the 1990s, when young immigrants returned from the United States, Puerto Rico, Panama, and Jamaica. *Merenrap* (aka merenhouse), a style that blends merengue, house music, Caribbean music, and hip hop music, also emerged in those two decades, with Billboard-, Emmy-, and Grammy Award–winning bands such as Proyecto Uno (Project One, 1989–), Ilegales (1995–), and Fulanito (1996–).

Rap Dominicano is a youth-led musical style that began around 1996 in barrios and hip hop clubs and is based on East Coast American rap. Early rappers included El Lápiz Conciente (The Concious Pencil, Avelino Figueroa Junior Rodriguez, 1983–) and Vakero (Manuel Baret Martes, 1979–). Early Dominican rap was concerned with braggadocio and feuding. Since then, rap has stayed localized but has become more socially conscious as rappers protest squalor, violence, and drug use in their urban neighborhoods.

Current Dominican rap acts include Black Point (Jonás Joaquín Ortiz Alberto, 1989–), El Cata (Edward E. Bello Pou, n.d.), Ingco Crew (n.d.), Don Miguelo (Miguel Ángel Valerio Lebron, 1981–), and Redimi2 (Willy Cruz, 1979–), the latter being a Christian music rapper. La Materialista (Yameiry Infante Honoret, 1985–), who raps about sex and female empowerment, is the most famous female rapper. Dominican diaspora rappers include New York City–based rappers Sensato del Patio (William Reyna, n.d.), who was born in San Cristóbal; Spkilla (aka SPK, Edwin Almonte, n.d.); Arcángel (Austin Agustín Santos, 1985–), who moved to Puerto Rico in 2002 to form the reggaetón duo Arcángel and De La Ghetto

(2002–); and Mangú (Jimmy Flavor, n.d.), who was born in Santiago, Dominican Republic, and raised in the United States. American rapper Cardi B (Belcalis Almanzar, 1992–) also has Dominican roots on her father's side.

Anthony J. Fonseca

See also: Puerto Rico; The United States

Further Reading

McGill, Lisa D. 2005. "'Diasporic Intimacy': Merengue Hip Hop, Proyecto Uno, and Representin' Afro-Latino Cultures." In *Constructing Black Selves: Caribbean American Narratives and the Second Generation*, chap. 5. New York: New York University Press.

Sellers, Julie A. 2004. "Merengue and Transnational Identities." In *Merengue and Dominican Identity: Music as National Unifier*, chap. 9. Jefferson, NC: McFarland.

Further Listening

Proyecto Uno. 2013. *Original.* Diameter International Group.

Doug E. Fresh

(Douglas E. Davis, 1966–, Christ Church, Barbados)

Doug E. Fresh was a New York–based beatboxer, rapper, dancer, radio personality, and restaurateur who was musically active during the 1980s. Known as the human beatbox, he emulated the sounds of drum machines, tap dancing, percussions, and synthesizers using only his mouth, throat, and a microphone. He appeared in the American film *Beat Street* (1984) and later was the founder of Doug E. Fresh and the Get Fresh Crew (1985–2003), which included Slick Rick (aka Rick the Ruler, MC Ricky D, Richard Martin Lloyd Walters, 1965–). He also originated the Dougie, a dance craze based on his signature vogue move, a swipe of the hand past the ear on the same side to indicate nonchalance.

FROM POET TO RAPPER AND BEATBOXER

Doug E. Fresh started out not as a rapper or beatboxer but as a poet, styling himself after the jazz poems of Langston Hughes (James Mercer Langston Hughes, 1902–1967). He turned to beatboxing and ended up performing at an event with Kurtis Blow (1959–) when the rapper's crew accidentally misplaced his (Kurtis Blow's) turntables; Doug E. Fresh, who had already developed a reputation for his skills, was recruited to provide backing sounds. He was then signed as a solo artist to New Jersey–based Sound Makers Records (1983–1986). His single "Just Having Fun" was used in the film *Beat Street* (1984).

The Get Fresh Crew was signed to Reality Records (1983–1993), and its first single, "The Show" (1985), was a hit, achieving Gold certification, but Slick Rick left to pursue a solo career and was later incarcerated. Nonetheless, the group's first album, *Oh, My God!* (1986), referencing a line from one of its singles, "La Di Da Di," established Doug E. Fresh as one of the premiere beatboxers in rap, rivaled mainly by Buffy (Darren Robinson, 1967–1995) of the Fat Boys (1982–1991,

2008–). "La Di Da Di" featured Doug E. Fresh's beatboxing for its entire five minutes. The Get Fresh Crew's next album, *The World's Greatest Entertainer* (1988),
led to tour dates with Tony! Toni! Toné! (1988–1997, 2003–). The album's lacklus-
ter sales ended the group's stint with Reality Records.

Doug E. Fresh later signed with MC Hammer's (1962–) Bust It Records (1990–
1996) and released *Doin' What I Gotta Do* (as Doug E. Fresh and the New Get Fresh
Crew) in 1992, but it was a commercial failure. As a result, Doug E. Fresh moved
to Gee Street, a subsidiary of Island Records (1959–), but his career faltered.

The Dougie (the dance move that Doug E. Fresh originated) became popular in
2007 when Dallas rapper Lil' Wil (Wil Martin, 1987–) released "My Dougie," and
the Dougie became a household phrase when Cali Swag District (2009–2015)
released the 2010 Billboard Top 10 R&B/hip hop and hot rap charts single "Teach
Me How to Dougie." Also in 2010, Doug E. Fresh opened Doug E's Chicken and
Waffles, a Harlem restaurant. In 2013, he debuted the classic hip hop show, "The
Show," on 107.5 WBLS; it lasted until 2016. A believer in Scientology, he holds
the distinction of being one of the few hip hop performers included on a Scientology music album, *The Joy of Creating* (2001). As of 2018, he is rumored to be working on a comeback album.

Anthony J. Fonseca

See also: Barbados; Beatboxing; Slick Rick; The United States

Further Reading

Price, Emmett George. 2006. "Doug E. Fresh." In *Hip Hop Culture*, pp. 48–49. Santa
    Barbara, CA: ABC-CLIO.

Shanks, David. 2010. "Uptown, Baby! Hip Hop in Harlem and Upper Manhattan." In *Hip
    Hop in America: A Regional Guide*, edited by Mickey Hess, vol. 1, chap. 2. Santa
    Barbara, CA: Greenwood.

Further Listening

Doug E. Fresh and the New Get Fresh Crew. 1992. *Doin' What I Gotta Do.* Bust It
    Records.

Dr. Dre

(Andre Romelle Young, 1965–, Compton, California)

Dr. Dre began his career as a DJ and rapper but has since established himself as
one of hip hop's leading record producers and savviest executives. As both a performer and a producer, he helped define and promote the West Coast sound, and
he is also responsible for launching the careers of numerous other performers, in
both hip hop and related genres. He has been the founder of several successful record companies, and his business acumen has made him one of the wealthiest entertainment executives in the world. Beyond recording and producing music, Dr. Dre
has ventured successfully into other fields, starting with motion pictures. He has
appeared on screen in a handful of minor roles, and his music has been used in
well over 100 motion pictures, television shows, and video games.

As a natural extension of his work in the recording studio, Dr. Dre has also
directed a few music videos and served as a producer, notably for the recent N.W.A.

biopic *Straight Outta Compton* (2015). His most significant nonmusic business venture has been the development and marketing of a line of headphones, Beats by Dr. Dre, that have sold well primarily as fashion accessories. The purchase of the Beats brand by Apple in 2014 reportedly made Dr. Dre the richest hip hop individual in the world, surpassing Puff Daddy (1969–). Purely as a musical figure, Dr. Dre is one the most important American hip hop musicians. While his own recorded output is limited, the individuals who have worked in his studio include most of the major figures of the past two decades, and his style is emulated widely.

EARLY YEARS

Dr. Dre was born as Andre Romelle Young to teenage parents of modest means, who separated when their son was three; they divorced in 1972. He was then raised by his single mother. He attended the public schools in Compton but transferred several times because of poor grades and to avoid gang activity. He attempted to enroll in an apprenticeship program in the aviation industry but was denied entry because of his grades. He later attended Chester Adult School in Compton before dropping out to focus on a career in music. He developed his interest in music at a popular upscale dance club in Compton, Eve after Dark (1979–1990). Although he was underage, he was able to convince management to add him to the stable of DJs who provided nonstop music from 9 p.m. to 5 a.m.

He first appeared under the stage name Dr. J, after his favorite basketball player, Julius Erving (1950–), but quickly conflated that with his own first name to become Dr. Dre. With numerous DJs on staff, the club had enough equipment for a modest recording studio in a back room, and there, working with DJ Yella (Antoine Carraby, 1967–), Dr. Dre recorded and produced his first song, "Surgery" (1984). That track would become a modest local hit in Compton. About that same time, he joined the R&B and hip hop group World Class Wreckin' Cru (1983–1988), and he and DJ Yella also appeared on KDAY, a radio station serving South Central Los Angeles, all of which helped to make Dr. Dre an emerging local celebrity.

FOUNDING N.W.A.

In the late 1980s, Dr. Dre began to work primarily as a producer for Eazy-E's (1964–1995) recording label, Ruthless Records (1987–). There he collaborated with Ice Cube (1969–) to create much of the material that Dr. Dre, Eazy-E, Ice Cube, and a few others would record as the group N.W.A. (1986–1991) on its debut album, *Straight Outta Compton* (1988). While Dr. Dre did perform one solo rap and appeared as a performer on four other tracks, most of his work was behind the scenes as the album's producer, a duty he shared with DJ Yella.

Following Ice Cube's departure from the group in a dispute over royalties, Dr. Dre took on a larger role as a songwriter and performer on N.W.A.'s second album, *Efil4za—n* (1991), and he again shared producing duties with DJ Yella. This second effort was noteworthy for its shift from the aggressive gangsta rap sound of *Straight Outta Compton* to a more relaxed and smoother sound that would be known as G-funk (gangsta-funk). While Dr. Dre has been credited with inventing this new sound, it is more likely that he picked up the elements of this style while working with another Ruthless Records artist, the rapper Cold 187um (Gregory Fernan Hutchinson, 1967–).

As head of production for Ruthless Records, Dr. Dre had begun to feel pressure to produce artists and hits for the label, and he also believed that he was being cheated out of royalties through questionable accounting practices. For those reasons, in 1991 he agreed to join with the D.O.C. (Tracy Lynn Curry, 1968–) and Suge Knight (Marion Hugh Knight Jr., 1965–) to form a new label, Death Row Records (1991–2009); Knight, who was notorious for his strong-arm tactics, was able to convince Eazy-E to release Dr. Dre and several other Ruthless artists from their contracts.

In 1992, Dr. Dre, working with those new Death Row performers, issued his own debut solo album, *The Chronic*, which reached triple Platinum in sales, earned a Grammy for one of its singles, and ignited a craze for G-funk. He was also responsible for producing Snoop Dogg's (1971–) debut album, *Doggystyle* (1993), and several of Tupac Shakur's (1971–1996) first tracks and album on the label. By 1995, however, Suge Knight had begun to run the Death Row label with increasingly thuggish behavior. What had been general insults on a few tracks aimed at rival hip hop artists had now become public verbal threats of physical violence, and gun-carrying associates of Knight, who had run-ins with the law, became common sights. Knight's questionable business practices, the death of Tupac Shakur, and the rising conflict between East and West Coast hip hop sent the label into a downward spiral and led to Dr. Dre's departure from Death Row late in 1996.

AFTERMATH AND BEYOND

His new company, Aftermath Entertainment (1996–), was to be a boutique label that stressed quality over quantity. Through 2015, only 22 albums were issued, of which 17 have achieved sales of Platinum or higher. All were produced in whole or part by Dr. Dre. The label's first release was a compilation album, *Dr. Dre Presents the Aftermath* (1996), which received mixed reviews but still reached Platinum sales. Dr. Dre would disown this album in his 1999 single "Still D.R.E." That same year, he released his second solo album, *2001*, which continued to develop his G-funk sound, but with lyrics that reverted to the images of violence, drugs, and misogyny of his earlier tracks. Dr. Dre remarked that he had been motivated by questions about his creative abilities in the seven years since *The Chronic*. In reaching sextuple Platinum sales, *2001* silenced most of his critics.

With the success of *2001*, Dr. Dre shifted his interests to producing the music of other performers, especially new talent that was brought to Aftermath, where his perfectionist tendencies served everyone well. He was responsible for Eminem's (1972–) major-label debut, *The Slim Shady LP* (1999); his landmark *The Marshall Mathers LP* (2000), which would become the highest-selling hip hop album in history; and three additional albums. Dr. Dre also oversaw the very successful debut and three follow-up albums by 50 Cent (1975–) as well Kendrick Lamar's (1987–) debut album. Dr. Dre also worked with a number of young hip hop performers who never completed albums and were either dropped from the Aftermath roster or left of their own accord. Elsewhere, he collaborated widely with such performers as

Mary J. Blige (1971–), Missy Elliott (1971–), Gwen Stefani (1969–), Justin Timberlake (1981–), and Jay-Z (1969–). He also worked on projects with former colleagues Ice Cube and Snoop Dogg, and occasional reports of reunion albums surfaced, but nothing ever came to fruition.

Dr. Dre's own third album, tentatively titled *Detox*, occupied him for well over a decade. Between 20 and 40 songs were recorded, and at least 300 beats were left incomplete over the years. Despite occasional announcements that the album would be released, Dr. Dre officially cancelled the project in August 2015, commenting that it did not meet his standards. He announced days later the release of an entirely new, unrelated album, inspired by the motion picture biography of N.W.A., *Straight Outta Compton*. Dr. Dre's *Compton* was not the motion picture's soundtrack, despite a misleading subtitle on the album, but it undoubtedly benefited from its indirect association with the motion picture. Critical reception was good, and sales were strong, though not spectacular.

Scott Warfield

See also: Eminem; 50 Cent; Gangsta Rap; G-Funk; N.W.A.; Snoop Dogg; The United States

Further Reading

Borgmeyer, John, and Holly Lang. 2007. *Dr. Dre: A Biography.* Westport, CT: Greenwood Press.

Ro, Ronin. 2007. *Dr. Dre: The Biography.* New York: Thunder's Mouth Press.

Further Listening

Dr. Dre. 1992. *The Chronic.* Interscope/Death Row Records.

Dr. Dre. 1999. *2001.* Aftermath Entertainment.

Further Viewing

Robin Block, dir. 2003. *Dr. Dre: The Attitude Surgeon.* A Focal Point television production for Chromedreams Media. New Malden, Surrey, England: Leftfield Media.

Drake

(Aubrey Drake Graham, 1986–, Toronto, Canada [possibly Memphis, Tennessee])

Drake is a Canadian rapper, songwriter, producer, and actor who has four No. 1, certified-Platinum albums on the Canadian and Billboard 200 album charts; two certified-Platinum mixtapes; 20 Top 10 singles in the Hot 100; 16 No. 1 singles on the Billboard Hot R&B/Hip-Hop/Rap Songs chart, a record; and 17 No. 1 singles on the Hot Rap chart. He also released a chart-topping album, *More Life* (2017), as a playlist.

At seven weeks, Drake is tied for the second most consecutive weeks simultaneously topping the Hot 100 and Billboard 200 (the others being Michael Jackson and The Monkees), second to the Beatles (1960–1970) and Whitney Houston (1963–2012), who topped both charts for 12 consecutive weeks. Drake has been in the Top 10 of the Billboard Hot 100 for 51 consecutive weeks, ranking him third behind Katy Perry (Katheryn Elizabeth Hudson, 1984–), at 69, and the Chainsmokers (2012–), at 61. He also ranks fourth on the all-time Billboard Top 40 list, with 56, the second highest among rappers, behind Lil Wayne (1982–), who has 69. Drake has the second most (to the Glee Cast) total Hot 100 entries at 155. In 2017, Drake had 24 entries on the Billboard Hot 100 simultaneously, breaking his own 2016 record of 20.

Because he split his childhood between urban and affluent Toronto neighborhoods (with his mother) and urban Memphis (with his father), his raps portray both urban ("the hood") and middle-class existence. The son of a drummer who once worked with Jerry Lee Lewis (1935–) and nephew of famous bassist Larry Graham Jr. (1946–), Drake was a teen actor on the Canadian television program *Degrassi: The Next Generation* (2001–2015), portraying a popular athlete who becomes wheelchair bound and decides to become a rapper. His own interest in rap began through a friendship with his once incarcerated father's cellmate, who was a rapper.

He began as Drizzy Drake, with three self-released mixtapes (2006, 2007, 2009), two on his October's Very Own (aka OVO Sound, 2007–) label. His third mixtape, *So Far Gone* (2009), produced "Best I Ever Had," a No. 2 hit on the Billboard Hot 100 and Grammy nominee. Drake toured with Lil Wayne in 2008, appeared on the cover of *Vibe* (1993–) in 2009, and was signed by Ca$h Money Records (1991–) and its imprint, Young Money Entertainment (2005–).

His debut album, *Thank Me Later* (2010), hit No. 1 on the Billboard 200, the R&B/hip hop, and the Hot Rap charts, breaking records by Kanye West (1977–) and Eminem (1972–) for rap debut first-week sales. His second studio album, *Take Care* (2011), won a Grammy Award. Drake's third, *Nothing Was the Same* (2013), was followed by two Ca$h Money mixtapes in 2015, *If You're Reading This It's Too Late* and *What a Time to Be Alive*, all certified Platinum.

Drake's fourth studio album, *Views* (2016), like his previous albums, reached No. 1 in the United States and Canada as well as in Australia, the United Kingdom, and New Zealand. The album won two Grammy Awards, and one of its singles, "One Dance," became Drake's sole No. 1 Hot 100 song as featured artist, although it did hold the top spot for 10 weeks and topped the R&B/hip hop chart for a record-tying 18 weeks.

Anthony J. Fonseca

See also: Canada; The United States

Further Reading

Pope, Amara. 2016. "Musical Artists Capitalizing on Hybrid Identities: A Case Study of Drake the 'Authentic' 'Black' 'Canadian' 'Rapper.'" *Stream: Inspiring Critical Thought* 8, no. 2: 3–22.

Singh, Kris, and Dale Tracy. 2015. "Assuming Niceness: Private and Public Relationships in Drake's *Nothing Was the Same.*" *Popular Music* 34, no. 1: 94–112.

Further Listening

Drake. 2016. *Views.* Young Money Entertainment.

Drake. 2017. *More Life: A Playlist by October Firm.* Young Money Entertainment.

D12

(aka The Dirty Dozen, 1996–, Detroit, Michigan)

D12 is an American hip hop group featuring Eminem (Marshall Bruce Mathers III, 1972–), one of the world's top-selling rappers, who has had six No. 1 solo studio albums on the Billboard 200 and five chart-topping Billboard Hot 100 singles. Other original members in the band included Proof (DeShaun Dupree Holton, 1973–2006), Bugz (Karnail Pitts, 1978–1999), and Bizarre (Rufus Arthur Johnson, 1976–). Kuniva (Von Carlisle, 1976–), from the Detroit hip hop duo Da Brigade (2000–2006), was invited to join by Proof after Eminem got his first solo deal, as was producer Kon Artis (Denaun Porter (1978–). Swift (aka Swifty McVay, Ondre Moore, 1976–) joined after Bugz's death by gunshot in an altercation. Achieving mainstream success after Eminem rose to international fame, D12's studio albums on the Shady Records (1999–) label, *Devil's Night* (2001) and *D12 World* (2004), have both reached the top spot on the Billboard 200.

D12's original recording and touring lineup consisted of the band's six members and their alter egos, including Eminem's Slim Shady alter ego. The other alter egos were Proof's Dirty Harry, Bizarre's Peter S. Bizarre, Kuniva's Hannz G./Rondell Beene, Kon Artis's Mr. Porter, and Bugz's Robert Beck. The band's two albums spawned two Top 40 singles, "Purple P—" (aka "Purple Pills," also released as the censored single "Purple Hills") and "My Band," the latter peaking at No. 6 on the Hot 100. The band has virtually folded since 2006, due to Eminem's solo success and subsequent hiatus and the death of band member Proof, also by gunshot, in 2006.

D12's first release was a self-released EP called the Underground EP, which was recorded between 1996 and 1998 but released in 2000. Its cover features the D of D12 shaped like the logo for the Detroit Tigers baseball team, showing the band's affinity for its home city. D12 became a side project after Dr. Dre (1965–) persuaded Eminem to pursue a solo career around 1999. In addition, D12's other members began establishing solo reputations. Bizarre and Bugz each released an EP, *Attack of the Weirdos* (1998) and *These Streets* (1999), respectively, the former going on to have a prolific recording career of seven albums. Bugz's tragic death in 1999 brought Eminem back to the group (to honor his friend's memory), and the new lineup of Proof, Bizarre, Kuniva, Kon Artis, Swift, and Eminem became the D12 known by most fans.

Both D12's *Devil's Night* and Eminem's *The Marshall Mathers LP* (2000) are dedicated to Bugz. *Devil's Night* went on to sell four million copies worldwide. *D12 World* featured production by Proof, Eminem, Dr. Dre, and Kanye West (1977–). D12 toured without Eminem for the *D12 World* tour, as he was busy with a solo project. A mixtape, *Return of the Dozen, Vol. 2*, was released in 2011, but Eminem participated in only one song. Bizarre and Kon Artis left the group in 2012.

Anthony J. Fonseca

See also: Eminem; The United States

Further Reading

Esling, Isabelle. 2012. "The Dirty Dozen: The Story behind the D12 Group." In *Eminem and the Detroit Rap Scene: White Kid in a Black Music World*, chap. 2. Phoenix, AZ: Colossus Books.

Stubbs, David. 2004. "D12-Devil's Night." In *Cleaning out My Closet: Eminem, The Stories behind Every Song*, pp. 141–60. New York: Thunder's Mouth Press.

Further Listening

D12. 2004. *D12 World.* Shady Records.

Dubstep

Dubstep is an electronic dance music genre that began in 1990s South London at the Big Apple Record Shop. It consists of experimental remixes that deemphasize vocals and place the breakbeat, drums, and bass in the foreground. As the 1990s progressed, more variations of the sound, played by a growing number of DJs, could be heard in nightclubs such as Plastic People (1994–2015), known for its stellar sound system. By 2000, dubstep could be heard on radio. The defining characteristics of today's dubstep are a syncopated rhythm, 138 to 142 beats per minute (bpm), and a wobble bass, also called the wub—an extended bass note that is manipulated rhythmically by using a low-frequency oscillator; the effect is an oscillating bass that sounds as if it is being played on a wah pedal.

London-based producers Benga (Adegbenga Adejumo, 1986–) and Skream (Oliver Dene Jones, 1986–), Digital Mystikz (n.d.), and Loefah (Peter Livingston, n.d.), started an evolution in dubstep that resulted in a darker, more clipped, and minimalist sound, and by 2005, more dubstep DJs were getting airplay on radio shows such as "Dubstep Warz" on BBC Radio 1. Baltimore-based English dubstep DJ Joe Nice (2002–) helped with cultivating and promoting dubstep in the United States. Nightclubs and dance clubs started dubstep nights, featuring the new imports, and DJs started infusing dubstep into their sets. Dubstep then began influencing mainstream popular music genres, gaining further worldwide recognition, and by 2010 it had infiltrated the pop charts.

By 2011, dubstep had grown in American markets with the rise of a subgenre, the brostep, with American producer Skrillex (Sonny John Moore, 1988–) at the DJ helm. Brostep is a variation of dubstep that stresses the middle register and medium fields of sound, employing musical shifts that seem either automated or robotic, as well as a sense of aggression experienced in heavy metal.

Dubstep dance is informed by an impulse of movement that seems to start in one body part and then travels throughout the body, similar to the way electricity would flow and rebound. Much of the movement is tight

Skrillex has become a central figure for popularizing electronic dance music (EDM) and dubstep. He's earned Grammy wins, has multiple Platinum-certified EPs and singles, and his live shows are hugely popular with fans. (Featureflash/Dreamstime.com)

and uses small, detailed gestures. Origins of this type of movement can be traced back to the development of modern dance, when Isadora Duncan (1877–1927) created a dance technique that moved and radiated outward from an impulse starting in the solar plexus region. The dancer looks as if a film editor, slowing movement and accelerating it at different points in the music, is manipulating the body. When performing to dubstep, a dancer can look as fluid as water or like stop-motion animation. Overall, the dance style is a derivative of breaking, freehand, and liquid (aka liquid and digits—a gestural interpretative form that involves aspects of pantomime); it is a toprock-based dance, with elements of b-boy poses and pauses of balance. Marquese Scott (1981–), originating from Inglewood, California, and one of dubstep's preeminent dance performers, is known for his popping/breaking style. Tecktonik, another dance style linked to dubstep, originated in France and is predominately about arm movement and using the hips and knees to gently shuffle across the floor. This dubstep-related dance style has movements reminiscent of disco but performed at a much more frantic pace.

Paige A. Willson

See also: France; Hip Hop Dance; The United Kingdom

Further Reading

Stirling, Christabel. 2016. "'Beyond the Dance Floor?' Gendered Publics and Creative Practices in Electronic Dance Music." *Contemporary Music Review* 35, no. 1: 130–49.

Sullivan, Paul. 2014. *Remixology: Tracing the Dub Diaspora.* London: Reaktion Books.

E

East Timor

East Timor is a sovereign island nation of over one million people in Southeast Asia, made up of the eastern half of the island of Timor and a few nearby islands whose official language is Portuguese. This predominantly Christian nation was colonized by Portugal in the 16th century and was known as Portuguese Timor until 1975, when it was invaded and occupied by Indonesia until 1999. Its music, influenced by Portugal and Indonesia, includes styles such as *gamelan* music and *fado*, although the most widespread form of music is native—folk music such as the *likurai* post-war dance, which is also now used by women in courtship. Popular East Timorese music followed its turn-of-the-century independence movement, with songs that encouraged people to register to vote or advocated independence. Music and poetry were both used by East Timorese performers resisting the Indonesian occupation. Chants are often used in East Timorese popular music.

The most famous East Timorese popular musician is diaspora singer Teo Batiste Ximenes (n.d.), who grew up in Australia but uses East Timorese folk rhythms. Recent Western influences on popular music include genres such as rock, reggae, and hip hop. More research is needed on hip hop in East Timor, particularly on the protest songs and poetry that took place there as an underground activity during the Indonesian occupation.

Hip hop, including rap, is new to the nation. Since 2013, the Australian government has been sending emissaries to teach East Timor youth breakdancing and hip hop culture through workshops, building makeshift music studios. At this time, East Timor is still suffering from ongoing terrorist attacks and third-world development issues, such as lack of access to clean running water and a disengaged youth culture that has resorted to rebellion and crime. As of 2018, numerous b-boy and b-girl dance crews exist in East Timor's capital city, Dili, and elements of rock, country, reggae, hip hop, and rap have made their way into the country's musical social gatherings.

Anthony J. Fonseca

See also: Breakdancing; Indonesia; Portugal

Further Reading

Dunphy, Kim, Meredith Elton, and Alex Jordan. 2014. "Exploring Dance/Movement Therapy in Post Conflict Timor-Leste." *American Journal of Dance Therapy* 36, no. 2: 189–208.

Myrttinen, Henri. 2013. "Resistance, Symbolism, and the Language of Stateness in Timor-Leste." *Oceania* 83, no. 3: 208–20.

Eazy-E

(Eric Lynn Wright, 1963–1995, Compton, California)

Eazy-E was a gangsta and West Coast hip hop rapper and record producer, best known for his cofounding of Ruthless Records (1987–) with Jerry Heller (Gerald E. Heller, 1940–) in Los Angeles and his membership in the Compton, California, rap group N.W.A. (aka N— wit Attitudes, 1986–1991). A driving force behind the popularization of gangsta rap, Eazy-E was a high school dropout who did a short but profitable stint as a drug dealer before becoming a rapper and producer. Along with Dr. Dre (1965–), Ice Cube (1969–), and Arabian Prince (Kim Nazel, 1965–), Eazy-E formed N.W.A. following the success of his single "Boyz-n-the-Hood" (1987), written by Ice Cube and Dr. Dre, in which he raps about the violence of daily life in Compton. Eventually the N.W.A. lineup included DJ Yella (Antoine Carraby, 1967–) and MC Ren (Lorenzo Jerald Patterson, 1969–), all portrayed in the American biographical film *Straight Outta Compton* (2015). N.W.A.'s 1988 double-Platinum album *Straight Outta Compton* is one of rap music's benchmark recordings, and its follow-up, *Efil4za—n* (aka *N—az4life,* 1991), went to No. 1 on the Billboard 200 without a single or video, going Platinum in two weeks.

Eazy-Duz-It, Eazy-E's debut solo album, was released in 1988 and peaked at No. 41 on the Billboard 200. Produced by Dr. Dre and Yella, it sold over 2.5 million copies. Eazy-E's rap delivery is distinctive in that it has a breathless quality juxtaposed against his highly enunciated narrative lines that generally tell an involved story using a descending melodic contour. His starting off lines with higher notes so that each phrase ends lower than it begins, similar to the style of Will Smith's (1968–) Fresh Prince, creates drama and prevents monotony, especially when he incorporates singsong-sounding and tightly rhymed bridges and refrains. His music is also known for its personal attacks on other musicians. After Dr. Dre left N.W.A. and Ruthless because of contract and artistic disputes with Heller and Eazy-E, he released *The Chronic* (1992), which contained a song that insulted Eazy-E. In response, the entirety of Eazy-E's *It's On (Dr. Dre) 187um Killa* (1993), insulted Dr. Dre (as did videos from the EP). A second EP, *5150 Home for tha Sick*, was released in 1993, and Eazy-E's final album, *Str8 off tha Streetz of Muthaphukkin Compton* (1995), was released posthumously after he died of AIDS.

Anthony J. Fonseca

See also: Dr. Dre; Ice Cube; N.W.A.; The United States

Further Reading

Heller, Jerry, and Gil Reavill. 2006. *Ruthless: A Memoir.* New York: Simon Spotlight Entertainment.

Leonard, David J. 2007. "Ice Cube." In *Icons of Hip Hop: An Encyclopedia of the Movement, Music, and Culture*, edited by Mickey Hess, vol. 2, pp. 293–316. Westport, CT: Greenwood.

Further Viewing

Gray, Gary, dir. 2012. *Ruthless Memories: Preserving the Life and Legend of Eric (Eazy E) Wright.* Los Angeles: New Line Cinema.

Ecuador

Ecuador, a South American democratic republic, has an ethnically diverse population and a diverse music that ranges from indigenous dance styles and indigenous and Spanish sentimental styles to Andean and African Ecuadorian styles based on flutes and marimbas, respectively. It has been a sovereign Spanish-language state of over 15 million people since 1830 (although 13 Amerindian languages are recognized). Hip hop activity takes place mostly in the capital city, Quito, and the most populated city, Guayaquil. Ecuador is one of the most ecologically friendly nations in the world, as exemplified in its most popular current hip hop singer, spoken-word artist, and rapper Mateo Kingman (1991–), who debuted in 2016 with *Respira*. Kingman's Spanish lyrics examine life and spirituality in the rain forest through raps and chants within a mix of African drums and traditional instruments from the Ecuadorian Pacific, sometimes run through a synthesizer.

Other hip hop artists include Kingman's rap crew EVHA (aka El Viejo Hombre de los Andes, the Old Man of the Andes, 2014–), Andean electronica musician Nicola Cruz (1987–), and rapper Guanaco (aka Guanaco MC, Juan Pablo Cobo, 1980–), a 20-year rapper and member of Sudakaya (2002–) who raps in Spanish. Guanaco has released four albums, including *Blasfemia* (2016), 10 songs and spoken-interlude tracks influenced by French-born Spanish alternative Latin rock, reggae, and ska singer-songwriter and musician Manu Chao (José-Manuel Thomas Arthur Chao Ortega, 1961–) that pay tribute to musical styles such as *rocera* and *canteen* and use indigenous music loops, all juxtaposed against turntablism and hip hop rhythms, to achieve a global sound. The band Swing Original Monks (2010–), which formed in Quito and comprises of Ecuadorian, other South American, European, and American musicians, employs some hip hop elements (e.g., rap, loops, samples, and beatboxing) in its music, which is an eclectic combination of alternative rock, electronic cumbia, ska, and gypsy swing jazz.

Among diaspora rappers, the most famous is singer, rapper, record executive, and pastor Gerardo (Gerardo Mejía, 1965–), who is from Guayaquil but grew up in Glendale, California; Gerardo had a Top 10 hit in 1991 with "Rico Suave," which peaked at No. 7 on the Billboard Hot 100.

Anthony J. Fonseca

See also: Colombia; Peru; Reggae

Further Reading

Lara, Francisco, and Diana Ruggiero. 2016. "Highland Afro-Ecuadorian Bomba and Identity along the Black Pacific at the Turn of the Twenty-First Century." *Revista de Música Latinoamericana* 37, no. 2: 135–64, 262–63.

Wong, Ketty. 2012. *Whose National Music? Identity, Mestizaje, and Migration in Ecuador.* Studies of Latin American and Caribbean Music. Philadelphia: Temple University Press.

Further Listening

Kingman, Mateo. 2016. *Respira.* AYA Records.

Eedris Abdulkareem

(Eedris Turayo Abdulkareem Ajenifuja, 1974–, Kano, Nigeria)

Sometimes known as Mr. Remedy, Eedris Abdulkareem is a Nigerian hip hop artist who claims Kano State, Nigeria, as his state of origin. Part of his name, Abdulkareem, loosely translates to "servant of the generous God." His music career began in 1996 with the hip hop band the Remedies, and his first solo album, *P.A.S.S.* (*Pains and Stress = Success*) was released in 2002 on Kennis Music (1998–), a label he remained with until 2005. The album features what is arguably the first ever diss track by a Nigerian rapper, "Wackawickee MCs." His second album, titled *Mr. Lecturer* (2002), spawned his first video hit, "Mr. Lecturer," which is about abuses in the Nigerian educational system. As of 2018, *Mr. Lecturer* is his best-selling album. His third album, *Jaga Jaga* (2004), was banned from radio airplay (it continued to be played in nightclubs) because it focused on political corruption in Nigeria.

In 2004, he gained international attention and was subsequently blacklisted after a scuffle with American rapper 50 Cent (1975–): To protest how poorly local artists were treated when compared to foreign artists, Eedris Abdulkareem took 50 Cent's seat on an ADC Airlines plane going from the Murtala Muhammad Airport in Lagos to Port Harcourt, Nigeria. This resulted in a fight between both rappers' entourages. Eedris Abdulkareem publicly apologized in 2007.

In 2005, he launched his own record label, La Kreem Music (2005–), in Lagos and released his fourth album, *Letter to Mr. President*. Since then he has released *King Is Back* (2007*) and *Unfinished Business* (2010*), and as of 2018 he is reportedly working on a new album. His music is informed by synthesized beats combined with traditional instrumentation, which is fused with Jamaican and reggae rhythms. His raps often take the form of dialogues between himself and guest rappers, as in "Mr. Lecturer," which is structured completely as a prosaic dialogue between a female student and her professor. His vocal delivery is measured and carefully articulated, and he often makes use of vocal effects such as autotuning. He is the founder of the Eedris Abdulkareem Foundation, a fundraising organization dedicated to fighting the spread of HIV and AIDS in sub-Saharan Africa.

Anthony J. Fonseca

See also: Nigeria; Political Hip Hop

Further Reading

Shonekan, Stephanie. 2011. "Sharing Hip Hop Cultures: The Case of Nigerians and African Americans." *American Behavioral Scientist* 55, no. 1: 9–23.

Shonekan, Stephanie. 2012. "Nigerian Hip Hop: Exploring a Black World Hybrid." In *Hip Hop Africa: New African Music in a Globalizing World*, edited by Eric Charry, chap. 7. Bloomington: Indiana University Press.

Egypt

Egypt had a youth scene that was first exposed to hip hop in the 1990s. DJs began playing American rap in nightclubs in the early 2000s, and an underground Egyptian hip hop scene that blended hip hop rhymes with historic Arabic instruments such as the *oud* (a lute) and the Egyptian flute, as well as sampling from classical and traditional Egyptian music, emerged. The group Asfalt, featuring Ibrahim Farouk (n.d.), Mohamed Gad (n.d.), and Mohamed El Deeb (1984–), formed in 2005; Asfalt intentionally distanced itself from mainstream popular (*habibi*) music culture, which band members considered a vapid distraction, choosing instead to raise social awareness about issues such as unemployment, poverty, drugs, sexual harassment, religious discrimination, governmental oppression, and the economy.

THEMES, CENSORSHIP, AND REVOLUTION

Arabian Knightz, which formed in 2005 with members Rush (Karim Adel, 1986*–), Sphinx (Hesham Abed, 1982*–), and E-Money (Ehab Adel, 1981*–), performed despite a dictatorship that actively sought to quash underground protest music and flooded public spaces with pro-regime pop music. Arabian Knightz and other underground hip hop acts received frequent warnings from and were often censored by the Egyptian Ministry of Culture, though it was able to release some music on the Internet. When the January 2011 revolution that led to the ousting of President Hosni Mubarak (1928–, in office 1981–2011) erupted, Arabian Knightz released "Rebel," an unmixed song with raw lyrics that went viral on the Internet. With its extensive sampling of American rapper Lauryn Hill's (1975–) song "I Find It Hard to Say (Rebel)" (2002) and lyrics in both Arabic and English, "Rebel" energized Egyptian revolutionaries and made their cause international. After the revolution, Arabian Knightz was able to release a long-awaited debut LP (delayed since 2008 by censors), *Uknighted State of Arabia* (2012), a product of an extensive collaboration with musicians known as the Arab League (2000–2010)*, with the assistance of American producer Fredwreck (aka Fredwreck Nassar, Farid Karam Nassar, 1972–).

Egyptian rappers have frequently rapped about hegemonic powers, both international and local. Prior to the revolution, any references to President Mubarak were subtle or indirect for fear of reprisals, whereas direct references to the leaders of foreign nations could be bitingly sarcastic, as in "Obama" (2009) by Ahmed Tharwat (aka Zap, n.d.), in which he derided the Egyptian people for welcoming President Barack Obama (1961–, in office 2009–2017), thereby not maintaining their cultural dignity. After the revolution, Egyptian rappers have rapped more freely about the Egyptian government, as in Arabian Knightz's 2013 hit "We Are the Government," which expresses opposition to all forms of government along with the desire for the Egyptian people to take governmental power into their own hands.

Since the 2011 revolution, Egyptian hip hop has expanded tremendously with the growing popularity of acts such as F Killa (aka Flow Killer, Al Moukatel, n.d.), MC Ahmed Amin (n.d.), MTM (1999–2004*), Y Crew Family (2005–), and Wara2a B-100 (2011–). As Egyptian hip hop edges closer to the mainstream, its artists continue to shape their messages to expose prevailing social and political realities and inspire their audiences to imagine new alternatives.

Jennifer L. Roth-Burnette

See also: France

Further Reading

Aidi, Hishaam. 2011. "The Grand (Hip Hop) Chessboard Race, Rap and *Raison d'Etat*." *Middle East Report* 260: 25–39.

Gana, N. 2012. "Rap and Revolt in the Arab World." *Social Text* 30, no. 4 (113): 25–53.

Robertson, Craig. 2015. "Whose Music, Whose Country? Music, Mobilization, and Social Change in North Africa." *African Conflict and Peacebuilding Review* 5, no. 1: 66–87.

Swedenburg, Ted. 2012. "Egypt's Music of Protest from Sayyid Darwish to DJ Haha." *Middle East Report* 265: 39–43.

Weis, Ellen R. 2016. "Egyptian Hip Hop: Expressions from the Underground." *Cairo Papers in Social Science*, Vol. 34, no. 1. Cairo: American University in Cairo Press.

Further Listening

MTM. 2004. *My Phone Is Ringing!* Kelma Records.

EL

(aka E.L., LOMI, Elom Adablah, 1986–, Accra, Ghana)

EL is a Ghanaian rapper and sound-recording engineer, producer, and executive whose musical styles include hip hop, hiplife, *azonto*, and R&B. He raps in English, Ga (spoken in southeastern Ghana and in the capital, Accra), Twi, Ewe, and pidgin English. His debut album, *Something Else* (2012), and his second solo album, *ELOM (Everybody Loves Original Music)* (2016) received critical acclaim, and EL has had several hit songs, including "Obuu Mo" ("You Don't Respect" in Ga), "Kaalu" ("Behave"), "One Ghana," "Mame Wossop," and "Auntie Martha," from his debut album alone. EL's voice is in the baritone range, though frequently he is autotuned. He is nevertheless known for effortlessly switching between several languages while rapping, as well as for composing memorable melodic lines. His themes range from the musical experience to romantic breakups, from praising God and those who support him to sexual fantasies and street life.

EL grew up in Dansoman, a suburb in Accra, Ghana. He was an academically strong student who exhibited musical talent as a teen. From 2002 to 2005, EL joined Ghanaian rapper and singer Jayso's (Paul Nuamah Donkor, 1983–) collective Skillions (Skills in a Million, aka the Skillions, 1999*–). In 2008, during his freshman year at the University of Ghana, Legon, while working on economics and political science degrees, EL signed to Skillions Records (2008–), Jayso's independent record company in Accra. Skillions produced the mixtape *Skillionaires* (2009), the first Ghanaian hip hop mixtape. EL stayed with the label until he graduated and pursued a solo career as a rapper and producer. In 2012, EL owned his first studio in Asylum Down, back in Accra, and released the hip hop single "Chale (So Fli)" ("Friend [So Fly]" in Ga); that same year, he took a risk by investing all his funds into new equipment and acquired a studio in Osu, close to Accra's central business district and livelier nightlife.

Something Else, released and globally distributed by Akwaaba Music (2008–) in 2013, earned EL the Ghana Music Awards Album of the Year. This highly successful album was followed in 2014 and 2015 by *B.A.R. (The Best African Rapper*

Album) and *B.A.R. 2*, which featured some of the most prominent Ghanaian rappers of the 2010s, including Sarkodie (1985–), Edem (Denning Edem Hotor, 1986–), and Joey B (Darryl Paa Kwesi Bannerman-Martin, 1989–). In *ELOM*, EL collaborated with both Ghanaian and Nigerian rappers. The latter included American-born Banky W (Oluwabankole Wellington, 1981–) and Phyno (Chibuzor Nelson Azubuike, 1986–).

In 2015, EL received the Ghana Music Awards Rapper of the Year, followed in 2016 by the Ahana Music Awards Hiplife/Hip Hop Artist of the Year and Producer of the Year. Even more notable is EL's production career; in just one year (2011), he produced such works by Ghanaian hip hop and hiplife artists as Sarkodie's "You Go Kill Me" (also featuring EL), D-Black's (Desmond Kwesi Blackmore, 1986–) "Get on da Dance Floor" and the "Godfather of Hiplife," and Reggie Rockstone's (Reginald Yaw Asante Ossei, late 1960s–) "Rockstone's Office" (1990*).

Melissa Ursula Dawn Goldsmith

See also: Ghana

Further Reading

Collins, John. 2012. "Contemporary Ghanaian Popular Music since the 1980s." In *Hip Hop Africa: New African Music in a Globalizing World*, edited by Eric Charry, chap. 10. Bloomington: Indiana University Press.

Shipley, Jesse Weaver. 2013. "Transnational Circulation and Digital Fatigue in Ghana's Azonto Dance Craze." *American Ethnologist* 40, no. 2: 362–81.

Further Listening

EL. 2012. *Something Else.* Akwaaba Music.

El Salvador

El Salvador is a small but densely populated Central America nation of over six million, consisting largely of indigenous and European mestizos, including the Cuzcatlecs, the Lenca, and the Maya. After being a Spanish and then a Mexican colony, it became sovereign in 1841, but with a history of political and economic instability as well as authoritarian rulers, ultimately leading to the Salvadoran Civil War (1979–1992), the result being a multiparty constitutional republic. It continues to struggle with poverty and crime. Salvadoran music is influenced by indigenous peoples (Lenca, Cacaopera, Pipil, and Mayans) and the Spanish, with popular styles being *cumbia* and rock as well as traditional music. Hip hop was introduced after 1992 as a result of diaspora, immigration, and deportation from the United States.

Salvadoran hip hop emerged in the late 1990s in the United States with groups such as Reyes del Bajo Mundo (aka RDBM, 1992–) and Crooked Stilo (1991–). New York City–based Reyes del Bajo Mundo was the first Salvadoran-born hip hop group heard on mainstream radio in El Salvador, and East Los Angeles–based brother duo Crooked Stilo created a hybrid form of rap based on music of their Spanish heritage. These early rap crews inspired rappers in El Salvador, leading to groups such as Pescozada (Slap or Punch, 1998–) and Mecate (literally "rope," not to be confused with El Mecate, 1998–). The duo Pescozada, from Chalatenango, is produced by San Francisco-based Salvadoran Omnionn (Agustin Anaya, n.d.), who became a band member. Its members rap in Spanish about politics and the aftermath of the Salvadoran Civil War. A controversial and censored group, Mecate infuses its socially conscious rap with humor and has achieved fame with the drum-and-bass rap "En Directo" (n.d.), about an underage gangsta style killer.

Anthony J. Fonseca

See also: Cumbia Rap; Gangsta Rap; Guatemala; Political Hip Hop; The United States

Further Reading

Alejandro, Jacky. 2014. "Hip Hop Is Not Dead: The Emergence of Mara Salvatrucha Rap as a Form of MS-13 Expressive Culture." *Alternativas: Latin American Cultural Studies Journal* 2, no. 1: 1–19.

Almeida, Paul, and Ruben Urbizagastegui. 1999. "Cutumay Camones: Popular Music in El Salvador's National Liberation Movement." *Latin American Perspectives* 26, no. 2: 13–42.

Further Listening

Pescozada. 2010. *Anarquía Club Social.* Istmo Urban.

eLDee

(aka eLDee the Don, Lanre Dabiri, 1977–, Kaduna, Nigeria)

eLDee is a Nigerian rapper, record producer, activist, and architect (he studied architecture at the University of Lagos) known for both his solo career and his membership in Trybesmen (aka Da Trybe, 1998–2005), a band considered to be one of the pioneers of Nigerian hip hop, with two 1999 hit singles, "Trybal Marks" and "Shake Bodi," and two 2002 hits, "Work It Out" and "Oya," as well as the 2005 album *BIG Picture.*

He has released five solo albums, *Long Time Coming* (2004), *Return of the King* (2006), *Big Boy* (2008), *Is It Your Money* (2010), and *Undeniable* (2012). He also founded his own independent label, Trybe Records, at first to support Trybesmen, but eventually supporting new artists. His Afropop music is a blend of African beats, reggae, and hip hop. His songs are about a variety of issues, but all of them, including his protest songs such as "One Day" (2010), are upbeat, synthesizer-based melodies.

His vocals are mainly in English and are gentle when sung and soft-spoken when rapped, and he makes liberal use of vocal processors, especially with doubling and autotuning. Some of his hits include "Bosi Gbangba" (2010), "Category" (2012), "Champion" (2006), "Higher" (2012), and "I Go Yarn" (2006). In 2002, elDee moved to Atlanta, where he recorded his first two solo albums. He supports various causes, such as African sustainability and gay rights in Nigeria (and Africa). He views discrimination against gays as equivalent to discrimination against particular races or religions.

Anthony J. Fonseca

See also: Nigeria; Political Hip Hop

Further Reading

Clark, Msia Kibona. 2013. "Representing Africa! Trends in Contemporary African Hip Hop." *Journal of Pan African Studies* 6, no. 3: 1–4.

Shipley, Jesse Weaver. 2017. "Parody after Identity: Digital Music and the Politics of Uncertainty in West Africa." *American Ethnologist* 44, no. 2: 249–62.

Shonekan, Stephanie. 2012. "Nigerian Hip Hop: Exploring a Black World Hybrid." In *Hip Hop Africa: New African Music in a Globalizing World*, edited by Eric Charry, chap. 7. Bloomington: Indiana University Press.

Further Listening

eLDee. 2012. *Undeniable.* Trybe Records.

The Electric Boogaloos

(1977–, Fresno, California)

The Electric Boogaloos were an early West Coast funk and hip hop dance crew. Boogaloo Sam (Sam Solomon, 1959–) created the crew after watching late-1960s television dancers who were using the locking technique in their moves. His idea was to combine the dime-stopping moves of locking and the associated stiff, rigid moves of roboting (aka botting) with moves that were so smooth, relaxed, and flowing that they gave the impression the dancer had no bones. His new dance, which he debuted around 1975, the boogaloo (aka boog or electric boogaloo), named after the song called "James Brown's Boo-Ga-Loo" (1966) by James Brown (1933–2006), was part of the illusory styles of dance that were becoming vogue at the time, such as locking, roboting, strobing, and tutting (moving the arms and hands in an angular fashion to create the illusion of Egyptian hieroglyphs). Boogaloo Sam's new style was loose and fluid, designed to mimic cartoons and animated movies through circular rolls of the hips, knees, and head.

Once he polished the moves, Boogaloo Sam decided to create a dance crew, which he originally called the Electronic Boogaloo Lockers. He recruited and trained his brother Timothy (1961–), who then took the stage name Pop'in Pete. Along with a few other dancers, the brothers went to Hollywood and danced on the streets to boombox music they supplied themselves. The crew made little in tips but were approached by an agent who told them to audition for Jeff Kutash (1945–), a dancer and choreographer who ran a traveling Las Vegas–type show. The Electric Boogaloos immediately impressed Kutash and were hired. The original Electric Boogaloos were Boogaloo Sam, Pop'in Pete, Robot Dane (Dane Parker, n.d.), Puppet Boozer (Marvin Boozer, n.d.), Creep'n Sid (Cedric Williams, 1959–), and Scarecrow Scalley (Gary Allen, n.d.). Boogaloo Sam's cousin, Stephen Nichols (n.d.), was already a locker (a dancer who uses the locking technique) who wanted to join the crew, so he trained in popping, joined the crew, and took the stage name Skeeter Rabbit. Other dancers who joined the crew in later years included the Bronx-based and ex–Rock Steady Crew dancer Mr. Wiggles (Steffan Clemente, n.d.) and liquid animation dance specialist Boogaloo Shrimp (Michael Chambers, 1967–).

The Electric Boogaloos are known for their costumes and showmanship, as some members dance both in highly choreographed unison and as soloists, solos being performed while other members strike a freeze pose (typically with all dancers frozen in a geometric pattern). The solos are designed to emphasize each member's individual skills and strengths as well as serve as a signature move, normally telegraphed by the dancer's stage name (e.g., "Boogaloo" for a dancer who specializes in boogaloo, "Pop'in" for a popper/locker, "Robot" for a dancer who bots, and "Creep'n" for a dancer who specializes in floating or the moonwalk). The Electric Boogaloos helped popularize not only the dance they called electric boogaloo but also the techniques of popping, locking, creeping (aka floating or the moonwalk), and puppeting. The techniques of the electric boogaloo, however, differ from most of these other dances' techniques, which are based on flexing the muscles and using stiff, dime-stop moves that usually emphasize upper body movements.

The electric boogaloo is based on the idea of using fluid movements that emphasize the lower body, since the dance is leg oriented, with emphasis on hip rolling while the knees remain loose and bent and the feet continually slide. The head is often involved in the rotation as well. Some of its characteristic moves had names such as Crazy Legs, Neck-o-flex, Twist-o-flex, and the Walk-out (which has become common in popping).

Anthony J. Fonseca

See also: Hip Hop Dance; Popping and Locking; The Robot; The United States

Further Reading

Fuhrer, Margaret. 2014. "Urban and Commercial Dance." In *American Dance: The Complete Illustrated History*, chap. 10. Minneapolis, MN: Voyageur Press.

Guzman-Sanchez, Thomas. 2012. *Underground Dance Masters: Final History of a Forgotten Era*. Santa Barbara, CA: Praeger.

Elliott, Missy

(aka Missy "Misdemeanor" Elliott, Melissa Arnette Elliott, 1971–, Portsmouth, Virginia)

Missy Elliott is an American hip hop record producer, recording artist, rapper, and dancer. She is best known for her collaboration with Norfolk, Virginia, native producer, music mixer, and rapper Timbaland (Timothy Zachery Mosley, 1972–). Their musical partnership netted five consecutive Platinum and multi-Platinum albums, including Elliott's debut, *Supa Dupa Fly* (1997), released on Goldmind (1997–), her independent label in partnership with Elektra Records (1950–). Aside from her own albums, Elliott has produced for various musicians over three decades: Aaliyah (Aaliyah Dana Haughton, 1979–2001), Monica (Monica Denise Brown, 1980–), Tweet (Charlene Keys, 1972–), Blaque (1996–2005), Fantasia (Fantasia Monique Barrino, 1984–), and Jazmine Sullivan (1987–), to name just a few. Elliott has had six songs reach the Top 10 of the Billboard Hot 100 chart, and she was featured on six other Top 10 songs by various artists. Overall, she has had 17 solo singles and 25 singles where she is a featured guest rapper hit the Hot 100. Elliott is also known for a shyness that is uncharacteristic of hip hop and rap performers, although she possesses a great camera presence and a willingness to don oddball costumes and makeup for performances and videos.

EARLY MUSIC CAREER

Elliott did not start out as a solo act. Her first band was a female R&B group called Sista (1993–1994), which produced one album on the Elektra label in 1994, *4 All the Sistas around da World*, and one single, "Brand New." It was on *4 All the Sistas around da World* that Elliott began working with Timbaland, as well as hip hop artists and groups from Hampton, Virginia, such as Jodeci (1988–1996, 2014–) member and producer DeVante Swing (Donald Earle DeGrate Jr., 1969–), for whom Sista (then called Fayze) performed a cold a cappella audition after a concert; Elliott would later pen lyrics on two Jodeci albums.

Missy Elliott is a Grammy Award–winning American hip hop record producer, recording artist, rapper, and dancer, who is also known for her appearances in music videos. Five of her six albums have been certified Platinum. (Gary Gershoff/Getty Images for VH1)

Elliott became a member of the Swing Mob Collective (aka Da Bassment Cru, 1991–1995), a group of artists working in Norfolk, Virginia, with Swing, including the rap duo Timbaland and Magoo (1989–), singers Ginuwine (Elgin Baylor Lumpkin, 1970–) and Tweet, and hip hop band Playa (1990–2003, 2007–), among others. This collaboration allowed her to work on recordings for artists such as Aaliyah and SWV (Sisters with Voices, 1990–1998, 2005–). By the end of 1995, Swing Mob had dispersed, but Elliott and Timbaland worked together as a songwriting and production team, cowriting and coproducing nine tracks for Aaliyah's multi-Platinum *One in a Million* (1996), with Elliott contributing vocals and rapping to various tracks. She was also a featured vocalist for Puff Daddy's (1969–) Bad Boy Records (1993–), performing on remixes and songwriting and acting as arranger, composer, executive producer, performer, mixer, and vocalist on Nicole's (Nicole Monique Wray, 1981–) certified-Gold album *Make It Hot* (1998), released on Elliott's Goldmind label (1997–). Elliott finally went solo in 1997 with *Supa Dupa Fly*, produced by Timbaland, which reached No. 3 on the Billboard 200 and spawned a hit single, "Sock It 2 Me," which peaked at No. 12 on the Hot 100 and was her second Top 10 hit in New Zealand. The album was certified Platinum and was Grammy nominated for Best Rap Album.

Timbaland produced her next three albums, *Da Real World* (1999), *Miss E . . . So Addictive* (2001), and *Under Construction* (2002), which all went Platinum in the United States, with *Under Construction* being certified double Platinum. The three spawned four Top 10 singles on the Hot 100, including "Hot Boyz" (No. 5), "Get Ur Freak On" (No. 7), "Work It" (No. 2), and "Gossip Folks" (No. 8), as well as "One Minute Man" (No. 15). "Get Ur Freak On," "Work It," and another single, "Scream (aka Itchin')" earned her Grammies for Best Female Rap Solo Performance (Elliott has been nominated 21 times and has won five Grammies). The latter two albums charted in Australia, Belgium, Germany, Ireland, the Netherlands, New Zealand/Aotearoa, Sweden, Switzerland, and the United Kingdom, making Elliott an international star.

Elliott also became a music video fixture, not only in her own videos but as a featured artist in videos for other artists. Among her videos was a double music video directed by David Meyers (1980–) for the songs "Take Away" and "4 My People," the former serving as a moving tribute to Aaliyah, with dancers and Elliott dressed in funereal white, and the latter containing post-9/11 scenes of hundreds of dancers wearing various hues of red, white, and blue dancing in front of a red-and-white-striped flag with a blue "M" in the middle and Elliott dressed in pastel versions of red, white, and blue. Also in 2001, she coproduced "Lady Marmalade" for *Moulin Rouge! Music from Baz Luhrmann's Film*; the song reached No. 1 on the Billboard Hot 100. *Under Construction* became her best-selling album and received Grammy nominations for Best Rap Album and Album of the Year.

FIRST SELF-PRODUCED ALBUM

In 2004, Elliott costarred in a commercial for the clothing company Gap, Inc., with Madonna (1958–) and performed with her, Britney Spears (1981–), and Christina Aguilera (1980–) at the 2003 MTV Video Music Awards. Her fifth album, *This Is Not a Test!* (2003), was also certified Platinum and produced the Top 40 hit "Pass That Dutch," which peaked at No. 27. In 2005, she released the certified-Gold album *The Cookbook*, her first solo album not produced by Timbaland (it spawned the hit "Lose Control," which peaked at No. 3 on the Billboard Hot 100), and she tried her hand with a (short-lived) reality show on the UPN Network (1995–), *The Road to Stardom with Missy Elliott*. *The Cookbook* received five Grammy nominations, and the "Lose Control" video won a Grammy. She won Best Female Hip Hop Artist at the 2005 American Music Awards and was nominated for Best International Female Artist at the 2006 BRIT Awards (the British Phonographic Industry's annual pop music awards).

Since *The Cookbook*, Elliott has taken a hiatus from recording solo albums, although in 2016 she released the single "WTF (Where They From)" with the promise of an upcoming album. Since 2005, she has concentrated on writing and production, with songs that have reached No. 1 on the Hot R&B/Hip-Hop Songs charts: "Let It Go" (2007) by Keyshia Cole (1981–), "Need You Bad" (2008) by Jazmine Sullivan, and "Everything to Me" (2010) by Monica. Since 2008, she has written and/or produced Grammy-nominated songs for Cole, Fantasia, Jennifer Hudson (1981–), Monica, and Sullivan, and in 2013, she received a Grammy nomination for the collaborative song "Without Me." In 2015, Elliott performed at the Super Bowl XLIX halftime show. Elliott's temporary hiatus has also been explained as a result of her being diagnosed with Graves' disease in 2008.

MUSICAL STYLES

Elliott's musical style has changed throughout her career. She began with more of an R&B version of hip hop, as with her hit "The Rain," which samples "I Can't Stand the Rain," a hit for Ann Peebles (1947–) in 1973, or "Sock It 2 Me," which features Elliott's singing in a typical R&B style; Elliott's rapping style at that point was laid-back and low-key. In *Da Real World*, she and Timbaland experiment with a harsher, urban sound that has more sexual energy, and the album and individual songs include her trademark song intros, which usually include ad-libbed talking and erotic vocalizations. The album's hits, "Hot Boyz" and "She's a B—," prefigure the sound she would perfect in *Miss E . . . So Addictive* and *Under Construction*. In fact, "She's a B—" marks one of Elliott's earliest uses of nonsense rhymes and humorous vocalizations (sometimes called cartoons) juxtaposed against a driving beat and syncopated rhythms created between synthesizer and drum, techniques that inform many of the songs on her next albums.

Her rapping style also became more breathless and included much more profanity, often for comic effect. *Miss E . . . So Addictive* begins with a humorous R&B profanity-laden intro ballad that morphs into a club beat that borrows from funk; the remainder of the album is mainly funk-infused rap songs intended for club dancing, with humorous interludes and comic lyrics, as in "Minute Man." The album shows her experimentation with beats, as in "Get Ur Freak On," which borrows from Eastern music and uses a synthesized, sped-up *tumbi* voice to create its beat, as well as her use of musical surprises, in this case vocalizations to fill space and create comic moments, such as an operatic voice singing profanity and the refrain of "Hello!" The tracks "4 My People" and "Watcha Gonna Do" feature breathing, screams, growls, and grunts, which help establish the beat early and then become part of the instrumentation. In addition, her rapping becomes faster and her voice more sultry, using deeper vocal registers in "Scream (aka Itchin)" and "Watcha Gonna Do."

Miss E . . . So Addictive's lyrics tell of her musical dominance. Many of the same techniques, especially the use of spoken intros, appear on *Under Construction*, which begins with references to East Coast versus West Coast feuding, Aaliyah's death, and the 9/11 tragedy. The intro morphs into a club beat with the phrase "Let the show begin," which introduces "Go to the Floor." In "Work It," Elliott and Timbaland experiment with lyrics in reverse, and in "Gossip Folks," with children's voices. *The Cookbook* shows even more experimentation with beats, as in "Lose Control," which contains synthesized video game sounds in an ascending scale, combined with frenetic vocal layering. The album also reintroduces old-style hip hop techniques, such as scratching and the use of R&B.

Anthony J. Fonseca

See also: Dirty Rap; Timbaland; The United States

Further Reading

Bezdecheck, Bethany. 2009. *Missy Elliott*. Library of Hip Hop Biographies. New York: Rosen.

Lane, Nikki. 2011. "Black Women Queering the Mic: Missy Elliott Disturbing the Boundaries of Racialized Sexuality and Gender." *Journal of Homosexuality* 58, nos. 6–7: 775–92.

Witherspoon, Nia O. 2017. " 'Beep, Beep, Who Got the Keys to the Jeep?': Missy's Trick as (Un)Making Queer." *Journal of Popular Culture* 50, no. 4: 871–95.

Further Listening

Elliott, Missy. 2001. *Missy E . . . So Addictive*. Elektra.

Elliott, Missy. 2003. *This Is Not a Test!* Elektra.

Elliott, Missy. 2005. *The Cookbook*. Atlantic.

Eminem

(Marshall Bruce Mathers III, 1972–, St. Joseph, Missouri)

Eminem is one of the best-known and most successful rappers in the United States, with a transatlantic following and a consecutive series of chart-topping and award-winning albums. Based in Detroit, he is also well known as a record producer and an actor, and as a white rapper has become a central figure in the public and academic conversation on the negotiation of race in rap as well as the conversation on homophobia, misogyny, and violence. *The Slim Shady LP* (1999) launched a long string of successes accompanied by international fame. Since then, Eminem has earned 15 Grammy Awards, including six for Best Rap Album: *The Slim Shady LP*, *The Marshall Mathers LP* (2000), *The Eminem Show* (2002), *Relapse* (2009), *Recovery* (2010), and *The Marshall Mathers LP2* (2013). He has also earned four for Best Rap Solo Performance: "My Name Is" (1999), "The Real Slim Shady" (2000), "Lose Yourself" (2002), and "Not Afraid" (2010), and "Lose Yourself" won Best Male Rap Solo Performance. Despite the controversies that surround his music, Eminem has been wildly successful as a performer and producer, and Billboard lists him as the best-selling artist of the first decade of the 21st century.

FROM DROPOUT TO SUCCESSFUL RAPPER

Eminem dropped out of high school after he had been held back several times in ninth grade, and instead devoted his time to his rapping career. Though his first album, *Infinite* (1996), performed poorly, his lyrical dexterity in the 1997 Rap Olympics in Los Angeles won him the mentorship of Dr. Dre (1965–), who signed him to his record label, Aftermath Entertainment (1996–), and coproduced *The Slim Shady LP*. His 2010 Recovery Tour took him around the globe to Europe, Australia,

Asia, and South Africa as well as North America, and his 2014 Rapture Tour traveled Australia, New Zealand, South Africa, and England.

In 1999, Eminem created his own record label, New York City–based Shady Records, and has since produced records for 50 Cent (1975–), Obie Trice (1974–), and his band D12 (aka the Dirty Dozen, 1996–). As an actor, he gave a critically acclaimed performance as Jimmy "B-Rabbit" Smith in the American film *8 Mile* (2002). He also won an Academy Award for Best Original Song for the single he wrote for this movie ("Lose Yourself"), the first hip hop track to earn this distinction.

LYRICAL CONTENT AND PERSONAL ISSUES

Eminem's lyrics tend toward the extremely violent, misogynistic, and homophobic. In fact, when *The Slim Shady LP* was released, it raised concerns not only in conservative circles but also in the wider public sphere. The lyrics to "Guilty Conscience," for instance, unambiguously encourage men to kill their wives if they cheat. Eminem attempted to quell these concerns by insisting that he was performing as his delinquent alter ego named Slim Shady, but his subsequent releases were informed by the same themes; he continues to illustrate intimate-partner violence in his songs and to employ homophobic and transphobic slurs, although his friendship and artistic partnership with Elton John (Reginald Kenneth Dwight, 1947–) has silenced some of his critics in this area. Eminem's relationship with these issues, however, is more complex than surface criticisms suggest, and he has demonstrated a high degree of self-awareness.

In 2000, Eminem acknowledged the negative influence his music could have on fans in his single "Stan," featuring the British singer Dido (Florian Cloud de Bounevialle Armstrong, 1971–). "Stan" is the story of an obsessed fan who unravels when Eminem doesn't respond to his letters, acting out some of the same violence found in Eminem's albums. The song ends with Eminem's responding to Stan, but realizing too late that Stan has already killed himself and his pregnant girlfriend. "Love the Way You Lie" (2010), recorded with guest artist Rihanna (1988–), who had in 2009 weathered a very public domestic violence incident, presents the destructive cycle of abuse through the guise of Eminem's relationship with his ex-wife, Kimberly Anne Scott (n.d.). In 2000, he released the single "Kim," in which he vividly imagines killing her. In contrast, his "Love the Way You Lie," which perpetuates society's tendency to blame the victim and exonerate the abuser, is a carefully considered commentary on the escalation and negotiation of abuse. It has been embraced by some as a song that opened up a public space for addressing the complexities of intimate-partner violence. In both songs, however, Eminem refuses responsibility—in "Stan," he tells Stan that he shouldn't follow the examples found in music, since musicians adopt personae in songs; this places the onus squarely on Stan.

Ironically, these very issues of misogyny, violence, and homophobia may have fueled much of Eminem's success. White rappers have historically had a difficult time breaking into the industry, often charged with appropriating and fetishizing black culture. Eminem has counteracted this accusation by fully engaging with rap's quest for personal authenticity. He simultaneously accepts that rap is black music, without attempting to sound or act black, and instead embraces his whiteness. His single "My Name Is" explicitly references numerous tropes and icons from white culture: the teacher, the doctor, a disdain for parents, a love of Nine Inch Nails (1988–), and the Incredible Hulk. Further, he has forged a white identity of his own that puts him outside the mainstream, stressing his hard-earned street credentials, his abusive and violent tendencies (he has amassed several assault charges), his crude and offensive lyrics, and his white trash background. These traits have imbued him with a level of authenticity that other white rappers have been unable to achieve, earning him an impressively large and autonomous place in the rap community. In 2017, he was greeted with both accolades and criticism when he dissed current president Donald Trump (1946–) in one of his live performances.

Jessica Leah Getman

See also: Dr. Dre; D12; Gangsta Rap; The United States

Further Reading

Kajikawa, Loren. 2009. "Eminem's 'My Name Is': Signifying Whiteness, Rearticulating Race." *Journal of the Society for American Music* 3, no. 3: 341–63.

Thaller, Jonel, and Jill Theresa Messing. 2014. "(Mis)Perceptions around Intimate Partner Violence in the Music Video and Lyrics for 'Love the Way You Lie.'" *Feminist Media Studies* 14, no. 4: 623–39.

Further Listening

Eminem. 1999. *The Slim Shady LP.* Aftermath Entertainment/Interscope Records.

Eminem. 2000. *The Marshall Mathers LP.* Aftermath Entertainment/Interscope Records.

Eminem. 2010. *Recovery.* Aftermath Entertainment/Interscope/Shady Records.

Enow, Stanley

(aka Bayangi Boy, Stanley Ebai Enow, 1986–, Bamenda, Cameroon)

Stanley Enow is a Cameroonian rapper, record label owner, voice actor, and radio and TV presenter. His best-known hit single "Hein père" ("Hey/All Right, Father," 2013) fuses hip hop, high life, EDM, and traditional music from Cameroon. It reached No. 1 on ReverbNation's Cameroon list and on Trace Africa's Top 10 Songs. Enow sings and raps in French, English, and pidgin languages. Most active musically with rapping, Enow has a background in writing and earned a bachelor's degree in journalism from the University of Douala in Cameroon. He also has some dancing background, having studied breakdancing in his teens.

In 2013, he won Male Artist of the Year and Urban Artist of the Year at the first Cameroon Academy Awards, and in 2014 he was the first Cameroonian to win Best New Act at the MTV Africa Music Awards. Both awards were also for "Hein père." His second single, "TumbuBoss," from an EP of the same title (2014), was also a hit.

In 2015, he released his first album, *Soldier Like Ma Papa*, which was produced by his co-owned record label, Motherland Empire (2013*–) in Douala, Cameroon.

The album is a tribute to his father, who was in the Cameroon Army. The album combines ragamuffin music, R&B, and rap and features hip hop artists from Cameroon, the Dominican Republic of Congo, Ghana, Nigeria, and South Africa, including Sarkodie (1985–) from Ghana and Ice Prince (1986–) from Nigeria. Enow's acclaim has been on the rise since "Hein père" and his follow-up hit single "TumbuBoss."

Melissa Ursula Dawn Goldsmith

See also: Cameroon

Further Reading

Anon. 2017. "Stanley Enow: His Eyes on Nigerian Market." *The Day* (Lagos, Nigeria), July 23.

Mofokeng, Lesley. 2017. "Hot Artist Making Sweet Music." *Sowetan* (Johannesburg, South Africa), December 1.

EPMD

(1986–1993, 2006–, Brentwood, Long Island, New York)

EPMD, an acronym for Erick and Parrish Making Dollars, is an American hip hop duo consisting of MC Erick Sermon (aka Green-Eyed Bandit, 1968–) and MC PMD (aka Parrish the Microphone Doctor, Parrish Smith, 1968–). The band was originally called EEPMD, for Easy Erick and Parrish the Microphone Doctor, but the name was changed to EPMD to be more marketable and to avoid any confusion with Eazy-E (1964–1995). Sermon and PMD have worked with various DJs (turntablists), but since 2012 they have been touring with Grammy-nominated producer DJ Scratch (George Spivey, 1968–). The band had six certified-Gold albums, and its biggest hit was the satirical "Crossover" (1992), about rappers who sold out. EPMD's sound can be categorized by the term cool funk, in that both rappers used a laid-back delivery; Sermon's heavy accent, which is sometimes confused with slurring; the liberal use of samples, loops, and heavy bass or synth beats; and a slow to moderate tempo.

The duo started rapping together in 1986 after meeting in high school and debuted in 1988 with the certified-Gold album *Strictly Business* ("business" is used in every one of the duo's album titles), which reached No. 80 on the Billboard 200 and included two songs that charted on Billboard's Hot R&B/Hip-Hop Songs chart: "You Got's To Chill" (No. 22) and "Strictly Business" (No. 25). The album sold 300,000 copies in one day and established the duo's mastery for funk and rock sampling; on one song alone they sampled from Public Enemy (1982–), the Steve Miller Band (1966–), Kool and the Gang (1964–), and ZZ Top (1969–). The album, distributed by Priority Records (1985–), also introduced their "Jane" sequence of songs about a troublesome relationship. Having signed with Sleeping Bag Records (1981–), they were produced by Kurtis Mantronik (Kurtis el Khaleel, 1965–), and their touring was managed by Russell Simmons (1957–) of Def Jam Recordings (1983–) and RUSH Communications (1991–), which resulted in rave reviews and high-profile appearances.

Their second album, *Unfinished Business* (1989), was also on Sleeping Bag; EPMD then moved to Def Jam for *Business as Usual* (1990) and *Business Never Personal* (1992), adopting a more aggressive, gangsta rap–influenced style. EPMD broke up briefly from 1993 to 1997 but reunited for the Gold records *Back in Business* (1997) and *Out of Business* (1999), the latter containing remixes with new vocals and new material; a second breakup and reunion led to *We Mean Business* (2008), which did not do as well. Both members of EPMD have released solo albums: MC Erick Sermon's *No Pressure* (1993), *Double or Nothing* (1995), *Def Squad Presents Erick Onasis* (2000), *Music* (2001), *React* (2002), *Chilltown, New York* (2004), and *E.S.P.* (2015), and MC PMD's *Shade Business* (1994), *Business Is Business* (1996), *Underground Connection* (2002), *The Awakening* (2003), and *Welcome to the Goondox* (2013), as well as MC PMD's collaboration with Tokyo's DJ Honda (Hōnda Katsuhiro, 1965–), *Underground Connection* (2002). MC Erick Sermon also created Def Squad Productions (1993–) in New York and recorded as part of the New York–based collective Def Squad and the Hit Squad (1990–1993, 2006–).

Anthony J. Fonseca

See also: The United States

Further Reading

Coleman, Brian. 2007. "EPMD: *Strictly Business*." In *Check the Technique: Liner Notes for Hip Hop Junkies*. New York: Villard.

Siblin, Eric. 1998. "These Rappers Mean Business: Erick and Parrish Are Back Chillin' Together—and EPMD Is Making Dollars Again." *The Gazette* (Montreal), February 19, F5.

Further Listening

EPMD. 1999. *Out of Business*. Def Jam Records.

Equatorial Guinea

Equatorial Guinea's capital city, Malabo, has hosted an International Hip Hop Festival, which celebrates African and European hip hop (using French and Spanish texts), since 2006. The festival promotes tourism, offering hip hop performances and workshops; however, Equatorial Guinea, which is isolated geographically, rarely produces popular music, so musicians usually travel to neighboring Cameroon or to Europe to record.

Hip hop likely emerged in Malabo in the early 1990s, where traditional music is part of everyday life and foreign popular music, including American rock, Jamaican reggae, Cameroonian *makossa*, Congo Basin's *soukous*, and Spanish acoustic guitar music, is popular. Traditional Bubi music is also popular not only to the largest minority, the Bubi, but also to Equatorial Guinea's majority, the Fang. The internationally known Equatoguinean duo Hijas Del Sol (Daughters of the Sun, 1992–) sing in Bubi and Spanish. This female duo is best known for their traditional, Afropop-, jazz-, and Latin-influenced recordings, and their album *Kchaba* (1999), produced in Madrid, employs turntablism. Female singer and rapper Yuma (Yolanda Ayingono, 1980–) was born in Evinayong and resides in Malabo. She raps primarily in the Fang language but at times weaves Spanish texts into songs about street life, sexuality, and self-improvement. Her album *La vida es tranki* (*Life Is Chill*, 2005) fuses hip hop with reggae, gospel, jazz, rhythm and blues, and traditional Central African music.

RAPPERS IN EXILE IN SPAIN

Several Equatoguinean rappers are born or reside in exile in Madrid. Jota Mayúscula (Jesús Bibang González, n.d.), of Equatoguinean and Spanish descent, is a turntablist, producer, and radio host. Since 1998, Mayúscula has collaborated with mostly Spanish hip hop artists in Spanish texts. In 2000, he pursued a solo career, with lyrics focusing on hardships in general and racism in particular. Female rapper and singer Mefe (anonymous, n.d.) used Spanish texts, though she is originally from Malabo. She combined hip hop with reggae and traditional West African music. Her debut, *Fuego: Street Album* (*Fire*, 2002), addressed social issues. The rapper El Negro Bey (Black Is Beautiful, anonymous, 1984–) was born in Bata, another hip hop center in Equatorial Guinea. His rapping texts are in Fang and criticize the atrocities of the Equatoguinean government, human-rights violations, and crime. El Negro Bey fuses hip hop with pan-African rhythms, such as from the Central African rumba, and uses slam poetry. His efforts include *Erosión* (*Erosion*, 2009) and *Reliquia* (*Relic*, 2011).

Ironically, former Vice President Teodoro Nguema Obiang Mangue (1969–, in office 2012–), the son of President Teodoro Obiang Nguema Mbasogo's (1942–, in office 1979–), is also a rapper; however, Mbasogo's regime is notorious for banning Equatoguinean rappers for criticizing the government.

Melissa Ursula Dawn Goldsmith

See also: Spain

Further Reading
Rice, Xan. 2005. "President's Playboy Son Splashes Out Pounds 1M(illion) in Luxury Car Spree." *The Times* (London), July 21, 35.
Seone, Nora Sala. 2011. "'Welcome to the Eccentric Circus': Youth, Rap Music, and the Appropriation of Power in Malabo (Equatorial Guinea)." *Scientific Journal of Humanistic Studies* 3, no. 5: 12–21.

Further Listening
Yuma. 2005. *La vida es tranki* (*Life Is Chill*). Rhythm and Flow.

Eric B. and Rakim

(1986–1993, 2016–, New York City, New York)

Eric B. and Rakim are a legendary American hip hop duo consisting of turntablist Eric B. (Louis Eric Barrier, 1965–) and MC Rakim Rakim (aka Rakim, The God MC, Kid Wizard, Rakim Allah, William Michael Griffin, 1968–). The duo is considered integral to the early development of rap music, especially during the latter half of the 1980s, heavily influencing the next wave of hip hop artists.

Eric B. grew up as a musician, playing trumpet, drums, and turntables while in high school in Queens, New York. He became a radio disc jockey under the moniker Eric B, and one of his jobs included promotions. On a promotional assignment, he inquired about available rappers and was introduced to Rakim, an 18-year-old jazz saxophone player and a member of the Nation of Gods and Earths (aka the Five Percent Nation, 1964–), who had been writing raps under the name Kid Wizard since he was a teenager in Wyandanch, a Long Island neighborhood. Rakim's brother worked at a plant where bootleg albums were pressed, so the duo had access to the fresh, new music it needed to DJ at parties. The two also sought a mentor, the legendary Marley Marl (1962–), whom Eric B. hired to engineer the duo's first single, "Eric B. Is President" (1986). After Def Jam Recordings (1983–) founder Russell Simmons (1957–) heard the single, he signed Eric B. and Rakim to Island Records (1959–), which owned the 4th and Broadway Records (aka 4th and B'way Records, 1984–) imprint.

ALBUMS AND SOUND

The duo's debut album, *Paid in Full* (1987), was characterized by Eric B.'s solid beats, heavy on the tom and kick drums, his sampled funk loops, and his liberal use of reverb and hiccups (the album contains three instrumentals), as well as Rakim's even, methodical vocal delivery and freestyle handling of rhythm; he introduced the idea of eschewing singsong, overly rhythmic rapping for raps that were independent of musical phrasing and contained frequent use of enjambment and were highly intricate and articulate. The album was released on 4th and Broadway Records and made it into the Top 10 on Billboard's Top R&B/Hip-Hop Albums chart, peaking at No. 8. The duo signed with MCA Records (1934–2003), for whom they released two albums, in 1990.

The duo's next two albums, *Follow the Leader* (1988) and *Let the Rhythm Hit 'Em* (1990), showed the duo's evolution from minimalism and was well received in the hip hop world, but it was their guest appearance on Jody Watley's (1959–) "Friends" (1989) that gave the duo their first Hot 100 Top 10. Their albums did not do well commercially, but their talent for innovation and improvisation, as well as their encyclopedic knowledge of jazz and funk, did not go unnoticed, nor did their insistence on producing quality work over commercial work. Their next album, *Don't Sweat the Technique* (1992), included two singles that were used in the 1991 comedy *House Party 2*. The personality differences that had worked well for the duo until that time began to work against them, which led to a breakup and both members' solo careers.

SEPARATE EFFORTS

The duo began the process of dissolving in 1992, but Eric B. had taken precautionary legal steps that tied Rakim's hands, forcing him to keep a low profile, limiting him to only one notable musical appearance for years, on the soundtrack to the 1993 American film *Gunmen*. Eric B. went on to produce his solo album *Eric B.*

(1995) and various other artists, and Rakim released *The 18th Letter* in 1997 and *The Master* in 1999. Afterward, Rakim made guest appearances with hip hop legends such as Jay-Z (1969–) and KRS-One (1965–). Rakim had secured a deal with Universal Records for *The 18th Letter* in 1996, and originally he enjoyed some success, as the album reached No. 4 on the Billboard 200 and was certified Gold.

He then signed with Dr. Dre's (1965–) Aftermath Entertainment (1996–) record label in 2000, but left that label in 2003. He went into semiretirement but retained the masters he had made with Dr. Dre. In 2009, he released *The Seventh Seal* three years after his originally planned launch date. The album spawned two singles, "Holy Are You" and "Walk These Streets." As time has passed, Rakim has become widely acknowledged as one of the best—if not the best—rap lyricists of all time, and he is regarded as one of the most skilled MCs in all of the rap world. He is consistently ranked in the Top 5 of all MCs by media outlets such as MTV (which ranked him No. 4) and *The Source* (which ranked him No. 1 on its list of MC lyricists).

Although the duo went on to enjoy critical success over four albums, it has yet to be inducted into the Rock and Roll Hall of Fame, despite being announced as one of the finalists in 2011. Since 2016, rumors of a reunion have been announced on the duo's website, but as of 2018, no details have emerged.

Anthony J. Fonseca

See also: Five Percent Nation; The United States

Further Reading

Coleman, Brian. 2007. "Eric B. and Rakim: *Paid in Full.*" In *Check the Technique: Liner Notes for Hip Hop Junkies*, pp. 200–209. New York: Villard.

Rausch, Andrew J. 2011. "Eric B." In *I Am Hip Hop: Conversations on the Music and Culture*, chap. 10. Lanham, MD: Scarecrow.

Further Listening

Eric B. and Rakim. 1987. *Paid in Full.* 4th and Broadway.

Eric B. and Rakim. 1988. *Follow the Leader.* MCA-UNI Records.

Erykah Badu

(Erica Abi Wright, 1971–, Dallas, Texas)

Erykah Badu debuted in 1997 with her album *Baduizm*, a neo soul offering that introduced her own particular fusion of jazz, R&B, and classic soul; her trademark message of female empowerment; and her sensual, mystical Earth-mother image. The term "Baduizm" has since come to refer to the arcane worldview expressed through her lyrics and videos, a mixture of Islamic, Christian, and Buddhist symbols and beliefs that her fans have embraced. She has since produced five studio albums and has toured worldwide, through Europe, Australia, South America, and Asia. She has also appeared in American films such as *Blues Brothers 2000* (1998) and *The Cider House Rules* (1999) as well as in collaborative music videos such as "You Got Me" (1999) with the Roots (1987–) and "Q.U.E.E.N." (2013) with Janelle Monáe (Janelle Monáe Robinson, 1985–). Her singles and records have regularly placed on the charts and have won awards both in the United States and internationally.

BEGINNINGS, THEMES, AND SOUND

Erykah Badu changed her name in high school and college, first invoking, in her first name, the sound "kah," a reference to the Egyptian word *ka*, referring to a person's spirit and her transcendent inner self, and later adopting the sound "badu," a representation of her musical identity, as she often used that sound in her improvised scat solos. Before going mainstream, she performed as part of a hip hop duo and spent some time in the Memphis music circuit. Since *Badiuzm* (1997), she has embraced soul as a genre essential for black expression, working to revitalize it at the turn of the 21st century. Her music invokes folk ritual, intimacy, and spirituality, blending tradition and modernity to empower black women. Her lyrics are outspoken, promoting solidarity, sisterhood, love, and self-sufficiency, both challenging and embracing stereotypes about femininity and sexuality.

Draped over a laid-back hip hop groove and jazz-inflected harmonies, the lyrics for Erykah Badu's first hit single, "On and On" (1996), exemplify the reason her voice and phrasing are often compared to Billie Holiday's (Eleanora Fagan, 1915–1959). The song's lyrics exemplify her major themes, the cyclical nature of life, the interdependence of humanity and the Earth, and the equation of the human spirit with God. The word "cipher" in the chorus represents her sense of self, which is tied to the image of the rolling stone, which represents Earth. The song not only establishes her personal mythology but also references the teachings of the Five Percent Nation (1964–), a sect of the Nation of Islam (1930–), as well as secular cosmology, both of these being concerned with promoting knowledge of and respect for the self. The music video for "On and On" emphasizes Erykah Badu's embracing of both tradition and modern sensuality by presenting her as two primary characters from Alice Walker's (1944–) novel *The Color Purple* (1982), as depicted in Steven Spielberg's 1985 film version. By embodying the character Celie, Erykah Badu identifies as traditional, rural, common, and domestic; by embodying Shug, she identifies as a sophisticated, sensual jazz singer. In this way, she contends with the duality of the black woman's experience.

AWARDS

Eminently successful in creating a public image that reflects her messages of self-empowerment and black feminism, as well as in producing venerated musical projects both live and recorded, Erykah Badu has amassed a number of awards. *Baduizm* (1997) made it in the Top 10 on both the U.S. and Swedish charts and won a Grammy Award in 1998 for Best R&B Album; the single "On and On" garnered a Grammy that same year for Best Female R&B Vocal Performance. *Live*, Erykah Badu's live album released later in 1997, reached the top of the Billboard chart for R&B/Hip-Hop Albums in the United States, and her following studio albums, *Mama's Gun* (2000), *Worldwide Underground* (2003), *New Amerykah Part One (4th World War)* (2008), and *New Amerykah Part Two (Return of the Ankh)* (2010), charted globally, all peaking at No. 3 or higher on the Billboard R&B/Hip-Hop Albums chart. She has received two further Grammy Awards for collaborations with other artists, for the Roots' "You Got Me" and for Common's (1972–) "Love of My Life (An Ode to Hip Hop)" (2002). In 2015, she released her mixtape *But You Caint Use My Phone*.

Jessica Leah Getman

See also: Five Percent Nation; Neo Soul; The United States

Further Reading

Bibi Khan, Khatija. 2012. "Erykah Badu and the Teachings of the Nation of Gods and Earths." *Muziki: Journal of Music Research in Africa* 9, no. 2: 80–89.

King, Jason. 1999. "When Autobiography Becomes Soul: Erykah Badu and the Cultural Politics of Black Feminism." *Women and Performance: A Journal of Feminist Theory* 10, no. 1–2: 211–43.

Further Listening

Erykah Badu. 1997. *Baduizm*. Universal Records.

Erykah Badu. 2010. *New Amerykah Part Two (Return of the Ankh)*. Universal Motown.

Estelle

(Estelle Fanta Swaray, 1980–, London, England)

Estelle is a West London singer, rapper, songwriter, and producer who since 2004 has lived in Los Angeles. She is best known for her mainstream hit single "American Boy" (2008), which reached No. 1 on singles charts in the United Kingdom and landed in the Top 10 on various international charts; it also reached No. 9 on the Billboard Hot 100 in the United States. Estelle cowrote this certified-Platinum single with will.i.am (1975–) and John Legend (John Roger Stephens, 1978–), among others. Will.i.am produced the song, which featured Kanye West (1977–). In 2009, it won the Grammy Award for Best Rap/Sung Collaboration. In addition, Estelle has earned critical acclaim and awards for her albums *Shine* (2008), *All of Me* (2012), and *True Romance* (2015). Her music combines hip hop, grime, neo soul, pop, R&B, and reggae.

EARLY YEARS, INFLUENCE, AND *SHINE*

Part Senegalese and Granadino, Estelle grew up in Hammersmith, London, in a religious household listening to American gospel, traditional West African music, and reggae. Listening to Ella Fitzgerald (1917–1996) and later Mary J. Blige (1971–) influenced her singing and rapping. Like both, Estelle is a soprano.

Estelle began her music career while working at London's hip hop record store Deal Real. In London's clubs, her open-mic appearances drew attention and led to collaborations on sound recordings. Her debut was the 12-inch single "Excuse Me" (2003). While on a trip to Los Angeles, she approached West at a restaurant and asked to be introduced to Legend, who soon after produced two songs on her debut album, *The 18th Day* (2004). The single "1980" reached No. 14 on the U.K. pop chart, and Estelle became the first artist to sign to Legend's label Homeschool Records (2007–), a joint venture with Atlantic (1947–). Her follow-up, *Shine* (2008), featured "American Boy." Her first album released in the United States, *Shine* is also her most critically acclaimed work, having reached No. 38 on the Billboard 200, become certified Gold, and made it to the short list for the 2008 Mercury Prize.

RECORD PRODUCTION AND LATER ALBUMS

While recording *The 18th Day,* Estelle formed her own record label, Stellarents, which signed new artists from the West London scene. Her 2009 self-standing single, "Star," was used in Crystal Light beverage commercials in the United States. After *Shine,* she recorded *All of Me* on Legend's label, and in 2010 she released the critically acclaimed single "Freak" with Canadian rapper Kardinal Offishall (Jason D. Harrow, 1976–). Parisian EDM DJ and remixer David Guetta (Pierre David Guetta, 1967–), with whom she worked on "One Love" (2009), produced this song. Estelle also released "World Go Round" (2009) with American rapper Busta Rhymes (1972–).

In 2015, she released *True Romance* on her new Los Angeles–based record label, Established 1980 Records (2015–), in partnership with BMG (2008–). A guest appearance on Fox's television show *Empire* (2015–), in which she sang her single "Conqueror," led to the song's reaching No. 42 on the Billboard Hot 100 and No. 15 on Billboard's R&B singles chart.

Melissa Ursula Dawn Goldsmith

See also: The United Kingdom; West, Kanye

Further Reading

Trilling, Daniel, and Harry Williams. 2008–2009. "A Woman of Conviction." *New States-man* 137–38, nos. 4928–30, December 22, 2008–January 9, 2009, 72–74.

Zachariah, Natasha Ann. 2011. "Live Life to Write Songs: Rapper-Singer Estelle Is Taking Her Time between Albums to Build Up Material for Her Songs." *The Straits Times* (Singapore), October 24.

Further Listening

Estelle. 2008. *Shine.* Atlantic/Homeschool Records.

Estelle. 2015. *True Romance.* BMG/Established 1980 Records.

Estonia

The Republic of Estonia is a Baltic state that became independent in 1991 after the fall of the Soviet Union. Hip hop, first in English and Russian and then, from the mid-2000s on, primarily in Estonian, quickly became popular in the years following Estonian independence. The founders of Estonian rap are Tartu-based Cool D (Priit Kolsar, 1976–) and Tallinn-based G-Enka (Henry Körvits, 1974–), DJ Paul (aka Tallinn Funk, Paul Oja, 1979–), Revo (Revo Jõgisalu, 1976–2011), Kozy (Anonymous, 1975*–), and DJ Critikal (Bert Prikenfeld, 1996*–).

The first Estonian hip hop album was Cool D's *O'Culo* (1995*). Other Estonian rappers and groups include Toe Tag (Revo, G-Eenka, and Oja's one-time band, 1996–); Rakvere-based Tommyboy (Toomas Tilk, 1976–), Chalice (Jarek Kasar,

1983–), and Öökülm (2010–), consisting of MC Lord (Mart Rauba, n.d.) and DJ Melkker (Martin Tutt, n.d.); and Talinn-based Suur Papa (1989–) from Tallinn, Metsakutsu (Rainer Olbri, 1987–), and DVPH (2008–), consisting of Dragan Volta (n.d.) and Põhjamaade Hirm (Nordic Fear, Johan Kullerkup, 1985–). Other hip hop acts include Kuuluud (2008–), consisting of Hirm and producer Tatmo Savvo (n.d.); Külalised (2006*–); Tartu's 5Loops (2010–); and Talinn's Reket (Racket, Tom Olaf Urb, 1985–) and Abraham (Lennart Lundve, 1988–). The cities Tallinn and Tartu are the most important centers of Estonian rap, and annual Estonian hip hop festivals have taken place since 2006 in the town of Elva, near Tartu. The Estonian MC Battle was held annually from 2000 to 2010.

Because Estonia is a nation with a history of centuries of dominance by foreign powers (Denmark, Germany, Sweden, the Soviet Union, and briefly Nazi Germany), personal and political freedom are common issues in hip hop. Cool D, who won Best Male Performer of the Year and Best Performance at the 2004 Estonian Music Awards, raps about Estonia's uneasy relationship with Russia and remarks that Estonians have been compelled to learn a foreign language and customs in "Eestlased" (Estonians). Further, the use of sexually charged lyrics and profanity in Estonian hip hop is part of this expression of personal freedom, as this would never have been allowed under the heavy censorship of the Soviet Union.

Rapping in Estonian became widespread with the rise of Cool D, whose early work was influenced by American rappers such as Ice Cube (1969–) and Public Enemy (1982–). In 1998, Kozy brought Cool D, G-Eenka, DJ Critikal, and Revo together to form the supergroup A-Rühm (1998–), which agreed to rap exclusively in Estonian. That year, A-Rühm cut "Popmuusik" ("Pop Musicians"), bringing hip hop to national fame. The shift to Estonian language in Estonian rap by the early 2000s brought themes of nationhood, personal freedom, and Estonian identity to the fore. In 2006, Chalice was commissioned to write the Estonian nationalist anthem "Minu inimesed" ("My People"), which was performed at a presidential concert that celebrated Estonian Independence Day and in 2007 at the Tenth Youth Song Festival (with a full symphony and a choir of 30,000).

Although most Estonian rap includes beats and sustained chords in addition to using similar technology to American rap, "My People," a spoken-word poem with pizzicato strings and soft wind melodies, demonstrates Estonians' generous definition of rap: as long as a song consists of spoken rhymes over music, it is considered rap.

Terry Klefstad

See also: Political Hip Hop

Further Reading

Kobin, Maarja, and Airi-Alina Allaste. 2009. "Hip Hop in Rakvere: The Importance of the Local in Global Subculture." In *Subcultures and New Religious Movements in Russia and East-Central Europe*, edited by George McKay, Christopher Williams, Michael Goddard, Neil Foxlee, and Egidija Ramanauskaitė, chap. 4. Oxford, England: P. Lang.

Vallaste, Triin. 2017. "Music, Technology, and Shifts in Popular Culture: Making Hip Hop in e-Estonia." In *Hip Hop at Europe's Edge: Music, Agency, and Social Change*, edited by Milosz Miszczynski and Adriana Helbig, chap. 7. Bloomington: Indiana University Press.

Further Listening
G-Enka and Paul Oja. 2014. *Genka/Paul Oja*. Legendaarne Records.

Ethiopia

Ethiopia, the second most populous country in Africa next to Nigeria, is located in Northeast Africa, known as the Horn of Africa. Its history is intertwined with the history of reggae and hip hop. Ethiopia has a generally pious and traditionalist atmosphere, with musical preferences favoring Ethiopian traditional music and popular music such as American jazz and rock as well as Jamaican reggae—all of which Ethiopian musicians have stylized into their own unique sound, despite a lack of recording studios and copyright royalty collection issues. Ethiopian musicians have also found it difficult to choose a rapping text, not only because Ethiopia is so linguistically diverse but also because strong cultural pride limits the audience. The emerging preferred rapping language is Amharic; Oromo, Tigrinya, and English are less used.

Horrible environmental conditions as well as sociopolitical corruption have also had a limiting effect on the development of Ethiopian hip hop. During the Derg Era (1974–1991), over one million people died due to the 1983–1985 famine and government-imposed genocide. Diaspora rappers were the result of mass deportations. The Eritrean-Ethiopian War (1998–2000) economically drained the country further. Government censorship during the Derg Era and into the present Federal Democratic Republic Era (1991–) thwarted political rap's existence. Rappers also censored themselves because some were government sponsored; many opted for lyrical content that focused on Ethiopian historical and cultural pride, morality, everyday life, and youth struggles and ambitions. One source of Ethiopian historical and cultural pride is rooted especially in the 19th century, when Ethiopia was the only African country to resist European colonization. Another source is that in the 20th century, Ethiopia had a popular emperor, Haile Selassie I (Ras Tafari Makonnen Woldemikael, 1892–1975, reign 1930–1974), who helped modernize the country. Selassie became famous for an international reason as well: according to Rastafarianism, his reign fulfilled Biblical prophecy. This belief strongly ties Jamaica and its music to Ethiopia—Jamaican deejays, who toast mainly in English or Jamaican patois, sometimes add Amharic lines as a tribute to Selassie.

A small hip hop scene exists in Ethiopia's capital city, Addis Ababa. Rappers work under aliases to protect themselves from threats and punishment. One pioneering rapper is Lij Michael (aka Faf, Michael Taye, n.d.), who raps in Amharic and English. Like other Ethiopian musicians since the 2000s, Lij Michael disseminates his music through streaming services, which has led to opportunities to tour worldwide. A later act, DJ Same (anonymous, n.d.), fuses hip hop with traditional Amharic music called *fukera*, beatboxing to its oration. DJ Same uses an Apple iPhone to play samples and loops during live concerts. Other rappers using Amharic are Ella Man (Elias Hussen, 1993–), Woah (anonymous, 1982–), Yoni Yoye (anonymous, 1988–), and Jukebox the Illustrious (anonymous, 1975–).

Woah and Jukebox the Illustrious attended college in Texas and collaborated, but many acts outside Ethiopia focus away from the country's issues and use languages that appeal to broader audiences. Feven (Feven Ghebremicael, 1975–), born in Massawa, Ethiopia (now Eritrea), raps in Swedish and English as a member of GFX (Greenhouse FX, 2000*–) as well as other groups and is a notable Ethiopian/Eritrean hip hop act with chart success in Sweden. In her videos and rap texts, Feven has addressed her status as an Ethiopian expatriate and a Muslim. Another result of diaspora, Willy William (1981–) is a Champagné, France–born DJ of Ethiopian Guadeloupean descent who produces house music, R&B, dancehall, and *zouk* as well as hip hop. He belongs to the French hip hop band Collectif Métissé (2009–).

Women rappers have yet to emerge aboveground in Ethiopia. Reasons for this lack of public participation are rooted in religious beliefs and the perception that the exercise of women's rights is political protest.

Melissa Ursula Dawn Goldsmith

See also: Jamaica; Reggae

Further Reading

Mekonnen, Danny A. 2010. "Ethio-Groove on the World Stage: Music, Mobility, Mediation." *Callaloo* 33, no. 1: 299–313, 368.

Shabby, Malka. 2003. "'RaGap': Music and Identity among Young Ethiopians in Israel." *Critical Arts: A South-North Journal of Cultural and Media Studies* 17, nos. 1–2: 93–105.

F

Fab Five Freddy

(aka Fab 5 Freddy, Fred Brathwaite, 1959–, Brooklyn, New York)

Fab Five Freddy is an American graffiti artist, rapper, filmmaker, cinematographer, producer, painter, actor, and video jockey. He is known for having introduced elements of hip hop such as street art, dancing, and rapping to both mainstream culture and the art world. He is best known as the original host of MTV's *Yo! MTV Raps* (1988–1995); however, from his Fab 5 graffiti tags and uses of Andy Warhol's (Andrew Warhola, 1928–1987) pop art painting *Campbell's Soup Cans* (1962) that appeared on the sides of subway cars in New York City to his producing the American classic breakdancing film *Wild Style* (1983), from his being a reference in Blondie's No. 1 hit single "Rapture" (1981) to his own rap recording "Change the Beat," which contains one of the most scratched samples in hip hop history, he has become more than a television host—he has reached cult icon status.

Fab Five Freddy began as a graffiti artist from the Bedford-Stuyvesant section of Brooklyn. He took his name in 1979 after joining the graffiti crew The Fabulous 5. Before his involvement with the film *Wild Style* (1983) and hosting *Yo! MTV Raps* in 1987, he helped bridge graffiti art culture with the downtown New York art world as well as hip hop with the contemporary punk movement. (Johnny Nunez/WireImage for Rush Philanthropic Arts Foundation/Getty Images)

MUSICAL AND ARTISTIC BEGINNINGS

Born as Fred Brathwaite and raised in the Bedford-Stuyvesant section of Brooklyn, New York, Fab Five Freddy's earliest exposure to music was likely jazz, since his parents were avid jazz listeners and record collectors.

His godfather was drummer, percussionist, and composer Max Roach (1924–2007)—one of the prominent figures of bebop and cool jazz in the 1950s and 1960s. Since high school, he and Roach have been close friends. Roach had purchased a large house in Brooklyn, where he would invite Brooklyn jazz musicians for jam sessions and discussions on jazz as well as entertain his jazz aficionado friend and godson. His father also knew jazz pianist Thelonious Monk (1917–1982), a prominent figure of bebop, cool jazz, and hard bop and his earliest musical obsession.

Though he loved music, he pursued art and developed an interest in graffiti with the belief that it descended from 1960s pop art. His primary medium for his own graffiti was spray enamel. While studying art and pop culture at Medgar Evers College in Brooklyn in 1979, he joined the graffiti crew the Fabulous 5 (1970s*), in which he developed his tag and stage name. He also became interested in both the emerging hip hop scene in the Bronx, New York, and in the punk and new wave scene on the Lower East Side of Manhattan.

BUILDING BRIDGES TO THE MAINSTREAM

In 1978, Fab Five Freddy found work as a camera operator on American art, fashion, and music journalist Glenn O'Brien's (1947–2017) public-access cable show *TV Party* (1978–1980), on which he was also a guest. In 1980, O'Brien cast him alongside Puerto Rican–born graffiti artist Lee Quiñones (George Lee Quiñones, 1960–) in his documentary film *Downtown 81*, formerly titled *New York Beat*, on Brooklyn graffiti and neoexpressionist artist Jean-Michel Basquiat (1960–1988). Although the film was not released until 2000, this experience led to Fab Five Freddy's cocreating, filming, and producing *Wild Style* (1983), director Charlie Ahearn's (1951–) American film. Fab Five Freddy also acted in it and showcased Quiñones's art. In the meantime, Fab Five Freddy and graffiti artist Futura 2000 (aka Futura, Leonard Hilton McGurr, 1955–) became cocurators of the art show *Beyond Words* at Manhattan's Mudd Club, the first art exhibit that drew members of the Bronx hip hop scene to the downtown New York City art world. This show featured the duo's graffiti as well as the artwork of Basquiat and Keith Haring (1958–1990), among others.

After this exhibit, Fab Five Freddy appeared on hip hop photographer and videographer Henry Chalfant's (1940–) *Graffiti Rock* show with Rock Steady Crew (RSC, 1977–) and later on shows with Afrika Bambaata (Kevin Donovan, 1957–), including the popular *Wheels of Steel Show*. In the same year, within the hip hop scene, he met the punk and new wave band Blondie (1974–1982, 1997–), who already had Billboard Hot 100 No. 1 hits. The band showed him their rap text to "Rapture" (1981), which mentioned him in its namechecking. "Rapture" became both a No. 1 hit on the U.S. Billboard Hot 100 and an international hit, bringing his name to the fore of hip hop culture's global recognition. That same year, he rapped with Blondie on two EPs that were released in the United Kingdom through England's *Flexipop!* (1980–1983) magazine. In addition, in 1982 he rapped on the A side of the 12-inch single "Change the Beat" in both English and French; the B side featured female rapper BeSide (Anne Marie Boyle, n.d.), nicknamed "Fab Five Betty," who raps the song in French. On this rendition, Fab Five Freddy added the line "Ahhhhh, this stuff is really fresh," which became one of the most scratched samples in hip hop history. Most famously, Herbie Hancock used it in "Rockit" (1983). The same year as "Change the Beat," Fab Five Freddy continued rapping and went on the first rap tour in Europe with Afrika Bambaataa, Grand Mixer D.ST (aka GrandMixer DXT, Derek Showard, 1960–), Rock Steady Crew (RSC, 1977–) and Futura 2000 (Leonard Hilton McGurr, 1955–), among others. He then collaborated with the German punk band Die Toten Hosen (The Dead, Boring Event, 1982–) to produce "Eisgekühlter bommerlunder" ("Hip Hop Bommi Bop," 1983), which became the first hip hop–punk coproduction.

In 1987, he was asked by MTV to become the main host of *Yo! MTV Raps*. Freddy was the main host from 1988 to 1989, sharing the host responsibilities with American radio personality Doctor Dré (André Brown, 1963–) and radio personality, rapper, actor, and musician Ed Lover (James Roberts, 1963–). The television show introduced Americans to the music of the most successful hip hop recording artists of the time. He concurrently served as associate producer for Wesley Snipes's (1962–) film *New Jack City* (1991), and he directed hip hop videos for Queen Latifah's (1970–) "Ladies First" (1989), Snoop Dogg's (1971–) "Who Am I? (What's My Name?)" (1993), and Nas's (1973–) "One Love" (1994), among others. Since the 1990s, Fab Five Freddy has returned to painting and has been creating media art. From 2009 to 2013, he created a series of paintings and video essays; among these are the *Crystal Punch* pictures and the *Abstract Remix* paintings—both inspired by the remixing and sampling techniques found in hip hop music.

Melissa Ursula Dawn Goldsmith

See also: Blondie; Graffiti Art; Hancock, Herbie; Hip Hop Dance; The United States

Further Reading

Chang, Jeff. 2005. *Can't Stop Won't Stop: A History of the Hip Hop Generation.* New York: Picador.

Jenkins, Willard. 2011. "Fab 5 Freddy: A Jazz Upbringing at the Roots of Hip Hop." Interview with Fab Five Freddy. *JazzTimes*, May 19.

Fashion

Fashion is a big part of hip hop culture. As dancers, musicians, and DJs became popular and achieved star status, the styles of clothes they wore on the streets and in clubs spread. Hip hop fashion embraces a specific culture at a specific time and is an outgrowth of the larger pop culture fashion movements of the 1960s and 1970s, when people began emulating the clothing worn by their favorite artists and musicians. Hip hop street culture created its unique variation by experimenting with color, fit, and fashion accessories.

In the 1970s, dance crews such as the Lockers (aka the Campbell Lockers, 1971–1982) from Los Angeles, founded by Toni Basil (1943–) and Don Campbell (1951–), wore costumes rather than clothing. The same can be said of the Electric Boogaloos (1977–), who were from Fresno, California. These dance crews were easily identified by their large, colorful beret-style hats, colorful knickers, large suspenders, and

Lesbian rapper-songwriter Young M.A. is known not only for her hardcore freestyle talents, but also for her eclectic style: bling, full neck tattoos, and double braids. With her baggy jeans, backwards baseball hats, and hoodies, Young M.A.'s fashion sense challenges gender-normative conventions. (Michael Tullberg/Getty Images)

striped socks as well as black hats and white gloves, clothing that resembled that worn by artists who study mime. The predominant color combination was black and white, although the groups sometimes adopted matching variations of colors. Such costuming influenced a lot of the West Coast funk fashion. Television series such as *Soul Train* (1971–2006) and *What's Happening*! (1976–1979, featuring one of the original Lockers, Fred Berry, 1951–2003) highlighted these Los Angeles fashions. *Soul Train* in particular featured performances of not only R&B, soul, jazz, disco, and funk but hip hop as well, propelling not just the music and dance moves but also its fashion into the mainstream.

By contrast, the New York crews were simpler in their fashion choices. Early New York breakers wore more athletic clothing—tracksuits were popular, along with the new name-brand tennis shoes, especially Nike, Adidas, and Keds. Kangol hats were also favored. The most popular color combinations (into the early 1980s) were red and black. Many crews wore leather jackets and incorporated punk accessories, such as zippers and chains. More stylized versions of these hip hop fashions were made famous through pop music videos, such as Michael Jackson's (1958–2009) "Bad" (1987) and "Thriller" (1983).

As the 1980s drew to a close, hair and accessories became more pronounced (more voluminous and bigger) as the popularity of hip hop and rap culture grew. Popular rap artists set a new trend, wearing oversized jewelry, chains especially, but also watches and rings. Gigantic hoop earrings made their way into women's fashion. Shirts and jackets incorporated the large-shoulder, small-waist look, and pants ranged from very tight leather to a very baggy "Harem" pant (parachute pants) that was nicknamed "MC Hammer pants" due to early rapper MC Hammer's (1962–) popularizing them in his videos. In time, a new variant emerged as a cultural shift toward roots pride occurred, leading to the inclusion of traditional African prints and colors and Rastafarian accessories and hairstyles, such as dreadlocks.

FROM THE 1990s INTO THE 21st CENTURY

The 1990s saw the rise of fashion that has become associated with hip hop as it is known today, with clothing emphasizing a softer and baggy look and bright colors (including neon) being popular with young rappers such as the Fresh Prince (Will Smith, 1968–), Kid n' Play (Christopher Reid, 1964–, and Christopher Martin, 1962–), and the all-female group TLC (1991–). TLC set the tone for many women's fashions. In addition, musicians continued to embrace designer clothing, such as Hilfiger, Ralph Lauren, Calvin Klein, Nautica, and FUBU (originally an acronym for Four Urban Brothers United, it became For Us By Us).

Designers who embraced hip hop culture employed rappers in their runway shows. Sports jerseys (sometimes described as throwback jerseys) and sport team hats, always a favorite of the hip hop culture, continued to be prominent. The emphasis on large clothing earned a nickname for the style, "Balla." Flashy gold, diamond jewelry, and other expensive accessories, known as "bling," also became popular—bling led to ultimate fashion excess, most notably the "grill," capping the full front row of teeth in gold or platinum. Women embraced masculine fashion and wore the same clothing, but with the added touch of makeup to feminize themselves. Rappers such as Lil' Kim (1975–) and Foxy Brown (Inga DeCarlo Fung Marchand, 1978–) popularized a new, sexier look for women that accented the female silhouette. In addition, mainstream fashion had a hip hop undercurrent, sometimes embracing a boxy look that resembled prison wear, but worn baggy and limited to very achromatic variations of black, white, and gray (this color scheme was embraced by the hardcore or gangsta rappers that were emerging in the 1990s as a way to preserve the street origins of hip hop).

By the turn of the century, hip hop artists, rappers, and music producers were branching into the fashion scene themselves, with labels and designs of their own. In 1998, Sean John Combs (1969–), known then as Puff Daddy, Puffy, or P. Diddy, began his award-winning clothing line, Sean John, which was especially known for its tailored dress jackets. That same year, Queens, New York–based Def Jam Recordings (1983–) cofounder Russell Simmons (1957–) created Phat Farm (1992–) and followed up a year later with a children's hip hop clothing line, Baby Phat (1993–). In 2002, the Southern hip hop group OutKast (1992–) started their own clothing line, OutKast Clothing, but it soon folded due to a lack of sales. With less success than earlier, Simmons created new clothing lines in the 21st century: Argyleculture (2008) and Tantris (2012). For the most part, labels started by musicians have folded, as the trends change so quickly that it is hard for one clothing line to keep pace.

Since the 2010s, Starter Clothing Line has produced vintage sporting wear and starter jackets that revamp the looks of the 1980s and 1990s; even established shoes and clothing lines such as Reebok and Adidas embrace the snapback trends today. Recently, hip hop fashion has merged with other trends, such as skateboarding and surfing, embracing the printed T-shirt and more tapered pant leg, Vans shoes, knit caps, and more fitted clothing. Tattoos are also a new trend, ranging from fully sleeved to tribal work on the neck and face. Chest pieces, wherein the whole chest is a complete work of art, are now being seen. International hip hop fashions are very similar to American ones, with the added element of the indigenous culture—always toeing the line of what is considered an urban or street trend.

Paige A. Willson

See also: Campbell, Don; The Electric Boogaloos; Gangsta Rap; Hip Hop Dance; Puff Daddy

Further Reading

Penney, Joel. 2012. "'We Don't Wear Tight Clothes': Gay Panic and Queer Style in Contemporary Hip Hop." *Popular Music and Society* 35, no. 3: 321–32.

Romero, Elena. 2012. *Free Stylin': How Hip Hop Changed the Fashion Industry.* Santa Barbara, CA: Praeger.

Fatback Band

(aka Fatback, 1970–, New York City, New York)

The Fatback Band is a popular American 1970s and 1980s funk, disco, and R&B band that was best known for a long string of hit singles that peaked on Billboard's Hot R&B Songs (which later became Hot R&B/Hip-Hop Songs), including "(Do the) Spanish Hustle" (1976) and "I Like Girls" (1978), which barely missed the Billboard Hot 100 by charting at 101. Hits such as "(Are You Ready) Do the Bus Stop" (1975), "(Do the) Spanish Hustle," and the second re-release of "I Found Lovin'" (1986) peaked in the Top 20 positions on the United Kingdom's Singles Chart. Another hit song, "King Tim III (Personality Jock)" (1979), contained rapped passages by the persona King Tim, who used braggadocio as well as an invitation for listeners to clap. "King Tim III," a B side, became more popular than "You're My Candy," the record's A side. Its label, New York City–based Spring Records (1967–1990*), in association with Polydor (1913–), released the seven-inch single album in March 1979, whereas Englewood, New Jersey–based Sugar Hill Records (1979–1985) released the 12-inch single album, the Sugarhill Gang's (1979–1985, 1994–) "Rapper's Delight," in August 1979. Based on release dates, "King Tim III" is the first commercially released song with rap; however, publication dates show that "King Tim III" had its copyright registered on August 29, 1979, whereas "Rapper's Delight" had its copyright registered on September 24, 1979, with a publication date of August 25, 1979, given in its copyright registration documents. In addition, "Rapper's Delight" used the words "hip hop" and was a full rap single—and more importantly, it overshadowed "King Tim III" with its success.

Bill Curtis (William Curtis, 1932–), the founder of the Fatback Band, was born and raised in Fayetteville, North Carolina, served in the army, and moved to New York City in 1955, ultimately becoming a session drummer. In 1970, Curtis formed the Fatback Band to fuse the "fatback" beat of New Orleans Mardi Gras parade band music (derived from Dixieland's rhythm section) and emerging 1970s funk. The initial instrumentation also shows some cool jazz and jazz-rock fusion influences: trumpet, saxophone, and flute, as well as electric guitar, electric bass, electric piano, and drums. In the early 1970s, the band played street funk, but eventually it expanded its sound to include congas, vocals, saxophone, and electric guitar. The Fatback

Band's first hit, "Street Dance" (1973), peaked at No. 26 on Billboard's Hot R&B Songs. The band adapted and changed its sound as disco, R&B, and soul became popular in the 1970s and 1980s and songs were usually geared toward dancing.

Lyrical content often focused on aspects of urban life and dance, with some double meanings, wordplay, and humor. Hits had titles such as "Street Dance," "Keep on Steppin'" (1974), "The Booty" (1976), "Master Booty" (1978), "Party Time" (1976), "All Nite Party" (1988), "Double Dutch" (1978), and "Gotta Get My Hands on Some (Money)" (1980). By the mid-1980s, the Fatback Band's string of hits had stopped in the United States, but the band continued releasing hits in the United Kingdom until 1988, when it released "All Nite Party." There were several personnel changes over the years, but as of 2018, drummer Curtis and the Fatback Band still perform concerts and tour.

Melissa Ursula Dawn Goldsmith

See also: The Sugarhill Gang; The United States

Further Reading

Charnas, Dan. 2010. "Album One: Number Runners." In *The Big Payback: The History of the Business of Hip Hop*, chap. 1. New York: New American Library.

George, Nelson. 1998. "Hip Hop Wasn't Just Another Date." In *Hip Hop America*, chap. 2. New York: Viking Press.

Further Listening

Fatback Band. 1973. *People Music.* Spring Records.

Fatback Band. 1979. *Fatback XII.* Spring Records.

50 Cent

(Curtis James Jackson III, 1975–, Queens, New York)

Curtis James Jackson III, better known as 50 Cent, has lived a life that is almost a cliché of hip hop culture. He has been involved with drugs and has had brushes with the law—and his professional career has been marked by his own shooting and frequent feuds. Throughout his career, 50 Cent has engaged in numerous public feuds with other rappers, including Ja Rule (Jeffrey Atkins, 1976–), the Game (Jayceon Terrell Taylor, 1979–), Eedris Abdulkareem (1974–), and Rick Ross (William Leonard Roberts II, 1976–). It is not always clear, however, how genuine such disagreements are, or if they have been staged for their publicity value. Nonetheless, his music has been incredibly popular, and the synergy between his music and business enterprises has made 50 Cent one of hip hop's wealthiest individuals.

EARLY LIFE TO SUCCESSFUL HIP HOP CAREER

Born to a 15-year-old single mother who worked as a cocaine dealer and was murdered when he was eight, 50 Cent was raised by his grandparents in Queens, New York. From age 12, he became involved in selling drugs and other illegal activities, which culminated in several arrests in 1994. Jackson avoided a longer sentence by spending six months in a boot camp, during which time he earned his GED. He also adopted the nickname 50 Cent from a 1980s Brooklyn thief who would steal from anyone, as a reminder that through rap music he would support himself legally.

A self-taught rapper, 50 Cent was introduced in 1996 to Jam Master Jay (Jason William Mizell, 1965–2002), DJ of Run-D.M.C. (1981–2002), who taught him the basics of counting measures and creating songs. In particular, 50 Cent learned how to write strong melodic hooks for his own raps, and he also began to appear uncredited on recordings by other rappers. Meanwhile, he worked on his own first album. "How to Rob" (1999) was 50 Cent's controversial debut single; in it he named more than 40 rap and pop performers as his potential victims. Although he later claimed that the track was meant to be humorous and not disrespectful, response to it was mixed, even among the rappers he named. In April of the following year, 50 Cent was shot nine times in front of his grandmother's house in Queens. Speculation by authorities and others was that the shooting was in retaliation for "How to Rob," but this was quickly dismissed. Nonetheless, the incident marked the beginning of 50 Cent's public image as a hip hop performer with frequent feuds and criminal connections.

Because of the shooting, 50 Cent's intended debut album on the Columbia label, *Power of the Dollar* (2000), was never released, but its bootlegged track "Ghetto Qur'an," which told in great detail the story of ruthless Queens, New York, drug dealer Kenneth "Supreme" McGriff (1960–), became an underground sensation. Authorities later believed that McGriff, who laundered drug money through the hip hop label Murder Inc. Records (1999–), was involved in the murder of Jam Master Jay, who had defied an informal industry ban by continuing to work with 50 Cent. Against this background, 50 Cent's *Get Rich or Die Tryin'* (2003), his actual debut, became the most highly anticipated hip hop release in years, and the album first appeared on many Billboard charts, including on the Billboard 200, at No. 1. From *Get Rich or Die Tryin'*, 50 Cent's "In da Club" became his first single to reach No. 1 on the Billboard Hot 100, remaining there for nine weeks. The album's second single, "21 Questions," also peaked at No. 1. *Get Rich or Die Tryin'* earned 50 Cent a Grammy nomination for Best Rap Album. His follow-up album, *The Massacre* (2005), which contained the diss track "Piggy Bank," directed at Ja Rule, Jadakiss (1975–), and many other rappers, did even better, selling over one million copies in its first four days in release and earning five Grammy Award nominations; his subsequent albums have all sold nearly as well.

The success of his own releases led his label Interscope (1989–) to give 50 Cent control of his own division, G-Unit Records (2003–), which featured other rappers from his Queens neighborhood. His recent albums include *Bulletproof* (2006), *Curtis* (2007), *Before I Self Destruct* (2009), and *Animal Ambition: An Untamed Desire to Win* (2014), among others. In 2010, 50 Cent won a Grammy Award for Best Rap Performance by a Duo or Group for "Crack a Bottle" with Eminem and Dr. Dre (1965–).

Quick to leverage his celebrity to sell numerous products beyond music, 50 Cent's first ventures included beverages, fragrances, condoms, luxury clothing, and headphones. He has also produced films and television shows, especially those aimed at black audiences, and he has developed a large-scale philanthropic project that sends food to Africa. His latest investments involve branded precious metals and boxing promotion. His name and his companies, such as headphone company SMS Audio (2011–), are partnered with many well known brands such as Disney (1923–) and Lucasfilm (1971–). In 2015, a personal judgment against him by the ex-girlfriend of rapper Rick Ross and the resulting high legal fees led 50 Cent to file for Chapter 11 bankruptcy.

Scott Warfield

See also: Fashion; Gangsta Rap; Jam Master Jay; The United States

Further Reading

50 Cent. 2004. *From Pieces to Weight: Once upon a Time in Southside Queens.* London: MTV Books.

Williams, Justin. 2013. "Borrowing and Lineage in Eminem/2Pac's *Loyal to the Game* and 50 Cent's *Get Rich or Die Trying.*" In *Rhymin' and Stealin': Musical Borrowing in Hip Hop Music*, chap. 5. Ann Arbor, MI: University of Michigan Press.

Further Listening

50 Cent. 2003. *Get Rich or Die Tryin'.* Interscope Records/Shady Records/Aftermath Entertainment.

50 Cent. 2005. *The Massacre.* Aftermath Entertainment.

Fiji

Fiji, a nation of over 330 South Pacific islands located in Melanesia, has a hip hop scene that began in the early 1990s, when American hip hop arrived via tourists and Fijians with dual citizenship. Fiji's population is about half indigenous people of Polynesian or Melanesian descent (iTaukei) or from surrounding Pacific Islands and about half Fijian Indian. Although the two main populations speak Fijian or Fijian Hindi, Fiji's official language is English.

Hip hop initially found fertile ground in Fiji's capital city, Suva. Fijians have modified all aspects of hip hop, from introducing Pacific themes in graffiti art and breakdancing moves to localizing rap lyrics about economic hardship and unemployment. Fiji's first rappers were Sammy G (anonymous, n.d.) and Mr. Grin (David Lavaki, n.d.). Sammy G's debut single, "Liquid Poison" (1999), is about alcohol abuse. His mixtape *House Party* (2010, but self-released about a year earlier through SoundCloud) was circulated through Fijians residing worldwide. He later founded Underdawg Productions (2008–) to benefit unsigned Fijian hip hop artists and to document hip hop in Fiji. Mr. Grin recorded "Suva City" (2008) with Sammy G. Other notable Fijian hip hop acts are Mynlessme (Faga Timote, n.d.) and his group the Brown Street Boys (BSB, n.d.), Lil Leps (Lepani Raiyala, n.d.), Nemoney (Nemani Borando, n.d.), Rabbit (Kurt Ram, n.d.), and JDeuce (Sekove Qiolevu, 1983*–), who is from Kaba, in the Fijian province of Tailevu (but was raised in Los Angeles).

What catapulted hip hop's popularity in Fiji was instability: despite tourism and one of the most highly developed economies in the Pacific, Fiji has experienced government corruption, military coups, and ethnic conflict since its independence from the United Kingdom in 1970, including five coups since 2006. Ultimately, this unrest has led some Fiji-born rappers to find national and international success. Singer-songwriter Fiji (George Veikoso, 1970–) was born in Tailevu but grew up in Hawaii. He fuses hip hop with reggae, jazz, ska, R&B, traditional Hawaiian, and Fijian music, and his lyrics are in English and Fijian. Female rapper, singer, and hip hop activist MC Trey (aka Trey, Thelma Thomas, n.d.) is from Lami, though her hip hop career and residence are in Sydney. Trey was an MC for the Australian hip hop band Foreign Heights (2006–2008). Her solo studio albums *Daily Affirmations* (2000) and *Tapastry Tunes* (2003) incorporate hip hop, funk, and jazz. Her lyrics are in English and focus on feminism, self-protection, and romance.

Melissa Ursula Dawn Goldsmith

See also: Australia; The United Kingdom

Further Reading

Kabutaulaka, Tarcisius. 2015. "Re-presenting Melanesia: Ignoble Savages and Melanesian Alter Natives." *Contemporary Pacific* 27, no. 1: 110–46.

Lal, Brij V. 2011. "Where Has All the Music Gone? Reflections on the Fortieth Anniversary of Fiji's Independence." *Contemporary Pacific* 23, no. 2: 412–37, 553.

Webb, Michael, and Camellia Webb-Gannon. 2016. "Musical Melanesianism: Imagining and Expressing Regional Identity and Solidarity in Popular Song and Video." *Contemporary Pacific* 28, no. 1: 59–95, 279.

Further Listening

Fiji. 1999. *Grattitude.* Ricochet Records.

MC Trey. 2003. *Tapastry Tunes.* Tapastry Toons.

Filmmaking (Documentaries)

A documentary film contains nonfictional subject matter and is made for the purpose of historical documentation, instruction, and education. Documentaries tend to have a straightforward narrative; however, many may also consist of experimental or abstract cinematography. Documentaries are usually shot on a much lower budget and are shorter than full-length feature motion pictures. They are also less distributed and shown in smaller venues than motion pictures. Rarely do they reach large markets, even once they have received awards, strong critical reception, or cult status. With its cutting-edge subject matter and artistic uses of cinematography (e.g., a straightforward one-take or an uncut shot of a subject, handheld filming techniques, and extreme close-up shots to have a fragment represent the whole object), documentary filmmaking nevertheless influences motion picture and music video filmmaking. Hip hop documentaries are no different from other films in these respects. As with other kinds of documentaries, there is a pattern of use of subject matter that seems constant. Because less funding is required than for motion pictures, lower production values are acceptable. There is a much stronger global output of hip hop documentaries than hip hop feature films. As of 2018, full-length hip hop films that have originated from the United States strongly dominate the entire hip hop motion picture output.

Early hip hop documentaries may be credited for sparking interest in producing hip hop films. For example, *Right On! Poetry on Film* (1971), from the United States, features music by members of the Last Poets (1968–), credited as the Original Last Poets. Originating from Harlem, the Last Poets may have been the world's first group that performed hip hop. The United States–produced New York City gang crime thriller *The Warriors* (1979) is often considered a proto–hip hop film because its narrative and urban themes resemble later hip hop dramas, though its soundtrack contains no hip hop. Just after hip hop music's earliest formative years, director Tony Silver (1935–2008) and hip hop photographer/videographer Henry Chalfant's (1940–) created the American documentary *Style Wars*, which aired in 1983 on PBS and premiered in theatres in 1984.

Often credited as the first hip hop documentary, *Style Wars* introduced audiences worldwide to hip hop culture. Its main approach was that graffiti was both a form of creative expression and an art, as opposed to being viewed as vandalism. The film included interviews and the work of some of the most prominent New York City graffiti artists, such as Dondi (Donald Joseph White, 1961–1998), Futura (aka Futura 2000, Leonard Hilton McGurr, 1955–), Iz the Wiz (Michael Martin, 1958–2009), Seen UA (Richie Mirando, 1961–), and ZEPHYR (Andrew Witten, n.d.). *Style Wars* also featured breakdancers Crazy Legs (1966–) and Frosty Freeze (1963–2008), as well as a soundtrack of mostly old-school songs, such as the Sugarhill Gang's (1979–1985, 1994–) "8th Wonder" (1980), Grandmaster Flash and the Furious Five's (1976–1982, 1987–1988) "The Message" (1982), and Treacherous Three's (1978–1984) "Feel the Heartbeat" (1981). Coinciding with *Style Wars*' release were the American 1983 full-length hip hop feature films *Wildstyle* and *Flashdance* as well as 1984's *Breakin'* and *Breakin' 2: Electric Boogaloo*. The American documentary *Beat This: A Hip Hop History* (1984) immediately followed.

From the mid-1980s into the early 1990s, American hip hop documentaries and just a few non-American documentaries were released. Like *Style Wars*, these films explored at least one aspect of hip hop. Just one example is America's *Wreckin' Shop from Brooklyn* (1992), which focused on breakdancing. An early documentary on hip hop in England was *Electro Rock* (1985), a music video–based documentary that offered some of the earliest footage of b-girl activity outside the United States. Hip hop dancer Bubbles (1969–) was captured on film. Twenty years later she became the subject of another documentary, *Redder Than Red* (2005), produced in England, Germany, and the United States. The Dutch-made *Big Fun in the Big Town* (1986) was filmed in New York City. Its first half focused on proto-punk and rock singer Iggy Pop (James Newell Osterberg Jr., 1947–) and his band the Stooges (1967–1971, 1972–1974, 2003–2016); its second half focused on the New York hip hop scene, with interviews and some performances of pioneering American acts such as the Last Poets, Grandmaster Flash (1958–), Roxanne Shanté (1969–), Doug E. Fresh (1966–), Run-D.M.C. (1981–2002), LL Cool J (1968–), and Schoolly D (Jesse Bonds Weaver Jr., 1962–).

Te Kupu (aka D Word, Dean Hapeta, 1966–), a founding member of the Wellington, New Zealand/Aotearoa band Upper Hutt Posse (UHP, 1985–), codirected *Solidarity* (1992), a documentary on UHP's visit to the United States. Some full-length feature motion pictures that coincided with these documentaries include the

United States' *Krush Groove* (1985), *Colors* (1988), *Tougher Than Leather* (1988), *Straight out of Brooklyn* (1991), *Boyz n the Hood* (1991), *Juice* (1992), and *New Jack City* (1991), as well as Spike Lee (Shelton Jackson Lee, 1957–) films such as *Do the Right Thing* (1989). Lee's documentary directorial filmography includes *4 Little Girls* (1997), *Bad 25* (2012), and *Michael Jackson's Journey from Motown to "Off the Wall"* (2016).

Rusty Cundieff's (George Arthur Cundieff, 1960–) United States—and United Kingdom–produced *Fear of a Black Hat* (1993) is a mockumentary, much in the same comic vein as the American hard rock and heavy metal mockumentary *This Is Spinal Tap* (1984). *Fear of a Black Hat* parodies real hip hop artists, such as the members of Public Enemy (1986–) and N.W.A. (1986–1991), as well as Tamra Davis's (1962–) American film *CB4* (1993), which also parodies N.W.A. *CB4* also included segments that featured actual hip hop artists, such as Eazy-E (1964–1995), Ice Cube (1969–), Flavor Flav (1959–), and Ice-T (1958–), with performance footage.

By the mid-1990s and into the 21st century, documentary topics included a focus on elements of hip hop, much in the same way they were presented in *Style Wars*, as well as on artist biographies, behind-the-scenes glimpses of concerts and recordings, concert or battle performances, hip hop's influence, and outsider/insider perceptions of hip hop. By the time these films were made, old- and new-school were becoming history, Tupac Shakur (1971–1996) was dead, and Suge Knight (Marion Hugh Knight Jr., 1965–) was serving prison time. Just a few of these documentaries include the United States' *The Show* (1995), *Rhyme and Reason* (1997), *Jails, Hospitals, and Hip Hop* (2000), *Welcome to Death Row* (2001), *Tupac: Resurrection* (2003), the *Beef* films (2003, 2004, 2005, and 2007), *And You Don't Stop: 30 Years of Hip Hop* (2004), *Jay-Z: Fade to Black* (2004), *Just for Kicks* (2005), and *Rize* (2005); Australia's *Basic Equipment* (1998); the Netherlands and Tanzania's *Hali halisi* (*The Real Situation*, 1999); and the United Kingdom's *Biggie and Tupac* (2002).

In 2000, the American films *Downtown 81* (aka *New York Beat*, shot in 1980) and *Stations of the Elevated* (shot in 1981) were released. *Downtown 81* focused on graffiti artist Jean Basquiat (1960–1988) and featured graffiti artists Lee Quiñones (George Lee Quiñones, 1960–) and Fab Five Freddy (1959–). This film experience led to Fab Five Freddy's cocreating, filming, and producing *Wild Style*, director Charlie Ahearn's (1951–) American film, which showcased Quiñones's art. *Stations of the Elevated* has no voice-over narration and consists of a visual style reminiscent of early experimental films, such as Germany's *Berlin: Die sinfonie der großstadt* (*Berlin: Symphony of a Great City*, 1927–) and the Soviet Union's *Chelovek s kinoapparatom* (*Man with a Movie Camera*, 1929).

Female rappers became subjects of documentaries during this time. Petra Mäussnest's German (1967–) rap documentary *Will einmal bis zur sonne* (*I Want to Go to the Sun*, 2002) focuses on Brixx (Ildiko Basa, 1976–), an American-influenced Hungarian female MC who was raised in Kassel, Germany, and is based in Cologne, Germany. It also contains footage of German rappers Cora E. (aka Zulu-Queen, Sylvia Macco, 1968–) and Pyranja (Anja Käckenmeister, 1978–). Contemporary documentaries, such as Israel's *Arotzim shel za'am* (*Channels of Rage*, 2003), explore rap within the context of politics and culture. Instructional documentaries, such as the New York City turntablist crew the X-Ecutioners' (formerly X-Men, 1989–) U.S. film *Built to Scratch* (2004), have helped to place hip hop artists in the role of instructor. Turntablist skills in the United States and Europe are also highlighted in documentaries such as Canada's *Hang the DJ* (1998) and the United States' *Scratch* (2001); rap battles were the focus of the United States' *Freestyle: The Art of Rhyme* (2000), and beatboxing was featured in *Breath Control: The History of the Human Beat Box* (2002). Meanwhile, the United States' *The Freshest Kids: A History of the B-Boy* (2002) featured Crazy Legs (1966–) breakdancing.

From the mid-2000s into 2018, documentaries have exhibited increasing global collaboration. They also explore how hip hop has developed in countries outside the United States, as in Kenya's *Hip Hop Colony* (2006), Uganda's *Diamonds in the Rough: A Ugandan Hip Hop Revolution* (2007), Tanzania and Kenya's *Ni wakati!* (*It's Time*, 2010), Zimbabwe's *Zim Hip Hop Documentary* (2013), Argentina's *Buenos Aires Rap* (2014), and Germany's *Black Tape* (2015). Confronting stereotypes and facing obstacles have been covered in documentaries such as the United States' *Bad Rap* (2016) and *The Hip Hop Fellow* (2012), which focus, respectively, on Asian rappers and record producer, DJ, and recording executive 9th Wonder's (1975–) year as a fellow teaching courses at Harvard University. More documentaries focus on female involvement in hip hop, such as South Africa's *Counting Headz: South Afrika Sistaz in Hip Hop* (2007); Senegal's *Sarabah* (2012), about Senegalese rapper and anti–female genital mutilation activist Sister Fa (Fatou Diatta, 1982–); Afghanistan's *Hip Hop Kabul* (2013); Switzerland's *Sonita* (2015), about the Afghani rapper Sonita Alizadeh (1997*–); and the Czech Republic's *Girl Power* (2016).

Humor is frequently employed, as exemplified in the United Kingdom's *The Great Hip Hop Hoax* (2013), which focuses on a Scottish duo with made-up identities and affected Californian accents who become "the rapping Proclaimers" (1983–) and pursue a recording career in the United States. Other hip hop documentary-comedies include the United States' *Dave Chappelle's Block Party* (2006), the United Kingdom's *Exit through the Gift Shop* (2010), and New Zealand's *Hip Hop-eration* (2014). In addition to humor, documentaries such as Luxembourg's *Hamilius: Hip Hop Culture in Luxembourg* (2010), Mongolia and Australia's *Mongolian Bling* (2012), and the United States' *Shake the Dust* (2014) use irony to explore hip hop found in unlikely locations. Another theme in hip hop documentaries is copyright. Examples include the United States' *Alternative Freedom* (2006) and *Copyright Criminals* (2009) and Denmark's *Good Copy, Bad Copy* (2007).

Though these new themes have emerged in hip hop documentaries, older themes remain popular. Hip hop history is constantly being updated and readdressed in documentaries such as the United States' *Planet B-Boy* (2007), *I Am Hip Hop: The Chicago Hip Hop Documentary* (2008), *History and Concept of Hip Hop Dance* (2010), and *Uprising: Hip Hop and the L.A. Riots* (2012) and Canada's *Hip Hop Evolution* (2016). Documentaries that follow hip hop acts, providing historical or political context, include the United States and Palestine's *Slingshot Hip Hop* (2008), Switzerland's *Moi c'est moi—Ich bin ich* (*I Am I*, 2011), the United States and China's *Underground Hip Hop in China* (2011), and the United States' *Beats, Rhymes, and Life: The Travels of A Tribe Called Quest* (2011). Behind-the-scenes concert preparations and reunions continue in documentaries such as the United States' *Rock the Bells* (2006), about Wu-Tang Clan's intended final concert performance, and the United States and Morocco's *I Love Hip Hop in Morocco* (2007).

Biographical documentaries continue, including U.S. films such as *Notorious B.I.G.: Bigger Than Life* (2007), *2 Turntables and a Microphone: The Life and Death of Jam Master Jay* (2008), *The Wonder Year* (2011), and *Ruthless Memories: Preserving the Life and Legend of Eric (Eazy-E) Wright* (2012). Several of these documentaries coincide with or precede biopics such as American films *Notorious* (2009), on the Notorious B.I.G. (1967–1997), and *All Eyez on Me* (2017), on Tupac Shakur. The documentary *2 Turntables and a Microphone*, however, appeared years after *Tougher Than Leather* (1988), the American musical crime drama and blaxploitation/spaghetti western parody motion picture starring Run-D.M.C. (1981–2002). Related to biographical documentaries are documentaries that focus on hip hop music studios, such as the United States and France's *Our Vinyl Weighs a Ton: This Is Stones Throw Records* (2013), and those covering emerging movements or aesthetics, such as the United States' *Nerdcore for Life* (2008) and *Nerdcore Rising* (2008). Documentaries that investigate hip hop and crime continue. These include U.S. films *Rap Sheet: Hip Hop and the Cops* (2006) and *Rhyme and Punishment* (2011).

Other recent films continue to explore graffiti (e.g., the U.S. films *Overspray 1.0* [2006], *Bomb It* [2007] and *Bomb It 2* [2010] and the Netherland's *Kroonjuwelen: Hard Times, Good Times, Better Times* [*Crown Jewels*, 2006]), fashion (e.g., the United States' *Fresh Dressed* [2015]), beatboxing (e.g., the United States' *Beatboxing: The Fifth Element of Hip Hop* [2011]), and breakdancing (e.g., the United Kingdom's *Turn It Loose!* [2009] and the United States' *Bomb It, Bomb It 2*, and *Bouncing Cats* [2010]). At times, hip hop artists have turned film projects into labors of love. An example is the Welfare Poets's (WP, 1997–) *No Human Being Is Illegal: The Story and Struggle of the Other Hidden People of Iceland* (2013), which was inspired by the group's work in Iceland assisting refugees. Another example is Chuck D's (1960–) commissioned film about the Last Poets, *Hustler's Convention* (2015, United Kingdom).

Melissa Ursula Dawn Goldsmith

See also: Battling; Breakdancing; Filmmaking (Feature Films Made in the United States); Filmmaking (Feature Films Made outside the United States); Graffiti Art; Hip Hop Dance; Turntablism

Further Reading

Donalson, Melvin Burke. 2007. *Hip Hop in American Cinema.* New York: Peter Lang.

George, Courtney. 2016. "From Bounce to the Mainstream: Hip Hop Representations of Post-Katrina New Orleans in Music, Film and Television." *European Journal of American Culture* 35, no. 1: 17–32.

Monteyne, Kimberley. 2013. *Hip Hop on Film: Performance, Culture, Urban Space, and Genre Transformation in the 1980s.* Jackson: University Press of Mississippi.

Raimist, Rachel, Kevin Epps, and Michael Wanguhu. 2007. "Put Your Camera Where My Eyes Can See Hip Hop Video, Film, and Documentary." In *Total Chaos: The Art and Aesthetics of Hip Hop*, edited by Jeff Chang, chap. 31. New York: Civitas Books.

Watkins, S. Craig. 1998. *Representing: Hip Hop Culture and the Production of Black Cinema.* Chicago: University of Chicago Press.

Filmmaking (Feature Films Made in the United States)

Filmmaking, both in the United States and across the globe, has been greatly influenced by hip hop music and culture—from soundtrack choices to story content, character development, and cinematic style. In a mainstream and American example, Darren Aronofsky's (1969–) film π (aka *Pi,* 1998), adopted a form of audiovisual editing he called "hip hop montage." This technique featured visual and sonic ruptures, fractures, and repetitions inspired by the backspinning, punch phrasing, and scratching employed in hip hop music. Screen productions more specific to the hip hop genre and culture range from feature films to music videos (though it took years for MTV [1981–] to fully embrace hip hop videos) and documentaries. Hip hop filmmaking is usually associated with the hip hop musicals of the early 1980s in the United States and the related tradition of Hollywood-style gangsta films produced into the 1990s and beyond.

EARLY EFFORTS

The hip hop films of the early 1980s include such American works as *Wild Style* (1983), *Beat Street* (1984), and *Krush Groove* (1985). In light of African American cinematic practices that came directly before and after them, these films are often considered unremarkable. Some of the previous African American genres included blaxploitation films, a genre that in the 1970s produced iconic visual experiences such as *Shaft* (1971) and *Foxy Brown* (1974). In addition, New Jack Cinema, which stretched from the mid-1980s onward, produced classics such as *New Jack City* (1991). The early 1980s hip hop films were later dubbed hip hop musicals because, like traditional musicals, they feature celebrities (rappers, playing themselves) who perform on screen. *Krush Groove*, for instance, featured Run-D.M.C. (1981–2002), LL Cool J (1968–), and Beastie Boys (1980–2012). These musicals also maintain narrative elements from traditional stage and film musicals, including both ensemble performances and the entanglement of a budding but endangered heterosexual romance with on-screen musical numbers. More important for the tradition of hip hop filmmaking, however, is that these musicals introduced key tropes from urban youth culture into film practice, including the centralization of rap celebrities and other markers of hip hop culture such as graffiti art, breakdancing, and hip hop fashion. In these films, the city (often New York, and more specifically the Bronx) becomes a primary space of meaning, a fact that has powerfully impacted hip hop filmmaking over the ensuing decades.

PLACE AS FILM SPACE: SPIKE LEE AND NEW JACK CINEMA

The focus on place is evident in the films of Spike Lee (Shelton Jackson Lee, 1957–), one of the more influential African American directors of the late 20th and early 21st centuries. Financed by the Hollywood studio system but still able to retain impressive autonomy, Lee had the freedom to control his own narratives and to experiment with form, all while marketing extensively. His films, which include *She's Gotta Have It* (1986), *Do the Right Thing* (1989), *Malcolm X* (1992),

Bamboozled (2000), and *Inside Man* (2006), are highly reflexive, interrogating the role of history and of the city—in his case Brooklyn—in shaping black culture. Film techniques borrowed from the Italian neorealists (1944–1952), the French new wave (1958–1969), and early Soviet filmmaking (1920–1930) are woven through his films, including a focus on location shooting, a preference for ordinary characters, and the use of montage and visible editing strategies such as jump cuts. He is also known for making documentaries and for employing this documentary style in his dramatic feature films. *Do the Right Thing*, for instance, explored racism by representing a 24-hour period in a single block of Bed-Stuy (Bedford-Stuyvesant), a neighborhood in Brooklyn, New York, illuminating the conflicting pressures of the inner city. Lee's use of hip hop music in this film demonstrated that the genre could be used to depict a wide array of associations, including location, emotional and mental states, historical setting, generational perspectives, and black male and female subjectivity.

Films such as *Do the Right Thing* provided a powerful model for the burgeoning New Jack Cinema (named after the highly successful *New Jack City* and also referred to as New Black Realism). This brand of filmmaking continues the focus on young black men in the inner city of Brooklyn or Los Angeles; they are usually gangsta-type characters who clash over drug culture on one hand and community regeneration on the other. These films tend to be violent and visually realistic, and they demonstrate how women, children, the elderly, the unemployed, and systems of belief are implicated in—or are victims of—such conflicts. Films such as *Boyz n the Hood* (1991), *Straight out of Brooklyn* (1991), *Menace II Society* (1993), and *Above the Rim* (1994) portray real anxieties over rising unemployment in black communities, the criminalization of young black men, and a growing sense of helplessness. Hip hop and rap continue to be prominent in these works as part of a network of signifiers that provide the audience with access to the cultures on screen. Such films are often criticized for their misogynistic messages and for portraying a one-dimensional black youth culture, playing off of African American guilt regarding the tension between cultural authenticity and upward mobility. A related hip hop–film tradition has emerged in France, where movies such as *Banlieue 13* (*District B13*, aka *B-13*, 2004) demonstrate the influence of hip hop culture and New Jack Cinema and where the French *banlieue* (suburb) stands in place of the United States' hood.

HOLLYWOOD IN THE 2000s

Hip hop film in Hollywood has diffused over time, broadening in genre and style, and focusing less on the inner city and black cultural themes. Films such as *Dead Presidents* (1995) and *Eve's Bayou* (1997) fall under historical realism; *The Best Man* (1999) and *Love and Basketball* (2000) are romances; and *Don't Be a Menace to South Central While Drinking Your Juice in the Hood* (1996) is a parody of the New Jack genre.

Since the 2000s, hip hop film has taken the form of other genres, such as opera adaptations (for example, *Carmen: A Hip Hopera*, 2001). But older genres, such as the youth dance flick (*Save the Last Dance*, 2005), the coming-of-age and achieving-your-dreams film (*Feel the Noise*, 2007; *Step Off*, originally *Battle*, 2011), the horror movie (the *Blade* series, 1998–2004), and the crime drama (*Ill Manors*, 2012), continue to be made as well. Documentary filming techniques have been employed more than ever in several popular hip hop biopics, as exemplified in *Straight Outta Compton* (2015), on N.W.A. (1986–1991), and *All Eyez on Me* (2017), on Tupac Shakur (1971–1996).

Jessica Leah Getman

See also: Fashion; Gangs (United States); Gangsta Rap; Graffiti Art; Hip Hop Dance; Filmmaking (Documentaries); Filmmaking (Feature Films Made outside the United States); New Jack Swing; The United States

Further Reading

Harkness, Geoff. 2015. "Thirty Years of Rapsploitation: Hip Hop Culture in American Cinema." In *The Cambridge Companion to Hip Hop*, edited by Justin Williams, chap. 12. Cambridge, England: Cambridge University Press.

Massood, Paula J. 2003. *Black City Cinema: African American Urban Experiences in Film*. Philadelphia: Temple University Press.

Monteyne, Kimberley. 2013. *Hip Hop on Film: Performance, Culture, Urban Space, and Genre Transformation in the 1980s*. Jackson: University Press of Mississippi.

Filmmaking (Feature Films Made outside the United States)

Few full-length motion pictures on hip hop are made outside of the United States, the country that originated seminal hip hop motion pictures such as *Wild Style* (1983), *Breakin'* and *Breakin' 2: Electric Boogaloo* (1984), and *Beat Street* (1984), as well as documentaries such as *Style Wars* (1983). A few European documentaries such as the United Kingdom's *Electro Rock* (1985) followed, but it took some time before more full-length hip hop motion pictures were made outside the United States.

Two of the earliest examples of such full-length hip hop films were Hong Kong's *Ching fung dik sau* (*Mismatched Couples*, 1985) and Sweden's *Stockholmsnatt* (*Stockholm Night*, aka *The King of Kungsan*, 1987). The main character in *Ching fung dik sau* is Eddie, a teenage b-boy who meets an acrobat and contortionist named Mini, a poor opera performer who works on the street as a busker and hawker. Complications begin when Eddie convinces his sister to allow Mini to stay with them for a while and to help at her fast food restaurant. *Ching fung dik sau* is a romantic comedy that was released the same year as the American film *Krush Groove* in the United States, but breakdancing in the film is used much more the way it was used in *Flashdance* (1983) in that breakdancers are featured. Though the main character can breakdance, hip hop dance is just a backdrop. *Stockholmsnatt* is an urban crime drama starring legendary American record producer, composer, musician, and film producer Quincy Jones (1933–), who costars as part of an ensemble named Bezerk; he also scored the film's music. The film takes place in Stockholm's park, the Kungsträdgården, which in the movie is taken over by violent teenagers, and its protagonist is Paolo, an Italian in Sweden who develops a passion for Kung Fu films and ultimately inflicts violence on innocent people.

The film, with its violence, urban themes, and hip hop–inspired music (including beatboxing), became a cult classic in Sweden.

The 1990s saw some American collaboration with other countries on films such as *Fear of a Black Hat* (1993), produced in both the United States and the United Kingdom, and *Whiteboyz* (1999), produced in France and the United States, but both films are perceived as American hip hop films with elements of American, not European, hip hop. *Fear of a Black Hat* was the first hip hop mockumentary that parodied well known American hip hop acts such as Public Enemy (1986–) and N.W.A. (1986–1991), whereas *Whiteboyz* focuses on a protagonist named Flip, who lives in an all-white town in Iowa and dreams of being a hip hop music star who can hang out with Dr. Dre (1965–) and Snoop Dogg (1971–). The film features Dr. Dre and Snoop Dogg as themselves, as well as beatboxer Doug E. Fresh (1966–) and rapper Slick Rick (1965–), who are credited as Parking Lot Rappers #1 and #2, and rapper Big Pun (1971–2000), who is an uncredited member of the fictional Don Flip crew. Meanwhile, India's *Kadhalan* (1994) and Japan's *'Hood* (1998), both with very few hip hop dance and music moments, were released. The first Tamil motion picture that featured rap was *Baba* (2002), which featured rapper–turned–playback singer Blaaze singing "Baba Rap."

The 2000s involved a continuation of collaborations, with hip hop motion pictures such as the United States and France's *Brooklyn Babylon* (2001) and the United States and Thailand's *Province 77* (2002). While American directors shot both films on location in the United States, they touch on the protagonist's outsider status, as seen in *Stockholmsnatt*. Filmed by Marc Levin (n.d.), the son of documentary filmmaker and journalist Alan Levin (1926–2006), as part of his hip hop trilogy, which began with the American basketball film *Slam* (1998) and *Whiteboyz*, *Brooklyn Babylon* is a *Romeo and Juliet* love story between Sara, a woman betrothed to Judah in her Jewish Lubavitch community, and hip hop songwriter Sol, who is black. The film also focuses on tensions between the Lubavitch community and West Indian Rastafarians and other black neighbors. Members of the Roots (1987–) play members of the Lions; the Roots' beatboxer, Rahzel (Rahzel Manely Brown, n.d.), is the film's narrator. *Province 77* is shot in Los Angeles and focuses on Thai town, called Thailand's 77th Province for the expatriate Thais who settle there. The main characters are conflicted between maintaining their Thai culture and embracing an urban life that consists of hip hop, street violence, and drugs. The Thai American hip hop group Thaitanium (2000–) scored the film's soundtrack.

Other films taking place during the first decade of the 2000s were France's *Banlieue 13* (*District B13*, aka *B-13*, 2004), Finland's *Tyttö sinä olet tähti* (*Beauty and the Bastard*, 2005), and the United Kingdom's *Ali G Indahouse* (2002) and a series of films known as *Kidulthood* and *Adulthood* (2006 and 2008) that were later followed by *Brotherhood* (2016). *Ali G Indahouse* showcases internationally known English comedian Sacha Baron Cohen's (1971–) character Ali G (Alistair Leslie Graham) as a white English rude boy who has a penchant for hip hop, reggae, and other kinds of urban music. *Banlieue 13*, as well as *Kidulthood* and *Adulthood*, in contrast, were dramas. *Banlieue 13* resembles New Jack Cinema thrillers such as *New Jack City* (1991), where the French *banlieue* (suburb) stands in place of the United States hood.

By the 2010s, there was greater global variety in hip hop motion pictures, with films such as Ghana's *Coz ov Moni: The First Pidgin Musical Film in the World* (2010) and *Coz ov Moni 2 (FOKN Revenge)* (2013), Vietnam's *Sài gòn yo!* (*Saigon Electric*, 2011), Japan's *Tokyo Tribe* (2014), New Zealand's *Born to Dance* (2015), Israel's *Junction 48* (2016), and India's *Meesaya murukku* (*Twirl Your Moustache*, 2017), as well as European films or American European collaborations such as the United Kingdom's *Anuvahood* (2011) and *Ill Manors* (2012), the Netherlands' *Body Language* (2011), France's *Qu'Allah bénisse la France!* (*May Allah Bless France*, 2014), and the United States and Germany's *Morris from America* (2016). Hip hop music is in the foreground of *Coz ov Moni*, which takes place in Ghana. The sequel features the Ghanaian hip hop group FOKN Bois (2008–).

Following the previous decade's *Tyttö sinä olet tähti*, romance films in which the couple share a mutual talent or love for hip hop, such as *Junction 48*, have increased in the 2010s. Hip hop dancing also remains popular, as shown in *Sài gòn yo* and *Born to Dance*. *Morris from America* focuses again on the outsider theme, this time more lightheartedly as a fish-out-of-water comedy. What remains clear in this decade is that global hip hop films are strongly inspired by American ones, though they are increasingly giving a stronger sense of place as identity.

Melissa Ursula Dawn Goldsmith

See also: Breakdancing; Filmmaking (Documentaries); Filmmaking (Feature Films Made in the United States); Hip Hop Dance

Further Reading

Bluher, Dominique. 2001. "Hip Hop Cinema in France." *Camera Obscura* 16, no. 1: 77–96.

Orlando, Valerie. 2003. "From Rap to Raï in the Mixing Bowl: Beur Hip Hop Culture and Banlieue Cinema in Urban France." *Journal of Popular Culture* 36, no. 3: 395–416.

Shary, Timothy, and Alexandra Seibel. 2007. *Youth Culture in Global Cinema*. Austin: University of Texas Press.

Finland

Finland is a Nordic Scandinavian country with a population that is majority Finnish (followed by Finland-Swedes and other minority populations). Hip hop, called *Suomiräp* (*Suomârâp* in Sámi) or just *Räp* (*Râp*), emerged in Finland in the mid-1980s; however, popular music preferences leaned toward rock, pop, heavy metal, and experimental metal. Though many early Finnish rappers rapped in English, later rappers have used mainly the Finnish language, though Helsinki slang and dialects have made their way into the music. Although the first recorded Finnish rap song was General Njassa's (Jyrki Leo Jantunen, n.d.) "I'm Young, Beautiful and Natural" (1983) and pioneer humorous rap group Raptori (1989–) was founded in Hyvinkää six years later, Finnish rap did not catch on until the 2000s. Raptori's first album, *Moe!*, sold over 80,000 copies.

Most Finnish people reside in the capital, Helsinki, or other southern cities such as Tampere, Oulu, and Turku. The national languages of Finland are Finnish and Swedish, with Swedish being taught to most Finns at an early age. A much less common recognized language is Sámi, spoken not only by the Inari Sámi people in North Finland but also by the Sámi people in Norway, Sweden, and Russia. Traditional Finnish music includes Karelian songs about Finnish heroic mythology (for example, *Runonlaulanta*, a kind of chanting called *poem singing*), Nordic folksongs with Scandinavian influence (such as Pelimanni music played first on fiddle and clarinet, then on harmonium and accordion), Germanic or Swedish ballads called *Rekilaulu* (sleigh songs), and Sámi music (spiritual songs known as *Jolk*). Finland also has an established history of classical music, most notably producing composers such as Jean Sibelius (Johan Julius Christian Sibelius, 1865–1957), Yrjö Kilpinen (1892–1959), and Esa-Pekka Salonen (1958–). Nationalist tendencies favored folk and classical music until the 1930s, but by the 1940s, light popular songs called *Iskelmä* (meaning hits) were being played on the radio, followed by American rock in the 1950s.

The late 1990s saw the emergence of the Helsinki duo Fintelligens (1997–), the most successful hip hop band in Finland, which released three highly successful albums and cofounded the record label Rähinä Records (2003–). Other popular rap artists included Asa (aka Avain, Matti Salo, 1980–) and Paleface (Karri Pekka Matias Miettinen, 1978–), who both wrote socially conscious lyrics; Ruudolf (Rudy Frans Kulmala, 1983–), known for downbeat music, calm delivery, freestyle skills, and self-improvement lyrics; ex-Fintelligens rapper and producer Elastinen (Kimmo Ilpo Juhani Laiho, 1981–); rapper Cheek (Jare Henrik Tiihonen, 1981–), who has released nine albums; Stig (Pasi Siitonen, 1978–), a crossover act between hip hop, R&B, and country music; and rap crew Notkea Rotta (2001–), which infuses its lyrics with comedy. Inari-based Amoc, an acronym for Aanaar Master of Ceremony (Mikkâl Antti Morottaja, 1984–), raps in Sámi.

As of 2018, the Finnish rap scene is divided between underground and mainstream acts, the former opting for more socially conscious rap.

Melissa Ursula Dawn Goldsmith and Anthony J. Fonseca

See also: Sweden

Further Reading

Leppänen, Sirpa, and Sari Pietikäinen. 2010. "Urban Rap Goes to Arctic Lapland: Breaking through and Saving the Endangered Inari Sámi Language." In *Language and the Market*, edited by Helen Kelly-Holmes and Gerlinde Mautner, chap. 12. Basingstoke, England: Palgrave Macmillan.

Tervo, Mervi. 2014. "From Appropriation to Translation: Localizing Rap Music to Finland." *Popular Music and Society* 37, no. 2: 169–86.

Further Listening

Amoc. 2007. *Amok-kaččam*. Tuupa Records.

Fintelligens. 2008. *Lisää* (*More*). Rähinä Records.

Five Percent Nation

(1964–, Harlem, New York)

The Five Percent Nation is an Islamic organization that is sometimes also referred to as the Nation of Gods and Earths. It was founded by a former member of the

Nation of Islam, Clarence 13X (Clarence Edward Smith, 1928–1969), in the early 1960s, and in its early years it comprised mostly other former Nation of Islam (1930–) members. The term Five Percenters, as practitioners are called, refers to the belief that the world's population is divided into three categories: the first and largest group (85 percent) are ignorant of both themselves and God; the second group (10 percent) are the elite who know the truth but do not share it with others, lying to the 85 percent in order to benefit themselves; the third group (5 percent) comprises those who know the truth and seek to educate and enlighten the ignorant 85 percent. They also refer to themselves as the Poor Righteous Teachers, whose spiritual responsibility is to teach others the doctrine of their faith. Five Percenter men are referred to as Gods and Five Percenter women as Earths, which gave rise to the more recent name for the organization, Nation of Gods and Earths. Five Percenters believe that God and the universe can be understood through science and mathematics.

Like the Nation of Islam, Five Percent Nation theology posits that the original race consisted of black- and brown-skinned people and that all other races are descended from them. Members of the Nation of Islam and Five Percenters believe that God is a man but differ on who that man is. Nation of Islam members believe that their organization's founder, Wallace Fard Muhammad (Wallace Dodd Fard, 1877–1934*), is Allah reincarnate. Clarence 13X rejected this idea, claiming that because Fard was most likely Arab and not black, he could not be Allah, since it is the black man that is God personified.

The Five Percent Nation shares most of their doctrine with the Nation of Islam, including the style of passing on doctrine through lessons that students, or initiates, learn by rote memorization through a series of questions and answers. The first two lessons that the Five Percenters use differ from those of the Nation of Islam and are called the "Science of Supreme Mathematics" and the "Supreme Alphabet." The Five Percenter lessons end with another additional set, called "Solar Facts," which are also unique to them. Together these three lessons emphasize the role of science and numerology in Five Percenter doctrine. In the Science of Supreme Mathematics, each number is given a symbolic meaning (for example, 1 = Knowledge, 2 = Wisdom, 0 = Cipher), as is each letter in the Supreme Alphabet (A = Allah, G = God, U = You or Universe). Five Percenters use the Science of Supreme Mathematics and the Supreme Alphabet to explain God and the universe and to share knowledge with the unenlightened.

ROLE IN HIP HOP

Five Percenters have played an influential role in hip hop from its earliest days. During the mid-1970s, they gained a reputation for being peacekeepers at hip hop parties, keeping rival gang activity away from events and allowing performers such as DJ Kool Herc (1955–) to focus on music and dancing. Many artists openly claimed affiliation or membership with the group, and during the late 1980s into the 1990s, as socially conscious rap gained traction and some commercial success, artists such as Rakim (1968–), of Eric B. and Rakim (1986–1993), and Chuck D (1960–), of Public

Enemy (1982–), brought teachings from the Five Percent Nation to black American youth through their music. Brand Nubian (1989–), Wu-Tang Clan (1992–), Poor Righteous Teachers (1989–1996), Big Daddy Kane (1968–), Nas (1973–), Mos Def (1973–), Gang Starr (1986–2006), the Roots (1987–), and Erykah Badu (1971–) are all artists or groups who are either former or current members of the Five Percent Nation and/or have referenced Five Percenter ideology in their music.

Musicologist Felicia Miyakawa identifies four main tools through which hip hop artists disseminate Five Percenter theology: lyrics; flow, layering, and rupture; sampling and musical borrowing; and album packaging and organization (p. 37). For example, some rappers use Supreme Mathematics and/or the Supreme Alphabet to embed their lyrics with references to Five Percenter lessons and teachings. In "Soul Controller," for instance, Brand Nubian's Grand Puba (Maxwell Dixon, 1966–) refers to Supreme Mathematics when he raps about terms such as "Knowledge Cipher," "Power," and "Wisdom" and associates each with numerology. He also refers to Five Percenter ideology earlier in the song, when he offers peace to all the Gods and Earths. Additionally, he observes the power of being black, noting that the black man comes first.

Lauron Jockwig Kehrer

See also: Big Daddy Kane; Black Nationalism; Brand Nubian; Chuck D; Eric B. and Rakim; Erykah Badu; Gang Starr; Mos Def; Nas; Nation of Islam; Poor Righteous Teachers; The Roots; The United States; Wu-Tang Clan

Further Reading

Hakeem Grewal, Sara. 2013. "Intra- and Interlingual Translation in Blackamerican Muslim Hip Hop." *African American Review* 46, no. 1: 37–54.
Miyakawa, Felicia. 2005. *Five Percenter Rap: God Hop's Music, Message, and Black Muslim Mission.* Bloomington: Indiana University Press.

Flavor Flav

(aka Flav, William Jonathan Drayton Jr., 1959–, Long Island, New York)

Flavor Flav is an American rapper, comic actor, restaurateur, and reality television show personality who was the first and quintessential hype man in early American rap, when he served in that capacity for Public Enemy (1982–). As a multi-instrumentalist, he plays piano, guitar, bass, saxophone, clarinet, drums, and percussion. He got his start with Chuck D (1960–), who cofounded and then fronted Public Enemy. Flavor Flav's role was to provide comic relief and color for the band's performances, which he would do through exaggerated, elongated yells such as his benchmark "Yeah boy!"

After a successful run with Public Enemy, he had legal and financial troubles, spent time in jail, and ended up living in a small Brooklyn apartment, only to resurface not as a rapper but as a comic personality in various VH1 (1985–) reality series. On the advice of MC Hammer (1962–), Flavor Flav appeared in the third season of *Surreal Life* (aka *The Surreal Life*, 2003–2006), the short-lived *Strange Love* (2005), and the hit *Flavor of Love* (2006–2008). He is best known as the hype man, appearing publicly in oversized, brightly colored caps turned sideways, top hats, Viking horns and crowns, oversized plastic glasses, and a wall clock dangling on a chain from his neck. He typically wore brightly colored tracksuits; large neon jackets or, conversely, dark gang jackets; or unnaturally brightly colored ties and tails. He would also jump around or dance outrageously on stage.

As a five-year-old, he started teaching himself piano and was recognized as a musical prodigy, singing and playing piano, drums, and guitar. Unfortunately, he was also extremely mischievous, accidentally setting a house on fire. By his junior year of high school, he had been in jail; he dropped out of school. After straightening out his life, he began attending Adelphi University and met Chuck D. The duo became friends and coworkers, working for Chuck D's father, and collaborated on Chuck D's hip hop college radio show, then began rapping. The two cofounded Public Enemy in 1982, and the group released a track, "Public Enemy #1," which caught Def Jam Records' (1983–) Rick Rubin's (Frederick Jay Rubin, 1963–) attention and was released by Def Jam in 1987.

The two, as Public Enemy, were signed to Def Jam in 1986, even though Rubin originally wanted Chuck D as a solo act. The band's first album, *Yo! Bum Rush the Show* (1987), included "Public Enemy #1" (as "Public Enemy No. 1") and made it clear that Flavor Flav was essential as Chuck D's comic relief, to better sell his serious, urgent rapping style. Public Enemy's next album, *It Takes a Nation of Millions to Hold Us Back* (1988), was certified double Platinum, and the Spike Lee–commissioned single "Fight the Power" (1989) made Chuck D and Flavor Flav household names, the latter serving as the band's public face and promotional voice. As a rapper, Flavor Flav usually rapped higher harmonies to Chuck D's lead, but he was given a few rap leads, on songs such as "911 Is a Joke," from the classic album *Fear of a Black Planet* (1999). In 2006, he released his only solo album, *Flavor Flav*.

Anthony J. Fonseca

See also: Chuck D; Flavor Flav; Public Enemy; The United States

Further Reading

Grierson, Tim. 2015. *Public Enemy: Inside the Terrordome.* London: Omnibus Press.

Radford, Benjamin. 2016. "Bad Clowns of the Song." In *Bad Clowns*, chap. 7. Albuquerque: University of New Mexico Press.

France

France is a Western European presidential republic that includes overseas regions and territories such as French Guiana (South America) and several ocean islands, adding up to a total population of 67 million people, many of whom live in its urban centers: Paris, Marseille, Lyon, Lille, Nice, Toulouse, and Bordeaux. French hip hop had emerged by 1983, following the New York City Rap Tour that traveled to France and England. French rappers and DJs such as David Guetta (Pierre David Guetta, 1967–), Lionel D (Lionel Eguienta, 1959–), and French Senegalese–Chadian MC Solaar (1969–), who had moved to France in 1970 and became the first certified-Platinum French hip hop artist, imported the music style from New York City; it soon became an underground-scene music.

France's music exemplifies diversity: classical, romantic, folk, popular, *chanson*, and *cabaret* styles are found throughout the country. In 1857, Paris-based Édouard-Léon Scott de Martinville (1817–1879) patented the earliest-known sound-recording device, the *phonautograph*. The country's music industry has produced many internationally renowned artists. Notated French music dates back to the 10th century with the Notre Dame School of composers and the songs of troubadours and trouvères, continuing on through Western art music history with the ars nova and Burgundian Schools of composers and beyond. Music ranges from concert music during the Baroque era through the postmodern era to various region-specific folk and popular styles such as the *chanson* and electronica.

Traditional instrumentation includes the bagpipe, the hurdy-gurdy, the accordion, the lute, the mandolin, and various horns. Between France and Spain live the Basques, an indigenous ethnic group whose improvised poetry as bards expressed the concerns of the people and was critical to Basque culture. Another ethnic group, Corsicans from the Mediterranean island of Corsica (a territorial collectivity of France), developed monophonic and polyphonic songs as well, the last with intricate harmonies that led to improvised polyphonic singing. These polyphonic songs nearly went out of practice until the 1970s, when they were revived for the purpose of stressing Corsican national identity as well as political protest for Corsican independence.

Throughout the 20th century, benchmark French singers included Édith Piaf (Édith Giovanna Gassion, 1915–1963), Juliette Gréco (1927–), Mireille Mathieu (1946–), Gilbert Bécaud (François Gilbert Léopold Silly, 1927–2001), and Charles Aznavour (Shahnour Vaghinag Aznavourian, 1924–). During the 1970s, new artists modernized the *chanson française* until it became the *nouvelle chanson*, which opened the door for rock and pop music, including punk and electronic dance, setting the stage for French house music in the late 1990s with bands such as Paris-based Daft Punk (1993–). Earlier, Moroccan-born French composer, singer-songwriter, arranger, and producer Jacques Morali (1947–1991) and French producer Henri Belolo (1936–) founded the internationally successful dance band the Village People (1977–1985, 1987–) in the United States. Since the early 1980s, France has had one of the largest hip hop markets, including *zouk*, *bouyon*, and *raï* musics produced and purchased in Martinique, Guadeloupe, Haiti, Dominican Republic, and parts of Africa.

In 1984, French rapper, DJ, and producer Dee Nasty (Daniel Bigeault, 1960–) released the rap album *Paname City Rappin'*, and in 1991, MC Solaar's *Qui sème le vent récolte le tempo* became a hit (the title is a pun of the French translation of the Biblical proverb from Hosea 8:7, *Qui séme le vent récolte la tempête*, meaning "He who sows the wind reaps the whirlwind").

Around 1983, hip hop radio shows began to be heard in Paris. Guadeloupean DJ Sidney (Patrick Duteil, 1955–) began hosting the show *Rapper Dapper Snapper*, and later in 1984, he hosted the show *H.I.P. H.O.P.* (1984), becoming the first black man in France to host a weekly television show. Meanwhile, Dee Nasty hosted Funk à Billy, and by 1987 he was well received at the DMC World DJ Championships. Although some French hip hop is informed by a mellow, downtempo style, hardcore rap performers are also popular. The group Assassin (1985–2006) is a hardcore rap

Assuming their robot personas, Paris-based French house-music duo Daft Punk stand next to Beyoncé at the Tidal launch event, which took place in 2015 at Skylight at Moynihan Station in New York City. Like Beyoncé and her husband Jay-Z, Daft Punk was identified as one of several artist co-owners of the music streaming service. (Jamie McCarthy/Getty Images for Roc Nation)

act that began in the underground scene doing sociopolitical rap. Suprême NTM (aka NTM, 1989–2001, 2008–), which has infused some of its songs with soul and reggae beats, performs violent, gangsta-style antipolice, antiracist rap. Marseille-based IAM (1989–) performs pro-Africa, pro-immigrant music with an Egyptian flair; its 1997 album *L'école du micro d'argent* (*The School of Microphone Money*) received Platinum certification.

Many hardcore rappers set themselves up in opposition to what they considered to be a sellout mainstream style. These include multi-Platinum-status rapper Booba (Elie Yaffa, 1976–), Africa- and Caribbean-born hip hop group 113 (1999–2010), Madagascar-born rapper Rohff (aka Roh2f, Housni Mkouboi, 1977–), four-man rap group La Rumeur (1995–), Paris-based hip hop duo Lunatic (1994–2003), and Moroccan-born rapper Kamelanc' (aka Kamelancien, Kamel Jdayni Houari, 1980–). More mainstream rappers include Kery James (aka Daddy Kery, Alix Mathurin, 1977–), Médine (Medine Zaouiche, 1983–), Youssoupha (Youssoupha Mabiki, 1979–), and Fonky Family (1994–2007). Guadeloupe-born to Haitian parents, Kery James is a rapper and singer-songwriter as well as a hip hop dancer and record producer. He is also part of French hip hop and rap collective Mafia K-1 Fry (1995–). Kabyle (Algerian) rapper Médine is a Muslim rapper whose songs tend to the political, protesting poverty, oppression, and religious persecution. Congo-born Youssoupha is the son of musician and Congo-Kinshasa political figure Tabu Ley Rochereau

(Pascal-Emmanuel Sinamoyi Tabu, 1937–2013). Marseille-based group Fonky Family was one of the original French hip hop bands of the early 1990s.

Overall, French hip hop music has evolved from being imitative of Americans to music that infuses cultural and ethnic traditions. For example, African-based French hip hop artists write songs about African poverty and use African instruments such as the *kora, balafon, ngoni, djembe, gwo ka drums,* and *bèlè drums*; French Antilles hip hop is infused with Caribbean themes and rhythms. In addition to music, France has a vibrant b-boy and b-girl scene, including champions such as Lilou (Ali Ramdani, 1984–), an Algerian French member of the all-star LEGION X (n.d.) crew, and popping expert Salah (aka Spider Salah, Salah Benlemqawanssa, 1979–), who infuses animation, boogaloo, and effects into his style. Breakdancing emerged in the early 1980s with the Paris City Breakers (1981–), and DJ Duteil made France the first country to broadcast a television series with a focus on b-boying.

Anthony J. Fonseca

See also: Algeria; Belgium; Breakdancing; Egypt; Guadeloupe; Haiti; Martinique; MC Solaar; Paris City Breakers; Tijoux, Ana

Further Reading

Bretillon, Chong J. 2014. "'Ma face vanille': White Rappers, 'Black Music,' and Race in France." *International Journal of Francophone Studies* 17, nos. 3–4: 421–43.

Hammou, Karim. 2016. "Mainstreaming French Rap Music: Commodification and Artistic Legitimation of Othered Cultural Goods." *Poetics* 59: 67–81.

Further Listening

Fonky Family. 2006. *Marginale musique* (*Marginal Music*). Sony BMG Music Entertainment.

Suprême NTM. 1998. *Suprême NTM*. Epic.

Youssoupha. 2015. *NGRTD* (aka *Négritude*). Bomayé Musik.

Franti, Michael

(1966–, Oakland, California)

Michael Franti is an American rapper, spoken-word artist, guitarist, and singer-songwriter known for his sociopolitical lyrics and strong stance for Middle East peace and nonviolence in general. He leads the hip hop, funk, reggae, jazz, folk, and rock band Michael Franti and Spearhead (aka Spearhead, 1994–) and participates in other project bands such as Beatnigs (1986–1990), a San Francisco–based industrial and punk spoken-word band that used a dancer and percussionist, and the Disposable Heroes of Hiphoprisy (1990–1993), a fusion band that performed hip hop rhythms with industrial music. With Michael Franti and Spearhead, he had four albums chart in the Billboard 200, with *The Sound of Sunshine* (2010) peaking at No. 17.

Franti is also an environmental activist and a promoter of African education and veganism. In 2001, he was awarded the Domestic Human Rights Award by Global Exchange (1988–), an international NGO (nongovernmental association) based in

San Francisco, for his work to end war. Franti's musical style can best be described as acoustic guitar-based indie that fuses hip hop and African or world beats. He usually sings in a laid-back style, and his raps take the form of carefully articulated spoken-word phrases.

Franti was born to an interracial couple, but because his mother feared her family's racism, she put him up for adoption. A Finnish American couple with four children, including an adopted African American son, adopted Franti. His family moved briefly to Canada, then back to San Francisco. Franti started writing poetry in high school and formed two bands, but his big break came when the Disposable Heroes of Hiphoprisy was picked by U2 (1976–) to open for their Zoo TV Tour (1992). The Disposable Heroes of Hiphoprisy then collaborated with American spoken-word artist and writer William S. Burroughs (1914–1997) on the album *Spare Ass Annie and Other Tales* (1993).

Franti then formed Spearhead in San Francisco. Rather than continuing with political rap, Franti switched to funk and soul music and signed with Capitol Records (1942–) for two albums before changing the band's name to Michael Franti and Spearhead and creating its own label, Boo Boo Wax (2000–). With the album *Stay Human* (2000), Franti began writing sociopolitical lyrics again, with an emphasis on capital punishment, mass media monopolization, the prison-industrial complex, and corporate globalization. The band's songs have been used in television, film, and video games.

Anthony J. Fonseca

See also: Political Hip Hop; The United States

Further Reading

Franti, Michael. 1997. "Discovering Rasta Roots by Way of New Zealand." In *Inside the Music: Conversations with Contemporary Musicians about Spirituality, Creativity, and Consciousness*, edited by Dimitri Ehrlich, chap. 9. Boston: Shambhala.

Franti, Michael. 2006. *Food for the Masses: Lyrics and Portraits*. San Rafael, CA: Insight Editions.

Odell, Michael. 2001. "You're Tuned to Death Row: Hip Hop Hero Michael Franti Has Made a Concept Album about Capital Punishment. He Tells Micheal Odell Why." *The Guardian*, April 30, 2.10.

Further Listening

Michael Franti and Spearhead. 2010. *The Sound of Sunshine*. Boo Boo Wax.

Frosty Freeze

(aka The Freeze to Please, Mr. Freeze, Wayne Frost, 1963–2008, Bronx, New York)

Frosty Freeze is a b-boy hip hop dancer associated with Rock Steady Crew (RSC, 1977–), an American old-school breakdancing group from his home city, the Bronx, New York. His style was comedic and acrobatic, and often incorporated extremely dangerous flips and dance moves such as his signature moves—what he called the

Dead Man Drop, in which he dropped directly onto his back from one leg, and the Suicide, in which he flipped in the air and landed flat on his back. Both were usually followed by a kip-up or a series of semi-kip-ups (a rising handspring either from a fully supine or prone or partially supine or prone position that is often prepared in the fully supine position by rolling forward to gain speed). Generally, he concentrated on rapid footwork (floor rock) and balance in his jumpstyle and shuffle repertoire, incorporating moves from the traditional Cossack dance as well. Since b-boy dance phrases end with a freeze, Frost nicknamed himself Frosty Freeze.

Frosty Freeze was featured in the American films *Flashdance*, *Wild Style*, *Style Wars* (all 1983), and *The Freshest Kids: A History of the B-Boy* (2002), as well as hip hop music videos for Afrika Bambaataa and the Soulsonic Force's (1980–2003) "Planet Rock" (1982), where he breakdances against an urban background, and Malcolm McLaren's (1946–2010) "Buffalo Gals" (1982), which featured hip hop fused with square dance. In 1981, he was also pictured on the cover of *The Village Voice* (the article was titled "Physical Graffiti: Breaking Is Hard to Do")—the first article written on b-boying. In 2004, the RSC was honored at the VH-1 Hip Hop Honors. In 2008, Frosty Freeze died unexpectedly from an undisclosed illness.

Anthony J. Fonseca

See also: Breakdancing; Hip Hop Dance; Rock Steady Crew; The United States

Further Reading

Banes, Sally, and Martha Cooper. 1981. "Physical Graffiti: Breaking Is Hard to Do." *Village Voice*, April 22, 31–33.

Fuhrer, Margaret. 2014. "Urban and Commercial Dance." In *American Dance: The Complete Illustrated History*, chap. 10. Minneapolis, MN: Voyageur Press.

Schloss, Joseph G. 2009. *Foundation: B-Boys, B-Girls, and Hip Hop Culture in New York*. New York: Oxford University Press.

Further Viewing

Lee, Benson, dir. 2007. *Planet B-Boy*. New York: Mental Pictures.

Fugees

(1992–1997, South Orange, New Jersey)

Fugees was an American group that fused hip hop with reggae and neo soul. It was best known for the album *The Score* (1996), which hit No. 1 on the Billboard 200, was certified sextuple Platinum, and won a Grammy for Best Rap Album. *The Score* also consists of Fugees' hip hop rendition of "Killing Me Softly (with His Song)" (1971), composed by Charles Fox (1940–) and Norman Gimbel (1927–), which was a hit in 1974 for soul singer Roberta Flack (1939–). This rendition won a Grammy Award for Best R&B Performance by a Duo or Group with Vocals. Fugees included American singer-songwriter Lauryn Hill (Lauryn Noelle Hill, 1975–), Haitian singer-rapper Wyclef Jean (Nel Ust Wyclef Jean, 1969–), and American rapper-songwriter-producer Pras (Prakazrel Samuel Michél, 1972–).

At the height of its career with *The Score* (1996), Fugees was one of the earliest hip hop acts to have success with fusing hip hop with reggae and neo soul in the United States. The Grammy Award–winning trio consisted of rapper-songwriter-producer Pras, singer-songwriter Lauryn Hill, and singer-songwriter and rapper Wyclef Jean. (Jeff Kravitz/FilmMagic/Getty Images)

While attending Columbia High School (1989–1993) in Maplewood, New Jersey, Hill met Pras (Prakazrel Michel, 1972–) and formed Tranzlator Crew (aka Rap Translators, 1989–1997). Pras introduced Hill to his cousin Wyclef Jean, who joined the group. In 1993, the trio recorded demos and signed on the Ruffhouse Records label (1989–1999, 2012–). The trio changed its name to Fugees, inspired by the derogatory name given to Haitian Americans. In addition to its name change, the group shifted musical direction from pop and R&B to hip hop for its debut studio album, *Blunted on Reality*, on which it explored message rap, some political hip hop, jazz rap, and neo soul. Difficulties between the group and Ruffhouse began to emerge. Although the album was recorded in 1992, it was not released until two years later. Though it received a mostly favorable reception, *Blunted on Reality*'s best-charting position was at No. 62 on Billboard's Top R&B/Hip-Hop Albums, with its top single, "Nappy Heads," peaking at No. 49 on the Billboard Hot 100.

Despite *Blunted on Reality*'s lack of success, Ruffhouse Records gave Fugees an advance that would enable it to record a second album in a relaxed atmosphere. The group purchased studio equipment and set up recording in Wyclef Jean's uncle's basement, which members called the "Booga Basement." Fugees' second and final album, *The Score*, featured the group at its best, fusing hip hop, dubstep, and reggae. In addition to "Killing Me Softly," the album featured a rendition of Bob Marley and the Wailers' (1963–1981) reggae classic "No Woman No Cry" (1974). Another rendition, the Delfonics' (1965–) R&B and soul song "Ready or Not Here I Come (Can't Hide from Love)" (1968), appeared on the album with a sample from Irish new age composer Enya's (1961–) "Boadicea" (1987). The sample was taken without Enya's credit, so Enya threatened lawsuit; however, the dispute was quickly settled when Enya realized the group did not comprise of gangsta rappers and that she would receive songwriter credit and royalties from the use of the sample. In addition, the sample-heavy album was full of memorable melodic hooks that appealed to the mainstream public.

BREAKUP AND SOLO EFFORTS

Despite success, the group disbanded in 1997. Hill began to pursue her successful solo career and her solo album; *The Miseducation of Lauryn Hill* (1998) made her the first female artist to win five Grammys in one night. The album's lyrics touched on her strained relationship with Fugees and on her everyday struggles. This strained relationship included a turbulent romantic relationship between Hill and Wyclef Jean; creative differences between Hill, Wyclef Jean, and Pras; an initial lack of support from other members for her solo endeavor (by the time Jean offered to produce her album, Hill turned him down); and outside factors such as the stress of performance schedules and handling notoriety.

Wyclef Jean and Pras also continued with solo endeavors. The former's debut album *The Carnival* (1997) was certified double Platinum, and his follow-up album *The Ecleftic: 2 Sides II a Book* (2000) was certified Platinum. His third studio album, *Masquerade* (2002), peaked at No. 6 on the Billboard 200, and a string of critically and commercially successful albums followed, including *Welcome to Haiti: Creole 101* (2004), a world music album in English, French, Haitian Creole, and Latin, and the concept album *From the Hut, to the Projects, to the Mansion* (2009). He has collaborated with many artists, including participating in the production of Latin rock band Santana's (1966–) Grammy Award–winning album *Supernatural* (1999) and making an appearance as a featured rapper in Latin pop singer Shakira's (1977–) "Hips Don't Lie" (2007). He has also appeared in several films, most notably in *Carmen: A Hip Hopera* (2001, United States) and *Black November* (2012, Nigeria). Meanwhile, Wyclef Jean became politically active, filing for candidacy in 2010 in the Haitian presidential election and getting involved in philanthropic efforts for Haiti. His latest album is *Carnival III: The Fall and Rise of a Refugee* (2017), which peaked at No. 112 on the Billboard 200 and No. 8 on Billboard's Rap Album Sales but was critically unsuccessful.

Pras's first solo studio album, *Ghetto Supastar* (1998), peaked at No. 55 on the Billboard 200 and charted internationally. The title track, featuring Mýa (Mýa Marie Harrison, 1979–) and Wu-Tang Clan's (1992–) Ol' Dirty Bastard (aka ODB, Russell Tyrone Jones, 1968–2004), peaked at No. 15 on the Billboard Hot 100. He released a second album, *Win, Lose, or Draw* (2005), but since 1999, Pras has pursued acting and film production. Some of his acting credits include the American films *Mystery Men* (1999), *Go for Broke* (2002), *Nora's Hair Salon* (2004), and *The Mutant Chronicles* (2007). His film production work includes full-length films and documentaries. The latter includes *Paper Dreams* (2009), about real-life piracy off the coast of Africa, and *Sweet Micky for President* (2015), which chronicles *compas* (dance music) musician Michel Martelly's (1961–) rise to the Haitian presidency.

An attempt at a Fugees reunion took place between 2004 and 2006; however, the experience drew members further apart. Despite its small output, the Fugees' albums and tours influenced other hip hop artists. Though other parts of the world have warmly received the fusion of rap and reggae, this kind of fusion had to compete with harder-sounding East Coast and West Coast rap in the United States. To its credit, Fugees were successful in popularizing this fusion sound.

Melissa Ursula Dawn Goldsmith

See also: Haiti; Hill, Lauryn; Neo Soul; Reggae; The United States

Further Reading

Hardy, Ernest. 2003. "Fugees: *The Score*; Wyclef Jean: *The Carnival*; Lauryn Hill: *The Miseducation of Lauryn Hill*." In *Classical Material: The Hip Hop Album Guide*, edited by Oliver Wang, pp. 74–77. Toronto: ECW Press.

Lipsitz, George. 2006. "Breaking the Silence: The Fugees and *The Score*." *Journal of Haitian Studies* 12, no. 1: 4–23.

Further Listening

Fugees. 1994. *Blunted on Reality*. Ruffhouse Records.

Fugees. 1996. *The Score*. Columbia Ruffhouse Records.

G

Gabon

Gabon is a Central African country located on the western coast (the Gulf of Guinea) and on the equator. In 1960, Gabon gained its independence from France and became a dominant-party presidential republic. Since then, politics and music have often become intertwined. In 1986, the second wife of Gabon's second president, Omar Bongo (1935–2009, in office 1973–2009), Josephine Bongo (1944–), divorced him and resumed her Afropop and *soukous* singing career as Patience Dabany. Dabany eventually toured in 2004 with legendary American funk singer-songwriter, dancer, and bandleader James Brown (1933–2006) in Europe. The Bongos' son, current President Ali Bongo Ondimba (1959–, in office 2009–), as Alain Bongo released the funk and soul album *A Brand New Man* (1977). His 2009 presidential campaign strategy included rapping onstage as Le Candidat des Jeunes (The Candidate of Youth), releasing "Paroles aux jeunes" ("Words to Young People") with the English title "Youth, Have Your Say."

Ondimba's victory was also the result of music industry and hip hop involvement: in 2005, the music label Eben Entertainment (2002–) motivated youth to vote with its campaign "Bouge ton vote" ("Get Your Vote Moving"). Gabonese rappers Ba'Ponga (Franck Stéphane Dibault, n.d.), Jojo (Moussirou Josias Ariel, 1995–), Tina (aka Miss Tina, Chirstine Mboumba, 1989–), Hay'oe (1990s*), and Kôbe Building (aka Black Kôba, Ndong Ronny, 1979–) supported and campaigned for Ondimba.

By the late 1980s, American and French hip hop, in addition to the Cameroonian *makossa* and *soukous* (Congolese rumba), had become popular in Gabon on both global and local hip hop air on Libreville radio stations such as Radio Africa No. 1 (1981–) and later 104.5 Urban FM (2010–). Preferred rapping texts are in French and Fang with some English, reflecting Gabon's official and common language, French, and its dominant national language, Fang. Not only does the government sponsor hip hop artists and concerts, but it also uses hip hop for political messages such as unity, youth encouragement, self-improvement, and societal improvement; however, pioneering Gabonese hip hop took place not in Gabon, but in Paris. Omar Bongo's nephew Klaus (Gervais Mpouho, n.d.) and his hip hop group V2A4 (Vis Tout et Fort, Live Out Loud, 1990s*) released *African Revolution* (1989), a studio album that criticized African dictatorships, including Klaus's uncle's regime because he exercised despotlike powers and because Gabon, though the fourth-wealthiest country in Africa because of oil, suffers from tremendous economic disparity.

Hip hop acts of the 1990s include the duo Movaizhaleine (1992–), the female rapper and R&B singer Naneth (Nanette Pauline Nkoghé, 1974–), Hay'oe, and

Ba'Ponga. Later acts include Masta Kudi (Claude Mboumba, n.d.), Secta'a (1998–), Aurélil (aka TIGA, Aurélien Tigalekou, 1990–), Communauté Black (1999–), Lomé, Togo-based SIH (Son Injecté Hardcore, Sound-Injected Hardcore, 2002*–), and Kôbe Building. Having grown up in Gabon and France, hardcore political rapper Kôbe Building focuses on government corruption and antidrug messages. He uses his music for fundraising to support orphanages and prevent child prostitution and trafficking.

Melissa Ursula Dawn Goldsmith

See also: Cameroon; France; The United States

Further Reading

Aterianus-Owanga, Alice. 2015. "'Orality Is My Reality': The Identity Stakes of the 'Oral' Creation in Libreville Hip Hop Practices." *Journal of African Cultural Studies* 27, no. 2: 146–58.

Auzanneau, Michelle. 2002. "Rap in Libreville, Gabon: An Urban Sociolinguistic Space," translated by Ralph Schoolcraft. In *Black, Blan, Beur: Rap Music and Hip Hop Culture in the Francophone World*, edited by Alain-Philippe Durand, chap. 9. Lanham, MD: Scarecrow.

Further Listening

Ba'Ponga. 2016. *Best of Ba'Ponga.* Eben Entertainment.

The Gambia

The Gambia is (except for its coastline on the Atlantic Ocean) a West African country that is entirely surrounded by Senegal. In 1965, it gained its independence from the United Kingdom, but has since experienced political unrest, government corruption, and a weakened economy. Musically, the Gambia shares interests with Senegal: popular music includes their own *mbalax* as well as Dominican *merengue* and Jamaican reggae, ragga, and dancehall. Like Senegal, the Gambia has an eight-century history of griot culture with storytelling praise-singers. Senegalese hip hop inspired Gambian hip hop, and both employ storytelling or message rap, fusing hip hop with reggae, ragga, and dancehall in addition to mbalax, Hispanic American salsa, and other kinds of traditional music.

Initially, the Gambia kept its ties as a Commonwealth of Nations (1949–) member state that recognized Great Britain's Queen Elizabeth II (1926–, reign 1952–) as queen of the Gambia. In 1970, it became the Republic of The Gambia, but an unsuccessful coup attempt in 1981 resulted in the Senegambia Confederation (1982–1989) as a unification effort. Finally, a 1994 Gambian coup d'état under Yahya Jammeh (1965–), chair of the Armed Forces Provisional Ruling Council, led to a 2015 name change for the country, to Islamic Republic of The Gambia. In 2017, the newly elected President Adama Barrow (1965–) returned the name to Republic of The Gambia.

Gambian hip hop began around 1995, when Gambia Radio and Television Services was established and began broadcasting global hip hop from the capital city, Banjul, and the two largest cities, Serekunda and Brikama. Gambian lyrical themes include peace (antiwar), God (Allah), love, and tolerance, and rappers are critical of government corruption, which has led to poverty and prostitution. Rapping texts are in Wolof (also spoken in Senegal) and English; Mandinka is used but rarely. Performing ragga-rap, Black Nature (1995–) was the Gambia's first rap group. Another early act was the Gambian-Senegalese band Pencha B (aka Pencha Bi, Penchabi, 1996*–), whose lyrics stood out for the use of folklore and whose sound included traditional instruments such as the *kora, djembe, balafong*, and xylophone.

Other early acts were Da Fugitivz (1997–), Dancehall Masters (1998–), and Masla Bi (1998–). Originally from Banjul, Da Fugitivz moved to Stockholm, though the crew still raps in English and Wolof. Also from Banjul but now based in London, the reggae group Born Africans (1998–) employed rap and had several hit songs such as "No More War" (2001) and "Praises" (2002).

Recent acts have had more diverse lyrical content; subgenres such as rap-mbalax have emerged. Two rap-mbalax acts are Gee (Gibril Bala Gaye, 1987–) and VYPA (Amadou Secka, 1985–). VYPA's diverse songs have romantic, apocalyptic, and gangsta themes. Female rappers include Debbie Romeo (Ibinado Deborah Romeo, 1987–), a Nigerian who grew up in the Gambia, and Nancy Nanz (Nancy Waggeh, 1986–), the "Gambian Beyoncé," from Bajul. Nancy Nanz's debut single, "Baby Boy" (2004), is a Wolof version of American R&B, pop, and hip hop singer Beyoncé's (1981–) song of the same title (2003). In 2007, Nancy Nanz released her debut album, *Xalel* (*Children*).

Melissa Ursula Dawn Goldsmith

See also: Griot; Senegal

Further Reading

Charry, Eric. 2000. *Mande Music: Traditional and Modern Music of the Maninka and Mandinka of Western Africa.* Chicago: University of Chicago Press.

Juffermans, Kasper. 2012. "Multimodality and Audiences: Local Languaging in the Gambian Linguistic Landscape." *Sociolinguistic Studies* 6, no. 2: 259–84.

Further Listening

Nancy Nanz. 2007. *Xalel.* Gamcel.

Gamblerz

(2002–, Seoul, South Korea)

Gamblerz, a b-boy dance crew best known for winning top international breakdancing competitions, hails from Ulsan, a metropolitan suburb of Seoul. In 2004 and 2009, Gamblerz won first place at the Battle of the Year (BOTY) in Braunschweig, Germany, the premier annual international b-boying competition; in 2003, after being together for less than a year, Gamblerz had won third place in the same competition. In 2008 and 2014, the crew won first place in R-16, a Korea-based international breakdancing tournament and urban arts festival. In 2014, crewmember the End/KYS (Kim Yeon-Soo, 1987–) served as a judge for the Red Bull BC One, another major international b-boy competition. The crew's power moves include one-leg swipes and one-hand chair flares.

With Korean contemporaries such as T.I.P. Crew (1996–) and Jinjo Crew (2001–), both from Seoul as well, and Morning of Owl (2002–) from Suwon, South Korea,

Gamblerz has represented South Korea as a strong competitor in b-boy champion-ships worldwide. In 2002, B-Boy Music (Jung-dae Kim, n.d.) established the crew as Gambler (the original name) with six members. The same year, B-Boy Dark-ness (Kyung-ho Chang, n.d.), its first leader, changed the name to Gamblerz.

In 2008, after leadership challenges and other conflicts, Darkness left to pursue other dreams (the group's motto had been "Happy b-boying"). With two other mem-bers, he started a new crew under the original Gambler name; the crew now dances as MoSt mOdeRn (2009–).

In 2010, Gamblerz and other b-boy crews received international notoriety after members were arrested for refusing to serve in the South Korean army. As of 2018, B-Boy Sick (Chung Hyun-Sik, 1981–) leads the 13-member crew.

Melissa Ursula Dawn Goldsmith

See also: Battling; Breakdancing; Hip Hop Dance; Korea

Further Reading

File, Curtis. 2013. *Korean Dance: Pure Emotion and Energy.* Korea Essentials No. 15. Seoul: Korea Foundation.

Tudor, Daniel. 2014. "Korea's Music Scene." *Geek in Korea: Discovering Asia's New King-dom of Cool*, part 8. North Clarendon, VT: Tuttle.

Gang Starr

(1986–2003, Boston, Massachusetts)

Gang Starr was a college-educated East Coast hip hop duo that became notable for pioneering New York City's hardcore hip hop as well as its alternative hip hop albums and music videos. The duo released six studio albums: *No More Mr. Nice Guy* (1989), *Step in the Arena* (1991), *Daily Operation* (1992), *Hard to Earn* (1994), *Moment of Truth* (1998), and *The Ownerz* (2003). All charted on Billboard's Top R&B/Hip-Hop Albums chart; starting with Gang Starr's second album, *Step in the Arena,* five of six albums charted on the Billboard 200, most notably with *Moment of Truth* peaking at No. 6 and attaining Gold certification. Its only two songs that charted on the Billboard Hot 100 were "Mass Appeal" (1994), which peaked at No. 67, and "You Know My Steez" (1997), which peaked at No. 76. Gang Starr's best-charting success was on Billboard's Hot Rap Singles, topping the chart once with "Take It Personal" (1992) but reaching No. 5 with "Just to Get a Rep," (1990), "Ex Girl to the Next Girl" (1992), and "You Know My Steez." Gang Starr also had a large cult fol-lowing. Its first music video, "Jazz Thing" (1990), was directed by Spike Lee (Shel-ton Jackson Lee, 1957–) for his American film *Mo' Better Blues* (1990). Fab Five Freddy (1959–) directed Gang Starr's second video, "Just to Get a Rep." In 2002, Gang Starr composed "Battle" for the American hip hop motion picture *8 Mile,* which starred Eminem (1972–) and was based on the rapper's early life.

Gang Starr originally began in Roxbury, located in Boston. At the time, it was a group consisting of rapper Guru (Gifted Unlimited Rhymes Universal, Keith Edward Elam, 1961–2010), at the time known as MC Keithy E; 1, 2 B-Down (aka Mike Dee, n.d.); rapper and producer Donald D (aka Microphone King Donald-D,

Dondee, Donald Lamont, n.d.); DJ, producer, and turntablist the 45 King (Mark Howard James, 1961–); and several others. The group's earliest recordings took place in 1986. In 1987, the group relocated to Brooklyn, New York, where it recorded 12-inch singles on Wild Pitch Records (1987–), such as "The Lesson" and "Believe Dat!" (both 1987) as well as "Movin' On" (1988). This group disbanded in 1989.

As the only artist to continue with the Gang Starr name, Guru contacted DJ Premier (Christopher Edward Martin, 1966–), who was then known as Waxmaster C, recording for Wild Pitch, and living in Brooklyn. After Waxmaster C made him a beat tape that he liked, Guru invited him to join Gang Starr. In 1989, Gang Starr released its debut studio album, *No More Mr. Nice Guy*, on Bellaphon (1963–) and then signed onto the Chrysalis Records label (1968–). Gang Starr released *Step in the Arena*, *Daily Operation*, and *Hard to Earn* while performing and touring frequently. Guru's lyrics often focused on street themes but with narrative twists, at times alluding to and incorporating Five Percent Nation (1964–) teachings. His lyrics often juxtaposed chains of polysyllabic words, which gave his rap flow a complex sound. DJ Premier was a suitable match to Guru for his depth of knowledge, in selecting jazz, funk, and soul recordings as well as in writing hip hop lyrics, which informed his turntablism. By 1993, both Guru and DJ Premier were working extensively on other projects. DJ Premier became a prolific music producer, and Guru began recording the first of his four-volume jazz rap projects, *Guru's Jazzmatazz*, which received critical acclaim. In 1999, Gang Starr's compilation album *Full Clip: A Decade of Gang Starr* went Gold. By this time, the two were working less frequently together. Despite such positive reception of Gang Starr's album's, Guru's debut solo album, *Baldhead Slick & da Click* (2001), was poorly received. It nevertheless peaked at No. 22 on Billboard's Top R&B/Hip-Hop Albums chart, and Guru followed the album with the better-received *Version 7.0: The Street Scriptures* (2005) and *Guru 8.0: Lost and Found*. Like DJ Premier, Guru collaborated with countless other hip hop artists. His solo albums outside the *Jazzmatazz* series show a continuation toward more intelligent alternative hip hop. In 2010, Guru died of cancer.

In addition to its music, Gang Starr's legacy includes the Gang Starr Foundation, a collective that began in 1993 in Boston, partly formed by American rapper, singer, and actor Big Shug (Cary Guy, n.d.). Along with producer DJ Premier, members of the collective once supported Bahamadia (1976–) and as of 2018 still include Big Shug, rapper Bumpy Knuckles (aka Freddie Foxxx, James Campbell, 1969–), Jeru the Damaja (Kendrick Jeru Davis, 1972–), and the duo M.O.P. (Mash Out Posse, 1992–).

Melissa Ursula Dawn Goldsmith

See also: Bahamadia; Five Percent Nation; Political Hip Hop; The United States

Further Reading

Price-Styles, Alice. 2015. "MC Origins: Rap and Spoken Word Poetry." In *The Cambridge Companion to Hip Hop*, edited by Justin Williams, chap. 1. Cambridge, England: Cambridge University Press.

Williams, Justin. 2010. "The Construction of Jazz Rap as High Art in Hip Hop Music." *Journal of Musicology* 27, no. 4: 435–59.

Further Listening
Gang Starr. 1998. *Moment of Truth.* Noo Trybe Records.

Gangs (United States)

Gangs are organizations that operate off the grid of any legal or economic system. They range from transnational crime syndicates, such as the Mafia or Yakuza, to more localized street and area gangs, such as the Bloods (1972–) and the Crips (1969–) in Los Angeles. Though they are not terrorist organizations nor hate groups, gangs serve many of the same purposes: protecting a subculture, uniting youth into a common cause, and striking out against perceived and real enemies. Local street gang activity has played a major role in the development of hip hop. Gang culture is one of the informing forces within the communities from which many rap artists emerged, often providing rappers with subject matter; gang culture also has influenced many elements of hip hop style. In the United States in particular, the origins of hip hop are deeply connected to urban street gangs, beginning in the 1970s and continuing to the present time.

STREET GANGS AFTER THE CIVIL RIGHTS MOVEMENT

Societies are defined by their organization—people in a society organized themselves for a common good, through legal and economic systems. This in turn leads to the creation of organizations of those who, due to unhappiness within the legal system, collectively operate outside it. Gangs typically generate income through illegal means: bootlegging, drug dealing, and/or trafficking. Gangs settle disputes not through lawsuits but through violence. One way to understand gang culture is to view gangs as for-profit businesses, with the crucial caveat being that they do not typically work through recognized economic and legal means such as banks, shareholders, or courts.

Hip hop's origins in New York City during the late 1970s coincided with a significant peak in gang activity in poor and working-class minority areas. By the late 1970s, many heavily influential antiracist groups such as the African American Black Panther Party (originating from Oakland, California), the Latino Brown Berets (originating from Los Angeles), and the Puerto Rican Young Lords (from Chicago) had been weakened or entirely eliminated due to governmental intervention and internal leadership problems. This left a power vacuum at a time when urban areas were experiencing intense economic hardship due to white flight, discriminatory city planning, and diminishing employment opportunities. Under such conditions, young people became attracted to variant means of financial success— illegal activities such as drug dealing, for example. Though lucrative, drug dealing is a dangerous business, so the organizational structure provided by gangs offered protection as well as an otherwise lacking sense of belonging. In many urban areas, the emergence of crack cocaine, a cheap and highly addictive drug, made gang activity very lucrative. While several street gangs, such as the Crips, emerged with the expressed purpose of combating the spread of drugs in their communities, ironically, even they eventually engaged in illegal drug activity, which also led to execution-style murders.

GANGS IN HIP HOP

Early on, hip hop pioneers sought to harness their work to draw young people of color away from gangs. Afrika Bambaataa (1957–) formed what would become the Universal Zulu Nation (1973–) with the expressed intent of providing young people who might be attracted to gangs an alternative; his goal was to use music to help youth express themselves and find community. Public Enemy's (1982–) politically charged lyrics and use of Black Nationalist themes also advanced ways of organizing people of color independent of the gang scene.

Gangsta rap's relationship to the gang scene was complex. Early gangsta rappers such as Schoolly D (Jesse Bonds Weaver Jr., 1962–) and N.W.A. (1986–1991) drew heavily on the gang scene for the stories they told and the public personas they crafted; however, few of these artists were directly involved with gangs. Although N.W.A.'s Eazy-E (1964–1995) engaged in small-time drug dealing before cofounding the group, the band's other members were never directly involved in gang life. They did, however, live in communities that were deeply affected by gang activity, making gang culture a significant influence on their lyrics. In 1990, amid growing public backlash against gangsta rap and increased public anxiety about gang violence, several West Coast rappers, under the name West Coast Rap All-Stars, released the single "We're All in the Same Gang" to promote an antiviolence message.

Death Row Records' (1991–2008) connection to gangs was much more direct. Snoop Dogg (1971–), one of the label's most successful artists, was a member of the Crips in Long Beach, California, and he faced murder charges at the time of his debut album's release. Death Row's cofounder, Suge Knight (Marion Hugh Knight Jr., 1965–), also had gang ties, and his rivalry with the Crips led (directly or indirectly, yet to be determined) to the 1996 shooting death of Tupac Shakur (1971–1996); however, the G-funk sound that Death Row helped develop in the early 1990s was itself part of the post–Los Angeles riots (1992) gang peace movement, with an emphasis on outdoor parties and other leisure activities widely associated with the peace movement.

Many contemporary local American hip hop scenes are directly related to gang activity. For example, several Chicago-based artists have been injured or killed or have played a direct role in much of the city's recent surge in violence. As a result, many commentators have claimed that lyrics from Chicago rappers such as Chief Keef (1995–) contribute to the city's high violent-crime rate by promoting, rather than reflecting, violence. In Baton Rouge, native rapper Boosie Badazz (Torrence Hatch, 1982–) served time in prison for a drug conviction and was charged with, but acquitted of, first-degree murder. Furthermore, as rapper and sociopolitical activist Killer Mike (Michael Render, 1975–) and scholar Erik Nielson (1976–) noted in a 2014 editorial in *USA Today* criticizing the practice, prosecutors routinely introduce rap lyrics penned by (almost always poor black) defendants as evidence of violent behavior; thus, the relationship between rap and gang violence is enshrined in public culture and certain sectors of our legal system.

The bottom line is that gangs are complex organizations. While they undoubtedly engage in often-violent criminal activities, they function as sources of deep identification and social support for historically marginalized communities, and in many cases provide the only financial opportunities for youth. It should therefore be unsurprising that overall, hip hop's relationship to gangs has been complex. Though some artists, such as Missy Elliott (1971–), have attempted to use their work to direct young people away from gangs, others, such as Geto Boys (1986–), have drawn on the sensationalism of gang life to craft their own public personas and, more importantly, to sell records.

Bryan J. McCann

See also: Crip Walk; Gangsta Rap; G-Funk; Mafioso Rap; The United States

Further Reading

Chang, Jeff. 2005. *Can't Stop Won't Stop: A History of the Hip Hop Generation.* New York: Picador.

Davis, Mike. 2006. *City of Quartz: Excavating the Future in Los Angeles.* London: Verso.

Nielson, Erik, and Michael Render. 2014. "Rap Suffers Poetic (In)justice: Supreme Court Is Finally Getting Schooled in Hip Hop: Music Is Not a Threat to Safety." *U.S.A. Today,* December 1.

Williams, Stanley Tookie. 2004. *Blue Rage, Black Redemption: A Memoir.* New York: Touchstone-Damamli.

Further Listening

N.W.A. 1988. *Straight Outta Compton.* Ruthless Records/Priority Records.

West Coast Rap All Stars. 1990. *We're All in the Same Gang.* Warner Bros. Records 12.

Gangsta Rap

Gangsta rap is a subgenre of rap music that rose to prominence in the late 1980s. Emerging largely out of South Central Los Angeles, at the height of public anxieties about crime, drugs, and street gang violence, gangsta rap artists came to embody what many characterized as some of the worst stereotypes of African American men. The music was aggressive and informed by a heavy bass beat, and gangsta rap lyrics emphasized hypermasculinity, aggressive sexual practices, violence, abuse of drugs and alcohol, and unapologetic materialism (often referred to as "bling"). While gangsta rap was incredibly popular with minority youth, it also appealed to white American teens. The music quickly became the target of intense criticism by elected officials, law enforcement, and self-proclaimed culture warriors.

ORIGINS

As with many rap subgenres, there is no definitive or clear starting point for gangsta rap. In fact, lyrical engagement in aggressive masculinity and criminality in popular culture predates hip hop. Following the end of chattel slavery and the collapse of Reconstruction (1863–1877), tales of badly behaved and even criminal men began proliferating in African American folklore. Figures such as the career criminal Stag-O-Lee (Lee Shelton, 1865–1912), as well as oral narrative and blaxsploitation mainstays such as Pimpin' Sam and Dolomite, appeared with growing regularity from the late 19th century on. Often loosely based on real people and events, these stories found expression in both oral and written traditions; this included a sharing through folksongs such as "Stack-a-Lee" (1890*), which emerged into the musical mainstream by the 1900s through versioning and covers. Such men were typically violent and sexually aggressive—and they often met tragic ends. In other words, they were not heroes in any traditional sense of the word.

When viewed through the prism of post-Emancipation, when racism in the Jim Crow South and industrial North was increasingly predicated on fashioning black masculinity as inherently violent and criminal, creating stories and songs allowed African American communities to take ownership of their stereotypes. As they did so, they created new meaning through identification and implication. In addition, blues musicians penned songs during the early- and mid-20th-century that prefigured gangsta rap in their lyrical content, and during the early 1970s, the emergence and popularity of American blaxploitation films such as *Sweet Sweetback's Baadasssss Song* (1971) and *Superfly* (1972) signified another moment in black popular culture, the exaltation of the black male criminal, basically a continuation of the rebel criminal, similar to white culture's exaltation of Billy the Kid (Henry McCarty, 1859–1881) or the British reverence of the folkloric Robin Hood (1377*–).

Many early rap acts, including Schoolly D (Jesse Bonds Weaver Jr., 1962–), Boogie Down Productions (1985–1992), and Ice-T (1958–), drew on gangsta themes in their work; however, what most Americans understand as gangsta rap found its most complete expression with the release of N.W.A.'s (1986–1991) *Straight Outta Compton* (1988). In addition to the album's title track, songs such as "F— the Police" and "Gangsta, Gangsta" had an aggressive tone and contained lyrics that indulged in tropes widely associated with criminality.

In the opening verse of "Straight Outta Compton," Ice Cube (1969–) brags that he is crazy and boasts that when he is disrespected, he grabs a sawed-off shotgun (which is illegal), squeezes the trigger, and creates a trail of bodies. The song's music video portrays the members of N.W.A. as a roaming band of marauders through Compton's impoverished streets. There they are harassed, chased, and arrested by police. At the time of the album's release, Compton and other municipalities in South Central Los Angeles were targets of intense police surveillance, which included drug raids, so the area developed an international reputation as a gang- and drug-fueled war zone that embodied many people's worst fears about crime and violence. Crime was a central element of electoral and cultural politics during the 1980s—and it was most frequently associated with poor and working-class urban communities of color such as Compton. Gangsta rappers such as N.W.A., Geto Boys (1986–), Compton's Most Wanted (1987–), and Snop Dogg (as Snoop Doggy Dogg, 1971–) found commercial success and public notoriety by repackaging and celebrating this association.

GANGSTA RAP AND THE CULTURE WARS

Gangsta rap came to prominence alongside an increasingly influential cultural conservative movement. It celebrated criminality and therefore attracted unfavorable attention from law enforcement at a time when crime prevention figured prominently in politics. Many law enforcement officials and police unions spoke out forcefully against "F— the Police." N.W.A. claimed the track was simply a revenge fantasy that should not be taken literally; however, in 1989, the politically influential Fraternal Order of Police (1915–) adopted a resolution boycotting the concerts of any artists whose music they believed promoted violence against police officers, and in a historically unprecedented move, the F.B.I.'s Office of Public Affairs sent a letter to Priority Records (1985–), the company that distributed *Straight Outta Compton*, expressing its belief that the song encouraged violence against police. Many concert venues therefore required the group to omit the song from their set lists, but during a 1989 concert in Detroit, N.W.A. began performing the controversial track; police chased the group offstage. Law enforcement and elected officials also spoke forcefully against rapper Ice-T's thrash metal band Body Count's (1990–2006, 2009–) song "Cop Killer" (1992), which the band removed from their album following the backlash. In addition, in 1992, a young black man claimed he was inspired to fatally shoot a Texas state trooper by Tupac Shakur's (1971–1996) debut album *2Pacalypse Now* (1991).

Many cultural conservatives also targeted gangsta rap, claiming its violent and hypersexual content posed a significant threat to the health of civil society. Groups such as the Parents Music Resource Center (1985) and the American Family Association (1977–), the latter labeled a hate group by the Southern Poverty Law Center (1971–), targeted many music artists who performed what they called obscene lyrics, including rappers and gangsta rappers. Such organizations penned newspaper editorials, appeared on television, and testified before Congressional committees to argue that such music was harmful to teenagers and children. Activists such as Tipper Gore (1948–) and Jack Thompson (1951–) argued that record companies should be more responsive to parental concerns when distributing music. They ultimately created the idea of requiring the Parental Advisory sticker to be placed on controversial albums. These stickers still adorn CD covers. In addition, the activists' efforts led to the designation of albums and singles with the Parental Advisory label as "Explicit."

Black cultural conservatives played an especially important role in the backlash against gangsta rap. Veterans of the Civil Rights Movement in the United States (1954–1968), such as Reverend Calvin Butts (1949–) and C. Delores Tucker (1927–2005), became prominent voices against artists such as Dr. Dre (1965–) and Snoop Dogg. They claimed that gangsta rap encouraged black youth to choose a life of crime and violence out of the desire to emulate their rapper heroes. Tucker, who founded the National Political Congress of Black Women (1984–), also emphasized the degradation of women in many gangsta rap songs and videos. During testimony before Congress, Tucker declared that gangsta rap lyrics and music videos portrayed women as objects of disdain. In the speech, she invoked Dr. Martin Luther King Jr. (1929–1968). Objecting to lyrics that routinely referred to women in derogatory terms, Tucker and her allies drew on the memory of the American civil rights battle to portray gangsta rappers as traitors to the black community and as mercenaries who made millions by promoting violence and insulting African American women.

Tucker's campaign against gangsta rap prompted her, a lifetime Democrat, to campaign with 1996 Republican presidential candidate Bob Dole (1923–) and conservative activist William Bennett (1943–) in an effort to encourage consumers to boycott gangsta rap and pressure recording companies to cease signing gangsta artists. Although figures such as Gore and Tucker won some victories against gangsta rap, they never managed to threaten the genre's bottom line. Gangsta artists continued to produce best-selling albums that made millions of dollars.

DEATH ROW RECORDS AND GANGSTA'S TWILIGHT

After leaving N.W.A. over financial disputes with group founder Eazy-E (1964–1995) and music producer Jerry Heller (1940–2016), Dr. Dre formed Death Row Records (1991–2008) with former bodyguard Suge Knight (Marion Hugh Knight Jr., 1965–). Death Row quickly became one of the most successful record companies in the country and helped cement gangsta rap's status as one of America's most lucrative musical genres. In addition to Dre's solo debut *The Chronic* (1992), Death Row released Snoop Dogg's hugely successful *Doggystyle* (1993). The latter figured significantly into the antigangsta crusades of Tucker and her allies. Largely due to Dr. Dre's producing style, Death Row brought a more relaxed aesthetic to gangsta rap. Whereas the work of N.W.A., the Geto Boys, and other gangsta acts was often aggressive in tone, Dr. Dre heavily sampled soul, R&B, and funk tracks from the 1960s and 1970s. Unlike the work of N.W.A. and Ice Cube's solo recordings, Death Row artists' work rarely referenced violence against police and other figures of authority. Rather, tracks such as "F— wit' Dre Day" and "Gin and Juice" focused on partying, cruising around South Central Los Angeles in lowriders, and committing violence against other black men.

Many Death Row artists experienced high-profile legal problems. Snoop Dogg, a former member of the Crips street gang, stood trial for murder during the release of *Doggystyle*. Dr. Dre faced assault charges after physically assaulting a journalist. In 1995, Tupac Shakur joined Death Row while on release awaiting the appeal of his recent rape conviction. Furthermore, Suge Knight had a reputation for gang connections and aggressive business tactics, including physical violence against competitors. While Death Row artists were not the only rappers to encounter legal trouble, the fact that their most successful artists had been accused or convicted of violent crimes figured significantly in the label's reputation for crossing the line between fantasy and reality. On November 29, 1993, the cover of *Newsweek* featured a photograph of Snoop Dogg accompanied by the text, "When is rap 2 violent?"

Death Row also played a central role in fomenting tension between East and West Coast rappers. Before the ascent of gangsta rap, New York was widely regarded as the home of hip hop. In addition to being rap's point of origin, New York, and other East Coast cities, produced artists such as Afrika Bambaataa (1957–), Grandmaster Flash (1958–), the Sugarhill Gang (1979–1985, 1994–), LL Cool J (1968–), Run-D.M.C. (1981–2002), Beastie Boys (1980–2012), and Public Enemy (1982–), whose work enjoyed commercial success and often critical acclaim. West Coast rap, in comparison, appeared amateurish; however, following the release of *Straight Outta Compton*, West Coast gangsta rap became the most successful subgenre of hip hop. The proprietary claims over hip hop that emerged from these shifts in coastal dominance resulted in significant bitterness between artists and fans. Suge Knight was especially aggressive in aggravating the feud, likely in hopes that the resulting notoriety would positively affect record sales.

The most notable expression of this feud occurred between Death Row Records and Bad Boy Entertainment (1993–). Both labels' producers and artists publicly antagonized each other through lyrics, comments to media, and occasional physical confrontations. The feud between Tupac Shakur and Bad Boy's the Notorious B.I.G. (1972–1997) was especially volatile following the former's claim that the Notorious B.I.G. and Puff Daddy (1969–) played a role in his 1994 shooting at Quad Recording Studios (1977–) in New York City. After the fatal shooting of Tupac Shakur in 1996 and the Notorious B.I.G. less than one year later, many rappers, music journalists, and fans came to believe the feud had gone too far. After Tupac Shakur's death, most of Death Row's most successful artists left the label, and Suge Knight was sentenced to prison for a parole violation the same year.

During the late 1980s and early 1990s, gangsta rap was the most successful rap subgenre of hip hop. At the end of the 20th century and during the 21st century, the designation gangsta rap has become less useful, as the subgenre has enjoyed increasing crossover success in mainstream hip hop markets. Highly successful contemporary rappers such as Lil Wayne (1982–), Kevin Gates (Kevin Jerome Gilyard, 1986–), and 50 Cent (1975–) frequently incorporate gangsta themes into their work. Furthermore, N.W.A. and Tupac Shakur were inducted into the Rock and Roll Hall of Fame in 2016 and 2017 respectively, suggesting that the stigma that once marked gangsta rap has, at least to an extent, abated. Emerging at a time when many mainstream politicians and culture warriors emphasized law and order as a top public-policy priority, gangsta's celebration of black criminality made it one of the 20th century's most controversial forms of music. Although the term *gangsta rap* has lost most of its traction in recent years, its themes remain an important element of contemporary rap.

Bryan J. McCann

See also: Gangs (United States); G-Funk; N.W.A.; Snoop Dogg; Tupac Shakur; The United States

Further Reading

Chang, Jeff. 2005. *Can't Stop Won't Stop: A History of the Hip Hop Generation*. New York: Picador.

McCann, Bryan J. 2017. *The Mark of Criminality: Rhetoric, Race, and Gangsta Rap in the War-on-Crime Era*. Tuscaloosa: University of Alabama Press.

Quinn, Eithne. 2005. *Nuthin' but a "G" Thang: The Culture and Commerce of Gangsta Rap*. New York: Columbia University Press.

Further Listening

N.W.A. 1988. *Straight Outta Compton*. Ruthless/Priority Records.

Schoolly D. 1985. *Schoolly D*. Schoolly D Records.

Germany

Germany is a European parliamentary republic of 82 million inhabitants, making it the most populous member of the European Union and the second most popular immigration destination in the world. Its capital, Berlin, is also its largest city, but Germany boasts many major cities, such as Hamburg, Munich, Cologne, Frankfurt, Stuttgart, Düsseldorf, Leipzig, Bremen, Dresden, Hannover, and Nuremberg. Hip hop made its way into Germany in the early 1980s, practiced first through graffiti and breakdancing. The first rap song in German was "Rappers Deutsch," a 1980 parody song by a three–radio DJ project band, GLS United (1980–1981), and rap was made a popular music format in 1991 when the German music label Bombastic Records (1990–2002) released the 15-track album *Krauts with Attitude: German Hip Hop Vol. 1.*

The pioneer rap crew in Germany was Advanced Chemistry (1987–), from Heidelberg. It featured members from Italy, Ghana, and Haiti. Advanced Chemistry localized American socially conscious rap, combining it with the Native Tongues movement, to create rap songs in German that challenged discrimination against immigrants. Other hip hop acts of the 1980s included Kiel-based Cora E. (Sylvia Macco, 1968–), an early underground female rapper who wrote her own lyrics and had a hit in 1996 with "Schlüsselkind" ("Latchkey Kid").

One of the first mainstream pop-influenced hip hop bands was Die Fantastischen Vier (The Fantastic Four, aka Fanta 4, 1986–), which originated in Stuttgart. It eschewed what it considered to be the cliché, American gangsta rap, and in 1996 it created its own record label in Stuttgart, Four Music. Frankfurt-based rap duo Rödelheim Hartreim Projekt (Rödelheim Hard-Rhyme Project, aka RHP, 1995–), in contrast, was influenced by American gangsta rap. A contemporary of RHP was the pop, soul, and hip hop band Söhne Mannheims (Sons of Mannheim, 1995–). One of its founding members, Kobra (Xavier Kurt Naidoo, 1971–), was a backing vocalist for RHP and had a highly successful solo career beginning with his debut album *Nicht von dieser welt* (*Not from This World*, 1998), which sold over a million copies. The Mannheim-born artist has South African parents and is also of German, Irish, and Indian descent. Before his success in Germany, he had recorded an English hip hop album, *Seeing Is Believing* (1994), in the United States.

Some exchanges between Austrian and German hip hop took place during this time. Germany's hip hop scenes provided the strongest influence for Austrian ones. One reason for this influence was their shared language: Austria's official language, Austrian Standard German, shares syntax, words, and phrases with South German speakers. In 1993, the Viennese group Schönheitsfehler (Blemish, 1992–2005) had the first commercially successful hip hop act when its single "F—You" charted in Germany. The Bavarian band Blumentopf (Flowerpot, 1992–2016), from Freising, was popular in Austria and collaborated with other Austrian hip hop acts, such as Texta (1993–) from Linz and Total Chaos (1993–) from Innsbruck, to form the supergroup Kaleidoskop (2001–2002).

Many German hip hop artists are of Turkish German descent, mainly a product of the later 1990s and early 2000s when immigrants were moving to Germany and started creating rap music influenced by both German and American hip hop scenes.

With music infused by the Arabesque style and samples, they rapped songs about immigration, discrimination, and racism as well as the plight of the migrant worker. In 1991, Nuremberg-based King Size Terror (1990–1994), a hip hop group of Turkish, Peruvian, and African American origin, produced the first Turkish-language rap with the single "Bir yabancinin hayati" ("The Life of the Stranger"), which portrayed Turkish youth as strangers in mainstream German culture. King Size Terror led to the creation of Cartel as the first successful Turkish hip hop group. Cartel had problems with violence and incarceration and at one point was forbidden to perform together, and the band's first album, which contained both German and Turkish rapping, was banned.

Berlin-based rapper Kool Savaş (Savaş Yurderi, 1975–) cofounded the rap duo Westberlin Maskulin (1997–2000) as well as the crew Masters of Rap (1996–). Kool Savaş has collaborated with 50 Cent (1975–), among others. Turkish German rapper Eko Fresh (aka Elektro Eko, Ekrem Bora, 1983–) was born in Cologne, grew up in Mönchengladbachand, and began rapping when he was 14 years old. He first achieved fame through the wrestling world but eventually released the hit diss track "Die Abrechnung" ("The Settlement [of Accounts]," 2004), named after the first part of Hitler's *Mein Kampf* (*My Story*, 1924). Eko Fresh continued his music career by producing 10 studio albums. Other notable acts from between the 1990s and 2000s are A.i.d.S. (Alles ist die Sekte, Everything Is the Sect, aka RoyalTS, 1997–), Die Sekte (The Sect, 1998–), Hungary-born Brixx (Ildiko Basa, 1976–), Cora E. (aka Zulu-Queen, Sylvia Macco, 1968–), and Pyranja (Anja Käckenmeister, 1978–), the last three being female rappers.

THE 2000s AND BEYOND

The 21st-century German hip hop scene still has prominent migrant hip hop activity; however, more recent hip hop has had an increasingly American influence. Turkish rappers, who are generally darker than Germans, have often perceived themselves as blacks in Germany and therefore relate to the African American experience. As in the United States, issues of authenticity and appropriation have emerged in Germany, with Turkish rappers viewing themselves as more authentic than whiter-looking German rappers. Turkish interest in gangsta rap, as exemplified by Die Sekte from Berlin, has been diminishing since the 2000s. Since white German rappers have become more intrigued by gangsta rap, Turkish and other German immigrant rappers are focusing on how to use other kinds of rap. Hypermasculinity remains present in German hip hop, including Turkish hip hop from Germany. In this kind of Turkish hip hop, there has been increased use of traditional Arabesk music and Arabic scales such as *makams* (rules of composition) and instruments such as the *bağlama* (lute), *zuma* (horn), *kanun* (zither), and *kemençe* (bowed fiddle).

In Berlin, *oriental hip hop*, which emerged in the early 1990s, combined elements of American hip hop with Turkish and Arabic traditional music. It is far more popular in the 2010s. Microphone Mafia (1989–) from Cologne exemplifies this sound, rapping in German, Turkish, Spanish, and Italian. The group performs concerts and records with German Sephardic Jewish singer and musician Esther Béjarano (Esther Loewy, 1924–), one of the last survivors of the Women's Orchestra of Auschwitz, who sings antifascist songs. Their albums include *Per la vita* (*For Life*, 2009) and *La vita continua* (*Life Goes On*, 2013).

As of 2018, with the largest music market in Europe and the fourth-largest one in the world, just after the United States, Japan, and the United Kingdom, hip hop thrives in Germany and is accepted into the mainstream with earlier innovative styles such as Neue deutsche Welle (German new wave), disco, metal, punk, electronica, techno, and indie music. Notable recent acts include Bushido ("The Way of the Warrior" in Japanese, aka Sonny Black, Anis Mohamed Youssef Ferchichi, 1978–); Die Sekte's MOK (aka Muzik oder Knast, Music or Prison, Tarkan Karaalioğlu, 1976–) and Alpa Gun (Alper Sendilmen, 1980–); Fler (aka Frank White, Patrick Losensky, n.d.); and Kitty Kat (aka Kitten Ket, Katharina Löwel, 1982–). Immigrant rappers include Tony D (aka Tony Damager, Muhamed Ayad, 1983–), of Lebanese descent, and Spain-born Farid Bang (Farid El Abdellaoui, 1986–), of Moroccan descent.

Anthony J. Fonseca and Melissa Ursula Dawn Goldsmith

See also: Austria; Gangsta Rap; Turkey; The United States

Further Reading

Güney, Serhat, Cem Pekman, and Bülent Kabaş. 2014. "Diasporic Music in Transition: Turkish Immigrant Performers on the Stage of 'Multikulti' Berlin." *Popular Music and Society* 37, no. 2: 132–51.

Putnam, Michael, and Juliane Schicker. 2014. "Straight Outta Marzahn: (Re)Constructing Communicative Memory in East Germany through Hip Hop." *Popular Music and Society* 37, no. 1: 85–100.

Further Listening

Kool Savaş. 2015. *Rap Genius.* Essah Media.

Microphone Mafia. 2006. *Testa nera* (*Black Head* in Italian). Al Dente Recordz.

Schönheitsfehler. 2000. *SexDrugsAndHipHop.* Motor Music.

Geto Boys

(aka Ghetto Boys, 1986–, Houston, Texas)

Geto Boys is an American rap group which, through nine albums, became influential in the southern rap subgenre, sometimes nicknamed the Dirty South. Unlike most rap bands, the Geto Boys rotated its lineup throughout its history, with the stabilizing influence being Lil' J, aka J Prince or James Prince (James A. Smith, n.d.), producer and owner of Rap-A-Lot Records (1986–) in Houston, who conceived of a rap group that could dramatize the problems of Houston's impoverished Fifth Ward.

By the first album, *Making Trouble* (1988), the only original member left from the original lineup, called Ghetto Boys, was Sire Jukebox (Keith Rogers, 1972*–). For that album, the lineup consisted of him, two members from Trenton, New Jersey—DJ Ready Red (Collins Leysath, n.d.) and Prince Johnny C (anonymous, n.d.)—and Little Billy, a rapper/dancer dwarf who soon became famous as Bush-wick Bill (Richard Stephen Shaw, 1966–). Bill was born in Kingston, Jamaica, and raised in Brooklyn, New York.

The group again broke up, this time because of contract disputes with J Prince, and its most successful lineup was created, consisting of DJ Ready Red, Bushwick Bill, and two members from Houston—Scarface (Brad Terrence Jordan, 1970–) and Willie D (William James Dennis, 1966–). The new quartet broke ground with *Grip It! On That Other Level* (1989), but the band began to flourish with its next album, *The Geto Boys* (1990), which saw its sales expand after pressure from the Parents Music Resource Center (PMRC) and the onset of Parental Advisory labels. The album's violent content (misogyny, gore, psychotic experiences, and necro-philia) not only increased sales but prompted Geffen Records (1980–) to balk as distributor, forcing a switch of the album's label, Def American Recordings (now American Recordings, 1988–), to Warner Bros. Records (1958–).

The band's next album, *We Can't Be Stopped* (1991), marked the replacement of DJ Ready Red with DJ Domantion (Michael Poye, n.d.) and the move back to Rap-A-Lot Records; the label used a highly publicized Bushwick Bill incident to boost its sales and those of the hit single "Mind Playing Tricks on Me," a hip hop classic that also peaked at No. 23 on the Billboard Hot 100. Bushwick Bill, while under the influence, tried to get his girlfriend at the time to shoot him, and after a strug-gle, he was shot in his right eye. The album cover features a graphic photograph of his sitting on a hospital gurney, flanked by Scarface and Willie D. Bushwick Bill would also do a solo song about the incident, "Ever So Clear," on the album *Little Big Man* (1992).

Willie D left the group for a solo career, and Big Mike (Michael Barnett, 1971–) joined Scarface and Bushwick Bill for the album *Till Death Do Us Part* (1993). The album was certified Gold and spawned the hit "Six Feet Deep" (No. 40 on the Billboard Hot 100), but fans did not like Big Mike, so Willie D returned and replaced him to record *The Resurrection* (1996) and *Da Good da Bad and da Ugly* (1998). *The Foundation* and *The Resurrection Screwed and Chopped A-Lot* were both released in 2004, after the band reunited following a slight hiatus. Scarface, origi-nally known as DJ Akshen, signed with Rap-A-Lot Records to join Geto Boys in 1989 and until 2005 remained with the group while releasing a series of solo albums; he also created his own label (Face II Face Records, 1993*–) in Houston and was coordinator and president of Def Jam South (1999–) in New York; he was influen-tial in signing and popularizing Ludacris (1977–).

The band's sound prioritizes raps over music. Songs have a consistent rhythm, which is usually in the background so that vocals stand out, which is important since all members of the band take turns rapping—foreground vocals emphasize each rapper's unique vocal quality and style as well as lyrical contribution. Slower songs usually sample R&B loops, typically keyboard or jazz guitar riffs, which add to the laid-back quality of the downtempo drum loops, and here Geto Boys vocalists use a quiet, almost understated method of rapping, juxtaposed against little background singing. In angrier songs, typically songs about killers and pro-test songs such as "We Can't Be Stopped" and "Crooked Officer," rappers use more immediate and breathless rapping styles in a higher range, and these in later albums may be juxtaposed against Jamaican rhythms and/or accompanied and complemented by background singing.

Anthony J. Fonseca

See also: Dirty South; Gangsta Rap; Hardcore Hip Hop; Horrorcore; The United States

Further Reading

Scarface and Benjamin Meadows Ingram. 2015. *Diary of a Madman: The Geto Boys, Life, Death, and the Roots of Southern Rap.* New York: HarperCollins.

Westoff, Ben. 2011. "Geto Boys: Paranoia, Insanity, and Rap-A-Lot Records." In *Dirty South: OutKast, Lil Wayne, Soulja Boy, and the Southern Rappers Who Reinvented Hip Hop*, chap. 2. Chicago: Chicago Review Press.

G-Funk

G-funk is the common name for gangsta-funk, a subgenre of rap that emerged from West Coast gangsta rap during the early 1990s. Drawing heavily on samples from funk albums of the 1970s, G-funk's tone was far less aggressive than the work of gangsta rap groups such as N.W.A. (1986–1991) and Geto Boys (1986–) or that of Ice Cube (1969–). Rather, it is characterized by a laid-back rhythm and vocal delivery; instrumentation such as synthesizer, bass, and brass; and sampling of Afrocentric funk groups such as Plainfield, New Jersey's Parliament (1968–1970, 1974–1980) and Funkadelic (1968–) as well as Ohio Players (1959–2002) from Dayton. While G-funk's lyrics sometimes expressed the same violent fantasizing, its lyrics emphasized leisurely practices such as drinking, smoking marijuana, partying, cruising (in lowriders), and engaging in promiscuous sex.

Although there is some debate over its origins, N.W.A.'s Dr. Dre (1965–) is widely regarded as G-funk's chief pioneer. Dr. Dre experimented with Funkadelic samples since Funkadelic's sound, which rose to prominence during the 1970s as a less vacuous alternative to disco, possessed a psychedelic, neo soul aesthetic. Like funk, live G-funk uses elaborate stage theatrics, featuring costumes and props. Dr. Dre's first distinct foray into funk sampling occurred on N.W.A.'s final album, *Efil4za—n* (1991), on the Ruthless label. After leaving N.W.A. and forming Death Row Records (1991–2008) with producer Suge Knight (Marion Hugh Knight Jr., 1965–), Dr. Dre began perfecting his style while working on his first solo album, *The Chronic* (1992), which was released on the Death Row label.

G-FUNK AND THE POST–LOS ANGELES RIOTS ERA

In addition to Dr. Dre's own artistic curiosities, the racial climate during the early 1990s in the United States figured significantly into G-funk's resonance and success. Death Row released *The Chronic* in the same year as the Los Angeles riots, following the acquittal of four police officers in the videotaped beating of black motorist Rodney King (1965–2012). The riots had a profound impact on the United States, as they ignited long-standing racial tensions between police and the African American community. Following the riots, however, several of Los Angeles's largest gangs entered a peace agreement in the name of community rebuilding. Although a notable reduction of local gang-related violence followed the truce, law enforcement suspected the peace agreements were a post-riot ploy among gangs to collectively target police officers; thus, when gangs would hold outdoor parties that came to symbolize the peace movement, police would often arrive and force the crowds to disperse. Los Angeles and other cities also passed increasingly punitive ordinances targeting loitering, listening to boomboxes, and cruising. These new policies disproportionately impacted black and Latino youth and gave expression to post-riot anxieties about young racial minorities occupying public space.

Understanding the criminalization of black leisure following the Los Angeles riots is crucial for appreciating the context of G-funk's emergence as a popular rap subgenre. Iconic G-funk tracks such as Dr. Dre's "Let Me Ride" (1993), Warren G (Warren Griffin III, 1968–) and Nate Dogg's (Nathaniel Dwayne Hale, 1969–2011) "Regulate" (1994), and Snoop Doggy Dogg's (1971–) "What's My Name?" (1993) celebrated many of the leisure activities urban police were targeting. "Regulate" tells the story of Warren G and Nate Dogg as they endeavor to go on a date; however, early in the track, a group of men mug Warren G, stealing his gold rings and Rolex watch. After he and Nate Dogg retaliate and kill a couple of the muggers, Nate Dogg declares that the two will now enjoy their evening of leisure, which includes (in both the lyrical narrative and the music video) going to an East Los Angeles motel to party with women (characterized as "hoes").

While few G-funk tracks directly address police, partially due to the industry-wide stigma regarding antipolice lyrics following the backlash against N.W.A.'s "F— tha Police" (1988) and Body Count's (1990–2006, 2009–) "Cop Killer" (1992), some music videos make subtle references to law enforcement. For example, in "What's My Name?," Snoop Dogg and his posse transform from human to Dober-man pinschers and back again. Throughout the video, bumbling white dogcatchers chase the group to prevent them from causing havoc and arriving at a party. But by the video's end, they arrive, and even the dogcatchers end up dancing to the beat. The narrative arc is strikingly similar to that of the video for N.W.A.'s "Straight Outta Compton" (1988), which portrays the group eluding Los Angeles police. In these songs and videos, G-funk's investment in the leisurely practices of black youth is apparent, and G-funk rappers portray violence from fellow community members or law enforcement as a barrier to pleasure. Because minority leisure was increasingly under police scrutiny, G-funk possesses a distinctly political element, perfect for an audience eager to consume music that validated their leisure practices.

GENERATIONAL DIVIDE

While G-funk's emergence in the post-riot period suggests a degree of political content reminiscent of the 1960s and 1970s, many G-funk artists distanced themselves from older generations of African Americans while also drawing heavily on their music. In the popular *Chronic* track "Let Me Ride," Dr. Dre eschews stereotypical medallions (old-school bling), dreadlocks (Rastafari culture), and the raised black fist (Black Panther Party and the Black Power Movement). Afrocentric medallions and dreadlocks, as well as the iconic Black Power fist were symbols of the antiracist struggle between the early years of the United States' Civil Rights Movement (1954–1968) and the 1980s. Dr. Dre's production style, however, drew heavily on the very musical acts that provided the soundtrack for this era of racial struggle, specifically musicians such as George Clinton (1941–), directors of blaxploitation films (1970s–1990s), and black artists widely associated with Black Power.

This central tension in G-funk helps explain why it was a source of intense anxiety for many elder voices in the black community. It was difficult for cultural figures such as Jesse Jackson Sr. (1941–) and C. Delores Tucker (1927–2005), who frequently spoke out against gangsta rap in general and G-funk in particular, to hear lyrics that they believed denigrated black men and women accompanied by funk tracks that many of them likely held in their own record collections.

Bryan J. McCann

See also: Dr. Dre; Gangsta Rap; The United States

Further Reading

Chang, Jeff. 2005. *Can't Stop Won't Stop: A History of the Hip Hop Generation.* New York: Picador.

Diallo, David. 2010. "From Electro-Rap to G-Funk: A Social History of Rap Music in Los Angeles and Compton, California." In *Hip Hop in America: A Regional Guide,* edited by Mickey Hess, vol. 1, chap. 10. Santa Barbara, CA: Greenwood.

Quinn, Eithne. 2005. *Nuthin' but a "G" Thang: The Culture and Commerce of Gangsta Rap.* New York: Columbia University Press.

Further Listening

Dr. Dre. 1992. *The Chronic.* Death Row Records.

Snoop Doggy Dogg. 1993. *Doggystyle.* Death Row/Interscope Records.

Ghana

Ghana is a West African country whose south coast borders the Atlantic Ocean with the Gulf of Guinea, and it borders Burkina Faso, Togo, and the Ivory Coast. In the 1980s, Ghanaian hip hop (called GH rap) emerged in the capital city, Accra, shortly after the arrival of American hip hop. Most GH Rap is in English with American vernacular, though pidgin English (combining English with Ghanaian dialects), Twi, and Ga are often used. Ghana's first rap crew, Chief G and the Tribe (1989–1997), was started by a 10-year-old New York–born rapper and singer-songwriter of Fante and Canadian descent, Jay Ghartey (Kweku Gyasi Ghartey, 1979*–).

Ghana's main population is Akan, but significant ethnic groups include Dagbani, Mossi, Ewe, Ga-Adangbe, Gurma, and Fulani peoples; minority populations include Guan/Gonja, Gurunsi, and Bissa/Mande peoples. English remains the official language, though many national languages exist, including Akan, Asante and Akuapem Twi, Dagbani, Mòóre, Ewe, Ga, Adangme, Gourmanché, Fula, Guang, Gonja, Hausa, Sisaala, Frafra, Wasa, Nzema, and Kasem, as well as French, Portuguese, and Arabic.

Ghana has a rich music history. Aspects of many musical genres and styles originated in the nation, considered the home of West African drumming and improvisation: polyrhythm and systematic cross-rhythm (found in European classical music and Afro-Cuban music); collective improvisation (as in American Dixieland, where several members of the frontline—clarinet, cornet, and trombone—improvise together); bebop; and cool jazz. Traditional music is regionally divided between the north (connected to Sahelian music and performed by people who speak Gur and Mande) and coastal south (performed by people who speak Kwa languages, including Akan). Polyrhythms, defined as at least two simultaneously played pattern of rhythms, occur in both regions' music.

Northern traditions include *gyll music*, played on the *balafon* (a kind of xylophone), and griot singing traditions, whereas southern traditions include drumming, dance music, and songs in Akan. Both regions use what are called "talking drums" (called *dondo* or *odondo* in Akan, Fante, Twi, and Baoule; *kalangu* or *dan kar'bi* in Hausa) in music and communication. The talking drum has an hourglass shape and skin drumheads on both ends that are connected through tension by leather cords that are banded in the middle. The drums' talking takes the form of the sound of humming or mimicking tone patterns of speech created by changes in pitch as the drummer squeezes the cords between the arm and the body. A hooked stick is used to hit the drums. Both regions also use clapping as percussion. Ghanaian drumming includes other drums, such as the *adowa* and *kete*, as well as bells. The northern region uses string instruments (chordophones) such as the *kologo* (a lute) and *gonjey* (fiddle) as well as wind instruments (aerophones) such as flutes and horns.

HIGHLIFE

Caribbean music has been influential to Ghanaian popular music, which includes Afrobeat, Afrorock, palm wine music (known as *maringa* in Sierra Leone, with roots going back to the 1880s and employing Trinbagonian calypso melodies and rhythms), and highlife (a guitar band musical style that fuses American swing jazz and rock with Jamaican ska and Congolese *soukous*, derived from Congolese *rumba*). Highlife emerged in the 1920s. It uses Akan rhythms and is played with multiple Western instruments, such as lead and rhythm guitar, horns, and vocals. By the 1940s, guitar band highlife and dance band highlife had developed; the latter dominated in urban areas. By the 1950s and 1960s, rock had been incorporated. With acts such as A. B. Crentsil (Alfred Benjamin Crensil, 1943–) and Nana Ampadu (1945–), and later with Amakye Dede (aka Iron Boy, Highlife Maestro, Abrantie, Dan Amakye Dede, 1958–) and Bisa Kdei (Ronald Kwaku Dei Appiah, 1986–), highlife's popularity had spread to Nigeria, Gambia, Liberia, Sierra Leone, the United States, the United Kingdom, and Germany. George Darko (1951–), Charles Kwadwo Fosuh (1964–), and Nana Acheampong (aka Champion Lover boy, Ernest Acheamponng, n.d.) established the subgenre *burger highlife* in Germany.

GH RAP AND HIPLIFE

Other pioneering artists, Native Funk Lords (NFL, 1992*–1997, including members of Chief G and the Tribe), who rapped in pidgin English, and Talking Drums (1990–1994)* and Nananom (meaning in Asante Kings and Queens, 1994–2001*), who rapped in Twi, began combining highlife (especially its heavy use of rhythm guitar) with American hip hop. This new hip hop style became known as hiplife. Though it emerged in the 1990s, hiplife's roots can be traced further back to the 1970s, when Ghanaian musicians experimented with fusing rap with highlife, reggae, rock, and gospel. For example, in 1973, multi-instrumentalist, singer, songwriter, and later record producer Gyedu Blay Ambolley (1947–) released "Simigwa-do" (a title based on his fusion of highlife and jazz), fusing Fante and English rap passages with Fante-style highlife. In 1993, Talking Drums released the first hiplife single, "Aden?"

In 1994, Reggie Rockstone (Reginald Yaw Asante Ossei, 1967*–) came to Accra from New York City to perform at the Panifest, an event that celebrated both Ghana and the African diaspora. He was so impressed by Accra's GH rap scene that he recorded with his cousin Sidney Ofori (n.d.) of Nananom. Reggie Rockstone, who was born in England and grew up in the United States, was already an established rapper. The former member of the London group PLZ (Parables, Linguistics, and Zlang, 1992–1993) produced successful early hiplife studio albums such as *Makaa maka* (*I Said It Because I Said It*, 1997), *Me na me kae* (*I Was the One Who Said It*, 1999), and *Me ka* (*I Will Say*, 2000), and became known as "the Godfather of Hiplife." Shortly afterward, Buk Bak (pidgin English for School Books, 1996*–2006, 2011–2013), became the first successful hiplife rapping crew that used Ga texts. Buk Bak also rapped in Twi and pidgin English. Contemporary acts included Black Monkz (1995–), VVIP (formerly Vision in Progress, 1997–), Akyeame (1997–2016*), Lord Kenya (Abraham Philip Akpor Kojo, 1978–), and Jay Q (Jeff Tennyson Quaye, 1977–). The last produced Buk Bak and VIP, highlife acts such as Daddy Lumba and Nana Acheampong, and post-2000 hiplife acts such as Castro (Theophilus Tagoe Castro, 1982–2014)*. Jay Q also incorporated into hiplife a 1960s urban recreational dance music from Ga communities called *kpanlogo*.

In 1999, Hammer (aka Tony Starks, Edward Nana Poku Osei, 1976–), as part of the production duo the Last Two (1999–), produced Obrafour's (The Executioner, Michael Elliot Kwabena Okyere Darko, 1976–) *Pae mu ka* (*To Proclaim the Truth* in Akan), the best-selling hiplife album in Ghana. Shortly afterward, the duo broke up, and Hammer became Hammer of the Last Two. At the time, the language tendency leaned toward Akan and pidgin English (for example, by 2004, Reggie Rockstone had opted to rap in pidgin English only). Meanwhile, the London-born producer Panji Anoff (aka Uncle Panji, Panji Marc Owoof Anoff, n.d.) produced GH rap and hiplife in pidgin English. In contrast, Hammer of the Last Two produced and promoted GH rap and hiplife acts in languages other than Akan. Such acts included Kwaw Kese (aka Abodam or Craziness, Emmanuel Botway, 1977–), Tinny (Nii Addo Quaynor, 1982–), Edem (Denning Edem Hotor, 1986–), and Sarkodie (1985–). All rap and sing in Twi and use pidgin English; Tinny and Edem also use Ewe, while Kwaw Kese and Edem also use Ga. The exception, Kwaw Kese, also uses Akan.

Since the 2000s, Sarkodie has been one of the most critically acclaimed GH rappers. He also records hiplife and *azonto*, the latter being a Ghanaian musical genre that employs fast-paced dance beats to accompany a dance characterized by hand movements that pantomime everyday activities to amuse and relay coded messages to an audience. Sarkodie's lyrics focus on romance, praising God, friendship, and street life. The single "Baby" from his debut album *Makye* (2009) became a national hit. In 2011, Sarkodie collaborated with producer and rapper EL (1986–) and had a hit with "You Go Kill Me," which employed azonto beats, and he released his second and most successful album, *Rapperholic* (2011). EL raps in pidgin English, Ga, Twi, and Ewe on his albums *Something Else* (2012) and *ELOM* (*Everybody loves original music*, 2016). His lyrical content is similar to Sarkodie's. EL's career began in 2002 when he joined producer, keyboardist, and pidgin English rapper-songwriter Jayso's (Paul Nuamah Donkor, 1983–) collective Skillions (aka Skills in a Million, The Skillions, 1999*–), which included rapper and producer Ball J (aka Ball J Beat, Albert Ayeh-Hanson, 1984–). EL signed onto Jayso's label, Skillions Records (2008–), which produced the first GH rap mixtape, *Skillionaires* (2009). By 2011, EL had become Ghana's most successful hiplife producer, working with Reggie Rockstone, Sarkodie, D-Black (Desmond Kwesi Blackmore, 1986–), and C-Real (1984–). Contemporary hiplife acts often record GH Rap and fuse other genres such as R&B, dancehall, reggae, African jazz, and Afropop. These acts include R2Bees (2007–), Appietus (Appiah Dankwah, 1977–), KluMonsta (Jeffrey Klu, n.d.), Samini (aka Batman Samini, meaning Rain God in Dagaare or Waale, Emmanuel Andrews Samini, 1981–), Trigmatic (aka Trig Ma Dollar, Enoch Nana Yaw Oduro-Adjei, 1984–), Guru (aka Gurunkz, Maradona Yeboah Adjei, 1987–), StoneBwoy (Livingstone Etse Satekla, 1988–), Kojo Cue (Linford Kennedy Amankwaa, 1989–), Joey B (aka Beezy, Darryl Paa Kwesi Bannerman-Martin, 1989–), MzVee (Vera Hamenoo-Kpeda, 1992–) and her producer Richie (Richie Mensah, 1986–), Asumadu (Solomon Asumadu Mensah, 1993–), Pappy Kojo (aka Fante Van Damme, Realer, No, Jason Gaisie, 1989–), Ruff n Smooth (2009–), and Fancy Gadam (Mujahid Ahmed Bello, 1988–).

In the 2010s, hip hop artists have shown interest in combining spoken-word arts, as exemplified in Mutombo da Poet's (aka Mutombo the Poet, anonymous, n.d.) debut studio album *Photosentences* (2012) in pidgin English, Standard English, and Twi. *Banku music*, a fusion of Ghanaian highlife and bounce with Nigerian chord progressions, has also emerged and is pioneered by Nigerian singer-songwriter Mr Eazi (Oluwatosin Oluwole Ajibade, 1991–).

DIASPORA ACTS

Ghana's diaspora acts have concentrated in Europe as well as the United States. Several Ghanaian hip hop artists were born and live in London and focus on English hip hop and grime, including D-Black, Sway (1982–), Stormzy (aka Wicked Skengman, Michael Ebenazer Kwadjo Omari Owuo Jr., 1993–), Tinchy Stryder (aka The Star in the Hood, Kwasi Danquah, 1987–), and Fuse ODG (Nana Richard Abiona, 1988–). In addition, MC and producer Kobi Onyame (Kwame Barfour-Osei, 1982–)

is based in Glasgow, Scotland, and FOKN Bois (2008–) is based in Budapest, Hungary. Diaspora acts in the United States include M.anifest (Kwame Ametepee Tsikata, 1982–), of Minneapolis; Akwadaa Nyame (Kwame Aduse Poku, n.d.), of the Bronx, New York; Blitz the Ambassador (Samuel Bazawule, 1982–), of Brooklyn, New York; Kursa Chyld (1985–, anonymous), of Cedar Rapids, Iowa, and Atlanta; N-Dex (Dexter Owusu, 1986–), of Oklahoma City; and Coptic (Eric Matlock, n.d.), of New York City. Coptic produced music for notable American hip hop acts such as the Notorious B.I.G. (1972–1997), Puff Daddy (1969–), KRS-One (1965–), and Jermaine Dupri (1972–).

Melissa Ursula Dawn Goldsmith

See also: EL; Nigeria; Reggae; Sarkodie; The United Kingdom

Further Reading

Collins, John. 2012. "Contemporary Ghanaian Popular Music since the 1980s." In *Hip Hop Africa: New African Music in a Globalizing World*, edited by Eric Charry, chap. 10. Bloomington: Indiana University Press.

Osumare, Halifu. 2012. *The Hiplife in Ghana: West African Indigenization of Hip Hop*. New York: Palgrave Macmillan.

Shipley, Jesse Weaver. 2012. "The Birth of Ghanaian Hiplife: Urban Style, Black Thought, Proverbial Speech." In *Hip Hop Africa*, edited by Eric Charry, chap. 1. Bloomington: Indiana University Press.

Further Listening

Blitz the Ambassador. 2016. *Diasporadical*. Jakarta.

D-Black. *Lightwork*. 2016. Black Avenue Muzik.

Fancy Gadam. 2017. *All Eyes on Me*. 5M Music.

Mutombo da Poet. 2012. *Photosentences*. Pidgin Music.

Sarkodie. *Makye*. 2009. Duncwills Entertainment.

Glitch Hop

Glitch hop is a subgenre of both electronica and hip hop. It blends breakbeats, hip hop bass grooves, and rap samples with the sounds, techniques, and looping practices of glitch music, which is music that deliberately incorporates errors or glitches, such as audio malfunctions—skips, hums, distortion, noise, even incorrect bit rate use. Like hip hop and electronica in general, glitch hop has an ever-shifting nature, which results in a variety of techniques and styles. It can lean more toward electronic dance music than hip hop, but this is not always the case, and it may or may not include rap. Glitch hop is international, with the majority of artists representing the United States, the United Kingdom, Australia, New Zealand, and Japan.

ORIGINS AND SOUNDS

Glitch music, as a parent genre to glitch hop, grew out of the practice of validating aural error. With the proliferation of digital media in the 1990s, the sounds of error changed from record scratches and garbled tape to CD skips and computer blips. These sonic disturbances—electronic hums, clicks, distortions, and bleeps—came to be referred to as glitches. Some digital musicians embraced these sounds, just as analog musicians and sound artists in earlier decades had validated similar process errors in turntables and magnetic tape. Glitch music became popular internationally (though particularly in Japan, Northern Europe, and North America), with composers conceptualizing their music as a series of these incidents merged into a unified whole using digital processing. Sometimes it involves the concepts of "sound mangling" or "crunching," the generation and programming of microsounds, which are sounds lasting less than one-tenth of a second. These microsounds are then combined as coherent pulses and rhythms. Sometimes it involves the transformation of synthesized or sampled sound through techniques such as warping, frequency sweeping, timestretching, layering, pitch shifting, and bit reduction. Given this approach, it should be no surprise that glitch music as a genre is often viewed as residing in a space somewhere between popular electronic dance music and the intellectual avant-garde.

Given hip hop's reliance on sampling, it is no surprise that glitch and hip hop merged in the late 1990s with the band often cited as the earliest glitch hop act, Miami-based Push Button Objects (aka PBO, 1997–2003). PBO's EP *Cash* (1997) demonstrates that the first gestures in this direction were more heavily influenced by hip hop than are the current trends. PBO—like most hip hop and electronica artists—relied on a drum machine to create breakbeats, using the machine's looping and layering functions as inspiration for the formal structure of compositions. PBO's Edgar Farinas (n.d.) synthesized electronic sounds and keyboard pads, crunching, stretching, shifting, and warping them into the experimental timbres and iterations found in glitch music. He also sampled preexisting sounds and vocal passages or statements, usually transforming them digitally as well, but often doing so in a way that mimicked the short repetitions and scratching effects created on turntables by analog DJs.

Cash loops heavy backbeats and bass grooves, layers glitch sounds and melodies, and inserts grainy, spliced vocals. These traits remain influential in PBO's subsequent releases and are especially potent in PBO's best-known single, "360°" (2000), created with Del the Funky Homosapien (Teren Delvon Jones, 1972–), Mr. Lif (Jeffrey Haynes, 1974–), and DJ Craze (Aristh Delgado, 1977–). The song goes further, however, in its representation of the hip hop style, not only sampling and transforming short, rapped vocal passages but presenting more complete and complex raps by guest artists. This approach is also found in the first album by Prefuse 73, the project band of Guillermo Scott Herren (1976–), *Vocal Studies + Uprock Narratives* (2001).

INFLUENCES OF LO-FI AND TECHNOLOGY

Glitch hop artists initially embraced a lo-fi aesthetic that connected them to their roots in hip hop and early glitch music, but as time passed, the sound of glitch hop became more refined, incorporating modern electronica aesthetics and prioritizing a cleaner, more exacting sound. This can be attributed to prodigious advances in digital tools, such as the inexpensive Akai Music Production Controller series, and computer processing speeds. Glitch hop continues to rely on looping and layering for its form, and as is the case for most subgenres of electronica, the differences between glitch hop and its related styles are often ambiguous.

Although hip hop elements such as breakbeats and sampled rap vocals have remained, these elements do not necessarily need to be present for a track to be identified as glitch hop. "Vice" (2013) by Dodge (Rob Talbot, n.d.), Fuski (Christopher Allen, n.d.), and Culprate (John Hilsop, n.d.), for instance, emphasizes hip hop–style vocal intrusions and synthesizer melodies, while glitch hop tracks by David Tipper (1976–) tend more fully toward electronica. His track "Bubble Control" (*Bubble Control*, 2011), for instance, arguably references the warped sub-bass of dubstep and the floating atmospheres of ambient music but retains its glitch hop label through its prominent breakbeat and its imitation turntable scratches. "Bubble Control" exemplifies Tipper's prioritization of experimentation in timbre and rhythm in glitch sound design as he blurs boundaries across several areas of electronica.

Additional glitch hop artists and groups include Dabrye (Tadd Mullinix, n.d.), the Glitch Mob (2006–), Autechre (1987–), Taylor Deupree (1971–), Flying Lotus (1983–), and Pretty Lights (1981–). As demonstrated by Tipper's "Bubble Control," contemporary glitch hop artists tend to conceive of their music as part of a constellation of subgenres, a web of stylistic relationships that engulf glitch hop but can also include IDM (intelligent dance music), ambient, wonky, neurohop, electrogaze, trip hop, and dubstep, among many others.

Jessica Leah Getman

See also: Industrial Hip Hop; Nerdcore

Further Reading
D'Errico, Mike. 2015. "Off the Grid: Instrumental Hip Hop and Experimentation after the Golden Age." In *The Cambridge Companion to Hip Hop*, edited by Justin Williams, chap. 22. Cambridge, England: Cambridge University Press.
Vanhanen, Janne. 2003. "Virtual Sound: Examining Glitch and Production." *Contemporary Music Review* 22, no. 4: 45–52.

Further Listening
Prefuse 73. 2001. *Vocal Studies + Uprock Narratives.* Warp Records.
Push Button Objects. 1997. *Cash EP.* Schematic.
Tipper, David. 2011. *Bubble Control EP.* Tippermusic.

Graffiti Art

Graffiti art can be found in almost any urban environment and in some rural communities, as well as in railways (on train cars) and on other public transportation. It can take the form of vandalism—of buildings, cars, and trains, as spray-painted symbols, words, and images. This vandalism, known as graffiti, has a rich history, accented by significant cultural and political movements and designed to be viewed

The use of spray paint is the most popular technique used in graffiti, a major aspect of hip hop culture. Inexpensive and easily accessible, spray paint has been used in graffiti that had been considered vandalism, as with bombing (spray painting graffiti images) trains or subway cars. Recently, graffiti has been re-classified as art, as exhibited in the works of Fab Five Freddy, and many others. Some cities even contract graffiti artists for beautification projects. (Mirko Vitali/Dreamstime.com)

openly by the public, whether desired or not by governmental entities or private businesses. Graffiti has certainly been around longer, but for at least the last five decades, this practice of marking public spaces has developed into a profound art form, utilizing professional-grade techniques and expressing deep meaning for the artist and sometimes the viewer. Graffiti art has evolved to become many cities' most beloved art form, with large neighborhoods and metropolitan areas embracing and encouraging more works, some even being commissioned by private companies and city leaders.

Graffiti's history can be traced back to ancient Egypt and Greece, cultures that encouraged public renderings of images of ships, battles, and religious symbols. Such images' being considered a public art form notwithstanding, modern culture's perception of these images has been less about art and more about historical context, especially since poetry was a significant part of these ancient art forms. It wasn't until World War II (1939–1945) that graffiti was used as a symbol of defiance (beyond the individual acts of painting people's dwellings with racial slurs or incendiary accusations of treason to intimidate them). The emergence of the rallying cry "Kilroy was here," tagged on walls throughout Europe to strike fear into the Germans, implying that the Allied forces could be anywhere and everywhere, made symbolic and cultural graffiti more common. This Kilroy image of the bald-headed man with a large nose peaking over a wall became iconic during World War II and for many years afterward. During the United States Civil Rights Movement (1954–1968), many images were drawn in public areas to express anger and frustration over the racial inequality in America. This trend continued into the 1970s, and can be seen today with the Black Lives Matter movement (2013–). As of 2018, graffiti has multiple functions, from expressing the artist's individuality and prowess to protesting war and calling attention to significant political issues in America and abroad. Graffiti has also kept its ties to pop culture iconography, gang symbols, and psychedelic drug hallucinations.

The term *graffiti art* shows a cultural acceptance of graffiti as a legitimate art form, based on the artist's intent and his or her mastery of specialized techniques. Most graffiti artists use spray paint as their primary medium, and some use stencils and markers to help in graffiti creation. Specialized nozzles created for spray paint cans make possible different spray patterns, aiding in the creation of straight edges or wide gradations and helping artists blend different colors and patterns. Spray paint became the popular medium because of ease of access, as well as its ability to adhere to most surfaces and dry quickly and efficiently; spray paint manufacturers also provide a wide array of colors and textures. Other techniques include bleach or acid marking, wheatpasting and paste-ups, letter pressing or rubbing, street poster art, sculpture, and installations. Many artists illegally paint or tag buildings and therefore need to make a quick escape from the scene of the crime, so the need for a fast-drying medium is paramount, especially since much gang-related tagging (including artist symbols—images that artists use as their signatures) are painted on highway overpasses, train cars, public concrete walls, and government buildings and grounds. But not all graffiti is simple tagging. Large-scale murals are now a significant part of graffiti art, and many artists are being commissioned by cities, neighborhoods, and businesses to create these murals, helping to establish community identities in urban environments. The Denver RiNo District is one of these areas in the United States—here businesses are embracing the individuality of various artists and their viewpoints. The area was the old warehouse district just off the railway lines where goods were housed before being sent on to stores. Now the area is being converted into urban housing, bars and breweries, and restaurants, which have large areas of wall space for the creation of these murals. Houston's Third Ward is another example of a warehouse district going through the same kind of conversion. Its large walls offer ideal spaces for artists to create larger-than-life pictorials and community pride.

Internationally, graffiti art is highly respected, especially in Europe and South America, with large-scale works on the sides of skyscrapers and monuments. Just a few internationally renowned graffiti artists of the hip hop era include Fab Five Freddy (1959–), who along with graffiti artists such as Jean-Michel Basquiat (1960–1988) and Puerto Rican–born Lee Quiñones (George Lee Quiñones, 1960–) helped introduce and connect the New York art world to graffiti art; Banksy (anonymous, n.d.) of England; Blek le Rat (Xavier Prou, 1952–) and Jef Aérosol (Jean-François Perroy, 1957–) of France; Faith47 (anonymous, 1979–) of South Africa; Rone (Tyrone Wright, 1980–) of Australia; and Anti-Nuke (anonymous, n.d.) of Japan. The Berlin Wall contains a two-mile stretch of graffiti artwork after artwork, each with its own perspective on the history of the wall itself, including German ancestral and Nazi atrocities committed against Jews, other people, and other countries during World War II. In Poland, Lithuania, Spain, the United Kingdom, Puerto

Rico, and other countries, artists have been commissioned by apartment building owners to create works that exceed 10 stories high, giving entire neighborhoods a glimpse into the mind of the artist, whose storytelling is relevant to the community in which his or her graffiti piece is painted. In contrast, it is difficult to find graffiti in some countries that have oppressive governments (for example, Afghanistan, Democratic Republic of Congo, and North Korea) or maintain restrictions against it for reasons such as promoting tourism or perceptions of cleanliness (for example, Brunei, Mauritius, and Singapore).

Matthew Schlief

See also: Fab Five Freddy; Gangs (United States)

Further Reading

Christensen, Miyase, and Tindra Thor. 2017. "The Reciprocal City: Performing Solidarity—Mediating Space through Street Art and Graffiti." *International Communication Gazette* 79, nos. 6–7: 584–612.

Merrill, Samuel. 2015. "Keeping It Real? Subcultural Graffiti, Street Art, Heritage and Authenticity." *International Journal of Heritage Studies* 21, no. 4: 369–89.

Grandmaster Flash

(Joseph Saddler, 1958–, Bridgetown, Barbados)

Grandmaster Flash is best known for his association with the Furious Five (1976–1982), a hip hop group founded in the Bronx, New York, in the mid-1970s. Born in Barbados, he emigrated as a child (with his family). He grew up with not only a keen interest in electronics and audio circuitry but also the experience of his father's extensive record collection, consisting largely of Caribbean and African American music. Although the group disbanded in the 1980s, they have reunited for performances.

EARLY TECHNIQUES

Grandmaster Flash began DJing as a teen, modeling his sound system and style after pioneering hip hop artist DJ Kool Herc (1955–) and studying the techniques of Pete Jones (n.d.) and Grandmaster Flowers (Jonathan Cameron Flowers, d. 1992*), considered the first American mobile DJ by many scholars. Grandmaster Flash was a celebrated party DJ in the 1970s, working with Kurtis Blow (1959–) and Lovebug Starski (Kevin Smith, 1960–). Flash relied on his DJ experience, his knowledge of popular music, and his expertise in electronics to create the technology and techniques that would allow him not only to mix, but also to make his own beats. To that end, he introduced the beatbox, a manually operated, custom-rigged drum machine, and custom-built much of his equipment as he developed his innovative approach to turntablism.

Flash pioneered what he called the quick-mix method, which incorporated cutting, backspin, and double-back, using the turntables in innovative ways, such as a counterpoint to vocals. Flash worked closely with colleague GrandWizard Theodore (1963–), who is credited with developing turntable scratching.

GRANDMASTER FLASH AND THE FURIOUS FIVE

Grandmaster Flash's crew grew around him. By the mid-1970s, he was performing with three MCs who rapped while he DJed: The Kidd Creole (Nathaniel Glover, 1960–), Melle Mel (Melvin Glover, 1961–), and Cowboy (Keith Wiggins, 1960–). Calling themselves Grandmaster Flash and the 3 MCs, they began performing in 1976 at Disco Fever in the Bronx; the group became one of the first hip hop groups to secure a regular engagement in a well known venue. Later, the group added Scorpio (aka Mr. Ness, Eddie Morris, n.d.) and Rahiem (Guy Todd Williams, n.d.) to form the Furious Five.

Grandmaster Flash and the Furious Five signed with Enjoy Records (1962–1995) and in 1979 released their first single, "Superappin," in which the five MCs introduce themselves and their styles over Flash's high-energy, funk beats that sample "Seven Minutes of Funk" by the short-lived band the Whole Darn Family (1976). The following year, the group signed with Sugar Hill Records (1979–) and released "Freedom," which showcased Flash's extraordinary mixing skills—his sampling of Freedom's (1977–1984) "Get Up and Dance" (1979) with the high energy of the Furious Five at the mic—conveying all the creativity and excitement of a jam in a recording.

To their emerging hip hop style, the Furious Five added rap routines, nonimprovised rhymes in which the rappers would finish one another's lines, moving text delivery rapidly around the group. As a lead innovator of turntable technique and hip hop style, Grandmaster Flash became the first DJ to make an entire recording based on mixing other records: in 1981, Sugar Hill Records produced "The Adventures of Grandmaster Flash on the Wheels of Steel" (referring to his dual turntables). Here Grandmaster Flash showcased his mixing skills and demonstrated the growing possibilities of intertextuality and intermusicality in hip hop as he combined elements of various iconic songs with his group's own "Freedom" (1980).

The socially conscious lyrics delivered by Melle Mel in "The Message" (1982) and "New York, New York" (1983) ushered in message rap, a new kind of rap that forcibly shed light on social and political issues. The narrative of "The Message," delivered in Melle Mel's gritty, powerful style, focused on endemic poverty, violence, a lack of positive role models, and the nearly inexorable trajectory toward the prison system for many African American young men. Grandmaster Flash's beat undergirds the text with an understated, tense, midtempo, synthesized motif. This spare sound would pervade other hip hop beats of the early 1980s.

Live performances of "The Message" often featured all of the Furious Five MCs taking turns on the verses. Because of both its skilled musicianship and its demonstration of the power of rap as a sociopolitical vehicle for expressing the realities faced by many African Americans, the song won significant honors: it reached No. 4 on Billboard's R&B chart before going Platinum; the *Village Voice* (1955–) and *Rolling Stone* (1967–) named it single of the year; and it was one of 50 recordings chosen by the Library of Congress in 2002 for the National Recording Registry (the first hip hop recording to receive this honor).

Flash and Melle Mel continued recording message rap, releasing "White Lines (Don't Don't Do It)" (1983), warning of the dangers of cocaine. In an ironic musical metaphor, Flash's backup singers provide vocal samples, between verses, of the harmonic bridge of the Beatles' (1960–1970) "Twist and Shout" (1963), lines from white music to represent white lines. In "Beat Street Breakdown" (Sugar Hill Records, recorded for the 1984 American film *Beat Street*), Melle Mel delivers a message about violence and poverty while imagining a brighter future for African Americans; as a DJ, Grandmaster Flash offers an exquisite example of virtuosic turntablism, with a scratching technique that takes on a rhetorical, almost verbal quality.

In 2007, Grandmaster Flash and the Furious Five were inducted into the Rock and Roll Hall of Fame in a ceremony presided over by Jay-Z (1969–). The 21st century has also seen the group honored in the Grammy Hall of Fame (2011). As of 2018, Grandmaster Flash has continued to DJ and remains a key figure in legitimizing the notion of DJ as musician and turntable as instrument.

Jennifer L. Roth-Burnette

See also: GrandWizard Theodore; Melle Mel; Turntablism; The United States

Further Reading

Chang, Jeff. 2005. *Can't Stop, Won't Stop: A History of the Hip Hop Generation.* New York: Picador.

Ewoodzie, Joseph C. Jr. 2017. *Break Beats in the Bronx: Rediscovering Hip Hop's Early Years.* Chapel Hill: UNC Press Books.

Forman, Murray, and Mark Anthony Neal, eds. 2004. *That's the Joint: The Hip Hop Studies Reader.* 2nd ed. New York: Routledge.

Reeves, Marcus. 2008. "The New Afro-Urban Movement." In *Somebody Scream! Rap Music's Rise to Prominence in the Aftershock of Black Power*, chap. 2. New York: Faber and Faber.

Williams, H. C. 2007. "Grandmaster Flash." In *Icons of Hip Hop: An Encyclopedia of the Movement, Music and Culture*, edited by Mickey Hess, vol. 1. Westport, CT: Greenwood Press.

GrandWizard Theodore

(aka Grand Wizzard Theodore, Theodore Livingston, 1963–, Bronx, New York)

GrandWizard Theodore is a pioneering American hip hop turntablist and DJ who was credited for creating scratching, moving an album forward and/or backward to create rhythmic sounds, either unaccompanied (solo) or accompanying another album, in 1975. Scratching later became the basis of all turntablist techniques. Shortly afterward, he developed and specialized in record needle drops, which were done without cuing up the record (marking spots on an album with small stickers or wax pencils).

THE STORY OF THE SCRATCH

Born Theodore Livingston, GrandWizard Theodore at a young age became a Bronx house party DJ who formed the L Brothers (aka The Love Brothers,

1970s–1980s*) with his two older brothers (the L Brothers would later become part of the Fantastic Five). In 1975, after returning from school, he was playing albums on a record player in his bedroom and practicing his DJ skills for local parties when he was told by his mother that his playing was too loud. To pay attention to her, he tried to hold the album he was playing in place with his hand but accidentally moved it forward and backward (this technique later would become known as a rub, though it became the first scratch). From that point on, he took interest in this accidental sound and began to explore its musical potential, planning to introduce rubbing (as well as scratching) as part of his DJ sets for house parties in the Bronx.

The L Brothers were friends with and sometimes worked with pioneering turntablist Grandmaster Flash (1958–), who had already developed the backspin technique (aka quick-mix theory) to extend the instrumental breaks of a song. GrandWizard Theodore worked with him to further develop the scratching technique. Combining mixing and scratching (using the regular, or forward, hand-moving style) with needle drops and other techniques, GrandWizard Theodore soon used turntablism as musical accompaniment as well as solo musical performance.

GRANDWIZARD THEODORE AND THE FANTASTIC FIVE

In 1979, he became the leader of the American old-school hip hop and disco group GrandWizard Theodore and the Fantastic Five (aka Fantastic Five, Fantastic Freaks, The Fantastic Romantic 5, 1979*–). In 1980, the group released the 12-inch single "Can I Get a Soul Clap (Fresh out the Pack)," which consisted of the five MCs rapping against GrandWizard Theodore's rhythmic scratches.

GrandWizard Theodore and the Fantastic Five were best known for appearing in the American hip hop feature film *Wild Style* (1983). Later the group appeared with American old-school hip hop group the Cold Crush Brothers (1978–) on the track "Stylewild '94," from Public Enemy's (1986–) DJ Terminator X's (Norman Rogers, 1966–) last solo studio album *Super Bad* (1994). The group also recorded on *Harlem World 1981* (1998), a 1981 live MC battle tape between Cold Crush Brothers and the Fantastic Five that was released nearly 20 years later. As of 2018, stylizing his name with a second *z* and adding a space, Grand Wizzard Theodore still performs and teaches turntablism classes, most notably at Jam Master Jay's (Jason William Mizell, 1965–2002) Scratch DJ Academy (2002–).

In 1998, GrandWizard Theodore was inducted into the Technics DJ Hall of Fame, and in 2014 he was among the first DJs to have his handprints immortalized in a cement square on Guitar Center's (1959–) RockWalk in Hollywood.

Melissa Ursula Dawn Goldsmith

See also: Grandmaster Flash; Turntablism; The United States

Further Reading

Katz, Mark. 2010. "The Turntable as Weapon: Understanding the Hip Hop DJ Battle." In *Capturing Sound: How Technology Has Changed Music*, chap. 6. Rev. ed. Berkeley: University of California Press.

Katz, Mark. 2012. *Groove Music: The Art and Culture of the Hip Hop DJ.* New York: Oxford University Press.

Webber, Stephen. 2008. "The Rise of the Hip Hop DJ: Featuring Original Interviews with Rob Swift and DJ Shadow." In *DJ Skills: The Essential Guide to Mixing and Scratching*, chap. 4. Burlington, MA: Focal Press.

Greece

Greece's hip hop scene emerged slightly later than those of most European countries, with the earliest bands forming in the mid-1980s. This is a surprisingly slow development, considering how urban Greek culture embraced graffiti, subversive Greek popular music (such as *rebetika*, *entelina*, or the *new wave laika*), and way-of-life countercultures such as *zamanfou* (aka *ochaderfismos*), centered on social loafing. Preferences for Greek popular and folk music, American rock, and Jamaican reggae, as well as a general anti-American sentiment, made it difficult for American-style rap to take hold. American hip hop first became interesting to Greeks through films such as *Wild Style* and *Flashdance* (both 1983) as well as *Beat Street, Breakin'* and *Breakin' 2: Electric Boogaloo* (all 1984).

Space FM 93.9 was one of the earliest Greek radio stations to play local hip hop. MC Dimitris Mentzelos (1968–), of the hip hop group Imiskoúmbria (aka Imiz or The Semi Sardines, 1996–), formerly Tar 'n' Feathers and Hemisphere, hosted the radio show *Breathless* on the station from 1992 to 1993. MTV (1981–) and the Greek music channel MAD TV (aka MAD, 1996–) also aired American hip hop. MAD TV's show *StreetBeat* (1997*–) introduced Greek youth to global and local hip hop, and tourists and immigrants brought hip hop music with them, especially to Athens, which by the 1990s had a hip hop dance club, Sussex, and a hip hop roller rink, the Roxy. Athens became the center of Greek hip hop, though hip hop activity existed in a few places such as Thessaloniki, Greece's second-largest city; however, by the late 1980s, hip hop had reached the Greek islands, resulting in Cypriot hip hop.

Pioneering groups in Athens included Imiskoúmbria, FF.C (FortiFied Concept, 1987–2005), Terror X Crew (1992–2002), Active Member (1992–2015, 2017–), and the first commercially successful Greek act, Goin' Through (1993–). Several early Greek hip hop musicians began their interest in hip hop as either graffiti artists, such as Terror X Crew's Artémis (Artémis Fanourgiákis, n.d.), or breakdancers, such as FF.C's Kostis Kourmentalas (n.d.), Terror X Crew's Efthýmis Bilios (n.d.), and Goin' Through's Michalis Papathanasiou (n.d.). Early rap MCs favored English, but by the late 1980s, Greek texts had become favored. In 1992, Active Member released the first hip hop album in Greek, *Protest*. The early hardcore hip hop group Terror X Crew continued to rap in English as well (and have rapped in Ancient Greek). Some pioneering hip hop artists fused hip hop with other kinds of music. For example, FF.C fused political hip hop with rock, and Terror X Crew fused hardcore hip hop with punk. Imiskoúmbria gained an international reputation through pioneered comedy rap. Other early acts included Razastarr (1993–2010, 2016–), Frontal Attack (aka Psi, 1995–), and Stíchoima (Lyrics, 1999–).

Later hip hop acts included the duo Artémis/Efthýmis (A/E, 2002–), consisting of ex–Terror X Crew members. After leaving Active Member, rapper X-ray (aka Xray, Cheap Science, Nikitas Klint, 1975–) formed the band Rodes (2002–2010), which fused hip hop with traditional Greek music, rock, dubstep, and electronica. San Diego, California–born Greek rapper, music producer, and tattoo artist Táki Tsan (Panagiótis Stravaléxis, 1979–), known variously as Waze, Paidí Thávma (Whiz Kid), Tymvorýchos (Tambourine), and Tay Chan, formed and fronted Zontani Nekri (ZN, Living Dead, 1997–), Greece's first gangsta rap group. ZN released the first Greek gangsta rap album, *The First Volume* (1998). Tay Chan later formed Tigré Sporákia (Tiger Snakes, 2003–) with Eisvoléas (Invader, Ilías Papanikolós, 1985–) of the hardcore hip hop group Alfa Gama (1990s*). Paremvolés (Interferences, 1990s*) released the first hardcore rap album, *En opsi* (*In Consideration Of*, 1999). Since the 2000s, Greek hip hop has entered mainstream popularity. Notable examples include rappers Stereo Mike (Mihalis Exarchos, 1978–), Katachthónios (Infernal, Lázaros Karakóstas, 1978–), and Sifu Versus (Nikos Domvros, 1980–). Notable bands include Warriorz (2002–), Stavento (2004–), Trendy Hooliguns (2004–), and FlyByWire (2009–). Supergroups also emerged, such as La Klikária (The Clique, 2000–2001), which consisted of Imiskoúmbria, Dr. Dreez (Chrístos Alexandrís, 1971–), and Mamaletta (Mariletta Konstantara, n.d.) of the multinational group Endangered Speeches (2009–) and was formed at Berklee College of Music in Boston.

LOW BAP

In the early 2000s, *Skliropyrinikó* (hardcore) and low bap became dominant hip hop subgenres in Athens. Low bap uses a slower tempo as well as a quieter and gentler approach to rap than hardcore, alluding to the boombap production sound—a kick drum "boom" sound followed by a snare drum "bap" sound, looped, plus throbbing bass. Active Member transformed into a low bap collective and led the Low Bap Movement, which is committed to promoting leftist social and political change. Original members included X-ray; rapper, hip hop producer, and sampler BDFoxmoor (Michalis Mitakidis, 1967–); and DJ MCD (aka a dog named Rodriguez, Dimitris Kritikos, 1973–). Its leader from 2002 to 2015, BDFoxmoor, and his wife Sadahzinia (aka Broken Code, Yolanda Tsiampokalou, 1977–), the first female Greek rapper, founded the independent low bap label 8ctagon (2003–).

The low bap sound was created during the making of Active Member's third album, *To megálo kólpo* (*The Great Gulf*, 1995). A popular low bap song is Active Member's "Páme (Guantanamo)," translated as "Let's Go (Guantanamo)" (urging the shutdown of the United States' Guantanamo Bay detention camp), from the album *Pérasma st' Akróneiro* (*Crossing the Acropolis*, 2002). Devoted hardcore and low bap fans came to dislike Imiskoúmbria for its levity. Hip hop tastes have also become divided between hardcore and low bap. Other low bap acts include Vavylóna (Babylon, 1997–), 843 (1999–), Prohja (1998), Kaká Mantáta (1986–), Michális Kouinélis (aka Michail Kouïnélis, 1979), Pýrines Lachés (Fire Spells, aka Pýrina Fengária [Fire Moons], 2003–), and Thirio (Beast, Kóstas Drakoúlas, 1980–).

Melissa Ursula Dawn Goldsmith

See also: Cyprus; Hardcore Hip Hop; Political Hip Hop

Further Reading

Elafros, Athena. 2013. "Greek Hip Hop: Local and Translocal Authentication in the Restricted Field of Production." *Poetics* 41, no. 1: 75–95.

Elafros, Athena. 2013. "Mapping the Hip Hop Transnation: A Brief History of Hip Hop in Athens, Greece." In *Hip Hop in Europe: Cultural Identities and Transnational Flows*, edited by Sina A. Nitzsche and Walter Grünzweig, chap. 2. Zürich, Switzerland: LIT Verlag.

Hess, Franklin L. 2010. "From American Form to Greek Performance: The Global Hip Hop Poetics and Politics of the Imiskoúmbria." In *The Languages of Global Hip Hop*, edited by Marina Terkourafi, chap. 7. New York: Continuum.

Further Listening

Active Member. 2002. *Pérasma st' Akróneiro*. Warner Music Greece/Freestyle Productions.

Various Artists. 1999. *Low Bap Sessions, Vol. 1*. Warner Music Greece/Freestyle Productions.

Various Artists. 1999. *Low Bap Sessions, Vol. 2: Ta Demos*. Warner Music Greece/Freestyle Productions.

Grime

Grime is a hip hop and EDM music style that originated around the turn of the century in London on pirate radio stations such as Rinse FM (1994–), which not only played grime music but released various mixtapes of it. It is a hybridization of African and Caribbean musical elements and music styles such as electronic dance, garage, jungle, dancehall, and ragga with uptempo, syncopated breakbeats (usually around 130 or 140 beats per minute) in 4/4 (quadruple) meter and double-time rhythm; early grime had eight-bar verse patterns (which became 16- and 32-bar patterns in time) and low bassline frequencies. Raps tend to be about the griminess or grittiness of urban life, hence the style's name.

Grime left the underground scene and went mainstream around 2003, owing to efforts by musicians such as Dizzee Rascal (Dylan Kwabena Mills, 1984–) with the album *Boy in da Corner* (2003) and Wiley (Richard Cowie, 1979–) with the album *Treddin' on Thin Ice* (2004), both on XL Recordings (1989–); Kano (Kane Brett Robinson, 1985–) with the album *Home Sweet Home* (2005), on 679 Recordings (aka 37 Adventures, 2001–); and Lethal Bizzle (Maxwell Owusu Ansah, 1984–) with the album *Against All Oddz* (2005), on his short-lived J Did Entertainment label. Other early musicians included Ghetts (Justin Clarke, 1984–), Jme (Jamie Adenuga, 1985–), Skepta (Joseph Junior Adenuga, 1982–), Bugzy Malone (Aaron Davis, 1990–), Akala (Kingslee James Daley, 1983–), and Stormzy (Michael Ebenezer Kwadjo Omari Owuo Jr., 1993–), as well as bands such as the Streets (1994–2011, 2017–), Boy Better Know (2005–), Newham Generals (2004–), Roll Deep (aka Roll Deep Entourage, 2002–2013), and Ruff Sqwad (2001–). Grime became more popular when television stations such as Channel AKA (aka Channel U, 2003–), a digital satellite channel owned by All around the World Productions (1991–), began broadcasting it and other styles of hip hop such as dubstep, reggae, dancehall, and Afrobeat.

Dizzee Rascal has had the most mainstream success of all grime rappers, with 10 Top 10 hits on the U.K. Singles Chart, including four No. 1 songs: "Dance wiv Me" (2008), "Bonkers" (2009), "Holiday" (2009), and "Dirtee Disco" (2010). Wiley and Lethal Bizzle have also charted often, the former having racked up six Top 10 U.K. singles, including one No. 1, "Heatwave" (2012), and the latter having reached the Top 10 with "Oi!" (2002) and produced three songs that peaked at No. 11: "Pow!" ("Forward," 2004), "Rari Workout" (2014), and "Fester Skank" (2015). In 2016, the Ministry of Sound (1991–) media group released a grime compilation titled *Grime Time*, and Skepta's fourth studio album, *Konnichiwa*, entered the U.K. Albums Chart at No. 2. In 2017, Stormzy's *Gang Signs & Prayer* became the first grime album to reach No. 1 on the U.K. Albums Chart.

The next-largest grime scene is based in Birmingham. Although grime is basically a male-dominated style, female rappers such as Solihull-based Lady Leshurr (Melesha O'Garro, 1989–) and London-based Lady Sovereign (Louise Amanda Harman, 1985–) have become popular. The grime scene has stayed mainly in the United Kingdom, but the style has achieved minor popularity in the United States since 2010.

Anthony J. Fonseca

See also: Chopper; The United Kingdom

Further Reading

Barron, Lee. 2013. "The Sound of Street Corner Society: U.K. Grime Music as Ethnography." *European Journal of Cultural Studies* 16, no. 5: 531–47.

Bramwell, Richard. 2015. *U.K. Hip Hop, Grime, and the City: The Aesthetics and Ethics of London's Rap Scenes.* New York: Routledge.

Stirling, Christabel. 2016. "'Beyond the Dance Floor?' Gendered Publics and Creative Practices in Electronic Dance Music." *Contemporary Music Review* 35, no. 1: 130–49.

Further Listening

Dizzee Rascal. 2003. *Boy in da Corner.* XL Recordings.

Various Artists. 2016. *Grime Time.* Ministry of Sound.

Griot

(aka *Jali, Jeli, Djeli*)

A griot is a performer whose role—serving nobility and tribal communities by orally transmitting through music and spoken word the histories and genealogies of a culture—can be traced back over 800 years. Like bards, who perform by singing or speak-singing, they often accompany themselves on an instrument, sometimes adding pantomime. Hip hop scholarship often compares the griot's verbal arts to rap or Jamaican toasting, but a better comparison would be to the skills of rappers and bolon players, who historically have had the power to publicly criticize regimes and individual people (more research is needed to determine how the griot's verbal arts served as a precursor to rap). Specifically, African rap, which more often than American rap or rap of other cultures has lyrical content that concentrates on political and social issues, demonstrates a closer connection to the griot's verbal arts. Focusing on the griot as a precursor to the rapper supports the notion that rap and hip hop have African roots, continuing African musical aesthetics, although the contribution of other kinds of oral and storytelling traditions in Europe, the Middle East, Asia, and the United States to rap development must be considered. Also needing further study is the fact that griots were victims of slave trade and diaspora, which would have affected not only their location but also their performances.

Despite having lesser status today than during the Mali Empire (1235*–1670), griots continue performing, most notably in West Africa, communicating news and praising their patrons. Today's griots are most prominently found in Mandé, followed by Dagomba, Fulbe, Hausa, Mauritanian Arab, Mossi, Songhai, Tukulóor, Serer, Songhai, and Wolof cultures; therefore, modern griots exist in West African in Maghreb countries such as Chad, Ivory Coast, the Gambia, Ghana, Mali, Senegal, Guinea, Mauritania, Burkina Faso, Niger, and northern Nigeria. In countries such as Mali, where over 70 percent of the population is illiterate as of 2018, reliance on griots is essential.

The position of griot is an acquired role—not just anyone can be a griot; in fact, historically griots could not marry outside their artistic group, and training was passed down within the family. In addition, griots tend to be skilled musicians who play instruments such as the *kora*, *balafon*, *goje*, *ngoni*, or *xalam*—instruments that have made their way into some West African hip hop, as in Tim Winsey's (Tim Winsé, 1973–) "Zessa" (2004), which features the kora. The role and concept of the griot is used often in hip hop. Examples include Freestyle Fellowship's (1991–1993, 1998–) studio album *Innercity Griots* (1993), Positive Black Soul's (PBS, 1989–) griot-point-of-view song "Return of da Djelly" (1995), and dälek's *From Filthy Tongue of Gods and Griots* (2002).

Influential Senegalese *mbalax* singer-songwriter Youssou N'Dour's (1959–), who fuses *mbalax* with hip hop and other kinds of music, has a maternal lineage comprising griots. Though he did not grow up within that tradition, N'Dour learned enough from his siblings and surroundings to self-identify as a modern-day griot. Senegalese American singer-songwriter Akon (1973–) also has a connection to griot tradition: he is the son of Dogon griot percussionist Mor Thiam (Mor Dogo Thiam, 1941–) from Dakar, Senegal.

Melissa Ursula Dawn Goldsmith

See also: Bolon and Bolon Player; Burkina Faso; The Gambia; Ghana; Guinea-Bisseau; Ivory Coast; Mali; Niger; Nigeria; Senegal

Further Reading

Sajnani, Damon. 2013. "Troubling the Trope of 'Rapper as Modern Griot.'" *Journal of Pan African Studies* 6, no. 3: 156–80.

Tang, Patricia. 2012. "The Rapper as Modern Griot: Reclaiming Ancient Traditions." In *Hip Hop Africa: New African Music in a Globalizing World*, edited by Eric Charry, chap. 5. Bloomington: Indiana University Press.

Further Listening

dälek. 2002. *From Filthy Tongue of Gods and Griots.* Ipecac Recordings.

Freestyle Fellowship. 1993. *Innercity Griots.* 4th and Broadway.

Guadeloupe

Guadeloupe, islands in the French Antilles in the Caribbean, has a hip hop scene informed by Antillean Creole texts and popular music. Along with Martinique, Guadeloupe is the home of *zouk*, a fast-tempo music heard during Carnival (a Christian festive season that focuses on celebrations such as parades, musical performances, and feasts before the liturgical season of Lent, a solemn period of prayer, penance, forgiving, and self-denial). The word *zouk* means to shake incessantly and to party or be festive, but a softly played, slowed-down subgenre of zouk, known as *zouk-love*, focuses on romance. Guadeloupean hip hop adopts elements of zouk and *gwo ka moderne*, which features traditional drums and adds conga or *djembe*, chimes, and electric bass guitar, and is used as jump-up music. Guadeloupean musicians have also modified Trinbagonian calypso, Dominica's *cadence-lypso*, Haiti's compas/cadence, and Jamaica's reggae and dancehall, in addition to American hip hop and jazz. In addition, by 1984, several years after France developed its hip hop scene, American hip hop had reached Guadeloupe and influenced its music. Guadeloupean musicians also used elements of live French Antilles hip hop: limited technology, rapping over previously composed American beats, and call-and-response.

Since the late 1990s, prominent Guadeloupean hip hop artists have fused several musical styles. These include singer-songwriter, producer, and actor D. Daly (Didier Daly, 1978–); ragga artist Nuttea (aka Daddy Nuttea, Olivier Lara, 1968–); rapper and producer LM Star Jee (aka Starjee, n.d.); singer-songwriter, slam poet, and novelist TiMalo (Thierry Malo, 1974–); *zouk R&B* and new jack swing singer-songwriter and producer Jean-Michel Rotin (1970–); and female rapper and singer-songwriter Swé (anonymous, n.d.). Guadeloupean hip hop lyrics focus on poverty, aspiration, and social injustice, at times with a sense of humor.

Once established, French Antilles hip hop became popular

Since the late 1990s, musicians like ragga artist Nuttea have contributed to Guadeloupean hip hop's sound; a fusion of many musical styles like ragga, reggae, dancehall, zouk R&B, and new jack swing. Nuttea was raised by his grandparents in Guadeloupe before moving to Paris at age six, though he remains musically connected to his motherland. (Eric Fougere/VIP Images/Corbis via Getty Images)

in France. Guadeloupean-born rapper, musician, DJ, and television/radio host Sidney Duteil (Patrick Duteil, 1955–) was a pioneer of Paris's hip hop scene in the early 1980s. Duteil was the first black man in France to host a weekly television show, *H.I.P. H.O.P.* (1984), which was broadcast in Guadeloupe. By the late 1980s, Guadeloupe had several of its own hip hop radio programs. Martinican rappers' use of Antillean Creole inspired Guadeloupean rappers to follow suit. Rapper F—ly (aka Missié GG, Joseph Régis, 1977–) released the first commercially successful hip hop album, *L'indiscipliné* (*The Unruly*, 2001). Other pioneers were rappers Exxòs (Christophe Sophy, n.d.) from Les Abymes and Nèg Lyrical (Rodolphe Richefal, 1976–) from Martinique. Nèg Lyrical's *Kimannièoupédimwenanbagaÿkonsapé fèt?!* (the title, which is based more on sound than meaning, is a compound wordplay; 1996) was the first Antillean Creole rap album recorded in Martinique.

Melissa Ursula Dawn Goldsmith

See also: France; Martinique; Reggae

Further Reading

Gadet, Steve. 2012. "The Creole Hip Hop Culture: Between Tradition and Modernity, Orality, and Scriptuality." In *Marronnage and Arts: Revolts in Bodies and Voices*, edited by Stéphanie Melyon-Reinette, chap. 9. Newcastle upon Tyne, England: Cambridge Scholars.

Gadet, Steve. 2015. "Hip Hop Culture: Bridging Gaps between Young Caribbean Citizens." *Caribbean Quarterly* 61, no. 1 (March): 75–97.

Further Listening

F—ly. 2001. *L'indiscipliné.* Riko Rekords.

Guatemala

Guatemala, a Central American representative democracy that borders both the Pacific Ocean and the Caribbean, is the most populated state in Central America with about 16 million citizens. Guatemalans have a diverse sense of musical styles, and an alternative popular music and underground music movement cropped up in the 1990s, leading to a growing rap scene. Most rap is imported from the United States, although a few local hip hop artists are beginning to attract international attention.

These artists include singer-rapper Rebeca Lane (Rebeca Eunice Vargas Tamayac, 1984–) and rap groups Bacteria Sound System (2005–) and Balam Ajpu (Jaguar Warrior or Warrior of Light, 2010–). Balam Aipu raps in both Spanish and the ancient Mayan Tz'utujil language, using hip hop and reggae to teach ancestors' stories and ways of life. The six-man group Bacteria Sound System Crew fuses elements of hip hop, reggae, and dancehall. Its lyrical content ranges from romance to social awareness, and it tends to inject humor into them.

Trasciende is a hip hop academy that offers art workshops as a means of drawing youth away from violence and into a peaceful environment. In 2009, a group of b-boys (breakdancers) founded the academy. Trasciende creates new opportunities for youth in a country that struggles with high rates of poverty, crime, and drug trading. Because of these poor conditions, Guatemala ranks 31st out of 33 Latin American and Caribbean countries on the Human Development Index.

As of 2018, Guatemala's most popular new hip hop artist is poet, sociologist, and rapper-songwriter Rebeca Lane, who uses hip hop to promote feminism and social justice and to encourage communities to know their histories. Her song "Mujer lunar" ("Lunar Woman," 2013) has become an anthem for women throughout Guatemala. In 2017, she released her debut studio album, *Alma mestiza* (*Mestizo Soul*).

Anthony J. Fonseca

See also: El Salvador; Mexico

Further Reading

Barrett, Rusty. 2016. "Mayan Language Revitalization, Hip Hop, and Ethnic Identity in Guatemala." *Language and Communication* 47 (March): 144–53.

Bell, Elizabeth R. 2017. "'This Isn't Underground; This Is Highlands': Mayan-Language Hip Hop, Cultural Resilience, and Youth Education in Guatemala." *Journal of Folklore Research* 54, no. 3: 167–97.

Further Listening

Lane, Rebeca. 2017. *Alma mestiza* (*Mestizo Soul*). Flowfish Records.

Guinea-Bissau

Guinea-Bissau saw hip hop emerge in the 1990s and quickly spread from urban to rural areas as a tool of underground resistance, protesting the West African country's political unrest and use of military force that had resulted in violence, corruption, economic disparity, social injustice, and widespread drug use and human trafficking. Bissau-Guinean *raperu* (rappers) often live in fear and face threats, censorship, and possible military beatings. Despite this, rapping texts are usually in Upper Guinea Creole, the common language for nearly 70 percent of Guinea-Bissau's diverse population, though occasionally texts are in Portuguese, the official language. Music is inspired by reggae and *kuduro* (aka *kuduru*), an Angolan popular music that developed in the late 1980s and samples Caribbean *zouk* and soca, adding African percussion with house beats and techno.

As of 2018, hip hop is popular, though American and European hits dominate airplay. Though hip hop has been more prominent in Bissau-Guinean culture since the 2010s, events have revealed that performing hip hop critical of the government is still unsafe. In 2013, Masta Tito (Tito Marcelino Morgado, 1983–) recorded his best-known song, "No kansa golpe" ("Endless Coup," 2013), which criticized the governing military. In the same year, he was abducted, beaten, and threatened not to rap again. As of 2018, Masta Tito nevertheless continues recording and performing in Buba, the largest city in southern Guinea-Bissau.

EMERGING FROM THE SUPPRESSED UNDERGROUND

Because early hip hop was driven underground and mostly included live, unrecorded activities, it is extremely difficult to verify the existence of numerous pioneering Bissau-Guinean hip hop artists through recorded songs or albums. One of the earliest hip hop songs, Naka B's (Ramiro Naka, n.d.) "Coli-sensa" ("Please," 1999), criticized the government and post-independence hardships. An internationally known acoustic guitarist and singer, Naka B was not just a hip hop artist, having since 1981 recorded traditional Bissau-Guinean music as well as Latin and Caribbean music and jazz. In 2001, Shivani Ahlowalia (n.d.), who fronts the American-Bengali-Punjabi-Danish live electronic music band Alo Wala (2013–), cofounded the Washington, DC–based Cobiana Records and Cobiana Communications and Culture, which also has a digital radio website. After seeing numerous hip hop artists perform, such as the first hip hop collective, Big Up GB Hip Hop Movement (n.d.), Ahlowalia became inspired to give such acts a distribution outlet. Cobiana Records is devoted not only to hip hop artists but also to releasing recordings of iconic *gumbé* (aka *goombay* or *gumbay*) bands such as Super Mama Djombo (1964*–) and Cobiana Djazz (aka Cobiana Jazz, 1970–1977*). This effort is a major reason that, regardless of political repression, hip hop is growing in Guinea-Bissau.

Among the pioneering hip hop raperus, Masta Tito is the most famous. Masta Tito started rapping in 2002 with the song "Vampiro" ("Vampire"). He incorporates reggae and dancehall in his hip hop music, often autotuning his singing and rapping. Texts are often against military atrocities to civilians in Guinea-Bissau. Another notable artist, rapper N'Pans (Pansau Natchanda, 1975–), also uses hip hop to criticize Guinea-Bissau's regime. N'Pans's "Conversa di bardadi" ("True Conversation," 2008) was released several years after he settled in Moscow. He is currently one of few black rappers living in Russia, is now collaborating with Russian rapper Ligalize (Andrey Vladimirovich Menshikov, 1977–), and has joined the project band Legal Busine\$\$ (2000–2012*). After releasing four solo studio albums in Moscow, N'Pans started his own label, Force Records (2010–).

In 2011, Hasan Salaam (1981–), the first American rapper to perform a concert in Guinea-Bissau, worked closely with Baloberos Crew (n.d.), who after the release of "Seven Minutes of Truth" (2009) were brutally beaten, jailed, and threatened by Guinea-Bissau's military intelligence. Prior to the concert in Guinea-Bissau, Salaam performed the song's verses at an installment of the Impossible Music Sessions (2010–) in Brooklyn, New York—an event that stages banned music, usually performed live by collaborating musicians, and focuses on the nonappearance of the artists at risk. He sang in English but kept the Portuguese refrain. In 2011, Baloberos Crew released the anti–drug trafficking song "Bo obi mas" ("Listen Again").

Melissa Ursula Dawn Goldsmith

See also: Angola; Political Hip Hop; Reggae

Further Reading

Borszik, Anne-Kristin. 2013. "Telling the Truth and Commenting Reality: 'Harsh Criticism' in Guinea-Bissau's Intervention Music." In *The Routledge History of Social Protest in Popular Music*, edited by Jonathan Friedman, chap. 24. New York: Routledge.

Lupati, Federica. 2016. "An Introduction to Hip Hop Culture in Guinea-Bissau: The Guinean *Raperu*." *Journal of Lusophone Studies* 1, no. 1: 139–52.

H

Haiti

Haiti is a country with a population of nearly 11 million that makes up the western part of the Caribbean island of Hispaniola; the Dominican Republic makes up the eastern part of the island. Haiti's citizens are descendants of the aboriginal Taíno people, the Spanish who colonized it, the French who were deeded the colony in the early 17th century, and slaves brought in from Africa to work on its sugarcane plantations. After the French Revolution (1789–1799), a successful slave revolt took place, leading to Haiti's independence in 1804. Haitian music is influenced by African rhythms, French and Spanish elements, and Taíno traditions. Its traditional styles include ceremonial music such as *vodou* and *rara*, dance music such as *compas* (aka *kompa*), *meringue*, *zouk*, and *mizik rasin* (roots music), ballads in the *twoubadou* style, and *mini-jazz* (a combination of *compass*, jazz, and two types of *kreyòl* music), as well as rock and hip hop.

The most popular Haitian song is the patriotic anthem "Haïti Chérie" (aka "Souvenir d'Haïti," 1920), by Othello Bayard de Cayes (1885–1971), and its most popular vocalist is Croix-des-Bouquets–born Wyclef Jean (Nel Ust Wyclef Jean, 1969–), who performs alternative hip hop. The 1970s brought about the reggae-influenced Sanba Movement, with musicians such as Port-au-Prince–born singer Eddy François (n.d.) influencing 1990s mizik rasin through his bands Boukman Eksperyans (1978–) and Boukan Ginen (1990–), who combined reggae, rock, and funk with traditional forms. Haitian hip hop, or *rap kreyòl*, typically addresses social and political topics, though some songs extol the virtues of partying and materialism.

As early as the 1980s, street rappers performed rap kreyòl, but most of these musicians faded into obscurity, with the exception to the originator of Haitian hip hop music and culture, Master Dji (George Lys Herard, 1961–1994), a former radio host who rapped in English, French, and Haitian Creole. He became a music pioneer who united rara, rasin, compas, rap, and reggae and was instrumental in getting rap music aired. In 1982, Master Dji penned the first Haitian Creole rap song, "Vakans." Recent popular hip hop acts include Port-au-Prince–based bands Barikad Crew (2002–) and RockFam Lame-a (aka Rockfam, 2004–) and rappers Dug G. (aka Dug G. Born, Jean-Hubert Valcourt, n.d.), and Jimmy O (Jean Jimmy Alexandre, 1974–2010). Barikad Crew has three albums as of 2018; RockFam Lame-a released four. A political rap act, the six-member Barikad Crew mixes hip hop beats with traditional roots culture to encourage youth to better society. Ex—RockFam Lame-a member Dug G. raps to encourage youth to excel, especially in business; he has released an album, two mixtapes, and a compilation. Jimmy O, who rapped in Haitian Creole, was one of the rappers killed during the Haitian earthquake; he was about to release a much-anticipated debut album.

Among Haitian diaspora hip hop acts, the best known are the Brooklyn, New York–based Kangol Kid (Shaun Shiller Fequiere, n.d.) of U.T.F.O. (Untouchable Force Organization, 1984–1992); New York–based CaRiMi (2002–2016); Montreal-based Muzion (1996–2014); and Muzion's leader, Imposs (Stanley Rimsky Salgado, n.d.), who went solo in 2007. By far, the best-known Haitian hip hop artists are Wyclef Jean and his cousin Pras (Prakazrel Samuel Michél, 1972–), both members of the Grammy Award–winning band Fugees (1992–1997).

Anthony J. Fonseca

See also: France; Reggae; The United States

Further Reading

Jean-Charles, Régine Michelle. 2014. "The Myth of Diaspora Exceptionalism: Wyclef Jean Performs *Jaspora*." *American Quarterly* 66, no. 3: 835–52.

Melyon-Reinette, Stéphanie. 2016. "Homosexuals, Hemophiliacs, Heroin Addicts, and Haitians: How Hip Hop Transformed Haitian Stigmatization into a Source of Pride." In *La Verdad: An International Dialogue on Hip Hop Latinidades*, edited by Melissa Castillo-Garsow and Jason Nicholls, chap. 16. Columbus: Ohio State University Press.

Further Listening

RockFam Lame-a. 2012. *Afiche'w.* RockFam Records.

Hancock, Herbie

(Herbert Jeffrey Hancock, 1940–, Chicago, Illinois)

Herbie Hancock is a jazz composer, keyboardist, bandleader, and sometime actor. His most famous connection to hip hop is his hit song "Rockit" (1983), which has the distinction of being the first mainstream hit fusion between hip hop and jazz that featured turntablism (scratching). Other connections to hip hop also exist in his work, for Hancock's music has served as source music for samples, and Hancock himself worked later in his career with hip hop artists such as Kanye West (1977–), the X-Ecutioners (1989–), GrandMixer DXT (aka Grand Mixer D.ST, Derek Showard, 1960–), and Rob Swift (Robert Aguilar, 1972–). Hancock has also been responsible for creating collaborations between jazz musicians and composers, acting as a go-between to introduce musicians who would then work together on hip hop projects.

EARLY JAZZ CAREER

At age seven, Hancock began studying classical piano. His interest in jazz and sense of complex harmonies developed during his teenage years as he listened to the vocal group the Hi-Lo's (1953–). He dropped out of Grinnell College (Iowa) briefly to work with notable jazz musicians Donald Byrd (1932–2013) and Coleman Hawkins (1904–1969) but eventually graduated with a bachelor's degree in music and mechanical engineering. In 1962, he recorded his first album, *Takin' Off,* which featured his song "Watermelon Man." After hearing the album, eminent jazz composer-trumpeter Miles Davis (1926–1991) was so impressed that he wanted to work with him, and in 1963, Hancock joined his quintet. Hancock's work in Davis's Second Great Quintet (1964–1969) resulted in a more prominent rhythm section that became used increasingly in post-bop as well as in jazz-rock fusion.

Hancock was one of the first keyboardists who shifted between piano, electric pianos, and synthesizers, exploring ways to fuse jazz (from cool to avant-garde) with funk, electronica, and ultimately hip hop. In the 1970s and 1980s, Hancock also scored films, receiving an Academy Award for Best Original Score for *'Round Midnight* (1986), a film in which he also had a supporting actor's role.

"ROCKIT" CONNECTIONS TO GLOBAL HIP HOP

Though Hancock's work is primarily in jazz, jazz fusion, and electronica, his discography since the 1970s and 1980s, when he was exploring jazz-funk fusion, which incorporates Afro-Caribbean and Latin percussion instruments and rhythms, shows connections between his music and global hip hop. For his critically acclaimed *Head Hunters* (1973), he assembled a new band called the Headhunters, partly so that he could compose funk. At the time, *Head Hunters* was the best-selling jazz album in history. It featured "Chameleon," which became a jazz standard with its funk-inspired ARP Odyssey analog synthesizer bass. Reissued in 1992 as a CD, *Head Hunters* became influential to subsequent funk, soul, and hip hop artists. It was followed by *Thrust* (1974) and then the jazz-funk album *Man-Child* (1975).

In 1983, Hancock composed "Rockit," which was was recorded, edited, and engineered at several sound-recording studios. Hancock worked with bass guitarist Bill Laswell (1955–), drum machine and synthesizer programmer Michael Beinhorn (n.d.), and turntablist Grand Mixer D.ST. "Rockit" entered mainstream popularity and encouraged interest in hip hop turntablism and breakdancing; in addition, it reached No. 1 on Billboard's Hot Dance Club Play, No. 6 on Hot Black Singles, and No. 64 on the U.S. Cashbox charts. Although it reached only No. 71 on the Billboard Hot 100, *Future Shock* (1983), the album on which the single later appeared, went Platinum.

The music video helped catapult its success and became famous in its own right. Godley and Creme (1977–1988), an English and London-based rock duo who became successful and influential music video directors, directed the video, which featured action shots and jump cuts of English installation artist and inventor Jim Whiting's (1951–) movable and danceable sculptures—hybrids of broken mannequins and robots—filmed to appear as though they are dancing within a house in London. Hancock appears on keyboard, on a television that is smashed by the end of the video. At the first MTV Video Music Awards, the video won in five categories, including Best Special Effects and Best Concept Video. In 2001, Hancock, Laswell, and Rob Swift collaborated again on a remix of "Rockit" for Hancock's album *Future 2 Future*. This time, Rob Swift and A Guy Called Gerald (Gerald

Simpson, 1968–) programmed beats. The remix expands on the original hit's use of electronica. Hancock later went on tour with Rob Swift and the X-Ecutioners, who performed a new concert version of "Rockit."

SAMPLES

Several of Hancock's most popular songs have been used as samples in hip hop music. Close to the time of its first release, "Rockit" was used numerous times by Grand Mixer D.ST, as well as generously in Knights of the Turntables's (1983–1986) "Techno Scratch" (1984) and as a hook or riff in the B-Boys's (1983–1985) "Cuttin' Herbie." Into the 1990s, it continued to be sampled by band's such as De La Soul (1987–), in "En Focus" (1993); by cult West Coast hip hop duo Charizma (Charles Edward Hicks Jr., 1973–1993) and Peanut Butter Wolf (Chris Manak, 1989*–), in "Pacin' the Floor" (2003); by Janet Jackson (1966–), in her hip hop and dance single "So Excited" (2006); and by Neeraj Shridhar (n.d.) and Suzanne D'Mello (aka Suzie Q, 1976–), in the Bollywood song "Prem ki naiyya" ("The Boat of My Love"), used in the romantic comedy film *Ajab Prem ki ghazab kahani* (aka *Unique Love Insatiable Story*, 2009).

In 2011, it was used as the hook in the Evolution Control Committee's (1986–) parody-mashup "Fock It," and in 2012, it was employed as a sound effect in Canadian turntablist A-Trak's (Alain Macklovitch, 1982–) "Disco Nap (Q Bert's Rocketcockpet Mix)." In addition, "Watermelon Man" has been sampled often in hip hop, most notably by LL Cool J (1968–), in "1-900 L.L. Cool J" (1989); by Digable Planets (1987–1995, 2005–), in "Escapism (Getting' Free)" (1993); by J Dilla (1974–2006), in "Zen Guitar" (2005); and by Massive Attack (1988–), in "Dead Editors" (2016). "Chameleon" has also been sampled, most notably by Public Enemy (1982–), in "Can't Do Nuttin' for Ya Man (Dub Mixx)" (1990); by Tupac Shakur (1971–1996), in "Words of Wisdom" (1991); and by DJ Shadow (1972–), in "Basic Mega-Mix" (1992). Most recently, it has been sampled by Beck (Bek David Campbell, 1970–) in his hip hop effort "Cellphone's Dead" (2006), which employs the bass riff of "Chameleon."

LATER CAREER

Hancock's further hip hop activities can be found on his albums *Sound-System* (1984), a Grammy Award winner on which he is backed by the Rockit Band and Grand Mixer D.ST; *Perfect Machine* (1988), also with the Rockit Band; and *Dis Is da Drum* (1994), an acid-jazz album that employs samples and loops. Hip hop is also used in the final track, "Hale Bopp, Hip Hop," on his collaboration with tenor/soprano saxophonist, composer, and fellow Buddhist musician Wayne Shorter's (1933–) album *1 + 1* (1997).

In 2008, Hancock helped produce "RoboCop," the seventh track of Kanye West's fourth studio album, *808s and Heartbreak*. That same year, Hancock won the Grammy Award for Album of the Year for *River: The Joni Letters* (2007), his tribute to folk, pop, and jazz singer-songwriter Joni Mitchell (Roberta Joan Anderson, 1943–). This was only the second jazz album to have won this award. In 2010,

Hancock released *The Imagine Project*, an album that featured many collaborations and performances with John Lennon (1940–1980), Peter Gabriel (1950–), Bob Dylan (Robert Allen Zimmerman, 1941–), and Sam Cooke (1931–1964), as well as international hip hop and R&B artists K'naan (1978–) and John Legend (John Roger Stephens, 1978–).

In 2014, Hancock was featured in "Tesla" and "Moment of Hesitation," two tracks on Flying Lotus's (aka FlyLo, Steven Ellison, 1983–) experimental jazz, electronica, and hip hop album *You're Dead!* These activities in hip hop all took place while Hancock pursued collaborations with jazz musicians, released jazz recordings, toured and performed, taught, and pursued humanitarian efforts in fundraising.

In 2013, Hancock taught jazz in the Music Department at the University of California, Los Angeles, and in 2014, he delivered six lectures titled "The Ethics of Jazz" as the Charles Eliot Norton Professor of Poetry chair at Harvard University. He has also won multiple awards for his music, including a 2013 Kennedy Center Honors Award; at the ceremony, Snoop Dogg (1971–) and the Beastie Boys' (1981–2012) turntablist Mix Master Mike (Michael Schwartz, 1970–) performed his music.

Melissa Ursula Dawn Goldsmith

See also: Turntablism; The United States

Further Reading

Hancock, Herbie, with Lisa Dickey. 2014. *Possibilities.* New York: Viking.

Price, Emmett G. III. 2006. *Hip Hop Culture.* Santa Barbara, CA: ABC-CLIO.

Further Listening

Hancock, Herbie. 1983. *Future Shock.* Columbia.

Hancock, Herbie. 1988. *Perfect Machine.* CBS.

Hancock, Herbie. 1994. *Dis Is da Drum.* Mercury.

Hancock, Herbie. 2001. *Future 2 Future.* Transparent Music.

Hardcore Hip Hop

Hardcore is an umbrella term for hip hop that is confrontational, expresses anger, and describes inflicting violence. It specifically includes not only gangsta rap but also horrorcore, crunkcore, and metal rap, styles that contain hip hop's most aggressive lyrics and sound. Hardcore is most often thought of as gangsta rap, beginning with East Coast hip hop acts such as Run-D.M.C. (1981–2002), Schooly D (Jesse Bonds Weaver Jr., 1962–), Boogie Down Productions (1985–1992), and Public Enemy (1986–). It eventually influenced West Coast acts such as Ice-T (1958–), who was from Newark, New Jersey, before he moved to South Los Angeles; N.W.A. (1986–1991); Compton's Most Wanted (1988–2007); and Cypress Hill (1988–). As it made its way South, it influenced Houston's horrorcore mainstays, Geto Boys (1986–). Acts such as Brotha Lynch Hung (1969–) from Sacramento, California, were also creating horrorcore as a gory and gratuitously violent style of gangsta rap. While gangsta rap remained successful into the 1990s, Ice-T explored hardcore hip hop further with metal-rap, creating his heavy metal rap band Body Count

(1990–2006, 2009–). Celtic band House of Pain (1991–1996, 2017–), from Los Angeles, is an early example of an act that focused away from gangsta rap themes and instead aggressively rapped about the Irish American experience. Another variation of hardcore hip hop was Lil' Kim's (1975–) sexually aggressive style, as exhibited on her debut album, *Hard Core* (1996).

GLOBAL ACTIVITY

Though hardcore hip hop caught on globally, it had its biggest impact in Europe. In other words, Africa and Oceania, as well as South America and the Caribbean, generally favored a gentler, more reggae-influenced sound of hip hop. In Asia, hardcore hip hop has a cult status. In many countries that practice censorship, this preference has as much to do with musical taste as it does with restrictions. Hardcore hip hop in Europe sometimes models itself on American hardcore, but instead of gang activity, it tends to focus on the related subject of street violence. Lyrics tell of political assassination (and the desire to do so), threaten violence as a revenge response to racism or social inequality, and simply describe horror, gore, and vulgarity in loving detail. Outside the United States, some countries that have hardcore hip hop scenes include Bosnia-Herzegovina, Denmark, France, Germany, Greece, Hungary, Ireland, Macedonia, the Netherlands, Norway, Romania, Serbia, Sweden, Switzerland, and the United Kingdom. Generally, there is no geographical predictor for hardcore's success, only limits imposed by regimes. Nevertheless, countries such as Albania, Croatia, Russia, and Turkey, which have stricter restrictions imposed on hip hop activity than other European countries, still have some hardcore political hip hop. Just a few European hardcore acts include Croatia's Ugly Leaders (1988–2001); Denmark's Suspekt (1997–); France's Assassin (1985–2006) and Suprême NTM (aka NTM, 1989–2001, 2008–); Greece's Terror X Crew (1992–2002); Macedonia's the Most Wanted (1991–1996); the Netherlands' DAMN (Don't Accept Mass Notion, 1989–1993) and Osdorp Posse (OP, 1989–2009); and Romania's R.A.C.L.A. (aka Rime Alese Care Lovesc Adânc, Handpicked Rhymes with a Deeper Meaning, 1993–2007, 2014–), B.U.G. Mafia (aka Black Underground, Bucharest Underground Mafia, 1993–), and La Familia (1996–).

When lyrics are perceived as going too far, even countries that have been the most supportive of freedom of expression have been known to investigate hardcore hip hop groups. For example, after creating a website that offered a bounty on then–American president George W. Bush's (1946–, in office 2001–2009) head and releasing a video titled "Antiamerikansk Dans" ("Anti-American Dance," 2004) with Swedish rapper Promoe, also known as Mårten Edh, (Nils Mårten Ed, 1976–), Oslo hip hop group Gatas Parlament (Street Parliament, aka Kveldens-Høydepunkt or "Highlight of the Evening," 1993–) were investigated briefly by the Secret Service and Norwegian police. Though the case was dropped, their website was taken down.

Africa has had a few emerging hardcore acts, which include Cape Verde and the Netherlands' Cabo Funk Alliance (1992–), Mali's Tata Pound (1995–), Kenya's MC Goreala (Eric Mukunza, 1992*–), South Africa's Major League Djz (2008–), and Zambia's Zone Fam (2009–). Diaspora acts have emerged, enabling hardcore hip hop artists such as the United States–based hardcore hip hop collective Nas-Jota (aka Jota, 2003*–), from Khartoum, to rap safely against Sudanese government corruption, including election rigging. NasJota consists of Sudanese and Arab rappers who perform in Arabic and English, and it created a Sudanese-Arabic label called NasJota (2003–). One example of a European hardcore hip hop act that is now based in Africa is the Lomé, Togo–based SIH (Son Injecté Hardcore, Sound-Injected Hardcore, 2002*–), with members from France.

Asia has a few emerging hardcore hip hop scenes, most notably in Bangladesh, Hong Kong, Mongolia, and the Philippines, with acts such as Bangladesh's Deshi MCs (aka E.N.L. ["Enlightenment"] Crew, 2005–); Hong Kong's LMF (aka Lazy Mutha F—a, 1993–2003, 2009–); Mongolia's Gee (Tugsjargal Munkherdene, 1984–), Ice Top (1996–), and Quiza (Quiza Battsengel, 1981–); and the Philippines' Death Threat (1993–2003, 2010–). Many of these acts are strongly influenced by American gangsta rap and come from localized gangsta rap scenes. Despite restrictions on hardcore hip hop in China, LMF is popular there. Once perceived as remote from Western popular culture, Mongolia's hip hop scene is small, yet developing, and has included some hardcore hip hop.

Hardcore hip hop has made its way to Oceania, though it is no surprise that it is most present in Australia and New Zealand. The few popular acts include Australia's internationally known 1200 Techniques (1997–2005), as well as Australian acts KidCrusher (Shawn Montague, 1986–), who is also an actor that uses a cannibal clown persona, and Kerser (Scott Barrow, 1987–); and New Zealand's Young Sid (Sidney Diamond, 1986–). Though tastes have been directed toward fusing hip hop with reggae, R&B, pop, or electronica in Oceania, politics have played more of a role in the paucity of hardcore acts in South America. Still, hardcore hip hop has managed to exist even in some South American countries where it's most restricted, as with the all-female Argentinian quintet Actitud María Marta (aka Hardcore, 1995–).

Melissa Ursula Dawn Goldsmith

See also: Crunkcore; Gangsta Rap; Horrorcore

Further Reading

Chang, Jeff. 2005. *Can't Stop Won't Stop: A History of the Hip Hop Generation.* New York: Picador.

Cramer, Jennifer, and Jill Hallett. 2010. "From Chi-Town to the Dirty-Dirty: Regional Identity Markers in U.S. Hip Hop." In *The Languages of Global Hip Hop*, edited by Marina Terkourafi, chap. 10. New York: Continuum.

Diallo, David. 2010. "From Electro-Rap to G-Funk: A Social History of Rap Music in Los Angeles and Compton, California." In *Hip Hop in America: A Regional Guide*, edited by Mickey Hess, vol. 1, chap. 10. Santa Barbara, CA: Greenwood.

Morgan, Marcyliena, and Dionne Bennett. 2011. "Hip Hop and the Global Imprint of a Black Cultural Form." *Daedalus* 140, no. 2: 176–96.

Further Listening

KidCrusher. 2007. *Cannibal Clown.* Victim Gear.

Gatas Parlament. 2004. *Fred, Frihet, & Alt Gratis (Peace, Freedom, and Everything Free).* Tee Productions.

Lil' Kim. 1996. *Hard Core.* Big Beat.

Ugly Leaders. 1994. *Prisoners of Pain.* Croatia. Records/Denyken Music.

Zone Fam. 2011. *The Business (Foreign Exchange).* Slam Dunk Records.

Heap, Imogen

(Imogen Jennifer Heap, 1977–, London, England)

Imogen Heap is a singer-songwriter, composer, producer, and engineer, as well as a highly sought after collaborator who is known for her combination of musical styles. In addition, her music, which includes elements of ambient, electronica, synthpop, indie rock, and hip hop, has been sampled and featured by many hip hop artists. Heap established her own record company, Megaphonic Records (2003–) in London, so that she could hold creative control and production rights over her work.

MUSICAL BEGINNINGS

Heap began studying classical piano and cello at an early age, and at 12 she was sent to boarding school, where she began experimenting with music technology, teaching herself the basics of sound engineering and audio production. Heap later attended the BRIT School for Performing Arts and Technology in Croydon, South London. After school, Heap signed her first contract at the age of 18, and in 1996, she met English composer, songwriter, and producer Guy Sigsworth (1960–), who became one of the collaborators and producers for her first album, *iMegaphone* (1998). In turn, Heap provided backing vocals for his London experimental rock band project, Acacia (1994–1997). Heap continued collaborating with Sigsworth, working with him on the U.K. single "Meantime" (1999). She also also collaborated with the English hip hop band Urban Species (1988–2000, 2008–). Appearing on the album *Blanket* (1998), she cowrote and sang the title track and U.K. single "Blanket."

FROU FROU

In 2001, Heap formed Frou Frou (2002–2004) with Sigsworth, named after their first album (2001), a project recording that consisted of tracks composed by Sigsworth. The name Frou Frou was suggested by Sigsworth, who was a Francophile, and it is based on the sound of a swishing skirt, Arthur Rimbaud's (1854–1891) poem "Ma Bohème" ("My Bohemia"), and a character's name in Leo Tolstoy's (1828–1910) *Anna Karenina* (1878). Even though *Frou Frou* was technically the duo's first album, *Details* (2002) was the first one on which Sigsworth and Heap were equally responsible for the instrumentation, writing, and production. Although it was not a commercial success immediately after release, it did earn popularity in the United States two years later after the single "Let Go" was featured in the film *Garden State* (2004). In 2003, Frou Frou disbanded after it failed to get a contract renewal for a second album.

Two months before the release of her second album, *Speak for Yourself* (2005), the track "Hide and Seek" was featured on the television show *The O.C.* (2003–2007) and was an immediate success through digital downloads in the United States and United Kingdom. A few years later, American singer Jason Derulo (Jason Joel Desrouleaux, 1989–) sampled "Hide and Seek" in his song "Whatcha Say" (2009), which hit No. 1 on the Billboard Hot 100. More hip hop tracks sampling Heap's work followed.

Other Heap songs sampled from *Speak for Yourself* included "Just for Now," sampled on the song "I'm God" (2009) by Lil B (aka The BasedGod, Brandon McCartney, 1989–), and the bonus track to the Japanese release of the album, "Speeding Cars," sampled on the song "Textbook Stuff" (2011), by XV (Donavan LaMond Johnson, 1985–). Hip hop artists also sampled songs by Frou Frou, namely "Let Go" and "Psychobabble." Since *Speak for Yourself,* Heap has released two more albums, *Ellipse* (2009) and *Sparks* (2014).

Though Frou Frou amicably disbanded in 2004, Heap and Sigsworth intended to collaborate again. But in 2018, Frou Frou is scheduled to appear on Heap's Mycelia World Tour. Mycelia is Heap's creative concept for artists to share music and form contracts by using open-source block chain–based technology such as Ethereum (2015–).

Lindsey E. Hartman

See also: The United Kingdom

Further Reading

Anderman, Joan. 2006. "Imogen Heap Revels in the Glorious Solitude of Electronic Pop." *The Boston Globe*, January 13, E16.

Gordon, Kylee Swenson. 2012. "Imogen Heap." In *The Recording Secrets behind 50 Great Albums*. Milwaukee, WI: Backbeat Book.

Morris, Jeremy Wade. 2014. "Artists as Entrepreneurs, Fans as Workers." *Popular Music and Society* 37, no. 3: 273–90.

Further Listening

Frou Frou. 2001. *Frou Frou.* Universal.

Imogen Heap. 1998. *iMegaphone.* Almo Sounds.

Imogen Heap. 2005. *Speak for Yourself.* Megaphonic Records.

Further Viewing

Pearsall, Justine, dir. 2010. *Imogen Heap: Everything In-Between: The Story of Ellipse.* New York: Sony Legacy.

Hieroglyphics

(aka Hieroglyphics Crew, 1991–, Oakland, California)

Hieroglyphics is an American hip hop collective founded by Oakland, California, rapper and producer Del the Funky Homosapien (sometimes stylized as Del The Funkee Homosapien, Teren Delvon Jones, 1972–). Considered primarily an underground act known more for its popular live concerts than its albums, Heiroglyphics has marketed itself well, from forming its own label, Hiero Imperium (1997–); to

The group Hieroglyphics performs in 2012 in San Bernardino, California. Established in Oakland, California, the hip hop collective focuses on live performance and music production with its own label, Hiero Imperium, and has achieved more of a cult following than a commercial one through its eclectic musical style that employs hip hop, jazz, and funk. (Akpanudosen/Getty Images)

creating iconography (a circle containing three eyes and a straight line for a mouth, the third eye representing metaphysical/spiritual understanding); to podcasting its performances as Hierocasts; to creating its own organization, the Hiero Nation. Del the Funky Homosapien, whose father was an artist, created the third eye logo, which is based on Mayan numerology and is associated with the symbol for infinity. In addition to Hieroglyphics, Hiero Imperium has produced work by each of its members, both as solo artists and in other groups, such as Extra Prolific (1993–1998) and Souls of Mischief (1991–).

Hieroglyphics sound incorporates various influences, as its members hail from the West Coast (Oakland), the South (Mississippi), and Jamaica. Its songs use elements of jazz and funk, through both original beats and samples. Hieroglyphics have released three studio albums: *3rd Eye Vision* (1998), which references the band's logo and aesthetic; *Full Circle* (2003); and *The Kitchen* (2013). Although the albums have had only modest success on the rap charts, *Full Circle* broke into the Billboard 200, peaking at No. 155.

The band's success at creating a cult following on limited commercial success make Hieroglyphics comparable in rock music circles to the Grateful Dead (1965–1995) or Phish (1983–2004, 2009–). Hieroglyphics's main message is best summed up in the first track on *3rd Eye Vision*, which opens with a voice over saying that the band it "trying to make something better" every time they take the stage.

As of 2018, the collective is composed of Del the Funky Homosapien; rapper Casual (Jon Owens, 1973–); rapper and vocalist Pep Love (Pallo E. Peacock, 1974–); DJ, producer, and manager Domino (Damian Siguenza, 1970–); producer and songwriter DJ Toure (Toure Batiste Duncan, n.d.); and the four individual members of Souls of Mischief—rapper and producer Phesto (aka Phesto Dee, Damani Thompson, 1974–); rapper and producer A-Plus (Adam Carter, 1974–); Opio (Opio Lindsey (1974–); and rapper and producer Tajai (Tajai Massey, 1975–).

Anthony J. Fonseca

See also: Five Percent Nation; Jamaica; Political Hip Hop; The United States

Further Reading

Bradley, Adam, and Andrew Dubois, eds. 2010. "Hieroglyphics." Under "Part 3: 1993–99: Rap Goes Mainstream" in *The Anthology of Rap*, pp. 404–9. New Haven, CT: Yale University Press.

Ciccariello-Maher, George, and Jeff St. Andrews. 2010. "Between Macks and Panthers: Hip Hop in Oakland and San Francisco." In *Hip Hop in America: A Regional Guide*, edited by Mickey Hess, vol. 1, chap. 11. Santa Barbara, CA.

Further Listening

Hieroglyphics. 1998. *3rd Eye Vision.* Hiero Imperium.

Hieroglyphics. 2003. *Full Circle.* Hiero Imperium.

Hill, Lauryn

(Lauryn Noelle Hill, 1975–, South Orange, New Jersey)

Lauryn Hill is an American singer-songwriter whose five Grammy award winning solo album, *The Miseducation of Lauryn Hill* (1998), and whose membership in the Fugees (1992–1997) has been extremely influential on hip hop. Known for blunt and honest lyrics that speak out against sexism, racism, and prejudice, she helped pave the way for socially conscious hip hop. *The Miseducation of Lauryn Hill,* a collection of songs that bridge the gap between hip hop, soul, and R&B, was the first hip hop album to win Album of the Year, and Hill was the first female artist to win five Grammys in one night.

Hill began both singing and acting at a young age, singing for Amateur Night at the Apollo in 1988 and acting in an Off-Broadway hip hop musical, *Club XII,* in 1990. She met and performed with MC Lyte (1971–) and Wyclef Jean (1969–). She had an important role in *Sister Act 2: Back in the Habit* (1993). While attending Columbia High School (1989–1993) in Maplewood, New Jersey, Hill met Pras (Prakazrel Michel, 1972–) and formed Tranzlator Crew (aka Rap Translators, 1989–1997). Jean joined the group soon after, and the new lineup changed their name to the Fugees. After the release of a successful second album, *The Score* (1996), the group disbanded; Hill began to pursue her solo career.

The inspiration for the title of *The Miseducation of Lauryn Hill* came from the book *The Mis-Education of the Negro* (1933) by Carter G. Woodson (1875–1950). Hill's frank lyrics touched on her strained relationship with the Fugees and on her everyday struggles. This strained relationship included a turbulent romantic relationship between Hill and Jean, creative differences between Hill and other members of the group, an initial lack of support from other members for her solo endeavor (by the time Jean offered to produce her album, Hill turned him down), and outside factors such as the stress of performance schedules and handling notoriety. Hill's other source of stress was becoming pregnant (not with Jean's child) in between 1997 and 1998 while working on her own successful career.

The songs "I Used to Love Him" and "To Zion" refer to Hill's deteriorated relationship with Wyclef Jean and to loving her first child, respectively. The first single, "Doo Wop (That Thing)," became a Billboard Hot 100 No. 1, while "Ex-Factor" and "Everything Is Everything" peaked at Nos. 21 and 35, respectively. Hill then took a brief hiatus from the pressures and scrutiny that came with fame and the music industry. In 2001, she recorded new songs for *MTV Unplugged* (1989–). Her second album, *MTV Unplugged No. 2.0* (2002), was recorded live for a small audience. Songs for the album were based on her experiences and struggles with the music industry and within her personal life. The *Unplugged* session featured all new material that followed a folk and soul style, with numerous spoken social commentaries as interludes between songs.

Hill has also performed and collaborated on various projects, including a 2004 to 2006 reunion with the Fugees. Other projects include the Grammy nominated track "So High (Cloud 9 Remix)" (2005) with John Legend (John Stephens, 1978–), narration for the documentary *Concerning Violence* (2014), songs for the soundtrack to *What Happened, Miss Simone?* (2016), and performances at the Coachella Valley Music and Arts Festival (2011) and the New Orleans Jazz and Heritage Festival (2011 and 2016).

Lindsey E. Hartman

See also: Fugees; Neo Soul; Political Hip Hop; The United States

Further Reading

Bradley, Adam, and Andrew Dubois, eds. 2010. "Lauryn Hill." Under "Part 3: 1993–1999: Rap Goes Mainstream" in *The Anthology of Rap*, pp. 410–16. New Haven, CT: Yale University Press.

Bruce, La Marr Jurelle. 2012. "'The People Inside My Head, Too': Madness, Black Womanhood, and the Radical Performance of Lauryn Hill." *African American Review* 45, no. 3: 371–89.

Further Listening

Hill, Lauryn. 1998. *The Miseducation of Lauryn Hill.* Ruffhouse Records/Columbia.

Hilltop Hoods

(1994–, Adelaide, Australia)

Hilltop Hoods, one of Australia's most internationally successful and highly acclaimed hip hop groups, incorporates jazz, funk, electronica, rock, and punk into its music. Five of its seven studio albums, *The Calling* (2003), *The Hard Road* (2006), *State of the Art* (2009), *Drinking from the Sun* (2012), and *Walking under Stars* (2014), were ARIA-certified Platinum and have charted in Australia, with the last two charting in New Zealand. With *The Hard Road*, the Hilltop Hoods became the first Australian hip hop group to have a No. 1 on the ARIA Albums

Chart, and its subsequent four studio albums peaked at No. 1 as well. In addition, two remix albums that use a symphonic orchestra, *The Hard Road: Restrung* (2007) and *Drinking from the Sun, Walking Under Stars: Restrung* (2016), have peaked on the ARIA Albums Chart at Nos. 8 and 1, respectively.

The Hilltop Hoods have also released several EPs. Its hit singles include "The Nosebleed Section" (2004), "Chase that Feeling" (2009), "I Love It" (2011), "Cosby Sweater" (2014), "Higher" (2015), and "1955" (2016). Beyond recording and touring worldwide, the Hilltop Hoods have been involved in many other projects, beginning in the early 2000s with the collaborative-turned-collective Certified Wise Crew, which links its members to other Adelaide hip hop artists and groups such as Vents (aka Vents One, Vents Uno, Joseph Lardner, 1983–) and Funkoars (1999–).

FORMATION

In 1994, rappers Suffa (Matthew David Lambert, 1977–) and MC Pressure (Daniel Howe Smith, n.d.) met at Blackwood High School in Adelaide, South Australia. Shortly afterward, they recruited producer, audio engineer, and turntablist DJ Next (Ben John Hare, n.d.). Around 1995, the Hilltop Hoods made its first demo, *Highlanders*, on cassette. Its first EP, *Back Once Again* (1997), and debut studio album, *A Matter of Time* (1999), were self-released. During this time, DJ Next departed and was replaced by DJ Debris (Barry John M. Francis, n.d.), part of the Cross Bred Mongrels (aka CBM, 1990*–2005, 2009–) duo.

In 2001, the Hilltop Hoods self-released its second album *Left Foot, Right Foot*. Before its third studio album, *The Calling*, the Hilltop Hoods signed onto Australian rapper Pegz's (aka MC Pegasus, Tirren Staaf, 1977–) Melbourne, Australia–based Obese Records label (1995–2007), whose parent company was the Warner Music Group (aka WEA, 1958–). *The Calling* was recorded almost entirely on DJ Suffa's mother's computer and had an unusual monaural sound. From that point on, the Hilltop Hoods had a string of hit albums and singles, as well as national awards.

LYRICAL CONTENT

The band's lyrical content is highly diverse. Members melodically rap, chant, and sing in English about street life, social and economic injustice, racial inequality, and biographical details, but, more interestingly, also about slow-paced suburb living, concert going, performing music, poking fun at American celebrity, age differences, and antiwar sentiments.

In 2005, the band created the Hilltop Hoods Initiative with Arts SA to financially assist new South Australian hip hop artists to manufacture and distribute a recording on compact disc. The group established its own label in 2008, Golden Era Records, in Adelaide. From *State of the Art* on, the Hilltop Hoods have produced the rest of its albums.

Melissa Ursula Dawn Goldsmith

See also: Australia; Political Hip Hop

Further Reading

Mitchell, Tony. 2007. "The DIY Habitus of Australian Hip Hop." *Culture and Policy* 123, no. 1: 109–22.

Rodger, Dianne. 2016. "Creating the Right 'Vibe': Exploring the Utilization of Space at Hip Hop Concerts in Adelaide and Melbourne." In *Emotions, Senses, and Spaces: Ethnographic Engagements and Intersections*, edited by Alison Dundon and Susan R. Hemer, chap. 3. Adelaide, Australia: University of Adelaide Press.

Further Listening

Hilltop Hoods. 2003. *The Calling.* Obese Records.

Hip Hop Dance

Hip hop dance had become its own specific form, alongside ballet, modern, tap, and jazz dance by the early 1970s. As a style, however, hip hop dance can be traced back to a freeform style of street dancing that was performed as far back as 1724, with African dance gatherings in historic Congo Square in New Orleans. On Sundays, enslaved Africans held meetings in which they played music and dance. West African ritualistic dance styles incorporated a low center of gravity, bent knees, and percussive movement, styles of dance that have carried over into hip hop (as well as other kinds of African American dance). As blacks from the South migrated both north and west, street dance from Congo Square spread its influence. By the 1920s and 1930s, Harlem saw street dancing at rent parties, in the form of the Lindy Hop. By the 1940s and 1950s, stylized moves from street dancing were found in many kinds of popular dancing performed in shanties and jazz clubs nationwide. The dancing of Chuck Berry (1926–) as well as white rockabilly musicians such as Elvis Presley (1935–1977) and Jerry Lee Lewis (1935–) were inspired by these street dancing moves.

EARLY VERSIONS

Like with all dance styles, tracing hip hop dance moves to an authoritative original source is virtually impossible. Nonetheless, most scholars agree that what is known today as hip hop dance began in the early 1970s. In addition to his influence on early rapping, James Brown (1933–2006) influenced dance. Recordings of his dancing while singing the funk song "Get on the Good Foot" (1972) inspired early hip hop moves. For example, Brown's camel walk influenced the moon walk; his boogaloo was a precursor to the electric boogaloo as well as popping. In general, funk, which originated in the 1960s and 1970s in California, became an important influence on both hip hop music and dance. The Lockers (1971–1982), a dance group established by dancers and choreographers Toni Basil (Antonia Christina Basilotta, 1943–) and Don Campbell (1951–) in Los Angeles, promoted street dance as an art form and were a precursor to hip hop dance crews. The earliest hip hop dance was more upright and contained, as seen with the boogaloo, popping, and locking. Performers took turns showing their moves, which meant that there was a need for a repetition of drum solo interludes, requiring a breakbeat, or segments of music that DJs looped until each dancer was finished.

In 1973, ex–disc jockey and producer Afrika Bambaataa (1957–) formed the Zulu Nation (which later became the Universal Zulu Nation) in the Bronx, New York, which focused on elements of hip hop culture. He was one of the early champions of hip hop, which became the umbrella term that included the new street dancing styles of the 1970s and 1980s. In the beginning, most hip hop dance was performed by buskers, but it could also be seen on television shows such as *Soul Train* (1971–2006) and in American films such as *Flashdance* and *Wild Style* (both 1983), as well as *Breakin'* and *Beat Street* (both 1984). In addition, in *Footloose* (1984), which is set in a small, religious, predominately white town, the two main characters join a breakdancing street performance.

Hip hop dance crews began forming in New York City: The first was within the Zulu Nation, but soon other early breakdancing or b-boy crews emerged, such as Rock Steady Crew (RSC, 1977–) in New York and the Electric Boogaloos (1977–) in Fresno, California. Competitions, eventually known as battles, began to arise between rival crews who focused on breaking or breakdancing, which had become the foundation for all hip hop dance. Regional variants were apparent in early hip hop dance moves, but most attention focused on the West and East Coasts. Moves became more standardized due to early 1980s media exposure.

NEW-SCHOOL HIP HOP

By the mid-1980s, some hip hop dance moves had entered the mainstream, such as the Roger Rabbit, the Cabbage Patch, the Worm, the Humpty dance, and the Running Man. Many of these moves were performed to companion songs. In some cases, dance moves developed from popular television shows. For example, *The Fresh Prince of Bel-Air*'s (1990–1996) Carlton Banks, played by Alfonso Ribeiro (1971–), comically butchered hip hop steps, and a dance called "The Carlton" became famous.

The same time period saw hip hop dance morph into more floor work, feats of balance and agility that incorporated martial arts and acrobatics, especially in breakdancing. Dance moves such as freezes or breaks became standard ways to signify sudden changes, and competitions began to focus on freezing, breaking, and power moves. Other styles that derived from breaking emerged in the late 1990s. For example, styles such as the Memphis jookin, turfing, jerkin', clowning, and krumping became popular. Significant changes to freestyle form came with the addition of counts, a technique credited to Basil, a system of tracking movement to music that had been developed in court dances (that transitioned into ballet). Basil's work on 1980s videos with many hip hop groups introduced the new way of structuring hip hop.

MAINSTREAMING

Hip hop dance instruction also underwent a major change. In 1989, Buddha Stretch at the Broadway Dance Center started hosting classes, formally bringing hip hop into the dance studio. Hip hop dance has since become an amalgamation of the street, party, pop and lock, breaking, and structured technique styles. Purists argue that hip hop dancing after the late 1980s became commercialized and watered down, that dance teachers were responsible for diluting hip hop dance moves. This was compounded by choreographers with backgrounds in jazz and modern dance who studied hip hop, teaching lyrical hip hop, by relating the moves to their knowledge of dance. So-called pseudo–hip hop incorporates jazz and modern dance moves and to some appears disconnected from hip hop culture and its street origins.

In 1992, what was called New Style Hip Hop dance (hip hop dance in New York) became an influence on French and Japanese dancers, as shown in the American documentary films *Wreckin' Shop from Brooklyn* (1992) and *History and Concept of Hip Hop Dance* (2010). New style, returned to the traditional West African dance's low center of gravity, with the feet grounded and the body remaining loose. A bent and a lowered chest leave the pelvic region and legs to be the focal point, and the dancer chooses to either emphasize the beat or move through it. Dancers can perform freestyle as long as they remain true to foundation movements. The core of New Style Hip Hop is to remain loose and free and improvisational.

Though not part of the breakdancing scene, twerking has also become an important element of hip hop dance. Twerking, based on African dance, is normally performed by female dancers (although male dancers have twerked both for humor and in serious competitions), and involves dropping the body down, with knees bent, and then dancing mainly by flexing and relaxing the buttocks, with additional shakes and pseudo sexual grinding. Skilled twerkers use speed, balance, body part isolation, and control to create routines that contain freezes and the lowest possible body positioning.

Since the early 1990s, hip hop dance has increasingly become main stream because of American television series such as *The Party Machine with Nia Peeples* (1991) and *In Living Color* (1990–1994). Organizations such as Hip Hop International (2002–) have created the World Hip Hop Dance Championship, a televised hip hop dance competition in which all-male and all-female crews battle and showcase their power moves. Some American hip hop dance crews who have competed in the World Hip Hop Dance Championship include Jabbawockeez (2004–) from San Diego, California, the all–Asian American Quest Crew (2006–) from Artesia, California; Poreotics (2007–) from Westminster, California; and the all-female Beat Freaks (2003–) from Los Angeles.

Paige A. Willson

See also: Battling; Breakdancing; Dubstep; The Electric Boogaloos; Lyrical Hip Hop; Popping and Locking; The Robot; Uprock

Further Reading

Guzman-Sanchez, Thomas. 2012. *Underground Dance Masters: Final History of a Forgotten Era.* Santa Barbara, CA: Praeger.

Pabon, Jorge Popmaster Fabel. 2004. "Physical Graffiti: The History of Hip Hop Dance." In *That's the Joint: The Hip Hop Studies Reader,* edited by Murray Forman and Mark Anthony Neal, 2nd ed., chap. 5. New York: Routledge.

Schloss, Joseph G. 2009. *Foundation: B-Boys, B-Girls, and Hip Hop Culture in New York.* New York: Oxford University Press.

Hip Hop Diplomacy

Hip Hop Diplomacy is a term that refers to the use of hip hop cultural practices to cultivate and encourage good will and diplomatic relationships between countries, especially between the United States and other nations. Since the mid-20th century, the State Department has used music as a diplomatic tool on the world stage, and it began to incorporate hip hop into its diplomacy programs beginning in the early 2000s.

The State Department began engaging American musicians in cultural diplomacy in 1955, during the Cold War (1947–1991), when it sent jazz artists such as Louis Armstrong (1901–1971), Duke Ellington (1899–1974), and Benny Goodman (1909–1986) on tour in parts of Eastern Europe and the Soviet Union. These tours of the so-called "Jazz Ambassadors" were designed to promote a positive image of Americans and American life, and to win support for the American government. The emphasis on jazz and on African American musicians was intended to encourage the view that the American government and American culture promoted equality between all citizens, and to showcase the skills of the top musicians in one of the country's native idioms. The tours were primarily one-directional, meaning that artists came to perform for audiences in other countries, but did not necessarily engage with musicians or musical traditions of those places.

In 1961, the United States Congress passed the Fulbright-Hayes Act, officially known as the Mutual Educational and Cultural Exchange Act, the purpose of which is to use such a cultural exchange to increase mutual understanding the United States and other countries, with the result being friendly, sympathetic, and peaceful multinational relations. To help achieve this goal, the Bureau of Educational and Cultural Affairs (ECA) was founded within the State Department during that same year. Today, the ECA is responsible for several programs and initiatives, including the American Music Abroad (2005–), Center Stage (2012–), Next Level (2014–), and One Beat (2012–), all of which send American musicians to other countries to engage in cultural diplomacy.

In 2005, the State Department began sending groups of hip hop artists, including rappers, DJs, and dancers, to parts of Europe, African, Asia, and the Middle East in an attempt to combat the radicalization of Muslim youth in those areas. Hip hop was identified as a musical genre with which global youth, especially Muslim youth, could identify because of its roots as protest music in marginalized communities in the United States, as well as its international popularity.

The United States government has also tried to counteract the radical and potentially violent ideologies to which Muslim youth in Europe and other parts of the world may be exposed by offering a more moderate view of Islam through hip hop. These programs endorse a view of American culture as inclusive and supportive of its Muslim citizens, a position that is designed to gain support for the government and weaken fundamentalist sects that oppose Western involvement and influence. These programs differ from earlier, Cold War–era State Department efforts in that the target is now more likely to be friendly European states, or nonallied nations, not necessarily enemy states; however, the goal of garnering good will and support for the United States and promoting peaceful relationships through cultural exchange remains the same.

POST-9/11 HIP HOP DIPLOMACY

Through these more recent, post–September 11, 2001, programs, the American government has emphasized the role and influence of Muslim artists in hip hop. Indeed, Islam has been an important aspect of hip hop from its beginning, especially as rappers who were members of the Five Percent Nation (1964–) and the Nation of Islam (1930–) achieved a wide level of success with music that incorporated phrases and ideologies of their faith. Artists such as Rakim (1968–), Public Enemy (1982–), Poor Righteous Teachers (1989–1996), and others incorporated aspects of Islam in their music, and as other Muslim-identified rappers, such as Lupe Fiasco (Wasalu Muhammad Jaco, 1982–) and Busta Rhymes (1972–), became famous, they brought increased visibility to their faith and its role in the genre. Through hip hop, foreign youth can learn about African American history, including the role of pivotal figures such as Malcolm X (1925–1965), whose speeches are sometimes sampled into hip hop tracks.

Working with the Department of Music at the University of North Carolina at Chapel Hill, in 2014 the ECA began Next Level, an arts-based exchange using multidisciplinary hip hop collaborations in order to address conflict resolution. The program sends groups of beatmakers, DJs, dancers (b-boys and b-girls or those who specialize in other hip hop dance styles) and/or MCs to lead exchange programs that last from four to six weeks in various countries. Unlike the earliest State Department initiatives, Next Level is designed to be a collaboration that engages youth and artists from the countries with which it is involved. In addition to concerts, Next Level offers other activities, including interactive performances with local musicians, lecture demonstrations, workshops, and jam sessions.

The emphasis on education and musical entrepreneurship allows for a deeper level of cultural engagement with local communities, not just one-directional performances. Next Level 1.0 (2014–2015) organized exchange programs in Bangladesh, Bosnia and Herzogovina/Montenegro, India, Senegal, Serbia, and Zimbabwe. Next Level 2.0 (2015–2016) has organized exchanges with El Salvador, Honduras, Tanzania, Thailand, and Uganda. Additionally, through the Global Next Level residency program, artists from participating countries are brought to the United States in a true cultural and musical exchange. In April 2016, for example, a group of Next Level participants, including a b-girl from Kampala, Uganda, a b-boy from Thailand, rappers from Tanzania and Honduras, and a DJ and turntablist from El Salvador, appeared together at American University. The emphasis on collaborative creative processes, education, and conflict resolution created a genuine cultural exchange where local musicians, not just American artists, are celebrated and included.

Lauron Jockwig Kehrer

See also: Black Nationalism; Eric B. and Rakim; Five Percent Nation; Nation of Islam; Poor Righteous Teachers; Public Enemy

Further Reading

Aidi, Hisham D. 2014. *Rebel Music: Race, Empire, and the New Muslim Youth Culture.* New York: Pantheon Books.

Katz, Mark. 2017. "The Case for Hip Hop Diplomacy." *American Music Review* 46, no. 2: 1–5.

Hip Hop Pantsula

(aka HHP, Jabba, Jabulani Tsambo, 1980–, Mafikeng, now Mahikeng, South Africa)

Hip Hop Pantsula, or HHP, is a South African *motswako* rapper and singer-songwriter who is best known for his influence on rappers living not only in South Africa but also in other countries on the continent. *Motswako* is a subgenre of hip hop that emerged in the mid-1990s in Mafikeng, South Africa (now Mahikeng), a major city located near Botswana. HHP's studio albums include *Introduction* (1999), *Maf Town* (2001), *O Mang?* (*Who Are You*, 2003), *YBA 2 NW* (2005), *Acceptance Speech* (2007), *Dumela* (*Thank You*, 2009), *Motswafrika* (2011), and *Motswako High School* (2014).

HHP's rapping texts are mostly in Setswana, mixed with some English, which is typical for *motswako*, but he also raps in Zulu and Sesotho. Active since 1997, he helped popularize motswako, which emerged in the mid-1990s in his hometown of Mafikeng, South Africa, close to the Botswana border. He has collaborated with many rappers, including Tuks Senganga (aka Tuks, Tumelo Kepadisa, 1981–), Tumi Molekane (1981–), and Cassper Nyovest (Refiloe Maele Phoolo, 1990–), from South Africa; M.anifest (Kwame Ametepee Tsikiata, 1982–), from Ghana; Naeto C (1982–), from the United States and Nigeria; and Nas (1973–), from the United States. HHP also has successful remix albums, including *O Mang Reloaded* (2004), *Special Edition Mega Mixes* (2007), and *Acceptance Speech Rewritten* (2008). In 2009, he won an MTV Africa Music Award for best video for "Mpitse" ("Miss Me").

He wrote rapping texts while in high school at St. Alban's College in Pretoria, South Africa. As lead MC in the group Verbal Assassins (1996*–1997), he and his high school friends recorded Verbal Assassins' debut and only studio album, *Party* (1997). After the group's breakup, he started his solo career after meeting South African gospel, R&B, new jack swing, and Afrobeat singer-songwriter and producer Isaac Mthethwa (n.d.).

HHP's debut album *Introduction* used Setswana, Zulu, and Sesotho texts, with lyrical content that focused on partying and romance. For a post-Apartheid (1948–1991) South Africa and Botswana, his laid-back rap, accompanied by hip hop beats and a musically softer sound than kwaito and American hip hop, made *Introduction* a success. He followed with *Maf Town*, the frequently used nickname for his hometown, Mafikeng.

His lyrical content would become much more serious in subsequent albums, starting with *O Mang* in 2003, when he gained creative control and ownership of his masters. In subsequent albums he folded in autobiographical content, described personal hardship and ambitions, and protested violence, xenophobia, economic disparity, and social injustice not only in South Africa, but in other African countries as well. In fact, social activism is another aspect of HHP's career. In 2013, he supported the pan-African unity initiative Daraja Walk, a long-distance walk from South to East Africa that was intended as a unifying and social outlet for African youth. Part of his social activism is performing live concerts in countries with still developing scenes, such as Lesotho.

Melissa Ursula Dawn Goldsmith

See also: Motswako; Political Hip Hop; South Africa

Further Reading

Anon. 2009. "The Heavy Sounds of HHP." *The Argus* (Cape Town), March 29, 3.

Künzler, Daniel. 2011. "South African Rap Music, Counter Discourses, Identity, and Commodification beyond the Prophets of da City." *Journal of Southern African Studies* 37, no. 1: 27–43.

Masemola, Michael Kgomotso, and Pinky Makoe. 2014. "Musical Space as Site of Transculturation of Memory and Transformation of Consciousness: The Re-affirmation of Africa in the Black Atlantic Assemblage." *Muziki: Journal of Music Research in Africa* 11, no. 1: 63–70.

Puleng, Segalo. 2006. "The Psychological Power of Rap Music in the Healing of Black Communities." *Muziki: Journal of Music Research in Africa* 3, no. 1: 28–35.

Further Listening

HHP. 2003. *O mang? (Who Are You)*? ccp Record Company.

HHP. 2004. *Omang Reloaded.* ccp Record Company.

Hip House

Hip house is a combination of house music, normally associated with dance-oriented nightclubs, and hip hop. It is sometimes called *rap house* or *house rap*, and it became popular in the late 1980s, appearing first in large urban areas such as New York and Chicago. Due to the popularity of both musical genres, it quickly caught on as a style in both the United States and the United Kingdom. One of the earliest bands to popularize hip house was the Beatmasters (1986–), who, working with the pop crossover female rap duo Cookie Crew (1983–1992), released the hit "Rok Da House" (1987) on Rhythm King Records (1986–).

Other early recordings included Tyree (Tyree Cooper, n.d.) and Afrika Bambaataa's (1957–) cousin Kool Rock Steady (Edward Rudolph, 1968–1996), whose "Turn up the Bass" was released in 1988; the Beatmasters and rapper Merlin's (Justin Mark Boreland, n.d.) "Who's in the House" (1988); and Vitamin-C's (Clarence J. Carter, n.d.) 1990 club hit "The Chicago Way," released on the Chicago-based Jack Street (1988–1990) label; however, the two songs that made hip house ubiquitous with clubbing were by jazz and hip hop trio Jungle Brothers (1987–) and the duo of Rob Base and DJ E-Z Rock (1985–). Jungle Brothers' "I'll House You," from their debut album *Straight Out of the Jungle* (1988), reached No. 22 on the U.K. Singles Chart, and Rob Base and DJ E-Z Rock's "It Takes Two," from the 1988 album of the same name, hit No. 36 on the Billboard Hot 100 and went Platinum. These hip house songs were featured in various DJ shows, such as those of Manchester, England-based DJ Chad Jackson (Mark Chadwick, n.d.), whose own "Hear the Drummer (Get Wicked)" was a 1990 U.K. Top 10 hit.

Hip house since 2000 has evolved into a sound called electro hop, which is hip house combined with electropop, a style of synth-pop featuring a harder sound and which became influential on iconic pop performers such as Lady Gaga (1986–). These hip house artists were mainstream, in fact indistinguishable from dance and pop musicians. They included Los Angeles electronic dance duo LMFAO (2006–2012); Los Angeles dance, pop, and EDM groups the Black Eyed Peas (1995–),

Hyper Crush (2006–), and Far East Movement (2003–); San Luis Obispo, California turntablist and producer Wolfgang Gartner (Joseph Thomas Youngman, 1982–); Miami rappers Pitbull (1981–) and Flo Rida (Tramar Lacel Dillard, 1979–); Harlem, New York singer-songwriter, rapper, and actress Azealia Banks (1991–); Tupelo, Mississippi singer-songwriter and producer Diplo (Thomas Wesley Pentz, 1978–); Birmingham, England electronic music multi-instrumentalist, producer, and rapper-songwriter Mike Skinner (Michael Geoffrey Skinner, 1978–), who records with the project band the Streets (1994–2011, 2017–); London rapper-songwriter and producer Example (Elliot John Gleave, 1982–); Breda, Netherlands producer and turntablist Tiësto (Tijs Michiel Verwest, 1969–); Stockholm progressive and electro house group Swedish House Mafia (2008–2013); and Paris-born Euro-dance DJ and producer David Guetta (Pierre David Guetta, 1967–). Hip house is related to other musical styles such as U.K. garage (R&B, garage band, and hip hop) grime (garage band, hip hop, and rap), and grindie (grime, drum and bass, and alternative dance).

Anthony J. Fonseca

See also: Brick City Club; The United States

Further Reading

Hanson, Carter F. 2014. "Pop Goes Utopia: An Examination of Utopianism in Recent Electronic Dance Pop." *Utopian Studies* 25, no. 2: 384–413.

Soojin Park, Judy. 2015. "Searching for a Cultural Home: Asian American Youth in the EDM Festival Scene." *Dancecult: Journal of Electronic Dance Music Culture* 7, no. 1: 15–34.

Further Listening

Flo Rida. 2008. *Mail on Sunday.* Poe Boy Entertainment/Atlantic.

Tiësto. 2009. *Kaleidoscope.* Ultra Records.

Horrorcore

Horrorcore is an American rap subgenre or style whose defining elements are exaggerated violence, imagery that relates to the occult or to the supernatural, realistic portrayals of violence that are described so that they are disturbing or disquieting, references to the dark side of the human mind, obsession with mental illness, and references to altered states of consciousness through drug abuse. Other themes might include the macabre, psychosis/schizophrenia, Satanism, mutilation and self-mutilation, cannibalism, rape or sexual crime, even necrophilia; however, many horrorcore songs profess a sort of "honor among thieves," whereby the bond between the violent narrators and their friends is sacred—and they protect each other, as do members of Insane Clown Posse's (aka ICP, 1989–) "Homies" (2002).

Musically, horrorcore has no one defining sound, although some of its practitioners, such as the Memphis-based Three 6 Mafia (aka Triple 6 Mafia, 1991–), use steady, slow-paced beats and a gradual buildup, often set against a steady, eerie, and almost monotone syllabic setting of rap that sounds like chanting, to create a sound reminiscent of horror films. Most horrorcore bands, however, do not incorporate elements of filmic horror, and not all mentions of horror make a song

Performing in gothic or evil clownface, Insane Clown Posse (ICP) is horrorcore's most influential and commercially successful hip hop act. At concerts and festivals, ICP's most dedicated fans (who are primarily white), known as Juggalos, emulate the duo's makeup and make "whoop, whoop" calls. (Michael Ochs Archives/Getty Images)

horrorcore, as with, for example Jimmy Spicer's (James Bromley Spicer, n.d.) "Adventures of Super Rhyme" (1980) an early recording on Dazz Records (1980–1991), Dana Dane's (Dana McLeese, 1965–) "Nightmares" (1985), and Michael Jackson's (1958–2009) "Thriller" (1982) mention characters from horror films, but they are all comic or lighthearted in tone, and in parts are experiments in non sequitur and wordplay, rather than forays into dark psychology. In other words, horrorcore has to possess a threat. The most famous rapper associated with horrorcore is Eminem (1972–). Among strictly horrorcore performers, Insane Clown Posse and Twiztid (1997–) have sold well.

Horrorcore utilizes gratuitously graphic images to portray violence; in addition, some horrorcore is known for its aggrandizement of ultraviolent behavior, such as beating or stabbing an unsuspecting victim, and some acts write images of demons and other monsters, usually metaphorically, into their lyrics. At its essence, horrorcore is about celebrating the status of the outsider to society, especially if that person is not just murderous, but transgressive. In many ways it is a natural progression from gangsta rap, with the main difference being victimization—gangsta rap victims of violence tend to be either other gang members or police, while in horrorcore, an MC might rap about robbing and killing his elementary school teacher, a prostitute, a fast-food manager who he finds annoying, or even an innocent bystander.

Horrorcore is sometimes characterized as hardcore gangsta rap, although some of its practitioners also owe a debt to hardcore metal. The other source of horrorcore is not associated with hip hop or metal, but with folk and country music. The outlaw song, such as Johnny Cash's (1932–2003) "Folsom Prison Blues" (1955) or the traditional murder ballad, such as "Pretty Polly" (aka "The Cruel Ship's Carpenter"), contain references to random murder for the sheer pleasure of the experience or the premeditated killing of a pregnant woman, respectively. Although mainstream rock music generally has no version of this type of transgressive music, some of its more unusual acts such as Nick Cave and the Bad Seeds (1983–), an Australian rock band, visit themes of serial killing, spree killing, and torture in albums such as *Murder Ballads* (1996), where songs describe these acts in loving detail.

The quintessential horrorcore band, Insane Clown Posse, cites as its influence an early song by the Houston-based Geto Boys (1986–), "Assassins" (off of *Making Trouble*, 1988). Geto Boys's "Mind Playing Tricks on Me" (off of *We Can't Be Stopped*, 1991) is a horrorcore classic, complete with nightmare imagery, mysterious presences, drug trips, dark psychology, and random ultraviolence. Later groups such as the short-lived Flatlinerz (1992–1995, 2014–) and Gravediggaz (1991–2002, 2011–) popularized the word "horrorcore" to describe the style of music.

FIRST AND SECOND WAVE

Some scholars argue that horrorcore gained prominence in 1994 with the release of Flatlinerz' *U.S.A.* and Gravediggaz' *6 Feet Deep* (released in Europe as *N—amortis*), but one of the earliest, if not the earliest example of horrorcore, is solo rapper/songwriter Ganksta N-I-P (Lewayne Williams, 1969–). A Houston rapper who often wrote songs for Geto Boys, Gangksta N-I-P in 1982 released his debut album, *The South Park Psycho*, which contained keyboard riff samples from the film *Halloween* (1978), set against lyrics expressing the need to act violently, perhaps even go on a killing spree. The album also includes exaggerated violence, such as the rapper's threat to make an intended random victim beat himself up if he (the rapper) is too tired to do it.

A second wave of horrorcore bands included New York's guru of musical weirdness Kool Keith (Keith Matthew Thornton, 1966–) and Santa Ana, California–based short-lived trio KMC (1991). Kool Keith, known for jarring images and absurdity, was arguably performing horrorcore beginning with his tenure with Ultramagnetic MCs (1984–2001, 2006–) and their album *Critical Beatdown* (1988, 1997) and continuing into his solo career. KMC's 1991 album *Three Men with the Power of Ten* does not have quite the same scare factor as *The South Park Psycho*, but it does serve as an early of example of using frenetic beats and horror stingers (instances of sudden sound in horror to scare the audience) in a rap album; the songs are also violent, though not extremely graphic.

In Sacramento, fellow California act Brotha Lynch Hung (1969–) debuted in 1992 and by 1995 had fully embraced horrorcore with the gory and graphic *Season of the Siccness*, which was certified Platinum. About the same time as Kool Keith,

Detroit-based Esham (Rashaam Smith, 1973–) made a huge local splash by exploring both horrorcore themes, funk and rap samples, and unsettling rhythms in 1989, with his teenaged debut album *Boomin' "Words from Hell 1990."* Esham's style, which he called acid rap, was a huge influence on a local rap band called Inner City Posse, which later became Insane Clown Posse.

HORRORCORE AROUND THE WORLD

Though hardcore has some strong international scenes, horrorcore has far less presence outside the United States. Many international acts are especially inspired by ICP and Brotha Lynch Hung. Examples from North America and Europe include Swollen Members (1992–), from Canada; Die Vamummtn (The Dummies, 2006–2016), from Austria; Suspekt (1997–), from Denmark; and Terror X Crew (1992–2002), from Greece. Die Antwoord ("The Answer" in Afrikaans, 2008–), from South Africa, sometimes uses horrorcore elements, whereas Horrorshow (2006–), from Australia, despite its name, is not a horrorcore act at all. Allen Halloween (Allen Pires Sanhá, 1980–), an alternative and horrorcore immigrant rapper, singer, and producer from Guinea, resides in Portugal and performs hip hop Tuga (Portugese hip hop). Perhaps horrorcore's existence is most surprising in Kazakhstan, where the popularity of Post Mortem (2007–) is possible, despite hip hop's being restricted.

Anthony J. Fonseca

See also: Brotha Lynch Hung; Geto Boys; Hardcore Hip Hop

Further Reading

Hess, Danielle. 2007. "Hip Hop and Horror." Under "Wu-Tang Clan" by Jessica Elliott and Mickey Hess. In *Icons of Hip Hop: An Encyclopedia of the Movement, Music, and Culture*, edited by Mickey Hess, vol. 2, pp. 365–90. Westport, CT: Greenwood Press.

Radford, Benjamin. 2016. "Bad Clowns of the Song." In *Bad Clowns*, chap. 7. Albuquerque: University of New Mexico Press.

Further Listening

Esham. 1989. *Boomin' Words from Hell 1990*. Reel Life Productions.

Ganksta N-I-P. 1992. *The South Park Psycho*. Rap-A-Lot Records.

Insane Clown Posse. 1997. *The Great Milenko*. Hollywood Records.

KMC. 1991. *Three Men with the Power of Ten*. Priority Records.

Hungary

Hungary is a Central European country whose population is mostly Hungarian, with small minority populations that are German and Roma. Once part of the Austro-Hungarian Empire (1867–1918), Hungary became the Kingdom of Hungary from 1920 to 1946. Until 1989, Hungary had been an Eastern Bloc country under communism, but near the turn of the century, Hungary experienced a fairly smooth transition to democracy. Just after the departure of the communist regime, underground radio stations and music clubs surfaced. Hungary's capital city

Budapest had popular music scenes that included rock, electronic music, punk, metal, and hip hop, including Animal Cannibals (1989–), a pioneering rap act that employed comedy, coding, and Hungarian wordplay.

Hungary possesses a rich music history. By the 20th century, its best-known composers, Béla Bartók (1881–1945) and Zoltán Kodály (1882–1967), contributed simultaneously to modern music and to Hungarian folk music's popularity and preservation. Although Hungary's communist regime censored popular music, American jazz and rock became extremely popular by the 1950s and 1960s, as Hungarian rock bands carefully navigated the suppression of freedom of speech.

In 1995, Animal Cannibals released *Fehéren fekete, Feketén fehér* (*White to Black, Black to White*). In the meantime, the hip hop group Membran (Membrane, early 1990s–) fused dubstep, electronica, and jazz, and HIP HOP BOYZ (1993–) and Happy Gang (1993–) fused hip hop with pop. Hungarian hip hop localized typical American lyrical content, particularly that associated with gangsta rap. The most successful pioneering act was gangster rapper Ganxsta Zolee (aka Döglögy, Zana Zoltán, 1966–) and his rapping collective Ganxsta Zolee És a Kartel (1995–). Their single "BOOM A Fejbe!" ("Boom to the Head!"), from the debut album *Egyenesen a gettóbói* (*Straight Out the Ghetto*, 1995–) and produced by Epic Records (1953–), was a national hit. Later, the collective's album, the Latin-influenced *Helldorado* (1999), was certified Platinum in Hungary. Other early groups were Rapülők (1992–1994, 2006*–), Az Árral Szemben (Against the Current, 1995–2004), and Fekete Vonat (Black Train, 1997–). Despite Ganxsta Zolee És a Kartel's success, Hungarian hip hop failed to thrive and has had limited commercial success outside the country.

Speak (Tamás Deák, 1976–) was the first Hungarian rapper to become internationally famous when the video for his antiwar song "Stop the War" (2003) went viral on the Internet, with unintentionally comical aspects, for in 2017, the video was parodied as "World Peace Rap" on the American television show *Saturday Night Live* (1975–). Another Hungarian hip hop act that gained notoriety outside Hungary was rapper Brixx (Ildiko Basa, 1976–), a female MC who raps in English. Her debut album *Everything Happens for a Reason* (1999) was released on the Columbia Records label (1887–). The 2000s demonstrate that Hungarian hip hop is focused on musical diversity, if not diverse lyrical content: The electronica group the Balkan Fanatik (2002–) fuses folk rock with hip hop; Irie Maffia (2005–) and Eccentrics (2004–2006)* fuse hip hop with funk, rock, reggae, and dancehall; and beatmaker Mujo (aka mujo beatz, anonymous, n.d.), originally from Japan, fuses lo-fi hip hop with ambient chillout music. Pioneering acts continue as well. Membran included Hungarian folk music instruments such as the cimbalom, in addition to acoustic instruments such as the saxophone and sitar, in its debut studio album *Closed* (2007). DJ Cadik (Chef, Pál Séfel, n.d.), who led Membran, has had his own solo career and released the experimental hip hop and trip hop (downtempo) albums *Basic* (2008), *Just* (2011), and *ALMA* (2012), incorporating drum and bass and glitch music. Ganxsta Zolee És a Kartel still records, and Animal Cannibals recently released *1111* (2016).

Melissa Ursula Dawn Goldsmith

See also: Austria; Germany

Further Reading

Miklody, Eva. 2004. "A.R.T., Klikk, K.A.O.S., and the Rest: Hungarian Youth Rapping." In *Blackening Europe: The African American Presence*, edited by Heike Raphael-Hernandez, chap. 11. New York: Routledge.

Simeziane, Sarah. 2010. "Roma Rap and the *Black Train:* Minority Voices in Hungarian Hip Hop." In *The Languages of Global Hip Hop*, edited by Marina Terkourafi, chap. 4. New York: Continuum.

Further Listening

Animal Cannibals. 2016. *1111.* Magneoton.

Ganxsta Zolee És a Kartel. 1999. *Helldorado.* Epic.

Mujo and BluntOne. 2015. *Reel Street Jazz.* Vinyldigital.de.

Hype Man

A hype man is a kind of MC or toaster whose job involves engaging the audience or crowd through wild fashion and side commentary on a song's main lyrics, with exclamations and interjections and attempts to increase the audience's excitement with call-and-response chants. The hype man may also serve as a vocal harmonizer. The prototype for the hype man is Bobby Howard Byrd (1934–2007), an American R&B/soul singer songwriter who helped develop soul and funk musician James Brown (1933–2006). Byrd would interject vocalizations into Brown's songs, giving him a counterpoint to his lead vocals. A possible origin of the hype man is the Jamaican act of toasting, or talking/chanting over a rhythm to create comedy, boastful commentaries, and rhymed storytelling.

The most famous use of a hype man in rap is Public Enemy's (1982–) Flavor Flav (1959–), the American rapper, comic actor, restaurateur, and reality television show personality who provided comic relief and color for MC Chuck D (1960–). The Hype man often improvises through interventions, while also drawing attention to the words of the rapper. In a practical sense, the hype man gives the main rapper places where he can take a breath, sometimes by just interjecting one or two words within a line. Early hype men were used by Grandmaster Flash and the Furious Five (1976–1982, 1987–1988) and Kool Moe Dee (1963–). Flavor Flav established many of the conventions of the hype man, such as an outlandish sense of fashion and a vocal style that contrasted dramatically with that of the rapper. Another significant hype man was Jay-Z (1969–), who began his career as a hype man for Big Daddy Kane (1968–).

Anthony J. Fonseca

See also: Flavor Flav; Jamaica; Jay-Z; MC; Public Enemy

Further Reading

Danielsen, Anne. 2008. "The Musicalization of 'Reality': Reality Rap and Rap Reality on Public Enemy's *Fear of a Black Planet.*" *European Journal of Cultural Studies* 11, no. 4: 405–21.

Grierson, Tim. 2015. *Public Enemy: Inside the Terrordome.* London: Omnibus Press.

I

Ice Cube

(O'Shea Jackson, 1969–, Los Angeles, California)

Ice Cube is an American rapper, producer, actor, and filmmaker who was one of the central figures in the rise of gangsta rap. As a member of N.W.A. (1986–1991), he helped create the landmark *Straight Outta Compton* (1988). His solo debut, *Ameri-KKKa's Most Wanted* (1990), continued the controversies that had begun with his lyrics for N.W.A., as did *Death Certificate* (1991) and *The Predator* (1992), which were very well received. His popularity declined somewhat with subsequent albums, as his sound mellowed somewhat. He made his motion picture debut in John Singleton's (1968–) critically acclaimed *Boyz n the Hood* (1991), and he has subsequently appeared in more than 30 other films. He has also found success as a screenwriter of American comedy films. As a hip hop writer, he is best known for lyrics that include explicit language and blunt references to drugs, violence, misogyny, and images of the crumbling inner city; conversely, he is the creator and producer of the family-friendly television comedy *Are We There Yet?* (2010–2013).

FOUNDING N.W.A.

Ice Cube was born in the Crenshaw neighborhood of Los Angeles. His middle-class parents expressed strong values that included educational accomplishment, so Ice Cube studied architecture in college, completing his degree in drafting in only one year. He had developed an interest in hip hop music while in high school, where he had written his first songs, including one he sold to Eazy-E (1964–1995), a future member of N.W.A. With K-Dee (aka Kid Disaster, Darrel Johnson, 1969–) and Sir Jinx (Anthony Wheaton, n.d.), he formed the group C.I.A. (Cru in Action, 1984–1987). His gift for lyrics attracted the attention of Dr. Dre (1965–), who hired him as a ghostwriter for several groups.

By 1987, Ice Cube was working virtually full time with N.W.A., writing raps for Dr. Dre and Eazy-E, and performing on their breakout debut album *Straight Outta Compton*. Despite the extraordinary success of that recording, Ice Cube left in a contract dispute over compensation for his lyrics on both that album and an Eazy-E solo album. The animus between N.W.A. and Ice Cube would resurface in raps by both sides in years to come.

SOLO CAREER

AmeriKKKa's Most Wanted made clear that the explicit language, misogyny, and racism that informed Ice Cube's N.W.A. lyrics would be present in his solo projects, though even critics noted that *Death Certificate* and *The Predator* were a prescient commentary on the conditions that precipitated the 1992 Los Angeles riots. His lyrics remained raw and defiant throughout his solo albums, and his delivery retained the convincing and authoritative manner that helped to define gangsta rap.

After his performance in *Boyz n the Hood* (1991), he became a hot property in film, as both an actor and screenwriter. His successful writing projects include *Friday* (1995), *Barbershop* (2002), and *Are We There Yet?* (2005), all three of which did well at the box office and spawned lucrative sequels. *Are We There Yet?* also became the basis of a successful television situation comedy (2010–2013).

Scott Warfield

See also: Dr. Dre; Eazy-E; Gangsta Rap; N.W.A.; The United States

Further Reading

Leonard, David J. 2007. "Ice Cube." In *Icons of Hip Hop: An Encyclopedia of the Movement, Music, and Culture*, edited by Mickey Hess, vol. 2, pp. 293–316. Westport, CT: Greenwood Press.
Woldu, Gail Hilson. 2008. *The Words and Music of Ice Cube.* Westport, CT: Praeger.

Further Listening

Ice Cube. 1990. *AmeriKKKa's Most Wanted.* Priority Records.

Ice Prince

(Panshak Henry Zamani, 1986–, Minna, Nigeria)

Ice Prince is a Nigerian rapper, singer-songwriter, and actor whose rap career began in 2004. He is most famous for one of his early songs, "Oleku" (a song with multiple meanings, from strong to cool, 2010), which featured rapper Brymo (Olawale Ashimi or Olawale Olofo'ro, 1986–), and was also released on his debut album *Everybody Loves Ice Prince* (2011). Ice Prince is a tenor who went from rapping to singing in church choirs, later returning to rap, and his songs use simple electronica dance beats and heavily autotuned R&B vocals, in addition to rapping. He cites many American hip hop acts, including the Notorious B.I.G. (1972–1997), Rakim (1968–), Talib Kweli (1975–), and Lauryn Hill (1975–), as well as fellow Nigerian rappers M.I. (1981–) and Jesse Jagz (1984–), as his influences.

When he was two years old, his Ngas (aka Angas, a tribal people found mainly in the state of Plateau in central Nigeria) family, which was very poor, moved to Jos, a mining city of about a million residents which had a burgeoning hip hop scene. At age 13, he began writing and performing rap songs as a way to raise money for new clothes, and by 15, he began recording. Within a year he formed the short-lived hip hop group Ecomog Squad (2002–2003).

In 2004, he began singing in a church choir and joined the production crew called the Loopy Crew, which featured future solo rappers M.I. and Jesse Jagz. The three had become his roommates after his parents died in 1999 and 2000. M.I. became his mentor, and Ice Prince released his debut single "Extraordinary" and his follow-up single, the M.I.-produced "Rewind," both of which saw local airplay in

Abuja, the capital city of Nigeria, and Lagos, the largest metropolitan area in Nigeria. Both also became minor hits. He then signed with Chocolate City, which released his two albums.

His single "Oleku" eventually became one of Nigeria's most remixed songs. The album *Everybody Loves Ice Prince* spawned four singles, including hits "Aboki" ("Friend") and "More." A remix of "Aboki" featuring Ghanian rapper Sarkodie (1985–) became a hit. Ice Prince has been featured on other hip hop artists' singles, the most notable being "Super Sun (Remix)" (2011) by Bez (Emmanuel Bez Idakula, 1983–), a Nigerian alternative soul multi-instrumentalist, singer-songwriter, and composer.

Over his career, he has won various awards, including the 2013 BET Award for Best International Act: Africa, for his second studio album, *Fire of Zamani* (2013), and the 2014 Nigeria Entertainment Award for Best Rap Act of the Year. In 2015, he began serving as vice president of the Chocolate City (2005–) recording label.

Anthony J. Fonseca

See also: Jesse Jagz; M.I.; Nigeria

Further Reading

Gbogi, Michael Tosin. 2016. "Contesting Meanings in the Postmodern Age: The Example of Nigerian Hip Hop Music." *Matatu* 48, no. 2: 335–62.

Shonekan, Stephanie. 2013. "'The Blueprint: The Gift and the Curse' of American Hip Hop Culture for Nigeria's Millennial Youth." *Journal of Pan African Studies* 6, no. 3: 181–98.

Further Listening

Ice Prince. 2011. *Everybody Loves Ice Prince.* Chocolate City.

Ice Prince. 2013. *Fire of Zamani.* Chocolate City.

Iceland

Iceland is a North Atlantic Ocean island country whose population is almost entirely Icelandic, with very small Polish and other minority populations. Icelandic culture is rooted in Scandinavian culture, though current residents also descend from Germanic and Gaelic populations who settled on the island since the Middle Ages. Hip hop reached Iceland in the early 1980s, though at the time popular music tastes were focused on the new wave pop and synth-pop, alternative rock, heavy metal, post-punk, and folk-infused indie rock that emerged in the capital city, Reykjavík.

Iceland is notable for its literature, including medieval sagas, which are historically based narratives that were written mostly in the 13th century about conflicts during the Saga Age (870–1056). Other notable literature includes Eddic poetry (medieval stories from the Scandinavian mainland) and Skaldic poetry (composed by Icelandic poets called *skalds*, these poems, sometimes satirical, were inserted within stories that honor nobility), sacred verse, autobiographical prose, and *rímur*. The last is a Germanic alliterative epic poem with stanzas of two to four lines that has its earliest extant examples from the late 15th century. Icelandic modern literature, which includes romantic, naturalist, expressionist, and post-expressionist prose, has at times revived earlier epic poetry, particularly the rímur, which became sung a cappella despite being banned for many years by the National Church (Evangelical Lutheran Church of Iceland, 1540–). Rímur has also found its way into popular music, including Icelandic hip hop.

POPULAR MUSIC AND WAVES OF HIP HOP

As early as 1983 breakdancing and graffiti were underground activities, followed by rap; however, internationally successful bands such as the Sugarcubes (1986–1992), followed by lead singer Björk (Björk Guðmundsdóttir, 1965–) as soloist, dominated local airwaves. By the early 1990s, graffiti as art gained popularity in Reykjavík. Prominent graffiti crews were CAN Crew (Can Armed Ninjas, 1997–) and Team 13 (later Twisted Minds Crew [TMC], 1997–), the latter rapping in English. Prominent b-boy crews included Shakers Crew (1997*–) and Element Crew (aka 5th Element Crew, 1998–). Rap battle festivals emerged in the 1990s, including Rímnaflæðl, an onstage freestyle rapping competition in Miðberg.

The earliest hip hop acts opted for the English language to reach beyond the Icelandic audience. These early acts informed Iceland's first wave of hip hop and included Hip Hop Elements (later Kritikal Mazz, 1997–), Bounce Brothers (1997*–), and Multifunctionals (1997*–). Quarashi (1996–2005, 2016–) was the first Icelandic hip hop group to experience national success; 500 copies of its EP *Switchstance* (1996) sold in one week. Quarashi opened for internationally known American groups such as the Fugees (1992–1997), released the Iceland-certified Gold album *Xeneizes* (1999), and attained a recording contract with a major American label, Columbia Records (1887–). Meanwhile, the Subterraninan (Subterranean, 1997–1999) released its successful debut, *Central Magnetizm* (1997). The group included female rapper, producer, and sound engineer CELL7 (Ragna Kjartansdóttir, n.d.). The Reykjavík-based, East Coast–influenced duo Antlew/Maximum (1997–2005*), consisting of Icelandic producer Maximum (aka Earmax, B.L.A.K.E., Gnúsi Yones, Magnús Jónsson, n.d.) and Brooklyn, New York rapper Antlew (aka Lefty Hooks, Anthony Lewis, n.d.), was the earliest Icelandic act to fuse hip hop with R&B and neo soul. Meanwhile, Multifunctionals, a group that usually rapped in English, released "Númer 1" (1997), the first single to contain rap in Icelandic.

By 2000, a second wave of Icelandic hip hop had begun, characterized by success with recording in Icelandic. The earliest to do so were brothers Sesar A (Eyjólfu Eyvindarson, 1975–) and Blaz Roca (aka Johnny National, Erpur Eyvindarson, 1977–), who had been rapping since 1993, growing up in Denmark. With Trió Óla Skans (1997–1999*) and the Subterraninan, they formed the band SupahSyndikal (1999–). In 2001, Sesar A released the first full hip hop album in Icelandic, *Stormurinn á eftir logninu* (*The Storm after the Calm*). A year later, he produced the first rap compilation, *Rímnamín* (a portmanteau using "rhyme" and "vitamin," 2002), recording with his brother as the rapping duo Sækópah (2001*–2002)—the first duo to use Icelandic texts. He also helped produce Blaz Roca's debut solo album *Kópakabana* (2010). Blaz Roca became the most popular and prolific Icelandic rapper, fronting the band XXX Rottweiler Hundar (aka 110 Rottweiler Hundar,

Rottweiler Dogs, 2000–). Blaz Roca also rapped on *Rímur & Rapp* (2002), a compilation featuring Icelandic rappers, folk singers, and traditional rímur musicians. Contemporary acts included Forgotten Lores (2000–), who released the critically acclaimed albums *Týndi hlekkurinnn* (*Lost Lick*, 2003) and *Frá Heimsenda* (*From Heimsenda*, 2006), and Skytturnar (The Marksmen or The Shooters, 2001*–2005, 2012–).

Since 2002, a large number of Icelandic acts have emerged, some using American-inspired lyrical content such as gangsta rap and braggadocio, but most focusing on diverse topics such as political corruption, women's rights, gender equality, fantastic or apocalyptic narratives, Icelandic literature or culture, and everyday life. Some acts included Bæjarins bestu (The Best Town, 2002–), Móri (Magnús Ómarsson, n.d.), Emmsjé Gauti (Gauti Þeyr Másson, 1989–), Poetrix (Sævar Daníel Kolandavelu, n.d.), Afkvæmi Guðanna (The Offspring of the Gods, 2002–), Bent og 7Berg (Bent and 7Berg, 2002–), and Hæsta Hendin (The Highest Hand, 2003*–). Pioneering acts such as Cell7 also made successful comebacks. Maximum continued on to establish the electronica hip house band GusGus (1995–), which later recorded trip hop on the album *This Is Normal* (1999). Other trip hop (downtempo) acts include Emilíana Torrini (Emilíana Torrini Davíðsdóttir, 1977–), TMC's Beatmakin Troopa (Pan Thorarensen, 1981–), Hermigervill (Sveinbjörn Thorarensen, 1984–), Samaris (2011–), and IntrObeatz (aka Introbeats, Ársæll Ingason, n.d.).

In the 2010s Icelandic hip hop continues its diversity of topics and musical fusion, embracing trap music, which marks the beginning of the third wave. Successful trap, trap hop, or trap pop acts include Geisha Cartel (2012*–), $igmund (Sigmundur Páll Feysteinsson, 1997*–), Aron Can (1999–), and Los Angeles–raised Gísli Pálmi (Gísli Pálmi Sigurðsson, 1991–). Other acts include Kött Grà Pje (aka Kött G P, Gray Cat, Atli Sigþórsson, 1983–), Lord Pusswhip (Þórður Ingi Jónsson, 1993–), STNY (aka Stony, Stony Blyden, Thorsteinn Sindri Baldvinsson Blyden, 1993–), GKR (Gaukur Grétuson, 1994–), Herra Hnetusmjör (Árni Páll Árnason, n.d.), Þriðja Hæðin (The Third Floor, 2008–), Shades of Reykjavík (2011–), Úlfur Úlfur (2011–), and Reykjavíkurdætur (Daughters of Reykjavik, 2013–). The last is an all-female band whose feminist topics, at times through use of metaphor or coding, include protesting rape culture and victim blaming, expressing pride in sexuality and maternity, countering the male gaze, and advocating for gender equality and women's rights.

Melissa Ursula Dawn Goldsmith

See also: Quarashi; The United States

Further Reading

Mitchell, Tony. 2015. "Icelandic Hip Hop from 'Selling American Fish to Icelanders' to Reykjavíkdætur (Reykjavík Daughters)." *Journal of World Popular Music* 2, no. 2: 240–60.

Patrick, Brian Anse. 2008. "Vikings and Rappers: The Icelandic Sagas Hip Hop across *8 Mile*." *Journal of Popular Culture* 41, no. 2 (April): 281–305.

Further Listening

Afkvæmi Guðanna. 2016. *Hættu að hringja í mig* (*Stop Calling Me*). Gemsar.

Shades of Reykjavík. 2017. *Rós* (*Fighters*). Self-released.

Ice-T

(Tracy Lauren Marrow, 1958–, Newark, New Jersey)

Ice-T, a highly successful early 1980s hip hop performer, helped to establish West Coast rappers as equal to their New York rivals. He is also one of the founders of gangsta rap culture. In the last two decades, he has also been a popular motion picture and television actor, especially in roles that promote hip hop identities. In the 1980s he made occasional film appearances. Beginning with the American motion picture *New Jack City* (1991), in which he played an undercover narcotics detective, he appeared in over two dozen motion pictures in the next decade, usually as a gang member, drug dealer, or law enforcement figure. Since 2000, he has starred in the long-running *Law and Order: Special Victims Unit* (1999–), as Odafin "Fin" Tutuola, a former undercover narcotics officer.

EARLY YEARS

Born Tracy Lauren Marrow and raised in suburban middle-class New Jersey until the deaths of his parents left him orphaned at the age of 12, Ice-T lived briefly with various relatives in Los Angeles. During his high school years, he acquired the nickname Ice-T as a reflection of his interest in the novels of pimp Iceberg Slim (aka Robert Beck, Robert Lee Maupin, 1918–1992), whose works he memorized and recited to his friends. Although not a gang member himself, he did associate with members of the Crips (1969–) and engaged in some illegal activities.

At 17 and living on his own, he was unable to support himself and his girlfriend on a Social Security check, and so he sold marijuana and stolen car stereos. He also became involved with music in a vocal group at Crenshaw High School and eventually enlisted in the U.S. Army, where he first became interested in hip hop music. At this time, he purchased stereo equipment, which he used to learn turntablism and MCing (rapping). Following his discharge, he adopted the stage name Ice-T and began to work as a DJ, but found that he attracted more attention as a rapper. About that same time, he returned to his criminal activities, until a serious car accident put him in a hospital as a John Doe, because he carried no identification while committing crimes. Shortly after his release, he decided to become a professional rapper and give up his illegal activities.

SUCCESS AT RAPPING

Beginning in the mid-1980s, Ice-T's recordings helped to shift hip hop's center of gravity away from its New York origins. In 1983, he recorded his first single, "Cold Wind Madness," and despite its lack of airplay due to its hardcore lyrics, the track achieved some commercial success. As Ice-T's reputation grew in clubs in Los Angeles, similar tracks followed. Upon hearing Schoolly D's (Jesse Bonds Weaver Jr., 1962–) "P.S.K. What Does It Mean?" (1985), Ice-T composed his own rap about gang life, "6 in the Mornin'" (1986), a track that is cited frequently as perhaps the first example of gangsta rap. On the success of this and other singles, he signed with Sire Records (1966–), acquired by Warner Bros. Records (1958–) in 1978, which released his first two studio albums, *Rhyme Pays* (1987) and *Power* (1988), both of which achieved Gold status. His fourth album, *O.G. Original Gangster* (1991), earned a Grammy and is considered one of gangsta rap's defining albums. The single "Body Count" is noteworthy for its introduction of Body Count (1990–2006, 2009–), his heavy metal band, metal being a musical genre that had interested him since high school.

His next project was Body Count's self-titled debut album. *Body Count* (1992) spawned the provocative single "Cop Killer," written by Ice-T to convey the frustrations of individuals, chiefly minorities, who have been the victims of police brutality and therefore wanted to seek revenge; the track immediately drew nationwide protests from police, the National Rifle Association (NRA, 1871–), and numerous prominent politicians. In an interview for the *Los Angeles Times*, Ice-T observed that motion picture fans were not troubled by the numerous police killed by Arnold Schwarzenegger's (1947–) character in the American motion picture *The Terminator* (1984), and he contrasted that mindset with the racist attitudes that sought to censor a black man to keep him from writing about a cop killer.

Following those controversies, Ice-T retook control of his recordings by reactivating his own label, Rhyme $yndicate Records (1987–2011), named after the hip hop collective, which issued his next two albums so he could avoid having every aspect of his work monitored by record company executives. During the 1990s, he made three albums with Body Count, but since 2000, Ice-T made only three new albums of any kind, as he switched to acting.

Scott Warfield

See also: Gangsta Rap; Hardcore; Political Hip Hop; The United States

Further Reading

Bradley, Adam, and Andrew Dubois, eds. 2010. "Ice-T." Under "Part 2: 1985–92: The Golden Age" in *The Anthology of Rap*, pp. 187–93. New Haven, CT: Yale University Press.

Ice-T and Douglas Century. 2001. *Ice: A Memoir of Gangster Life and Redemption—from South Central to Hollywood*. New York: One World/Ballantine Books.

Philips, Chuck. 1992. "Cover Story: 'Arnold Schwarzenegger Blew Away Dozens of Cops as the Terminator, But I Don't Hear Anybody Complaining': A Q&A with Ice-T about Rock, Race, and the 'Cop Killer' Furor." *Los Angeles Times*, July 19, 7.

Further Listening

Ice-T. 1991. *O.G. Original Gangster*. Sire/Warner Bros. Records.

Iggy Azalea

(Amethyst Amelia Kelly, 1990–, Sydney Australia)

Iggy Azalea is an Australian rapper known for combining hip hop with electronica, trap, pop, and drum and bass music. She uses a variety of Southern hip hop rapping styles as well, from gangsta rap to crunk. Between 2012 and 2015 she became the focus of several hip hop controversies, which included accusations of white appropriation of black music, of hyper sexualization, and of not possessing the attributes that make a good hip hop artist. She started out self-releasing music, but by 2014 she had found a distributor for her album *The New Classic*, which spawned a No. 1 hit, "Fancy," and went Platinum.

FROM AUSTRALIA TO THE UNITED STATES

Though raised by her nonmusical family in Mullumbimby, Australia, she began rapping at age 14. By age 16 she dropped out of high school and earned enough money to move to the United States, where she lived in Miami, Houston, and Atlanta. During these years, she studied Southern hip hop, created her stage name based on a childhood pet's name and a home street name, and had a false start with forming her own group.

In 2010, Interscope Records (1989–) managed her, and she moved to Los Angeles; however, she began her hip hop career with *Ignorant Art* (2011) and *TrapGold* (2012), self-released mixtapes. "Pu$$y," from *Ignorant Art*, along with its video, led to widespread international attention and collaborations with well known hip hop and pop artists, as well as concert appearances and a worldwide tour. She also self-released videos for "My World" and "The Last Song."

DEBUT ALBUM

In 2012, issues with Interscope developed when it prevented Southern rapper T.I. (Clifford Joseph Harris Jr., 1980–) from working with Azalea on her debut album *The New Classic*. To continue under his artistic direction, Azalea signed with T.I.'s independent label Grand Hustle Records (2002–). In the meantime, her 2011 remix of Kendrick Lamar's (1987–) "Look Out for Detox" (2010), titled "D.R.U.G.S.," was widely criticized; she had to apologize for adapting Kendrick Lamar's lyrics that referenced being a runaway slave.

Azalea's albums *The New Classic* and *Reclassified* were released in 2014 on the Virgin EMI Records label. At this point, she was internationally known: She appeared with artists on MTV, issued singles and EPs online, and toured worldwide. In 2013, she had signed with Virgin EMI (2013–) in the United Kingdom and Def Jam Recordings (1983–) in the United States, as she was working on nonalbum Billboard Hot 100 hits such as "Bounce," "Work," and "Change Your Life." As of 2018, Azalea continues studying Southern hip hop in the United States in addition to her music career.

Melissa Ursula Dawn Goldsmith

See also: Australia; Banks, Azealia; Dirty Rap; Dirty South; Trap

Further Reading

Eberhardt, Maeve, and Kara Freeman. 2015. "'First Things First, I'm the Realest': Linguistic Appropriation, White Privilege, and the Hip Hop Persona of Iggy Azalea." *Journal of Sociolinguistics* 19, no. 3: 303–27.

Morrissey, Tara. 2014. "The New Real: Iggy Azalea and the Reality Performance." *PORTAL: Journal of Multidisciplinary International Studies* 11, no. 1: 1–17.

Williams, Melvin L. 2017. "White Chicks with a Gangsta' Pitch: Gendered Whiteness in United States Rap Culture (1990–2017)." *Journal of Hip Hop Studies* 4, no. 1: 50–93.

Further Listening
Iggy Azalea. 2014. *The New Classic.* Virgin EMI Records.

India

India possesses a vibrant hip hop scene that is relatively new, beginning in the 1980s, but has produced a distinctive sound which has now spread to other countries, including those in the Western Hemisphere. By some reports, there are today some 2,000 rappers in India, rapping in different languages such as Bhojpuri, English, Haryanvi, Hindi, Khasi, Punjabi, and Tamil, among others. As of 2018, producer, singer, and actor YoYo Honey Singh (aka Honey Singh, Hirdesh Singh, 1983–) is the most popular hip hop artist in India. His music completely eschews any Indian influence and is indistinguishable from American hip hop in its style or approach; however, he prefers to sing in Hindi and his native Punjabi rather than English. Singh has become widely popular in Bollywood, where he rose to fame in late 2013. Other popular current Indian hip hop artists include soloists Badshah (Aditya Prateek Singh Sisodia, n.d.) and Raftaar (Dilin Nair, 1988–), and bands Machas with Attitude (2008–2017) and Hiphop Tamizha (2005–).

BEGINNINGS

When hip hop reached India, it found a fertile musical ground, since many classical and popular Indian musicians have had a longtime fascination with black music, initially modeling their solo work after the improvisations of jazz; in addition, extramusical racial issues strengthened their identification with black music. By the mid-1980s, with access to American breakdancing motion pictures such as *Wild Style* (1983) and *Beat Street* (1984), Indian youth started to create a hip hop culture that became extremely popular in India's major urban cities in both the North and the South, especially in Mumbai, Delhi, Chennai, Bangalore, and Kolkata. Though these cities created hip hop undergrounds that included house parties and various kinds of battles, Kolkata was striking in that it was host to many aboveground hip hop dance workshops and academies that emerged by the late 1980s. In contrast, rap was a larger focus of development in Mumbai, Delhi, Bangalore, and Chennai. American rapping styles were emulated before Indian hip hop artists turned to using their own languages in the 1990s. Regardless of any Indian preference toward its own languages, English, which is an official language of India (as well as Hindi), was often used in Indian hip hop, with a unique feature being that both American and British English vernacular are used.

Baba Sehgal (Harjeet Singh Sehgal, 1965*–) holds the distinction of being India's first rapper, and its first Hindi rapper, releasing his debut and second albums *Dilruba* and *Alibaba* in 1991. Most of his songs are tongue-in-cheek raps about cultural foibles and everyday life, and most are based on Western rap music conventions, despite his music's being quintessentially Indian in instrumentation. His videos show both Western and Indian influences, as he wears American style form fitting shirts—whose colors are so unnatural that they are reminiscent of Bollywood costumes. A natural in front of the camera, he tried his hand at acting, making his debut in the Bollywood romance thriller *Miss 420* (1998), also appearing on the movie soundtrack, which was released earlier in 1994; however, it was the Tamil film *Kadhalan* (1994) which caused hip hop to catch on. It featured the electronic hip hop song "Pettai Rap," in a scene which featured Bollywood versions of various hip hop and gymnastic dance moves, as well as a colorful, androgynous character who references Flavor Flav (1959–) in his comic dress style and vocal choices.

Meanwhile, English Indian film and music producer Bally Sagoo (1964–), from Delhi, but raised in Birmingham, England, had been active in the recording industry since 1989, when as a DJ he remixed the Punjabi song "Hey Jamalo," which became a hit. Its music and video foreshadows the *bhangra-beat* scene which would become India's unique contribution to hip hop. Sagoo combined hip hop with ragga and eventually bhangra-beat music. In 1994, he signed with Sony Records (1929–) and became the first Indian artist to be played on national mainstream radio. He later toured India with Michael Jackson (1958–2009) on the HIStory Tour (1996–1997), and launched his own U.K. label, Ishq Records (1999–). In 2003, at the U.K. Asian Awards, he won the award for Outstanding Achievement. Attesting to the popularity of Indian hip hop, London-based the Rishi Rich Project (2003–), led by producer Rishi Rich (Rishpal Singh Rekhi, 1976–), began working with artists in the South Asian Underground scene, including those involved in the R&B-bhangra fusion scene, popularizing Indian hip hop in both the U.K. Asian underground scene and in India.

Chennai-born and Zambian-raised rapper-turned-playback-singer Blaaze (Lakshmi Narasimha Vijaya Rajagopala Sheshadri Sharma Rajesh Raman, 1975–) is a notable contemporary of Sagoo. Once a breakdancing pioneering act in Zambia, Blaaze, who was raised there and educated in England and the United States, performed and produced Zambia's first music video, "Advice 4 Livin'" (1991). A decade later, Blaaze relocated to Chennai and relaunched his career there as a rapper and playback singer, first singing "Baba Rap" for the Tamil fantasy action motion picture *Baba* (2002). The film's composer A. R. Rahman (Allah-Rakha Rahman, b. Dileep Shekhar, 1967–) has since worked with Blaaze numerous times. Blaaze has worked on numerous internationally made films, sometimes writing his own rap lyrics, including "Gangsta Blues" for *Slumdog Millionaire* (2008, United Kingdom).

MODERNIZATION

Among the current cache of Indian rappers, Badshah stands out. He is a rapper, producer, and composer/lyricist known for his Hindi, Haryanvi, and Punjabi songs. He came onto the scene in 2006 with the group Mafia Mundeer (along with YoYo Honey Singh), and since he went solo in 2012, his songs have been featured in Bollywood soundtracks. His 2015 single, "DJ Waley Babu," was ranked No. 1 on Indian iTunes charts within 24 hours of its release and received over 168 million

YouTube views. Raftaar is a rapper, singer, and lyricist, as well as a dancer who since 2009 has produced music either with Mafia Mundeer, or as a solo act; he has also moved on to producing music for Bollywood. Machas with Attitude is a hip hop trio whose songs were primarily in English, although they feature lyrics in Hindi, Tamil, Telugu, Kannada, and Malayalam. The American rapper group N.W.A.'s (1986–1991) name and music were the inspiration for Machas with Attitude. Hiphop Tamizha is a duo that pioneered Tamil hip hop in India. The group started as an underground phenomenon until the commercial success of "Club le Mabbu le" (2011). Its debut album *Hip Hop Tamizhan* was India's first Tamil hip hop album.

Since the early 2000s, female women rappers have emerged, though with less success in general than their male contemporaries. Sofia Ashraf (1987–) from Chennai, India is a well known Tamil rapper whose themes include protesting against corporations who fail to clean up after their disasters, particularly the Dow Chemical Company, an American corporation who ultimately purchased Union Carbide India Limited in 2001, about 17 years after the Bhopal gas tragedy; she also protest raps about the treatment of Muslims since the terrorist attacks of September 11, 2001. In 2015, she released the music video "Kodaikanal Won't" to protest against the British Dutch company Unilever (1930–) for mercury found in the Tamil Nadu city Kodaikanal. Emerging from Mumbai's hip hop scene was MC Dee (Deepa Unnikrishnan, 1997*–), who writes her own rap texts in English and Marathi and whose themes include protesting against gender inequality and supporting women's empowerment.

HYBRIDIZATION: BHANGRA-BEAT AND FUSION

Coming from the Punjab region, which includes most of North India and Pakistan, *bhangra-beat* music has been produced mainly in the last two decades in the United Kingdom, Canada, and the United States, rather than in India. Bhangra-beat is a hybrid music genre that has much in common with hip hop and rap, as well as the folk dance and music of Punjabi farmers. Rap, hip hop, and bhangra-beat share lyrical concerns, as well as performance practices: an obsession with materialism, or an expressed desire or boasting about jewelry, wealth, and/or clothing; cultural identity politics; aggrandizement of alcohol and drugs; sexuality; and masculinity. The songs also shared hip hop's call to dance. In addition, bhangra-beat embraces remix culture, and it shares with hip hop the influence of reggae and trance music. Sometimes called *urban desi*, it shows a Western hybridization that incorporates older, classical Indian music. Bhangra-beat is related to, but vastly different from, Bollywood-influenced dance music, which is more house music influenced. Although a second-generation music, bhangra-beat is more tradition-influenced than earlier Indian hip hop, incorporating both the traditional vocals in Punjabi and the traditional drum instrumentation (particularly the *dhol*) of Punjabi folk music, juxtaposed against Western hip hop rhythms and rap. By 1997, the sound had become popular in the underground dance club circuit. From the late 1990s into today, Bollywood films that are first released in India have also employed the sound, so bhangra-beat music is well known and appreciated in India as well.

The cross-borrowing between bhangra-beat and U.S., U.K., and Canadian hip hop musicians began in 2002, with Jay-Z (1969–) and Panjabi MC's (Rajinder Singh Rai, 1973–) megahit "Beware of the Boys" ("Mundian To Bach Ke"). In addition to Jay-Z, M.I.A (1975–), Timbaland (1972–), and Snoop Dogg (1971–) have all used the bhangra-beat conventions that had emerged from club scenes in London, New York City, Chicago, Seattle, Toronto, and other urban areas due to the influence of the Indian diaspora. Neither the Westernization of India-based music with hip hop nor the introduction of classical Indian music into Western hip hop music was a new phenomenon in the 1990s. The most famous example of Western and Indian music crossover is the music of sitar player Ravi Shankar (Rabindra Shankar Chowdhury, 1920–2012), who influenced the Beatles (1960–1970), the Rolling Stones (1962–), the Moody Blues (1964–), and the Cyrkle (1961–1968).

Fusion between Indian music and pop music had a resurgence in popularity in the United States, the United Kingdom, and abroad in the 1990s, with bands such as Thievery Corporation (1995–) from Washington, DC; Cornershop (1991–) from Leicester and Wolverhampton, England; and MIDIval Punditz (1997–) from New Delhi. By the 1990s, underground DJ remixes found their way into hip hop because of the heavy dhol beat, the repetitive melody of the single-stringed *tumbi*, and on occasion, the sounds of the *tabla*, the *iktar* (or *ektara*), and the *chimta*. The music's high energy fits well with rap and hip hop music conventions. In addition, cultural similarities between urban Punjabi youth and ethnic youth in the United Kingdom, the United States, and Canada, led to a tougher urban sound. Both bhangra-beat and fusion also gained a boost in appeal in the West in the 2000s and 2010s with Chennai's A. R. Rahman's (Allah-Rakha Rahman (1967–) award-winning and popular score to Danny Boyle's (1956–) award-winning box office smash *Slumdog Millionaire* (2008).

Eventually, by the late 1990s into the 2000s, women such as underground DJ Rekha (Rekha Malhotra, 1971–) in New York City and rapper Ms Scandalous (Savita Vaid, 1985–) in London began to produce rap and hip hop hits, moving beyond the role of the video vixen and featured musical guest in Bollywood hip hop songs of prominent artists and producers. Panjabi Hit Squad's (2002–) "Hai Hai" featured Ms Scandalous and became a YouTube phenomenon. Rapper Nindy Kaur (1975–), born in Birmingham, England, has been involved in spreading bhangra-beat to the United States through her bhangra-beat band RDB's (Rhythm, Dhol, Bass, 1997–2013) tours and the band's collaboration with Snoop Dogg, and has influenced Indian music through the band's appearances on soundtracks for Bollywood films. Kaur and her spouse, RDB lead singer and songwriter Manj Musik (Manjeet Singh Ral, 1985–), both have worked with Raftaar.

DANCE

Indian dancers adopted some of the moves of hip hop dancers, but added to these techniques the elaborate costuming and highly choreographed gymnastic moves of Bollywood dance, as well as the choreography of traditional bhangra (which also became gymnastic because of its martial arts influences). Today, many bhangra dance competitions are held in universities and colleges worldwide, especially in the United States. These feature a hybridization of bhangra-beat and Punjabi folk dance moves and require intense training to produce dances that are of a stunt show quality. The competitiveness of the dancers has led to faster tempos and an increase in the number of stunts involved. Competitions involve flips, tumbles, and even pyramids. In bhangra-beat videos, Bollywood influences can be seen: in many cases, singers are backed by a group of dancers in traditional clothing or by chorus dancers doing choreographed hip hop and/or jazz dance moves together, as in the music video for "Jaan Panjabi," by Punjabi By Nature, from the 2007 CD *Jaan Panjabi: The Album*. The video features a hip hop and jazz dance chorus, bhangra dancers in traditional clothing, dhol players, and martial arts dancing, in addition to members of PBN, who also add hip hop hand movements.

Anthony J. Fonseca and Melissa Ursula Dawn Goldsmith

See also: Canada; Filmmaking (Feature Films Made outside the United States); Pakistan; Panjabi Hit Squad; Panjabi MC; The United Kingdom; The United States

Further Reading

Diethrich, Gregory. 2000. "Desi Music Vibes: The Performance of Indian Youth Culture in Chicago." *Asian Music* 31, no. 1: 35–61.

Gapinath, Gayatri. 1994. "Bombay, U.K., Yuba City: Bhangra Music and the Engendering of Diaspora." *Diaspora* 4, no. 3: 303–21.

Goldsmith, Melissa, and Anthony J. Fonseca. 2013. "Bhangra-Beat and Hip Hop: Hyphenated Musical Cultures, Hybridized Music." In *Crossing Traditions: American Popular Music in Local and Global Contexts*, edited by Babacar M'Baye and Alexander Charles Oliver Hall, chap. 9. Lanham, MD: Scarecrow.

Maire, Sunaina. 1998. "Desis reprazent: Bhangra Remix and Hip Hop in New York City." *Postcolonial Studies* 1, no. 3: 357–70.

Warwick, Jacqueline. 2000. "'Make Way for the Indian': Bhangra Music and South Asian Presence in Toronto." *Popular Music and Society* 24, no. 2: 25–44.

Zumkhawala-Cook, Richard. 2008. "Bollywood Gets Funky: American Hip Hop, Basement Bhangra, and the Racial Politics in Music." In *Global Bollywood: Travels of Hindi Song and Dance*, edited by Sangita Gopal and Sujata Moorti, chap. 12. Minneapolis: University of Minnesota Press.

Further Listening

Bally Sagoo. 1992. *Wham Bam 2 (The Second Massacre)*. Star Records.

Panjabi Hit Squad featuring Ms Scandalous. 2003. *Hai Hai*. Def Jam U.K.

RDB. 2003. *Unstoppable*. Untouchables Records.

Various Artists. 2015. *The Asian Collection*. Sony Music.

Indonesia

Indonesia arrived late on the hip hop scene, with best-selling Indonesian rapper Iwa K (Iwa Kusuma, 1970–), from Bandung, West Java, Indonesia, performing in the late 1980s and recording in the early 1990s with albums *Kuingin kembali* (*I Want Back*, 1992), *Topeng* (*Mask*, 1993), and *Kramotak* (*Brain Cramps*, 1996). Iwa K won many awards, including the Indonesian Music Award for Best Rap Performance in

1999. He has been listed in *Rolling Stone Indonesia* among both the 150 greatest Indonesian albums and songs. Most early Indonesian hip hop groups incorporated local culture, including tribal beats, into their music, even though rhymes were in Indonesian and English. Lyrics often combined formal Indonesian with street slang and were informed by regionally nuanced pronunciations, regional idioms (usually in Javanese, Sundanese, or Betawi), and expressions of youth code. Most of the songs protested the state-imposed Indonesian cultural identity, which was implemented by Indonesia's second president, Hajji Suharto (1821–2008), who ruled the country from 1967 to 1998. Themes included youth frustration, love, working conditions, and cultural identity. Early Indonesian hip hop, such as recordings by Iwa K and Denada (1994–), were often mixed with heavy metal, producing what is called hip-metal.

Since the 1990s, Indonesian hip hop has flourished. Homicide (1994–), was founded by Morgue Vanguard (aka Ucock, Heri Sutresna, n.d.), who is both a musician and an activist in Bandung; thus, Homicide's music is about politics. Its albums include *Tha Nekrophone Dayz* (2006) and *Illurrekshun* (2008), and other recordings include the *Godzilla Necronometry* EP (2005), *Split 12-inch* (2008), and *Barisan Nisan* (2015). NEO (1999–) is a five-member hip hop group from Jakarta which has won awards including the 1999 and 2000 Anugerah Musik Indonesia. Its albums include *Borju* (1999), *Bahagia* (*Happy*, 2000), *Tu La Lit* (2002), *NEO* (2004), *Boss* (2007) and *Positive* (2013), and its sound includes individuated rapping, sometimes over a lyrical R&B instrumental melody and contrasting programmed beats and a turntablist.

Batik Tribe (2007–) is a four-member hip hop band from Jakarta consisting of Della MC (Havis, n.d.), Cool B (Budi, n.d.), Wizzow (Wisnu, n.d.), and DJ S'tea (Sonu, n.d.). The band performs wearing Batik, which links them with Indonesian iconography (DJ S'tea frequently covers his turntables with a batik cloth). The band's rapping style incorporates R&B and reggae, and some singles employ the Javanese gamelan. Batik Tribe focuses on current social and cultural issues. Its first album, *Melangkah* (*Stepping*, 2008), especially the song "Indo Yo Ey" ("Indonesia Rap," 2008), combines electronic hip hop beat with gamelan. Balikpapan's Saykoji (aka Igor, Ignatius Penyami, n.d.), who has rapped with Batik Tribe, has become a popular Indonesian rapper since 2006. His albums include *Saykoji* (2005), *Musik hati* (*Music Heart*, 2006), *Switch* (2008), *Jesus Rock Live* (2013), and he has released singles such as "Online" (2009), "Apa Ku Bilang" ("What Did I Say," 2012), "Move On" (2013), and "Gece Dong" (2014).

Recent hip hop bands include Young Lex (2014–), which features Ucok Munthe (n.d.), a senior rapper from Medan. Young Lex's albums include *Aku dan Diri Ku* (*Me and Myself*), and its hits include "Satu Microphone" ("One Microphone," 2014), the Missy Elliott (1971–) influenced "O Aja Ya Kan" (2015), and "Goyang Bos" ("Rocking Boss," 2015). Other recent hip hop acts include Bondan Prakoso (1984–) and Fade to Black (2004–), Kungpow Chicken (2004*–), Ebith Beat A (2004*–), 8 Ball (Muhammed Iqbal, n.d.), Soul ID (2002–), Mizta D (anonymous, 1979–), the Law and Amank (2008–), and Mr. Ginting (Andreanus Ginting, n.d.).

Kheng Keow Koay

See also: Reggae

Further Reading

Nilan, Pam. 2015. "Youth Culture in/beyond Indonesia: Hybridity or Assemblage?" In *A Critical Youth Studies for the Twenty-First Century*, edited by Peter Kelly and Annelies Kamp, chap. 5. Boston: Brill.

Varela, Miguel Escobar. 2014. "Wayang Hip Hop: Java's Oldest Performance Tradition Meets Global Youth Culture." *Asian Theatre Journal* 31, no. 2: 481–504.

Industrial Hip Hop

Industrial hip hop is a style which fuses hip hop beats or rap vocals with industrial music, which is typically experimental electronic music that draws on harsh, discordant, metallic-sounding beats, noise, and power chords and generally features transgressive or provocative topics. *Techno*, a kind of concurrent electronic dance music that originated in Detroit, shares many of these source sounds with industrial hip hop, which emerged in the 1980s with acts such as Bristol, England vocalist Mark Stewart (1960–); Salem, Illinois-born and Detroit- and New York City–based bassist and producer Bill Laswell (William Laswell, 1950–); and London keyboardist and producer Adrian Sherwood (1958–).

In 1985, Stewart, working with a group of musicians that included Sherwood on keyboards and musicians associated with Sugar Hill Records (1978–), released one of the most important early industrial hip hop albums, *As the Veneer of Democracy Starts to Fade*, on Mute Records (1978–). The next year, Oakland, California, guitarist, rapper-songwriter, and spoken-word artist Michael Franti (1966–) cofounded the Beatnigs (1986–1990), a band which combined hardcore punk, industrial, jazz, and hip hop. Meanwhile, Sherwood cofounded the band TACK>>HEAD (aka Fats Comet, 1987–1991, 2004–), working with Sugar Hill musicians Doug Wimbish (Douglas Arthur Wimbish, 1956–), Keith Leblanc (n.d.), and Skip McDonald (Bernard Alexander, 1949–). The pioneering work by Stewart, Laswell, and Sherwood paved the way for early industrial hip hop bands such as Meat Beat Manifesto (1987–), Franti's the Disposable Heroes of Hiphoprisy (1990–1993), and Consolidated (1990–2005), as well as rapper MC 900 Ft. Jesus (Mark Griffin, 1957–).

Roedermark, Germany (near Frankfurt) record label Mille Plateaux (1993–), created by Achim Szepanski (n.d.), helped popularize and further develop the style with a series of five compilations called Electric Ladyland (1995–1998). Second generation industrial hip hop acts included the project band Scorn (1991–1997, 2000–2011), fronted by grindcore mainstay Mick Harris (Michael John Harris, 1967–), who had worked with Laswell. Scorn member Justin Broadrick (1969–), who then founded the industrial hip hop and metal band Godflesh (1988–2002, 2010–). Other notable industrial hip hop acts include Steril (1990–), an Oldenburg, Germany–based band that combines hip hop beats, turntablism, and rap with industrial elements; Antipop Consortium (1997–2002, 2007–), a New York–based alternative hip hop group notable for its stream-of-consciousness rapping, spoken word, and metatextuality; Death Grips (2010–), a Sacramento, California, experimental hip hop band that fuses hip hop, punk rock, and industrial; and dälek (1998–), a Newark, New Jersey, alternative hip hop band music which creates atmospheric, complex industrial music.

Industrial hip hop is related to some styles of trip hop, dubstep, digital hardcore, and breakcore, and *illbient* (the last is a style of ambient music that emerged in the 1990s that is called *ill*, which is American slang to describe something that is good or cool).

Anthony J. Fonseca

See also: Germany; Glitch Hop; The United Kingdom; The United States

Further Reading

Collins, Karen. 2005. "Dead Channel Surfing: The Commonalities between Cyberpunk Literature and Industrial Music." *Popular Music* 24, no. 2: 165–78.

Spencer, Zoe, and Molefi Kete Asante. 2011. *Murda', Misogyny, and Mayhem: Hip Hop and the Culture of Abnormality in the Urban Community.* Lanham, MD: University Press of America.

Further Listening

Various Artists. 1995. *Electric Ladyland.* Mille Plateaux.

Intik

(1988–2006, Algiers, Algeria)

Intik was an Algerian hip hop quartet whose members go by the DJ names Youss (Youcef Seddas, n.d.), Rhéda (Rhéda Chetoui, n.d.), Samir (Samir Djoudi, n.d.), and Nabil (Nabil Bouaiche, n.d.). The four have released two albums of rap songs in both Darija (Algerian Arabic creole) and French and have appeared on compilation albums. The band's name loosely translates, ironically, as "everything's going great" (sometimes also represented as "no problem"). The irony in its translation lies in the group's rap themes, such as the violent upbringing of Algerian youth during the 1980s and 1990s.

Intik's music is a combination of a synthesized version (not using traditional instruments) of traditional Algerian music (*chaâbi*), funk, hip hop, rap and reggae, with a bit of *raï* (Creole Algerian folk music based on traditional rural songs by shepherds) mixed in as well. Intik's music tends to be melodic and laid back, with raps that are delivered in an even tone, interspersed with Jamaican style reggae interludes. Often Algerian melodies are juxtaposed against a hip hop beat.

Lyrics, though delivered with measured vocals, tell of Algeria's political unrest and its effects on the nation's youth. The band's musical hybridization came about because Youss was chiefly interested in reggae and ragga, a fusion of dancehall music and reggae (although he started with a rap trio called YBG), while Nabil, Samir and Reda were already experimenting with Arabic versions of rap. The result is that the songs are catchy and engaging, with thematic concerns that are powerful and moving.

Youss points to a police action against protestors in October 1988 and his (and other members') decision to leave Algiers for France due to what Intik explained was politico-economic unrest as a result of outside and interior interests in oil, gas, and uranium—unrest in Algeria was responsible for the nations's lowering gasoline prices. Inspired by Public Enemy (1982–), which used words instead of violence to protest, Intik began writing and performing raps and was soon discovered when one of its cassette tapes was sent to Algiers-born Imhotep (Pascal Perez, 1960–) of the Marseille, France–based rap group IAM (1989–) by French journalist Hélène Lee (n.d.). IAM often performed songs about Africa, with a great emphasis on Egypt, and slavery (IAM's first hit was "Les tam-tam de l'Afrique" ["The Tam-Tam of Africa"] in 1991).

IAM invited Intik to perform at Logic Hip Hop in Marseilles. On the quality of its song "Va le dire a ta mére" ("Go Tell It to Your Mother"), Intik was signed to the Sony label Saint George Records (1993–), for which it produced two albums, *Intik* (1999) and *La victoire* (*Victory*, 2001), although in its own country Intik was not allowed on television for some time and some songs were omitted from itsalbums because they were critical of the government. Afterward, Youss left the band to pursue other projects.

Anthony J. Fonseca

See also: Algeria; France; Political Hip Hop

Further Reading

Davies, Eirlys E., and Abdelali Bentahila. 2006. "Code Switching and the Globalisation of Popular Music: The Case of North African Rai and Rap." *Multilingua* 25, no. 4: 367–92.

Spady, James G., H. Samy Alim, and Samir Meghelli. 2006. "Interview with Youcef aka Youss (Intik)." In *Tha Global Cipha: Hip Hop Culture and Consciousness*, pp. 656–67. Philadelphia: Black History Museum Publishers.

Invisibl Skratch Piklz

(1989–2000, 2014–, San Francisco, California)

Invisibl Skratch Piklz is a pioneering American turntablist crew cofounded child-hood friends DJ QBert (Richard Quitevis, 1969–), Mix Master Mike (Michael Schwartz, 1970–), and DJ Apollo (Apollo Novicio, n.d.), who left the group in 1993. They originally used the names Shadow DJs, Rock Steady DJs, and Shadow of the Prophet, before deciding on Invisibl Skratch Piklz. The trio won the international Disco Mix Club (DMC) World DJ Championships three years in a row, before retiring in 1994 after DMC asked them to encourage other turntablist crews to enter competitions. The crew nevertheless continued scratching and later added other personnel, including DJ Disk (Luis Quintanilla, 1970–), Shortkut (Jon Cruz, 1975–), D-Styles (Dave Cuasito, 1972–), DJ Flare (Sean Moran, n.d.), Yogafrog (Ritchie Desuasido, 1974–), and A-Trak (Alain Macklovitch, 1982–). Many members are Filipino American.

From the crew's start, individual members had perfected both foundational skills and advanced turntablist techniques. DJ QBert is often credit as being the innovator of the hamster scratching technique (moving the record album on a turntable backward, then forward). The technique eases one's reach for the mixer and adds speed between scratching and mixing. DJ Flare invented the flare scratch, in which the crossfader is left open so the album playing is heard—the mixer is then quickly closed and reopened, which gives the effect of the album's sound being cut into two separate sounds. Invisibl Skratch Piklz was also the first to apply the band concept to turntablism, where each member treats his turntable as a musical instrument with a specialized sonic role that participates within the larger ensemble.

After its competitive years, Invisibl Skratch Piklz began showcasing its newly created combinations and teaching them to others. In 1996, the crew won a showcase battle with former rival and legendary turntablist crew X-Men (now the X-Ecutioners, 1989–) of New York City. From 1995 to 2000 Invisibl Skratch Piklz assisted in designing products for DJs made by the Danish audio and turntable equipment company Ortofon (1918–) and the Japanese turntable, audio equipment, and musical instrument company Vestax (1977–2014). In addition, the crew developed a DJ tool called a "break record," on which samples are cut up to create ready-made breaks for live performances.

Together, the crew made numerous turntablist instruction videos and websites, as well as participated in turntablist documentaries such as the American film *Scratch* (2001). Shortkut and D-Styles became members of Beat Junkies (aka World Famous Beat Junkies, 1992–). In 1996, Mix Master Mike began working as an added member of the legendary American hip hop group Beastie Boys (1981–2012). Out of his many solo recording endeavors, QBert had a critically acclaimed debut album, *Wave Twisters: Episode 7 Million: Sonic Wars within the Protons* (1998), which marked the beginning of the Invisibl Skratch Piklz's recording label, Galactic Butt Hair Records. But the crew went on a lengthy hiatus starting in 2000.

In contrast to World Famous Beat Junkies, who have a prolific label, the company has since released just one other album, D-Styles' *Return to Planetary Deterioration/Clifford's Mustache* (2001). In 2009, QBert launched QBert Skratch University, an interactive online school and community for DJs, which gives feedback to students learning turntablism. After core members Qbert, Shortkut, and D-Styles reunited under the crew's name, the Invisibl Skratch Piklz released the instrumental/cut-up studio album *The 13th Floor* (2016).

Melissa Ursula Dawn Goldsmith

See also: Battling; DJ QBert; Mix Master Mike; The Philippines; Turntablism; The United States

Further Reading

Katz, Mark. 2012. *Groove Music: The Art and Culture of the Hip Hop DJ.* New York: Oxford University Press.

Wang, Oliver. 2015. *Legions of Boom: Filipino American Mobile DJ Crews in the San Francisco Bay Area.* Durham, NC: Duke University Press.

Further Listening

Invisibl Skratch Piklz. 2016. *The 13th Floor.* Alpha Pup Records.

Iran

Iran has a hip hop scene which is defined by *Rap-e Farsi* (Farsi-language rap), which fuses Western hip hop styles with ancient Persian poetic traditions. *Rap-e Farsi* is part of an underground scene that circumvents religious and governmental restrictions on music production and performance. Though Iranian youth were exposed to Western hip hop in the 1990s through audio recordings, Iran's own form of hip hop emerged in Tehran around 2000, becoming one of the most popular genres for the under-30 demographic that constitutes two-thirds of the Iranian population. Though the Iranian government presently limits performance and production of rap music, a growing number of underground hip hop artists are expanding the artistic potentials of the genre. Bahram Nouraei (1988–), whose breakthrough hit in 2008 directly criticized then-president Mahmoud Ahmadinejad (1956–, in office 2005–2013), is now known for using chronology as a storytelling device, as in his abstract track "Lady Sunshine" (2011) and in the album *Good Mistake* (2015), which is organized according to a reverse chronology. Also part of the underground rap scene are Erfan Hajrasuliha (1983–), Pishro (Mohammad Reza Naseri Azad, 1986–), Ho3ein (Hossein Eblis, 1987–), Ali Sorena (1990–), Shayea (Mohammad Reza, 1982–), Sadegh Vahedi (1990–), and Ashkan Fadaei (1989–).

GROWTH IN THE 2000s

In the early 2000s Hichkas (aka Nobody, Soroush Lashkari, 1985–) began rapping in Tehran. He combined Western urban beats and Iranian instrumentation with lyrics that highlighted social injustice. Considered the father of Iranian hip hop, Hichkas is the lead rapper of the Persian rap supergroup 021 (1990s*), named for Tehran's area code, and he has collaborated with American artist Kool G Rap (Nathaniel Thomas Wilson, 1968–). Authorities arrested Hichkas after the release of his first album, *Jangle Asfalt* (*Asphalt Jungle*, 2006), and he subsequently decided to leave Iran after his release. The first rapper authorized by the Iranian government to perform publicly was Yas (Yaser Bakhtari, 1982–), who claims Tupac Shakur (1971–1996) as a major influence; Yas's lyrics rely heavily on classical Persian poetic imagery, though his delivery style can best be describe as a ferocious torrent of words that communicate uplifting messages about Iranian culture and people.

According to London-based rapper Reveal (Mehrak Golestan, 1983–), the Internet has fostered a transnational community of hip hop artists inside and outside Iran who share music, collaborate, and avoid government censorship. While rappers within Iran often consciously avoid profane language, some of those outside, such as French-based Alireza JJ (Alireza Jazayeri, 1985–) of the pioneering Iranian gangsta rap group Zedbazi (2002–2014), challenges cultural norms by using profanity and coarse subject matter. German-based Shahin Najafi (1980–) has from his youth spoken out against the Iranian government and religious authorities. After the release of his satirical song "I Have a Beard" (2005), he was banned from returning to Iran. Najafi has released albums both independently and as a temporary member of the collective Tapesh 2012 (1998–). He has rapped in support of those killed while protesting the 2009–2010 Iranian elections.

THE 2010s AND CONNECTIONS TO PERSIAN POETRY

Salome MC (1985–), Iran's first female hip hop artist and producer, raps about Iranian political corruption and societal ills from locations in Japan and China. In

2014, she collaborated with Australian hip hop producer and rapper Bastian Killjoy (n.d.) on "Road to Nothing," which alternates texts written by the two with the classical Persian poetry of Omar Khayyám (1048–1131)* to create allegorical lyrics. The intertwining of past poetry and present rap is also seen in the music of Nazila (anonymous, 1987–2012), who made headlines as one of few female rappers in Iran. Her furious, hard-driving rhymes brought attention to the poor and abused, drawing on images from the works of the Persian poet Hafez (1325–1390)*.

Jennifer L. Roth-Burnette

See also: Political Hip Hop

Further Reading

Breyley, G. J. 2014. "Waking Up the Colors: Memory and Allegory in Iranian Hip Hop and Ambient Music." *Australian Literary Studies* 29, nos. 1–2: 107–19.

Shahshahani, Soheila. 2013. "The Sounds of Music in Tehran." *Anthropology of the Middle East* 8, no. 1: 24–39.

Iraq

Iraq has a hip hop scene that is relatively young, due to the suppression of anything associated with Western culture during the reign of Saddam Hussein (1937–2006) from 1979 to 2003, a period that overlapped with the early days of hip hop elsewhere in the world. Said to have sprung from influence of U.S. troops during its occupation of Iraq that began in 2003, Iraqi hip hop culture has been a recent development. Lyrics in Iraqi rap explore themes of violence and war, alienation and anger, ideas that are prominent in hip hop throughout the world. Iraqi rappers note that they have been drawn to the culture because it provides a constructive outlet for their fears and frustrations.

FIRST GULF WAR AND IRAQI HIP HOP

Prior to the United States–led invasion in 2003, particularly in the period following the Gulf War (1990–1991), government control and limitation of Internet and satellite services meant there were few avenues for exposure to outside music, and new music genres were not welcome. Iraqi popular music that predates 2003 is largely based in the folk and classical traditions of the country and is considered conservative compared to music of neighboring countries. State censorship and control set limitations on lyrics, further confining creative output. In stark contrast, some Western popular music, including, hip hop artists such as Eminem (1972–), was heard on Voice of Youth, a radio station owned by Hussein's eldest son, Uday (1965*–2003) and broadcast exclusively in English. While Voice of Youth was seen as Uday's attempt to pander to the youth, its content presented the first exposure to rap music for many young Iraqis. U.S. soldiers brought rap recordings (most predominantly gangsta rap), but they also brought performance; troops report gathering to let off steam through freestyle rapping, without DJs. As the conflict in Iraq escalated and U.S. forces withdrew behind blast walls, American servicemen interacted less frequently and less directly with Iraqi citizens, and the Iraqis were left to their own devices to explore Iraqi hip hop culture, but due to the resurgence of satellite broadcast that followed the overthrow of Saddam Hussein's regime in 2003, more Western culture became available.

FURTHER DEVELOPMENT

Iraqi hip hop is new enough that a canon of performers is still developing, but there are a few who have gained some prominence. In 2009, Danger Zone Killer (aka DZK, 2008*–), a trio of MCs made up of Mr. Passion (Hisham Sabbah, n.d.), J-Fire (Ahmed Farouq, 1986*–), and Nine-Z (anonymous, n.d.), performed at what was likely the first public hip hop concert at the National Theatre in Baghdad. An Arabic diaspora also includes influential rappers of Iraqi birth or descent. Timz (Tommy Hanna, 1985–) was born in El Cajon, California to parents who had fled persecution in Baghdad before his birth. His antiwar song "Iraq" (2007) garnered national attention in the United States. The Narcicyst (aka Narcy, Yassin Alsalman, 1982–) was born in Dubai to Iraqi parents; the family moved to Montreal when he was five. His works have been cited as providing inspiration in the Egyptian uprising during the Arab Spring (2010–2012).

Susannah Cleveland

See also: Kuwait

Further Reading
Arango, Tim, and Yasir Ghazi. 2011. "Baghdad Journal: An Embrace of the United States, Spun and Mixed by Iraqis." *New York Times*, October 13, A13.
Quail, Christine. 2008. "The Politics of Arab Hip Hop: An Interview with the Narcicyst." *Taboo* 12 (Spring): 111–18.

Further Listening
The Narcicyst. 2009. *The Narcicyst.* Paranoid Arab Boy Music.

Ireland

Ireland is known for its ability to keep its traditional music vibrant into the 21st century, despite globalization and influence from the United States and England. Pop and rock music have been part of the Irish music scene since the 1960s, when local Irish bands ("showbands") played American and English hits at dancehalls and clubs across the country, and in many ways Ireland's hip hop artists have followed in their footsteps, making their names locally—some achieve national or international success. Early Irish hip hop acts such as the Rubberbandits (2000–), Messiah J. and the Expert (2002–), and GMC (Garry McCarthy, n.d.), were known for the use of absurd and dark humor in their raps.

Limerick's the Rubberbandits is a highly successful comedy funk and rap duo who perform wearing white plastic bags over their heads. The duo's single "I Want to Fight Your Father" reached the Top 10 of the Irish charts and their YouTube videos routinely top a million views. Messiah J. and the Expert (2002–) is a hip hop duo out of Dublin who loop samples of strings and horns in music that is a fusion of hip hop, indie, reggae, and funk; the duo uses dark humor, creative rapping that includes stutters and groans, and chopper style rapping. GMC (Garry McCarthy,

Initially using an American accent in his R&B infused raps back in 2006, Irish rapper Lethal Dialect has since proudly opted for his working class accent to make socio-political commentary. Hailing from Cabra, a suburb on the northside of Dublin, Lethal Dialect's message rap focuses on Irish daily life and family, as well as cultural and class stereotyping. (C Brandon/Redferns via Getty Images)

n.d.) is a rapper who juxtaposes his lyrics against catchy electronic dance beats and pitch-adjusted vocals, as exemplified in "Not Tonight (The Bouncer Song)" (2004) and "The Whiskey Didn't Help" (2009).

Recent Irish hip hop acts such as Rusangano Family (2014–), Lethal Dialect (2016–), Rob Kelly (1978–), Rejjie Snow (Alex Anyaegbunam, 1993–), and Temper-Mental (aka MissElayneous, Elayne Harrington, 1988–) use rapping more for sociopolitical concerns. The last is a female rapper from the Dublin suburb Finglas who focuses on classism; Temper-Mental is also an advocate for the homeless. With members from Zimbabwe, Togo, and Ireland, Limerick's dance hall and grime trio Rusangano Family (2014–) were an instant hit with the debut album *Let the Dead Bury the Dead* (2016), with songs from the point of view of immigrants. Dublin-based rapper Lethal Dialect is known for his refusal to hide his Irish accent in his laid-back R&B-infused raps. Rob Kelly's debut album *Kel Jefe* (*Celtic Boss*, 2014, a wordplay on Celtic and the Spanish El Jefe, which means the boss) established him as a gangsta style rapper who is fond of metaphor and wordplay. Singer and rapper Rejjie Snow has introduced R&B and G-funk to the Irish scene with seven singles and one album, *The Moon and You* (2017).

Anthony J. Fonseca

See also: Reggae; The United Kingdom

Further Reading

Moriarty, Máiréad. 2015. "Hip Hop, LPP, and Globalization." In *Globalizing Language Policy and Planning: An Irish Language Perspective*, chap. 6. New York: Palgrave Macmillan.

O'Keeffe, Michelle. 2002. "Graffiti Woz 'ere: Irish Graffiti Artists—Or Vandals, Depending on Your Perspective—Or Work; But Then, That's Part of the Buzz." *Irish Times*, April 27, 74.

Further Listening

Rusangano Family. 2016. *Let the Dead Bury the Dead.* Self-released.

Israel

Israel, created in 1947 through a United Nations partition plan to create independent Arab and Jewish states, is a Middle East Mediterranean and primarily Jewish country of nearly nine million that borders various Arabic countries: Lebanon; Syria; Jordan; the Palestinian territories; and Egypt. The country's musical traditions are a hybridization of Jewish (especially Yemenite), other Middle Eastern, Russian traditional, and German cabaret, as well as American and British classical, jazz, pop, and rock, and world music. Israeli hip hop began in the 1980s with rap parody and caught on as Ethiopian youth migrated to and brought their musical traditions as well as the concerns of minority diaspora. A small number of artists perform hip hop with a Zionist message, whereas most Israeli hip hop focuses on urban concerns such as poverty and social equality.

After the Six Day War of 1967, Israel's cultural and economic standing increased drastically, and rock music became internationalized and popular with acts such as the Churchills (1965–1973) and Shalom Hanoch (1946–). Also in the 1960s, Mizrahi music, a genre that combines indigenous elements, Middle Eastern instruments, Greek bouzouki, rock guitars, Western instruments, melismas, ornamentation, minor keys, and the Western 12-tone scale (chromatic scale), became influential. In addition, the World War II (1939–1945) rise of cabarets led to music that was more upbeat and in a major key, which eventually gave rise to Israel's pop music scene and its stars, including folk singer-songwriters Etti Ankri (Esther Ankri, 1963–), Chava Alberstein (1947–), and Shlomo Artzi (1949–); pop singers David D'Or (David Nehaisi, 1965–), Ivri Lider (1974–), and Dana International (Sharon Cohen, 1945–); rock musicians Aviv Gefen (1973–) and Rita (Rita Yahan-Farouz, 1962–); electronica and world music composer-musician Idan Raichel (1977–); and metal and progressive acts HaYehudim (1992–), Danny Sanderson (1950–), and Arik Einstein (Arieh Lieb Einstein, 1939–2013).

Israeli hip hop began in 1986 when rock keyboardist Yair Nitzani (1958–) released an old-school hip hop parody single, "Hashem Tamid" (1986); in 1993, Nitzani produced the old-school rap album *Humus Metamtem*, with Jamaican Jewish MC Nigel Haadmor (Yehoshua Sofer, 1958–) and bassist and producer Yossi Fine (Joseph Thomas Fine, 1964–). By the 1990s, Ethiopian youth who had migrated to Israel were beginning to identify with reggae and hip hop as musical modes of expression for black youth. In 1995, after a Beastie Boys (1981–2012) tour, rock band Shabak

Samech (aka Shabak S, 1992–2000, 2007–) began rapping in Hebrew. In 1996, two Israeli radio DJs, Quami de la Fox (Eyal Freedman, n.d.) and Liron Teeni (n.d.), cocreated *Esek Shachor* (*Black Business*), the first hip hop radio show.

There are many contemporary hip hop acts in Israel: the rapper BOCA (1991–), a Soviet Israeli immigrant who released his first mixtape in 2010 and his first album, *I.H.H.A.*, in 2011; rap group Hadag Nahash (1996–), which has a sound infused by roots music, funk, jazz, and pop, and was the first Israeli mainstream rap success; rapper Subliminal (Ya'akov Kobi Shimoni, 1979*–), who is famous for popularizing Zionist hip hop, praising military service; producer and rapper SHI 360 (aka Supreme Hebrew Intelekt, Shai Haddad, n.d.), who spent his childhood in Montreal, where he began his rap career but returned to Israel to create sociopolitical rap songs; Jerusalem-based MC Sagol 59 (Khen Rotem, 1968–), who went from blues, funk, and rock to hip hop and has recorded five studio albums to datethe duo Strong Black Coffee (aka Café Shahor Hazak, 2014–); and actor Alon De Loco (Alon Cohen, 1974–), a music producer and DJ as well as breakdancer who has released three albums as of 2018.

Anthony J. Fonseca

See also: Ethiopia; Political Hip Hop; Russia

Further Reading
Dorchin, Uri. 2015. "Conservative Innovators: Reviving Israeli Spirit through Black Music." *Journal of Popular Music Studies* 27, no. 2: 199–217.
Korat, Yael. 2007. "Israeli Hip Hop as a Democratic Platform: Zionism, Anti-Zionism, and Post Zionism." *Anamesa* 5, no. 1: 43–58.

Further Listening
Hadag Nahash. 2010. *6.* Eighth Note.

Italy

Italy is a Southern European parliamentary republic of 61 million that juts out into the Mediterranean Sea, sharing land borders with countries such as France, Switzerland, Austria, and Slovenia. The Italian hip hop scene began between the late 1980s and early 1990s, as posse tracks (rap songs that have verses sung by various rappers) became popular with youth. Italy's pioneer hip hop acts included the American East Coast–influenced, Milan-based underground crew Articolo 31 (1990–2006) and singer-songwriter and rapper Jovanotti (aka Jova, Lorenzo Cherubini, 1966–), who united rap with Italian pop.

Having had such a lengthy history, Italian music ranges from classical and opera to traditional, sacred (Gregorian chants, used in Roman Catholic mass) to popular, with traditional Italian music being tied closely to ethnic identity, and Northern Italian music being Celtic-influenced while Southern Italian is Mediterranean. Traditional Italian instrumentation includes *organetto* (a type of accordion), guitar, mandolin, brass instruments, various flutes, clarinet, violin, *tammora* (a hand drum with bells, played like a tambourine), various percussions, and sometimes bagpipes.

Opera, as well as other Western art vocal and instrumental music, is historically a part of Italian identity, as are the folksy Neapolitan songs (*canzone napoletana*) and their associated *cantautori* (singer-songwriter) traditions.

Industrialization urbanized Italian culture, and immigration from Africa, Asia, and other European countries led to musical diversity. The French Café *chantant* was introduced in the 1890s, and American jazz and swing made its way into Italy in the 1910s as Italian musicians traveled abroad and returned with American and Latin American influences. Foreign music was censored during the Fascist regime, which ended after World War II. Protest music became popular in the 1960s, as did English rock and pop, including synthpop, rap, and techno, with Italy becoming influential in the electronic dance music scene, with *Italo disco* emerging and Academy Award winner Giorgio Moroder (Giovanni Giorgio Moroder, 1940–) coming to prominence in the late 1970s; about the same time, Italy saw the emergence of the progressive rock movement, and bands such as Goblin (1972–1982, 2005–) achieved international fame through film music.

Articolo 31 combined hip hop with funk, pop, and traditional Italian music, and its founders, rapper J-Ax (Alessandro Aleotti, 1972–) and DJ Jad (Vito Luca Perrini, n.d.), signed with BMG Ricordi (Bertelsmann Music Group, 1987–2008), which led to commercial success but resulted in diss tracks aimed at them by other underground rappers. Jovanotti evolved from a simple rap and disco sound toward a much more complex sound that included funk, ska, world music, and symphonic arrangements, and his raps became concerned with spiritual and political issues.

Also in 1990, the short-lived Italian rap band Sangue Misto (1990–1994) popularized raggamuffin and reggae music. Other popular early Italian hip hop acts include rappers Kaos One (Marco Fiorito, 1971–), Fabri Fibra (Fabrizio Tarducci, 1976–), Clementino (Clemente Maccaro, 1982–), and Noyz Narcos (aka White Zombie, Emanuele Frasca, 1979–), and groups such as Varese-based Otierre (OTR, short for Originale Trasmissione del Ritmo, or Original Rhythm Transmission, 1991–1997). More recently, two young rappers reached the peak of fame: Fedez and Emis Killa. Kaos One came onto the hip hop scene in 1985 as a dancer breakdancer and writer, but soon began rapping in both English and Italian and went on to release five solo albums.

Senigallia-born Fabri Fibra (1976–) recorded his demo in 1995 and formed the underground rap duo Uomini di Mare (1995–1999), going solo in 2000 and establishing a record label, Teste Mobili Records (Bobbing Head Records, 1996–), on which he released his debut album, *Turbe Giovanili* (2002). Avellino-born Clementino, who like Fabri Fibra came from the group Rapstar (2011–), is known for his freestyle. Rome-based Noyz Narcos, member of the collective TruceKlan (2008), started out in a grindcore group before becoming a rapper. More recent hip hop artists include Milan-born Fedez (Federico Leonardo Lucia, 1989–) and Vimercate-born Emis Killa (Emiliano Rudolf Giambelli, 1989–).

Anthony J. Fonseca

See also: Hip House; Industrial Hip Hop

Further Reading

Androutsopoulos, Jannis, and Arno Scholz. 2003. "Spaghetti Funk: Appropriations of Hip Hop Culture and Rap Music in Europe." *Popular Music and Society* 26, no. 4: 463–79.

Bordin, Elisa. 2013. "Graffiti Goes to Italy: Weaving Transnational Threads of All Sizes and Colors." In *Hip Hop in Europe: Cultural Identities and Transnational Flows*, edited by Sina A. Nitzsche and Walter Grünzweig, chap. 15. Zürich, Switzerland: LIT Verlag.

Santoro, Marco, and Marco Solaroli. 2007. "Authors and Rappers: Italian Hip Hop and the Shifting Boundaries of Canzone d'Autore." *Popular Music* 26, no. 3: 463–88.

Further Listening

Emis Killa. 2016. *Terza stagione* (*Third Season*). Carosello Records.

Fabri Fibra. 2010. *Controcultura* (*Counterculture*). Universal Music Group.

Noyz Narcos. 2013. *Monster.* Propaganda Records/Quadraro Basement.

Ivory Coast

The Ivory Coast is an independent West African republic that was at one time colonized by France, until 1960, when it achieved independence under tribal chief and French Parliament member Félix Houphouët-Boigny (1905–1993, in power, 1960–1993), though since his death the country has experienced one coup d'état, in 1999, and a new constitution, in 2000. The county's music is influenced by a variety of ethnic communities, many of which use vocal polyphony and polyrhythmic drums, and popular traditional music styles include the satirical political *zouglou* style, West African percussion and bass-based *coupé-décalé*, folk rhythm–based *gbégbé*, Caribbean-influenced *zouk*, R&B, reggae, pop, and to a lesser degree (because it is considered a foreign music), hip hop.

Since 1998, an annual battle event known as "Le Défi" ("The Challenge") takes place in the country's capital city, Abidjan. Ivorian popular music can be traced to Daloa-based guitarist Ernesto Djédjé (1948–1983), who used Congolese folk rhythms and the *dopé* style with modern instruments to create what would become a new subgenre called *ziglibithy*. Reggae became popular with the emergence of Dimbokro-based Alpha Blondy (Seydou Koné, 1953–) and Odienné-based Tiken Jah Fakoly (Doumbia Moussa Fakoly, 1968–), who both helped popularize Afro-reggae. Grand Bassam–based Freddy Meiway (Frederic Desire Ehui, 1962–) pioneered a new electronic dance sound called *zoblazo*. Ivorian hip hop, which began around the mid-1990s at the University of Abidjan, is highly influenced by American gangsta rap, which was localized to become *rap dogba*; however, as of 2018, no Ivorian rappers have achieved popularity beyond the local level.

Few diaspora acts have attained international celebrity. One example is rapper Dynamic Boobah Siddik (aka Mastah Boobah, Boobah Siddik, n.d.), who is from Abidjan, settled in Dakar, Senegal, and is a founding member of hardcore political hip hop and reggae fusion collective, Shadow Zu (1995–). Since 2003, he has had a solo career, switching from French to English in 2004 to reach a larger audience. Also from Abidjan, Rammy (Rammy Kouyaté, n.d.) is a female rapper, songwriter, and poet pursuing her career in Washington, DC, after having earned her master's in English from the University of Abidjan. Rammy records hip hop and R&B in both French and English, focusing on love as well as her own Mandinka heritage. Rapper, producer, and educator SΔmmus (aka Sammus, Enongo Lumumba-Kasongo, 1986–) was born in Ithaca, New York and is of Ivorian and Congolese descent; however her focus is on American nerdcore.

Anthony J. Fonseca and Melissa Ursula Dawn Goldsmith

See also: France; Reggae

Further Reading

Akombo, David. 2016. "The Music and Dance of Côte d'Ivoire." In *The Unity of Music and Dance in World Cultures*, chap. 3. Jefferson, NC: McFarland.

Reed, Daniel B. 2012. "Promises of the Chameleon: Reggae Artist Tiken Jah Fakoly's Intertextual Contestation of Power in Côte d'Ivoire." In *Hip Hop Africa: New African Music in a Globalizing World*, edited by Eric Charry, chap. 4. Bloomington: Indiana University Press.

Ivy Queen

(Martha Ivelisse Pesante Rodríguez, 1972–, Añasco, Puerto Rico)

Ivy Queen, also known as the Queen of Reggaetón, is a bilingual hip hop, R&B, *bachata*, and *reggaetón* singer and rapper, as well as a songwriter, record producer, and actor. She is known for her striking image, which includes long acrylic nails (which she emphasizes in her music videos), her alto vocal range, comparable to Missy Elliott (1971–) and Cher (1946–), her breathless and heavily syncopated vocal deliveries, and her use of unconventional instrumentation in her music. Her songs often incorporate a Caribbean influence, using traditional ethnic instruments such as kettledrums and accordions, as well as offbeat instruments such as harpsichords. Her lyrics encourage feminism, challenge the double standards of infidelity, and explore homosexuality and the power structures in male–female relationships.

Born in Añasco, Puerto Rico, she moved with her parents to New York City, where she studied at the New Jersey School of Performing Arts and lived until the age of 18. She then moved to San Juan, Puerto Rico, and met record producer DJ Negro (anonymous, n.d.)* and performed with the Noise (1992–2004), a rap group from San Juan that infused reggaetón with urban and gangsta rap. In 1996, she began a solo career; Sony distributed her debut and second albums *En mi imperio* (*In My Empire*, 1997) and *The Original Rude Girl* (1998). The label dropped her after sluggish sales, so she took a hiatus from music, and for her third album, *Diva* (2003), she signed with the short-lived Real Music, Inc. (2003–2004), an independent label out of Miami.

Follow-up studio albums *Diva, Flashback* (2005) and *Sentimiento* (2006) attained Gold and Platinum certification. Her seventh album, *Drama Queen* (2010) produced a Top 10 single, "La vida es así" ("Life Is So"). *Musa* (2012) earned a Grammy nomination. Ivy Queen's latest album, *Vendetta* (2015), was actually four separate simultaneously released albums (urban contemporary, hip hop, bachata, and salsa, with eight songs devoted to each genre).

Also known as The Queen of Reggaetón, singer-songwriter, rapper, record producer, and actor Ivy Queen performs in both Spanish and English. In 2005, the Puerto Rican musician, who also performs bachata, salsa, R&B, and hip hop, founded her own sound recording label, Filtro Musik, which is now known as Ivy Queen Musa Sound Corporation. (Scott Dudelson/Getty Images)

In 2005, Ivy Queen cofounded her own record label in San Juan, Filtro Musik (now Ivy Queen Musa Sound Corporation, 2005–), and Univision Records (2001–2008) signed Filtro Musik to promote *Flashback*. *Sentimiento* was a departure for her as it marked her move toward performing solo rather than in duets with guest singers and rappers. In 2010, she signed with Machete Music (2005–), a San Juan–based subsidiary of Universal Music Latin Entertainment (2008–). The resulting album, *Drama Queen*, peaked at No. 163 on the Billboard 200 and No. 3 on Top Latin Albums. In 2009, Ivy Queen launched a reggaetón doll through Global Trading Partners.

Anthony J. Fonseca

See also: Puerto Rico; Reggaetón; The United States

Further Reading

Báez, Jillian M. 2006. "En mi imperio": Competing Discourses of Agency in Ivy Queen's Reggaetón." *Centro Journal* 18, no. 2: 62–81.

Samponaro, Philip. 2009. "'Oye mi canto' ['Listen to my song']: The History and Politics of Reggaetón." *Popular Music and Society* 32, no. 4: 489–506.

J

J Dilla

(aka Jay Dee, James Dewitt Yancey, 1974–2006, Detroit, Michigan)

J Dilla was an American record producer and rapper who was best known for working with benchmark artists such as A Tribe Called Quest (1985–1998, 2006–2013, 2015–), De La Soul (1987–), Busta Rhymes (1972–), Erykah Badu (1971–), the Roots (1987–), the Pharcyde (1989–), and Common (1972–). He was also part of the Ummah (1996–1999), a production collective that included Q-Tip (Jonathan William Davis, 1970–), Ali Shaheed Muhammad (1970–), and Raphael Saadiq (1966–). He gained immediate recognition after producing seven songs for the Pharcyde's rap and hip hop album *Labcabincalifornia* (1995) and programming Poe's (Annie Decatur Danielewski, 1968–) electronic rock debut album *Hello* (1995), both under the name Jay Dee. He was also a member of the influential Soulquarians collective (late 1990s–2000s).

J Dilla was part of the underground hip hop scene in 1990s Detroit. The child of musicians, he was considered a music prodigy: at two years old he collected vinyl albums and would entertain others by playing the records at a park. Funk musician Amp Fiddler (Joseph Anthony Fiddler, 1965–) discovered J Dilla and encouraged his musical talents. By high school, though reclusive and artistic, J Dilla cofounded a rap group called Slum Village (1990–) and produced its first album, which got the attention of the local hip hop scene. It was the band's second effort, *Fantastic, Vol. 2*, which made J Dilla a star producer and MC.

He debuted as a soloist with 2001's *Welcome 2 Detroit*, under the name Jay Dee aka J Dilla. He moved to Los Angeles and cofounded the duo Jaylib in 2002, releasing *Champion Sound* (2003), which he produced. By this time, he was already very ill with a rare blood coagulation disease and lupus. He eventually performed in a wheelchair. J Dilla died three days after releasing *Donuts* (2006), a collection of beats created while in the hospital.

His sound is experimental and atmospheric, with liberal use of sound samples and musical hiccups (reverb, reversals, and the like). Reports circulated that over 100 beats he created before his death survived. *Champion Sound* was reissued in June 2007, and *Yancey Boys*, the debut album by younger brother Illa J (John Derek Yancey, 1986–), produced entirely by J Dilla, was released in 2008.

The Yancey Media Group (2013–), as well as the J Dilla Foundation (2010–), was founded by his mother in his honor. In 2014, J Dilla's family donated a significant number of artifacts, including his custom-made Minimoog Voyager synthesizer that he used to create beats, to the Smithsonian's National Museum of African American History and Culture. As of 2018, the number of hip hop acts which honor J Dilla's memory through verses that mention him and beats dedicated to him continues to grow.

Anthony J. Fonseca

See also: The United States

Further Reading

Bua, Justin. 2011. "J Dilla." *The Legends of Hip Hop.* New York: Harper Design.

Furguson, Jordan. 2014. *J Dilla's "Donuts."* New York: Bloomsbury.

Gholz, Carleton S. 2010. "Welcome to tha D: Making and Remaking Hip Hop Culture in Post-Motown Detroit." In *Hip Hop in America: A Regional Guide*, edited by Mickey Hess, vol. 2, chap. 16. Santa Barbara, CA: Greenwood.

Jaa9 and OnklP

(2003–, Lillehammer, Norway)

Jaa9 and OnklP is a Norwegian hip hop duo. Both Jaa9 (Johnny Engdal Silseth, 1982–) and OnklP (Pål Tøien, 1984–) are members of Dirty Oppland (2002–), a Lillehammer rap collective that combines elements of American East Coast gangsta and Southern rap, but with Norwegian texts. The duo's rap songs are concerned with consciousness raising in areas such as negative gangster behavior (e.g., thug life, womanizing, drugs, and battles or conflicts), Norwegian pride, selling out, and partying. Songs use wordplay, such as dual meaning, which makes English translations of the texts extremely challenging.

Jaa9 and OnklP's first full album-length recording was *Bondegrammatikk: The Mixtape* (*Peasants' Grammar: The Mixtape*, 2003), which included a cover of American rapper Busta Rhymes' (1972–) and pop singer Mariah Carey's (1970–) hip hop and R&B hit, "I Know What You Want" (2003). As of 2018, *Bondegrammatikk* is Norway's best-selling mixtape. The duo have released five subsequent albums, *Sjåre brymæ* (*Firm Breasts*, 2004), *Bondedramatikk: En gateplate* (*Peasants' Drama: A Street Record*, 2008), *Sellout!* (2009), *Føkk ferie* (*Take a Holiday*, 2015), and *Gamle hunder, nye triks* (*Old Dogs, New Tricks*, 2016). It has also produced the EPs *Lasse* (2011), *Geir* (2011), and *Diskoteket er stengt* (*The Disco Is Closed*, 2014). *Sellout!* and *Lasse* were recorded on contract for the Sony Music (1929–) labels and peaked on Norway's official hit albums chart, the VG-Lista, at Nos. 21 and 23, respectively. *Sellout!* was also recorded on the Columbia Records (1887–) label, as was *Geir*, which peaked at No. 31 on the VG-Lista.

The duo's most successful album, *Sjåre brymæ*, a combination of mostly hip hop with a little pop and some humorous skits, reached No. 3 on the VG-Lista. Following this success, the duo contacted 1970s pop singer Dag Spantell (1950–) from Oslo to make a hip hop cover of the verses from his hit Norwegian version of Ricky Nelson's (Eric Hilliard Nelson, 1940–1985) own Top 40 country-rock hit "Garden Party" (1972), titled "Kjendis-party" (1973). Spantell, whose voice resembles Freddy Fender's (Baldemar Garza Huera, 1937–2006) tenor, along with its treble, had a hit with "Kjendis-party," which reached No. 4 on Norsktoppen, an official list for Norway's top singles. Jaa9 and OnklP's version, released on *Sjåre brymæ*, also became a popular hit in Norway, peaking at No. 2 on the VG-Lista hit singles chart. It helped spark a comeback career for the retired Spantell, who at times performed with Jaa9 and OnklP in concert.

Since 2013, Jaa9 and OnklP have recorded on the Knirckefritt (2011*–) label in Oslo, which has a distribution agreement with Universal Music AS, Norway (1977*–). Jaa9 and OnklP's second most successful album, *Diskoteket er stengt*, peaked at No. 11 on the VG-Lista. Throughout their career as Jaa9 and OnklP, Engdal and Tøien have concurrently recorded with Dirty Oppland, separately. Tøien has also collaborated with pop and punk bands such as Oslo Ess (2010–).

Melissa Ursula Dawn Goldsmith

See also: Beastie Boys; Dirty South; Gangsta Rap; Norway

Further Reading

Brunstad, Endre, Unn Røyneland, and Toril Opsahl. 2010. "Hip Hop, Ethnicity and Linguistic Practice in Rural and Urban Norway." In *The Languages of Global Hip Hop*, edited by Marina Terkourafi, chap. 9. New York: Continuum.

Uberg Naerland, Torgeir. 2014. "Hip Hop and the Public Sphere: Political Commitment and Communicative Practices on the Norwegian Hip Hop Scene." *Javnost* 21, no. 1: 37–52.

Further Listening

Jaa9 and OnklP. 2004. *Sjåre brymæ (Firm Breasts)*. Beatservice Records/C+C Records.

Jam Master Jay

(Jason Mizell, 1965–2002, Brooklyn, New York)

Jam Master Jay is best known as the American DJ and turntablist for the legendary East Coast hip hop group Run-D.M.C. (1981–2002) from the Hollis neighborhood of Queens, New York. Run-D.M.C. was one of the earliest hip hop groups to cross over and have hits in the popular music mainstream. The trio, consisting of Jam Master Jay, with rappers and vocalists D.M.C. (Darryl Mc Daniel, 1964–) and Run (born Joseph Simmons, 1964–) became the first hip hop act to attain Gold, Platinum, and multi-Platinum album certifications in the United States, as well as the first Grammy nomination. Run-D.M.C. was also the first hip hop group to have music videos broadcast on MTV (1981–) and its image appear on the cover of *Rolling Stone* magazine. Jam Master Jay appears on all of Run-D.M.C.'s recording output. He also created his own label, Jam Master Jay Records (aka JMJ Records, 1989–2002), and mentored 50 Cent (1975–). Before his murder in 2002, he had founded the Scratch DJ Academy in New York, where he was committed to teaching others the art of DJing (turntablism) and music production. In 2009, he was inducted into the Rock and Roll Hall of Fame as part of Run-D.M.C.

EARLY YEARS

Born Jason Mizell, he took an early interest in music and began playing any musical instrument to which he had access, starting with the trumpet, at age three.

In 1975, his family moved from Brooklyn to Queens, where he learned to play guitar, bass, and drums. As a multi-instrumentalist, he was an especially talented guitarist. His other access to music was through church, where he performed in choirs and bands. Coincidentally, he was related to the successful Los Angeles music production duo, the Mizell Brothers (1970*–2011), consisting of Larry Mizell (1944–) and his older brother Fonce (Alphonso Mizell, 1943–2011). As jazz musicians who developed the sound of 1970s jazz-funk, the Mizell Brothers hit a successful stride when Motown moved to Los Angeles. This success, however, was at best a distant family story for Jason Mizell, who lived across the country.

By the time he was 13, he started playing turntables at parties and became interested in DJing and mixing. While living briefly in Atlantic City, New Jersey, he took mixing lessons from DJ Def Lou Hauck (n.d.), who taught him cross-fading skills (just one example of these skills includes fading out one album while fading another one in).

By the early 1980s, he played turntables at parties, parks, and some nightclubs, making enough money to purchase his first pair of Technics 1200s, which were the most sought after turntables for DJing, mixing, and scratching. He started using the name Jazzy Jase professionally and began wearing leather jackets, fedoras, gold link chains, and large gold rings to attract attention. He took a band approach to turntablism, thinking of himself as a band member, as he practiced and improved by performing with garage bands. He employed regular scratching and mastered cross-fading complex musical samples while playing albums. His style used a light touch, particularly on scratching.

RUN-D.M.C.

Meanwhile, two rappers who performed under the names Run and D.M.C. grew up together and had just finished high school. Run's older brother was Russell Simmons (1957–), who at the time was an aspiring hip hop promoter. With limited earlier recording experience, Simmons was looking to record again. In 1982, Mizell met both Run and D.M.C. at the Two-Fifths Park in Hollis, Queens. Run and D.M.C. rapped with him at the park and they became friends. With the encouragement of Simmons to recruit him and rename him Jam Master Jay, they joined together as a hip hop trio. Jam Master Jay had the idea for the trio's name: Run-D.M.C., and Simmons, who cofounded Def Jam Recordings (1983–) in New York City, began producing the trio. Run-D.M.C.'s first single "It's Like That (Sucker MCs)" (1983) peaked at No. 15 on Billboard's Hot R&B/Hip-Hop Songs chart. With the success of its first single and Simmons's help, Run-D.M.C. signed a major recording contract with Profile Records (1981–).

Run D.M.C.'s eponymous debut label was released a year later with some modest success. The album established the trio's style, which included Jam Master Jay's turntablism, Run and D.M.C.'s socially conscious rapping texts, and a hard rock edge and popular rock samples. The trio's follow-ups, *King of Rock* (1985) and *Raising Hell* (1986), brought far greater success with hit singles such as "King of Rock" and "Can You Rock It Like This." *King of Rock* attained Platinum status, but *Raising Hell* eventually attained triple Platinum certification, peaked at No. 6 on the Billboard 200 and No. 1 on Billboard's Top R&B/Hip-Hop Albums chart, and garnered strong critical acclaim. Run-D.M.C. also appeared in films at this time, including *Krush Groove* (1985), a fictionalized version of Simmons's efforts to start Def Jam. Though *Tougher Than Leather* (1988) was less successful than *Raising Hell*, the album attained Platinum certification. *Tougher Than Leather* was tied to the motion picture of the same title, directed by Rick Rubin (Frederick Jay Rubin, 1963–), which was a critical failure. The album was more sample-heavy than the previous albums and did not employ as much rap-rock, for which Run-D.M.C. became known. Instead, Jam Master Jay, who used his real name on album credits, opted for many funk and soul samples.

JAM MASTER JAY RECORDS

In 1989, he launched Jam Master Jay Records, which attained a half dozen notable hip hop artists, starting with the gangsta rap group Onyx (1988–) from Queens and rapper Jayo Felony (Jame Savage, 1969–) from San Diego, California. Meanwhile, Run-D.M.C. released its worst selling album, *Back from Hell* (1990), which incorporated new jack swing, and took a three-year hiatus. In 1993, Onyx had a hit single, "Slam," which reach No. 4 on the Billboard Hot 100. The same year, Onyx's debut studio album *Bacdaf—up* was certified Platinum and Run-D.M.C. released *Down with the King*, which was a return to the trio's earlier sound and was better received than *Back from Hell*.

For his label, Jam Master Jay wore several hats as producer, A&R (talent searching and developing), and mentoring. In 1996, he found his most famous recruit, 50 Cent (1975–). Like Jayo Felony (n.d.), who was a member of the Crips gang, 50 Cent had experienced a life of crime and violence, though had a talent as a rapper and writer. Jam Master Jay both mentored 50 Cent and gave him music lessons that taught him how to count measures and structure his songs. He remained on the JMJ Records label for just on year (1998–1999) before moving onto huge success with his debut studio album *Get Rich or Die Tryin'* (2003) on larger labels such as Eminem's (1972–) Shady Records (1999–) and Dr. Dre's (1965–) Aftermath Entertainment (1996–).

After another hiatus, Run-D.M.C. released *Crown Royal* (2001), its final album. Though the album peaked at No. 37 on the Billboard 200 and 22 on the Top R&B/Hip-Hop Albums chart, it attained mixed critical reception. Since *Back from Hell*, Run-D.M.C. had difficulties shaking an outdated old-school hip hop image, even though Run-D.M.C. inspired many new artists. In addition, both he and Simmons, who managed Run-D.M.C., were contributing to the development and success of new hip hop acts.

MURDER AND UNSOLVED MYSTERY

In 2002, Jam Master Jay was getting ready to begin another chapter of his life. As part of Run-D.M.C., which was responsible for giving hip hop mainstream recognition, he was inspiring public interest in turntablism. He had founded the Scratch DJ Academy in New York, teaching turntablism and music production. In October 2002 an unknown assailant shot and murdered Jam Master Jay at his recording studio in Queens. Another victim and witness to the crime, Urieco Rincon (1977–), survived his gunshot wound to the ankle. The most popular theory of the murder is that the shooting was a payback execution of some kind. In 2003, Supreme (Kenneth McGriff, 1960–), an American drug trafficker and friend of recording label Murder Inc.'s (1997–) cofounder Irv Gotti (Irving Domingo Lorenzo Jr., 1970–), was investigated for targeting Jam Master Jay because he had signed 50 Cent. In "Ghetto Qu'ran" (1999), 50 Cent had written about McGriff and his Queens gang, the Supreme Team. Another detail supporting the payback theory emerged in 2007 when federal prosecutors named rapper Tenad (Ronald Washington, n.d.) as an accomplice to the murder, claiming that he pointed his gun at the studio to cover for the murderer. Federal prosecutors also named him as a suspect in the 1995 murder of American hardcore rapper and producer Stretch (Randy Walker, 1968–1995), a close friend and collaborator of Tupac Shakur (1971–1996). Despite being named, Tenad was never convicted, and Jam Master Jay's murder remains unsolved.

This tragedy put an end to Run-D.M.C. and JMJ Records, though his Scratch DJ Academy continues with many locations in the United States today. Notable turntablists such as GrandWizard Theodore (now Grand Wizzard Theodore, 1963–) have taught there. In 2009, Run-D.M.C. became the second hip hop group to be inducted into the Rock and Roll Hall of Fame, after Grandmaster Flash and the Furious Five (1976–1982, 1987–1988). In 2012, *Spin* magazine named Jam Master Jay one of the greatest guitarists of all time because of his ability to transform sampled guitar sounds.

Melissa Ursula Dawn Goldsmith

See also: 50 Cent; Run-D.M.C.; Turntablism

Further Reading

Katz, Mark. 2012. *Groove Music: The Art and Culture of the Hip Hop DJ.* New York: Oxford University Press.

Ronin Ro. 2005. *Raising Hell: The Reign, Ruin, and Redemption of Run-D.M.C. and Jam Master Jay.* New York: Harper-Collins.

Thigpen, David E. 2003. *Jam Master Jay: The Heart of Hip Hop.* New York: Pocket Star Books.

Further Listening

Run-D.M.C. 1984. *Run-D.M.C.* Profile Records.

Run-D.M.C. 1986. *Raising Hell.* Profile Records.

Run-D.M.C. 2015. *Live at the Apollo.* Egg Raid.

Jamaica

Jamaica is a Caribbean island nation that gained its independence in 1962 from the United Kingdom. Because it is a tourist destination, American hip hop reached Jamaica in the early 1980s and grew in popularity in the 1990s, as access to

American television improved, despite the fact that the Jamaican music industry does not support local Jamaican hip hop; however, because it is home to reggae, ragga, dancehall, and dubstep, as well as toasting, Jamaica's influence on American hip hop is rich and plentiful. For example, toasting—improvised braggadocio poetry spoken into a mic to excite a dance crowd or a party audience—was influential to the development of rap and the role of the American hip hop DJ. A major distinction between Jamaican dancehall/reggae deejays and hip hop DJs is that the former do not select albums. Instead, Jamaican deejays are speech-singers who perform at parties, toasting to an instrumental accompaniment called *riddim* (Jamaica patois for "rhythm"). The speech-singing is often a monotone melody or chant that uses alliteration and vocal techniques such as stuttering. If singing is used, the deejay is called a *singjay*.

These riddims are the musical grooves found in reggae, ragga, dancehall, dubstep, soca, and other kinds of music, and they have classifications such as "Diwali," "Kopa," "Nanny Goat," and "Real Rock"; some are named after recorded songs. The idea of the riddim was essential in hip hop, dubstep, reggaetón, and grime. Jamaican deejays who choose particular riddims are selectors, and these Jamaican deejays, such as toasters King Stitt (Winston Sparkes, 1940–2012) and U-Roy (aka the Originator, Ewart Beckford, 1942–) began using the instrumental version side of popular 45 RPM records to make their own toasts, often in English or Jamaican patois, but sometimes adding Ethiopian Amharic lines as a tribute to former Ethiopian emperor Haile Selassie I (Ras Tafari Makonnen Woldemikael, 1892–1975), whose reign from 1930 to 1974, according to Rastafarianism, fulfilled Biblical prophecy.

But it was an American immigrant from Kingston, Jamaica, DJ Kool Herc (1955–), who originated hip hop. Starting in 1972, DJ Kool Herc employed aspects of dancehall deejaying, including toasting, incorporating salsa and African percussions, and using a sound system inspired by the Jamaican sound system. Including deejays, music engineers, and MCs who perform reggae, dancehall, ska, and rocksteady music, the Jamaican sound system emerged in the 1950s in Kingston, became popular in the 1970s, and would eventually be used in jungle, drum and bass, and EDM. Other Jamaican influences found in American hip hop culture include the notion of bling-bling (originally an anticolonial sentiment), which is American slang for elaborate or excessive jewelry, accessories, gold coins, money, and grillz (gold or diamond capping over teeth). In addition, lyrical topics such as (militant) pan-Africanism and smoking marijuana, as well as remix culture, existed in reggae and dancehall music long before hip hop.

Several Jamaican reggae musicians either perform or fuse reggae and dancehall with hip hop. Legendary reggae singer-songwriter and guitarist Bob Marley's (Robert Nesta Marley, 1945–1981) youngest son, Damian Marley (aka Jr. Gong, 1978–) has worked with American rapper Nas (1973–) on the collaboration studio album *Distant Relatives* (2010), which peaked at No. 5 on the Billboard 200 and No. 1 on Billboard's Top R&B/Hip-Hop Albums chart. Half brother Ky-Mani Marley's (1976–) studio album *Radio* (2007) marks the beginning of his fusing reggae with hip hop. Internationally known reggae singer-songwriter, rapper, and deejay Shaggy (1968–) has fused the two genres as well. Other Jamaican musicians who perform techno, house, and dancehall have been influenced by hip hop, including Echomatik (2016–), Redselector (Christopher Edmonds, n.d.), and Equiknoxx (aka Equiknoxx Music, 2000–).

One of the most successful Jamaican hip hop artists is Five Steez (Peter Wright, 1986–), who won critical acclaim for his debut studio album, *War for Peace* (2012). Rapping in English and Jamaican patois, Five Steez focuses on autobiography, Kingston daily life and pride, gorgeous women, attaining wealth, smoking marijuana, and protesting police brutality. He is one of the founders of Kingston's main hip hop event, Pay Attention (2012–), a showcase and party. Rapper, singer-songwriter, producer, and actor Sean Paul (Sean Paul Ryan Francis Henriques, 1973–), like Shaggy, raps and toasts in English and records reggae, dancehall, ragga, and hip hop. His second studio album, *Dutty Rock* (2004), won a Grammy Award for Best Reggae Album, peaking at No. 9 on the Billboard 200. Other Jamaican dancehall singer-songwriters who incorporate hip hop are Vybz Kartel (aka Worl' Boss, Adidja Azim Palmer, 1976–) and Elephant Man (Oneal Bryan, 1975–). Together, they have collaborated with American rappers and producers Jay-Z (1969–), Puff Daddy (1969–), and Swizz Beatz (1978–).

DIASPORA ACTS

Jamaica's independence led to a lagging economy. Between the 1960s and 1970s, many Jamaicans emigrated and settled primarily in North America and the United Kingdom for employment and more diverse opportunities. Through diaspora, many Jamaican artists have contributed to hip hop well beyond its formative years—when Jamaican rappers in Brooklyn, New York, rapped in their accents and wrote Jamaican subject matter. Just some Jamaican-born American hip hop artists include Bushwick Bill (Richard Stephen Shaw, 1966–), Canibus (Germaine Williams, 1974–) of the HRSMN (1996–), Pepa (Sandra Denton, 1964/1969–), Heavy D (Dwight Errington Myers, 1969–2011), Sean Kingston (Kisean Anderson, 1990–), Kurtis Mantronik (Kurtis el Khaleel, 1965–), MC Tee (Touré Embden, 1966–), and Chubb Rock (Richard Simpson, 1968–). Both Afrika Bambaataa (1957–) and Luke (1960–) were born to Barbadian and Jamaican immigrant parents. Notable American artists of Jamaican descent include the Notorious B.I.G. (1972–1997), Busta Rhymes (1972–), Joey Bada$$ (Jo-Vaughn Virginie Scott, 1995–), Pete Rock (Peter Phillips, 1970–), Elle Royal (formerly Patwa, Danielle Prendergast, 1989–), and will.i.am (1975–). English-born American citizen Slick Rick (1965–) is also of Jamaican descent. Some Jamaican immigrant artists have opted to record reggae, dancehall, ska, and reggae-infused punk, pop, and dance in Europe, especially in the United Kingdom.

Melissa Ursula Dawn Goldsmith

See also: Dubstep; Kool Herc; Reggae; Shaggy; Slick Rick; The United Kingdom

Further Reading

Marshall, Wayne. 2005. "Hearing Hip Hop's Jamaican Accent." *Newsletter—Institute for Studies in American Music* 34, no. 2: 8–9, 14–15.

Richardson, Elaine. 2006. "Crosscultural Vibrations: The Shared Language of Contestation of Jamaican Dancehallas and American Hiphoppas." In *Hip Hop Literacies*, chap. 2. New York: Routledge.

Further Listening
Five Steez. 2012. *War for Peace.* Self-released.

Japan

Japan, nicknamed Land of the Rising Sun, is a sovereign East Asian island nation (an archipelago consisting 430 inhabited islands) with a population of 127 million, located off the eastern coast of the Asian mainland. Japanese people make up 98.5 percent of the total population, with over nine million inhabiting Tokyo, the nation's capital. Japan today is one of the world's most highly educated nations, with the third-largest economy, making it fourth in the world in purchasing power. Musically, Japan is known for *J-pop*, which has some similarities to hip hop with a focus on R&B and a sound similar to that of American boy band/girl band music. Since the 1980s, hip hop music containing rap has become more popular, although it still faces resistence given the national preference for J-pop. As a way of diversifying, Japanese rappers have introduced pop elements into their songs, making their albums more marketable.

TRADITIONAL AND WESTERNIZED MUSIC

Japan is the second-largest music market in the world, including record label–owned karaoke venues. Traditional Japanese music includes *shōmyō* (Buddhist chanting), and *gagaku* (orchestral court music), as well as indigenous styles and imported musical forms such as *tōgaku* (court music introduced from China around the eighth century) and *komagaku* (dance music from China). In the 13th century, *honkyoku*, original solo pieces played by Buddhist priests for alms and enlightenment, emerged. Other styles include min'yō, or folk music, including work songs, religious songs, gathering/event songs, and children's songs, and modern ensemble taiko drumming, a recent traditional form that can be traced to the 1950s.

Westernized pop music, *kayōkyoku*, appeared around 1914 with the song "Kachūsha no uta" (aka "Katyusha's Song"), from a play based on Leo Tolstoy's (1828–1910) novel *Resurrection*, first published in 1899, sung by Sumako Matsui (1886–1919). By the 1990s, the term *Westernized pop* became known as *J-pop*, which had its roots more in 1960s pop and rock music than in Japanese forms. Bands such as Yellow Magic Orchestra (1977–1984, 2007–) and Southern All Stars (1974–2008, 2013–) began to record, and power trio and punk rock bands such as Shonen Knife (1981–), rock duo B'z (1988–), and funk-based hip hop hybrid bands such as Pizzicato Five (1979–2001) achieved commercial success in Japan and abroad.

SOUL AND HIP HOP

The success of Michael Jackson's (1958–2009) *Thriller* (1984), the first album by a Western artist to sell over one million copies in Japan, influenced the direction of J-pop, resulting in dance and hip hop–based idol and boy bands. Current J-pop stars include Hikaru Utada's (1983–), whose debut album, *First Love* (1999), sold over seven million copies; idol group Morning Musume (1997–), which remains one of the most well known girl groups in the Japanese pop music industry; idol group Momoiro Clover Z (2008–), whose live concerts have set attendance records; and boy band SMAP (1988–2016), at one time the best-selling band in Asia.

J-pop invariably opened the door for hip hop, a much more recent Japanese music scene, with Japanese rappers finally seeing commercial success in the late 1980s. The earliest Japanese hip hop occurred in 1981 when Yellow Magic Orchestra recorded "Rap Phenomena," a song remembered for its electronic beats and 808 drum machine. Hip hop was bolstered in the 1980s when soul, house, and break-dancing were introduced with the American television show *Soul Train* (1971–2006) and American films *Wild Style* (1983), *Flashdance* (1983), and *Beat Street* (1984); in addition, Rock Steady Crew (1977–) performed in Japan, and musician and producer Hiroshi Fujiwara (1964–) returned to Japan and started playing hip hop records (later in the decade). Tokyo's Yoyogi Park became a "pedestrian's paradise" every Sunday: traffic was shut down and youth would gather to break. In addition, Japanese youth began to identify with African American hip hop culture, its fashions, dance, and music—some even going so far as to invest in extreme tanning to change their skin color.

EMERGENCE OF RAP

The earliest Japanese turntablist was DJ Krush (Hideaki Ishi, 1962–), who started out at the Yoyogi Park breakdancing scene (1984–). Early rappers included Ito Seiko (Masayuki Ito, 1961–), Chikado Haruo (1951–), and Takagi Kan (1961–). Most of what they performed was old-school hip hop. By the 1990s, Platinum hip hop hits were possible, such as Kenji Ozawa (1968–) and Scha Dara Parr's (1988–) "Kon'ya wa būgi bakku" (Boogie Back Tonight, 1994). More recent Japanese hip hop groups, such as Rhymester (1989–), record issue-oriented rap, rather than the old-school party rap of their predecessors. These first rappers used English because it was easier than Japanese for scansion, but later rappers changed syntax and word order, and used slang, regional expressions, and English to make the language fit the rhythmic line and musical conventions. For many Japanese, the turning point for hip hop was Thumpin' Camp (1996), a street event attended by 4,000 hip hop fans. Japan's most famous graffiti artist, Anti-Nuke (anonymous, n.d.), also appeared, with slogans such as "I hate nuclear rain," next to an image of a small girl in a raincoat.

Recent hip hop stars include the aforementioned Rhymester and other pioneer artists, short-lived rap groups King Giddra (1993–1996) and Lamp Eye (1995–1996); long-standing pioneers Kick the Can Crew (1996–2004) and Tha Blue Herb (1997–); rappers Dabo (Daisuke Ashida, 1975–), Hime (anonymous, 1979–), Nujabes (Jun Seba, 1974–2010), singer Toshinobu Kubota (1962–). King Giddra's members had lived in the United States and felt that Japanese rap should be issue-oriented, a tool of social opposition. Lamp Eye was an underground rap group that released the classic single "Shōgen" ("Testimonial,"1996), attacking J-pop music for its insipid and imitative qualities. Tha Blue Herb is notable for its trip hop beats and reflective lyrics that are critical of celebrity and the Japanese music industry. Dabo, who based his style on American rap, was the first Japanese artist to be signed to Def Jam Japan (2000–); he is a former member of Nitro Microphone Underground (1998–2012), famous for the song "Still Shinin,'" from the album *Straight from the Underground* (2004), one of the most popular Japanese rap songs. Hime was a pioneer female rapper whose songs were about female empowerment. Kubota was a pioneer of soul music and reggae in Japan. Seba Jun excelled in many hip hop forms, including graffiti; a national hero, often compared to J Dilla (1974–2006), in the Japanese hip hop community, his death led to the production of many tribute albums.

The most recent wave of Japanese rappers includes Shing02 (Shingo Annen, 1975–), EVISBEATS (Akira Yoshimura, n.d.), and Daoko (anonymous, 1997–); rap groups include Monju (2008–), Suiyōbi no Campanella (aka Wednesday Campanella, 2012–), and Eccy (2007–). Artist and MC Shing02 raps in both Japanese and English against keyboard heavy beats and turntables. EVISBEATS is a downbeat Buddhist rapper who raps against laid back keyboard, string instruments, and snap beats. Beginning her career at age 17, Daoko bridges the gap between idol groups and hip hop, usually singing her lyrics, although she is known to rap, using a gentle

Performing in 2015 at the Lyric Theatre in Los Angeles, Shing02 is representative of the most recent wave of Japanese rappers who employ an eclectic sense of musical style. He raps in both Japanese and English and fuses hip hop with reggae, jazz, and traditional Japanese music. (Gabriel Olsen/Getty Images)

delivery. Underground group Monju is known for superior sampling work. Duo Suiyōbi no Campanella and Eccy are known for a J-pop, new age, and house-infused rap with idiosyncratic traditional instrumentation and beats, and both are known for chill out beats.

Anthony J. Fonseca

See also: Turntablism; The United States

Further Reading

Condry, Ian. 2006. *Hip Hop Japan: Rap and the Paths of Cultural Globalization.* Durham, NC: Duke University Press.

Manabe, Noriko. 2013. "Representing Japan: 'National' Style among Japanese Hip Hop DJs." *Popular Music* 32, no. 1: 35–50.

Manabe, Noriko. 2015. "Japanese Hip Hop: Alternative Stories." In *The Cambridge Companion to Hip Hop,* edited by Justin Williams, chap. 18. Cambridge, England: Cambridge University Press.

Further Listening

EVISBEATS. 2012. *Sketchbook.* Amida.

Nitro Microphone Underground. 2004. *Straight from the Underground.* Columbia Music.

Suiyōbi no Campanella. 2017. *Superman.* Warner Music Japan.

Jay-P

(Paul Omiria Epeju, 1987–, Kampala, Uganda)

Jay-P is a Ugandan rapper, record producer, and entrepreneur. Jay-P's rap style is mainly old-school, with emphasis on end rhymes. He also incorporates quickly articulated toasts and repetitive chants and is known for experimental techniques, such as having a young child rap the chorus in his single "Hustle Avenue" (2015).

Coming from a large family, Paul Omiria Epeju was the seventh of eight children who grew up in a housing project. His mother taught him to be a diligent learner and made sure he could speak fluent English. By age six, he showed an interest in music, and by nine, he was interested in hip hop. He performed in school, and later at parties and bars. At 18, he took the stage name Jay-P and created a bedroom music studio, which he named RX Records (aka Recipe Records, 2005*–). He eventually enlarged it into a garage studio.

Despite the makeshift nature of his studio, Jay-P's professional quality production values were demonstrated immediately on his debut album *Credibly Evident,* a diverse collection of moody and atmospheric, dramatic beats created by synthesizer, similar to the style made famous by New Orleans–based No Limit Records (1990–2003; revived as No Limit Forever Records, 2010–), which is owned by American rapper and hip hop sound recording producer Master P (1970–).

As of 2018, Jay-P has produced six albums in his DIY studio: *Credibly Evident* (2013), *The Best of Jay-P* (2014), *Orbis Unum in My Lifetime* (2014), *Hustle Avenue, Vol.2* (2015), *The Hits Collection* (2015), and *Modus Operandi* (2017).

Anthony J. Fonseca

See also: Dirty South; Uganda

Further Reading

Barz, Gregory F., and Gerald C. Liu. 2011. "Positive Disturbance: Tafesh, Twig, HIV/AIDS, and Hip Hop in Uganda." In *The Culture of AIDS in Africa: Hope and Healing in Music and the Arts*, edited by Gregory F. Barz and Judah M. Cohen, chap. 30. New York: Oxford University Press.

Odeke, Steven. 2014. "Jay-P's Rap Future Is Rapturous." *The New Vision* (Kampala, Uganda), May 23.

Slim MC. 2014. "Hip Hop and Social Change in Uganda." In *Hip Hop and Social Change in Africa: Ni Wakati*, edited by Msia Kibona Clark and Mickie Mwanzia Koster, chap. 10. Lanham, MD: Lexington Books.

Further Listening

Jay-P. 2015. *Hustle Avenue, Vol. 2*. Recipe Records.

Jay-Z

(Shawn Corey Carter, 1969–, Brooklyn, New York)

Jay-Z is one of the most successful hip hop artists of the present day. His skills as a rapper have generated an impressive string of critically praised albums that have also been commercial hits, earning him a fortune that he has used to build a financial empire that includes products ranging from fashion to entertainment to sports management. He rose from drug dealer to multi-Platinum-selling rapper and world-class businessman, married to one of R&B's leading stars, Beyoncé (1981–). As of 2018, Jay-Z is among the wealthiest hip hop artists and has translated success in the music industry into success in other businesses.

EARLY YEARS

Born Shawn Corey Carter and raised in the notorious Marcy Projects in Brooklyn, New York's Bedford-Stuyvesant neighborhood, Jay-Z faced a tough childhood. When he was 11, his uncle was murdered, which led his father to drugs and then to abandon his family, leaving his mother to raise him and his three siblings. He attended public schools in Brooklyn and Trenton, New Jersey, and though he was a good student in the lower grades, he did not graduate from high school. After his uncle's death, he became withdrawn and turned to dealing drugs, although he himself was not a user, and he credits music with giving him a way out of a difficult family situation.

As a child, he was exposed to various kinds of music from a record collection that contained a wide selection of popular styles. He enjoyed beating out rhythms on the kitchen table, and so he was given a boombox as a birthday present, which encouraged his interest in music. After watching *Soul Train* (1971–2006), he imitated performers such as Michael Jackson (1958–2009). He was also a strong reader and began to write down the rhymes that he heard, and then to write his own lyrics and even to freestyle. When he began to perform, his neighborhood nickname, Jazzy, became Jay-Z. He worked with another Brooklyn rapper, Big Daddy Kane (1968–), on tours. When Big Daddy Kane left the stage to change costumes, Jay-Z and another young rapper would freestyle until he returned.

EARLY RECORDINGS

Jay-Z's first single was "In My Lifetime" (1994), which he initially sold out of his own car when no major label would sign him to a contract. For that reason, Jay-Z cofounded the independent label Roc-A-Fella Records (1996–2013), which sold Jay-Z's music through a distribution deal with Priority Records (1995–), a West Coast label that specialized in hip hop. The first Roc-A-Fella release was Jay-Z's debut album, *Reasonable Doubt* (1996), which rose to No. 23 on the Billboard 200 and eventually reached Platinum sales. Critics praised the album for Jay-Z's vocal acrobatics, his stark honesty about the life of a street hustler, and a sound that was not compromised with obvious pop insertions. Many, including Jay-Z himself, consider *Reasonable Doubt* his finest work.

His second solo album, *In My Lifetime, Vol. 1* (1997), debuted at No. 3 and reached an even bigger audience, in part due to a new distribution deal with Def Jam Recordings (1983–). Some complaints were heard about the album's slicker, more commercial sound, which was the result of using several of Puff Daddy's (1969–) Bad Boy Records (1993–) label producers on this project, but most critics thought it was a strong continuation of his debut album.

Vol. 2 . . . Hard Knock Life (1998), Jay-Z's third album, opened at No. 1 on the Billboard 200. Sales eventually reached quintuple Platinum, making the album Jay-Z's biggest seller ever. Its success may owe something to a return to the less polished sound of *Reasonable Doubt*. The album also includes one of Jay-Z's most popular singles, the title track, "Hard Knock Life (Ghetto Anthem)," which samples the tune of the same name, "Hard Knock Life," from the Broadway musical hit *Annie* (1977). Most commentators point to that show's 1977 premiere as the point of origin for that sample, but in fact, *Annie* had just completed a modest run in revival in 1997, only months before Jay-Z's single was released, a synergy that hints at his already well-developed business sense.

SUBSEQUENT HITS

Over the next several years, Jay-Z delivered a remarkably consistent string of hit albums, all of which started at No. 1 on the Billboard 200 and reached Platinum sales or better in short order. During that same time, he also began to expand his business ventures; for example, he opened his first restaurant, the sports bar 40/40 Club, in 2003 and assumed the role of president of Def Jam Recordings in 2004, while also continuing to guide his Roc-A-Fella label. A feud with the rapper Nas (1973–) added yet another issue to his busy life.

Whatever the reasons, in late 2003, Jay-Z announced that a concert at Madison Square Garden during Thanksgiving week would be his retirement and that he planned to record no additional albums; however, he continued to perform and record as a guest artist on tracks by others, and in 2006, he released *Kingdom Come*, his ninth solo album. Its comeback single, "Show Me What You Got," was leaked on the Internet before its official release, which led to an FBI investigation.

Jay-Z continued to tour and perform live events, and he released two more successful albums, even as he continued to shift his attention to other business ventures. At the beginning of 2008, he gave up his position as the head of Def Jam, and in 2009, he joined with a consortium that included rapper Will Smith (1968–) and his wife Jada Pinkett Smith (1971–) to produce *Fela!*, a Broadway musical about the African musician and political figure Fela Kuti (Olufela Olusegun Oludotun Ransome-Kuti, 1938–1997). The show was a modest success, running for just over a year and winning a few awards. The most important personal event of those years was Jay-Z's marriage in 2008 to Beyoncé, an R&B singer whose musical accomplishments match her husband's, creating an entertainment supercouple.

In 2013, Jay-Z released his 12th solo album, *Magna Carta . . . Holy Grail*, which again started at No. 1 on the Billboard 200. Critical response to the album was generally less enthusiastic than for his previous releases. Nevertheless, the album reached double Platinum status in less than two months, confirming his continuing popularity with fans. South Korean business and technology conglomerate Samsung (1938–) used *Holy Grail* in a novel marketing deal with Jay-Z. The company purchased the rights to one million copies of the album, which could be downloaded for free by customers using a Samsung phone, and Jay-Z appeared in high profile ads broadcast during the NBA (National Basketball Association) Finals just before the album's physical release.

Jay-Z is one of the few legitimate multimillionaire businessmen who can credit his experience as a drug dealer for his professional successes. He has spoken honestly about how the lessons he learned in the streets have helped him in the music business, beginning with knowing with whom to associate and how to carry himself. Similarly, he compares his ability to negotiate a multi-million-dollar deal with bargaining between drug dealers and their suppliers. Despite his earlier unsavory activities, he has built an impressive diversified group of investments. Starting with his record companies, Jay-Z has branched out into clothing, cosmetics and fragrances, wine and spirits, media companies, restaurants, real estate, gambling, and sports. These last few categories also include an element of civic pride, with investments in the Barclays Center and its chief tenant, the Brooklyn Nets of the NBA, which have helped to revitalize the borough. Jay-Z's interest in sports has led him into sports management, which has given him the opportunity to advise athletes, many of whom have come from impoverished backgrounds similar to his own, on how to handle the outsized salaries and celebrity found in professional sports.

Jay-Z's fortune has also allowed him to engage in a variety of philanthropic activities, ranging from a scholarship fund to work for safe water around the world. Along with other superstar musicians, he contributed to relief efforts for the Hurricane Katrina disaster (2005), and his support of voter registration and similar political activities has made him a friend of President Barack Obama (1961–, in office, 2009–2017). One of Jay-Z's most recent business activities has been the 2015 acquisition of TIDAL, a subscription-based music streaming service that is run by a consortium of leading artists, including Jay-Z, who all provide exclusive content. In addition to providing its users with a higher fidelity sound at a premium price, TIDAL also claims to pay higher royalties to its artists. A few performers, however, have questioned the company's financial statements used to calculate royalties, as well as the number of subscribers.

Scott Warfield

See also: Beyoncé; Fashion; The United States

Further Reading

Bailey, Julius, ed. 2011. *Jay-Z: Essays on Hip Hop's Philosopher King*. Jefferson City, NC: MacFarland.

Greenburg, Zack O'Malley. 2015. *Empire State of Mind: How Jay-Z Went from Street Corner to Corner Office*. Rev. ed. New York: Portfolio/Penguin Press.

Jay-Z. *Decoded*. 2010. New York: Spiegel and Grau.

Further Listening

Jay-Z. 1996. *Reasonable Doubt*. Priority/Freeze/Roc-A-Fella Records.

Jay-Z. 2003. *The Black Album*. Roc-A-Fella Records.

Jay-Z. 2006. *Kingdom Come*. Roc-A-Fella Records.

Jay-Z. 2013. *Magna Carta . . . Holy Grail*. Roc-A-Fella Records.

Jean Grae

(Tsidi Ibrahim, 1976–, Cape Town, South Africa)

Jean Grae is a South African–born rapper, singer, music producer, and music engineer who was raised in New York City by jazz musician parents. She is known especially for her quick and smooth rap delivery and her varied intonation. She has also gained recognition for her musical explorations as a hip hop music engineer, at times playful with vocal processers; she also incorporates rap into musical layers in ways that resemble experimental performance artists and electroacoustic composers such as Laurie Anderson (1947–). Jean Grae's vocal range is coloratura soprano.

NEW YORK SCENE AND GROUND ZERO

Though she initially was more interested in dance, she studied vocal performance at Fiorello H. LaGuardia High School of Music and Art and the Performing Arts. Since 1995, she has been active in the New York hip hop scene. That year, she was discovered and recruited by hip hop pioneer and activist George "Rithm" Martinez (1974–) to record a five-song demo for his Brooklyn-based experimental hip hop group Ground Zero (1990–1998). The recording received critical acclaim, including "Unsigned Hype" honors in the March 1996 issue of the hip hop magazine *The Source*. Her first stage name was What? What? Since 1998, she has used the stage name Jean Grae (named after the X-Men character Jean Grey).

After Ground Zero, Jean Grae joined the New York–based hip hop group Natural Resource (1996*–1999). In 1996, Natural Resource released the following 12-inch records (represented here as A side / B side): "Negro League Baseball" / "They Lied" and "Bum Deal" on their own label, Makin' Records (2000–). She created her international fan base from her Ground Zero years by collaborating on Makin' Records recordings by Brooklyn-based acts such as Pumpkinhead (Robert Alan Diaz, 1975–2015), the Bad Seed (Corey Pierson, 1975–), and O. B. S. (Original Blunted Soldiers, 1999–), among others. She has also collaborated with Brooklyn-based acts such as Brooklyn Academy (1995–2008), Talib Kweli (1975–), and Mos Def (1973–), and has recorded with a large number of well known nonlocal hip hop artists and groups, including the Herbaliser (1995–), the Roots (1987–), Mr. Len (1975–), Phonte (Phonte Lyshod Coleman, 1978–), and 9th Wonder (1975–).

SOLO EFFORTS

Jean Grae's first solo album was *Attack of the Attacking Things* (2002), which was followed by *The Bootleg of the Bootleg EP* (2003), *This Week* (2004), and *The Orchestral Files* (2007). In 2004, she signed with Babygrande Records (2001–), but in 2005 she moved on to Talib Kweli's newly formed Blacksmith Records (2005–2012). She worked on the 9th Wonder album, *Jeanius with 9th Wonder* (2008), which was quickly followed by *The Evil Jeanius* (2008), a collaboration with the San Francisco–based alternative hip hop production duo Blue Sky Black Death (2003–).

In 2008, Jean Grae announced her intention to retire, but in the same year, she had also made the decision to self-release her music on her website, streaming and selling it through the service Bandcamp. She also began to advertise compositional services at a pay rate of 16 measures for $800. The decision to retire from the music industry to become independent was a statement against the treatment of musicians during the digital age. She eventually returned to performing live and songwriting.

As a result, her solo output since 2011 has been prolific. She released a free mix-tape, *Cookies or Comas* (2011), which has received critical acclaim and includes her rap as a vocal layer over R&B and hip hop beats. Tracks such as "Cakebasket" seem to reveal an experimental and humorous Jean Grae reminiscent of Anderson—whereas "Live Up," featuring lyrical R&B passages by Talib Kweli, includes infectious melodic hooks and her own singing.

In 2013, Jean Grae released *Dust Ruffle*, a 10-track retrospective album of unreleased songs recorded between 2004 and 2010, and *Gotham Down Deluxe*, a compilation of three of her *Gotham Down* Cycle EPs that included some lo-fi tracks. As of 2018, she has plans for another solo album, *Cake or Death*. In the meantime, Jean Grae has released multiple EPs, including *Ho x 3: A Christmas Thingy*, *Jeannie*, *#5*, and *That's Not How You Do That: An Instructional Album for Adults* (2014), as well as *That's Not How You Do That Either: Yet Another Instructional Album for Adults*, *iSweatergawd*, and *Saix* (2015). She has also released singles that are independent of albums and EPs, music for CD-ROM, a streamed audiobook titled *The State of Eh* (2014), and her online sitcom, *Life with Jeannie* (2013–), in which she both stars and directs.

Melissa Ursula Dawn Goldsmith

See also: South Africa; The United States

Further Reading

Smalls, Shanté Paradigm. 2011. "'The Rain Comes Down': Jean Grae and Hip Hop Heteronormativity." *American Behavioral Scientist* 55, no. 1: 86–95.

Walsh, Robert. 2006. "An Interview with Jean Grae." *Callaloo* 29, no. 3: 816–21.

Further Listening

Jean Grae. 2002. *Attack of the Attacking Things . . . The Dirty Mixes.* Third Earth Music.

Jean Grae and 9th Wonder. 2008. *Jeanius.* Blacksmith Music.

Jerkin'

(aka Doing the Jerk)

Jerkin' is a Los Angeles–based young adult and teen street dance that began gaining popularity on both the East and West Coasts around 2009, after a hip hop duo from Hesperia (about an hour east of Los Angeles), New Boyz (2009–2013), released the single "You're a Jerk." The music video featured the duo and its posse doing street dancing, using various versions of the Jerk. That same year, another hip hop duo, Audio Push (2006–), released the single "Teach Me How to Jerk," which uses a similar hiccupped/repeated chorus as Cali Swag District's (2009–2015) more famous Top 40 hit "Teach Me How to Dougie," also released in 2009. The music video for "Teach Me How to Jerk" shows the duo in a classroom, exhibiting to fellow students their moves as they all dance on desks, tables, and the floor, then move out into the hall and the gym, where the duo dance, encircled by the crowd. Other jerking hip hop crews include the Rej3ctz (2010–), whose 2011 dance single "Cat Daddy" made it into the Billboard Hot 100. Jerkin music is typically retro, heavy bass oriented, with lots of synthetic drum loops, handclaps, and heavy autotuning, and most of its practitioners are young. Dancers, however, will argue that jerkin' is a dance style, and that a dancer can jerk to any hip hop music.

THE MOVES

The Jerk is a bounce-oriented, loose-limbed dance that involves alternating between two moves, bent-knee hopping and a straight-leg kick out that transitions into a half kick back with a bent knee; dancers switch the moves from one leg to another—as one leg does the kicks, the other does the bent-knee hopping, mostly in place, though some jerkers move slightly forward. Some dancers will add a drop into the bent-knee hop, dropping to a crouching position on one or both legs. Arm movements are usually minimalized (for balance) and improvised (for style), although the wrist and hand can be used to strike various hip hop postures and to point to other dancers. Moves such as dips and pin drops can be incorporated, as well as the dance move Running Man (basically giving the illusion of rhythmically running/walking in place). More experienced jerkers will incorporate acrobatics into the dance, usually in the form of backflips or splits.

As time has progressed, the dance has evolved into more footwork oriented versions of itself, sometimes leaving the kick out altogether. In these versions, bent-knee hopping is accentuated with footwork moves, such as alternately crossing the feet in front of each other, doing a heel-toe alternation on one foot while hopping on the other (while alternating which leg hops and which foot does the heel-toe), and dropping down after sliding one leg under the body, giving the illusion that the dancer has collapsed.

In the aforementioned song's music video, other moves are incorporated, such as bending the knees inward alternately, rather than alternating the hop and kick. Dancers usually wear skinny jeans rather than baggy pants, as well as bright colors, retro T-shirts, and retro high-top shoes such as Chuck Taylors.

Anthony J. Fonseca

See also: Fashion; Hip Hop Dance; The United States

Further Reading

Guzman-Sanchez, Thomas. 2012. *Underground Dance Masters: Final History of a Forgotten Era.* Santa Barbara, CA: Praeger.

Kercher, Sophia. 2010. "Jerkin' Is Workin' for 'em: Kids Are Ditching the Gangsta Look for the Skinny Jeans and Neon Colors of a Dance and Music Style with a Grab-Bag of Retro Elements." *Los Angeles Times*, April 11.

Schloss, Joseph G. 2009. "From Rocking to B-Boying: History and Mystery." In *Foundation: B-Boys, B-Girls, and Hip Hop Culture in New York*, chap. 7. New York: Oxford University Press.

Jesse Jagz

(aka Jago, Jesse Garba Abaga, 1984–, Jos, Nigeria)

Jesse Jagz is a Nigerian hip hop and reggae rapper, singer-songwriter, and record producer who since 2004 has made a name for himself as the Nigerian Kanye West (1977–) through labels such as his imprint Jagz Nation (2012–) and Chocolate City (2005–), the latter being one of the most successful indigenous urban record labels in Africa and a subsidiary of Chocolate City Group, one of the biggest African entertainment conglomerates.

Jagz's parents were both members of the clergy, which allowed him access to music at an early age. By the time he was seven, he was active with the church choir and he was teaching himself on his parents' church's drum kit. He claims to be of the Taraba tribe and is known to be Jukun, part of a West African ethnic nation to which most of the tribes in North Central Nigeria trace their origin. He was raised in Jos (aka J-town), Nigeria, which has a population of nearly one million and is the administrative capital of the geographically centralized Plateau State, the 12th-largest state of Nigeria.

His first album (which went unreleased because the band dissolved) was one recorded around 2003 with a short-lived group called Gospel Insanity. He then formed his own band, Eleven Thirty (2004–2006) and enjoyed local success. His solo career came after a short-lived attempt at a record label. His debut hit was the single "Africa" (2006*), which topped local charts on northern Nigeria radio stations. Within a year, three of his singles found their way into the local Top 10. His debut album, *Jag of All Tradez* (2010*), was a critical success. Songs from the album, including "Wetin Dey" (2009*), "Pump It Up" (2009*), and "Nobody Test Me" (2010*) made him a national star, and since, he has been in high demand as a producer. His second and third albums, *Jagz Nation Vol 1: Thy Nation Come* (2013*) and *Jagz Nation Vol. 2: Royal Niger Company* (2014*), allowed him to showcase his production skills.

His music is informed by his willingness to experiment with incorporating different genres of music into his songs, juxtaposed against a solid hip hop beat; he uses various types of quirky instrumentation (for example, a chorus of bells, quirky keyboard voices, or full synthesized orchestra) and various degrees of autotuning and echo, and his rapping (usually in English) is soft and articulated. Reggae elements play an essential role in his music, present in virtually all his songs. His videos are highly influenced by Western hip hop, as he often dresses in leather jackets with dark sunglasses, T-shirts cut off at the sleeve, or dark hoodies, and he typically wears a large gold-linked chain around his neck.

By 2013, he was starting up his independent label, Jagz Nation, and that year he released the singles "Murder Dem" and "Redemption." In 2015, he re-signed with Chocolate City and released a new album, *The Indestructible Choc Boi Nation*. He had planned to release a new album, *Odysseus*, in 2016, but postponed the release.

Anthony J. Fonseca

See also: Ice Prince; M.I.; Nigeria; Political Hip Hop; Reggae

Further Reading

Clark, Msia Kibona. 2013. "Representing Africa! Trends in Contemporary African Hip Hop." *Journal of Pan African Studies* 6, no. 3: 1–4.

Olusegun-Joseph, Yomi. 2014. "Transethnic Alegory: The Yoruba World, Hip Hop, and the Rhetoric of Generational Difference." *Third Text* 28, no. 6: 517–28.

Shipley, Jesse Weaver. 2017. "Parody after Identity: Digital Music and the Politics of Uncertainty in West Africa." *American Ethnologist* 44, no. 2: 249–62.

Jinjo Crew

(2001–, Seoul, South Korea)

Jinjo Crew (the name roughly translates into "rising fire") is a b-boy dance crew from Seoul that is known for its power and speed moves, as well as incorporating team-oriented routines into dance battles. In 2010, Jinjo won the Battle of the Year against Japanese b-boy crew Mortal Combat (n.d.). Its members include international champion b-boy Hong10 (Kim Hong-Yeol, 1984*–), Wing (Kim Heon Woo, 1987*–), Skim (Kim Heon Jun, 1985*–), and Vero (Jang Ji Kwang, 1986*–).

The crew's routines are extremely intricate, with sometimes all five members getting involved in a soloist's entrance or exit from the center stage. B-boy Hong10's signature move, "the Hong10 Freeze" is a variation on a halo freeze, which involves a sudden stopping of motion with the freeze move as a headstand, supported by hands, with shoulders off the ground, and legs in the air. The crew is also known for its good-natured battle challenges and gestures during breakdance battles and its work ethic, as its members practice nine hours a day.

Jinjo Crew's earliest success was in 2004, when it placed second in the Beat-Walk. By 2007, the crew was winning important championships, including the CYON B-Boy Championships, the Converse Battle Move, the NICE Flavor Showcase Battle, and the WHAT Mixed Battle. In 2007 and 2008, Jinjo Crew won the LG Korean Nationals. In 2009, Jinjo won the National B-Boy Championships and the B-Boy All Star Battle, as well as the aforementioned Korean titles, and in 2010, it won the Floor Wars Korea Elimination and the Battle of the Year.

As of 2018, the crew still competes and wins championships in China, France, Germany, Denmark, Italy, Turkey, Taiwan, Belgium, and Korea, and it received a special award from the Korean Ministry of Culture, Sports, and Tourism.

Anthony J. Fonseca

See also: Battling; Breakdancing; Hip Hop Dance; Korea

Further Reading

Hong, Euny. 2014. "Why Pop Culture; or, Failure Is the Breakfast of Champions." In *The Birth of Korean Cool: How One Nation Is Conquering the World through Pop Culture*, chap. 6. New York: Simon and Schuster.

Song, Myoung-Sun. 2014. "The S(e)oul of Hip Hop: Locating Space and Identity in Korean Rap." In *The Korean Wave: Korean Popular Culture in Global Context*, edited by Yasue Kuwahara, chap. 7. New York: Palgrave Macmillan.

Usher, Charles. 2011. "South Korea: World Breakdancing Capital?" *The Christian Science Monitor*, July 5, 8.

Jones, Quincy

(aka Q, Quincy Delight Jones Jr., 1933–, Chicago, Illinois)

Quincy Jones is an American sound recording, film, and television producer, as well as composer, musician, conductor, magazine founder, entertainment executive, and philanthropist. Jones began a storied music career during the bebop era in the 1950s—now with 28 Grammy Awards, he has the most Grammys by any living musician. In 1964, Jones became the vice president of Mercury Records (1945–) and therefore the first black person to attain a top-leading administrative position within a white-owned sound recording company.

After working for other labels, he began his own recording label, Qwest Records (1980–2000, 2010–) in partnership with Warner Bros. Records (1958–) and later with Interscope Records (1989–). Among many other artists, Jones produced Michael Jackson's (1958–2009) most successful studio albums—*Off the Wall* (1979), *Thriller* (1982), and *Bad* (1987). By the 1990s, Qwest began producing hip hop recordings, though Jones focused on jazz, R&B, funk, and American and Brazilian pop. Jones was also the film producer of the American gangster thriller *New Jack City* (1991) who asked *Village Voice* writer (originator of the term

Since hip hop's early years, legendary American producer and musician Quincy Jones has been influential in developing its music and culture. His influence includes producing the American film *New Jack City* (1991), as well as producing numerous albums for a variety of artists across several decades. (Feature Flash/Dreamstime.com)

"new jack") Barry Michael Cooper (n.d.) to work on the screenplay. Jones composed the themes and developed, launched, and produced the American television sitcom series *The Fresh Prince of Bel-Air* (1990–1996), starring rapper-turned-actor named Will Smith (1968–), as well as *In the House* (1995–1998), starring rapper-turned-actor LL Cool J (1968–).

Among other hip hop acts, Jones produced albums for Canadian singer-songwriter Tamia (Tamia Marilyn Hill née Washington, 1975–), American rapper, singer-songwriter, producer, and actor Terrace Martin (1978–), and Australian singer-songwriter Grace (Grace Sewell, 1997–). He has also produced singles featuring American singer-songwriter or rappers and producers Al B. Sure! (Albert Joseph Brown III, 1968–), Babyface (1959–), T.I. (aka TIP, Clifford Joseph Harris Jr., 1980–), and B.o.B (Bobby Ray Simmons Jr., 1988–). In addition, Jones has produced studio albums featuring various hip hop and new jack swing artists such as Al B. Sure! and Big Daddy Kane (1968–), alongside legendary jazz, R&B, and pop musicians such as Sarah Vaughan (1924–1990) and Miles Davis (1926–1991) on *Back on the Block* (1989). Jones's studio album *Q: Soul Bossa Nostra* (2010) features various artists recording Brazilian music, R&B, jazz, and hip hop.

Jones has been influential on hip hop's development as an early advocate and mentor. Hip hop artists sample him often, as with "The Streetbeater" (1973, recorded in 1972), the theme from the American television comedy series *Sanford and Son* (1972–1977), which has been sampled in American rapper Masta Killa's (Jamiel Irief, born Elgin Turner, 1969–) "Old Man" (2004), English rapper and singer-songwriter M.I.A.'s (1975–) "U.R.A.Q.T." (2005), and Jones and T.I.'s "Sanford and Son" (2010). He also had a global impact on hip hop when he invited pioneering South African group Prophets of da City (1988–2001) to perform at the Montreux Jazz Festival in Switzerland in 1992, just a year before the end of apartheid. But Jones has also been critical of rappers-producers such as Kanye West (1977–) and Lil Wayne (1982–) when comparing them to jazz greats such as his mentor Ray Charles (Ray Charles Robinson, 1930–2004) or pop greats such as Jackson.

Jones' hip hop work has received several music industry awards. In 1990, *Back on the Block* won the Grammy Award for Album of the Year in addition to six other Grammys. One of those awards was for Best Rap Performance by a Duo or Group, which went to Jones and his collaborators who recorded on the album: Big Daddy Kane, Ice-T (1958–), Tevin Campbell (Tevin Jermod Campbell, 1976–), Kool Moe Dee (1962–), and Melle Mel (1961–).

Melissa Ursula Dawn Goldsmith

See also: The United States

Further Reading

Henry, Clarence Bernard. 2013. *Quincy Jones: His Life in Music*. Jackson: University Press of Mississippi.

Jones, Quincy. 2001. *Q: The Autobiography of Quincy Jones*. New York: Doubleday.

Further Listening

Quincy Jones. 2010. *Q: Soul Bossa Nostra*. Qwest/Interscope Records.

Jordan

Jordan is a Western Asian, Middle Eastern constitutional monarchy whose capital, Amman, is its most populous city and its cultural center. After being a British protectorate after World War I (1914–1918), it became an independent state in 1946. Sunni Islam is the dominant religion, practiced by 92 percent of the population, so rap is not widely popular. Hip hop began to gain some traction around 1998. Early Jordanian hip hop artists include DJ Shadia (Shadia Bseiso, 1986–), who showcased the genre in her radio show *The 5th Element* (2005–2008), and Amman-based Ostaz Samm (1984–).

The music of Jordan consists mainly of traditional forms; however, some pop styles have been successful, with stars such as Diana Karazon (1983–), Toni Qattan (Anton George Qattan, 1985–), and Hani Mitwasi (1983–). Rock music has become more popular in Amman in the last few decades, and the indie music scene gained some traction around 2008 with bands such as El Morabba3 (2009–), Autostrad (2007–), and Akher Zapheer (2007–).

Recent hip hop artists include rapper Satti (Ahmad Yaseen, n.d.) and group Torabyeh (2009–). Torabyeh gained worldwide attention after suing Israeli Prime Minister Benjamin Netanyahu (1949–, in office 2009–) for using one of its songs in his Likud campaign (1973–). Satti began his career in 2011 by rapping in English (he learned English from hip hop cassettes), but now opts for Arabic. His 19-track debut album was *Aress el shamal* (*The Groom of the North*, a wordplay on the city Irbid's nickname: Bride of the North, 2017). He was drawn to rapping because rap battles are similar to the traditional Haddaya, in which two poets engage in verbal sparring.

Anthony J. Fonseca

See also: Israel; Lebanon

Further Reading

Adely, Fida J. 2007. "Is Music Haram? Jordanian Girls Educating Each Other about Nation, Faith, and Gender in School." *Teachers College Record* 109, no. 7: 1663–81.

Hood, Kathleen, and Mohammad Al-Oun. 2014. "Changing Performance Traditions and Bedouin Identity in the North Badia, Jordan." *Nomadic Peoples* 18, no. 2: 78–99.

McDonald, David A. 2013. *My Voice Is My Weapon: Music, Nationalism, and the Poetics of Palestinian Resistance.* Durham, NC: Duke University Press.

Juice Crew

(aka Juice Crew All Stars, 1983–1991, Queens, New York)

Juice Crew was a hip hop collective consisting mostly of artists who were living in the Queensbridge Houses, a housing project in Long Island City, Queens, New York. Early members included Big Daddy Kane (Antonio Hardy, 1968–), Biz Markie (Marcel Theo Hall, 1964–), Masta Ace (Duval Clear, 1966–), Kool G Rap (Nathaniel Thomas Wilson, 1968–), MC Shan (Shawn Moltke, 1965–), and Roxanne Shanté (Lolita Shanté Gooden, 1969–), as well as producer and DJ Mr. Magic (John Rivas, 1956–2009). As founding producer of Cold Chillin' Records (1986–1998), pioneering American hip hop DJ, producer, house music production expert, and label owner Marley Marl (Marlon Lu'ree Williams, 1962–) established the Juice Crew starting in

1983 with Mr. Magic, his hip hop radio DJ colleague at New York City's WHBI (now WXNY, 1964–). Marley Marl also grew up living in the Queensbridge Houses.

Juice Crew's main rival was Boogie Down Productions (1985–1992), a South Bronx, New York hip hop band that served as a vehicle for KRS-One (Lawrence Krisna Parker, 1965–) during the early part of his rapping career. Its original lineup consisted of KRS-One, turntablist and producer DJ Scott La Rock (Scott Monroe Sterling, 1962–1987), and turntablist, beatboxer, and rapper D-Nice (Derrick Jones, 1970–). Boogie Down Productions was also responsible for one of the first diss rap feuds, the Bridge Wars. This began when Juice Crew released a 1985 song, "The Bridge," which seemingly expresses local pride in the borough as the place where rap began and attacked Queens, New York rapper LL Cool J (James Todd Smith, 1968–) for alleged plagiarism. In response, Boogie Down Productions released its debut single "South Bronx" (1986), which argued it was the birthplace of hip hop and contained lyrics that demeaned and threatened the Juice Crew, which responded with group member's MC Shan's "Kill That Noise" (1987). Boogie Down Productions, in turn, responded with the reggae-infused rap song "The Bridge Is Over" (1987). The feud, which has since been explained as KRS-One's jab at Mr. Magic, who once dissed his music, expanded to other New York rappers. KRS-One lost interest after the death of DJ Scott La Rock.

Anthony J. Fonseca

See also: Big Daddy Kane; Boogie Down Productions; KRS-One; LL Cool J; Marley Marl; Roxanne Shanté; The United States

Further Reading

Bradley, Adam, and Andrew Dubois, eds. 2010. "Big Daddy Kane." Under "Part 2: 1985–92: The Golden Age" in *The Anthology of Rap*, pp. 136–44. New Haven, CT: Yale University Press.

Danois, Ericka Blount. 2010. "From Queens Come Kings: Run-D.M.C. Stomps Hard out of a 'Soft' Borough." In *Hip Hop in America: A Regional Guide*, edited by Mickey Hess, vol. 1, chap. 3. Santa Barbara, CA: Greenwood.

Mshaka, Thembisa S. 2007. "Roxanne Shanté." *Icons of Hip Hop: An Encyclopedia of the Movement, Music, and Culture*, edited by Mickey Hess, vol. 1, pp. 51–68. Westport, CT: Greenwood Press.

Rausch, Andrew J. 2011. "Big Daddy Kane." In *I Am Hip Hop: Conversations on the Music and Culture*, chap. 3. Lanham, MD: Scarecrow.

Further Listening

Big Daddy Kane. 1988. *Long Live the Kane*. Cold Chillin'.

Biz Markie. 1988. *Goin' Off*. Cold Chillin'.

MC Shan. 1987. *Down by Law*. Cold Chillin'.

Roxanne Shanté. 1989. *Bad Sister*. Cold Chillin'/Reprise Records.

Jungle Brothers

(1987–, New York City, New York)

Jungle Brothers is a highly eclectic American hip hop group that fuses mostly old-school hip hop with jazz, funk, electronica, dance, house music, R&B, and

Afrobeat, in addition to other musical genres and world music. The group is best known as the founding and core members of the New York City hip hop collective Native Tongues (1988–1996) with their contemporaries: A Tribe Called Quest (1985–1998, 2006–2013, 2015–); De La Soul (1987–); and Black Sheep (1989–1995, 2000–2002, 2006–). All contributed to the sound of alternative and experimental hip hop during the Golden Age of Hip Hop (1986–1994). Members of Jungle Brothers are turntablist, guitarist, rapper, and producer Afrika Baby Bam (Nathaniel Phillip Hall, 1970–), rapper Mike Gee (aka Mike G, Michael Benton Small, 1969–), and DJ Sammy B (Sammy Burwell, 1968–). Jungle Brothers' main musical influences were James Brown (1933–2006), Marvin Gaye (1939–1984), and Afrika Bambaataa (1957–)—the last inspired Hall to use the stage name Afrika Baby Bam.

In the mid-1980s, Afrika Baby Bam and Mike Gee were friends in high school. DJ Sammy B was a family friend of Mike Gee's and was with the group from the beginning until 1997. In 1988, Jungle Brothers released its first studio album *Straight Out the Jungle* on the Warlock Records independent label (1985–2009). Some tracks featured A Tribe Called Quest's MC and producer Q-Tip (aka Kamaal Ibn John Fareed, b. Jonathan William Davis, 1970–). The album received strongly positive critical acclaim, though it was a commercial failure. But in 1989, Jungle Brothers signed to Warner Bros. (1958–), and the group released its second album, *Done by the Forces of Nature*, which also critically acclaimed with poor sales.

Both albums, however, had tracks that charted on the U.K. Singles Chart, most notably "I'll House You" (1988) which peaked at No. 22. In addition, "What U Waitin' 4?" (1990) peaked at No. 13 on Billboard's Dance Club Songs chart. Warner Bros. dropped Jungle Bros. shortly after poor sales on its third album, *J Beez Wit the Remedy* (1993), but by then Jungle Brothers was already active in the Native Tongues collective.

On its own Jungle Brothers released several subsequent studio albums: *Raw Deluxe* (1997), *V.I.P.* (2000), *All That We Do* (2002), *You in My Hut Now* (2003), and *I Got You* (2006). Jungle Brothers had a string of hit singles continue in the United Kingdom, most notably "Jungle Brother '98" (1998), "V.I.P." (1999), and "Breathe Don't Stop" (2004) peaking at Nos. 18, 28, and 21, respectively. The last was a version of Q-Tip's "Breathe and Stop" (1999).

Melissa Ursula Dawn Goldsmith

See also: De La Soul; Hip House; Native Tongues; A Tribe Called Quest; The United States

Further Reading

Anon. 2015. "Brothers Reignite Hip House Sound." *The Post* (Bristol, England), August 28, 26.

Danois, Ericka Blount. 2010. "From Queens Come Kings: Run-D.M.C. Stomps Hard Out of a 'Soft' Borough." In *Hip Hop in America: A Regional Guide*, edited by Mickey Hess, vol. 1, chap. 3. Santa Barbara, CA: Greenwood.

Rabaka, Reiland. 2012. "Remix 3: Jazzmatazz: From Classic Jazz and Bebop to Jazz Rap and Hip Hop." In *Hip Hop's Amnesia: From Blues and the Black Women's Club Movement to Rap and the Hip Hop Movement*, chap. 3. Lanham, MD: Lexington Books.

Further Listening

Jungle Brothers. 1988. *Straight out the Jungle.* Warlock Records.

Jungle Brothers. 1989. *Done by the Forces of Nature.* Warner Bros. Records.

Jungle Brothers. 1999. *V.I.P.* Gee Street/V2 Records.

Just D

(1990–1995, 2015–, Stockholm, Sweden)

Just D (meaning Just That) is a pioneering hip hop trio from Sweden that consists of Gura G (aka Speedbump, Gustave Lund, 1968–), Pedda Pedd (Peder Ernerot, 1967–), and Dr. C (Wille Crafoord, 1966–). The trio's first album *1 steg bak å 2 steg fram* (*1 Step Backward, 2 Steps Forward*, 1990) was the first rap album fully in Swedish at a time when early Swedish hip hop groups rapped and rhymed in English in order to gain international appeal. Interspersed with humorous skits, this album also layered Just D's rapping and beats with samples of various Swedish sound recordings. It sampled from entertainer, singer, pianist, and novelty/vaudeville songwriter Povel Ramel (1922–2007), rock and pop songwriter and ABBA (1972–1982) session guitarist Janne Schaffer (Jan Erik Tage Schaffer, 1945–), and jazz and folksinger Alice Babs (Hildur Alice Nilson, 1924–2014), among others.

Combining a mainstream pop sound with hip hop, the trio's appearance, use of humor, and sound resembled that of the Beastie Boys (1981–2012). Despite racial and/or socioeconomic differences between members and subsequent Swedish hip hop groups (members of Just D were from affluent nonimmigrant Swedish families, and Crafoord's family roots were Swedish nobility), Just D opened the doors for the second wave of Swedish hip hop artists such as the Latin Kings (TLK, 1991–2005), Infinite Mass (1991–), and Looptroop Rockers (aka Looptroop, 1991–).

Just D had a string of No. 1 hit singles in Sweden, which include "Juligen" ("Christmas," 1991); "Klåfinger and vart tog den söta lilla flickan vägen?" ("Meddler and Where Did That Sweet Little Girl Go?," 1993); "87–87" (1995); "Hubbabubba" (1995); "Sköna skor" ("Beautiful Shoes," 1995); and "Tre gringos" ("Three Gringos," 1996). Shortly after its first album was released on the then indie Ricochet Records label (1988–), Just D began working with Telegram Records Stockholm (1987–2006*), which reissued *1 steg bak å 2 steg fram*. In 1991, it released its second album, *Svenska ord* (*Swedish Words*), which had used similar sampling techniques and skits as its first album, this time utilizing samples from current television shows and commercials aired in Sweden. Swedish radio stations banned the penultimate track on this album, "Fortfarande hos J. Lindström" ("Still at J. Lindström"), because it consisted of a broadcast canceling signal.

Their subsequent albums *Rock n Roll* (1992), *Tre amigos* (*Three Friends*, 1993), and *Plast* (1995) not only contributed to the height of Just D's fame, but also to Swedish hip hop's acceptance by a larger audience, in Sweden as well as globally. Just D broke up in 1995; however, in 2000 and 2001, Lund and Ernerot worked together in the pop project group Sverige. From the late 1990s to 2000s, Crafoord had a solo recording career in jazz and pop.

Melissa Ursula Dawn Goldsmith

See also: Beastie Boys; Sweden

Further Reading

Berggren, Kalle. 2012. "'No Homo': Straight Insoculations and the Queering of Masculinity in Swedish Hip Hop." *NORMA* 7, no. 1: 51–66.

Berggren, Kalle. 2013. "Degrees of Intersectionality: Male Rap Artists in Sweden Negotiating Class, Race, and Gender." *Culture Unbound: Journal of Current Cultural Research* 5: 189–211.

Lindholm, Susan. 2017. "From Nueva Canción to Hip Hop: An Entangled History of Hip Hop in-between Chile and Sweden." *Scandia* 83, no. 1: 68–97.

Further Listening

Just D. 1990. *1 Steg bak å 2 steg fram* (*1 Step Backward, 2 Steps Forward*). Ricochet/Telegram.

Just D. 1992. *Rock n Roll.* Telegram.

K

Karpe Diem

(2000–, Oslo, Norway)

Karpe Diem is a rap duo that consists of Magdi Omar Ytreeide Abdelmaguid (1984–) and Chirag Rashmikant Patel (aka Chicosepoy, 1984–). One of the best-known Norwegian hip hop artists, it has recorded five hip hop albums that have reached the Top 10 of the VG-Lista chart: *Rett fra hjertet* (*Straight from the Heart*, 2006), *Fire vegger* (*Four Walls*, 2008), *Aldri solgt en løgn* (*Never Sold a Lie*, 2010), and *Kors på halsen, ti kniver i hjertet, mor og far i døden* (*Cross My Throat, Ten Knives in My Heart, and My Mother and Father Die If I Lie*, 2012), and *Heisann Montebello* (2016). *Aldri sogt en løgn* and *Kors på halsen, ti kniver i hjertet, mor og far i døden* reached No. 1. *Aldri sogt en løgn* was certified four-times Platinum in Norway. From these albums, Karpe Diem has had a string of 16 hits on the VG-Lista.

FORMATION AND WORDPLAY

Abdelmaguid and Patel, while students, established Karpe Diem initially because they wanted to participate in the 2000 Ungdommens kulturmønstring (UKM) Young Culture Meetings, a local-regional-national festival that focuses on the artistic expression of young people between 13 and 20. While Karpe Diem's rapping texts were primarily in Norwegian, the duo's creative output included Norwegian and English slang, Norwegian to English code switching, Arabic phrases, and a multiethnolectal style that employed loanwords that are not only from English, but also from Arabic and Hindi, as well as other languages found in prominent immigrant populations living in east Oslo. Deliberate mispronunciation of words, and the rolling of the letter "r," also takes place in the duo's rapping style, which is fast, smooth, and soft-spoken despite its strong messages about discrimination, inequality, otherness, identity, and stereotyping of immigrants in Norway. The duo also raps about family, upbringing, and world politics, since Abdelmaguid's father immigrated from Egypt, and his mother is Norwegian from Stryn, Sogn og Fjordane, Norway and Patel's father is Indian and immigrated from Uganda, and his mother was originally from Gujarat, India.

SUCCESS AND CONTROVERSY

Karpe Diem's first EP, *Glasskår* (wordplay for *Glass Shard/Cut*, 2004), focuses on the duo's multiethnic lives as Muslims in Oslo. It peaked at No. 9 on the

VG-Lista and was certified Gold in Norway. The duo won the Spellemannprisen, nicknamed the Norwegian Grammy Awards, for *Fire Vegger* and in the Pop Music category for *Kors på Halsen*, which is granted by the International Federation of the Phonographic Industry (IFPI) and represents the recording industry worldwide.

In 2011, Karpe Diem and DJ Marius Thingvald (1983–), who tours and sometimes records with the duo, was invited to perform "Tusen Tegninger" ("A Thousand Drawings"), a song about tolerance from the album *Aldri solgt en løgn*, at the national memorial ceremony for the victims of the 2011 Norway attacks. In 2016, Karpe Diem's song "Attitudeproblem," from the album *Heisann Montebello*, received widespread criticism and sparked debate on how the duo used the word "Jew" in the song, which was intended to protest Israel/Occupied Palestine Territories (1967–) and attack former Israel Prime Minister Ariel Sharon (Ariel Scheinermann, 1928–2014, in office 2001–2006).

Melissa Ursula Dawn Goldsmith

See also: Norway; Political Hip Hop

Further Reading

Nærland, Torgeir Uberg. 2015. "From Musical Expressivity to Public Political Discourse Proper: The Case of Karpe Diem in the Aftermath of the Utøya Massacre." *Popular Communication* 13, no. 3: 216–31.

Sandve, Birgitte. 2015. "Unwrapping 'Norwegianness': Politics of Difference in Karpe Diem." *Popular Music* 34, no. 1: 45–66.

Further Listening

Karpe Diem. 2010. *Aldri solgt en løgn* (*Never Sold a Lie*). Bonnier Amigo Music.

Karpe Diem. 2012. *Kors på halsen, ti kniver i hjertet, mor og far i døden* (*Cross My Throat, Ten Knives in My Heart, and My Mother and Father Die If I Lie*). Petroleum Records.

Kazakhstan

Kazakhstan is a Central Asian country that is mainly an Islamic constitutional republic. This nation of 18 million people was the last of the Soviet republics to declare independence during the dissolution of the Soviet Union in 1991. Traditional Kazakh music is usually instrumental. When vocals occur, texts depend on the style of music, whether it is epic singing, love songs, didactic songs, or musical dialogues between characters. Nontraditional music has therefore had a difficult time gaining popularity there. Modern, popular Kazakh music is heavily influenced by Russia, with little American influence—no R&B music made it to Kazakhstan until very recently, although a new style called Q-pop (*Qazaq pop*) has emerged based on the influence of *K-pop* (Korean pop) and *J-pop* (Japanese pop music). Q-pop's top stars are dance electronica singer-songwriters Kairat Nurtas (Kairat Nurtasuly Aidarbekov, 1989–), Galymzhan Moldanazar (1988*–), and Aikyn Tolepbergen (1982–).

The two most prolific hip hop acts are Rasiel (2009–) and Post Mortem (2007–), bands which have produced only four and two albums, respectively, although Post Mortem, a horrorcore band, has released many singles. Songwriter and producer

Jah Khalib (1993–) is considered the best beatmaker, and rap crew Da Gudda Jazz (n.d.) is a fan favorite.

Diaspora hip hop acts include rapper Scriptonite (Adil Oralbekovich Zhalelov, 1990–), who now lives in Russia. Kazakh rap ranges in topics from romance and sex, to gangster lifestyles, to immigrant issues.

Anthony J. Fonseca

See also: Russia

Further Reading

Adam, Sherwin. 2013. "Kanye West Accepted $3M(illion) to Perform for Despotic Kazakh Leader's Family." *The Independent*, September 2, 22.

Post, Jennifer C. 2014. "Performing Transition in Mongolia: Repatriation and Loss in the Music of Kazakh Mobile Pastoralists." *Yearbook for Traditional Music* 46: 43–61.

Tansug, Feza. 2009. "A Bibliographic Survey of Kazakh and Kyrgyz Literature on Music." *Yearbook for Traditional Music* 41: 199–220.

Keko

(Jocelyne Tracey Keko, 1987–, Tororo, Uganda)

Keko (aka Keko Town) is a Ugandan rapper who broke barriers when she was the first Ugandan artist to sign with a major label. Her breakthrough single, "How We Do It (Remix)," earned a 2011 Buzz Teeniez Award and 2011 Channel O Music Video Award, helping to launch her career.

In 2010, Keko signed with Platinum Entertainment. The first released track she appeared on was "Fallen Heroes" (2010), released through Hip Hop Canvas project (2005–). Keko soon began working with the recording label Supanova Music Group (2010–) to produce new music. Her first single released by Supanova was "Alwoo (Cry for Help)" (2010), a track whose lyrics address social issues such as domestic violence. Soon after, the track "How We Do It (Remix)," featuring the Ugandan music group Goodlyfe Crew (2008–), released as a single and video.

In 2011, she appeared on the grand finale of *Big Brother Africa 6* (also known as *Big Brother Africa: Amplified*). She signed an endorsement deal with Pepsi for Mountain Dew advertisements in East Africa. The song "How We Do It" was used featuring Keko rapping about Mountain Dew. In 2012, under Supanova, Keko collaborated with Just Jose (Joseph Mwima, 1987*–) and they released "Make You Dance," a chart-topping success. She was also beginning to work on her first album, but before completing it, Keko left Supanova for a major label, Sony Music Entertainment Africa, in an effort to further her career and reach international markets.

In 2012, she recorded a series of singles and videos that were supposed to have appeared on the track listing for Sony's release of *Kekonian*, the tentative title of her debut album. The singles released by Sony were "Let Me Go" (2012), "Naughty" (2013), "See Ya" (2013), and "Fly Solo" (2014). In 2014, Keko released a mixtape titled *P.A.R.A.N.O.I.D.* with Sony with guest artists from the Democratic Republic of Congo. In January 2015, the single "Mutima" and its accompanying video were released. In July 2015, Keko began filming for the third season of *Coke*

Studio Africa (2013–), but was kicked off the project and replaced after trashing a hotel room during her stay in Nairobi, Kenya.

After becoming frustrated with the management of her career, Keko announced in 2015 that she would once again be working with manager Shadrack Kuteesa (n.d.). A few weeks later, her video for the single "Ready" was released. Subsequently, the single "Facelift" (2015) was released, featuring Ghana hip hop duo R2Bees (2007–), under Sony Records. Keko's second mixtape, *Love from Venus*, was released in 2016.

It took several years and a title change, but Keko's debut album *Strides* was released in 2016 on RCA Records (1901–). The album contains the previously released singles that were intended for *Kekonian*. In 2017, Keko used Twitter to publicly come out as a lesbian and announced that she moved to Canada.

Lindsey E. Hartman

See also: Uganda

Further Reading

Manishimwe, Wilson. 2016. "Keko Makes a Comeback." *The New Vision* (Kampala, Uganda), September 12.

Ntarangwi, Mwenda. 2009. "Hip Hop and African Identity in Contemporary Globalization." In *East African Hip Hop: Youth Culture and Globalization*, chap. 2. Urbana: University of Illinois Press.

Slim MC. 2014. "Hip Hop and Social Change in Uganda." In *Hip Hop and Social Change in Africa: Ni Wakati*, edited by Msia Kibona Clark and Mickie Mwanzia Koster, chap. 10. Lanham, MD: Lexington Books.

Ken Swift

(Kenneth Gabbert, 1966–, New York City, New York)

Ken Swift is considered one of, if not, the most influential and talented b-boys. He is noted not only for his distinctive dance style but also for his contributions to education and preservation of hip hop dance. Described by many as the epitome of a b-boy, he started dancing in 1978 when he was 12, living in New York's Upper West Side; he learned to dance from observing other dancers in the parks. Today, Ken Swift is a dancer known for continuous development and innovation. Historically, he is credited with the development of many moves, including air tracks/flares, downrock, head and back spins, and windmills, all of which have become part of the standard b-boy repertoire. His unique style includes extremely precise, rapid footwork; successive kicks and landings; prolonged, tight, and precise curled-up backspins; and extremely quick and brief freezes.

Ken Swift's first crew was the Young City Boys (1978–1980s), but he soon joined the Manhattan branch of the Rock Steady Crew (RSC, 1977–). In 1981, when Crazy Legs (1966–) took over as president of RSC following a spectacular victory in a battle, he appointed Ken Swift as co–vice president with Frosty Freeze (1963–2008), a role Ken Swift maintained for years. With the RSC, Ken Swift had many opportunities to appear in film and on television, and he toured extensively as well. Much of his work has been aimed at maintaining the authenticity of breakdancing while helping to legitimize it as an art form.

An avid teacher, Ken Swift regularly judges dance competitions throughout the world. He has won many major awards, including the Universal Zulu Nation's (1973–) Achievement Award to the National Endowment for the Arts' American Master. In a 2011 poll, Ken Swift was named the second most influential dancer of the 20th century by the CNN Icon Series; he was the only b-boy on the list otherwise populated by ballet dancers.

He currently serves as president of the Breaklife Studios (2004–) in Brooklyn, New York, which houses the Ken Swift School of Hip Hop Fundamentals, and VII Gems, a break-off from RSC, originally formed as a subgroup devoted to battles, but has become a movement dedicated to the preservation of hip hop culture in all its forms.

Susannah Cleveland

See also: Battling; Breakdancing; Hip Hop Dance; Rock Steady Crew; The United States

Further Reading

Light, Alan, ed. 1999. *The Vibe History of Hip Hop.* New York: Three Rivers Press.

Schloss, Joseph G. 2009. *B-Boys, B-Girls, and Hip Hop Culture in New York.* New York: Oxford University Press.

Further Viewing

Ahearn, Charlie, dir. (1982) 2002. *Wild Style.* New York: Wild Style Productions.

Israel, dir. 2002. *The Freshest Kids: A History of the B-Boy.* Los Angeles: QD3 Entertainment.

Lathan, Stan, dir. (1984) 2003. *Beat Street.* Santa Monica, CA: MGM Home Entertainment.

Lee, Benson, dir. 2008. *Planet B-Boy.* New York: Elephant Eye Films.

Lyne, Adrian, dir. (1983) 2002. *Flashdance.* Hollywood: Paramount Pictures.

Silver, Tony, dir. (1983) 2004. *Style Wars.* Los Angeles: Public Art Films.

Kendrick Lamar

(Kendrick Lamar Duckworth, 1987–, Compton, California)

Kendrick Lamar is a socially conscious American rapper and songwriter who is both critically acclaimed and commercially successful. He frequently addresses institutionalized racism, gang culture, addiction, and depression in his lyrics, and demonstrates musical influences from spoken word, funk, and jazz. Outspokenly connected with West Coast rap, Kendrick Lamar's stylistic influences include Tupac Shakur (1971–1996), the Notorious B.I.G. (1972–1997), Jay-Z (1969–), Eminem (1972–), and Nas (1973–). In 2012, he made his major-label debut, jointly releasing *good kid, m.A.A.d City*; it was certified Platinum. He released the critically acclaimed *To Pimp a Butterfly* album in 2015, winning a Grammy for Best Rap Album.

Early on, he released four mixtapes under the moniker K-Dot: *Youngest N—a in Charge (Y.N.I.C.,* 2005), *Training Day* (2005), *No Sleep Till NYC* (2007), and *C4* (2009). His fifth mixtape, *O(verly) D(edicated)* (2010), was his first under the name Kendrick Lamar, released under the Top Dawg independent record label (Top Dawg Entertainment, aka TDE, 2004–), with which he had signed in 2005. With Top Dawg, he released his first full studio album, *Section.80*, in 2011. The debut single on the album, "HiiiPoWeR," refers to a self-empowerment movement previously referenced by Kendrick Lamar on "Cut You Off (To Grow Closer)" on the *O(verly) D(edicated)* mixtape. Along with Ab-Soul (Herbert Anthony Stevens IV, 1987–), the Watts, Los Angeles–based Jay Rock (Johnny Reed McKinzie Jr., 1985–), and Schoolboy Q (Quincy Matthew Hanley, 1986–), from Wiesbaden, Germany, he is a member of and frequent collaborator with the Top Dawg Entertainment collective Black Hippy (2009–).

Kendrick Lamar's *good kid, m.A.A.d City,* with Top Dawg, which was by then distributed by Interscope Records (1989–), was a concept album set in the Compton neighborhood of his youth during the summer of 2004. It is a pensive narrative that touches on addiction, gangs, love, and religion. Five singles were released off the album: "The Recipe," "Swimming Pools (Drank)," "B—, Don't Kill My Vibe," "Poetic Justice," and "Backseat Freestyle." A frequent guest on songs by both rap and pop artists, in 2013 he received attention for verses on A$AP Rocky's (Rakim Mayers, 1988–) "F—kin' Problems" and Big Sean's (Sean Michael Leonard Anderson, 1988–) "Control."

To Pimp a Butterfly (2015) delves further into political themes, but continues the introspection heard in Kendrick Lamar's previous work. In it he experiments with free jazz, avant-garde, soul, and funk sounds. Singles from the album include "i," "The Blacker the Berry," "King Kunta," "Alright," and "These Walls." "Alright" won 2015 Grammys for Best Rap Song and Best Rap Performance, and "These Walls" received a Grammy for Best Rap/Sung Collaboration. Kendrick Lamar also added a verse to the remixed version of Taylor Swift's (1989–) "Bad Blood," garnering another Grammy for the music video. In 2016, he released *untitled unmastered,* a compilation album of unreleased demos for *To Pimp a Butterfly.* In 2017, he released the album *DAMN,* which produced the No. 1 Billboard Hot 100 hit single, "Humble." Just two months after *DAMN*'s release, the album was certified double Platinum.

Katy E. Leonard

See also: Gangsta Rap; Political Hip Hop; The United States

Further Reading

Blum, Adam. 2016. "Rhythm Nation." *Studies in Gender and Sexuality* 17, no. 3: 141–49.

Graham, Natalie. 2017. "What Slaves We Are: Narrative, Trauma, and Power in Kendrick Lamar's 'Roots.'" *Transition* 122, no. 1 (2017): 123–32.

Further Listening

Kendrick Lamar. 2012. *good kid, m.A.A.d City.* Aftermath Entertainment.

Kendrick Lamar. 2015. *To Pimp a Butterfly.* Aftermath Entertainment.

Kenya

Kenya is an East African country that neighbors Ethiopia, Somalia, Tanzania, Uganda, and South Sudan. In 1963, Kenya gained its independence from the United Kingdom, and in 1964, the country became the Republic of Kenya. By a small margin, the Kikuyu is Kenya's largest population, followed by Luhya, Luo, Kalenjin,

Kamba, Kisii, Meru, and other African populations. Hip hop arrived in Kenya by the mid-1980s near the beginning of the Moi Era, but Kenyan hip hop did not emerge until the early 1990s in Nairobi, the country's capital city. Radio presenter, journalist, social activist, and underground rapper Mwafrika (now Mwa-free-ka, aka Mwaf, Makarios Ouma, n.d.) promoted early Kenyan hip hop at a time when popular music tastes included American soul, rock, and funk, Europop, Jamaican *reggae*, *soukous* (Congolese *rumba*), Guadeloupean *zouk*, Zanzibaran *taarab* music, and Swahili pop. Mwafrika later recorded and produced, with rapping texts mainly in Swahili and English—both official languages of Kenya—and at times in Sheng (slang) and tribal languages. Earliest Kenyan artists imitated American rapping styles and employed previously recorded American beats and samples. Nairobi-based Kalamashaka (aka K-Shaka, 1995–) was a pioneering rapping crew whose lyrical content focused on street violence, drugs, politics, tribalism, and HIV/AIDS. Kalamashaka's hit single "Tafsiri Hii" ("Interpret This" or "Read This," 1997) sparked the popularity of sociopolitical hip hop in Kenya. Kalamashaka's debut studio album was *Ni Wakati* (*It's Time*, 2001).

Kenyan rap contains a lot of political content, and it employs turntablism, sampling, spoken word, traditional chanting, and reggae-infused rhythms. Early acts were K-South (1995–), Ukoo Flani Maumau (1996–), Gidigidi Majimaji (1999–), and Necessary Noize (2000–). Nazizi (Nazizi Hirji, n.d.) of Necessary Noize is known as the First Lady of Rap. Some early Kenyan acts gained experience in the United States and then returned to Nairobi. These include producer Steve Ominde (n.d.) and the hardcore rapper MC Goreala (Eric Mukunza, 1992*–). Wawesh (Robert Wawero Kiboy, n.d.), an MC and producer from Nairobi, was based in Gothenburg, Sweden from 1984 to 2008 before returning. Others have been part of the Kenyan diaspora: Nairobi producer DJ Dona (Dona Ishike, n.d.), now based in Kansas City, Missouri, has collaborated with K-Nel (Nelson Muriuki, n.d.), a DJ and MC from Nairobi who was based in Cologne, for the compilation album *Kenyawood* (2008). As of 2014, K-Nel is based in Atlanta.

GENGE, BOOMBA MUSIC, KAPUKA RAP, AND RIFTSYDE FLAVA

By the late 1990s, the hip hop subgenre genge (meaning a group of people) emerged. Genge's lyrical content is more sexualized than early sociopolitical Kenyan hip hop. Since the 2010s, genge has become one of the dominant hip hop subgenres in Kenya. Using Sheng, Swahili, and local street dialects, genge gained popularity through Nonini (Hubert Mbuku Nakitare, 1982–), commonly known as the Godfather of Genge. He is the founding MC of the Nairobi genge crew P-Unit (Pro-habo Unit, 2003–15). Another rapper who popularized genge, Juacali (Paul Nunda, 1979–), established Calif Records (2000–) in Nairobi, and produced acts such as Jimwat (aka Jimw@t, Jimwizzy, James Wathigo Mburu, 1985–), as well as Nonini. Pilipili (Peter Gatonye, 1982–) is also a well known genge musician. Boomba music emerged around the same time as genge; however, it distinguishes itself by fusing hip hop with reggae and traditional pan-African music. Like genge, boomba uses Swahili and Sheng. Since the 2010s, it has become extremely popular in Kenya and Uganda. K-South is just one act that has recorded boomba music.

Another Kenyan hip hop subgenre is kapuka rap, having its roots with the Nairobi production team and label Ogopa Deejays (1990s*). The Nairobi group Camp Mulla (2009–) became one of the best-known kapuka rap artists with its release *FuNKYToWN* (2012). Kapuka rap employs dance and synthpop, in addition to some reggae. Another emerging Kenyan hip hop subgenre, Riftsyde flava (originating in Nakuru), has gained popularity in the 2010s. It features ostentatious rappers who use sexualized lyrics, accompanied by a prominent reggae bass line.

Melissa Ursula Dawn Goldsmith

See also: Political Hip Hop; Reggae; Tanzania; Uganda; The United States

Further Reading

Kidula, Jean Ngoya. 2012. "The Local and Global in Kenyan Rap and Hip Hop Culture." In *Hip Hop Africa: New African Music in a Globalizing World*, edited by Eric Charry, chap. 8. Bloomington: Indiana University Press.

Njogu, Kimani, and Maupeu, Hervé, eds. 2007. *Songs and Politics in Eastern Africa.* Dar es Salaam, Tanzania: Nyota Publishers.

Further Listening

Camp Mulla. 2012. *FuNKYToWN.* Sub Sahara.

K'naan

(Keinan Abdi Warsame, Keynaan Cabdi Warsame, 1978–, Mogadishu, Somalia)

K'naan is an internationally renowned Somali Canadian rapper, singer-songwriter, poet, writer, multi-instrumentalist, and philanthropist who fuses alternative hip hop with spoken word poetry, indie, R&B, neo soul, Ethiopian jazz, traditional Somali music, and Afrobeat. K'naan records in multiple musical roles: He raps, sings his own contrasting lyrical passages, and recites poetry—sometimes all in the same song. K'naan has won many awards, including Juno Awards for Rap Recording of the Year for *The Dusty Foot Philosopher* (2006), Artist of the Year (2010), and Single of the Year for "Wavin' Flag" (2011).

His four studio albums are *My Life Is a Movie* (2004), *The Dusty Foot Philosopher* (2005), *Troubadour* (2009), and *Country, God, or the Girl* (2012). *Troubadour* charted internationally, peaking at No. 32 on the Billboard 200 and No. 7 on the Canadian Albums Chart; *Country, God, or the Girl* peaked at No. 129 on the Billboard 200. K'Naan's top-charting hits include "Wavin' Flag (Celebration Mix)" (2010)—with its original version from 2009 peaking at No. 2 on the Canadian Hot 100 and the mix peaking at No. 82 on the Billboard Hot 100—and "Is Anybody Out There?" (2012). "Wavin' Flag (Celebration Mix) was Music Canada–certified triple Platinum and "Is Anybody Out There?" was Music Canada–certified Platinum—the "Celebration Mix" was performed with Young Artists for Haiti (2010), and proceeds went to Free the Children (now WE Charity), War Child Canada, and World Vision Canada.

EARLY YEARS IN SOMALIA

Born Keinan Abdi Warsame, K'naan came from a musical family. His aunt was the singer Magool (Halima Khaliif Omar, 1948–2004), a traditional Somali singer known for patriotic songs during the Ethio-Somali War (aka the Ogaden War, 1977–78), love songs, and Islamic protest songs against the late 1970s Somali government. While he was growing up in Mogadishu, Somalia's capital city, Magool sang to him and was part of his earliest exposure to songs, poetry, and lyric writing—Muslim Somali culture emphasizes poetry—in fact, Somalia is nicknamed the Nation of Bards or the Nation of Poets; however, growing resistance to the Siad-Barre regime led to the Somali Civil War (1986–), which continues as of 2018, despite the 1990 defeat of the Siad-Barre regime, as regional forces and clan militias compete for power still. Music was suppressed, and musicians such as Magool left Somalia in self-imposed exile. His father left for New York City when K'naan was a boy, and he spent his early teen years in war-torn Somalia, experiencing bloodshed firsthand when a teenager shot three of his close friends with a machine gun. By the time he was age 13, in 1991, most of his immediate family had moved to New York City and then settled in Toronto.

MUSICAL CAREER

His first language was Somali, so K'naan began studying English both in school and by listening to American rappers such as Rakim (1968–) and Nas (1973–). Learning poetry by ear is a frequently performed Somali cultural practice; before learning English, he memorized rap lyrics and studied patterns of internal and end rhymes. He began writing and rapping while growing up in one of Toronto's toughest neighborhoods, focusing not only on his experiences during the Somali Civil War, but also as a Somali immigrant often exposed to his new home's street violence. In 2000, as Keinaan, he released his debut studio album, *What Next?* Shortly afterward, he shortened his stage name to K'naan. His own first name means *traveler* in Somali. In 1999, K'naan did a spoken-word performance that criticized how the UN (United Nations) failed in its early 1990s missions to keep peace in Somalia. Senegalese mbalax singer-songwriter Youssou N'Dour (1959–) was so moved that he invited K'Naan to record two of his songs, "Drain My Gray Away" and "This Is My World" on his (N'Dour's) *Building Bridges* (2001), a UN-produced studio album. K'naan also toured with N'Dour, performing with Canadian singer-songwriter and hip hop artist Nelly Furtado (1978–), among others. K'naan continued performing and went on other UN-affiliated tours while recording studio, compilation, and live albums, singles, as well as the EP *More Beautiful than Silence* (2012).

MUSICAL TENDENCIES AND RECENT WORK

K'naan's texts favor English, but he also raps in Somali. Though often compared to the political and socially conscious music of legendary reggae singer-songwriter and guitarist Bob Marley (Robert Nesta Marley, 1945–1981), K'naan's texts and musical choices are strongly influenced by Nas, who also uses storytelling and message rap in versatile ways. For example, Nas uses gangsta rap braggadocio for an ironic twist in order to deliver a philosophical message, which is found in albums such as *Street's Disciple* (2004). K'naan uses the same device on "If Rap Gets Jealous" on *The Dusty Foot Philosopher* and *Troubadour*. In fact, his "Nothing to Lose" (2012) on *Country, God, or the Girl* featured Nas. K'naan also focuses on positive, uplifting messages, as found on "Take a Minute," also on *Troubadour*. His warm singing style and use of positive message rap is comparable to that of Chance the Rapper (1993–).

In 2011, K'naan visited Somalia; an opinion piece in his own words appeared in the *New York Times* Sunday Review. K'naan's latest album, the critically acclaimed *Country, God, or the Girl*, took on a different, more commercially oriented sound that included pop. Since its 2012 release, K'naan has not recorded an album; however, he has remained active performing, writing, directing, and engaging in peace activist work. In 2016, HBO (Home Box Office) picked up his pilot for *Mogadishu Minnesota*, directed and written by K'naan and produced by Kathryn Bigelow (1951–), the first and only woman who has won the Academy Award for Best Director. As of 2018, K'naan is the most famous Somali rapper and plans to return to recording.

Melissa Ursula Dawn Goldsmith

See also: Canada; Political Hip Hop; Somalia

Further Reading

Boutros, Alexandra. 2014. "'My Real'll Make Yours a Rental': Hip Hop and Canadian Copyright." In *Dynamic Fair Dealing: Creating Canadian Culture Online*, edited by Rosemary J. Coombe, Darren Wershler, and Martin Zeilinger, chap. 25. Toronto: University of Toronto Press.

K'naan. 2011. "A Son Returns to the Agony of Somalia." *New York Times*, September 25, SR5.

Sobral, Ana. 2013. "The Survivor's Odyssey: K'naan's 'The Dusty Foot Philosopher' as Modern Epic." *African American Review* 46, no. 1: 21–36.

Further Listening

K'naan. 2006. *The Dusty Foot Philosopher.* Sony BMG Music Entertainment Canada.

K'naan. 2009. *Troubadour.* AandM/Octone Records.

K'naan. 2012. *Country, God, or the Girl.* AandM/Octone Records.

Kool Herc

(aka Kool DJ Herc, DJ Kool Herc, Clive Campbell, 1955–, Kingston, Jamaica)

Kool Herc is recognized as the first hip hop DJ (turntablist). He originated the technique of stringing together the percussion breaks or breakdowns (when most instruments, except the rhythm section, drop out) from two copies of the same record by cross-fading, midsong, between discs on two different turntables. Not only did this technique create hip hop, but it extended the portion of the musical break that appealed most to dancers, which eventually led to a new term for the dancing that accompanied it, breakdancing (named after the isolated breakbeat). Often called the father or godfather of hip hop, Kool Herc's legacy extends beyond his invention of early DJ culture and addition to its evolution. Although there is still much debate about the use and origin of the term breakdancing, which was not attached to the art form by the hip hop community but rather by mainstream media, Kool Herc likely coined the earlier term b-boy, used to describe hip hop dancers (a shortening of break-boy, though there are alternative suggestions, such as Bronx-boy or beat-boy) and, by extension, created the act of dancing to breaks, or b-boying.

EARLY DJ GIGS

Kool Herc's family moved the 12-year-old from Jamaica to the Bronx in 1967, before reggae became a well known musical genre. His first foray into what developed into hip hop culture occurred when he drew graffiti as part of the 1970s and 1980s aerosol crew Ex-Vandals, or Experienced Vandals. It was during this stint with the Ex-Vandals that he got the nickname Kool Herc, a modification of a nickname he'd already garnered, Hercules, because of his prowess in high school sports. He soon quit graffiti out of fear of punishment from his strict father.

His public debut as a DJ was at a 1973 back-to-school party that he and his sister hosted in the community room of their apartment building to raise money for school clothes. Kool Herc continued hosting parties there and frequently had to move them outside to accommodate the influx of dancers. Within a year, he was spinning records at clubs such as the Twilight Zone and Hevalo, and he gained a loyal following, reportedly causing other DJ shows to shut down as dancers began attending only Kool Herc's shows.

HERCULOID

At this time, Kool Herc saw his role as providing entertainment that was deeply dependent on the accompanying dancing and not as a commercial music venture—he invested his earnings in the purchase of more equipment and records and an enormous sound system called the Herculoid, which he based on systems he had seen as a child in Jamaica. The Herculoid began as a turntable, an amplifier, and two large PA (public address) columns, but he continuously upgraded it; he eventually became famous for his system's volume and clarity, with a mix heavy in bass, aimed at getting dancers to feel the music. The records he spun included funk, soul, and Latin tunes, though he became so secretive about his source material that he (like many other DJs) reportedly soaked label demarcations off his discs to keep others from copying his set. Clubgoers respected the originality of his choices—all were in stark opposition to the disco songs that were on the radio at the time, and many of his selections, such as English progressive and blues rock band Babe Ruth's (1970–1976, 2007–) "The Mexican" (1972), James Brown's (1933–2006) "Give It Up or Turnit a Loose" (1968), and the Jimmy Castor Bunch's (1972–1980) "It's Just Begun" (1972), became b-boy anthems.

Kool Herc wanted to expand the DJ's role from just spinning records on two turntables, so he gradually introduced into his sets a tradition called toasting, something he had learned in Jamaica. This usually unrhymed practice involved calling out the names of guests to welcome, honor, or praise them. Eventually, as toasts became more elaborate, they called on traditions of African American poetry and traditions of call-and-response; they eventually developed into rapping, making MCs as integral to hip hop as DJs. The MC who worked most closely with Herc during this development was Coke La Rock (aka Coco La Rock, anonymous, 1955*–). Kool Herc was also joined by both male and female local MCs, as well as b-boy dancers; he referred to his entourage as the Herculords (1973–1980s).

LATER INVOLVEMENT IN HIP HOP

In 1977, Kool Herc was stabbed while he was playing at the Executive Playhouse. The incident caused both him and Coke La Rock to abandon the hip hop scene. Other DJs began to make names for themselves, and some asserted that Kool Herc was an inventor of a music genre but added that he did not possess the flashiness necessary for commercial success. DJs who came after him, such as Afrika Bambaata (1957–) and Grandmaster Flash (1958–), emphasized style and fashion, as well as music.

Since the early 2000s, renewed interest in the recording and preservation of hip hop culture have led to much interest in Kool Herc's life and work, and his name has been more prominent in popular culture studies. In 2007, the apartment building at 1520 Sedgwick Avenue, where DJ Herc and his sister began hosting parties, was recognized by New York state officials as the Birthplace of Hip Hop and placed on the national registers of historic places.

Susannah Cleveland

See also: Jamaica; Turntablism; The United States

Further Reading

Chang, Jeff. 2005. *Can't Stop, Won't Stop: A History of the Hip Hop Generation.* New York: Picador.

Fricke, Jim, and Charlie Ahearn. 2002. *The Experience Music Project Oral History of Hip Hop's First Decade: Yes Yes Y'All.* Cambridge, MA: Da Capo Press.

George, Nelson. 2004. (Reprinted 2012). "Hip Hop's Founding Fathers Speak the Truth." In *That's the Joint: The Hip Hop Studies Reader*, edited by Murray Forman and Mark Anthony Neal, 2nd ed., chap. 4. New York: Routledge.

Katz, Mark. 2012. *Groove Music: The Art and Culture of the Hip Hop DJ.* New York: Oxford University Press.

Further Viewing

Israel, dir. 2012. *The Freshest Kids: A History of the B-Boy.* Los Angeles, CA: QD3 Entertainment.

Lathan, Stan, dir. (1984). 2003. *Beat Street.* Santa Monica, CA: MGM Home Entertainment.

Kool Moe Dee

(Mohandes Dewese, 1963–, Harlem, New York)

Kool Moe Dee is an American rapper who started out his solo career in 1987 using an old-school style, comparable to the singsong delivery of Will Smith's the Fresh

Old-school rapper Kool Moe Dee was a member of the Harlem-based group Treacherous Three before having his own successful solo career. In 1987 he released the Platinum album *How Ya Like Me Now*, and in 1989 he was the first rapper to perform at the Grammy Awards. (Josh Brasted/FilmMagic/Getty Images)

Prince (1968–) or MC Hammer (1962–), but then made the successful transition in 1989 to a more raw delivery, with extended lines and uneven rhythms, with his third album, *Knowledge Is King*, which was certified Gold. In his own words, he was one of the few early rappers who found the right vibe at the right time, at one point changing his style after consulting fans, choosing to incorporate more dance rhythms, funk, and soul samples. He is also known as one-third of Harlem-based the Treacherous Three (1978–1984), which released three albums on Sugar Hill Records (1978–), including the song "The New Rap Language." The song featured Spoonie Gee (1963–), and serves as an early example in hip hop of using 16th-note rhythms with a lot of internal rhyme, a rapid vocal style still used in rap.

In 1986, after releasing his underground hit "Go See the Doctor," Kool Moe Dee signed with Jive Records (1981–) and released *Kool Moe Dee* (1987), featuring "I'm Kool Moe Dee," a song which introduced the rapper to the public. It was followed by his best-selling effort, the certified-Platinum *How Ya Like Me Now* (1987).

Kool Moe Dee is also famous for being involved in one of the earliest rap rivalries with LL Cool J (1968–), for being the first rapper to perform at the Grammy Awards in 1989, and for appearing in minor roles in various American films, such as *Panther* (1995), *Gang Related* (1997), *Storm Trooper* (1998), *Cypress Edge* (1999), *Out Kold* (2001), and *The New Guy* (2002). Kool Moe Dee went from being a high schooler who practiced his rapping and rhyming skills at house parties, to forming a seminal rap band, to taking a hiatus in order to earn a bachelor's degree in communications, to becoming what *Rolling Stone* called him one of the founders of rap.

Known primarily as an old-school rapper, his rhymes show a political consciousness, although he was just as likely to create lyrics of braggadocio and self-pride, along with a few party anthems. His songs spoke out against violence, drug abuse, and mistreatment of women, and he was a member of the Stop the Violence Movement (1987–). He claims that his influences included the verbal sparring of Muhammad Ali (Cassius Marcellus Clay Jr., 1942–2016), as well as the creative wordplay of Dr. Seuss (Theodor Seuss Geisel, 1904–1991).

Anthony J. Fonseca

See also: Chopper; Political Hip Hop; The United States

Further Reading

Bradley, Adam, and Andrew Dubois, eds. 2010. "Kool Moe Dee." Under "Part 2: 1985–92: The Golden Age" in *The Anthology of Rap*, pp. 201–8. New Haven, CT: Yale University Press.

Kool Moe Dee. 2003. *There's a God on the Mic: The True 50 Greatest MCs*. With a Foreword by Chuck D and photographs by Ernie Paniccioli. New York: Thunder's Mouth Press.

Further Listening

Kool Moe Dee. 1989. *Knowledge Is King*. Jive Records.

Koolism

(formerly Tribe Ledda L, 1992–, Canberra, Australia)

Koolism is a duo consisting of MC and lyricist Hau Latukefu (Langomi-e-Hau Latukefu, 1976–) from Queanbeyan, Australia, and producer, musician, and turntablist DJ Rampage (aka Danielsan Ichiban, Daniel Elleson, 1975–), from Auckland, New Zealand. Koolism is best known for its second album, *Part Three: Random Thoughts* (2004), which won an ARIA (Australian Recording Industry Association) Music Award for Best Urban Release.

In 1995, after recording the mixtape *These Front Door Keys* (1993), the duo, recording under the name Tribe Ledda L (1992–1995), changed its name to Koolism. It recorded its first mixtape, *Bedroom S—* (1996), in a home studio, using rap, singing, beats, and samples. The duo's rudimentary studio equipment allowed for limited editing only. The mixtape was simply handed from one person to the next, and despite the odds against its success, *Bedroom S—* was heard throughout the country, reaching Australian rapper, hip hop music journalist, publisher, sound recording distributor, and producer Blaze (Jason Murphy, 1968*–) from Sound Unlimited (aka Sound Unlimited Posse, Westside Posse, 1990–1994) and Dr. Phibes (anonymous, n.d.) of Next Level (aka The Next Level, 1990–2000*) in Sydney. Both had just formed the recording label Parallax View (1998–) and offered to release Koolism's first album, *Lift Ya Game* (1998). This album was followed by the EPs *Blue Notes* and *The Season* (both 2002). Both were intended as the first parts of a four-part series; however, in 2004, while Koolism was on tour, materials for *Butcher Shop* and *The Epic* were stolen in a car burglary. Koolism's album *Part One* (2002) consisted of some tracks previously recorded on mixtapes.

Since 2003, Koolism has toured, gaining more mainstream attention in Australia. *Part Three: Random Thoughts* (counting *Blue Notes* and *The Season* as Part Two), signified a shift to Invada Records (2002–) in Sydney, and has been the duo's best-selling album. Subsequent albums include *New Old Ground* (2006) and *The 'Umu* (*Underground Oven*, in Tongan, 2010). The themes in the duo's lyrics include Polynesian pride, family, war and terrorism, and braggadocio, and Koolism's lyrics often offer uplifting messages. Though the duo includes some electronica and other instruments, Koolism's sound often resembles American old-school hip hop.

In 2008, Latukefu began hosting the *Triple J Hip Hop Show*, a New Zealand radio program on the government-funded station Triple J (1975–). On his own, Latukefu released *Let It Be Known* (2014) and *The No End Theory* (2015), the latter fusing jazz, R&B, and new jack swing with hip hop. He has also collaborated with the Adelaide, Australian hip hop group Hilltop Hoods (1994–), among others, on EPs and mixtapes. As Dan Elleson, DJ Rampage has written, produced, and collaborated on tracks recorded by Australian hip hop artists such as Mnemonic Ascent (1999–2015). As of 2018, Koolism is still together, but has not released a recent album.

Melissa Ursula Dawn Goldsmith

See also: Australia; Political Hip Hop

Further Reading

Maxwell, Ian. 2003. *Phat Beats, Dope Rhymes: Hip Hop Down Under Comin' Upper.* Middletown, CT: Wesleyan University Press.

Mitchell, Tony. 2007. "The DIY Habitus of Australian Hip Hop." *Culture and Policy* 123, no. 1: 109–22.

Further Listening

Koolism. 2004. *Part Three: Random Thoughts.* Invada Records.

Korea

Korea is an East Asian peninsula that has been divided along political lines since 1945. It consists of two distinct sovereign states, the Democratic People's Republic of Korea (North) and the Republic of Korea (South). Political tensions led to the Korean War (1950–1953) and the tense current political climate. Due to strict government controls in North Korea, there is no known hip hop scene in the country. However, South Korea has a vibrant contemporary music scene that features electronic or hip hop music, known as K-pop, which emerged during the 1990s.

Traditional Korean music includes folk, religious/ceremonial, and ritual music styles. In contemporary Korea traditional music, called *gugak*, and Western music, called *yangak*, compete for popularity. Korean folk follows a set of rhythms and melodic modes, and their vocal styles and modes are limited (the degree being dependent on the region). Instruments include *gayageum*, *ajaeng*, and *geomungo* (zithers), *haegum* (a vertical fiddle), *daegeum*, *danso*, and various other flutes, *piri* (an oboe), *saenghwang* (a mouth organ), the *hun* (an ocarina), and various types of gongs, drums, and bells.

As of 2018, there is no known hip hop scene in North Korea. Both Kim Jong-il (1941–2011, supreme leader 1994–2011) and his son Kim Jong-un's (1983*–, supreme leader 2011–) totalitarian regimes employ self-imposed isolationism and do not allow freedom of speech, threatening punishment by jail sentence, beating, or death. The military-first regimes have the highest number of military and paramilitary personnel in the world, which polices on the street level for activities that are perceived as protesting against the government. Mass surveillance extends to monitoring all digital communications. By the 2010s, revolutionary operas are still promoted and state-financed. Since the 1980s, North Korea has had limited access to pop music, including South Korean K-pop—neither contain politicized content—and its own government-selected pop, which includes Pyongyang, North Korea's the Moranbong Band (aka Moran Hill Orchestra, 2012–), with members selected by Kim Jong-un.

Korean hip hop, or K–hip hop, is mainly associated with South Korea. It emerged as a musical form in the late 1980s once military rule had ended, becoming popular first in Korea and then internationally, as part of the Korean Wave, an increased global interest in South Korean culture that began around the 1990, with the emergence of social media and video sharing platforms. The first rapping to occur in any song was by rock singer Hong Seo-beom (n.d.), in his song "Kim Sat-gat" (1989), a tribute to Kim Byeong-yeon (aka Kim Sat-gat or Rainhat Poet, 1807–1863), and the first rapper was singer, dancer, and rapper Hyun Jin-young (Huh Hyun-seok, 1971–) of the band Wawa (1990–), whose solo album *New Dance* (1990) introduced hip hop to Korea. As of 2018, Hyun Jin-young has released five albums, including one that is jazz-influenced. Another early hip hop act was the hip hop and K-pop trio Seo Taiji and Boys (1992–1996), whose new jack swing song "Nan Arayo" (1992) incorporated American hip hop and R&B and whose first four albums sold four million copies and incorporated hard rock and gangsta rap. Other early hip hop groups included the K-pop dancer new jack swing duo Deux (1992–1995), whose members worked with Hyun Jin-young, and hip hop trio DJ DOC (1994–), whose "Dance with DOC" (1997) and "Run To You" (2000) are considered benchmark K-pop songs.

An expanding club scene and social media allowed hip hop music to gain popularity in the late 1990s, and rap groups such as Drunken Tiger (1999–2013) began to emerge. Drunken Tiger wrote its own lyrics, which were often explicit and critical of the government, and were therefore controversial. In 2001, the band topped the Korean charts with "Good Life," from the band's hit album, *The Legend of. . . .* In 2013, group leader Tiger JK (Seo Jung-kwon, 1974–) formed a new hip hop trio, MFBTY (2013–), an acronym for "My Fans Are Better Than Yours." The trio released a hit song, "Sweet Dream" (2013), and signed with Feel Ghood Music (2013–), Tiger JK's new label. In 2015, MFBTY released the album *Wondaland* on the label, and it peaked at No. 8 on Billboard's World Albums chart. Meanwhile, another record label, YG Entertainment (1996–), run by former Seo Taiji and Boys member Yang Hyun-suk (1969–), produced hip hop duo Jinusean (1997–), which had a hit song with "A-Yo" (2001). Important underground hip hop artists to emerge around the turn of the century included rapper-songwriter Verbal Jint (Kim Jin-tae, 1980–) and rap duo Garion (1998–). Verbal Jint began as an underground rapper and introduced rhyming into Korean rapping with his debut underground EP, *Modern Rhymes* (2001). In 2008, he formed the hip hop group Overclass and went mainstream with his solo album, *Framed*. Earlier, Garion's 2004 self-titled debut album, a compilation of the band's underground songs from the early 2000s, was notable for being rapped entirely in Korean. The band's 2005 single, "Mutu," won a Korean Music Awards.

Korean mainstream hip hop artists began to emerge around 2000. Dynamic Duo (2003–) achieved success with their 2004 debut album, *Taxi Driver*, which became the best-selling Korean hip hop album to date. Its *Double Dynamite* (2005) won a Korean Music Awards. The duo has released eight albums as of 2018. Epik High (2001–), known for its fusion of various hip hop music styles, became one of South Korea's music exports, touring North America in 2015 and playing Coachella in 2016. In addition, the success of comic rapper PSY's (1977–) "Gangnam Style" (2012) put Korean hip hop on the international map. The popularity of Korean hip hop was heightened with the 2012 TV reality series, *Show Me the Money* (2012–2017), which pitted rappers against one another and featured Verbal Jint in Season One.

The show brought female rappers to the attention of the public, with contestants such as chopper style rapper and pianist Tymee (aka E.via, Lee Ok-joo, 1985–) becoming popular. Her controversial videos and lyrics, which feature scantily clad females and twerking, with songs about female empowerment, have made her a fan favorite. Other current rappers include trap rapper Keith Ape (Lee Dongheon, 1993–), whose 2015 hit "It G Ma" became an international hit.

In addition to music, hip hop fashion has become popular with South Korean youth due to the influence of YG Entertainment's clothing sponsorships and its 2012 agreement with Cheil Industries (1954–) to launch a South Korean-based international fashion market, NONAGON. South Korea also has a vibrant b-boy scene, particularly in Seoul, that began in 2001 when hip hop dance crew Visual Shock (n.d.) performed well at Battle of the Year. In 2007, the Korean Tourism Organization founded an international b-boying competition called R-16 Korea.

Anthony J. Fonseca

See also: Breakdancing; Morning of Owl; PSY; T.I.P. Crew

Further Reading

Song, Myoung-Sun. 2014. "The S(e)oul of Hip Hop: Locating Space and Identity in Korean Rap." In *The Korean Wave: Korean Popular Culture in Global Context*, edited by Yasue Kuwahara, chap. 7. New York: Palgrave Macmillan.

Um, Hae-Kyung. 2013. "The Poetics of Resistance and the Politics of Crossing Borders: Korean Hip Hop and 'Cultural Reterritorialisation.'" *Popular Music* 32, no. 1: 51–64.

Further Listening

MFBTY. 2013. *Wondaland.* Feel Ghood Music.

KRS-One

(aka KRS, Blastmaster KRS-One, Teacha, Lawrence Parker, 1965–, Bronx, New York)

KRS-One is an American hip hop musician, rapper, turntablist, record producer, and social activist who began recording in 1986 as part of the hip hop group Boogie

Down Productions (BDP, 1985–1992), which he formed with DJ Scott La Rock (Scott Monroe Sterling, 1962–1987) and beatboxer D-Nice (Derrick Jones, 1970–) in South Bronx, New York.

Parker became KRS-One after he left his parents' home at age 16 to become an MC; while living in a homeless shelter he was given the nickname Krisna because of his interest in Hare Krishnas. While living in the shelter, he met Sterling, who was a counselor. Along with D-Nice and various guest musicians, they released BDP's debut album, *Criminal Minded* (1987) on the Bronx, New York, independent label B-Boy Records (1986–). The album reached No. 73 on Billboard's Top R&B/Hip-Hop Albums chart and sold over 200,000 copies; however, DJ Scott La Rock was shot and killed while attempting to intervene in a fight, causing KRS-One to retool the group, resulting in a series of solo projects until 1993, when he began releasing records as KRS-One.

Aside from his music, KRS-One is known for his political activism, including his helping to found the Stop the Violence Movement after the death of La Rock and his producing 1991 EP *H.E.A.L. (Human Education against Lies)*, featuring the song "Heal Yourself," with verses featuring Big Daddy Kane (1968–), LL Cool J (1968–), MC Lyte (1970–), Queen Latifah (1970–), and Run-D.M.C. (1981–), among others.

EARLY RECORDINGS

In 1985, under the name 12:41, KRS-One and La Rock contributed to a single, "$ucce$$ I$ the Word," released both by the New York independent labels Sleeping Bag Records (1981–) and Fresh Records (1985–1992), and by the U.K. label Streetwave Records (1980–1988), with the latter, as the B side to Just Ice's (Joseph Williams Jr., 1965–) "Put That Record Back On," but it did not chart. Boogie Down Productions came into being as an offshoot of a quartet that KRS-One and La Rock originally put together called Scott La Rock and the Celebrity Three (1986*); however, dissent among the band caused it to break up after it recorded its first single, "Advance" (1986).

With *Criminal Minded*, Boogie Down Productions helped usher in the era of gangsta and diss rap, as the album cover depicted the band wearing ammunition and brandishing guns and featured two early diss tracks called "South Bronx" and "The Bridge Is Over," songs considered part of the so-called Bridge Wars, an argument over the New York birthplace of rap, between BDP and radio DJ Mr. Magic (John Rivas, 1956–2009) representing the Bronx, and rapper MC Shan (Shawn Moltke, 1965–) with DJ and producer Marley Marl (1962–) representing Queens. KRS-One also engaged in an early live diss battle with MC Shan. BDP is also credited with helping to introduce rock music sampling and Jamaican rhythms into rap music, using a rhythm made famous by Yellowman (Winston Foster, 1956–) on "Remix for P is Free."

In 1988, without Scott La Rock, KRS-One released the second Boogie Down Productions album, *By All Means Necessary*, working with his wife, rapper Ms. Melodie (Ramona Scott, 1969–2012) and D-Nice, among others. With its next releases, BDP began to exhibit the didactic and political stances for which it would become known. Future albums such as *Ghetto Music: The Blueprint of Hip Hop* (1989), *Edutainment* (1990), *Live Hardcore Worldwide* (1991), and *Sex and Violence* (1992) made it clear that BDP was mainly KRS-One, as its music reflected his concerns with identity politics and social issues. Each of the four albums charted in the Billboard 200, at Nos. 75, 36, 32, and 42, respectively, and *Ghetto Music* and *Edutainment* both broke into the Hot R&B/Hip-Hop Songs chart Top 10. *Ghetto Music* produced two Top 10 singles on the Hot Rap Singles chart, "Jack of Spades" (No. 3) and "Why Is That?" (No. 5).

The first album released under the name KRS-One was 1993's *Return of the Boom Bap,* which peaked at No. 3 on the Hot R&B chart. His next two albums, *KRS-One* (1995) and *I Got Next* (1997) both hit No. 2 on the R&B chart, with the latter breaking into the Billboard 200's Top 10, peaking at No. 3. The former spawned his highest-charting solo single, "Outta Here," which reached No. 5 on the Hot Rap Singles chart, and the cult favorite "Sound of da Police." *KRS-One* featured Busta Rhymes (1972–) and Das EFX (1989–). Although his last seven albums had been with New York's Jive Records (1981–), in 1999 KRS-One became vice president of A&R at Reprise Records (1960–), which is now Warner Bros. Records (1958–).

2000s AND BEYOND

In 2001, KRS-One resigned and returned to recording on Koch Records (1987–2009, now known as Entertainment One Music or eOne Music, 2009), with *The Sneak Attack* (2001), and *Spiritual Minded* (2002). He founded the Temple of Hip Hop, a Ministry, Archive, School, and Society (M.A.S.S.) to maintain and promote hip hop culture, and recorded *Kristyles* (2003). He then switched to Grit (2002–2005)* and Antagonist Records (2002*–), respectively, for *Keep Right* (2003) and *Life* (2006). Of these, only *Kristyles* managed to break into the R&B Top 10; *The Sneak Attack* was the most successful on the Billboard 200, peaking at No. 43. In 2007, he collaborated with Marley Marl on *Hip Hop Lives* and has since released 11 albums as a solo act and as a collaborator, with only one solo project, *Adventures in Emceein* (2008), breaking into the Billboard 200. He has also appeared on several songs with other artists, ultimately earning nine Gold and seven Platinum records.

In 2004, KRS-One made controversial statements about the September 11, 2001 terrorist attacks, but he later claimed he had been misquoted. He has also crusaded for hip hop as a religion and has re-visioned the name KRS-One as standing for "Knowledge Reigns Supreme over Nearly Everybody," tying himself to the Five Percent Nation (1964–). He has also written four books, *The Science of Rap* (1996), *Ruminations* (2003), *The Gospel of Hip Hop* (2009), and *Knowledge Reigns Supreme* (2009), the last with novelist Priya Parmar (1974–)*, as well as a comic book, *Break the Chain* (1994); he has been invited to lecture at Yale and Harvard Universities.

Anthony J. Fonseca

See also: Boogie Down Productions; Five Percent Nation; Marley Marl; Political Hip Hop; Turntablism; The United States

Further Reading

Bua, Justin. 2011. "KRS-One." *The Legends of Hip Hop.* New York: Harper Design.

KRS-One and Michael Lipscomb. 1992. "Can the Teacher Be Taught?" *Transition,* no. 57: 168–89.

Further Listening

KRS-One. 1993. *Return of the Boom Bap.* Jive.

KRS-One. 1995. *KRS One.* Jive.

KRS-One. 2001. *The Sneak Attack.* Koch Records.

Krumping

Krumping, a hip hop dance style that originated in 1992 with Tommy the Clown (Thomas Johnson, n.d.) in Compton, California, is the immediate descendant of clowning, a dance that took place at parks and parties as an artistic expression intended to motivate youth to stay away from drugs and gangs. Although krumping and clowning originally shared their dancers and audiences, by the early 2000s, krumping did away with the clown paint and costumes and became aggressive, energetic, and competitive—it developed its own moves and approach to hip hop dance. For a brief, transitional time, krumping used costumes and face paint, but with dark clothing and at times gothic face paint that resembled African ceremonial war paint. Pioneering krumpers were Compton-based Big Mijo (Jo' Artis Ratti, 1985–) and Tight Eyez (Ceasare Willis, 1985–), followed by Los Angeles–based krumping innovator and choreographer Lil'C (Christopher Toler, 1983–). Tight Eyez became the leader of one of the best-known krump crews that as of 2018 still dances, Street Kingdom (2000–).

Krumping is an improvisational hip hop dance style that uses energetic, frenetic, and acrobatic moves. Here a dancer performs an unprepared leap as one of his freestyle krumping battle moves. (Sanches1980/Dreamstime.com)

MOVES AND GLOBAL POPULARITY

Krumping is improvisational, though it has some basic moves, such as chest pops, spine flexing, arm jabs and swings, stomps, and wobbles. Danced originally by teens looking for a creative outlet to express anger, aggression, agitation, or braggadocio, krumping moves are often acrobatic and extremely exaggerated, jerky, and frenetic. Like clowning, krumping employs popping, locking, pantomiming (storytelling), mocking, and ridiculing. Unlike clowning, krumping is supposed to be entirely improvisational, embracing freestyle and dancing in the moment. Krumping therefore focuses on the improvised battle for exhibition, unlike clowning, which focuses on staged choreography.

Preferred music for krumping has a fast tempo with lengthy rhythmic breaks or breakbeats. There is also a distinct culture at krumping battles: For example, not only may judges determine who wins the battle, but at any given time if a dancer or crew inspires the audience, a "kill-off" may ensue, meaning that the audience cheers and surrounds the dancer(s), the dancer(s) is then deemed the winner, thus killing off the opponent.

Although a battle dance, by the 2000s, krumping was featured on several American popular music videos such as Christina Aguilera's (1980–) "Dirrty" (2002), Missy Elliott's (1971–) "I'm Really Hot" (2003), and Madonna's (1958–) "Hung Up" (2005). Through these music videos, YouTube, social media, and hip hop dance workshops as global exchanges, krumping spread quickly worldwide. There are over 100 krumping crews in the Los Angeles area alone, while krump championship battles have taken place in Australia, Japan, Korea, Belgium, Germany, Ghana, Nigeria, and South Africa. From the very beginning with the formation of Street Kingdom in Los Angeles, the word "krump" was a backronym for Kingdom Radically Uplifted Mighty Praise—implying that krumping has roots in dancing to praise God or Jesus Christ, though not all krumpers dance for this reason. Using Christianity as a reason for krumping has nevertheless appealed to a new generation of krumpers and may make krumping acceptable to morally strict societies.

Despite the global spread, krumping battles, like other hip hop dance battles, include calling out for competitors, labbing (when crews get together to create moves), and accusations of biting (plagiarizing or stealing moves watching other dancers). As krumping moves have become combined with dubstep and other kinds of popular dance moves, it has also been fused with some dance styles that have traditional roots, such as Ghanaian krumping moves that have been combined with *azonto*, which features hand movements that pantomime daily life and uses storytelling and coded messages.

Melissa Ursula Dawn Goldsmith

See also: Battling; Clowning; Gangs (United States); Hip Hop Dance; The United States

Further Reading

Frazier, Robeson Taj, and Jessica Koslow. 2013. "Krumpin' in North Hollywood: Public Moves in Private Spaces." *Boom: A Journal of California* 3, no. 1: 1–16.

Todd, Megan Anne. 2011. "Aesthetic Foundations and Activist Strategies of Intervention in Rickerby Hinds' *Buckworld One*." *Journal of Pan African Studies* 4, no. 6: 148–70.

Further Viewing

LaChapelle, David, dir. 2005. *Rize*. Santa Monica, CA: Lionsgate.

Nassim, Shiri, dir. 2005. *The Heart of Krump*. West Hollywood, CA: Ardustry Home Entertainment/Krump Kings.

Kurtis Blow

(Kurt Walker, 1959–, Harlem, New York)

Kurtis Blow was instrumental in mainstreaming hip hop. As a result, he has become the hip hop artist known for breaking the most barriers. In 1979, Mercury Records (1945–) released his first major-label rap single, "Christmas Rappin'," which made the Billboard R&B chart in 1993, 1994, 1996, and 2000 and sold half a million copies. In 1980, he had the first certified-Gold rap single, "The Breaks" (also on Mercury) that peaked in the Top 5 on the R&B chart, and he became the first rapper to appear on the television variety and dance show, *Soul Train* (1971–2006). "The Breaks," a commentary on life and cultural types, sold over half a million copies. In 1985, he became the epitome of the hip hop artist who had achieved mainstream success: He became the first solo rapper to get an endorsement deal with Sprite. In the early 1990s, he was the first hip hop artist to collaborate on writing music for a soap opera, composing for *One Life to Live* (1968–) as an Internet soap series.

EARLY YEARS

Kurtis Blow first entered hip hop culture as a b-boy in the early 1970s. Around 1977, he began MCing and performing at clubs and parties as a turntablist, under the name Kool DJ Kurt. This took place about the same time he met Russell Simmons (1957–), who later cofounded Def Jam Recordings (1983–), while Simmons was at the City College of New York (CCNY). Simmons began to manage Kurtis Blow and following his success at clubs in the late 1970s, Simmons had him record "Christmas Rappin'." Major labels were at first hesitant to release a rap track, but on the heels of the Sugarhill Gang's (1979–1985, 1994–) chart success with "Rapper's Delight" in 1979, the commercial potential for rap and hip hop became clearer, and Mercury signed Kurtis Blow.

It is notable of his early success that though he was on a mainstream label and had crossover success in that context, his music was not modified to be marketed to a new audience, and thus was not considered crossover in itself. Unlike the Sugarhill Gang, who were, essentially, a studio-only act when they recorded "Rapper's Delight," Kurtis Blow's recordings were by a performer who had been active in the club culture and had been honing his style in front of an audience. The success of "The Breaks," still considered a major landmark of hip hop culture, solidified his reputation as the first solo rap superstar. His repeated success undermined earlier assumptions that rap was a novelty that would have no enduring commercial success or cultural influence.

CAREER FROM 1980s TO 2000s

Kurtis Blow had an early prolific recording career, but his early productivity was followed by a recording hiatus from 1990 through 2007, though other artists continued to sample and cover his earlier recordings. He released one album in 2008 and has had just a few singles since, making only a couple of guest appearances. His lyrical delivery can be described as singsong, a style that didn't maintain popularity past the early 1980s when other MCs aimed at a more aggressive style. As the 1980s progressed, he began producing and worked successfully with artists such as the Fat Boys (1982–1991, 2008–), Run-D.M.C. (1981–2002), Lovebug Starski (Kevin Smith, 1960–), Fearless Four (1977–1994), and Dr. Jeckyll and Mr. Hyde (1980–1987), to help them develop their styles. In the 1990s, he maintained his ties to hip hop by hosting a radio show on Los Angeles' KPWR-FM. He followed that with hosting an old-school rap program on Sirius Satellite Radio (1990–). He has been an activist on race issues, working with the Reverends Jesse Jackson (Jesse Louis Burns, 1941–) and Al Sharpton (1954–).

In the early 2000s Kurtis Blow cofounded the nondenominational Hip Hop Church in Harlem, New York, and became an ordained minister (for a long time he has been known as a devout Christian who avoids the use of profanity in his work). The church has since expanded to many other cities in the United States and has taken his career into a new direction.

Susannah Cleveland

See also: The United States

Further Reading

Bradley, Adam, and Andrew Dubois, eds. 2010. "Kurtis Blow." Under "Part 1: 1978–84: The Old School" in *The Anthology of Rap*, pp. 24–32. New Haven, CT: Yale University Press.

Pedersen, Birgitte Stougaard. 2013. "Aesthetic Potentials of Rhythm in Hip Hop Music and Culture: Rhythmic Conventions, Skills, and Everyday Life." *Thamyris/Intersecting: Place, Sex and Race* 26, no. 1: 55–70.

Further Listening

Kurtis Blow. 1980. *Kurtis Blow.* Mercury.

Further Viewing

Robbins, Brian, dir. 1995. *The Show.* Santa Monica, CA: Rysher Entertainment.

Schultz, Michael, dir. 1985. *Krush Groove.* Burbank, CA: Warner Home Video.

Spirer, Peter, dir. 1997. *Rhyme and Reason.* Burbank, CA: Buena Vista Home Entertainment.

Kuwait

Kuwait, with over four million people, has seen its population nearly double in the last decade, due in part to the 1991 expulsion of Iraqi troops and the fact that Kuwait, rich in oil, has the fourth highest GDP per capita of all nations. The country is also known for its cultural richness. Before the Gulf War (1990–1991), Kuwaitis often explored new forms of music and dance. Traditional Kuwaiti music is maritime-based, with lots of seafaring imagery, but the appeal of Western culture has made Kuwait a pioneer of contemporary music in the Gulf region. These tastes reflect changes to the population: Since the 1970s, two-thirds of Kuwait's population has been non-Kuwaiti. Still, with a small youth population between ages 15 and 24, Kuwaiti hip hop activity is minimal and concentrated mainly in its capital, Kuwait City.

Among pioneering hip hop efforts is Doss Al Eidani (Mohammed Al-Eidani, n.d.), dancer-instructor, popping expert, and hip hop activist, who emphasizes the positive qualities of hip hop to Kuwaiti youth, who were drawn to it prior to 1990 and are now involved in helping the hip hop scene make a comeback. Hip hop dance has become so popular in Kuwait that classes are offered for children who want to learn freestyle, rhythm, and creative movement through street dance. Graffiti is also popular, with artists such as internationally known calligrapher and painter Abdulaziz Alameer (n.d.), whose innovation to painting is working in typography. Music acts include trip hop and trance-electronica multimedia artist Zahed Sultan (n.d.), whose music has been licensed for television, film, and music compilations.

Among the top hip hop groups in Kuwait is brother duo Sons of Yusuf (2012–) and singer-rapper and producer Daffy (aka King Daff, Nawaf Fahed, n.d.). Sons of Yusuf, whose members have lived in Kuwait and California, produces music that blends Middle Eastern instrumentation and loops with old-school rap, reggae, gangsta, and chopper style. Sons of Yusuf's texts combine Arabic and English and lyrical themes often challenge outsiders' stereotypes of Muslims and Kuwaitis. Since 2004, Daffy has been active. He fuses hip hop with R&B, reggae, soul, jazz, and at times traditional Arabic music.

Contemporaries of Daffy include the brother duo Ya'koob and Humble (Ya'koob Al-Refaie, n.d., and Abdul'Rahman Al-Refaie, n.d.), who grew up in Los Angeles, developed their freestyle skills there, and have in the 2010s returned to Kuwait to pursue a hip hop career there. The duo's music embraces Islamic and Arabic culture, ideas, and philosophy, as well as confronts stereotyping of Islamic, Arabic, and Kuwaiti people. The duo, who is equally passionate about Los Angeles and Kuwait, raps in mostly English with some Arabic.

Anthony J. Fonseca

See also: Gangsta Rap; Hip Hop Dance; Reggae; The United States

Further Reading

Anon. 2013. "Ya'koob and Humble Abdul—Kuwaiti Brothers Blend Arabic Flavor with Rap." *Kuwait Times*, January 6.

Urkevich, Lisa. 2015. *Music and Traditions of the Arabian Peninsula: Saudi Arabia, Kuwait, Bahrain, and Qatar.* New York: Routledge.

Kwaito

Kwaito is a subgenre of house music that employs a slower tempo, deep resonating and prominent bass lines, rhythmic loops (employing a four-to-the-floor kick drum), samples of South African popular music, melodic hooks, and melodic speaking and shouting—with less emphasis on singing. Instruments used in kwaito include voice, sampler and drum machines, synthesizers, and percussion, sometimes including South African instruments. As with other South African popular and traditional music, kwaito employs call-and-response between the vocalist or group and listeners. Texts are in Zulu, Afrikaans (often an Afrikaans creole language such as Tsotsitaals or Camtho), and American vernacular.

In the late 1980s, kwaito emerged in Soweto, in Johannesburg, and fully developed into its own around 1993, after the end of Apartheid (1948–1991) and resulting worldwide sanctions against the country; this led to Nelson Mandela's (1918–2013, in office 1994–1999) becoming the country's first democratically elected president. Like hip hop, kwaito refers to music and to culture, so it is easy to draw comparisons between the two—and to mistakenly identify kwaito as either a subgenre of hip hop or a South African variety of American hip hop. As a form of expression that took place after South Africa's political liberation, kwaito's roots and history strongly belong to South Africa, though it has become popular by the late 1990s in neighboring Botswana and Namibia.

Kwaito artists have been concerned that kwaito remains authentic, arguing that it should resist the influences of American hip hop, even though they share some musical and extramusical elements. Famous South African kwaito artists are from Soweto, Cape Town, and Durban. They include groups such as Trompies (1995–), TKZee (TaKe It Eezy, 1996–), Bongo Maffin (1996–) and Big Nuz (2002–), as well as artists such as Pitch Black Afro (Thulani Ngcobo, 1976*–), Zola (Bonginkosi Dlamini, 1981–), and TKZee's Bouga Luv (Kabelo Mabalane, 1976–).

Sghubu, a hardcore subgenre of kwaito, emerged in the 2000s, and is performed by South African artists such as the duo Major League Djz (2008–). Botswana kwaito artists include Mapetla (Thabo Mapetla Ntirelang, n.d.) and Skazzo (Tlhotlhomiso Maruping, 1985–). Combining kwaito with *kwassa kwassa* beats and guitar, kwaito kwasa was developed in the mid-to-late-1990s in Botswana and performed by Motswana artists such as Vee (Odirile Vee Sento, 1983–) and Wizards of the Desert (1995–). Some Namibian kwaito artists include the Dogg (Martin Morocky, 1983–), Gazza (Lazarus Shiimi, 1990–), and Sunny Boy (Sunday Shipushu, 1983–). All also perform Namibian hip hop.

MUSICAL INFLUENCES AND EARLY DEVELOPMENT

In addition to house music, musical influences on kwaito include *imibongo* (traditional praise poetry), 1920s *marabi* and 1950s *kwela* rhythms, *mbaqanga* and *maskhandi* from South Africa, and reggae and dancehall from Jamaica. Kwaito began developing in Soweto in the late 1980s during the height of house music. As a post-apartheid ghetto, people in Soweto and in other townships in Johannesburg created the Camtho (Iscamtho means mixed languages) vocabulary based on Afrikaans words, but with different meanings. The Afrikaans word *kwaai*, which means strict or angry, came to mean cool, hot, or "kickin'." When people heard house tracks at parties that they liked, they would call the tracks *kwaai*. "Kwaito" was a term used for the new kind of music that had emphasized house beats. Another Camtho word for gangster, *amakwaitosi*, was also used, and kwaito's lyrical content typically focuses on having a good time, partying, or on localized street or ghetto topics. Kwaito was also influenced by contemporary popular music in South Africa that entered the main stream, such as disco, R&B, and funk.

Soweto-born Arthur Mafokate (Sello Arthur Mafokate, 1962–) had the first kwaito hit in South Africa in 1995 with "*Kaffir*," a song that protests racism by attacking the word *kaffir*, a derogatory term in Afrikaans for South African black people that traces back to white colonialism there. In "Kaffir," Mafokate addresses his *bass* (boss) by telling him that he would not like it if he called him a baboon. Though the song was banned from a few radio stations, the song catapulted Mafokate's career as a musician and producer and the popularity of kwaito. Mafokate later discovered and established the careers of other South African kwaito artists such as Mandoza (Mduduzi Edmund Tshabalala, 1978–2016).

Kwaito's very existence, as well as its entrance into mainstream popular music tastes in South Africa, reflected the freedom of expression experienced after Mandela came to power. Anti-apartheid chants and newly written refrains were used in kwaito songs, which continued describing ghetto life yet for some; these songs were not nearly as politically charged as hip hop came to be. Kwaito became so popular that schools in South African townships that could not afford music educators, instruments, or programs used kwaito instead to include music in the curriculum.

Among others, early successful kwaito artists included the first kwaito group Boom Shaka (1993–2000), as well as Thebe (Thebe Mogane, 1973–), Mdu Masilela (1970–), and Brenda Fassie (aka MaBrrr, 1964–2004). Fassie, nicknamed "Madonna of the Townships," had already established her career as an Afropop singer who sang anti-apartheid Afropop just after Mandela came to power. A year before Mafokate's success, Fassie's album *Abantu Bayakhuluma* (*People Speak*, 1994) included kwaito tracks in Zulu. Female kwaito artists remain rare, despite the fact that Fassie and Lebo Mathosa (1977–2006) of Boom Shaka helped popularize the music and paved the way for Lesh (Lesego Bile, 1984–), Botswana's first female kwaito singer.

Into the 2000s kwaito has remained popular and has been exported to Europe and the United States. Internationally known companies Reebok (1958–) and the Kia Motor Corporation (1944–) have used kwaito in commercials.

Melissa Ursula Dawn Goldsmith

See also: Botswana; Namibia; South Africa

Further Reading

Boloka, Gibson. 2003. "Cultural Studies and the Transformation of the Music Industry: Some Reflections on Kwaito." In *Shifting Selves: Post-Apartheid Essays on Mass Media, Culture, and Identity*, edited by Herman Wasserman and Sean Jacobs, chap. 5. Cape Town, South Africa: Kwela Books.

Steingo, Gavin. 2016. *Kwaito's Promise: Music and the Aesthetics of Freedom in South Africa*. Chicago: University of Chicago Press.

Further Listening

Bongo Maffin. 1998. *The Concerto*. Columbia.

Fassie, Brenda. 1994. *Abantu bayakhuluma* (*People Speak*). CCP Record Company.

Mafokate, Arthur. 1999. *Umpostoli* (*The Apostle*). 999 Music.

L

Laos

Laos is a communist-ruled, landlocked country in Mainland Southeast Asia that has been slowly loosening its censorship of hip hop. The government views hip hop as an attack on traditional culture, and still polices song lyrics and band clothing to make sure that no cursing occurs and no revealing clothes are worn. Nonetheless, radio stations have gone from playing neighboring Thai and Western music to playing rap songs in cities such as Vientiane, Savannakhet, and Pakse. Laotian teenagers, especially, have embraced the hip hop scene: grafitti art, breakdancing, fashion, and rap music. They wear baggy pants, long chains, use American urban slang, and some identify with the music's sociopolitical stance. To many Laotian teenagers, hip hop music is modern, and therefore a creative outlet that gives an opportunity for Laos to prove to the rest of the world that it is culturally progressive.

Vientiane-based Laobangfai (n.d.), the country's first hip hop and breakdancing troupe, has members who range in age from 8 to 20. Laotian rap has a strong connection to Minneapolis, which has a large, diasporic minority ethnic community and has spawned the country's three most famous rap acts: Gumby's (aka Pryce, anonymous, 1977*–) remix of Kai Punnipha's (n.d.) Thai hit "Goolaap Daeng" ("9999 Roses," 2008) made rap music ubiquitous among Laotian youth, getting a million downloads; Lila T. (Lila Thammavongsa, n.d.) and Lao Crimino (n.d.) are also part of the Laotian youth hip hop movement. As of 2018, Lila T. ranks among the best-known female rappers in Laos, and Lao Crimino is becoming the most famous Laotian hip hop band.

In addition to Laotian hip hop acts that have recorded music in the United States, since the late 1980s, Laotian immigrant youth have often participated in other hip hop activity, including open mic events not only in Minneapolis, but also in many Laotian communities in California. The Hmong—people who are from not only Laos, but also from Vietnam, China, and Thailand—are a part of this immigrant population. Storytelling attributes to rap are especially appealing to the Hmong and, since the 2000s, are used to help preserve Hmong culture and language for youth living in the United States.

Anthony J. Fonseca and Melissa Ursula Dawn Goldsmith

See also: Thailand

Further Reading

Poss, Nicholas. 2013. "'Reharmonizing' the Generations: Rap, Poetry, and Hmong Oral Traditional." In *Diversity in Diaspora: Hmong Americans in the Twenty-First Century*, edited by Mark Edward Pfeifer, Monica Chiu, and Kou Yang, chap. 10. Honolulu: University of Hawai'i Press.

Vue, Pao Lee. 2012. *Assimilation and the Gendered Color Line: Hmong Case Studies of Hip Hop and Import Racing.* The New Americans: Recent Immigration and American Society. El Paso, TX: LFB Scholarly.

Wong, Deborah. 2004. *Speak It Louder: Asian Americans Making Music.* New York: Routledge.

The Last Poets

(aka The Original Last Poets, 1968–, Harlem, New York)

The Last Poets is an umbrella name for groups of poets and musicians who began performing during the third period of Black Nationalism (post-1870s) and the Civil Rights Movement in the United States (1954–1968). Named after South African Bra Willie's (Keorapetse Kgositsile's, 1938–) political poems in *Spirits Unchained* (1969), which suggested that there would be a final era of poetry, hence last poets, the Last Poets became one of hip hop music's earliest influences. The group used rapping, the MC, beatboxing, and black consciousness raising. Gylan Kain (n.d.), David Nelson (n.d.), Abiodun Oyowele (Charles Davis, 1948–), and later Felipe Luciano (1947–), formed the group on Malcolm X's (1925–1965) birthday in 1968 in East Harlem, New York.

FORMATION AND EARLY ALBUMS

The group's origin is complicated because Luciano, Kain, and Nelson also recorded separately as the Original Last Poets, gaining notoriety for work on the soundtrack for Herbert Danska's (1926) documentary *Right On! Poetry on Film* (1971). In addition, the trio recorded live in 1972 for the album *Black Spirits—Festival of New Black Poets in America.* Alafia Pudim (aka Lightnin' Rod, 1944–) replaced Luciano after he left to start the Puerto Rican nationalist group the Young Lords (1968*–) in New York City, and he took over the Last Poets' leadership. One of the group's 1969 concerts was at Lincoln University in Pennsylvania and was attended by writer, poet, and spoken word artist Gil Scott-Heron (1949–2011), who became so inspired by the group that he spoke with them and then formed his first band, Black and Blues (1969–1970)*.

In 1970, the album *The Last Poets* peaked at No. 29 on Billboard's Top LPs (which became the Billboard 200), No. 3 on Billboard's Top Soul LPs, and No. 11 on Billboard Jazz LPs. The critically acclaimed eponymous album featured accompaniment by percussionist Nillaja Obabi (Raymond Hurrey, n.d.). The Last Poets' 1971 album *This Is Madness* followed, and established the recognizable sound of the group—a combination of jazz (bebop and cool) and funk with poetry, which the group termed "jazzoetry"—and a strong sociopolitical message about the condition of black people in the United States. As a result, the Last Poets was listed under President Richard Nixon's (1913–1994, in office 1969–1974) COINTELPRO (Counter INTELligence PROgram, 1956–1971), which meant he considered them dangerous. Regardless, the Last Poets recorded several albums:

Chastisment (1972), *Hustlers Convention* (1973), *At Last* (1974), and *Delights of the Garden* (1977).

RESURGENCE

Between the late 1970s and early 1980s, the Last Poets experienced a brief decline in popularity, but by the mid-1980s there was a resurgence of interest in the group and acknowledgement of its influence on hip hop—particularly *Hustlers Convention*—that corresponded to hip hop's own rise in popularity. *Hustlers Convention* was a project album that fused poetry with funk, jazz, and toasting. It is the story of two hustlers, Sport and Spoon, and their violent life in the ghetto. The album is a precursor to gangsta rap with its braggadocio passages made by the protagonists and descriptions of their crimes and blood on the streets.

Albums released between the 1980s and 1997 included *Oh, My People* (1984), *Freedom Express* (1988), *Retro Fit* (1992), *Holy Terror* (1993), *Scatterap/Home* (1994), and *Time Has Come* (1997). Though the compilation album *Jazzoetry* had been released in 1976 and 1984 had seen Celluloid Record's (1976–1989) reissue of *The Last Poets* and *This Is Madness*, there have been surprisingly few reissues. The most notable retrospective compilation was *The Prime Time Rhyme of the Last Poets—Best of Vol. 1 and Vol. 2* (1999). Subsequent albums by the Last Poets include compilation albums: *The Real Rap* (1999), *Poetry Is Black* (2002), and *On the Subway* (2006).

LEGACY

The Last Poets' legacy remains strongly present in hip hop. The use of rapped poetry over beats was the precursor to alternative hip hop and jazz rap, which found practitioners on both coasts of the United States, for example heard in music by Aceyalone (1970–) and his Project Blowed (1994–) collective and workshop on the West Coast and A Tribe Called Quest (1985–1998, 2006–2013, 2015–) on the East Coast. Tracks on *Hustlers Convention* have been sampled by Beastie Boys (1981–2001), Nas (1973–), and Wu-Tang Clan (1992–), among many others. In addition to peaking the interests of jazz trumpeter Miles Davis (1926–1991), who eventually fused jazz with hip hop on his posthumously released album *Doo-Bop* (1992), *Hustlers Convention* was a major influence on American hip hop pioneers such as Fab Five Freddy (1959–), Melle Mel (1961–), Grandmaster Flash (1958–), and Chuck D (1960–). Hip hop artists such as Common (1972–) and Tupac Shakur (1971–1996) were also inspired by the Last Poets' strong support of the Black Panther Party (1966–1982) and Malcolm X.

The Last Poets appeared on A Tribe Called Quest's *The Low End Theory* (1991), Nas's album *Untitled* (2008), and the Welfare Poets' (1997–) *Cruel and Unusual Punishment* (2010). Beyond American hip hop, the Last Poets' influence can be heard in Malik and the O.G.'s from Liverpool, England (2006–), who collaborated with the Last Poets and Scott-Heron in 2004, and shortly afterward on *Rhythms of the Diaspora, Vol. 1 and 2* (2015). In 2014, Chuck D commissioned the English documentary film *Hustlers Convention* (2015), which features this 2014 performance.

In 2016, an English translation of Christine Otten's novel in Dutch, *The Last Poets* (London: World Editions, 2011), by Jonathan Reeder, was published. The novel is based on the the Last Poets' lives and stories that Otten compiled during interviews with members and is a narrative on redemption.

Melissa Ursula Dawn Goldsmith

See also: Black Nationalism; Gangsta Rap; Political Hip Hop; Scott-Heron, Gil; The United States

Further Reading

Oyewole, Abiodun, and Umar Bin Hassan, with Kim Green. 1996. *The Last Poets on a Mission: Selected Poems and a History of the Last Poets.* New York: H. Holt.

Santoro, Gene. 1994. *Dancing in Your Head.* New York: Oxford University Press.

Stewart, James B. 2005. "Message in the Music: Political Commentary in Black Popular Music from Rhythm and Blues to Early Hip Hop." *Journal of African American History* 90, no. 3: 196–225.

Further Listening

The Last Poets. 1971. *This Is Madness.* Douglas Records.

The Last Poets. 1973. *Hustlers Convention.* Celluloid Records.

The Latin Kings

(TLK, 1991–2005, Stockholm, Sweden)

The Latin Kings were a pioneering Swedish hip hop group that emerged in Botkyrka, a southern suburbs of Stockholm that is part of the urban public housing project Miljonprogrammet (Million Programm, 1965–1974). Along with the Swedish hip hop trio Just D (1990–1995), they are one of the first to record a hip hop album in Swedish. They earned international attention through sound recordings on labels such as EastWest Records America (1990–2001, owned by Warner Music Group) and Mega Records (1983–2001). After believing that they were cheated by the recording industry, they worked with the Salazar Brothers (2009–) to produce TLK's later albums on Redline Records (2000–), their own Botkyrka-based recording label whose parent company is Virgin (1972–). TLK includes rapper MC Dogge Doggelito (Douglas Léon, 1975–) of Norra Botkyrka, Sweden, and the rapping-production duo known as the Salazar brothers, Salla (Christian Salazar, n.d.) and Chepe (Hugo Salazar, n.d.). Doggelito's father was from Venezuela, and the Salazar family roots are in Chile; this mutual connection to South America inspired the trio to name themselves after the largest Hispanic American street gang, the Chicago-based Latin Kings (Almighty Latin King and Queen Nation, 1954–).

The Latin Kings rap in their local Rinkeby Swedish, a pidgin language with loanwords from American English slang, as well as in Arabic, Kurdish, Italian, Persian, Spanish, and Turkish. Rinkeby Swedish is a youth vernacular language that is usually spoken in immigrant communities. At times using social realist humor, the trio's themes focus on Latino immigrant life in Stockholm, exposure to crime, racism, and poverty. Their sound typically combines East Coast hip hop with salsa, neo soul, and reggae.

After placing third in a 1992 national Rap-SM competition and being discovered by Swedish record producer Gordon Cyrus (1966*–), the trio released their first single, "Snubben Trodde Han Var Cool" ("The Guy Thought He Was Cool," 1993), which led to a contract with Warner Records. Their first album, *Välkommen till förorten* (*Welcome to the Suburb*, 1994), attained Gold certification and earned two Swedish Grammy Awards. Their subsequent albums are *I skuggan av betongen* (*In the Concrete Shade*, 1997), *Mitt kvarter* (*My Neighborhood*, 2000), and *Omerta* (2003, the title based on the Southern Italian Mafia term *Omertà*, a code of honor requiring either silence or nonparticipation with authorities, as well as not interfering with the crimes of certain other people), in addition to a compilation album, *Familia Royal* (2005).

The band broke up in 2005; however, as of 2018, Doggelito and the Salazar brothers are still active and successful in music.

Melissa Ursula Dawn Goldsmith

See also: Gangs (United States); Sweden

Further Reading

Cora, Lacatus. 2009. "Visual Identities of the Other Performance Art and the Public Sphere in Contemporary Sweden." *Scandinavian Studies* 81, no. 4: 475–500.

Gunlög, Sundberg. 2013. "Language Policy and Multilingual Identity in Sweden through the Lens of Generation Y." *Scandinavian Studies* 85, no. 2: 205–32.

Lindholm, Susan. 2014. "Representing the Marginalized Other: The Swedish Hip-Hop Group Advance Patrol." *Swedish Journal of Music Research/Svensk tidskrift för musikforskning* 96, no. 2: 105–125.

Lindholm, Susan. 2017. "Hip Hop Practice as Identity and Memory Work in and in-between Chile and Sweden." *Suomen Antropologi: Journal of the Finnish Anthropological Society* 42, no. 2: 60–74.

Further Listening

TLK. 1994. *Välkommen till förorten* (*Welcome to the Suburb*). EastWest/Warner Music Sweden.

TLK. 2003. *Omerta* (*Omertà*). Redline Records/Virgin.

Latvia

Latvia is a Baltic state that shares a border with Estonia, Lithuania, Russia, and Belarus. Like in other Baltic states, hip hop emerged in the early 1990s in Latvia. Early Latvian hip hop was influenced by the European disco and techno scenes, often consisting of nonsensical lyrics over a dance beat. Today, hip hop in Latvia is primarily sung in the Latvian language but includes some English and Russian lyrics, especially from groups who desire an impact in the larger Russian market.

Latvian rap, perhaps because of its origins, moves a little slower than most, with more space between the lines and words. It has a relaxed feel and a light spirit not common in other Slavic European nations. Also like the other Baltic States, Latvia has a long history of dominance by foreign powers, including Poland, Sweden, Russia, and briefly, Germany. Latvia was an independent republic in the 1920s and 1930s, but for most of the 20th century, Latvia was under Soviet control: it became an independent republic again in 1991 after the fall of the Soviet Union. Nonetheless, themes such as Latvian independence and anti-Soviet politics are not widespread in Latvian rap, but some rappers, such as Ozols (Girts Rozentals, 1979–), from Riga and Rays (Ravis Krams, 1985*–) have written songs on these issues. Latvian rap is a world apart from Russian rap, and Latvian rappers express that they are not Russian. The essential spirit of much Latvian rap is fun, laid-back, and not too serious.

The first Latvian hip hop artists include Mr. Tape (Modris Skaiskalns, 1966–), from Sigulda, Eastbam (Roberts Gobzins, 1978–) from Riga, and the band F—Art (1991–1996). In 1991, Mr. Tape achieved internet fame by mixing on reel-to-reel tapes instead of turntables at Disco Mix Club World Championship. By the 2000s, commercial and underground hip hop movements in Latvia had solidified. FACT (1995–), which included Ozols, Gustavo (Gustavs Butelis, 1978–) and Ciziks (Aivars Civzelis, 1975–), from Riga, and Gonza (Janis Kalnins, n.d.), was one of the country's most commercially successful hip hop groups. Ozols and Gustavo went solo and later clashed in the first recorded Latvian rap battle in the early 2000s.

Other important Latvian rap groups of the early 2000s include Armands (Armands Kincs, n.d.) and the band S'T'A (1998–). Gacho (aka MESA, Gatis Irbe, 1983*–), another emergent rapper in the 2000s, worked with Ozols and later reinvented himself in a new genre, electrohop, which made him one of the most popular rapping musicians in Latvia. Kreisais Krassts (Left Shore, 2002*–), which includes Arturs Skutelis (1986*–), Edavardi (Eduards Gorbunovs, 1990–), and ansis (Ansis Kolmanis, 1987–), is a group that is popular with urban youth; PKI is a group that incorporates Western influences, Latvian styles, and complicated battle-rap rhyming.

The record label Karaļūdens, launched by Dirty Deal Audio (DDA) in 2013, currently releases compilations of Latvian hip hop music. It is located in Latvia's capital city, Riga. In 2017, ansis was featured in Reinis Kapone's (n.d.) song "Gotham," which was released on the studio album *Katafalks* (*Hearse*, 2017), as well as in his music video. In addition, ansis produced this song, along with other songs, on the album and served as the album's music engineer at DDA.

Terry Klefstad

See also: Russia

Further Reading

Boiko, Martin. 2001. "The Latvian Folk Music Movement in the 1980s and 1990s: From 'Authenticity' to 'Postfolklore' and Onwards." *The World of Music* 43, nos. 2–3: 113–18.

Daugavietis, Jānos, and Ilze Lāce. 2011. "Subcultural Tastes in Latvia 2002–10: The Content of Style." *Studies of Transition States and Societies* 3, no. 2: 45–56.

Further Listening
ansis and Oriole. 2013. *Himnas.* Dirty Deal Audio (DDA).
Reinis Kapone. 2017. *Katafalks.* DDA.
Various Artists. 2013–2016*. *Compilations 01–08.* Karaļūdens.

Lebanon

Lebanon is home to a hip hop scene that emerged in the early 21st century, melding Western hip hop styles with Arabic rhymes and samples of traditional and popular Arab music styles. Rayess Bek (Wael Koudaih, 1979–), one of the first Lebanese rappers, spent his immigrant youth near Paris, learning French hip hop. On return to Lebanon, he founded the group Aks'ser (One-Way Street, 1996–2005*), and in 2003, he released his first solo career album, bringing social and political consciousness to Lebanese hip hop. Despite a lack of consistent market support, Lebanese hip hop has taken root—particularly in urban centers—where it is performed at clubs, weddings, private parties and festivals, and where street art and breakdancing are increasingly widespread.

ARTISTS, THEMES, AND SOUNDS

Lebanese Egyptian OMARZ (Amro Tome, 1981*–) sees a parallel between disaffected Arab youth and the similarly disadvantaged African American youth of

Lebanese rapper El Rass performs at a 2013 concert supporting the *Khat Thaleth* (*Third Rail*) project in Beirut, a compilation recording that features artists from Lebanon, Egypt, Jordan, Palestine, Syria, and Tunisia. El Rass raps in Arabic about social inequity, Islamic clerics, and Western-Arab relations. (ANWAR AMRO/AFP/Getty Images)

1980s U.S. hip hop culture. OMARZ worked with Syrian Lebanese Eslam Jawaad (Wissam Khodur, n.d.) in the transnational crew Desert Dragons (1998), speaking out violently against American and Israeli policies. By 2005, OMARZ was internationally known. His music was played on British radio, and he soon began work with Johnny Damascus (John Imad Nasr, n.d.) under the name Oriental Robotics, with DJ Lethal Skillz (Hussein Mao Atwi, n.d.), rapper Grandsunn (Ray Tannir, n.d.) and producer Scizzers (Sebou Pamboukian, n.d.). Oriental Robotics' hip hop tracks, such as "God Slave the Queen," combine audio clips as samples—often ironic—from famous political speeches, with stripped-down beats and rhymes that criticize British and American policies toward Arabs.

RGB (Rajab Abdel-Rahman, 1980*–) experienced firsthand the Lebanese Civil War (1975–1990), so he uses rap to express solidarity with those fighting tyranny across the Arab world. RGB joined in 1999 with MC Stress (anonymous, n.d.), MC Joker (anonymous, n.d.), and 6K (anonymous, n.d.) to form Kitaa Beirut (1999–2002*), bringing furious energy to the Lebanese underground scene until RGB's 2002 exile in France. These musicians regrouped in 2005 as Kita'youn (Boys of the Sector, 2005*–), touring Lebanon, Syria, and Jordan.

Twin brothers and graphic designers Mohamed (anonymous, n.d.) and Omar Kabbani (n.d.) formed the hip hop crew Ashekman (2001–) or "exhaust pipe"—symbolic both of their uncut style and their desire to expose the negatives in Lebanese society. The Kabbanis use light, varied beats as backdrops to controversial lyrics, and repeat their Arabic-language rap themes in their widely recognized street art, combining urban graffiti with Arabic calligraphy.

Malikah ("Queen," Lynn Fattouh, 1986–) is a role model for Arab young women limited by social stereotypes. She raps in Arabic, French, and English, delivering a message of Arab peace and unity. In 2007, she sealed her international reputation by opening for and later recording a track with Snoop Dogg (1971–).

In 2008, 11 male and female rappers of varied political and religious backgrounds performed and distributed copies of their album *Peace Beats*. In a society scarred by sectarian civil war, Lebanese hip hop artists continue to make statements by collaborating despite differing faith backgrounds, including Islam (Sunni and Shia), Christianity, Judaism, and Druze.

By the second decade of the 21st century, over 250 hip hop artists and groups, including 961 Crew (n.d.) Clotaire K (n.d.), FareeQ el Atrash (2006–), RAmez (Ramzi Khoury, 1978–), and Omar Zeineddine (n.d.), were active on the Internet, many offering potent sociopolitical messages. El Rass (Mazen El Sayed, n.d.) brings many of these themes together in his criticism—of Islamic clerics, the West, Arab governments, social injustice—delivered in a lively fusion of classical Arabic and contemporary street language. Both in his rap and in his speech he advances the idea of a new Arab cultural identity—a "digital bedouinism"—that goes beyond the norms of nationality, history or nostalgia.

Jennifer L. Roth-Burnette

See also: Egypt; Syria

Further Reading
Burkhalter, Thomas. 2013. *Local Music Scenes and Globalization: Transnational Platforms in Beirut. Routledge Studies in Ethnomusicology.* New York: Routledge.

Nassar, Angie. 2011. "Scratch the Past—This Is Our Soundtrack: Hip Hop in Lebanon." In *Arab Youth*, edited by Samir Khalaf and Roseanne Saad Khalaf, "Part 6: Popular Culture and Music." London: Saqi Books.

Les Nubians

(1998–, Paris, France)

Les Nubians is a smooth jazz, soul, and R&B hip hop sister duo from Paris, which was, at its popularity following its debut album, the most successful Francophone musical group in the United States. Its debut album, *Princesses Nubiennes* (*Nubian Princesses*, 1998), sold over 400,000 copies and was nominated for a Grammy Award; the band was also nominated for two NAACP Image Awards in 2000. Consisting of Hélène (1975–) and Célia (1979–) Faussart, Les Nubians began as an a cappella group with a jazz feel, but its sound has evolved over time.

The duo's music, which the two describe as "Afropean," is defined by a blending of African diaspora and European musical styles. This includes soul-inspired smooth jazz, which has as much in common with easy listening pop and warm R&B as it does with hip hop and dance. The sisters considered their sound an assimilated one, based on all the musical styles to which they had been exposed during their childhoods in Chad and France. Having traveled a lot as children, they embraced their African roots, as well as American jazz, funk, R&B, and the girl band Motown sound. Their songs also have a hint of British soul. The duo is best known for its single "Makeda," which reached No. 37 on the Hot R&B Singles and Tracks chart in 1999, and for its guest appearance on the Black Eyed Peas' (1995–) "On My Own," from its second album, *Bridging the Gap* (2000). The duo has been compared to British soul artists as Sade (Helen Folasade Adu, 1959–), Soul II Soul (1988–1997, 2007–), and Des'ree (Desirée Annette Weeks, 1968–).

The Faussart sisters began singing as a duo in 1992, when they moved to Bordeaux, France. They began singing to combat loneliness when their family moved to a rural area. At first they sang a cappella because they had trouble finding musicians willing to take a chance and perform with rookie singers, but they used the opportunity to hone vocals and create poetry slams; they also became session and backup singers for various artists. Hélène and Célia Faussart also helped create Les Nouveaux Griots (n.d.)—the term for an African storyteller and keeper of heritage—a cultural collective, which allowed them to interact with American jazz vocalist Abbey Lincoln (Anna Marie Wooldridge, 1930–2010). Their break came in 1998 when Virgin Records, France (1970–), signed them and produced their debut album.

Les Nubians' discography includes three other albums, *One Step Forward* (2003) also on Virgin, for which the duo sang in English, *Echos: Chapter One* (2006), which marked the duo's switch to its own Paris-based label, Nubiatik (2005–), and its African-influenced funk and neo soul hip hop album *Nü Revolution* (*New Revolution*, 2011) to the Shanachie label (1976), known for producing world music recordings). The later albums showed the duo venturing more into high energy dance rhythms. *Echos* featured both music and urban poetry.

Anthony J. Fonseca

See also: France; Griot

Further Reading

Bretillon, Chong J. 2014. "'Ma face vanille': White Rappers, 'Black Music,' and Race in France." *International Journal of Francophone Studies* 17, nos. 3–4: 421–43.

Hammou, Karim. 2016. "Mainstreaming French Rap Music: Commodification and Artistic Legitimation of Othered Cultural Goods." *Poetics* 59 (December): 67–81.

Harris, David L. 2003. "French Connection: The Sisters of Les Nubians Expand Their Hip Hop/R&B Domain with a New Album and a Move from Paris to Philadelphia." *Boston Globe*, August 15, C12.

Further Listening

Les Nubians. 1998. *Princesses Nubiennes* (*Nubian Princesses*). Virgin France S. A.

Les Nubians. 2011. *Nü revolution* (*New Revolution*). Shanachie.

Lesotho

Lesotho has had a struggling hip hop scene, despite the fact that by the mid-1980s American rap albums became available; popular music tastes favored reggae, jazz, Afropop, and *famo*, the latter a kind of Lesotho music that uses Sesotho (the country's official language) texts. With roots dating back to the 1920s, famo features a male or female singer, accordion, oil can drum, and sometimes bass. In addition, *kwaito*, a separate music consisting of some of the same elements as hip hop but using rap, slowed-down house music beats, drum loops, African music samples, and heavy bass, emerged in South Africa and found its way to popularity in Lesotho—a landlocked country within South Africa. Even in the 1990s, hip hop remained an underground culture in Lesotho, focusing on a capella rapping, since the country lacked its own music industry, so music production technology used to create beats was difficult to access.

Since 2000, the Lesotho hip hop scene has expanded in its capital, Maseru, where radio DJ Dallas T (Tello Leballo, n.d.) promoted Lesotho hip hop acts, including Kommanda Obbs (1998–)*, who released the mixtape *Complex Mind Set Volume 1* (2006), on Radio Lesotho's sister station Ultimate FM (2006–). Despite this English title, Kommanda Obbs raps in Sesotho and has coined "T'sepe" (Sesotho for iron or steel) for his hard-hitting rap with themes about hustling and surviving street life. Rapper Dunamis (Rets'elisitsoe Molefe, n.d.), who raps in English, resides in Maseru, where he started his label K.O.L. Music Productions (2007–). Dunamis sold over 1,000 copies of *Mastered Seed* (2007), which spawned the first Lesotho hip hop music video; he also sold over 100 copies of his second album, *The Glory and da Street* (2011), within the first two hours of the release. As of 2018, both Obbs and Dunamis still record mixtapes and aim to release more albums.

Melissa Ursula Dawn Goldsmith

See also: Kwaito; Reggae; South Africa

Further Reading

Boloka, Gibson. 2003. "Cultural Studies and the Transformation of the Music Industry: Some Reflections on Kwaito." In *Shifting Selves: Post-Apartheid Essays on Mass Media, Culture, and Identity*, edited by Herman Wasserman and Sean Jacobs, chap. 5. Cape Town, South Africa: Kwela Books.

Thorpe, Nick. 2008. "The High Life, Lesotho-Style." *Sunday Times* (London), February 17, 10.

Libya

Libya has recently gone through a sociopolitical change that has made the emergence of rap music not only possible, but also an indispensable feature of the current Arab music culture. Former Libyan Prime Minister Muammar Gaddafi (1942–2011, in power 1969–2011) had been broadcasting state-approved music in public spaces such as taxis, shops, and restaurants while isolating Libya from outside musical cultures. Nonetheless, Libyan hip hop was inevitable due to access to outside media beginning with the availability of satellite dishes in 1992 and the addition of public Internet access in 2000. As early as the 1990s, live performances by Libyan rappers who borrowed from mainstream Western hip hop showed the potential for songs about poverty, unemployment, corruption, autocracy, and oppression, especially since the lyrical and rhythmic qualities of hip hop, as well as its penchant for hyperbolic boasts, made the genre a good fit for Arabic poetic traditions. Hence, Libyan hip hop and rap artists have gravitated toward fusions of poetry, pop, traditional music, and rap, frequently used as a platform for political resistance. Libyan rap is characterized by an interweaving of new material with call-and-response chants, quotes from political speeches, and traditional instrumentation. Its rapid spread on the Internet solidified rap in Libya as a platform for self-expression and also a means for youth to communicate with one another across the country.

In February 2011 the Gaddafi regime fired on peaceful protestors in Benghazi and Al Bayda, galvanizing the public toward a government coup. During the ensuing "Day of Rage," the Gaddafi regime countered by implementing Internet blackouts, including blocks on social media sites, followed in March by a complete disconnection of Libya from the Internet. A cadre of amateur rappers emerged in public support of Libyan revolutionary efforts, bolstering fighters' morale and convincing people to join the revolution. Soon after the "Day of Rage," Revolution Beat recorded "Thawra" (Revolution) while anonymous rapper (to avoid persecution) Ibn Thabit (anonymous, n.d.) collaborated with MC Swat (anonymous, n.d.) on "Victory or Death." Thabit released his rap, with Arabic and Tamazight lyrics, on YouTube and on his own website. Following the liberation of Benghazi, rappers across Libya aired their work on stations such as Benghazi Free Radio and Libya FM, and distributed CD recordings of their music to Benghazi demonstrators. Khaled M (anonymous, n.d.), a Libyan American hip hop artist and son of a Gaddafi dissident, released, in collaboration with London-based Iraqi English artist Lowkey (Kareen Dennis, 1986–), the single "Can't Take Our Freedom."

Since the revolution, artists in Libya, such as the GAB Crew (2005–), continue to grapple with a newfound freedom of expression. The GAB Crew speaks for a growing community of Libyan rap artists—those mentioned as well as Sheeba (anonymous, n.d.), Street Souljahz (anonymous, n.d.), Malik L (anonymous, n.d.), Guys Underground (anonymous, n.d.), B-Way (anonymous, n.d.), and Music Masters (anonymous, n.d.)—who see hip hop as an authentic musical genre for a free Libya.

Jennifer L. Roth-Burnette

See also: Political Hip Hop

Further Reading

Ahmida, Ali Abdullatif. 2012. "Libya, Social Origins of Dictatorship, and the Challenge for Democracy." *Journal of the Middle East and Africa* 3, no. 1: 70–81.

Fedele, Valentina. 2014. "Singing the Revolution. North African Rap and the Story of the Arab Uprisings." *European Journal of Research on Social Studies* 1, no. 1: 24–28.

Lil' Kim

(Kimberly Denise Jones, 1975–, Brooklyn, New York)

Lil' Kim is an influential American rapper best known for her sexually explicit lyrics and provocative styles of dress. In the early 1990s she was the only female member of Junior M.A.F.I.A. (1992–1997), which was mentored and promoted by the Notorious B.I.G. (1972–1997) and which released a debut album, *Conspiracy* (1995) that was certified Gold. The album spawned three hit songs, "Player's Anthem," "I Need You Tonight," and "Get Money." The success of these tracks, which all included verses by Lil' Kim, helped launch the rapper's solo career.

Lil' Kim established her reputation early on with her debut album, *Hard Core* (1996). The title reflected the album's combination of hardcore rap lyrics and production style, as well as Lil' Kim's signature lyricism, based on explicitly sexual content. Even the album's cover was tantalizing, as it features Lil' Kim in a shear negligee, positioned on all fours on top of a bearskin rug. In other promotional materials, she appeared in a bikini with a fur-lined cover-up and heels, positioned in a squat facing the camera.

This hypersexual motif is also apparent in her lyrics, which are noteworthy for their raunchiness, as in her opening verse for "Big Momma Thang," where she uses explicit slang to express that she has gotten over her fear of male genitalia and anal intercourse. Though these kinds of lyrics were not new for hardcore rap, they were unusual in the work of female rappers at the time.

Hard Core was commercially and critically successful, peaking at No. 11 on the Billboard 200 and reaching double Platinum status. Singles from the album "No Time" and "Not Tonight (Ladies Night Remix)" each made it into the Top 20, at Nos. 18 and 6, respectively, on the Billboard Hot 100 charts. "No Time" reached the top spot on the Hot Rap Songs chart; "Not Tonight" peaked at No. 2.

Her second album, *The Notorious K.I.M.* (2000), was certified Platinum after just four weeks. In the following year, she was one of the vocalists on a cover of Labelle's (1962–1976) "Lady Marmalade," made for the film *Moulin Rouge!* (2001). The song stayed at No. 1 on the Billboard Hot 100 for five consecutive weeks, a record for female rappers at the time.

Many hip hop fans viewed Lil' Kim's explicit performances as an empowered approach to and expression of female sexuality, but critics questioned whether her raunchiness was exploitative. Civil rights activist C. Delores Tucker (1927–2005) objected to Lil' Kim's lyrics, calling her music "gangsta porno rap." Tucker criticized Warner Bros. Records for producing it.

Lil' Kim has a total of six studio albums, *Hard Core*, *The Notorious K.I.M.*, *La Bella Mafia* (2003), *The Naked Truth* (2005), *Ms. G.O.A.T.* (2008), and *Black*

Friday (2011). She also has her own label, International Rock Star Records (formerly Queen Bee Records), founded in 1999.

Lauron Jockwig Kehrer

See also: Dirty Rap; Gangsta Rap; Hardcore Hip Hop; The United States

Further Reading

McGlynn, Aine. 2007. "Lil' Kim." In *Icons of Hip Hop: An Encyclopedia of the Movement, Music, and Culture*, edited by Mickey Hess, vol. 2, pp. 439–56. Westport, CT: Greenwood Press.

Richardson, Elaine. 2006. "Ride or Die B, Jezebel, Lil' Kim, or Kimberly Jones and African Women's Language and Literacy Practices: The Naked Truf." In *Hip Hop Literacies*, chap. 4. New York: Routledge.

Further Listening

Lil' Kim. 1996. *Hard Core.* Big Beat.

Lil' Kim. 2003. *La bella mafia (Beautiful Mafia Woman).* Atlantic/Queen Bee Records.

Lil' Kim. 2008. *MS. G.O.A.T.* Queen Bee Records/Money Maker Records.

Lil Wayne

(Dwayne Michael Carter Jr., 1982–, New Orleans, Louisiana)

Lil Wayne is one of the major artists on the New Orleans–based label, Ca$h Money Records (1991–). In addition to being the founder and former CEO of his own imprint, Young Money Entertainment (2005–), he is one of the best-selling artists in any genre. Depending on how the Billboard Hot 100 is counted (if it is counted after 1958, and not retroactively adjusted to songs produced before the chart existed), he has surpassed Elvis Presley's (1935–1977) record for male artist with the most songs on the charts, with 133, as of 2018. Post 1958, he trails only one performer, the *Glee* Cast (2009–2015), for overall Hot 100 hits.

Lil Wayne has a distinctive rapping style; his delivery is slow, and his lyrics rely heavily on metaphors and similes. His lyrical content not only focuses on gangsta rap topics such as hustling, acquired wealth and material objects, respect, crime, and violence, but also social protest (including racial inequality and black peoples' exposure to violence and crime), romance (ranging from objectifying and demeaning women to romanticizing them), and autobiographical elements (growing up in New Orleans). His musical style shows some flexibility between hook- and almost drum-and-bass-driven hip hop, employing both fast (chopper style) as well as smooth, laid-back rap delivery styles, and eclecticism that fuses the unusual combination of gangsta with alternative hip hop and utilizing rock and R&B elements.

EARLY CAREER

Raised in the Hollygrove neighborhood of New Orleans, Lil Wayne began rapping at the age of eight, and by 1991 he was recording for Ca$h Money Records. He formed the duo the B.G.'z (1991–1996) with fellow New Orleans rapper B.G. (aka Lil Doogie, Christopher Noel Dorsey, 1980–). The duo recorded an album, *True Story*

(1995), which featured diss tracks toward fellow New Orleans rapper Mystikal (Michael Lawrence Tyler, 1970–) and competing New Orleans record label Big Boy Records (1992–2000). In 1996, he and B.G. joined Ca$h Money's band, Hot Boys (1997–2001, 2007–), which released its debut album, *Get It How U Live!* (1997). The group followed up in 1999 with a second, highly successful album, *Guerrilla Warfare,* produced by New Orleans native Mannie Fresh (Byron O. Thomas, 1969–). The group disbanded in 2001, but Ca$h Money released their third album, *Let 'Em Burn* (2003), comprising material recorded between 1998 and 2000, and members of the group continued to collaborate on each other's projects.

SOLO CAREER

In 1999, Lil Wayne released his first solo album, *Tha Block Is Hot.* It debuted on the Billboard 200 at No. 3 and was certified Platinum just two months after its release. The album features no explicit lyrics, reportedly because the rapper was a minor at the time, and his mother objected to his rapping extreme profanities. His second and third albums, *Lights Out* (2000) and *500 Degreez* (2002) were both certified Gold, but failed to reach the same level of success as *Tha Block Is Hot.* In 2004, he released his fourth studio album, *Tha Carter.* He followed with *Tha Carter II* in 2005 and a collaborative album with rapper and Ca$h Money cofounder, Birdman (1969–), titled *Like Father, Like Son,* in 2006. *Tha Carter III* was released in 2008, followed by the rock-influenced *Rebirth* in 2010 and *I Am Not a Human Being* in that same year.

Lil Wayne began recording material for *Tha Carter IV* in 2008, but the project was put on hold while he served a prison sentence for possession of an illegal weapon. Upon his release, he started rerecording new material, and the album was released in 2011 following several delays. It was one of his most successful releases, breaking records for number of iTunes downloads, reaching No. 1 on the Billboard 200, and it was certified double Platinum after just two months. *Tha Carter IV* spawned several well-performing singles, including "6 Foot 7 Foot," "How to Love," "She Will," "It's Good," and "Mirror." Featured guests on the album included Drake (1986–), Jadakiss (1975–), and Bruno Mars (Peter Gene Hernandez, 1985–).

Lil Wayne has continued to release studio albums every one to two years, including *I Am Not a Human Being II* (2013), *Free Weezy Album* (2015), and a collaborative album titled *ColleGrove* (2016). None have fared as well as *Tha Carter IV.* In addition to his studio albums, he has released many mixtapes, including the *Dedication* series (five releases), *Da Drought* series (three releases), *The Drought Is Over* series (five releases), and *Sorry 4 the Wait* (2011) and *Sorry for the Wait 2* (2015). These mixtapes often feature Lil Wayne's rapping new lyrics over the instrumental tracks from other rappers' songs.

In 2005, the same year he founded his own imprint, Young Money Entertainment, he was named the CEO of Ca$h Money Records. Ca$h Money Records has since released a number of commercially successful albums, including Drake's *Thank Me Later* (2010), Tyga's (Michael Ray Stevenson, 1989–) *Hotel California*

(2013), Nicki Minaj's (1982–) *Pink Friday: Roman Reloaded* (2012), and others. The label has also released a mixtape, *Young Money: The Mixtape Vol. 1* (2005) and three compilation albums that feature label artists, including *We Are Young Money* (2009), *Rich Gang* (with Ca$h Money Records, 2013), and *Rise of an Empire* (2014).

Lauron Jockwig Kehrer

See also: Birdman; Drake; Gangsta Rap; Nicki Minaj; The United States

Further Reading

Graham, Natalie. 2016. "Cracks in the Concrete: Policing Lil Wayne's Masculinity and the Feminizing Metaphor." *Journal of Popular Culture* 49, no. 4: 799–817.

Westoff, Ben. 2011. "Lil Wayne: Gangster Weirdo." In *Dirty South: OutKast, Lil Wayne, Soulja Boy, and the Southern Rappers Who Reinvented Hip Hop*, chap. 15. Chicago: Chicago Review Press.

Further Listening

Lil Wayne. 1999. *Tha Block Is Hot*. Ca$h Money Records/Universal Records.

Lil Wayne. 2011. *Tha Carter IV*. Ca$h Money Records.

Lithuania

Lithuania is a Baltic country with a population of nearly three million. It was occupied by the Soviet Union during World War II (1939–1945), and after; it declared its independence in 1990. Rock music developed there in the mid-1960s, first in illegal gatherings, via Radio Luxembourg (1933–1992) or smuggled vinyl albums, but by the 1980s, Lithuanians could openly perform in rock and hip hop bands. The most famous of these is Skamp (1998–), which in seven studio albums has combined hip hop with pop, rock, and reggae.

Skamp had a hit with a cover of George Gershwin's (1898–1937) "Summertime" (originally written for the American opera *Porgy and Bess* in 1934). The song, on the band's Koja Records (1995–2010) album *Angata* (1999), has a hip hop beat, and is sung in English, with rap in French and Lithuanian.

The main center for hip hop emerged in the 1990s in the capital, Vilnius. With seven studio albums, including three self-releases, G&G Sindikatas (1996–), from Vilnius, is the most popular rap act in the country. The five-man band's sound is based on American rap bands such as D12 (1996–) and Beastie Boys (1981–2012), which infuse rock, funk, and metal into their hip hop beats. G&G Sindikatas' songs include turntablism, heavy guitars and bass, funk drumming, brass, and synthesizer—and rappers take turn rapping verses and rap together in choruses. Helion (Tomas Matulevicius, n.d.) is a breakbeat Lithuanian DJ and producer known for popular mixes. The hip hop label Renegades of Bump (2010–) has taken on the task of producing Lithuanian rap samplers.

Hip hop dancing is extremely popular in Lithuania: The Low Air Urban Dance Theater (2012–) is an urban dance company, located in Vilnius, that specializes in lyrical hip hop.

Anthony J. Fonseca

See also: Hip Hop Dance; Lyrical Hip Hop; The United States

Further Reading

Bielinskiene, Asta, Zivile Casaite, and Julija Paliukenaite. 2015. "Music Publication in Lithuania after 1990: A Typological Analysis." *Fontes Artis Musicae* 62, no. 2:
110–17.

Droba, Krzysztof. 1993. "The History and the Present Day of Lithuanian Music (From
Čiurlionis to Landsgergis)." *Revista de Musicología* 16, no. 6: 3684–91.

Further Listening

G&G Sindikatas. 2001. *Gatvės lyga* (*Street League*). Bomba Records.

G&G Sindikatas. 2017. *Unplugged.* Self-released.

LL Cool J

(James Todd Smith, 1968–, Bay Shore, New York)

LL Cool J, whose name is a shortened version of Ladies Love Cool James, is an
American rapper, singer-songwriter, actor, writer, and entrepreneur. He fuses hip
hop with pop, performing pop rap. All of his albums have crossed over to the mainstream and charted on the Billboard 200, with *G.O.A.T. (Greatest of All Time)*
(2000) peaking at No. 1 and *10* (2002) peaking at No. 2.

His first eight studio albums, *Radio* (1985); *Bigger and Deffer* (1987); *Walking
with a Panther* (1989); *Mama Said Knock You Out* (1990); *14 Shots to the Dome*
(1993); *Mr. Smith* (1995); *Phenomenon* (1997); and *G.O.A.T*, have been certified at
least Platinum. His three subsequent studio albums, *10*; *The DEFinition* (2004);
and *Todd Smith* (2006), were certified Gold. His Top 10 hits on the Billboard Hot
100 include "Around the Way Girl" (1990), "Hey, Lover" (1995), "Doin' It" (1996),
"Loungin'" (1996), "Luv U Better" (2002), and "Control Myself" (2006). LL Cool
J's only Billboard Hot 100 No. 1 was as featured artist in Jennifer Lopez's (aka
J.Lo, 1969–) R&B and hip hop ballad "All I Have" (2002). He won two Grammy
Awards for Best Rap Solo Performance for "Mama Said Knock You Out" and "Hey,
Lover."

EARLY INTERESTS AND ALBUMS

Born James Todd Smith, he grew up with his grandparents in Hollis, Queens,
New York. His grandfather was a professional jazz saxophonist, and he lived at the
center of hip hop activity during its formative years. As a child, he discovered rap
and was inspired by the Sugarhill Gang's (1979–1985, 1994–) "Rapper's Delight"
(1979) and the Treacherous Three (1978–1984). At age 11, he was given a DJ system
by his grandfather so he could produce demos to send to New York City recording
companies.

In 1984, he dropped out of high school, began using the stage name LL Cool J,
and signed to a fledgling Def Jam Recordings label (1983–). That year, he released
the 12-inch single "I Need a Beat," which contains braggadocio and metatextuality (e.g., his expressing awareness of the elements of his backing beat and calling

for the break). Though it failed to chart, "I Need a Beat" sold over 100,000 copies. Its commercial success contributed to Def Jam's 1985 acquisition of a distribution deal with Columbia Records (1887–). More success and critical acclaim followed with LL Cool J's studio album debut, *Radio*, which made him one of the first rappers to achieve mainstream success. In 1986, he became the first hip hop act on the television show *American Bandstand* (1952–1989). His second album, *Bigger and Deffer*, went triple Platinum.

LATER ALBUMS AND ACTING CAREER

Though LL Cool J's *Walking with a Panther* also achieved commercial success, it was not as well received as his earlier albums. Its lyrical content focused on romance, missing some of the earlier albums' intelligent use of street themes, coding, braggadocio, and humor. Marley Marl (1962–) produced *Mama Said Knock You Out*, which brought back these devices and went double Platinum. The title track earned LL Cool J his first Grammy Award.

When he released *14 Shots to the Dome* in 1993, LL Cool J started to spend more time acting. Earlier, he made his acting debut as a rapper in the American hip hop film *Krush Groove* (1985), which was based on the early history of Def Jam. In the film, LL Cool J performed the love song "I Can't Live without My Radio" from his album *Radio*. He also played a rapper in the American football comedy *Wildcats* (1986). His films include *Toys* (1992), *In Too Deep* (1999), *S.W.A.T.* (2003 remake), *Last Holiday* (2006), and *Grudge Match* (2013), but his most notable acting roles have been on American television, starring in the situation comedy *In the House* (1995–1999) and in the crime drama *NCIS: Los Angeles* (2010–).

His concurrent successful recording output lasted into the 2000s with *Mr. Smith*, *Phenomenon*, *G.O.A.T*, *The DEFinition*, and *Todd Smith*. LL Cool J's final studio album with Def Jam was *Exit 13* (2008), which received mixed reception. After five years, LL Cool J released *Authentic* (2013) on the Santa Monica–based independent label 429 Records (under the Savoy Label Group, 2001–, a division of Nippon Columbia, formerly Columbia Music Entertainment, 1910–). Though it had mixed critical reception, it peaked at No. 23 on the Billboard 200, No. 7 on Billboard's Top R&B/Hip-Hop Albums, and No. 4 on Billboard's Independent Albums.

Melissa Ursula Dawn Goldsmith

See also: Boogie Down Productions; KRS-One; The United States

Further Reading

Lefty Banks. 2003. "LL Cool J: *Radio*; *Mama Said Knock You Out*." In *Classical Material: The Hip Hop Album Guide*, edited by Oliver Wang, pp. 108–110. Toronto: ECW Press.

LL Cool J, with Karen Hunter. 1997. *I Make My Own Rules*. New York: St. Martin's Press.

Further Listening

LL Cool J. 1985. *Radio*. Columbia/Def Jam.

LL Cool J. 1990. *Mama Said Knock You Out*. Def Jam Recordings.

The LOX

(aka The L.O.X., The Warlocks, 1994–, Yonkers, New York)

The LOX is an American hardcore hip hop trio consisting of rappers Sheek Louch (aka Donnie Def Jam, Donnie G, Sean Divine Jacobs, 1976–), Styles P (David Styles, 1974–), and Jadakiss (Jason Phillips, 1975–). The trio is known for collaborating with Puff Daddy (1969–) on "It's All about the Benjamins" (1997) and a multi-Platinum tribute single to the Notorious B.I.G. (1972–1997) titled "We'll Always Love Big Poppa" (1997). The LOX's certified-Platinum debut album, *Money, Power, and Respect* (1998), peaked at No. 3 on the Billboard 200 and No. 1 on Billboard's Top R&B/Hip-Hop Albums chart. Both the title track and "If You Think I'm Jiggy" peaked at No. 30 on the Billboard Hot 100. The LOX's second album, *We Are the Streets* (2000), received critical despite fewer sales, peaking at No. 5 on the Billboard 200 and No. 2 on Billboard's Top R&B/Hip-Hop Albums chart. In addition, the LOX appeared on numerous popular mainstream hits, including Jennifer Lopez's (aka J.Lo, 1969–) "Jenny from the Block" (2002).

In the early 1990s a trio of high school rapper friends called the Bomb Squad cut demos and performed locally. After appearing on the Toronto/New York City–based group Main Source's (1989–1994) track "Set It Off" (on *F—What You Think*, 1994) and building a following for its urban rap texts and self-released mixtapes, the trio became the Warlocks, eventually shortening it to the LOX. American hip hop singer-songwriter and fellow Yonkers, New York, resident Mary J. Blige (1971–) liked its sound and gave the trio's demo to Puff Daddy, who owned Bad Boy Entertainment (1993–).

Despite successful collaborations, hits, and huge sales on *Money, Power, and Respect*, the LOX wanted to move on from Bad Boy for a label that better represented its hardcore sound. Because the trio could not legally get a contract release, members of the LOX wore T-shirts at their concerts that read, "Let The LOX Go." Fans supported them and added pressure. The LOX then moved to the Ruff Ryders label (1988–) from 1999 to 2010, releasing *We Are the Streets* (2000), which was more hardcore than its debut album. It featured gangsta rap tracks with lyrics about enjoying violent nights out, committing crimes (including rape), and beating up enemies. The LOX's videos feature textbook objectification of women, often featuring video vixens.

After its second album, the LOX took a hiatus in which members pursued solo careers. In 2012, the LOX united to collaborate with Wu-Tang Clan (1992–) on *Wu Block*. The trio followed this project by releasing its first EP, *The Trinity*, on iTunes, touring worldwide to promote the EP, which was well received by critics and peaked at 141 on the Billboard 200 and No. 17 on Billboard's Top R&B/Hip-Hop Albums chart. The same year, the LOX formed their own recording label, D-Block (2013–). In 2016, the LOX released *Filthy America . . . It's Beautiful* on both the D-Block and Jay-Z's (1969–) Roc Nation (2008–) labels. It peaked at No. 42 on the Billboard 200 and No. 6 on Billboard's Top R&B/Hip-Hop Albums chart.

Melissa Ursula Dawn Goldsmith

See also: Blige, Mary J.; Gangsta Rap; Hardcore Hip Hop; The United States

Further Reading

Baker, Soren. 2000. "Hip Hop Report: More Grime Than Shine, the LOX Moves On." *Los Angeles Times*, January 23, CAL73.

Ogbar, Jeffrey. 2006. "Holla Black." *Radical Society* 32, no. 3: 67–74.

Quinn, Eithne. 2005. *Nuthin' but a G Thang: The Culture and Commerce of Gangsta Rap.* New York: Columbia University Press.

Further Listening

The LOX. 2000. *We Are the Streets.* Ruff Ryders.

Ludacris

(Christopher Brian Bridges, 1977–, Champaign, Illinois)

Ludacris is one of the most successful Dirty South rappers. His style, particularly as heard from 1998 to 2005, exemplifies the Dirty South sound: his lyrics are gleeful and humorous, and they highlight debauchery, hedonism, women, alcohol, drugs, and strip clubs; Ludacris lends to the sound his distinctive flowing vocals, a sense of creative wordplay, and an emphasis on exaggerated accentuation (of syllables).

Ludacris spent his childhood between his mother's home in the Chicago area and his father's, in the Atlanta area. He began rapping at age nine, and joined with other adolescent rappers to form short-lived groups named Tic Tac Toe and Loudmouth Hooligans. He moved to Atlanta full time at age 13, attending high school in College Park, Georgia, where he took part in rap battles in the lunchroom and the hallways. In the late 1990s, he briefly enrolled at Georgia State University to study music management. While still taking classes there, he joined Atlanta rap station Hot 97.5 as DJ Chris Lova Lova, working as a morning radio show intern, recording station promotions, and eventually cohosting a primetime show, "Future Flavors." He took advantage of his placement at 97.5 to promote his own music, eventually changing his rap moniker from Ludachris to Ludacris. Through his work in radio,

American rapper-songwriter Ludacris poses at the 2006 Independent Spirit Awards in Santa Monica, California. Though originally from the Midwest, Ludacris moved to Atlanta as a teen, where he honed his talents in rap battles and, by the 2000s, eventually became one of Dirty South's most successful and influential musicians and producers. (Carrienelson1/Dreamstime.com)

he met producer Timbaland (1972–) and rapped on Timbaland's track "Fat Rabbit," on the 1998 album *Tim's Bio: From the Motion Picture Life from da Bassment.*

EARLY CAREER

In 2000, Ludacris cofounded Disturbing tha Peace (DTP) records in Atlanta, which eventually became a subsidiary of Def Jam Recordings (1983–), and he independently produced his first album, *Incognegro*, in 2000 (it was subsequently released as *Back for the First Time* on Def Jam South in 2000). The success of his debut single, "What's Your Fantasy," featuring Shawnna (Rashawnna Guy, 1978–), led to his signing with Def Jam South (1999–), a regional division of Def Jam Recordings; the single sold over 30,000 copies and demonstrated Ludacris's distinctive style: lewd subject matter (similar to that of signifying, an early influence on rap), animated delivery, and heavily emphasized rhymes.

Back for the First Time, a repackaging of *Incognegro* with three new tracks, was nominated for a Grammy for Best Rap Album. It peaked at No. 4 on the Billboard 200 and No. 2 on the Billboard Top R&B/Hip-Hop Albums chart and was certified triple Platinum. Ludacris's Grammy-nominated second album for Def Jam, *Word of Mouf* (2001), included the lead single "Rollout (My Business)," as well as "Saturday (Oooh Oooh)," "Move B—," and "Area Codes." The album featured Southern rappers Sleepy Brown (Patrick Brown, 1970–), Mystikal (Michael Lawrence Tyler, 1970–), I-20 (Bobby Sandimanie, 1974–), and Nate Dogg (Nathaniel Dwayne Hale, 1969–2011). Ludacris's style and his choice of guests make *Word of Mouf* a quintessential Dirty South album.

ENDORSEMENT CONTROVERSY AND ACTING CAREER

In 2002, Ludacris recorded two Super Bowl commercial spots for Pepsi, but the ads were never shown. Pepsi revoked their endorsement deal with Ludacris after criticism from conservative news pundit Bill O'Reilly (1949–) that Ludacris was a thug who promoted antisocial behavior, which included violence, degradation of women, and substance abuse. After pressure from the Hip Hop Summit Action Network, Pepsi donated several million dollars to the Ludacris Foundation (2002–), but did not renew their relationship with Ludacris. The controversy may have in fact helped Ludacris, as his next album, *Chicken-N-Beer* (2003) was his first to top the Billboard 200 and the Top R&B/Hip-Hop Albums charts, although it sold fewer copies that *Word of Mouf.* The album boasted his first No. 1 single, produced by Kanye West (1977–) and featuring Shawnna, as well as blatantly sexualized singles "Splash Waterfalls" and "P-Poppin." Acknowledging his comments of the previous year, Ludacris took shots at O'Reilly in the songs "Blow It Out" and "Hoes in My Room."

In 2001, Ludacris (credited as Chris Bridges) began acting in films, playing Tej Parker in *2 Fast 2 Furious* and reprising the character in subsequent films in the franchise. He performed the Grammy-nominated "Act A Fool" for the film's soundtrack. Among his other acting credits, Ludacris played a supporting role in two Oscar-nominated films, *Crash* and *Hustle and Flow* (both 2005).

In 2004, Ludacris was featured on R&B singer Usher's (Usher Raymond IV, 1978–) internationally award-winning single "Yeah," produced by crunk popularizer Lil Jon (Jonathan Smith, 1971–). Also in 2004, Ludacris released *The Red Light District*, including singles "Get Back," "Number One Spot," "The Potion," and "Pimpin' All over the World." The album included a crossover remix of "Get Back," rerecorded with Canadian rock band Sum 41 (1996–). The album was certified Platinum but was not critically rated as highly as his previous albums.

Nominated for multiple awards over the years, Ludacris won his first Best Album Grammy for *Release Therapy* (2006) and was awarded Best Rap Song for the single "Money Maker." *Release Therapy* marked a shift to more serious lyrical themes as demonstrated by tracks such as "Runaway Love, featuring Mary J. Blige (1971–) and "Grew Up a Screw Up," featuring Young Jeezy (Jay Wayne Jenkins, 1977–), addressing topics such as violence against women and teen runaways.

Ludacris's later albums *Theater of the Mind* (2008) and *Battle of the Sexes* (2010) marked a return to the more partycentric, sexual rhymes of his earlier work, with the singles "What Them Girls Like," "One More Drink," "Nasty Girl," "How Low," "My Chick Bad," and "Sex Room." Guest musicians included Chris Brown (1989–), Sean Garrett (Garrett Hamler, 1979–), T-Pain (Faheem Rashad Najm, 1985–), Nicki Minaj (1982–), and Trey Songz (Tremaine Aldon Neverson, 1984–). Ludacris's most recent album, *Ludaversal* (2015) included more introspection in singles such as "Good Lovin'."

Katy E. Leonard

See also: Dirty South; The United States

Further Reading

Cramer, Jennifer, and Jill Hallett. 2010. "From Chi-Town to the Dirty-Dirty: Regional Identity Markers in U.S. Hip Hop." In *The Languages of Global Hip Hop*, edited by Marina Terkourafi, chap. 10. New York: Continuum.

Oliver, Richard, and Tim Leffel. 2006. "East Coast–West Coast–Gulf Coast: But Southern Rap? Ludacris!" In *Hip Hop, Inc.: Success Strategies of the Rap Moguls*, chap. 10. New York: Thunder's Mouth Press.

Richmond, Sanford K. 2013. "Paint the White House Black! A Critical Discourse Analysis Look at Hip Hop's Social, Cultural, and Political Influence on the Presidency of Barack Obama." *Western Journal of Black Studies* 37, no. 4: 249–57.

Further Listening

Ludacris. 2001. *Word of Mouf.* Def Jam South.
Ludacris. 2006. *Release Therapy.* Def Jam South.

Luke

(aka Luke Skyywalker, Luther Roderick Campbell, 1960–, Miami, Florida)

Luke is a controversial American record label owner, producer, Southern rap and Miami bass performer, band and song promoter, and actor, best known for his stint as leader of the 2 Live Crew (1982–91; 1994–98) from Miami. He is also known as a soloist for his debut solo album, *Banned in the U.S.A.* (aka *The Luke LP*, 1990).

His vocal style is best characterized as hyping through not carefully choreographed rapped rhymes, but a series of crowd shouts or sometimes chants, often to produce a call-and-response effect, a musical technique influenced by his Jamaican and Bahamian ancestry.

The 2 Live Crew was a California rap group fronted by DJ Mr. Mixx (David Hobbs, n.d.). The group released "Revelation" in 1985, and due to the song's popularity, was brought to Miami by concert promoter Luke, who as Luke Skyywalker became its manager and MC, getting the crew a record deal on his Miami-based Luke Skyywalker Records label (1985–, later changed to Luke Records in 1990). The new 2 Live Crew lineup released *The 2 Live Crew Is What We Are* (1986), a certified-Gold album which got attention because of the explicit sexual content of its lyrics. The band's second and third albums, *Move Somethin'* (1988) and *As Nasty as They Wanna Be* (1989), went Gold and Platinum, respectively, the latter resulting in the band's first No. 1 Rap song and Hot 100 hit, "Me So Horny" (which peaked at No. 26).

Luke's solo debut, *Banned in the USA* is actually credited as Luke, Featuring the 2 Live Crew, as Luke used the band's popularity to further sales, even though he paid the rest of the 2 Live Crew as performing musicians, giving them a flat fee, rather than royalties. Although the album was his highest Billboard 200, peaking at No. 21, and produced his highest-charting Hot 100 single, "Banned in the U.S.A." (1990), which reached No. 20, the song achieved only Gold status. "Banned in the U.S.A." was to be Luke's last charting single.

Mr. Mixx soon left the 2 Live Crew and all members of the group drew up a lawsuit against Luke; the result was the band's selling the 2 Live Crew name to Luke Skyywalker Records and Luke for a lump sum payment. Luke went on to do a few minor albums and star in the short-lived VH1 show *Luke's Parental Advisory* (2008). He was also sued unsuccessfully for copyright infringement in *Campbell v. Acuff-Rose Music, Inc.* (1994), which was argued in front of the U.S. Supreme Court and established the right of parody songs to exist. After retiring from rap, he became a minor sports figure via radio, inner city leagues, and involvement in a University of Miami football scandal when *The Miami Herald,* after a two-month investigation, reported in 1994 that Campbell paid football players at the University of Miami for making big plays in football games between 1986 and 1992—these game-day bounties included up to $500 for a touchdown. There was no involvement whatsoever of the University of Miami or its Athletics Department. The investigation found that Luke acted independently.

Anthony J. Fonseca

See also: Dirty Rap; Miami Bass; 2 Live Crew; The United States

Further Reading

Campbell, Luther. 2015. *The Book of Luke: My Fight for Truth, Justice, and Liberty City.* New York: Amistad.

French, Kenneth. 2017. "Geography of American Rap: Rap Diffusion and Rap Centers." *GeoJournal* 82, no. 2: 259–72.

Sanjek, David. 2006. "Ridiculing the 'White Bread Original': The Politics of Parody and Preservation of Greatness in Luther Campbell, aka *Luke Skyywalker et al. v. Acuff-Rose Music, Inc.*" *Cultural Studies* 20, nos. 2–3: 262–81.